ALEXANDER HAMILTON
JAMES MADISON
JOHN JAY

The Federalist

ALEXANDER HAMILTON

JAMES MADISON

JOHN JAY

The Federalist

EDITED WITH HISTORICAL AND LITERARY ANNOTATIONS,
AND INTRODUCTION, BY

J. R. POLE

FBA, FRHISTS: EMERITUS FELLOW OF ST. CATHERINE'S COLLEGE, OXFORD;
EMERITUS RHODES PROFESSOR OF AMERICAN HISTORY AND INSTITUTIONS,
UNIVERSITY OF OXFORD; HON. FOREIGN MEMBER OF THE
AMERICAN HISTORICAL ASSOCIATION

Hackett Publishing Company, Inc.
Indianapolis/Cambridge

For further information, please address:

Hackett Publishing Company, Inc.
P.O. Box 44937
Indianapolis, IN 46244-0937

www.hackettpublishing.com

Cover design by Abigail Coyle
Text design by Jennifer Plumley
Composition by Professional Book Compositors, Inc.
Printed at Sheridan Books, Inc.

Library of Congress Cataloging-in-Publication Data

The federalist / Alexander Hamilton, James Madison, John Jay; edited with historical and literary annotations and introduction by J. R. Pole.
    p. cm.
  Includes index.
  ISBN 0-87220-711-0 (pbk.) — ISBN 0-87220-712-9 (hardcover)
  1. Constitutional history—United States—Sources. I. Hamilton, Alexander, 1757–1804. II. Madison, James, 1751–1836. III. Jay, John, 1745–1829. IV. Pole, J. R. (Jack Richon)

KF4515.F4 2004
342.7302'9—dc22   2004004523

In Memory

Roy Porter

CONTENTS

— = *John Jay*

The Federalist

CONTENTS

EDITORIAL NOTE

This newly annotated edition of *The Federalist* relies on the dates in the New York newspapers established by Jacob E. Cooke's edition published by Wesleyan University Press of Middletown, Connecticut in 1961. That edition also includes many useful notes on historical events and identities, for many of which I make due acknowledgment. In common with other historians and political scientists I owe a great debt to that distinguished edition. Since Cooke's edition appeared there have been some advances in the science of literary attribution, and for these reasons as well as for further reflection on distinctions in style, I have proposed a handful of modifications of attribution. Although all three authors conformed to the conventions of literary English, my own feeling is that one can be somewhat more confident of Alexander Hamilton's style from internal evidence than other editors may have felt, and I have slightly differed from Cooke's attributions in a few cases. Cooke discusses these questions thoroughly in his own Introduction. Hamilton, James Madison, and John Jay were very well-educated men—in important respects better educated than most of their modern readers. To bring forward their educational background and assumptions will, I hope, enhance the meaning and significance of their work. My own purpose has thus been to make available to present-day (and future) readers a deeper and more substantial appreciation of the intellectual context of Publius's style and purpose by identifying all the historical references and (so far as I have caught them) all the unidentified literary allusions and quotations by which they sought to amplify their arguments and convince their readers. I have also hoped to clarify and explain important concepts (such as *sovereignty*) that play a significant part in the thinking both of the Founders and of their opponents; I have also noted changes in the meanings and values of certain linguistic terms and usages that have shifted since the 18th century. The intellectual world inhabited by Hamilton, Madison, and Jay has certain continuities with ours but significant differences; we can understand their meaning better if we can trace the sources of their knowledge and ideas. It is also worth pointing out to modern readers that, notwithstanding the standard view of *The Federalist* as a "classic" in political science, the authors were not always accurate or even well informed and were not above occasionally enforcing an argument with more emphasis than evidence. They could only work with the materials to hand, were engaged in a desperately serious exercise, and were in a considerable hurry. The permanent value of the essays is by no means diminished by the fact that they are very much products of their own time, needs, and limitations. It is by understanding these factors that we can best hope both to understand their work and appreciate their achievement.

Thanks are due:

A suggestion by Philip Bobbitt gave this work its initiating impulse. Over the years of research I have been sustained by grants from the law firms of Slaughter and May of London and of Getty, Meyer and Mayo of Lexington, Kentucky. I have incurred many debts to colleagues whom I have plagued with questions about historical minutiae, ancient, medieval, and early modern. Joyce Appleby, who generously read the whole text, has steered me away from some dubious interpretations and has averted errors I was about to commit. Warren Swain has given me the benefit of his knowledge of 18th-century English law. In grateful acknowledgment, I must add that I alone am responsible for the opinions expressed here and for any errors that may have survived.

For help in checking numerous details, for general research, and indispensable assistance in preparing the text it is a pleasure to acknowledge my debt to Juliana Dresvina.

The index was patiently compiled by Alison Adams.

Finally, it is a pleasure to acknowledge the dedication, enthusiasm, and expertise of Rick Todhunter, Brian Rak, and the entire editorial team at Hackett Publishing Company.

A NOTE ON THE TEXT
AND ANNOTATION

The text of *The Federalist* presented in this volume was provided by the Intelex Corporation and is based on the McLean edition, the first edition of *The Federalist* published in book form (1788), corrected in light of the critical edition edited by Jacob E. Cooke (1961). Variations between published editions of *The Federalist* have, in any case, little effect on our understanding of the essays; see Cooke for variants.

Notes provided by Hamilton, Madison, and Jay are marked with an asterisk (*).

My own annotation appears at the bottom of the page, referenced by line numbers. When not commenting on a specific word or phrase in the text (usually referenced by a single line number), my annotation should be read as referring to the sentence or group of sentences (often a complete paragraph) that begins and ends within the range of line numbers that appears in bold face type before the note.

INTRODUCTION

I

Political Background:
How The Federalist *Came to Be Written*

Independence dragged its way slowly into the lives of the peoples of the new United States. Viewed from the seats of power, the sense of achievement was great; leaders (and no doubt followers) knew that they had accomplished something of transcendent scale on the map of world history. But the experience had been costly. Except for one or two bursts of exhilaration, it was neither a sudden nor even, all too often, a joyful experience. The war, drawing men from their homes, disrupting both the human and animal life of farms and families, dividing neighbors and friends, and causing grievous deprivations, affected different regions in different ways and at different periods. Most of New England, for example, was free of warfare and virtually independent after 1775; New York was occupied by the British throughout the war. There were few who would have been able to record the moment at which they felt they had achieved the freedom they had fought for; and after that momentous transition, few would have been able to say that they felt very differently from the way they had felt the day before. So many of the hardships and difficulties that had strewn the paths of independence were unresolved and continued in much the same ways—or worse. Public demonstrations of joy were followed—or accompanied—by bitter internal struggles for political power, for direction of fiscal and economic policies, for disputed areas of settlement, and for control of vast but vaguely defined natural resources. Feelings of hope for higher standards of living and new opportunities of western settlements were clouded with apprehensions of debt and foreclosures resulting from internal conflicts. Above all, Americans, having fought for and attained their liberty, were at last on their own: they had taken upon themselves the heavy responsibility of self-government according to republican principles. They had overthrown patriarchal authority and hereditary right, which they had replaced by government based on voluntary consent and association. But as the authors of *The Federalist* were to show, independent republics did not have a very impressive record of survival; if they failed, Americans would have only themselves to blame.

The British, with all their experience, had failed to hold together the largest and most prosperous of European empires; it remained to be proved that the Americans could succeed in holding together a large, various, and potentially prosperous republic. They had constantly to bear in mind that they were far from being alone on their continent; Britain still dominated Canada and most of the West Indies, Spain owned Florida, claimed much of the vast and uncharted west, and controlled the outlet of the Mississippi, and numerous powerful Native

American tribes or kingdoms occupied much of the unexplored interior. When in the immediate wake of American Independence, Britain issued an order in council closing the British West Indies to American shipping, outraged Americans discovered that independence could have its costs as well as its liberties.

The Continental Congress, composed of delegations voting as equal units from the states, became a sort of pragmatic constitution through its own rules of procedure. The Congress had no president, only a current chairman. Yet from the beginning, the Congress took on itself many attributes of government. It appointed committees to raise supplies and to negotiate with foreign powers; it commissioned and approved a great seal; it appointed a commander-in-chief (a Virginia militia colonel called George Washington) with power to raise an army; it raised loans at home and abroad, issued its own currency, and intervened in an ugly dispute between rival settlers from Connecticut and Pennsylvania. In many ways it acted as the government of a sovereign power. But its internal powers were barely strong enough for its responsibilities. The continental currency depreciated steeply and had to be devalued at forty to one; and the Congress had no authority to raise taxes, only to impose requisitions on the states; when payments fell behind, the Congress had little effective power of enforcement. When, with military victory secured and independence established, individual states, beginning with Maryland and Pennsylvania, assumed responsibility for paying the Congress's debts owed to their citizens, it began to look as though the Confederation was losing its reasons for existence.

The political character of this new nation, whose name had not been formally established, and varied from "the united States of America" to simply "the u. States," was difficult to define in classical language. Protracted negotiations and bargaining among the states in the interests of creating a formal association were concluded only as late as 1781—and then under threat of French naval intervention. The Articles of Confederation, thus agreed, declared the union perpetual but did little to repair the critical weaknesses of the Congress. It was envisaged, for example, that one state might be at war without involving the others; citizens of individual states were to enjoy reciprocal rights but there was no judicial system to enforce them. The Congress's powerlessness had serious implications for its ability to conduct foreign affairs. Although its delegates had negotiated a generally satisfactory peace treaty with Britain—largely behind the backs of their French allies—the treaty imposed obligations on American citizens to pay outstanding pre-war debts still owed to British merchants. These fell heavily on Virginia planters. But civil actions could be pursued only in state courts; the Confederation had no collective judicial system, and local juries were so prejudiced in favor of their compatriots that the debts could seldom be collected. The Congress could offer no means of relieving this grievance, and the British government retaliated by refusing to evacuate certain forts in America's Canadian frontier.

The Confederation might, then, be said to lie somewhere between a league of sovereigns and a nation-state. State sovereignty was still reflected in the wording of the Articles, in the provision that any alteration required a unanimous vote, which, it was soon clear, would be virtually impossible to achieve; important measures would require approval of nine of the states. The failure of attempts to revive Congressional power by strengthening its control over imposts very soon proved the fragility of these arrangements when confronted by state power under the control of locally vested interests.

However, even before the war had ended, in the interest of facilitating the ratification of the Articles, New York and Virginia ceded their vast western land claims to the Congress. This made it obvious that there was no authority other than Congress to take charge of the planning of the West, where so many Americans were fixing their hopes and prospects and toward which indeed many were already on the move. Congress now owned more land than the existing states. The last act of the old Congress was one of its most sweeping: in a huge gesture toward the future, it passed the Northwest Ordinance of 1787, which provided for transitional territorial governments in stages leading to eventual statehood. This ordinance also contained a clause whose ultimate effect was intended to eliminate slavery from the Ohio Valley.

Stable economic management proved beyond the competence of many state governments. Customs wars among the states caused commercial instability, not to mention bad feeling. The reopening of trade with Britain brought a currency crisis; laws favoring debtors, passed by newfound popular majorities, were denounced as violations of faith by creditor and propertied interests. Six states issued their own paper currencies, with inflationary consequences (two, however, South Carolina and Pennsylvania, achieved some stability). Some states, notably New York and Virginia, were largely self-sufficient and felt little sense of urgency about subjecting themselves to a stronger union; these differences were to some extent reflected in attitudes to the new Constitution. In the late summer of 1786, farmers in western Massachusetts, driven to despair by the state's hard currency policies, rose in armed rebellion under the leadership of a revolutionary war captain named Daniel Shays. Their aim was not to seize power but to close the courts in order to avert foreclosures on their farms. But Massachusetts had adopted its own constitution by the votes of the towns as recently as 1780, and the rebellion sent shudders of alarm down the spines of the more substantial mercantile and propertied elements on a scale far wider than the boundaries of Massachusetts, and went far to convince state legislatures of the urgent need to respond to an invitation already received, to send delegates to Philadelphia to meet in convention. We shall notice that Alexander Hamilton calls Shays a "desperate debtor" (No. 6).

Wars are not generally a direct cause of internal revolutions, but they do tend to stimulate developments already in progress. One most important effect of the War of Independence was to bring forward and give continental status, interest, and self-consciousness to a relatively new upper- to middle-class leadership. Great merchants, like Robert Morris of Philadelphia, the "Financier" of the Revolution, numerous army officers from George Washington downwards, politicians who served in the Congress for a statutory three years and then returned to their states with a continental vision—these, some of them allied by marriage across state boundaries, formed an unofficial phalanx of leaders for whom America was greater than any individual state, and who were not prepared to stand aside and watch while the Confederation disintegrated into separate segments. For that was a new danger. People contemplated as a practical possibility that at least three new blocs of states might form themselves into separate federations, or that New York—"the Empire State"—might declare itself independent. If this happened, it was likely that they would collide with each other in the drive to settle the west; to use modern language, the American continent might become "balkanized." Europe would watch with predatory interest.

These were the circumstances that brought about a semi-official and poorly attended meeting in Annapolis in the summer of 1786. That meeting achieved little in itself, but issued a call to all the states to send delegations to assemble in Philadelphia in April 1787.

The official brief accepted by the state assemblies was limited to finding ways to improve the Articles of Confederation. There were those, like Patrick Henry, the famous Virginia orator of the Revolution, who deeply suspected the motives behind the call and refused to attend; but on the whole the Convention was made up of substantial landowners and merchants, many of them also lawyers; several also were former officers of the continental army, with experience of public life and its responsibilities, who had done some serious reading in history and political philosophy. The southern grandees, whether from the rice plantations of South Carolina and Georgia or the more mixed farms of the Chesapeake, were also substantial slave owners. George Washington was only one among several who traveled with an entourage of "unfree" personal servants and who brought them as a matter of course to Philadelphia—where slavery was in process of abolition.

The Convention decided to meet in secret in order to avoid the sudden and temporary storms that might blow up from public debate. This was not as strange a decision as it might now seem; none of the state assemblies met in public, and only that of Philadelphia permitted its debates to be reported in the press. But it had the countervailing effect of insulating the delegates from public opinion in their own states. The proposed constitution aroused many objections from different sectors. The most intense opposition was directed at the failure to include a federal bill of rights. There can be no doubt that the dispersing delegates were genuinely taken by surprise at the scale of the hostility to their work when it was submitted to the peoples of the states for ratification.

Two rival roads had lain before the Convention. One might have been labeled "ambition," the other, "self-protection." The so-called Virginia Plan, drawn up mainly by the Virginia delegation, who had arrived in Philadelphia before the others, proposed to scrap the entire scheme of the Articles and form a new government on a national basis.

After a two week's debate, a group led by the New Jersey delegation put forward a rival plan designed to retain the Articles in strengthened form. The

Virginia Plan prevailed to the extent of serving as an agenda for action; but it would be a mistake to regard the Constitution as a translation of the Virginia Plan. What emerged from four months of debate was a product of collisions, concessions, and often reluctant compromises. A debate about the rival interests of large and small states was transformed into a muted but ominous discussion of the rival interests of slave and free states.

It is altogether too easy and tempting to look back as though the Constitution was a logical result of these debates. But that conclusion fails in the course of a scrutiny of the debates themselves. There was nothing inevitable about the Constitution. A majority of delegates might well have been persuaded to approve different arrangements. The principle of separation of the branches or "powers" of government was generally approved, but no one could have foreseen the rigorous form it would take. Each branch of government is separately described, and its duties laid out, without any suggestion of priorities and with little guidance as to their interrelationships. Moreover, if the original Virginia Plan had prevailed, the system would have been more parliamentary, the president would have been drawn from the membership of Congress and would have been more accountable to it. Such nationalist leaders as Madison, Hamilton, and James Wilson, who secured a tactical point by calling themselves Federalists, suffered a severe strategic setback when the Convention insisted on equal representation for the states in the Senate. Madison viewed this rejection of his own project, of creating a national government based on proportional representation, as a defeat that the new Constitution could hardly survive.

Each state was to have a "republican" form of government although the term was nowhere defined. In fact, delegates relied heavily not on theory but on their long experience of a large measure of self-government through representative institutions. (It was this reliance on and affection for well-tried institutions that distinguished them from the French, who had very little such experience and were more easily attracted by the abstractions of theorists such as Rousseau and Condorcet). Montesquieu, the one great French authority who did impress the Convention, had insisted that the essential spirit of a republic was virtue. But virtue, again, lacked definition. At best, virtue was to be distilled from the concessions that self-interest was to make in the greater interest of the whole. And in the opinion of most of the makers of the Constitution, virtue was to be found among men of learning, leisure, and reflection.

But how could virtue tolerate slavery? The northern states were moving step by gradual step toward the elimination of slavery, an aim they hoped to achieve over time without in any way affecting their economic foundations. It was not so in the major southern states, where a large slave-owning class lived by exploiting the labor of African slavery to build what was virtually an alternative civil order. Such a Virginia slave owner as George Mason could denounce the immorality of slavery; Thomas Jefferson, in his recently published *Notes on the State of Virginia*, had observed its fatal effects on human conduct; but the bleak fact remained that the Convention possessed no power to prevent Georgia and South

Carolina from breaking away to form a separate republic. The Three-Fifths Compromise (see Brief Chronology, p. xl), built a flaw into the foundations of the Union, but was the price to be paid to secure their adherence. The Constitution, without defacing itself by using the word "slavery," included provision for the recovery of fugitive slaves. Twenty more years were to elapse before Congress could act to close the African slave trade.

The Union to be established under the Constitution would be led by a single executive possessed of more "energy" or power to act on its own initiative than would have been possible under the New Jersey Plan; it placed a series of restraints on the powers currently exercised by state governments; it provided for the creation of a general judiciary with specified powers and protections. In Madison's words, the Constitution proposed "a republican remedy" for the diseases most likely to afflict republican government. Yet it certainly placed great power in few hands. In the view of Anti-Federalists, many of whom were equally well educated and substantial, it betrayed the ideals of the Revolution.

Alarmed at the vituperation of the opposition, Alexander Hamilton secured the cooperation of John Jay and James Madison in expounding and explaining the series collectively signed "Publius" and published as *The Federalist.* The pseudonym, which was nowhere explained, presumably because readers were expected to recognize it, was taken from Roman history (or legend). Publius Valerius was credited with having restored the Roman Republic after the dictatorship of Tarquin.

The authors were well matched. Hamilton, born of unwed parents on the West Indian island of Nevis, showed such extraordinary promise as a boy that his neighbors collected the funds to send him to King's College—now Columbia University—in New York. (Its emblem is still a crown.) He qualified in law, but soon after the outbreak of armed conflict joined Washington's staff. He longed for military command, and astonished Washington by his intrepid leadership in storming a palisade. The French statesman Charles Maurice de Talleyrand, who met Hamilton in Philadelphia and later became French foreign secretary, once compared Hamilton favorably to William Pitt and Napoleon. John Jay (who was of French Protestant and Dutch—but not English—descent) was one of the leaders of the New York bar. He entered the Continental Congress and was appointed its foreign secretary; in that capacity, he negotiated a very unpopular agreement with Spain, which gained commercial advantages for Atlantic merchants at the expense of the closure of the outlet of the Mississippi. This raised a storm of protest in the Congress, which refused to ratify; it was just the sort of thing that many Anti-Federalists feared from the new regime. Madison, a Virginian who studied theology under the Rev. John Witherspoon at the College of New Jersey (now Princeton University; there is still a Witherspoon Street in Princeton), returned to take an active part in the political life of the state. He served three years as a representative in Congress, which widened his horizons, but his greatest achievement, as a member of the House of Delegates, was to steer Jefferson's bill for religious freedom through the legislature. Madison shared Jefferson's passionate belief in freedom of the individual conscience. His pamphlet, *A Memorial and Remonstrance* (see below), was reprinted by the dissenting justices of the Supreme Court in the church-and-state case of *Everson v. New Jersey* in 1947.

A good case can be made for claiming *The Federalist* as the culminating political classic of the Enlightenment. It remains in many ways a serene example of Enlightenment ideals. In the first place, it is a secular statement, which never appeals to religious faith or claims to base its reasoning on religious principles. Remove religion from human motivation and you find the structure of *The Federalist* standing, intact, systematic, clear-headed, and based fundamentally on frank appeals to self-interest. It is a product of the Enlightenment also in its conviction in the power of reason. And a classic — yes: it stands as a whole, complete and intelligible in the internal coherence of the arguments. (It can even be hinted that *The Federalist* is more coherent than the Constitution to which it is committed.) But in its modernity, its sense of urgency, its detailed application to working institutions, its frank appeal to the play of conflicting self-interests, it survives as a distinctly American classic.

A Note on Pseudonyms

Eighteenth-century controversialists usually published under the disguise of pseudonyms, which afforded two advantages — a form of personal protection, and at the same time a means of identifying the writer's standpoint. A classical pseudonym added a certain touch of grandeur to such claims. Hamilton had styled himself "Phocion," a Roman politician credited with magnanimity, when pleading for the restoration of confiscated loyalist estates in New York. It was assuredly Hamilton who hit on "Publius," an allusion, as we have seen, to the Publius Valerius who was supposed to have restored the Roman Republic after the tyranny of Tarquin, as the appropriate self-designation for the author of *The Federalist*. The classical style implied a certain hauteur — though the reputation of some classical heroes, such as Cato or Brutus, were common political currency. Cincinnatus was the legendary Roman democrat who returned to his plough after winning a crucial victory. (Washington may have wished he had followed this example!) A generation or so later it would have been "politically incorrect" to have excluded from one's audience those who lacked the appropriate education. The revolutionary period in America in fact revealed a very significant linguistic transition. In the late 1760s, John Dickinson, a wealthy Philadelphia lawyer and legislator, had presented himself as a humble "Farmer in Pennsylvania" in publishing the most widely read tract of that era. Some Anti-Federalist pamphleteers saw political advantage in identifying themselves as agrarians (though not as artisans); Melancton Smith went so far toward a posture of humility as to call himself "A Plebeian" although he was in fact a substantial New York merchant. After moving to America in 1792, the fiery English controversialist William Cobbett adopted with relish the name "Peter Porcupine." Thomas Paine, another English publicist who was equally at home in America, had published *Common Sense* anonymously, but put his name to *The Rights of Man*. The trend was in a democratic direction.

II

Introduction to the Historical Notes: The Meaning of History

The authors of *The Federalist* were aware that they were making history. To make history they had to invoke history. Their arguments are shot through with illustrations ranging chronologically from the Ancient World to their own times, and geographically from the Aegean and the Mediterranean to Europe and the Atlantic. Their historical knowledge, drawn from the classics and from much recent historical writing, mainly British and French, and occasionally from English and colonial records, was extensive, though varying in depth and accuracy; but they were not conducting a seminar in historiography and felt no need or obligation to explain their methods or to articulate a historical philosophy. If we want to discover their historical theory, as we need to do if we are properly to appreciate their text, we are left to extract it from their procedures.

The underlying concept of history, in its bearing on their own times, that emerges from this analysis is essentially utilitarian and two-dimensional; history resembles a chessboard on which past and present are interchangeable. In the relations between states, examples of which are developed at some length from the Ancient World and more recently from the German Empire, little has been altered by experience or by changes in time or circumstance. Historical knowledge was recorded in the sense in which Benjamin Franklin, in founding the American Philosophical Society, dedicated it to "useful knowledge." This perspective, which was current in Enlightenment thought, could be traced recently to David Hume's historical methods and more distantly to the historical culture of the Ancient World, as transmitted by Machiavelli to the political thought of the Italian Renaissance. Allowing for minor variations depending on where they stood in the historical cycle, at all times and places, men, societies, and states were subject to the same drives, ambitions, fears, and dangers. Hamilton and Jay, who are intensely interested in the causes of international or interstate conflict, show themselves to have been impressed by economic and navigational rivalries (ancient in the case of Carthage, modern in the Anglo-Dutch wars of the previous century) that drove states into conflict and war. But Hamilton was also impressed by the human lust for domination, transferring itself from the level of individual to that of political motivation.

This was not the only available long-distance perspective in the Founders' generation. The cyclical view, which was sometimes held in parallel with the "chessboard" view just described, conceived of civilizations and empires as emerging from small beginnings, rising to great heights of complexity, power, and luxury and then declining as a result of internal corruption and consequent military weakness. The greatest historical work in the English language was (and still is) Edward Gibbon's *Decline and Fall of the Roman Empire*, the first volume of which appeared in 1776. The cyclical view had considerable staying power and was exemplified in the 1830s by Thomas Cole's remarkable series of paintings *The Course of Empire*, which may now be seen in the New-York Historical Society on Central Park West. A great and imperial city rises to grandeur and power from pastoral beginnings but then yields to the corrupting influence of luxury, only to succumb to conquering invaders. At its height, the city is dominated by a statue of Mars; when all has crumbled to ruins, the standpoint from which the scene is viewed is taken from the empty base of that statue.[1]

Americans had had time to absorb the writings of Montesquieu, who took a more comparative view than many Enlightenment thinkers and saw different civilizations as being fundamentally influenced by climate and geography, giving rise to different systems of law and morals. It is clear that the authors of *The Federalist* believed that men—for it was men, not women, who directed public life—pursued *self-interest*. The lesson they drew from their historical studies was that self-interest was everywhere and at all times the same. Throughout their history men had striven for power, aggrandizement, and domination; although virtuous and public-spirited motives contributed to the cohesion and survival of societies, self-interest was the dominant force in the motives of men, and must therefore be controlled so as to make it serve as an instrument of self-preservation. "Ambition must be made to counter-act ambition," as Madison said, paraphrasing Montesquieu. At the same time the government must be endowed with *energy*, enabling it to act swiftly and decisively in the national interest when occasion called for executive action. It was Publius's guiding contention that the Constitution, taken as a whole, harnessed the dynamic qualities of human self-government and would turn them to creative courses, opening the way for the achievement of the best rather than the worst of human ambitions: a republican remedy, as we have seen Madison affirming, for the diseases most incident to republican government.

The Constitution that the authors set out to defend was not in fact their own ideal constitution, but they had to defend it, point by point, almost line by line, with a view to explaining how it was best adapted to serve the purpose of maintaining republican institutions intact against internal disruption and external power. Both were real dangers. As was observed in Part I above, the new Union was loosely knit and internally susceptible to conflicts of interest and principle, while major European powers still occupied huge swaths of American territory. The complex of checks and balances of which the Constitution was compounded was in part the outcome of the basic Virginia Plan, but owed more not to some carefully calculated theoretical scheme (as is often argued), but from the collision and interaction of proposals, demands, and concessions that had taken

---

[1] I owe this insight to John Hollander.

place during some four months of debate. The Constitution was created by men who spoke the same political language and shared certain general ideas that they ascribed to the concept of "republican government"—a generality encompassing wide and sometimes incompatible differences—but it was not the direct product of any one system of political thought. Yet in a sense Publius had to make the Constitution *look* as though it had emerged from a coherent plan, so that each part could be explained as integral to every other part.

The joint purpose of the three authors was facilitated by similarities of style. This is not to say that their styles were interchangeable. But they all addressed their readers in a measured, balanced prose that seemed to call for modulations in thought and action. They had read for the most part the same books and were steeped in the classics of the era dating from the late-17th century and known in Britain as Augustan.[2]

A number of claims and counterclaims as to the authorship of some of the essays were made both by Hamilton and Madison, by Hamilton's son, and by subsequent commentators in the 19th century. More recent scholarship had succeeded in reducing the area of doubt to the authorship of Nos. 49–58 and Nos. 62–63 when an important article by Douglass Adair in *The William and Mary Quarterly* (Third Series, vol. 3., nos. 2–3, 1944) resolved all these doubts in favor of Madison. Adair's finding was later confirmed by the application of a computerized methodology.[3] Jacob E. Cooke—writing before the arrival of the computer—observed that the prose styles of Hamilton and Madison were "remarkably similar," and of course they were advancing similar ideas. But there are revealing differences. Only Hamilton, I suggest, could have written the brilliant passage on the origins of Peloponnesian wars in No. 6, and his style seems to shine through No. 9; while an accumulated emphasis on measured but increasingly cogent argument is more characteristic of Madison's method, as found in Nos. 49–58.

As any reader of the text can see, the style called for reasonably sustained concentration, a capacity for holding different ideas in a sort of active suspense, and a conviction that historical knowledge together with a literary education would illustrate and reinforce the logic of the textual argument. The keynote was clarity. Clarity of thought was conveyed through clarity of expression. The style tells us something of the society that it was designed to influence. A high rate of literacy prevailed in many of the American colonies and early states, particularly in New England, New York, and Pennsylvania, whose farmers and artisans read widely in the polemics of the period in newspapers and pamphlets (it is interesting to note that Publius's literary allusions, which are principally from Shakespeare and from Pope's *Essay on Man*, are never attributed in the text,

---

[2] The allusion was to the stabilizing influence of the ascendancy of the Emperor Augustus after the Roman civil wars.

[3] Jacob E. Cooke, *The Federalist*, xx–xxx; and see David Epstein, *The Political Theory of The Federalist* (Chicago: University of Chicago Press, 1984), 199 n. 2.

presumably because they were expected to be familiar to the reader). Publius's measured cadences could be expected to percolate through to manual laborers, farm workers, or mariners (although many of these classes were probably qualified to vote under the property qualifications) from their better educated superiors in the social scale, and above all, from the "gentlemen of influence" as they were sometimes called—a land-owning or mercantile upper class whose social and economic standing was expected to exert its influence on their tenants or employees.

More than once during the debates at Philadelphia, the Greek lawgiver Solon had been quoted as saying that he had not given Sparta a perfect constitution, but the best the people could live with. It was the thrust of Publius's argument that the Constitution, which was in fact much weaker at the center and conceded more power to the states than the authors would have wished, was the best that Americans could live with while continuing to expand their civilization and live at peace with each other under a uniform system of laws. The federal structure that they had established was battered in the 19th century by sectional conflict, which the Founders had foreseen, feared, and sought to avoid. The Civil War subjected the Federal Union to its most extreme test of endurance; what Publius had helped to bring into existence in 1787–1788 had at length to be held together by force of arms rather than by argument and persuasion. But the Union, which survived the Civil War, retained (with considerable assistance from the Supreme Court) its basically federal structure—though qualified by successive amendments.

More than any other work of American political advocacy, *The Federalist* is cited not only by historians and political scientists but by judges and legal counsel as authority for the true meaning of the Constitution. This highly practical application would have gratified Publius, but does not always lead to definitive conclusions. Alternative meanings can be derived from the same text. The ambiguities that give rise to such alternatives sometimes make *The Federalist* problematic as an authority; Publius, like the Constitution itself, will always require interpretation. But interpretation will, one may hope, be formed in light of historical background; the resources, continuities, and divergences within Publius's memory are among the many reasons why his arguments will continue to be relevant long after the present day.

A BRIEF CHRONOLOGY

1215

Magna Carta conceded by King John.

"No Free-man shall be taken, or dispossessed, or imprisoned, of his free tenement or liberties or free customs, or be outlawed, or exiled, or in any way destroyed; nor will we condemn him, nor will we commit him to prison, save by the lawful judgment of his peers or by the laws of the land."

"To none will we sell, to none will we deny, to none will we delay, right or justice." (Revision of 1225)

1688

November: Glorious Revolution in England.

James II flees; though his intentions were unclear, declared by Parliament to have abdicated, leaving throne "vacant" (theoretically impossible).

William III and Mary (James's daughter) enthroned by Parliament as king and queen.

Mennonite Petition in Pennsylvania condemns slavery.

1689

February 13: Convention Parliament adopts and gains agreement of William to Declaration of Rights, later passed into legislation as Bill of Rights. Some items reappear in American Bill of Rights of 1791.

April 18: Overthrow of Dominion of New England; Leisler's rebellion in New York. Coode's rising makes Maryland a royal colony.

Other colonies follow; new charters granted by crown.

Act of Toleration eases condition of dissenters and extends same principle to colonies (without complete success).

1690

Anonymous publication of John Locke's *Two Treatises of Government.*

1691

Massachusetts receives new royal charter. Governor to be appointed by crown; council to be elected by outgoing assembly; political rights for Anglicans.

1692

March: Witch-hunt hysteria in Salem, Massachusetts; nineteen persons executed.

1693

February 8: College of William and Mary receives charter.

1694

Bank of England founded.
December 19: Triennial Act in England establishes three-year parliaments.

1695

Licensing Act expires (without debate), ending state censorship in England.

1696

Board of Trade founded with power to review colonial legislation; admiralty courts set up with jurisdiction over colonies.

1701

Act of Settlement confers tenure "during good behaviour" on English judges, giving independence from crown.

Foundation of Yale College (named Yale in 1718).

1704

Founding of *The Boston News-Letter*.

February 13: Victory of John Churchill, later Duke of Marlborough, at Blenheim. Major defeat for French power. British power in Europe strengthened.

1705

Virginia legislates to treat slaves as real property like land.

In *Smith v. Gould*, Chief Justice Holt declares, "As soon as a Negro comes into England, he becomes free: one may be a villein in England, but not a slave." But this judgment does not affect their status as a slave in the colonies.

1706

"Suspending clause" requires royal approval of certain classes of colonial legislation; later seen as anticipation of "judicial review."

1707

March 6: Act of Union joins Scotland with England, ends independent Scottish parliament (restored, 1999). Scotland retains own legal system; also Presbyterian Church order.

1708

Queen Anne exercises last royal veto.

1712

Board of Trade reverses attempt by Pennsylvania assembly to limit slave trade.

Act of Parliament founds post office, extended to colonies. (Office of Postmaster General will later be held by Benjamin Franklin.)

1713

Peace of Utrecht ends prolonged wars against France. Britain gains privilege in slave trade.

1714

Privy Council committee on colonial affairs revived. Board of Trade's powers diminish.

1716

Septennial Act extends life of a parliament from three to seven years.

1719

South Carolina converted into a royal province by a coup initiated in the Commons House.

Boston Gazette founded, later briefly edited by Benjamin Franklin.

1720

Counsel to Board of Trade gives opinion that Common Law extends to colonies, giving colonists protection of English rights.

John Trenchard and Thomas Gordon begin publication of *Cato's Letters*, exposing corruption in government, attacking privileges of Church of England; widely read in colonies, diffusing Lockeian and 17th-century "Commonwealth" ideas.

1726

January 26: As editor of *The New-England Courant*, Benjamin Franklin prints division list (roll call) in assembly vote on receiving Explanatory Charter.

1728

Benjamin Franklin begins to edit *The Pennsylvania Gazette*.

1729

Attorney General Sir Philip Yorke and Solicitor General Charles Talbot issue assurance to colonial slave owners that they will not lose their property in their slaves if they are baptized or taken with them to England, and that they may legally compel their slaves to return to the plantations.

1732

Franklin founds Library Company of Philadelphia.

Maryland assembly claiming English rights in controversy with Lord Baltimore.

1733

Franklin begins publication of *Poor Richard's Almanac*, popularizing useful knowledge, social satire, and commonsense ideas.

1735

John Peter Zenger, publisher of *New York Weekly Journal*, tried for seditious libel against Governor William Crosby, and acquitted by jury exercising claim to judge law as well as fact.

1736

William Parks founds *The Virginia Gazette*.

1740

Naturalization Act permits colonies to naturalize foreign Protestants after seven years' residence.

John Wesley and George Whitefield stir colonies, contributing to wave of religious revivals.

Land Bank founded in Massachusetts in response to currency shortage but amid strong merchant opposition.

1741

"Negro Conspiracy" terrifies New York and leads to brutal repression.

Parliament closes land bank by extending to colonies the "Bubble Act" forbidding corporations without parliamentary consent.

1743

Franklin founds American Philosophical Society held in Philadelphia for the Promotion of Useful Knowledge. Cofounds Academy of Philadelphia, later renamed University of Pennsylvania (1749).

1746

John Woolman begins travels to bring antislavery cause to fellow Quakers.

1748

Montesquieu's *De L'Esprit des Lois* published in France, translated and published in England as *The Spirit of the Laws* (1752); widely read in colonies.

1750

The Rev. Jonathan Mayhew's sermon in Boston, *A Discourse Concerning Unlimited Submission*, opposing tyranny on centenary of Charles I's execution (1749).

Iron Act controls intercolonial iron trade.

1751

Franklin publishes his *Observations Concerning the Increase of Mankind*, accurately estimating doubling of colonial population every 25 years.

1754

Boston printer Daniel Fowle publishes satirical account of conduct of the House, *A Monster of Monsters* (1754); is arrested and imprisoned for contempt. Publishes *A Total Eclipse of Liberty* (1755).

Albany Plan of Union, drafted by Franklin, agreed by meeting of Iroquois nations and representatives of New England, New York, Pennsylvania, and Maryland; rejected by colonial legislatures.

Philadelphia yearly Quaker meeting resolves against Quakers buying slaves.

King's College, later Columbia University, founded in New York City. (It still retains the crown as its symbol.)

Colonel George Washington opens fire on French in Ohio Valley: first shots in Seven Years War (French and Indian War). French advance on wide front.

1760

Death of George II; accession of youthful George III. Tutored and advised by Earl of Bute, arousing anti-Scottish prejudice.

1761

Writs of Assistance case, Boston, endorses crown officials' power of search without warrant. James Otis's speech inspires the young John Adams.

1763

George Grenville heads British ministry.

John Wilkes, M.P., attacks ministry and alleged Scottish influence on the king in No. 45 of his journal *The North Briton*. "45" becomes opposition symbol.

Ministry orders arrest of Wilkes and search of his premises under a general warrant, i.e., not specific as to items of search. Wilkes released on habeas corpus based on parliamentary privilege. Colonial newspapers report events, sympathetic to Wilkes.

In *Wilkes v. Wood*, Chief Justice of the Common Pleas Sir Charles Pratt, ruling for Wilkes, holds claims of the crown "fundamentally subversive of the liberty of the subject." Origin of American 4th Amendment.

Peace of Paris ends Seven Years War. Britain gains Quebec, East and West Florida, and all North America east of the Mississippi; debate over relative value of Canada and Guadeloupe leads to French retaining the latter.

Uprising led by Native American Chief Pontiac against encroaching British settlements narrowly put down; in response, by royal proclamation, no settlement to be permitted west of line drawn down the Alleghenies. Known as the Proclamation Line. (Readjusted at Fort Stanwyx, 1768.)

Paxton Boys massacre peaceful Conestoga Native Americans in western Pennsylvania.

1764

Parliament passes Revenue Act imposing taxes on colonial imports.

Parliament passes (tax-raising) "Sugar Act," replacing Molasses Act of 1733.

Currency Act withdraws paper money circulating in colonies, precipitating currency crisis. Boston merchants agree to impose nonimportation in retaliation.

James Otis publishes *Rights of the British Colonies Asserted and Proved.* Claims all British legal rights for colonists.

1765

Mutiny (Quartering) Act requires local accommodation for British troops, provoking vehement colonial protests.

Stamp Act passed by Parliament. Stamp duty imposed on nearly all formal transactions, including newspapers. Storm of protest throughout colonies; stamp collector Oliver hanged in effigy in Boston. Oliver resigns. Lt. Governor Thomas Hutchinson's house destroyed by mob.

Anti-Stamp Act publications include Otis's *Vindication of the British Colonies*; John Adams's *Dissertation on the Canon and Feudal Law*; Patrick Henry's "Treason" speech in Virginia House of Burgesses, and passage of protest resolutions.

In New York, Lt. Governor Caldwallder Colden stirs controversy by agreeing to receive appeal from a jury verdict in civil case, *Forsey v. Cunningham.*

In *Entick v. Carrington,* Sir Charles Pratt, now Lord Chief Justice Camden, denounces government claim of power to exercise prepublication censorship as "exorbitant," affirms common-law principle that officers of government are equally subject to law: "And as to the argument of state necessity, or a distinction that has been aimed at between state offences and others, the common law does not understand that kind of reasoning, nor do our books take notice of any such distinctions."

Camden denounces Stamp Act in House of Lords as contrary to principles of the Revolution (of 1688).

October 19: Stamp Act Congress.

New York nonimportation agreement followed by other colonies. Resolutions claim that taxation depends on consent, but colonists are not represented in Parliament. His Majesty's subjects in colonies have all entitlements of those at home. Recent restrictions on trade of colonies will cause hardships. Claim right to petition the crown for repeal.

1766

Soame Jenyns, *Objections to the Taxation of Our American Colonies . . . Briefly Consider'd.* Claims colonies are "virtually" represented in Parliament.

Grenville dismissed by George III: Rockingham, prime minister, promotes repeal of Stamp Act conditionally on passage of Declaratory Act, which asserts Parliament's right to legislate for colonies "in all cases whatsoever."

Second Quartering Act: New York won't comply.

Colonial Anglican appeal for an American bishopric gains support of Church in England. Colonial dissenters apprehensive of consequences.

Instigated by Samuel Adams, Massachusetts House erects a gallery for the public. (Enables Sons of Liberty to intimidate country members.)

March–April: Boston, *The Evening Post* and *The Gazette* under influence of Sons of Liberty begin to publish division lists of votes in House.

1767

Charles Townshend as chancellor of the exchequer introduces new colonial tariffs and creates Board of Customs Commissioners with powers to enforce collection.

Sons of Liberty reorganize in several colonies; raise disorders against customs collectors.

Massachusetts General Court adopts circular letter condemning Townshend acts.

Death of Townshend.

John Dickinson, Pennsylvania lawyer and legislator, writes *Letters from a Farmer in Pennsylvania.* Datelines first letter November 5, corresponding to date of William III's landing in 1688. Widely read throughout colonies, most influential colonial protest to date. Views separation as possibility but says only with extreme reluctance.

1768

Lord Hillsborough as secretary of new colonial department.

Boston mob riots after customs seize John Hancock's sloop *Liberty.*

General Thomas Gage restores order in Boston with British troops.

March: Creation of vice-admiralty courts in Boston. To sit without juries.

1768–1769

Regulator disorders in the Carolinas. Continue into 1771.

1769

Parliament revives a statute of Henry VIII for trials without juries of provincials brought to London.

Lord North forms ministry with confidence of the king.

Wilkes, elected to House of Commons for Middlesex, is expelled, reelected, declared noneligible, and arrested.

South Carolina assembly votes £1500 to assist Wilkes.

Colonies impose nonimportation of British goods.

1770

March 5: Boston massacre. Paul Revere, a silversmith, commemorates with a plate on which Crispus Attucks, an African American victim, is not clearly depicted.

April 12: Parliament repeals Townshend tariffs except on tea.

1771

January: Nonimportation ends. Normal trade relations resume.

May 16: North Carolina Regulators crushed by Gov. William Tryon at Alamance Creek.

September: Boston town meeting, followed by others, forms committee of correspondence.

1772

Rhode Island crowd burns Royal Navy schooner *Gaspée.*

1773

Exchange between Gov. Thomas Hutchinson and Massachusetts House on rival claims of Parliament and colonists.

Parliament confers distribution monopoly on East India Co. to relieve its financial difficulties, reduces tea tax to 3 pence. Colonial protests against taxation without representation and against monopoly.

December 16: Boston Tea Party: disguised as Mohawks, Boston Sons of Liberty board three ships, dump 90,000 pounds of tea (worth 9,000 pounds sterling) in Boston Harbor.

1774

Parliament passes "Intolerable Acts": Boston Port Act closes port of Boston; Massachusetts Government Act restricts towns to one meeting a year and makes members of council appointable by crown. Administration of Justice Act provides for trials of colonists in other counties or in England. Quartering Act. Quebec Act annexes Upper Canada to administration of Ohio Valley, recognizes Roman Catholic religion in formerly French provinces. Arouses alarm and hostility in (Protestant) New England.

"Solemn League and Covenant" on Scottish model drawn up by Boston committee of correspondence; call to subscribers to boycott British goods.

Colonial assemblies dissolved by royal governors.

August: James Wilson, Scottish-born and Edinburgh-educated lawyer practicing in Philadelphia, publishes *Considerations on the Nature and Extent of the Authority of the British Parliament.* On historical grounds, limited to British shores.

September 5: Continental Congress formed of delegates from all states except Georgia assembles in Philadelphia.

Thomas Jefferson writes A *Summary View of the Rights of British America* to instruct Virginia delegates. Asserts equality of Americans with British both as individuals and legally.

Congress receives, then rejects, Joseph Galloway's Plan of Union, which would create a continental parliamentary body to act in harmony with British Parliament.

September 28: Congress adopts Declaration and Resolves protesting against "Intolerable Acts."

October 7: Massachusetts House, meeting in Salem, having been dissolved by Gov. Hutchinson, declares itself a provincial congress.

October 14: Congress adopts Continental Association involving nonimportation to be enforced by local committees of inspection. Object is to put pressure on North government, but not to seek independence. Congress to reconvene the following May but only if Britain fails to comply.

In this period: pamphlet controversy between Daniel Leonard as "Massachusettensis" for crown sovereignty and John Adams as "Novanglus" for sovereignty based on consent; power of Parliament limited to regulation of external trade.

November: The king dissolves Parliament, calls general election, gets support from electors.

1775

March 23: Patrick Henry makes "liberty or death" speech in Virginia convention. Retains female slave as cook.

April 19: Battles of Lexington and Concord. British column severely harassed.

May 10: Second Continental Congress convenes in Philadelphia.

Massachusetts and South Carolina begin emissions of paper money.

Congress issues £200,000 in paper money.

May 23: Generals William Howe, Henry Clinton, and John Burgoyne arrive with British troops.

May 26: Congress resolves on state of defense. Seeks Canadian alliance (to which Canadians do not respond).

June 15: Congress forms a continental army with Washington as commander-in-chief (July 3).

July 6: Congress addresses "Olive Branch" petition to the king, blaming ministry. Publishes Dickinson's "Declaration of Causes for Taking Up Arms." Rejects conciliation proposal from Lord North as inadequate.

August 23: The king declares colonies to be in a state of rebellion.

September 12: Congress recommends colonies to write new constitutions.

September 25: Congress invades Canada; attack fails, with heavy losses.

November 7: Gov. Dunmore of Virginia offers freedom to slaves deserting masters to join British side.

November 16: Edmund Burke's speech in the Commons on Conciliation with the Colonies. Impossibility of keeping colonies permanently subdued.

November 29: Congress forms secret committee to conduct foreign affairs.

1776

January 10: Publication of Thomas Paine's republican *Common Sense* describes George III as "the royal brute of Britain." Powerful impact on American psychology. Frees Americans to consider independence; 120,000 copies distributed throughout colonies.

John Adams, *Thoughts on Government.* Influential in impressing republican principles with separation of powers in state debates on forming constitutions.

March 9: Adam Smith, *The Wealth of Nations* (London). Arguing against mercantilist view that natural resources are finite. Originates science of political economy.

May 10: Congress adopts resolution calling on states to form their own constitutions.

Secret negotiations with France. French court indicates that alliance and military aid will depend on American intentions on independence. French are not interested in assisting Americans to reach a settlement that strengthens them in the Empire, leaving Britain stronger. This affects timing of Declaration of Independence.

May 11: North Carolina adopts provisional constitution. Virginia instructs delegates to vote for independence (May 15). Richard Henry Lee proposes independence in Congress.

June 12: Virginia adopts declaration of rights and new constitution. Separation of church and state, later to become an American constitutional principle.

June 19: Radicals seize power in Pennsylvania.

July 2: Congress adopts Lee's resolution, forms committee to draft declaration; Jefferson entrusted with drafting.

Jefferson's denunciation of slavery struck out by committee; attack on slave trade retained, laying responsibility on George III.

July 4: Declaration of Independence adopted, proclaimed in Philadelphia on July 8; read in New York (July 9); "unanimous" added to preamble (July 15); engrossed (August 2); "United Colonies" altered to "United States" (September 9).

July 12: Committee presents draft of Articles of Confederation to Congress.

September 28: Pennsylvania adopts radical constitution.

October: Virginia House of Burgesses debates and passes Jefferson's bill against entails of estates.

1777

January: Vermont secedes from New York and adopts a radically democratic constitution.

April: Congress resumes consideration of proposed Articles of Confederation. Agrees to amendment of Gov. Thomas Burke of North Carolina guaranteeing state sovereignty.

June 12: Stars and Stripes flag approved.

July: Vermont constitution becomes first to outlaw slavery.

December: Washington establishes winter camp at Valley Forge.

1778

February: Treaty of Amity and Commerce with France. Diplomatic relations established. Franklin as minister.

Congress rejects offer of settlement brought by the Earl of Carlisle.

March: Massachusetts towns reject constitution proposed by the legislature.

March 6: South Carolina adopts constitution restricting public office to Protestants.

October: Virginia attempts statutory regulation of the market.

Winter 1778–1779: In England, with disaffection growing, movement for parliamentary reform based on redistribution of seats promoted in Yorkshire by Rev. Christopher Wyvill.

1779

January: Continental currency revalued at approximately 40:1.

October 22: New York legislation validates seizure of vast tracts of Loyalist property.

Winter 1779–1780: Massachusetts towns debate and vote on new draft constitution.

Dr. Benjamin Franklin FRS,[1] as minister to France, gets French ministry of marine and American Congress to issue orders to warships that if they intercept Captain Cook, who is believed (erroneously) to be returning from the South Seas, he is not to be treated as an enemy but is to be escorted to a British port with all marks of honor.

Pennsylvania attempts statutory regulation of economic activities.

1780

February 7: Congress creates executive departments of Finance, War, and Marine.

Congress puts plan to levy 5 percent impost on foreign imports, but fails to get agreement on necessary amendment of the Articles.

February 26: After New York and Virginia agree to cede western lands to Congress, Maryland ratifies Articles, bringing first U.S. Constitution formally into existence.

March 1: Pennsylvania passes the first Emancipation Act. Slaves' children born after the Act to serve to age 28. Other northern states follow with extreme gradualism. Process planned to culminate in 1850s.

March 19: Massachusetts legislature after some political arithmetic, declares constitution ratified. In force from following October (and, much amended, still in force).

May 4: American Academy of Arts and Science receives charter in Boston.

May 12: Robert Morris of the Philadelphia merchant firm of Willing and Morris is appointed superintendent of finance, known as "the Financier." Makes massive contribution to congressional finances, but his private interests arouse suspicion.

On Morris's initiative, Congress charters Bank of North America, to make short-term loans to Congress and pay interest on national debt. Also chartered by Pennsylvania.

August 22: In Massachusetts, Bett Freeman wins her freedom in *Brom and Bett v. Ashley* on basis of language of the bill of rights in constitution of 1780.

September 6: Congress calls on landed states to cede their claims to Congress for benefit of all. Congress would provide for division of these territories into new states. Maryland is holding up ratification of the Articles to exert leverage on Virginia and New York.

October: Cornwallis under siege at Yorktown by combined forces of French Admiral Rocheambeau and Washington. De Grasse provides naval cover and, lacking naval support, Cornwallis surrenders to Washington (October 18).

---

[1] Fellow of the Royal Society.

1782

March 6: Lord North resigns. Shelburne forms ministry, and following informal probes, formal peace negotiations open in Paris (September).

May: Virginia passes law permitting manumission, leading to eventual emancipation of 10,000 slaves.

June 19: Congress adopts Great Seal of United States.

July 27: Congress, fearing centralization, rejects Robert Morris's Report on Public Credit proposing (1) suspension of interest payments on national debt and (2) taking over by Congress of state debts.

October 8: Treaty of Amity and Commerce with the Netherlands and big loan negotiated by John Adams.

Chancellor George Wythe of Virginia declares principle that courts will intervene if legislature exceeds its powers under constitution.

November 29: Provisional agreement by which Britain recognizes American independence and makes concessions to American fisheries signed in Paris.

1783

March 10: Army officers near mutiny over lack of pay. Washington intervenes. Pausing to apologize for putting on spectacles, he says, "I have grown grey and almost blind in the service of my country." Discontent subsides.

April 11: Congress proclaims end of war.

April 18: Congress requests two changes in Articles: (1) power to raise duties, also (2) basing apportionment on population rather than land values (as now). Both rejected.

April 23: Last shiploads of Loyalists sail from New York, making 100,000 in all. Resettled in Canada and England. Those in permanent exile in England include Thomas Hutchinson, formerly chief justice and Lt. Governor of Massachusetts, and John Tabor Kempe, until 1776 attorney general of New York.

May 13: Society of the Cincinnati formed of officers and their descendants; Washington accepts presidency; widespread protests against "aristocratic" principles; Society of the Friendly Sons of St. Patrick formed in New York City.

May 30: Benjamin Towne begins first daily newspaper in America, *Pennsylvania Evening Post.*

September: Treaty of Paris.

December 23: Washington resigns his commission and presents his sword to Congress.

1784

Deepening economic crisis caused by flight of currency to pay for British imports.

March 25: Britain: Parliament dissolved. General election, in which Pitt, believed to wish peaceful settlement, gains large majority.

November 13: Samuel Seabury consecrated as first American Episcopal bishop.

1785

Maryland and Pennsylvania legislate to meet obligations of both state and Congress to their citizens.

March 24: Mount Vernon Conference promotes free navigation of rivers.

May 10: Publication of Jefferson's *Notes on the State of Virginia.*

October 27: Mathew Carey, Irish immigrant printer, starts to report assembly debates in his paper *The Pennsylvania Evening Herald.*

1786

Madison, in campaign for Jefferson's bill for religious freedom and in opposition to Henry's proposal to raise a tax in support of all Christian sects, writes pamphlet, *A Memorial and Remonstrance,* representing Enlightenment principle of separation of church and state. (Reprinted by dissenting justices in *Everson v. New Jersey,* 1947.)

January 16: Virginia passes Jefferson's Statute for Religious Freedom. (Jefferson's authorship engraved on his tombstone.) (1792: printed in *Encyclopédie Méthodique* in Paris.)

August: Shays's rebellion. Hard money policies driving Massachusetts farmers into debt. Capt. Daniel Shays, former army officer, leads movement beginning in western Massachusetts and spreading to east aimed at closing courts to prevent foreclosures. Shays's rebellion provokes extreme and widespread alarm among creditors; suppressed early 1787.

September 11: Annapolis Convention; commercial agenda, agrees to call for more far-reaching convention in Philadelphia.

United States defaults on interest payments to Spain, France, and (in August) the Netherlands.

1787

February 21: Congress joins call to states to send representatives to Philadelphia to revise Articles.

Madison privately drafts memorandum, "Vices of the Political System of the United States."

April–May 25: Fifty-five members of Constitutional Convention gather in Philadelphia. Convention agrees to meet in secret. Edmund Randolph introduces draft known as "Virginia Plan" proposing to scrap Articles and begin on new foundation.

May: Annual assembly elections in Massachusetts result in heavy defeat of sitting members.

June 14: William Paterson presents "New Jersey Plan" retaining Articles but with stronger powers of government in taxation and both foreign and interstate commerce.

Virginia Plan voted basis of discussion.

July 13: Congress adopts Northwest Ordinance providing for settlement and government under a federal governor of territories to be carved out of Ohio Valley; admissions to statehood to be based on population reaching 60,000 free inhabitants; after expiry of present generation, slavery to be excluded.

July 16: "Connecticut Compromise" adopted over objections of Madison and other nationalists. All states to be equally represented with two members in Senate. Representation according to population in House of Representatives, which is to control money bills. Outcome of prolonged debates: "Three-Fifth Compromise," allowing three-fifths of slaves to count for representation and taxation. Three branches—legislative, executive, and judicial—described and powers assigned separately, implying separation of powers, though this is not explicit. Two-year term for House with complete re-election; six-year term for Senate with one-third re-election. Electoral colleges in states to cast votes for president quadrienally. Provision for return of fugitive slaves; Congress not to close overseas slave trade until 1808. Preamble attributes Constitution to "We the People of the United States...." Congress to have power over foreign and interstate commerce. Constitution to be submitted to state conventions, and to become operative on nine approvals. Signed unanimously by delegates of twelve states (Rhode Island absent).

Gerry and Mason propose a bill of rights, agreed to in principle by Madison.

September 15: Convention closes. A lady at the door: "Dr. Franklin, what have you given us?" Franklin: "A republic, if you can keep it."

Alarmed at hostile reaction, Hamilton recruits Madison and Jay to join him in writing *The Federalist Papers*. Series runs from October 27, 1787 to May 28, 1788.

1788

January 2: Georgia ratifies.

January 9: Connecticut ratifies.

February 6: Massachusetts ratifies, proposing nine amendments.

February 19: French antislavery society, Les Amis des Noirs, founded in Paris.

March 24: Rhode Island rejects Constitution by referendum. Federalists abstain.

April 28: Maryland ratifies.

May 23: South Carolina ratifies.

June 21: New Hampshire (proposing twelve amendments) becomes ninth state; the Constitution is now in effect and elections can proceed.

June 25: Virginia ratifies, proposing twenty amendments.

July 21: North Carolina decides to withhold ratification pending a bill of rights.

July 24: New York ratifies.

September 13: Congress decides on New York as seat of government.

December 23: Congress accepts cession from Maryland of ten square miles for future District of Columbia.

1789

March: First Congress convenes in New York.

April 5: Ballots of electoral college counted. For president, Washington, 69; for vice president, John Adams, 34.

April 11: John Fenno founds and edits *Gazette of the United States*.

April 30: Washington inaugurated first president of the United States.

May 5–6: Proposals in Congress for a second convention. Opposed by Madison, who is appointed to chair drafting committee for amendments.

July 14: Storming of the Bastille in Paris.

August 13–24: House debates amendments. Madison prefers to integrate them into Constitution; House votes to add them. House sends amendments to Senate.

September 24: House accepts report of conference committee set up to work out differences; Senate concurs.

Judiciary Act establishes judicial system. Jay appointed chief justice.

Congress offers twelve possible amendments.

November 21: North Carolina ratifies.

1790

March 23: Franklin publishes attack on slavery and asks Congress to abolish it.

April 15: Franklin dies.

May 29: Rhode Island ratifies.

1791

June 25: Virginia ratifies ten amendments, making Bill of Rights part of the Constitution.

THEMES

No. 1: Jay   Sets out the plan for the whole project.

No. 2: Jay   Advantages conferred by providence on the Americans: their similarity in ancestry, in language, in religion, in principles of government. Importance of preserving these advantages. Wisdom of the Congress of 1774.

No. 3: Jay   Dangers facing the present Union. Discussion of causes of war.

No. 4: Jay   External dangers: Union the safeguard.

No. 5: Jay   Union of Scotland with England cited as example of advantages of union in principle. Need to avoid dangers of North-South antagonisms.

No. 6: Hamilton   On human nature. Men are seen to be ambitious, vindictive and rapacious. Delusions and dangers of expecting their relations to be harmonious. Causes of the Peloponnesian war. English wars against Louis XIV. First mention of Shays's rebellion as evidence of internal dangers. Republics are just as likely as other forms of government to go to war from material motives.

No.7: Hamilton   Dangers from rivalry between states, particularly in the west. Public debt seen as potential cause of conflict.

No. 8: Hamilton   Threatening consequences of internal wars. Dangers of standing armies.

No. 9: Hamilton   A firm Union is the best safeguard to peace and liberty of the states; a barrier against domestic factions and insurrections. Safety in distribution of power in departments of government. Answers the contention of Montesquieu that liberty is safest in small republics. The proposed constitution does not threaten state governments but makes them "constituent parts of the national sovereignty."

No. 10: Madison   Lists complaints about the present system. Dangers of faction; defines faction as a number of citizens united "by some common impulse of passion, or of interest, adverse to the rights of other citizens, or the permanent and aggregate interests of the community." Methods of removing causes of faction can be worse than the disease. Unequal distribution of property as cause of instability. Diversity of human passions and interests reflected in diversity of faculties, inequalities in society result from different and unequal faculties of acquiring property. Modern governments primary regulation is the regulation of conflicting interests. Differences between a Democracy and a Republic; a Republic filters popular passions by reposing authority in the wiser elements in society. The constitution offers "a Republican remedy for the diseases most incident to Republican Government."

No. 11: Hamilton   American interests in commerce call for vigorous national government. Importance to America of naval power.

No. 12: Hamilton Commercial prosperity will promote interests of revenue. One national government would be able to extend the duties on imports far more effectively than state governments.

No. 13: Hamilton Speculations on possibilities that America will divide into three confederacies.

No. 14: Hamilton A democracy will be confined to a small spot; a republic may be extended over a large region. America made the discovery of representation as basis of unmixed and at the same time extended republics. Prospect that the Union will facilitate domestic intercourse.

No. 15: Hamilton Need to confer energy on the powers of the government of the United States. Those who aim at augmenting the federal authority without diminishing that of the states are contending for incompatible principles, a political monster; an *imperio in imperium*. The nature of sovereign power is incompatible with restraint.

No. 16: Hamilton Continuation of the same argument. National authority will be asserted through the medium of the courts of justice. This essay anticipates the argument fully developed in No. 78, conferring on the courts the power to pronounce resolutions of the inferior authorities unconstitutional when contradictory to the supreme law of the land.

No. 17: Hamilton On the other hand, state governments will find it easier to encroach on national authority than for national authority to encroach on states. Compares separate governments in a confederacy with feudal baronies with the advantage that local governments will possess the confidence of the people.

No. 18: Madison Begins a long discourse on lessons to be learned from history of leagues and associations of republics in the ancient world. Case of Amphyctionic council which eventually collapsed through lack of adequate power. The argument develops through the experience of the Peloponnesian war and the Achaean league, illustrating the same principle.

No. 19: Madison Continues the same argument with reference to the history of the German empire, also invoking Poland and the Swiss cantons.

No. 20: Madison The argument developed with reference to the United Netherlands. A sovereign over sovereigns "as contradistinguished from individuals" is a solecism in theory and is subversive of civil order.

No. 21: Hamilton On government finance. State contributions by quotas a fundamental error, the result would be inequalities leading to the eventual destruction of the Union.

No. 22: Hamilton Importance of the power to regulate commerce. Cites British experience. Equal suffrage among states, which gives to Rhode Island the same power as Massachusetts, Connecticut, or New York is incompatible with republican principles. Republican government requires that the majority should prevail. Need for a judicial power capable of expounding the law and enforcing treaties. American government on the basis of the consent of the people, Hamilton here means the American people as a whole, not the people of the states.

No. 23: Hamilton   Necessity for powers of defense to exist without limitation; future exigencies cannot be foreseen.

No. 24: Hamilton   An objection to the proposed federal government in that it fails to forbid standing armies in peacetime. But only two state constitutions have that interdiction. United States needs a navy to protect its commercial interests.

No. 25: Hamilton   State governments cannot provide for common defense. Further reference to republics of the ancient world.

No. 26: Hamilton   Continues discussion of military establishments in times of peace with reference to medieval England and the Netherlands. But the militia will always be a safeguard.

No. 27: Hamilton   The general government will be better administered than state governments.

No. 28: Hamilton   In the event of emergency the force to be employed must be proportional to the extent of the danger.

No. 29: Hamilton   Continues discussion of the role of the militia as a republican safeguard.

No. 30: Hamilton   The importance of the control of the supply of money. In the Ottoman empire the sovereign had no power to impose a new tax, with disastrous consequences for the provinces. Anticipates that Americans will experience similar vicissitudes to other nations. Americans not exempt from vices of human nature.

No. 31: Hamilton   The federal government needs an unqualified power of taxation.

No. 32: Hamilton   Consolidation of the states into one complete sovereignty (seen by Anti-Federalists as aim of the Constitution) would imply subordination; but the plan of the convention only aims at a partial consolidation. State governments would retain rights of sovereignty not exclusively delegated to the United States.

No. 33: Hamilton   Problems arising from conflicts of laws. An anticipation of thesis on judicial power that will be developed in No. 78.

No. 34: Hamilton   Public expenses and public debt.

No. 35: Hamilton   Answers objections to the indefinite power of taxation in the Union. This leads to discussion on representation. Representation by class or by interests is visionary and impracticable. The legislature will be composed of superior members of each interest group.

No. 36: Hamilton   Representation of the people will consist of upper classes but not confined to them. Emphatic statement of equality of opportunity.

No. 37: Madison   Importance of energy in government. Impossible to define the boundaries between the legislature, executive, and judiciary; they are always overlapping just as the different branches of jurisdiction have not been finally established in Great Britain. Impossible to define law for the future. Language is imprecise even in the words of the almighty.

No. 38: Madison   Further invocation of ancient history. Replying to Anti-Federalists' objections, he contrasts the defects they discern to those which are being exchanged for it. Answers objection to the lack of a Bill of Rights.

No. 39: Madison   Concludes that the proposed constitution is neither wholly national nor wholly federal; it leaves a residual and inviolable sovereignty to the states in all matters not conceded to the government of the United States.

No. 40: Madison   Discusses the question of whether the convention was authorized to propose the constitution in this mixed form.

No. 41: Madison   Two general views of the constitution: first, relating to the power vested in the government; second, the particular structure of the government proposed. This essay deals with the powers of the government regulating commerce and maintaining harmony among states. All the powers conferred are necessary to the operation of the government.

No. 42: Madison   Powers relating to intercourse with foreign nations.

No. 43: Madison   Powers over residual issues. Contains a reference to slavery and the possibility of slave insurrection.

No. 44: Madison   Restrictions on the authorities of the states.

No. 45: Madison   All powers of the federal government have been shown to be necessary and proper to its legitimate purposes. Will the whole mass of them be dangerous to the authority left to the states? The state governments as constituent and essential parts of the federal government.

No. 46: Madison   Discusses the popularity with the people of the two forms of government, the federal and state. The powers to be lodged in the federal government do not threaten the states.

No. 47: Madison   On the separation of powers. Discusses views of Montesquieu and the British constitution and goes on to analyze state constitutions.

No. 48: Madison   Connections among branches of government are essential to its operation.

No. 49: Madison   Quotes Jefferson's notes on the state of Virginia; also quotes Hume that all government rests on opinion. Aggrandizement of the legislative at the expense of the other departments is a tendency of republican governments.

No. 50: Madison   Continues discussion on departments of governments.

No. 51: Madison   Each department must be given powers to resist encroachment by the others. "The interests of the man must be connected with the constitutional rights of the place." Legislative authority predominates in republican government. "Justice is the end of government."

No. 73: Hamilton   Adequate provision must be made for the support of the executive in order to give it sufficient vigor. The executive must be able to restrain the legislature.

No. 74: Hamilton   Further powers of the President.

No. 75: Hamilton   Power to make treaties with the advice and consent of the Senate.

No. 76: Hamilton   President's power to nominate to judicial and administrative offices.

No. 77: Hamilton   The Senate again: it will contribute to stability.

No. 78: Hamilton   Exposition of the principle of judicial review.

No. 79: Hamilton   The importance of providing the judiciary with a fixed provision for their support to secure their independence.

No. 80: Hamilton   The proper object of judicial power.

No. 81: Hamilton   Analysis of the judicial department. An attribute of state sovereignty is that it is not amenable to a suit without its own consent. Every state enjoys this protection.

No. 82: Hamilton   Only time can mature and protect this system.

No. 83: Hamilton   Objection to the Constitution on grounds that it lacks trial by jury in civil cases. This is spurious. The silence of the Constitution should not be taken to abolish trial by jury. The legislature is at liberty to adopt that institution. Trial by jury prevails in courts of common law. Discusses English and American principles of jurisprudence.

No. 84: Hamilton   Responds to a handful of remaining objections not already answered in the main body of the text.

No. 85: Hamilton   Expresses disgust at charges on the wealthy, the well-born, and the great in the American states. Publius admits that he may have expressed himself too forcibly in replying to some objections. Precarious state of national affairs. A nation without a national government is "an awful spectacle."

ONE

ALEXANDER HAMILTON
October 27, 1787
Introduction

To the People of the State of New York.

After an unequivocal experience of the inefficacy of the subsisting federal government, you are called upon to deliberate on a new constitution for the United States of America. The subject speaks its own importance; comprehending in its consequences, nothing less than the existence of the UNION, the safety and welfare of the parts of which it is composed, the fate of an empire, in many respects, 5
the most interesting in the world. It has been frequently remarked, that it seems to have been reserved to the people of this country, by their conduct and example, to decide the important question, whether societies of men are really capable or not, of establishing good government from reflection and choice, or whether they are forever destined to depend, for their political constitutions, on accident 10
and force. If there be any truth in the remark, the crisis, at which we are arrived, may with propriety be regarded as the aera in which that decision is to be made; and a wrong election of the part we shall act, may, in this view, deserve to be considered as the general misfortune of mankind.

This idea will add the inducements of philanthropy to those of patriotism to 15
heighten the solicitude, which all considerate and good men must feel for the event. Happy will it be if our choice should be directed by a judicious estimate of our true interests, unperplexed and unbiassed by considerations not connected with the public good. But this is a thing more ardently to be wished, than seriously to be expected. The plan offered to our deliberations, affects too many par- 20
ticular interests, innovates upon too many local institutions, not to involve in its discussion a variety of objects foreign to its merits, and of views, passions and prejudices little favourable to the discovery of truth.

Line 5 "Empire," which in this context refers to the sovereignty of the Union, does not connote what we would call "imperialism." The first English use of "empire" to define a self-contained polity acknowledging no higher authority occurred in the reign of Henry VIII in 1533 in the Act in Restraint of Appeals (to Rome), which severed England's connection with the Catholic Church—henceforth known in the English-speaking world as the *Roman* Catholic Church.
Line 6 "Interesting" is used in the modern sense of "important."

Among the most formidable of the obstacles which the new constitution will
25 have to encounter, may readily be distinguished the obvious interest of a certain
class of men in every state to resist all changes which may hazard a diminution of
the power, emolument and consequence of the offices they hold under the state-
establishments—and the perverted ambition of another class of men, who will
either hope to aggrandise themselves by the confusions of their country, or will flat-
30 ter themselves with fairer prospects of elevation from the subdivision of the empire
into several partial confederacies, than from its union under one government.

It is not, however, my design to dwell upon observations of this nature. I am
well aware that it would be disingenuous to resolve indiscriminately the opposition of any set of men (merely because their situations might subject them to sus-
35 picion) into interested or ambitious views: Candour will oblige us to admit, that
even such men may be actuated by upright intentions; and it cannot be doubted
that much of the opposition which has made its appearance, or may hereafter
make its appearance, will spring from sources, blameless at least, if not respectable, the honest errors of minds led astray by preconceived jealousies and
40 fears. So numerous indeed and so powerful are the causes, which serve to give a
false bias to the judgment, that we upon many occasions, see wise and good men
on the wrong as well as on the right side of questions, of the first magnitude to society. This circumstance, if duly attended to, would furnish a lesson of moderation to those, who are ever so thoroughly persuaded of their being in the right, in
45 any controversy. And a further reason for caution, in this respect, might be drawn
from the reflection, that we are not always sure, that those who advocate the truth
are influenced by purer principles than their antagonists. Ambition, avarice, personal animosity, party opposition, and many other motives, not more laudable
than these, are apt to operate as well upon those who support as upon those who
50 oppose the right side of a question. Were there not even these inducements to
moderation, nothing could be more ill-judged than that intolerant spirit, which
has, at all times, characterised political parties. For, in politics as in religion, it is
equally absurd to aim at making proselytes by fire and sword. Heresies in either
can rarely be cured by persecution.
55 And yet however just these sentiments will be allowed to be, we have already
sufficient indications, that it will happen in this as in all former cases of great national discussion. A torrent of angry and malignant passions will be let loose. To
judge from the conduct of the opposite parties, we shall be led to conclude, that
they will mutually hope to evince the justness of their opinions, and to increase
60 the number of their converts by the loudness of their declamations, and by the
bitterness of their invectives. An enlightened zeal for the energy and efficiency of

---

Lines 24–31 This paragraph addresses the problem of the entrenched interests of
state politicians fearing a loss of power under a constitution that diminished the
powers of the states. It also addresses those who expected to take advantage of widespread fiscal confusions in many states, a problem that more powerful federal government would resolve.

government will be stigmatized, as the off-spring of a temper fond of despotic power and hostile to the principles of liberty. An overscrupulous jealousy of danger to the rights of the people, which is more commonly the fault of the head than of the heart, will be represented as mere pretence and artifice; the bait for popularity at the expence of public good. It will be forgotten, on the one hand, that jealousy is the usual concomitant of violent love, and that the noble enthusiasm of liberty is too apt to be infected with a spirit of narrow and illiberal distrust. On the other hand, it will be equally forgotten, that the vigour of government is essential to the security of liberty; that, in the contemplation of a sound and well informed judgment, their interests can never be separated; and that a dangerous ambition more often lurks behind the specious mask of zeal for the rights of the people, than under the forbidding appearance of zeal for the firmness and efficiency of government. History will teach us, that the former has been found a much more certain road to the introduction of despotism, than the latter, and that of those men who have overturned the liberties of republics the greatest number have begun their carreer, by paying an obsequious court to the people, commencing demagogues and ending tyrants.

In the course of the preceeding observations I have had an eye, my fellow citizens, to putting you upon your guard against all attempts, from whatever quarter, to influence your decision in a matter of the utmost moment to your welfare by any impressions other than those which may result from the evidence of truth. You will, no doubt, at the same time, have collected from the general scope of them that they proceed from a source not unfriendly to the new constitution. Yes, my countrymen, I own to you, that, after having given it an attentive consideration, I am clearly of opinion, it is your interest to adopt it. I am convinced, that this is the safest course for your liberty, your dignity, and your happiness. I affect not reserves, which I do not feel. I will not amuse you with an appearance of deliberation, when I have decided. I frankly acknowledge to you my convictions, and I will freely lay before you the reasons on which they are founded. The consciousness of good intentions disdains ambiguity. I shall not however multiply professions on this head. My motives must remain in the depository of my own breast: My arguments will be open to all, and may be judged of by all. They shall at least be offered in a spirit, which will not disgrace the cause of truth.

Line 63 "Jealousy" in this period, in this political sense, does not refer to envy, but to a heightened concern for some right or interest. "Overscrupulous" means excessive.

Lines 69–70 ". . . the vigour of government is essential to the security of liberty." Liberty is secured by *strong* government; weak government leads to anarchy and loss of security. This will be a central theme of *The Federalist*.

Line 74 "History" for these writers usually means ancient Greek or Roman history. But as future essays will show, they are also conversant with much of early modern European history.

I propose in a series of papers, to discuss the following interesting particulars. — *The utility of the* UNION *to your political prosperity.* — *The insufficiency of the present confederation to preserve that union.* — *The necessity of a government at least equally energetic with the one proposed to the attainment of this object.* —

100 *The conformity of the proposed constitution to the true principles of republican government.* — *Its analogy to your own state constitution* — and lastly, *The additional security, which its adoption will afford to the preservation of that species of government, to liberty and to property.*

In the progress of this discussion I shall endeavour to give a satisfactory answer

105 to all the objections which shall have made their appearance, that may seem to have any claim to your attention.

It may perhaps be thought superfluous to offer arguments to prove the utility of the UNION, a point, no doubt, deeply engraved on the hearts of the great body of the people in every state, and one, which it may be imagined has no ad-

110 versaries. But the fact is, that we already hear it whispered in the private circles of those who oppose the new constitution, that the Thirteen States are of too great extent for any general system, and that we must of necessity resort to separate confederacies of distinct portions of the whole. This doctrine will, in all probability, be gradually propagated, till it has votaries enough to countenance an

115 open avowal of it. For nothing can be more evident, to those who are able to take an enlarged view of the subject, than the alternative of an adoption of the new constitution, or a dismemberment of the union. It will therefore be of use to begin by examining the advantages of that union, the certain evils and the probable dangers, to which every state will be exposed from its dissolution. — This

120 shall accordingly constitute the subject of my next address.

PUBLIUS.

The same idea, tracing the arguments to their consequences, is held out in several of the late publications against the new constitution.

Line 96–103 Here Publius outlines the general plan of the work—but only in very broad terms—that leave plenty of room for deviations and counterattacks on Anti-Federalist arguments as they might arise.

Lines 110–15 An implicit reference to the views of Montesquieu (see note, Line 59). Republican liberties are secure only in relatively small states. This theme will reappear with full annotation in No. 9.

TWO

JOHN JAY
October 31, 1787

Concerning Dangers from Foreign Force and Influence

To the People of the State of New York.

When the people of America reflect that they are now called upon to decide a question, which, in its consequences, must prove one of the most important, that ever engaged their attention, the propriety of their taking a very comprehensive, as well as a very serious view of it, will be evident.

Nothing is more certain than the indispensable necessity of government; and   5
it is equally undeniable, that whenever and however it is instituted, the people must cede to it some of their natural rights, in order to vest it with requisite powers. It is well worthy of consideration therefore, whether it would conduce more to the interest of the people of America, that they should, to all general purposes, be one nation, under one federal government, than that they should divide   10
themselves into separate confederacies, and give to the head of each, the same kind of powers which they are advised to place in one national government.

It has until lately been a received and uncontradicted opinion, that the prosperity of the people of America depended on their continuing firmly united, and the wishes, prayers, and efforts of our best and wisest citizens have been con-   15
stantly directed to that object. But politicians now appear, who insist that this opinion is erroneous, and that instead of looking for safety and happiness in union, we ought to seek it in a division of the states into distinct confederacies or sovereignties. However extraordinary this new doctrine may appear, it nevertheless has its advocates; and certain characters who were much opposed to it for-   20
merly, are at present of the number. Whatever may be the arguments or inducements, which have wrought this change in the sentiments and declarations of these Gentlemen, it certainly would not be wise in the people at large to adopt these new political tenets without being fully convinced that they are founded in truth and sound policy.   25

It has often given me pleasure to observe, that independent America was not composed of detached and distant territories, but that one connected, fertile, wide spreading country was the portion of our western sons of liberty. Providence has in a particular manner blessed it with a variety of soils and productions, and watered it with innumerable streams, for the delight and accommodation of its inhabitants.   30
A succession of navigable waters forms a kind of chain round its borders, as if to bind it together; while the most noble rivers in the world, running at convenient distances, present them with highways for the easy communication of friendly aids, and the mutual transportation and exchange of their various commodities.

35   With equal pleasure I have as often taken notice, that Providence has been
pleased to give this one connected country, to one united people, a people de-
scended from the same ancestors, speaking the same language, professing the
same religion, attached to the same principles of government, very similar in
their manners and customs, and who, by their joint counsels, arms, and efforts,
40   fighting side by side throughout a long and bloody war, have nobly established
their general liberty and independence.
      This country and this people seem to have been made for each other, and it
appears as if it was the design of Providence, that an inheritance so proper and
convenient for a band of brethren, united to each other by the strongest ties,
45   should never be split into a number of unsocial, jealous and alien sovereignties.
      Similar sentiments have hitherto prevailed among all orders and denomina-
tions of men among us. To all general purposes we have uniformly been one
people—each individual citizen every where enjoying the same national rights,
privileges, and protection. As a nation we have made peace and war—as a nation
50   we have vanquished our common enemies—as a nation we have formed alliances and made treaties, and entered into various compacts and conventions
with foreign states.
      A strong sense of the value and blessings of union induced the people, at a
very early period, to institute a federal government to preserve and perpetuate it.
55   They formed it almost as soon as they had a political existence; nay at a time,
when their habitations were in flames, when many of their citizens were bleed-
ing, and when the progress of hostility and desolation left little room for those
calm and mature enquiries and reflections, which must ever precede the formation of a wise and well balanced government for a free people. It is not to be won-
60   dered at that a government instituted in times so inauspicious, should on
experiment be found greatly deficient and inadequate to the purpose it was intended to answer.
      This intelligent people perceived and regretted these defects. Still continuing
no less attached to union, than enamoured of liberty, they observed the danger,
65   which immediately threatened the former and more remotely the latter; and
being persuaded that ample security for both, could only be found in a national
government more wisely framed, they, as with one voice, convened the late convention at Philadelphia, to take that important subject under consideration.

Lines 35–45 In view of the variety of peoples and sects already present in the United States, it is significant that the authors of *The Federalist* think of the people as so largely homogeneous—and regard this as a primary source of national strength. The theme recurs in Washington's *Farewell Address*.

Lines 47–48 We are already "one people," and equality of rights inheres in national citizenship; this subtly preempts American nationality for the nation rather than the states.

This convention, composed of men who possessed the confidence of the people, and many of whom had become highly distinguished by their patriotism, virtue and wisdom, in times which tried the minds and hearts of men, undertook the arduous task. In the mild season of peace, with minds unoccupied by other subjects, they passed many months in cool uninterrupted and daily consultations: and finally, without having been awed by power, or influenced by any passions except love for their country, they presented and recommended to the people the plan produced by their joint and very unanimous counsels.

Admit, for so is the fact, that this plan is only *recommended*, not imposed, yet let it be remembered, that it is neither recommended to *blind* approbation, nor to *blind* reprobation; but to that sedate and candid consideration, which the magnitude and importance of the subject demand, and which it certainly ought to receive. But, as has already been remarked, it is more to be wished than expected that it may be so considered and examined. Experience on a former occasion teaches us not to be too sanguine in such hopes. It is not yet forgotten, that well grounded apprehensions of imminent danger induced the people of America to form the memorable congress of 1774. That body recommended certain measures to their constituents, and the event proved their wisdom; yet it is fresh in our memories how soon the press began to teem with pamphlets and weekly papers against those very measures. Not only many of the officers of government who obeyed the dictates of personal interest, but others from a mistaken estimate of consequences, or the undue influence of ancient attachments, or whose ambition aimed at objects which did not correspond with the public good, were indefatigable in their endeavours to persuade the people to reject the advice of that patriotic congress. Many indeed were deceived and deluded, but the great majority of the people reasoned and decided judiciously; and happy they are in reflecting that they did so.

They considered that the congress was composed of many wise and experienced men. That being convened from different parts of the country, they brought with them and communicated to each other a variety of useful information. That in the course of the time they passed together in enquiring into and discussing the true interests of their country, they must have acquired very accurate knowledge on that head. That they were individually interested in the public liberty and prosperity, and therefore that it was not less their inclination, than their duty, to recommend only such measures, as after the most mature deliberation they really thought prudent and advisable.

These and similar considerations then induced the people to rely greatly on the judgment and integrity of the congress; and they took their advice, notwithstanding the various arts and endeavours used to deter and dissuade them from it. But if the people at large had reason to confide in the men of that congress, few of whom had then been fully tried or generally known, still greater reason have they now to respect the judgment and advice of the convention, for it is well known that some of the most distinguished members of that congress, who have been since tried and justly approved for patriotism and abilities, and who have grown old in acquiring political information, were also members of this convention, and carried into it their accumulated knowledge and experience.

115   It is worthy of remark that not only the first, but every succeeding congress, as well as the late convention, have invariably joined with the people in thinking that the prosperity of America depended on its union. To preserve and perpetuate it, was the great object of the people in forming that convention, and it is also the great object of the plan which the convention has advised them to adopt.
120 With what propriety therefore, or for what good purposes, are attempts at this particular period, made by some men, to depreciate the importance of the union? or why is it suggested that three or four confederacies would be better than one? I am persuaded in my own mind, that the people have always thought right on this subject, and that their universal and uniform attachment to the
125 cause of the union, rests on great and weighty reasons, which I shall endeavour to develope and explain in some ensuing papers. They who promote the idea of substituting a number of distinct confederacies in the room of the plan of the convention, seem clearly to foresee that the rejection of it would put the continuance of the union in the utmost jeopardy. That certainly would be the case, and
130 I sincerely wish that it may be as clearly foreseen by every good citizen, that whenever the dissolution of the union arrives, America will have reason to exclaim in the words of the Poet, "FAREWELL, A LONG FAREWELL, TO ALL MY GREATNESS."

    PUBLIUS.

Lines 132–33 "The Poet" is Shakespeare. "FAREWELL! A LONG FAREWELL TO ALL MY GREATNESS." *Henry VIII*, 3.2.352 (Cardinal Wolsey).

THREE

JOHN JAY
November 3, 1787
The Same Subject Continued

To the People of the State of New York.

It is not a new observation that the people of any country (if like the Americans intelligent and well informed) seldom adopt, and steadily persevere for many years, in an erroneous opinion respecting their interests. That consideration naturally tends to create great respect for the high opinion which the people of America have so long and uniformly entertained of the importance of their continuing firmly united under one federal government, vested with sufficient powers for all general and national purposes.

The more attentively I consider and investigate the reasons which appear to have given birth to this opinion, the more I become convinced that they are cogent and conclusive.

Among the many objects to which a wise and free people find it necessary to direct their attention, that of providing for their *safety* seems to be the first. The *safety* of the people doubtless has relation to a great variety of circumstances and considerations, and consequently affords great latitude to those who wish to define it precisely and comprehensively.

At present I mean only to consider it as it respects security for the preservation of peace and tranquility, as well against dangers from *foreign arms and influence,* as from dangers of the *like kind* arising from domestic causes. As the former of these comes first in order, it is proper it should be the first discussed. Let us therefore proceed to examine whether the people are not right in their opinion, that a cordial union under an efficient national government, affords them the best security that can be devised against *hostilities* from abroad.

The number of wars which have happened or will happen in the world, will always be found to be in proportion to the number and weight of the causes, whether *real* or *pretended,* which *provoke* or *invite* them. If this remark be just, it becomes useful to inquire, whether so many *just* causes of war are likely to be given by *united* America, as by *disunited* America; for if it should turn out that united America will probably give the fewest, then it will follow that, in this respect, the union tends most to preserve the people in a state of peace with other nations.

The *just* causes of war for the most part arise either from violations of treaties, or from direct violence. America has already formed treaties with no less than six

---

Lines 31–39 Nations with which the United States had treaties were France (1778), the Netherlands (1782), Great Britain (1783), Sweden (1783), and Prussia (1785).

foreign nations, and all of them, except Prussia, are maritime, and therefore able to annoy and injure us: She has also extensive commerce with Portugal, Spain, and Britain, and with respect to the two latter, has in addition the circumstance of neighbourhood to attend to.

It is of high importance to the peace of America, that she observe the laws of nations towards all these powers, and to me it appears evident that this will be more perfectly and punctually done by one national government, than it could be either by thirteen separate states, or by three or four distinct confederacies. For this opinion various reasons may be assigned.

When once an efficient national government is established, the best men in the country will not only consent to serve, but also will generally be appointed to manage it; for although town or county, or other contracted influence may place men in state assemblies, or senates, or courts of justice, or executive depart-ments; yet more general and extensive reputation for talents and other qualifica-tions, will be necessary to recommend men to offices under the national government—especially as it will have the widest field for choice, and never ex-perience that want of proper persons, which is not uncommon in some of the states. Hence it will result, that the administration, the political counsels, and the judicial decisions of the national government will be more wise, systematical and judicious, than those of individual states, and consequently more satisfactory with respect to other nations, as well as more *safe* with respect to us.

Under the national government, treaties and articles of treaties, as well as the laws of nations, will always be expounded in one sense, and executed in the same manner—whereas adjudications on the same points and questions, in thirteen states, or in three or four confederacies, will not always accord or be consistent; and that as well from the variety of independent courts and judges appointed by different and independent governments, as from the different local laws and interests which may affect and influence them. The wisdom of the convention in committing such questions to the jurisdiction and judgment of courts appointed by, and responsible only to one national government, cannot be too much commended.

Because prospect of present loss or advantage, may often tempt the governing party in one or two states to swerve from good faith and justice; but those temp-tations not reaching the other states, and consequently having little or no influ-ence on the national government, the temptation will be fruitless, and good faith and justice be preserved. The case of the treaty of peace with Britain, adds great weight to this reasoning.

Treaties with Denmark and Portugal were under negotiation, perhaps anticipating the sixth, which has not been identified.

Line 35 The reference to "neighbourhood" alludes to Britain's possession of Canada and Spain's possession of Florida, a situation that posed continuing diplomatic prob-lems for those states of the United States most susceptible to external threat.

If even if the governing party in a state should be disposed to resist such temp- *70* tations, yet as such temptations may, and commonly do result from circum- stances peculiar to the state, and may affect a great number of the inhabitants, the governing party may not always be able if willing to prevent the injustice meditated, or to punish the aggressors. But the national government, not being affected by those local circumstances, will neither be induced to commit the wrong themselves, nor want power or inclination to prevent, or punish its com- *75* mission by others.

So far therefore as either designed or accidental violations of treaties and of the laws of nations afford *just* causes of war, they are less to be apprehended under one general government, than under several lesser ones, and in that re- spect, the former most favors the *safety* of the people. *80*

As to those just causes of war which proceed from direct and unlawful vio- lence, it appears equally clear to me, that one good national government affords vastly more security against dangers of that sort, than can be derived from any other quarter.

Such violences are more frequently occasioned by the passions and interests *85* of a part than of the whole, of one or two states than of the union. — Not a single Indian war has yet been produced by aggressions of the present federal govern- ment, feeble as it is, but there are several instances of Indian hostilities having been provoked by the improper conduct of individual states, who either unable or unwilling to restrain or punish offences, have given occasion to the slaughter *90* of many innocent inhabitants.

The neighbourhood of Spanish and British territories, bordering on some states, and not on others, naturally confines the causes of quarrel more immedi- ately to the borderers. The bordering states, if any, will be those who, under the impulse of sudden irritation, and a quick sense of apparent interest or injury, will *95* be most likely by direct violence, to excite war with those nations; and nothing can so effectually obviate that danger, as a national government, whose wisdom and prudence will not be diminished by the passions which actuate the parties immediately interested.

But not only fewer just causes of war will be given by the national government, *100* but it will also be more in their power to accomodate and settle them amicably. They will be more temperate and cool, and in that respect, as well as in others, will be more in capacity to act with circumspection than the offending state. The pride of states as well as of men, naturally disposes them to justify all their actions, and opposes their acknowledging, correcting or repairing their errors and of- *105* fences. The national government in such cases will not be affected by this pride, but will proceed with moderation and candour to consider and decide on the means most proper to extricate them from the difficulties which threaten them.

Besides it is well known that acknowledgments, explanations and compensa- tions are often accepted as satisfactory from a strong united nation, which would *110* be rejected as unsatisfactory if offered by a state or confederacy of little consider- ation or power.

11

In the year 1685 the state of Genoa having offended Louis the XIVth. endeavoured to appease him. He demanded that they should send their *Doge* or chief magistrate, accompanied by four of their senators to *France* to ask his pardon and receive his terms. They were obliged to submit to it for the sake of peace. Would he on any occasion either have demanded or have received the like humiliation from Spain, or Britain, or any other *powerful* nation?

PUBLIUS.

FOUR

JOHN JAY
November 7, 1787
The Same Subject Continued

To the People of the State of New York.

My last paper assigned several reasons why the safety of the people would be best secured by union against the danger it may be exposed to by *just* causes of war given to other nations; and those reasons shew that such causes would not only be more rarely given, but would also be more easily accommodated by a national government, than either by the state governments, or the proposed little, confederacies. 5

But the safety of the people of America against dangers from *foreign* force, depends not only on their forbearing to give *just* causes of war to other nations, but also on their placing and continuing themselves in such a situation as not to *invite* hostility or insult; for it need not be observed, that there are *pretended* as well 10 as just causes of war.

It is too true, however disgraceful it may be to human nature, that nations in general will make war whenever they have a prospect of getting any thing by it, nay that absolute monarchs will often make war when their nations are to get nothing by it, but for purposes and objects merely personal, such as, a thirst for 15 military glory, revenge for personal affronts, ambition or private compacts to aggrandize or support their particular families, or partizans. These and a variety of motives, which affect only the mind of the sovereign, often lead him to engage in wars not sanctified by justice, or the voice and interests of his people. But independent of these inducements to war, which are most prevalent in absolute 20 monarchies, but which well deserve our attention, there are others which affect nations as often as kings; and some of them will on examination be found to grow out of our relative situation and circumstances.

With France and with Britain we are rivals in the fisheries, and can supply their markets cheaper than they can themselves, notwithstanding any efforts to 25 prevent it by bounties on their own, or duties on foreign fish.

With them and most other European nations, we are rivals in navigation and the carrying trade; and we shall deceive ourselves if we suppose that any of them will rejoice to see it flourish: for as our carrying trade cannot increase, without in

---

Lines 24–26 The principal rivalries were over the cod fisheries off New England, in which the American interest was supposed to be protected by the Treaty of Paris, 1783. Another major area of rivalry was in the whale trade.

30 some degree diminishing their's, it is more their interest and will be more their policy, to restrain, than to promote it.

In the trade to China and India, we interfere with more than one nation, inasmuch as it enables us to partake in advantages which they had in a manner monopolized, and as we thereby supply ourselves with commodities which we used
35 to purchase from them.

The extension of our own commerce in our own vessels, cannot give pleasure to any nations who possess territories on or near this continent, because the cheapness and excellence of our productions, added to the circumstance of vicinity, and the enterprize and address of our merchants and navigators, will
40 give us a greater share in the advantages which those territories afford, than consists with the wishes or policy of their respective sovereigns.

Spain thinks it convenient to shut the Mississippi against us on the one side, and Britain excludes us from the St. Lawrence on the other; nor will either of them permit the other waters, which are between them and us, to become the
45 means of mutual intercourse and traffic.

From these and such like considerations, which might if consistent with prudence, be more amplified and detailed, it is easy to see that jealousies and uneasinesses may gradually slide into the minds and cabinets of other nations; and that we are not to expect they should regard our advancement in union, in power
50 and consequence by land and by sea, with an eye of indifference and composure.

The people of America are aware that inducements to war may arise out of these circumstances, as well as from others not so obvious at present; and that whenever such inducements may find fit time and opportunity for operation, pretences to colour and justify them will not be wanting. Wisely therefore do they
55 consider union and a good national government as necessary to put and keep them in *such a situation* as instead of *inviting* war, will tend to repress and discourage it. That situation consists in the best possible state of defence, and necessarily depends on the government, the arms and the resources of the country.

As the safety of the whole is the interest of the whole, and cannot be provided
60 for without government, either one or more or many, let us inquire whether one good government is not, relative to the object in question, more competent than any other given number whatever.

Lines 32–35 The trade with India and China shows the erosion of mercantilist theory, which at its height was based on a belief in the existence of fixed amounts of national wealth. International competition was thus a zero-sum game. The theory had been undermined by Adam Smith (1723–1790) in *The Wealth of Nations* (1776).

Smith, one of the greatest luminaries of the Scottish Enlightenment and regarded by many as the founder of modern economic science, had been Professor of Moral Philosophy at the University of Glasgow. He was responsible for the concept of the "invisible hand" leading to economic and social progress.

Lines 42–44 The author might have added that Britain had also closed the British West Indies to American commerce by an order in council of 1783.

One government can collect and avail itself of the talents and experience of the ablest men, in whatever part of the union they may be found. It can move on uniform principles of policy. It can harmonize, assimilate, and protect the several parts and members, and extend the benefit of its foresight and precautions to each. In the formation of treaties it will regard the interest of the whole, and the particular interests of the parts as connected with that of the whole. It can apply the resources and power of the whole to the defence of any particular part, and that more easily and expeditiously than state governments, or separate confederacies can possibly do, for want of concert and unity of system. It can place the militia under one plan of discipline, and by putting their officers in a proper line of subordination to the chief magistrate, will in a manner consolidate them into one corps, and thereby render them more efficient than if divided into thirteen or into three or four distinct independent bodies.

What would the militia of Britain be, if the English militia obeyed the government of England, if the Scotch militia obeyed the government of Scotland, and if the Welch militia obeyed the government of Wales! Suppose an invasion, would those three governments (if they agreed at all) be able with all their respective forces, to operate against the enemy so effectually as the single government of Great Britain would?

We have heard much of the fleets of Britain, and the time may come, if we are wise, when the fleets of America may engage attention. But if one national government had not so regulated the navigation of Britain as to make it a nursery for seamen—if one national government had not called forth all the national means and materials for forming fleets, their prowess and their thunder would never have been celebrated. Let England have its navigation and fleet—let Scotland have its navigation and fleet—let Wales have its navigation and fleet—let Ireland have its navigation and fleet—let those four of the constituent parts of the British empire be under four independent governments, and it is easy to perceive how soon they would each dwindle into comparative insignificance.

Apply these facts to our own case. Leave America divided into thirteen, or if you please into three or four independent governments, what armies could they raise and pay, what fleets could they ever hope to have? If one was attacked would the other fly to its succour, and spend their blood and money in its defence? Would there be no danger of their being flattered into neutrality by specious promises, or seduced by a too great fondness for peace to decline hazarding their tranquillity and present safety for the sake of neighbours, of whom perhaps they have been jealous, and whose importance they are content to see diminished? Although such conduct would not be wise it would nevertheless be natural. The history of the states of Greece, and of other countries abound with such

---

Lines 83–84 The "one national government" dated from the union of England and Scotland by an agreement in the Act of Union of 1707. By an Act of the Westminster Parliament, Scotland regained its own Parliament in 2000. See above, No. 4.

instances, and it is not improbable that what has so often happened, would under similar circumstances happen again.

But admit that they might be willing to help the invaded state or confederacy. How and when, and in what proportion shall aids of men and money be afforded? Who shall command the allied armies, and from which of them shall he receive his orders? Who shall settle the terms of peace, and in case of disputes what umpire shall decide between them, and compel acquiescence? Various difficulties and inconveniences would be inseparable from such a situation; whereas one government watching over the general and common interests, and combining and directing the powers and resources of the whole, would be free from all these embarrassments, and conduce far more to the safety of the people.

But whatever may be our situation, whether firmly united under one national government, or split into a number of confederacies, certain it is, that foreign nations will know and view it exactly as it is; and they will act towards us accordingly. If they see that our national government is efficient and well administered—our trade prudently regulated—our militia properly organized and disciplined—our resources and finances discreetly managed—our credit reestablished—our people free, contented, and united, they will be much more disposed to cultivate our friendship, than provoke our resentment. If on the other hand they find us either destitute of an effectual government, (each state doing right or wrong as to its rulers may seem convenient), or split into three or four independent and probably discordant republics or confederacies, one inclining to Britain, another to France, and a third to Spain, and perhaps played off against each other by the three, what a poor pitiful figure will America make in their eyes! How liable would she become not only to their contempt, but to their outrage; and how soon would dear bought experience proclaim, that when a people or family so divide, it never fails to be against themselves.

PUBLIUS.

Lines 117–120 Militia training was often compulsory; states also subscribed to the idea of purchasing substitutes. State militia forces had contributed harassing actions against the British in the War of Independence and in that capacity were regarded as safeguards of liberty.

FIVE

JOHN JAY
November 10, 1787
The Same Subject Continued

To the People of the State of New York.

Queen Ann, in her letter of the 1st July, 1706 to the Scotch Parliament, makes some observations on the importance of the union then forming between England and Scotland, which merit our attention. I shall present the public with one or two extracts from it. "An entire and perfect union will be the solid foundation of lasting peace: It will secure your religion, liberty, and property, remove the animosities amongst yourselves, and the jealousies and differences betwixt our two kingdoms. It must encrease your strength, riches, and trade; and by this union the whole island, being joined in affection and free from all apprehensions of different interest, will be *enabled to resist all its enemies.*" "We most earnestly recommend to you calmness and unanimity in this great and weighty affair, that the union may be brought to a happy conclusion, being the only *effectual* way to secure our present and future happiness; and disappoint the designs of our and your enemies, who will doubtless, on this occasion, *use their utmost endeavours to prevent or delay this union.*"

It was remarked in the preceding paper, that weakness and divisions at home, would invite dangers from abroad; and that nothing would tend more to secure us from them than union, strength, and good government within ourselves. This subject is copious and cannot easily be exhausted.

The history of Great Britain is the one with which we are in general the best acquainted, and it gives us many useful lessons. We may profit by their experience,

5
10
15
20

Line 1 Jay says "Scotch." "Scottish" is now preferred, except for whiskey, and a road junction in Yorkshire called Scotch Corner.

Lines 19–28 Americans could acquaint themselves with British history through such works as: Gilbert Burnet (1643–1715, bishop of Salisbury and prominent in politics), *A History of My Own Time* (1723, 1734); David Hume, *History of England*, 8 vols. (1762); Henry St. John, Viscount Bolingbroke, *Remarks on the History of England*, in his periodical paper, *The Craftsman*, 1730–1731; Catherine Macaulay, *The History of England from the Accession of James I to that of the Brunswick Line*, 8 vols. (London, 1763–1783); and *The History of England from the Revolution to the Present Time in a Series of Letters to a Friend* (Bath, 1778); William Robertson, *History of Scotland During the Reigns of Queen Mary and King James the Sixth* [i.e., James I of England] (1759).

without paying the price which it cost them. Although it seems obvious to common sense, that the people of such an island should be but one nation, yet we find that they were for ages divided into three, and those three were almost constantly embroiled in quarrels and wars with one another. Notwithstanding their
25 true interest, with respect to the continental nations was really the same, yet by the arts and policy and practices of those nations, their mutual jealousies were perpetually kept enflamed, and for a long series of years they were far more inconvenient and troublesome, than they were useful and assisting to each other.

Should the people of America divide themselves into three or four nations,
30 would not the same thing happen? Would not similar jealousies arise; and be in like manner cherished? Instead of their being "joined in affection and free from all apprehension of different interests," envy and jealousy would soon extinguish confidence and affection, and the partial interests of each confederacy, instead of the general interests of all America, would be the only objects of their policy and
35 pursuits. Hence like most other *bordering* nations, they would always be either involved in disputes and war, or live in the constant apprehension of them.

The most sanguine advocates for three or four confederacies, cannot reasonably suppose that they would long remain exactly on an equal footing in point of strength, even if it was possible to form them so at first—but admitting that to be
40 practicable, yet what human contrivance can secure the continuance of such equality? Independent of those local circumstances which tend to beget and encrease power in one part, and to impede its progress in another, we must advert to the effects of that superior policy and good management which would probably distinguish the government of one above the rest, and by which their relative equal-
45 ity in strength and consideration, would be destroyed. For it cannot be presumed that the same degree of sound policy, prudence, and foresight, would uniformly be observed by each of these confederacies, for a long succession of years.

Whenever, and from whatever causes, it might happen; and happen it would, that any one of these nations or confederacies should rise on the scale of political
50 importance much above the degree of their neighbours, that moment would those neighbours behold her with envy and with fear: Both those passions would lead them to countenance, if not to promote, whatever might promise to diminish her importance; and would also restrain them from measures calculated to advance, or even to secure her prosperity. Much time would not be necessary to
55 enable her to discern these unfriendly dispositions. She would soon begin, not only to lose confidence in her neighbours, but also to feel a disposition equally unfavorable to them: Distrust naturally creates distrust, and by nothing is good will and kind conduct more speedily changed, than by invidious jealousies and uncandid imputations, whether expressed or implied.

60 The North is generally the region of strength, and many local circumstances render it probable, that the most Northern of the proposed confederacies would, at a period not very distant, be unquestionably more formidable than any of the others. No sooner would this become evident, than the *Northern Hive* would excite the same ideas and sensations in the more Southern parts of America, which it for-

merly did in the Southern parts of Europe: Nor does it appear to be a rash conjec- 65
ture, that its young swarms might often be tempted to gather honey in the more
blooming fields and milder air of their luxurious and more delicate neighbours.

They who well consider the history of similar divisions and confederacies, will
find abundant reason to apprehend, that those in contemplation would in no
other sense be neighbours, than as they would be borderers; that they would nei- 70
ther love nor trust one another, but on the contrary would be a prey to discord,
jealousy and mutual injuries; in short that they would place us exactly in the situations in which some nations doubtless wish to see us, viz. *formidable only to
each other.*

From these considerations it appears that those persons are greatly mistaken, 75
who suppose that alliances offensive and defensive might be formed between
these confederacies, and would produce that combination and union of wills, of
arms, and of resources, which would be necessary to put and keep them in a formidable state of defence against foreign enemies.

When did the independent states into which Britain and Spain were formerly 80
divided, combine in such alliances, or unite their forces against a foreign enemy?
The proposed confederacies will be *distinct nations.* Each of them would have its
commerce with foreigners to regulate by distinct treaties; and as their productions and commodities are different, and proper for different markets, so would
those treaties be essentially different. Different commercial concerns must create 85
different interests, and of course different degrees of political attachment to, and
connection with different foreign nations. Hence it might and probably would
happen, that the foreign nation with whom the *Southern* confederacy might be
at war, would be the one, with whom the *Northern* confederacy would be the
most desirous of preserving peace and friendship. An alliance so contrary to their 90
immediate interest would not therefore be easy to form, nor if formed, would it
be observed and fulfilled with perfect good faith.

Nay it is far more probable that in America, as in Europe, neighbouring nations, acting under the impulse of opposite interests, and unfriendly passions,
would frequently be found taking different sides. Considering our distance from 95
Europe, it would be more natural for these confederacies to apprehend danger
from one another, than from distant nations, and therefore that each of them
should be more desirous to guard against the others, by the aid of foreign alliances,
than to guard against foreign dangers by alliances between themselves. And here

---

Line 68 "The history of similar divisions and confederacies." These will be discussed in great detail in Nos. 18, 19, and 20.

Lines 99–104 The Romans, particularly in the eastern reaches of the Empire, made
a number of alliances with small states, which they used as buffers on their frontiers
but subsequently absorbed. Edward Gibbon, *The Decline and Fall of the Roman
Empire*, the first volume of which had appeared in 1776, is a likely source of
information.

100 let us not forget how much more easy it is to receive foreign fleets into our ports, and foreign armies into our country, than it is to persuade or compel them to depart. How many conquests did the Romans and others make in the characters of allies, and what innovations did they under the same character introduce into the governments of those whom they pretended to protect.

105 Let candid men judge then whether the division of America into any given number of independent sovereignties would tend to secure us against the hostilities and improper interference of foreign nations.

PUBLIUS.

SIX

ALEXANDER HAMILTON
November 14, 1787
Concerning Dangers from War Between the States

To the People of the State of New York.

The three last numbers of this paper have been dedicated to an enumeration of the dangers to which we should be exposed, in a state of disunion, from the arms and arts of foreign nations. I shall now proceed to delineate dangers of a different, and, perhaps, still more alarming kind, those which will in all probability flow from dissentions between the states themselves, and from domestic factions and 5
convulsions. These have been already in some instances slightly anticipated; but they deserve a more particular and more full investigation.

A man must be far gone in Utopian speculations who can seriously doubt, that if these states should either be wholly disunited, or only united in partial confederacies, the subdivisions into which they might be thrown would have fre- 10
quent and violent contests with each other. To presume a want of motives for such contests, as an argument against their existence, would be to forget that men are ambitious, vindictive and rapacious. To look for a continuation of harmony between a number of independent unconnected sovereignties, situated in the same neighbourhood, would be to disregard the uniform course of human 15
events, and to set at defiance the accumulated experience of ages.

The causes of hostility among nations are innumerable. There are some which have a general and almost constant operation upon the collective bodies of society: Of this description are the love of power or the desire of pre-eminence and dominion—the jealousy of power, or the desire of equality and safety. There 20
are others which have a more circumscribed, though an equally operative influence, within their spheres: Such are the rivalships and competitions of commerce between commercial nations. And there are others, not less numerous than either of the former, which take their origin entirely in private passions; in the attachments, enmities, interests, hopes and fears of leading individuals in the 25

Lines 17–55 Compare Hamilton's views of human nature with those associated with "benevolence," deriving from the moral philosophy of Lord Shaftesbury (1671–1713), and the essentially benign Scottish "common sense" school—both of which influenced Jefferson, but not Hamilton. It cannot be too strongly emphasized that although all exponents of the Enlightenment are committed to the use of reason, there is no single, unified "Enlightenment."

In discussing the motives for hostilities among states, Hamilton touches only lightly on economic rivalries.

communities of which they are members. Men of this class, whether the favourites of a king or of a people, have in too many instances abused the confidence they possessed; and assuming the pretext of some public motive, have not scrupled to sacrifice the national tranquility to personal advantage, or personal

30 gratification.

The celebrated Pericles, in compliance with the resentments of a prostitute,(*) at the expence of much of the blood and treasure of his countrymen, attacked, vanquished and destroyed the city of the *Samnians*. The same man, stimulated by private pique against the *Megarensians*,(†) another nation of Greece, or to avoid

35 a prosecution with which he was threatened as an accomplice in a supposed theft of the statuary *Phidias*,(‡) or to get rid of the accusations prepared to be brought against him for dissipating the funds of the state in the purchase of popularity,(§) or from a combination of all these causes, was the primitive author of that famous and fatal war, distinguished in the Grecian annals by the name of

40 the *Pelopponesian* war; which, after various vicissitudes, intermissions and renewals, terminated in the ruin of the Athenian commonwealth.

The ambitious cardinal, who was prime minister to Henry VIIIth. permitting his vanity to aspire to the tripple-crown,(**) entertained hopes of succeeding in the acquisition of that splendid prize by the influence of the emperor Charles

45 Vth. To secure the favour and interest of this enterprising and powerful monarch, he precipitated England into a war with France, contrary to the plainest dictates of policy, and at the hazard of the safety and independence, as well of the kingdom over which he presided by his councils, as of Europe in general. For if there ever was a sovereign who bid fair to realise the project of univer-

(*) ASPASIA, vide PLUTARCH'S life of Pericles.

(†) —Idem.

(‡) —Idem. Phidias was supposed to have stolen some public gold with the connivance of Pericles for the embellishment of the statue of Minerva.

(§) —Idem.

(**) Worn by the Popes.

Lines 35–36 ". . . a supposed theft of the statuary Phidias . . .": Hamilton describes the sculptor Phidias by the now archaic word "statuary," defined in Samuel Johnson's *Dictionary* (1773 edition) as "one who practices the art of making statues."

Line 42 The "ambitious cardinal" is Cardinal Wolsey (ca. 1475–1530), but "prime minister" is an anachronism, as that office came into existence in the 18th century. Wolsey's secular office was Lord Chancellor. Wolsey's lines, "Had I but serv'd my God with half the zeal/I served my king, He would not in mine age/Have left me naked to mine enemies," is from Shakespeare's *Henry VIII*, 3.2. Shakespeare, however, is ironical in the play. Wolsey is seen to serve only himself.

Line 43 The triple crown of the Roman Catholic Church is the pope's tiara.

sal monarchy it was the emperor Charles Vth. of whose intrigues Wolsey was at   *50*
once the instrument and the dupe.

The influence which the bigottry of one female,(*) the petulancies of another,(†)
and the cabals of a third(‡) had in the cotemporary policy, ferments and pacifica-
tions of a considerable part of Europe are topics that have been too often des-
canted upon not to be generally known.   *55*

To multiply examples of the agency of personal considerations in the production
of great national events, either foreign or domestic, according to their direction,

(*) Madame de Maintenon.

(†) Dutchess of Marlborough.

(‡) Madame de Pompadoure.

Lines 52–53 Madame de Maintenon, mistress to Louis XIV of France, was secretly
married to him in 1684; she formally dissociated herself from public policy, and exercised a pious influence at court; however, she was by far the most influential figure
with the king, and was partly responsible for Louis's policy of persecuting the
(Protestant) Huguenots. Sarah, Duchess of Marlborough (1660–1744), who survived
the duke (John Churchill, 1650–1722), was a turbulent and influential figure at the
court of Queen Anne until she lost favor with the queen; Madame de Pompadour
(1721–1764), mistress to Louis XV of France, was notorious for her influence at
court. It may be doubted whether Britain or France made war or peace on account
of these ladies' intrigues, but in many matters, particularly appointments to high
offices, they often exercised great influence.

Lines 56–65 The recent episode of Shays's rebellion in Massachusetts was in every-
one's mind and had done much to spur reluctant state legislatures into sending delegations to the Philadelphia Convention. The principal motive for the revolt, which
broke out in August 1786, and struggled on for several months before being suppressed in the spring of 1787, was to close the courts and thus prevent foreclosures
on the property of debt-ridden farmers. Although there is no evidence that Shays and
his followers aimed to seize control of the government, the outbreak caused great
alarm in other states, as well as in governing circles in Massachusetts itself, not least
because Massachusetts had a constitution that had been ratified by the people in
their towns as recently as 1780. For men like Hamilton, Jay, and Madison, who represented propertied interests, it raised the fundamental question, could republican
government work? (Jefferson, away in Paris, was far less troubled, and made a frivolous remark about watering the tree of liberty with the blood of tyrants to Colonel
William S. Smith, on November 13, 1787.) But the farmers' desperation was caused
in large part by hard-money policies on the part of the legislature. Hamilton's remark
is tendentious: Shays, a revolutionary war captain, did not "plunge Massachusetts
into civil war" for merely personal motives; he had a large following of "desperate
debtors" who could not pay their taxes, were threatened with loss of their liveli-
hoods, and felt betrayed by their representatives; their petitions went unanswered,
leaving them without remedy in normal politics. Fortunately, however, elections
were annual in Massachusetts, normal politics did afford redress, and most members
of the old assembly were turned out in 1787—with consequent changes in policy.

would be an unnecessary waste of time. Those who have but a superficial acquaintance with the sources from which they are to be drawn will themselves recollect a
60 variety of instances; and those who have a tolerable knowledge of human nature will not stand in need of such lights, to form their opinion either of the reality or extent of that agency. Perhaps however a reference, tending to illustrate the general principle, may with propriety be made to a case which has lately happened among ourselves. If SHAYS had not been a *desperate debtor* it is much to be doubted
65 whether Massachusetts would have been plunged into a civil war.

But notwithstanding the concurring testimony of experience, in this particular, there are still to be found visionary, or designing men, who stand ready to advocate the paradox of perpetual peace between the states, though dismembered and alienated from each other. The genius of republics (say they) is pacific; the
70 spirit of commerce has a tendency to soften the manners of men and to extinguish those inflammable humours which have so often kindled into wars. Commercial republics, like ours, will never be disposed to waste themselves in ruinous contentions with each other. They will be governed by mutual interest, and will cultivate a spirit of mutual amity and concord.

75 Is it not (we may ask these projectors in politics) the true interest of all nations to cultivate the same benevolent and philosophic spirit? If this be their true interest, have they in fact pursued it? Has it not, on the contrary, invariably been found, that momentary passions and immediate interests have a more active and imperious controul over human conduct than general or remote considerations of policy, util-
80 ity or justice? Have republics in practice been less addicted to war than monarchies? Are not the former administered by *men* as well as the latter? Are there not aversions, predilections, rivalships and desires of unjust acquisition that affect nations as well as kings? Are not popular assemblies frequently subject to the impulses of rage, resentment, jealousy, avarice, and of other irregular and violent propensities? Is it not
85 well known that their determinations are often governed by a few individuals, in whom they place confidence, and are of course liable to be tinctured by the passions and views of those individuals? Has commerce hitherto done any thing more than change the objects of war? Is not the love of wealth as domineering and enterprising a passion as that of power or glory? Have there not been as many wars
90 founded upon commercial motives, since that has become the prevailing system of nations, as were before occasioned by the cupidity of territory or dominion? Has not the spirit of commerce in many instances administered new incentives to the appetite both for the one and for the other?—Let experience the least fallible guide of human opinions be appealed to for an answer to these inquiries.

95 Sparta, Athens, Rome and Carthage were all republics; two of them, Athens and Carthage, of the commercial kind. Yet were they as often engaged in wars,

---

Lines 75–94 With this paragraph, Hamilton begins a nine-paragraph invocation of the long history of wars involving republics from the ancient world to that of the 17th and 18th centuries. The role of human nature is once again crucial. And the in-

offensive and defensive, as the neighbouring monarchies of the same times. Sparta was little better than a well regulated camp; and Rome was never sated of carnage and conquest.

Carthage, though a commercial republic, was the aggressor in the very war *100* that ended in her destruction. Hannibal had carried her arms into the heart of Italy and to the gates of Rome, before Scipio, in turn, gave him an overthrow in the territories of Carthage and made a conquest of the commonwealth.

Venice in latter times figured more than once in wars of ambition; till becoming an object of terror to the other Italian states, Pope Julius the Second found *105* means to accomplish that formidable league, which gave a deadly blow to the power and pride of this haughty republic.

The provinces of Holland, till they were overwhelmed in debts and taxes, took a leading and conspicuous part in the wars of Europe. They had furious contests with England for the dominion of the sea; and were among the most persevering *110* and most implacable of the opponents of Lewis XIV.

In the government of Britain the representatives of the people compose one branch of the national legislature. Commerce has been for ages the predominant pursuit of that country. Few nations, nevertheless, have been more frequently engaged in war; and the wars, in which that kingdom has been engaged, have in *115* numerous instances proceeded from the people.

There have been, if I may so express it, almost as many popular as royal wars. The cries of the nation and the importunities of their representatives have, upon various occasions, dragged their monarchs into war, or continued them in it, contrary to their inclinations, and, sometimes, contrary to the real interests of the *120* state. In that memorable struggle for superiority, between the rival houses of *Austria* and *Bourbon* which so long kept Europe in a flame, it is well known that

The LEAGUE OF CAMBRAY, comprehending the emperor, the king of France, the king of Arragon, and most of the Italian princes and states.

---

escapable inference, with important implications for republican political thought, is that republican government does not make men more virtuous; republics are just as subject to the vicious tendencies of humanity as monarchies. In this passage, economic motivation is introduced with reference to "commercial motives," of which the prime example was the three Anglo-Dutch wars of the mid-17th century.

Lines 108–11 Here, however, Publius runs together the commercial motives of the Dutch and the English with the power struggle in which they became allies against Louis XIV's France, after 1689, when William of Orange, Stadtholder of the Netherlands, became William III of England.

Hamilton's footnote The League of Cambrai against Venice was formed in 1508. Hamilton ranges widely through European history.

Lines 121–26 The War of the Spanish Succession, which sprang from the claims of the Bourbons to the thrones—and thence to the empires—of both France and Spain,

the antipathies of the English against the French, seconding the ambition, or rather the avarice of a favourite leader,* protracted the war beyond the limits
125 marked out by sound policy and for a considerable time in opposition to the views of the court.

The wars of these two last mentioned nations have in a great measure grown out of commercial considerations.—The desire of supplanting and the fear of being supplanted either in particular branches of traffic or in the general advan-
130 tages of trade and navigation; and sometimes even the more culpable desire of sharing in the commerce of other nations, without their consent.

The last war but two between Britain and Spain sprang from the attempts of the English merchants, to prosecute an illicit trade with the Spanish main. These unjustifiable practices on their part produced severities on the part of the
135 Spaniards, towards the subjects of Great Britain, which were not more justifiable; because they exceeded the bounds of a just retaliation, and were chargeable with inhumanity and cruelty. Many of the English who were taken on the Spanish coasts were sent to dig in the mines of Potosi; and by the usual progress of a spirit of resentment, the innocent were after a while confounded with the
140 guilty in indiscriminate punishment. The complaints of the merchants kindled a violent flame throughout the nation, which soon after broke out in the house of commons, and was communicated from that body to the ministry. Letters of reprisal were granted and a war ensued, which in its consequences overthrew all the alliances that but twenty years before had been formed, with sanguine ex-
145 pectations of the most beneficial fruits.

From this summary of what has taken place in other countries, whose situations have borne the nearest resemblance to our own, what reason can we have to confide in those reveries, which would seduce us into an expectation of peace and cordiality between the members of the present confederacy, in a state of

*The Duke of Marlborough.

---

was finally resolved in 1713 by the Treaty of Utrecht. At the battle of Blenheim (1704) John Churchill (1650–1722), later first Duke of Marlborough, won a major victory which changed the structure of power in Europe. From 1709, the principal allies, Britain, the Netherlands, and Austria, were engaged in a struggle to humiliate Louis XIV and cripple French power in Europe. To ascribe all this to the ambitions of the Duke of Marlborough is a tendentious use of history. It is arguable, however, that the war may have been "protracted beyond the limits marked out by sound policy." Blenheim Palace, at Woodstock in Oxfordshire, is the home built for Marlborough by a grateful nation. (Sir Winston Churchill, a direct descendant, was born there and is buried in the family graveyard at Bladon.) The Palace was designed by John Vanbrugh, playwright, architect, and man of letters, for whom another playwright, William Congreve, composed an epitaph closing with the lines: "Lie heavy on him, earth, for he / Laid many a heavy load on thee."

separation? Have we not already seen enough of the fallacy and extravagance of *150* those idle theories which have amused us with promises of an exemption from the imperfections, the weaknesses and the evils incident to society in every shape? Is it not time to awake from the deceitful dream of a golden age, and to adopt as a practical maxim for the direction of our political conduct, that we, as well as the other inhabitants of the globe, are yet remote from the happy empire *155* of perfect wisdom and perfect virtue?

Let the point of extreme depression to which our national dignity and credit have sunk—let the inconveniences felt every where from a lax and ill administration of government—let the revolt of a part of the state of North-Carolina— the late menacing disturbances in Pennsylvania, and the actual insurrections and *160* rebellions in Massachusetts, declare!— —

So far is the general sense of mankind from corresponding with the tenets of those, who endeavour to lull asleep our apprehensions of discord and hostility between the states, in the event of disunion, that it has from long observation of the progress of society become a sort of axiom in politics, that vicinity, or near *165* ness of situation, constitutes nations natural enemies. An intelligent writer expresses himself on this subject to this effect— "NEIGHBOURING NATIONS (says he) are naturally ENEMIES of each other, unless their common weakness forces them to league in a CONFEDERATE REPUBLIC, and their constitution prevents the differences that neighbourhood occasions, extinguishing that *170* secret jealousy, which disposes all states to aggrandize themselves at the expence of their neighbours. This passage, at the same time points out the EVIL and suggests the REMEDY.

PUBLIUS.

Vide Principes des Negotiations par L'Abbe de Mably.

Line 159 The reference to revolt in "a part of the state of North-Carolina" seems to refer to the Regulator rising of 1768–1771, before North Carolina was a state. The regulators, concentrated in the western section of the province, had grievances against unfair taxation, unequal administration of justice, and distant government in which they were not adequately represented. Their problems were partly redressed by assembly elections, but new disturbances soon broke out when Governor William Tryon dissolved the assembly after it had turned against the British government. A small army led by the governor eventually put down the rebels at the battle of Alamance Creek, with some loss of life, followed by hangings of the leaders. In Pennsylvania, disorders directed against claims of Connecticut settlers in the Wyoming Valley in 1775 had called for the intervention of the Continental Congress—evidence that the states could not be counted on to keep peace among themselves without a superior power. See further comment on No. 7, lines 53–60.

SEVEN

ALEXANDER HAMILTON
November 17, 1787
The Subject Continued and Particular Causes Enumerated

To the People of the State of New York.

It is sometimes asked, with an air of seeming triumph, what inducements, could the states have, if disunited, to make war upon each other? It would be a full answer to this question to say—precisely the same inducements, which have, at different times, deluged in blood all the nations in the world. But unfortunately for
5 us, the question admits of a more particular answer. There are causes of difference within our immediate contemplation, of the tendency of which, even under the restraints of a federal constitution, we have had sufficient experience to enable us to form a judgment of what might be expected, if those restraints were removed.

10 Territorial disputes have at all times been found one of the most fertile sources of hostility among nations. Perhaps the greatest proportion of the wars that have desolated the earth have sprung from this origin. This cause would exist, among us, in full force. We have a vast tract of unsettled territory within the boundaries of the United States. There still are discordant and undecided claims between
15 several of them; and the dissolution of the union would lay a foundation for similar claims between them all. It is well known, that they have heretofore had serious and animated discussions concerning the right to the lands which were

---

Lines 10–44 The states with claims on western lands were Massachusetts, Connecticut, New York, Virginia, North Carolina, South Carolina, and Georgia. Whether the lands in question devolved from the British crown upon these states as individual sovereignties, or whether all former crown lands devolved on the Continental Congress as representing the United States as a whole, was one of the more exacting constitutional problems of the new republic's earliest years—arising long before the Articles of Confederation had been drafted. It was resolved by voluntary cessions, the most important being from New York and Virginia, and the problem had been largely settled by the time the Convention met. In fact one of the dying Congress's final acts was one of its most important—passage of the Northwest Ordinance of 1787, which provided for the expansion of the Union by setting up territorial governments in the Ohio Valley, with procedure for admission of territories to the Union as states when certain requirements of population and government had been met. The Ordinance also provided for the gradual elimination of slavery in the vast northwestern territories affected. This Ordinance was reenacted under the Constitution by the first Congress of the United States.

ungranted at the time of the revolution, and which usually went under the name of crown-lands. The states within the limits of whose colonial governments they were comprised have claimed them as their property; the others have contended that the rights of the crown in this article devolved upon the union; especially as to all that part of the Western territory which, either by actual possession, or through the submission of the Indian proprietors, was subjected to the jurisdiction of the king of Great-Britain, till it was relinquished in the treaty of peace. This, it has been said, was at all events an acquisition to the confederacy by compact with a foreign power. It has been the prudent policy of congress to appease this controversy, by prevailing upon the states to make cessions to the United States for the benefit of the whole. This has been so far accomplished, as under a continuation of the union, to afford a decided prospect of an amicable termination of the dispute. A dismemberment of the confederacy however would revive this dispute, and would create others on the same subject. At present, a large part of the vacant Western territory is by cession at least, if not by any anterior right, the common property of the union. If that were at an end, the states which have made cessions, on a principle of federal compromise, would be apt, when the motive of the grant had ceased, to reclaim the lands as a reversion. The other states would no doubt insist on a proportion, by right of representation. Their argument would be that a grant, once made, could not be revoked; and that the justice of their participating in territory acquired, or secured by the joint efforts of the confederacy remained undiminished. If contrary to probability it should be admitted by all the states, that each had a right to a share of this common stock, there would still be a difficulty to be surmounted, as to a proper rule of apportionment. Different principles would be set up by different states for this purpose; and as they would affect the opposite interests of the parties, they might not easily be susceptible of a pacific adjustment.

In the wide field of Western territory, therefore, we perceive an ample theatre for hostile pretensions, without any umpire or common judge to interpose between the contending parties. To reason from the past to the future we shall have good ground to apprehend, that the sword would sometimes be appealed to as the arbiter of their differences. The circumstances of the dispute between Connecticut and Pennsylvania, respecting the lands at Wyoming, admonish us, not to be sanguine in expecting an easy accommodation of such differences. The articles of confederation obliged the parties to submit the matter to the decision of a federal court. The submission was made, and the court decided in favour of

---

Lines 51–60 The reference to "a federal court" may confuse, since no judicial system existed under the Articles of Confederation. The conflict arose from incursions by settlers from Connecticut, which was running short of land, into the western Wyoming Valley of Pennsylvania. In a region where conflicting claims were made on the basis of imperfect cartography, the two states contested each others' claims to jurisdiction. The "federal" court was established under the authority of the Congress,

Pennsylvania. But Connecticut gave strong indications of dissatisfaction with that
55   determination; nor did she appear to be entirely resigned to it, till by negotiation
and management something like an equivalent was found for the loss she supposed herself to have sustained. Nothing here said is intended to convey the
slightest censure on the conduct of that state. She no doubt sincerely believed
herself to have been injured by the decision; and states like individuals, acqui-
60   esce with great reluctance in determinations to their disadvantage.

   Those who had an opportunity of seeing the inside of the transactions, which
attended the progress of the controversy between this state and the district of Vermont, can vouch the opposition we experienced, as well from states not interested as from those which were interested in the claim; and can attest the danger
65   to which the peace of the confederacy might have been exposed, had this state
attempted to assert its rights by force. Two motives preponderated in that opposition—one a jealousy entertained of our future power—and the other, the interest of certain individuals of influence in the neighbouring states, who had
obtained grants of lands under the actual government of that district. Even the
70   states which brought forward claims, in contradiction to ours, seemed more solicitous to dismember this state, than to establish their own pretensions. These
were New-Hampshire, Massachusetts and Connecticut. New-Jersey and Rhode-
Island, upon all occasions discovered a warm zeal for the independence of Vermont; and Maryland, until alarmed by the appearance of a connection between
75   Canada and that place, entered deeply into the same views. These being small
states, saw with an unfriendly eye the perspective of our growing greatness. In a
review of these transactions we may trace some of the causes, which would be
likely to embroil the states with each other, if it should be their unpropitious destiny to become disunited.

80   The competitions of commerce would be another fruitful source of contention. The states less favourably circumstanced would be desirous of escaping

---

according to procedure laid down in Article IX of the Articles; it was composed of
judges nominated by delegations representing the two states. The court found in
favor of Pennsylvania in 1782, but in a manner that left many individual land claims
unsettled. This gave rise to continuing legal conflict, only resolved when Pennsylvania gave the settlers political recognition by forming Luzerne County in 1786. The
inefficiency of this method of addressing disputes among the states was itself an argument for creating a federal judiciary.

Lines 71–79 "This state" (line 71) is of course New York. The long-running conflict
over claims to independence from New York of residents in the Vermont region of
the state was finally resolved by the admission of Vermont to the Union in 1792.

   Later in the same paragraph, Hamilton draws on the confused conflict of territorial claims that had threatened the integrity of New York as a state. Vermont had
even indicated a possible preference for an alliance with Canada. All this demonstrated to many New Yorkers the fragility of their political security under the Articles
and the need for a stronger central government.

from the disadvantages of local situation, and of sharing in the advantages of their more fortunate neighbours. Each state, or separate confederacy, would pursue a system of commercial polity peculiar to itself. This would occasion distinctions, preferences and exclusions, which would beget discontent. The habits of intercourse, on the basis of equal privileges, to which we have been accustomed from the earliest settlement of the country, would give a keener edge to those causes of discontent, than they would naturally have, independent of this circumstance. *We should be ready to denominate injuries those things which were in reality the justifiable acts of independent sovereignties consulting a distinct interest.* The spirit of enterprise, which characterises the commercial part of America, has left no occasion of displaying itself unimproved. It is not at all probable that this unbridled spirit would pay much respect to those regulations of trade, by which particular states might endeavour to secure exclusive benefits to their own citizens. The infractions of these regulations on one side, the efforts to prevent and repel them on the other, would naturally lead to outrages, and these to reprisals and wars.

The opportunities, which some states would have of rendering others tributary to them, by commercial regulations, would be impatiently submitted to by the tributary states. The relative situation of New-York, Connecticut and New-Jersey, would afford an example of this kind. New-York, from the necessities of revenue, must lay duties on her importations. A great part of these duties must be paid by the inhabitants of the two other states in the capacity of consumers of what we import. New-York would neither be willing nor able to forego this advantage. Her citizens would not consent that a duty paid by them should be remitted in favour of the citizens of her neighbours; nor would it be practicable, if there were not this impediment in the way, to distinguish the customers in our own markets. Would Connecticut and New-Jersey long submit to be taxed by New-York for her exclusive benefit? Should we be long permitted to remain in the quiet and undisturbed enjoyment of a metropolis, from the possession of which we derived an advantage so odious to our neighbours, and, in their opinion, so oppressive? Should we be able to preserve it against the incumbent weight of Connecticut on the one side, and the co-operating pressure of New-Jersey on the other? These are questions that temerity alone will answer in the affirmative.

The public debt of the union would be a further cause of collision between the separate states or confederacies. The apportionment, in the first instance,

---

Lines 108–14 New Jersey, a state without a major Atlantic port, imported heavily through New York and Philadelphia, and had to pay prices reflecting duties levied by its great neighbors. Connecticut was in much the same position. Although this gave New York superior power, Hamilton appeals to the fears of New Yorkers from the resulting discontent and instability.

Lines 115–34 Hamilton anticipates the problem of public debts, either of state or confederation, which he later confronted in 1790 when he became secretary of the

and the progressive extinguishment, afterwards, would be alike productive of ill humour and animosity. How would it be possible to agree upon a rule of apportionment satisfactory to all? There is scarcely any, that can be proposed, which is
120 entirely free from real objections. These, as usual, would be exaggerated by the adverse interests of the parties. There are even dissimilar views among the states, as to the general principle of discharging the public debt. Some of them, either less impressed with the importance of national credit, or because their citizens have little, if any, immediate interest in the question, feel an indifference, if not
125 a repugnance to the payment of the domestic debt, at any rate. These would be inclined to magnify the difficulties of a distribution. Others of them, a numerous body of whose citizens are creditors to the public, beyond the proportion of the state in the total amount of the national debt, would be strenuous for some equitable and effectual provision. The procrastinations of the former would excite
130 the resentments of the latter. The settlement of a rule would in the mean time be postponed, by real differences of opinion and affected delays. The citizens of the states interested, would clamour, foreign powers would urge, for the satisfaction

---

treasury. As indicated in the text, certificates of credit were very unevenly distributed among the citizens of different states, being much more heavily concentrated from Pennsylvania northward. A compromise with Jefferson, who held the office of Secretary of State, over the location of the new federal capital (in which Jefferson, in self-exculpation, later claimed to have been duped) eased the settlement, and Hamilton met little resistance to his policy of paying the debts at the face value stated on the certificates. Controversy centered on the fact that these certificates had changed hands many times, effectively passing as a form of currency, and depreciating in the process; the political issue, therefore, was whether to distinguish between original holders and those who had subsequently bought securities on the market. Hamilton resolved these complex problems within a framework of specie payments that avoided discriminating against current holders. Avoiding such discrimination was an important point of both principle and policy: principle, because he would have regarded such discrimination as a violation of contract; policy, because it would have been subversive of public credit—particularly among supporters of the new government concentrated in the northern states. The politics of the issue was complicated by the objections of people in states that held only small proportions—generally southern states—to being taxed to reimburse the citizens of states (including Pennsylvania and New York, though he does not mention them by name) where heavy concentrations were held. For the time being, these problems lay in the future; Madison was then to oppose Hamilton by proposing discrimination in favor of original holders; but in writing *The Federalist*, the two could agree that in the absence of a stronger central government, there would be no way of resolving these conflicts, the Confederation not providing a mechanism.

A modern instance of the danger alluded to in lines 151–55 is that the operations of the United Nations have been impaired by financial stringencies caused by the prolonged failure of the United States to pay its dues.

of their just demands; and the peace of the states would be hazarded to the double contingency of external invasion and internal contention.

Suppose the difficulties of agreeing upon a rule surmounted, and the apportionment made. Still there is great room to suppose, that the rule agreed upon would, upon experiment, be found to bear harder upon some states than upon others. Those which were sufferers by it would naturally seek for a mitigation of the burthen. The others would as naturally be disinclined to a revision, which was likely to end in an increase of their own incumbrances. Their refusal would be too plausible a pretext to the complaining states to withhold their contributions, not to be embraced with avidity; and the non compliance of these states with their engagements would be a ground of bitter dissention and altercation. If even the rule adopted should in practice justify the equality of its principle, still delinquencies in payment, on the part of some of the states, would result from a diversity of other causes—the real deficiency of resources—the mismanagement of their finances, accidental disorders in the administration of the government—and in addition to the rest the reluctance with which men commonly part with money for purposes, that have outlived the exigencies which produced them, and interfere with the supply of immediate wants. Delinquencies from whatever causes would be productive of complaints, recriminations and quarrels. There is perhaps nothing more likely to disturb the tranquillity of nations, than their being bound to mutual contributions for any common object, which does not yield an equal and coincident benefit. For it is an observation as true, as it is trite, that there is nothing men differ so readily about as the payment of money.

Laws in violation of private contracts as they amount to aggressions on the rights of those states, whose citizens are injured by them, may be considered as

---

Line 156 This is the first reference in *The Federalist* to the question of contract. Several states had eased the distress of their large and politically influential debtor populations by passing "stay" laws, or their equivalent, which deferred payments owed on debts, or, as in South Carolina, made debts payable in worthless "pine barren" land, as well as by issuing paper money that tended to depreciate in value (though Pennsylvania and South Carolina supported fairly stable paper money policies). Paper money took the form of certificates of public debt, due to be redeemed at a given date, at a specified rate of interest; it did not circulate indefinitely as it does now. A debtor repaying a debt in devalued currency was obviously getting an unfair advantage, which when repeated wholesale damaged the interests of merchants and creditors as a class. Both these policies were denounced by creditors as violations of contractual obligations, whether private or public—though the reference to "private" contracts suggests that Hamilton had stay laws in his sights.

The Constitution forbade the states to pass laws "impairing the obligation of contracts" (Article 1, Section 9). This was a direct reply to such state policies, and was intended to limit the power of states over fiscal policy. The makers of the Constitution, however, overlooked the important point that states remained free to charter banks, whose bank notes would soon become a very effective form of paper money.

another probable source of hostility. We are not authorised to expect, that a more liberal or more equitable spirit would preside over the legislations of the individ-
160 ual states hereafter, if unrestrained by any additional checks, than we have heretofore seen, in too many instances, disgracing their several codes. We have observed the disposition to retaliation excited in Connecticut, in consequence of the enormities perpetrated by the legislature of Rhode-Island; and we may reasonably infer, that in similar cases, under other circumstances, a war not of
165 *parchment* but of the sword would chastise such atrocious breaches of moral obligation and social justice.

The probability of incompatible alliances between the different states, or confederacies, and different foreign nations, and the effects of this situation upon the

---

No treatise on English contract law existed in 1787—the first, by J. J. Powell, appeared in 1790; but from case law it may be said that a lawful contract came into existence when two independent parties made an agreement—which did not necessarily have to be signed and sealed: common law recognized verbal, or "parol," agreements. The assumption was that the parties entered into their mutual agreement freely, without fraud or deception, and without undue pressure or constraint on either side; in other words, they were equals in the market. Hamilton regarded the keeping of contracts as one of the cardinal principles of civilized society. What was novel in this situation was that in treating a state's promise to redeem state-issued money as in principle a contract, Hamilton was treating a state government as an equal in bargaining with a private citizen. But there is a legal difficulty: In Britain, the crown, being sovereign, could not be sued; under the Articles, the states retained their sovereignty: then could a sovereign state be sued under the Articles? And if not, could an unsuable party to an agreement be considered an equal? Hamilton, one of New York's leading lawyers, was aware of the question. In No. 81, he sought to reassure the states by confirming that a state could not be sued. (It soon appeared, however, that *The Federalist* had no authority with the Supreme Court, which ignored Hamilton's remark in the early case of *Chisholm v. Georgia* (1792), permitting a citizen of another state to sue Georgia; this led directly to the 11th Amendment, which protected the states from suits by private citizens of another state or of foreign states.) Hamilton's assurance is consistent with the language of Article 2 of the Confederation, protecting state sovereignty—still effective until the Constitution was ratified. However, the Constitution, by prohibiting any state from impairing the obligations of contract, appears in theory to deal a decisive blow at state sovereignty. Although Hamilton and Madison were later to divide on Hamilton's policies of repaying current holders of public debts at their original value, both men held that the contract clause would require that contracts be honored by the states. Madison resumes this theme in No. 44.

Lines 161–66 Rhode Island issued huge quantities of unstable paper that rapidly lost value and caused dismay and outrage among creditors in neighboring states; its behavior was the prime example of the sort of irresponsibility the contract clause was designed to check. Hamilton's reference to Connecticut's retaliation may allude to that state's tariff policies, though this is not clear.

peace of the whole, have been sufficiently unfolded in some preceding papers. From the view they have exhibited of this part of the subject, this conclusion is to   *170* be drawn, that America, if not connected at all, or only by the feeble tie of a simple league offensive and defensive, would by the operation of such opposite and . jarring alliances be gradually entangled in all the pernicious labyrinths of European politics and wars; and by the destructive contentions of the parts, into which she was divided, would be likely to become a prey to the artifices and   *175* machinations of powers equally the enemies of them all. *Divide et impera** must be the motto of every nation, that either hates, or fears us.

PUBLIUS.

---

*Divide and command.

Line 173 The word "entangled" anticipates the similar language of Washington's *Farewell Address*, which Hamilton helped to draft. (Washington, however, did not, as is often believed, speak of "entangling alliances.") *TTA 99, p. 102 His. U.S. Vol. 1 p. 294-296*

EIGHT

ALEXANDER HAMILTON

November 20, 1787

**The Effects of Internal War in Producing Standing Armies
and Other Institutions Unfriendly to Liberty**

To the People of the State of New York.

Assuming it therefore as an established truth that the several states, in case of disunion, or such combinations of them as might happen to be formed out of the wreck of the general confederacy, would be subject to those vicissitudes of peace and war, of friendship and enmity with each other, which have fallen to the lot of all neighbouring nations not united under one government, let us enter into a concise detail of some of the consequences that would attend such a situation.

War between the states, in the first periods of their separate existence, would be accompanied with much greater distresses than it commonly is in those countries, where regular military establishments have long obtained. The disciplined armies always kept on foot on the continent of Europe, though they bear a malignant aspect to liberty and economy, have notwithstanding been productive of the signal advantage, of rendering sudden conquests impracticable, and of preventing that rapid desolation, which used to mark the progress of war, prior to their introduction. The art of fortification has contributed to the same ends. The nations of Europe are encircled with chains of fortified places, which mutually obstruct invasion. Campaigns are wasted in reducing two or three frontier garrisons, to gain admittance into an enemy's country. Similar impediments occur at every step, to exhaust the strength and delay the progress of an invader. Formerly an invading army would penetrate into the heart of a neighbouring country, almost as soon as intelligence of its approach could be received; but now a comparatively small force of disciplined troops, acting on the defensive with the aid of posts, is able to impede and finally to frustrate the enterprises of one much more considerable. The history of war, in that quarter of the globe, is no longer a history of nations subdued and empires overturned, but of towns taken and retaken, of battles that decide nothing, of retreats more beneficial than victories, of much effort and little acquisition.

Lines 9–14 Frederick II ("the Great") of Prussia could be cited as a counterexample; one of the first acts of his reign was a sudden and unprovoked attack on Silesia in 1740. But there was substantial truth in Hamilton's account of the nature of war on the European continent since the end of the War of the Spanish Succession (1713).

In this country the scene would be altogether reversed. The jealousy of military establishments, would postpone them as long as possible. The want of fortifications leaving the frontiers of one state open to another, would facilitate inroads. The populous states would with little difficulty over-run their less populous neighbours. Conquests would be as easy to be made as difficult to be retained. War therefore would be desultory and predatory. Plunder and devastation ever march in the train of irregulars. The calamities of individuals would make the principal figure in the events, which would characterise our military exploits.

This picture is not too highly wrought, though I confess, it would not long remain a just one. Safety from external danger is the most powerful director of national conduct. Even the ardent love of liberty will, after a time, give way to its dictates. The violent destruction of life and property incident to war—the continual effort and alarm attendant on a state of continual danger, will compel nations the most attached to liberty, to resort for repose and security, to institutions, which have a tendency to destroy their civil and political rights. To be more safe they, at length, become willing to run the risk of being less free.

The institutions chiefly alluded to are STANDING ARMIES, and the correspondent appendages of military establishments. Standing armies, it is said, are not provided against in the new constitution, and it is thence inferred, that they would exist under it.* This inference, from the very form of the proposition, is, at best problematical and uncertain. But STANDING ARMIES, it may be replied,

*This objection will be fully examined in its proper place, and it will be shown that the only rational precaution which could have been taken on this subject has been taken; and a much better one than is to be found in any constitution that has been heretofore framed in America, most of which contain no guard at all on this subject.

Lines 43–57 Opposition to "standing armies" had been a cardinal principle of Whig doctrine since the overthrow of James II (1688), inherited by all shades of American opinion. The primary reason for this was obvious: a permanent army, maintained in peacetime, under the immediate control of the monarch, stood as a permanent threat to the liberties of parliaments and the people they represented. A secondary but important objection was that standing armies were expensive, and maintaining them was a permanent drain on the revenues, requiring taxation. Charles I had been obliged to summon a parliament in 1640 after eleven years of personal rule when he needed money for a Scottish war. England's history of very substantial freedom from a military establishment had contributed to English liberty, and was made possible by her island status; her freedom from the threat of foreign domination was due to the fact that she maintained a standing *navy*. But the Royal Navy never posed the same sort of threat to domestic liberties that an army was believed to do. Interestingly enough, the United States enjoyed the benefit of somewhat similar circumstances—protected by the Atlantic, and by the British navy, if diplomatic cards were shrewdly played. At a later date, the Monroe Doctrine (1823), proclaiming the autonomy of the American hemisphere, owed its practical efficacy to British

must inevitably result from a dissolution of the confederacy. Frequent war, and constant apprehension, which require a state of as constant preparation, will in-
50   fallibly produce them. The weaker states or confederacies, would first have re-course to them, to put themselves upon an equality with their more potent neighbours. They would endeavour to supply the inferiority of population and resources, by a more regular and effective system of defence, by disciplined troops and by fortifications. They would, at the same time, be necessitated to
55   strengthen the executive arm of government; in doing which, their constitutions would acquire a progressive direction towards monarchy. It is of the nature of war to increase the executive at the expence of the legislative authority.

The expedients which have been mentioned would soon give the states, or confederacies that made use of them, a superiority over their neighbours. Small
60   states, or states of less natural strength, under vigorous governments, and with the assistance of disciplined armies, have often triumphed over large states, or states of greater natural strength, which have been destitute of these advantages. Neither the pride, nor the safety of the more important states, or confederacies, would permit them long to submit to this mortifying and adventitious inferiority.
65   They would quickly resort to means similar to those by which it had been ef-fected, to reinstate themselves in their lost pre-eminence. Thus we should in a little time see established in every part of this country, the same engines of des-potism which have been the scourge of the old world. This at least would be the natural course of things, and our reasonings will be the more likely to be just, in
70   proportion as they are accommodated to this standard.

These are not vague inferences drawn from supposed or speculative defects in a constitution, the whole power of which is lodged in the hands of the people, or their representatives and delegates, but they are solid conclusions drawn from the natural and necessary progress of human affairs.
75   It may perhaps be asked, by way of objection to this, why did not standing armies spring up out of the contentions which so often distracted the ancient re-publics of Greece? Different answers equally satisfactory, may be given to this question. The industrious habits of the people of the present day, absorbed in the

---

domination of the Atlantic. Here Hamilton turns the conventional doctrine against the Anti-Federalists with the argument that the smaller states would need military forces to protect themselves against their stronger neighbors, in default of a Union strong enough to protect them.

Lines 59–62 Prussia's record in the Seven Years' War (1756–1763) would have been a prime example. So would that of Sweden both in the Thirty Years' War and, later, under Charles XII when he attacked Russia in 1700. (Charles's invasion ended disastrously at Poltava in 1709, however.)

Lines 75–86 A better reason why ancient Greek republics did not need standing armies was that the whole male citizenry was immediately available to be called to arms. Socrates (for example) served in the Athenian army as a patriotic and tough soldier.

pursuits of gain, and devoted to the improvements of agriculture and commerce are incompatible with the condition of a nation of soldiers, which was the true condition of the people of those republics. The means of revenue, which have been so greatly multiplied by the encrease of gold and silver, and of the arts of industry, and the science of finance, which is the offspring of modern times, concurring with the habits of nations, have produced an intire revolution in the system of war, and have rendered disciplined armies, distinct from the body of the citizens, the inseparable companion of frequent hostility.

There is a wide difference also, between military establishments in a country, seldom exposed by its situation to internal invasions, and in one which is often subject to them, and always apprehensive of them. The rulers of the former can have no good pretext, if they are even so inclined, to keep on foot armies so numerous as must of necessity be maintained in the latter. These armies being, in the first case, rarely, if at all, called into activity for interior defence, the people are in no danger of being broken to military subordination. The laws are not accustomed to relaxations, in favor of military exigencies—the civil state remains in full vigor, neither corrupted nor confounded with the principles or propensities of the other state. The smallness of the army renders the natural strength of the community an overmatch for it; and the citizens, not habituated to look up to the military power for protection, or to submit to its oppressions, neither love nor fear the soldiery: They view them with a spirit of jealous acquiescence in a necessary evil, and stand ready to resist a power which they suppose may be exerted to the prejudice of their rights.

The army under such circumstances, may usefully aid the magistrate to suppress a small faction, or an occasional mob, or insurrection; but it will be unable to enforce encroachments against the united efforts of the great body of the people.

In a country, in the predicament last described, the contrary of all this happens. The perpetual menacings of danger oblige the government to be always prepared to repel it—its armies must be numerous enough for instant defence. The continual necessity for their services enhances the importance of the soldier, and proportionably degrades the condition of the citizen. The military state becomes elevated above the civil. The inhabitants of territories, often the theatre of war, are unavoidably subjected to frequent infringements on their rights, which serve to weaken their sense of those rights; and by degrees, the people are brought to consider the soldiery not only as their protectors, but as their superiors. The transition from this disposition to that of considering them as masters, is neither remote, nor difficult: But it is very difficult to prevail upon a people under such impressions, to make a bold, or effectual resistance, to usurpations, supported by the military power.

The kingdom of Great Britain falls within the first description. An insular situation, and a powerful marine, guarding it in a great measure against the

---

Lines 117–34 Here Hamilton makes the point in our comment on lines 43–57, that Britain maintained a standing navy. And he does not fail to note its importance for British liberty; the comparison with continental nations is shrewd and relevant.

possibility of foreign invasion, supersede the necessity of a numerous army within
the kingdom. A sufficient force to make head against a sudden descent, till the
militia could have time to rally and embody, is all that has been deemed requisite.
No motive of national policy has demanded, nor would public opinion have tolerated a larger number of troops upon its domestic establishment. There has
been, for a long time past, little room for the operation of the other causes, which
have been enumerated as the consequences of internal war. This peculiar felicity
of situation has, in a great degree, contributed to preserve the liberty, which that
country to this day enjoys, in spite of the prevalent venality and corruption. If, on
the contrary, Britain had been situated on the continent, and had been compelled, as she would have been, by that situation, to make her military establishments at home co-extensive with those of the other great powers of Europe, she,
like them, would in all probability, be at this day a victim to the absolute power
of a single man. 'Tis possible, though not easy, that the people of that island may
be enslaved from other causes, but it cannot be by the prowess of an army so inconsiderable as that which has been usually kept up within the kingdom.

If we are wise enough to preserve the union, we may for ages enjoy an advantage similar to that of an insulated situation. Europe is at a great distance from us.
Her colonies in our vicinity, will be likely to continue too much disproportioned
in strength, to be able to give us any dangerous annoyance. Extensive military establishments cannot, in this position, be necessary to our security. But if we
should be disunited, and the integral parts should either remain separated, or
which is most probable, should be thrown together into two or three confederacies, we should be in a short course of time, in the predicament of the continental powers of Europe—our liberties would be a prey to the means of defending
ourselves against the ambition and jealousy of each other.

This is an idea not superficial nor futile, but solid and weighty. It deserves the
most serious and mature consideration of every prudent and honest man of whatever party. If such men will make a firm and solemn pause, and meditate dis-
passionately on the importance of this interesting idea, if they will contemplate
it, in all its attitudes, and trace it to all its consequences, they will not hesitate to
part with trivial objections to a constitution, the rejection of which would in all
probability put a final period to the union. The airy phantoms that flit before the
distempered imaginations of some of its adversaries, would quickly give place to
the more substantial prospects of dangers real, certain, and formidable.

PUBLIUS.

NINE

ALEXANDER HAMILTON
November 21, 1787

The Utility of the Union as a Safeguard Against Domestic Faction and Insurrection

To the People of the State of New York.

A firm union will be of the utmost moment to the peace and liberty of the states as a barrier against domestic faction and insurrection. It is impossible to read the history of the petty republics of Greece and Italy, without feeling sensations of horror and disgust at the distractions with which they were continually agitated, and at the rapid succession of revolutions, by which they were kept in a state of perpetual vibration, between the extremes of tyranny and anarchy. If they exhibit occasional calms, these only serve as short-lived contrasts to the furious storms that are to succeed. If now and then intervals of felicity open themselves to view, we behold them with a mixture of regret arising from the reflection that the pleasing scenes before us are soon to be overwhelmed by the tempestuous waves of sedition and party rage. If momentary rays of glory break forth from the gloom, while they dazzle us with a transient and fleeting brilliancy, they at the same time admonish us to lament that the vices of government should pervert the direction and tarnish the lustre of those bright talents and exalted indowments, for which the favoured soils, that produced them, have been so justly celebrated.

From the disorders that disfigure the annals of those republics, the advocates of despotism have drawn arguments, not only against the forms of republican government, but against the very principles of civil liberty. They have decried all free government, as inconsistent with the order of society, and have indulged themselves in malicious exultation over its friends and partizans. Happily for mankind, stupendous fabrics reared on the basis of liberty, which have flourished

---

Line 11 Among numerous references to alliances, wars, and political instabilities in the ancient world, this section's remark about "momentary rays of glory" is almost Publius's *only* recognition of Greek philosophy, literature, or art!

Lines 16–17 The "advocates of despotism" are not mentioned by name and one cannot be sure whom Hamilton had in mind. Hobbes, who might have qualified under that title, based his argument on human nature and on an original contract rather than on history. Machiavelli's use of Athens and Sparta in *The Prince*, chapter 5, occurs in a discussion of how to govern *foreign* cities that lived under their own laws before being annexed.

Lines 21–22 By "the stupendous fabrics reared on the basis of liberty" Hamilton presumably intends readers to understand the Roman Empire, which had "flourished for ages," but it seems likely that he was glancing at the British Empire as well.

for ages, have in a few glorious instances refuted their gloomy sophisms. And, I trust, America will be the broad and solid foundation of other edifices not less magnificent, which will be equally permanent monuments of their errors.

25   But it is not to be denied that the portraits, they have sketched of republican government, were too just copies of the originals from which they were taken. If it had been found impracticable, to have devised models of a more perfect structure, the enlightened friends to liberty would have been obliged to abandon the cause of that species of government as indefensible. The science of politics, how-
30   ever, like most other sciences has received great improvement. The efficacy of various principles is now well understood, which were either not known at all, or imperfectly known to the ancients. The regular distribution of power into distinct departments—the introduction of legislative ballances and checks—the institution of courts composed of judges, holding their offices during good behaviour—
35   the representation of the people in the legislature by deputies of their own election—these are either wholly new discoveries or have made their principal progress towards perfection in modern times. They are means, and powerful means, by which the excellencies of republican government may be retained and its imperfections lessened or avoided. To this catalogue of circumstances,
40   that tend to the amelioration of popular systems of civil government, I shall venture, however novel it may appear to some, to add one more on a principle, which has been made the foundation of an objection to the new constitution, I mean the ENLARGEMENT of the ORBIT within which such systems are to revolve either in respect to the dimensions of a single state, or to the consolidation
45   of several smaller states into one great confederacy. The latter is that which im-

---

Lines 29–37 This transition marks a significant departure toward recognition of what we now call "progress" in both political science and human institutions.

Lines 32–33 Hamilton here refers to "[T]he regular distribution of power into distinct departments . . . ," judicial tenure during good behavior, and representation through elections.

Line 40 "tend to the amelioration of the popular systems of civil government. . . " Human institutions are not doomed to failure or to be trapped in historical cycles; they can be improved by the application of enlightened intelligence. This type of reasoning sustains the claim of *The Federalist* to be an example of Enlightenment thinking.

Line 43 Note the astronomical imagery in "the ENLARGEMENT of the ORBIT within which such systems are to revolve . . . ." This type of metaphor, which had become familiar with the adoption of Newtonian mechanics, implied that political systems could be devised whose motions would follow permanent and unchanging laws, assimilating the laws of human behavior to the laws of natural motion. The further implication was that human nature could be subjected to such laws. This type of vision contrasts with the organic, developmental view that was to become popular in the 19th century, linking with Darwinian evolution; hints of these views appeared long before Darwin, and can be discerned in Chief Justice John Marshall's view of the Constitution. See also Publius's own implicit recognition of the organic character of the Constitution, No. 82.

mediately concerns the object under consideration. It will however be of use to examine the principle in its application to a single state which shall be attended to in another place.

The utility of a confederacy, as well to suppress faction and to guard the internal tranquillity of states, as to increase their external force and security, is in reality not a new idea. It has been practiced upon in different countries and ages, and has received the sanction of the most applauded writers, on the subjects of politics. The opponents of the PLAN proposed have with great assiduity cited and circulated the observations of Montesquieu on the necessity of a contracted territory for a republican government. But they seem not to have been apprised of the sentiments of that great man expressed in another part of his work, nor to have adverted to the consequences of the principle to which they subscribe, with such ready acquiescence.

When Montesquieu recommends a small extent for republics, the standards he had in view were of dimensions, far short of the limits of almost every one of these states. Neither Virginia, Massachusetts, Pennsylvania, New-York, North-Carolina, nor Georgia, can by any means be compared with the models, from which he reasoned and to which the terms of his description apply. If we therefore take his ideas on this point, as the criterion of truth, we shall be driven to the alternative, either of taking refuge at once in the arms of monarchy, or of splitting ourselves into an infinity of little jealous, clashing, tumultuous commonwealths, the wretched nurseries of unceasing discord and the miserable objects of universal pity or contempt. Some of the writers, who have come forward on the other side of the question, seem to have been aware of the dilemma; and have even been bold enough to hint at the division of the larger states, as a desirable thing. Such an infatuated policy, such a desperate expedient, might, by the multiplication of petty offices, answer the views of men, who possess not qualifications to

---

Lines 53–55 Montesquieu: Charles-Louis de Secondat, Baron de la Brède et de Montesquieu (1689–1755), was probably the Enlightenment author most frequently cited during the entire debate on the Constitution. His first major success, *The Persian Letters*, published in 1721, commented on French institutions obliquely, satirically claiming to adopt a comparative perspective by pretending to be letters home from a Persian prince. They quickly established his popularity. His greatest work, *The Spirit of the Laws (De L'Esprit des Lois)*, published in 1748, was soon translated into English and very widely read in Britain and America. Montesquieu argued that different types of legal systems, each accompanied by its own distinct ethos, were adapted to different climates and circumstances; it followed that different ethical principles were fitted for different types of government. Observe that this view contrasted sharply with Jefferson's moral universalism. (Once again, there is no single Enlightenment!) Montesquieu's view that republican forms of government were adaptable only to small territories was based on the conviction that a government strong enough to rule over a large area would inevitably be too strong for the liberties of the people—a conviction that was meat and drink to Anti-Federalists and thus a challenge that had to be answered. Hamilton is here concerned to show that the objection does not apply to the states of America, and that in fact the argument can be reversed.

extend their influence beyond the narrow circles of personal intrigue, but it could never promote the greatness or happiness of the people of America.

75   Referring the examination of the principle itself to another place, as has been already mentioned, it will be sufficient to remark here, that in the sense of the author who has been most emphatically quoted upon the occasion, it would only dictate a reduction of the SIZE of the more considerable MEMBERS of the union; but would not militate against their being all comprehended in one con-
80 federate government. And this is the true question, in the discussion of which we are at present interested.

    So far are the suggestions of Montesquieu from standing in opposition to a general union of the states, that he explicitly treats of a CONFEDERATE RE-PUBLIC as the expedient for extending the sphere of popular government and
85 reconciling the advantages of monarchy with those of republicanism.

    "It is very probable (says he*) that mankind would have been obliged, at length, to live constantly under the government of a SINGLE PERSON, had they not contrived a kind of constitution, that has all the internal advantages of a republican, together with the external force of a monarchial government. I mean
90 a CONFEDERATE REPUBLIC.

    "This form of government is a convention, by which several smaller *states* agree to become members of a larger *one*, which they intend to form. It is a kind of assemblage of societies, that constitute a new one, capable of encreasing by means of new associations, till they arrive to such a degree of power as to be able
95 to provide for the security of the united body.

    "A republic of this kind, able to withstand an external force, may support itself without any internal corruption. The form of this society prevents all manner of inconveniences.

    "If a single member should attempt to usurp the supreme authority, he could
100 not be supposed to have an equal authority and credit, in all the confederate states. Were he to have too great influence over one, this would alarm the rest. Were he to subdue a part, that which would still remain free might oppose him with forces, independent of those which he had usurped, and overpower him before he could be settled in his usurpation.

105   "Should a popular insurrection happen, in one of the confederate states, the others are able to quell it. Should abuses creep into one part, they are reformed by those that remain sound. The state may be destroyed on one side, and not on the other; the confederacy may be dissolved, and the confederates preserve their sovereignty.

110   "As this government is composed of small republics it enjoys the internal happiness of each, and with respect to its external situation it is possessed, by means of the association of all the advantages of large monarchies."

    I have thought it proper to quote at length these interesting passages, because they contain a luminous abrigement of the principal arguments in favour of the

---

Spirit of Laws, Vol. I. Book IX. Chap. I.

union, and must effectually remove the false impressions, which a misapplica- *115*
tion of other parts of the work was calculated to produce. They have at the same
time an intimate connection with the more immediate design of this paper;
which is to illustrate the tendency of the union to repress domestic faction and
insurrection.

A distinction, more subtle than accurate has been raised between a *confeder-* *120*
acy and a *consolidation* of the states. The essential characteristic of the first is said
to be, the restriction of its authority to the members in their collective capacities,
without reaching to the individuals of whom they are composed. It is contended
that the national council ought to have no concern with any object of internal
administration. An exact equality of suffrage between the members has also been *125*
insisted upon as a leading feature of a confederate government. These positions
are in the main arbitrary; they are supported neither by principle nor precedent.
It has indeed happened that governments of this kind have generally operated in
the manner, which the distinction, taken notice of, supposes to be inherent in
their nature — but there have been in most of them extensive exceptions to the *130*
practice, which serve to prove as far as example will go, that there is no absolute
rule on the subject. And it will be clearly shewn, in the course of this investigation, that as far as the principle contended for has prevailed, it has been the cause
of incurable disorder and imbecility in the government.

The definition of a *confederate republic* seems simply to be, an "assemblage of *135*
societies" or an association of two or more states into one state. The extent, modifications and objects of the federal authority are mere matters of discretion. So
long as the separate organization of the members be not abolished, so long as it
exists by a constitutional necessity for local purposes, though it should be in perfect subordination to the general authority of the union, it would still be, in fact and *140*
in theory, an association of states, or a confederacy. The proposed constitution,
so far from implying an abolition of the state governments, makes them constituent parts of the national sovereignty by allowing them a direct representation

---

Lines 120–34 Anti-Federalist critics repeatedly asserted that the aim of the Constitution was *consolidation* of the Union, destroying the liberties of the states; it was important to *The Federalist* to answer this objection by showing that the states would
retain many privileges that only the Constitution could effectively preserve. Hamilton sagaciously argues that the historical evidence is inconclusive and that "there is
no absolute rule on the subject" (lines 131–32). (If Madison had been writing this
essay he would probably have entered into an analysis of the Roman Republic, the
Dutch Republic and the Swiss Confederation; Hamilton makes his point without
citing examples.)

Lines 132–34 According to the plan of *The Federalist*, Madison will illustrate this
point about confederacies in great detail in Nos. 18–20.

Lines 142–43 The reference to making the states "constituent parts of the national
sovereignty" reappears in slightly altered form but similar strategic purpose in No.
45, lines 77–78, where "The state governments may be regarded as constituent and

145 in the senate, and leaves in their possession certain exclusive and very important portions of sovereign power. This fully corresponds, in every rational import of the terms, with the idea of a federal government.

---

essential parts of the federal government." The present phraseology flatters the aspirations of the states by hinting that they will be entering into a share of a larger sovereignty than they could claim on their own. At the same time they are given a reassurance that by entering into the "national" they will retain powers that they fear may be threatened. It is Publius's first hint that sovereignty might in some subtle way be divided between the nation and the states. This was sensitive territory. The concept of sovereignty carried a momentous rhetorical charge, involving the most fundamental issues of the right to govern and the obligations of the governed. In western political thought it was first expounded at length by the French jurisprudential philosopher Jean Bodin in his *Six Books of the Commonwealthe (Six Livres de la République)* (1576). This work was born of the turmoil of the French Wars of Religion; Bodin had nearly lost his life in the massacre of St. Bartholomew's Day in 1572, and the experience impressed on him the supreme importance of the state as the agent of lawful order. The central principles are that sovereignty is absolute: there is no appeal to a higher authority; but that to be valid, sovereignty must also bear the stamp of legitimacy. To be *absolute*, however, is not to be arbitrary: an absolute sovereign is *absolved* from the laws of men, but not from the laws of God. The concept was developed with extraordinary power by Thomas Hobbes in *Leviathan*, which, appearing in 1651, was also a product of the turmoil of civil war. Hobbes's theory, unlike Bodin's, was based on the concept of a primary—but irreversible— contract. In truth, however, no absolutist theory could be made to fit either British or American institutions, which in both cases rested both historically and jurisprudentially on a large measure of consent and participation. But when colonial lawyers debated the question of how power was distributed in the British Empire, they did recognize that a vast, loosely coordinated imperial structure could only be regulated from the center: in *some* respects, a form of British sovereign power had to be acknowledged, though not so much as to infringe on the internal liberties of the colonies. These ambiguities were never resolved, though attempts to resolve them threw up hints of divided authority, which would not have been compatible with the British principle that sovereignty over the empire rested in Parliament alone. After independence, the Articles of Confederation reverted to the conventional concept in Article 2, which confirmed the *individual* sovereignty of the states. In other words, the sovereignty of Parliament had devolved onto the states. The Continental Congress was a "congress" in the European sense—a coming together of sovereigns; by subscribing to the Articles, the states conferred only certain specified powers on the Congress. The Congress could neither tax nor make laws for individuals; it represented the states and it dealt with the states. The Congress could make treaties but it could not enforce them within the states; it could make requisitions on the states but could not enforce payment. These and other structural weaknesses in the system produced the paradox that the makers of the new Constitution found themselves facing problems somewhat similar to those of the British before them. The Federalists believed in principle that sovereignty could not be divided. In No. 20, Madison will state in cogent language the principle that the notion of "a sovereignty over sovereigns" (lines 127–28) is "a solecism in theory" (line 128) and subversive of order and civil polity in practice. Significantly, there is no disagreement

In the Lycian confederacy, which consisted of twenty-three CITIES or republics, the largest were intitled to *three* votes in the COMMON COUNCIL, those of the middle class to *two* and the smallest to *one*. The COMMON COUNCIL had the appointment of all the judges and magistrates of the respective CITIES. This was certainly the most delicate species of interference in their internal administration; for if there be any thing, that seems exclusively appropriated to the local jurisdictions, it is the appointment of their own officers. Yet Montesquieu, speaking of this association, says "Were I to give a model of an excellent confederate republic, it would be that of Lycia." Thus we perceive that the distinctions insisted upon were not within the contemplation of this enlightened civilian, and we shall be led to conclude that they are the novel refinements of an erroneous theory.

    PUBLIUS.

150

155

---

with Anti-Federalism on this point. The Virginia Anti-Federalist publicist calling himself "The Impartial Examiner," writing on February 20, 1788, used conventional language in describing the idea of two sovereignties existing in the same community as "a perfect solecism." Anti-Federalists, of course, didn't want to give up state sovereignty; the basic Federalist position, on the *same* view of sovereignty, was that the states must relinquish their claims, if the Union was to survive. But from Publius's point of view, the issue was fraught with political dangers arising from local attachments to the states, and from *localist* fears of just the sort of centralized power that the Americans had so recently escaped, and at such heavy cost. Madison's thinking was not as absolutist as his language in No. 20 would suggest; in a memorandum entitled "Vices of the Political System of the United States," drafted in April 1787, he observed that, "the great desideratum in Government is such a modification of the sovereignty as will render it sufficiently neutral between the different interests and factions, to control one part of the society from invading the rights of the other, and at the same time sufficiently controlled itself, from setting up an interest adverse to that of the whole Society." This anticipates arguments in Nos. 10 and 51. In fact, however, the concept of sovereignty was to be significantly modified during *The Federalist's* prolonged encounter with the opposition; further references occur and will be annotated in Nos. 15, 19, 20, 32, 33, 39, 40, 42, 43, 45, 62, 64, and 81.

Lines 147–58 The Lycians, who occupied a territory in southwest Anatolia (now the Asian area of Turkey), appear in the 8th century B.C. as a prosperous people confederated in about twenty cities and enjoying considerable freedom from powerful neighbors. The principle of the Lycian confederation that appeals to Hamilton is the proportional vote of the cities according to population. This resembles the principle applying to the system of voting under the new Constitution. So little is known of the Lycian confederation, however, that it is not mentioned by Herodotus (who does note that Lycian men took their surnames from their mothers). Montesquieu, who cites Strabo, refers to Lycia in a few lines of *The Spirit of the Laws,* book XI, chapter iv.

Lines 156–57 The phrase "this enlightened civilian" refers to Montesquieu's profession as a civil lawyer.

TEN

JAMES MADISON
November 22, 1787
The Same Subject Continued

To the People of the State of New York.

Among the numerous advantages promised by a well constructed union, none
deserves to be more accurately developed than its tendency to break and control
the violence of faction. The friend of popular governments, never finds himself
so much alarmed for their character and fate, as when he contemplates their
propensity to this dangerous vice. He will not fail therefore to set a due value on
any plan which, without violating the principles to which he is attached, provides a proper cure for it. The instability, injustice and confusion introduced into
the public councils, have in truth been the mortal diseases under which popular
governments have every where perished; as they continue to be the favorite and
fruitful topics from which the adversaries to liberty derive their most specious
declamations. The valuable improvements made by the American constitutions
on the popular models, both ancient and modern, cannot certainly be too much
admired; but it would be an unwarrantable partiality, to contend that they have
as effectually obviated the danger on this side as was wished and expected. Complaints are every where heard from our most considerate and virtuous citizens,
equally the friends of public and private faith, and of public and personal liberty;
that our governments are too unstable; that the public good is disregarded in the
conflicts of rival parties; and that measures are too often decided, not according
to the rules of justice, and the rights of the minor party; but by the superior force
of an interested and over-bearing majority. However anxiously we may wish that
these complaints had no foundation, the evidence of known facts will not permit
us to deny that they are in some degree true. It will be found indeed, on a candid
review of our situation, that some of the distresses under which we labor, have
been erroneously charged on the operation of our governments; but it will be
found, at the same time, that other causes will not alone account for many of our
heaviest misfortunes; and particularly, for that prevailing and increasing distrust
of public engagements, and alarm for private rights, which are echoed from one
end of the continent to the other. These must be chiefly, if not wholly, effects of
the unsteadiness and injustice, with which a factious spirit has tainted our public
administration.

By a faction I understand a number of citizens, whether amounting to a majority or minority of the whole, who are united and actuated by some common
impulse of passion, or of interest, adverse to the rights of other citizens or to the
permanent and aggregate interests of the community.

There are two methods of curing the mischiefs of faction: the one, by remov- *35* ing its causes; the other, by controling its effects.

There are again two methods of removing the causes of faction: the one by destroying the liberty which is essential to its existence, the other, by giving to every citizen the same opinions, the same passions, and the same interests.

It could never be more truly said than of the first remedy, that it is worse than *40* the disease. Liberty is to faction, what air is to fire, an aliment without which it instantly expires. But it could not be a less folly to abolish liberty, which is essential to political life, because it nourishes faction, than it would be to wish the annihilation of air, which is essential to animal life, because it imparts to fire its destructive agency. *45*

The second expedient is as impracticable, as the first would be unwise. As long as the reason of man continues fallible, and he is at liberty to exercise it, different opinions will be formed. As long as the connection subsists between his reason and his self-love, his opinions and his passions will have a reciprocal in- *50* fluence on each other; and the former will be objects to which the latter will attach themselves. The diversity in the faculties of men from which the rights of property originate, is not less an insuperable obstacle to an uniformity of interests. The protection of these faculties is the first object of government. From the protection of different and unequal faculties of acquiring property, the possession *55* of different degrees and kinds of property immediately results: and from the influence of these on the sentiments and views of the respective proprietors, ensues a division of the society into different interests and parties.

The latent causes of faction are thus sown in the nature of man; and we see them every where brought into different degrees of activity, according to the different circumstances of civil society. A zeal for different opinions concerning religion, *60* concerning government and many other points, as well of speculation as of practice; an attachment to different leaders ambitiously contending for pre-eminence

---

Lines 46–57 This passage suggests the influence of David Hume's essays, "That Politics May Be Reduced to a Science," and "Of the First Principles of Government." Madison's remarks about property struck a chord with Charles Beard, who had noticed as a boy growing up on his father's midwestern farm in the 1880s that when local farmers gathered in his parents' parlor on Sundays, they talked a lot about the prices of hogs and cereals but very little about political principles.

Lines 51–53 Notice Madison's curious statement that *rights* to property originate in the *diversity* of men's faculties; one might have expected him to say that men (for which, read persons) had a *property* in their faculties; he continues by saying that the first object of government is the protection of these faculties. According to conventional psychology, the mind was made up of differing faculties, such as reason, will, passion, and imagination. These were differently represented in different persons, resulting in unequal distribution of goods. *That*, in Madison's view, is what government is instituted to protect.

and power; or to persons of other descriptions whose fortunes have been interesting to the human passions, have in turn divided mankind into parties, inflamed
65   them with mutual animosity, and rendered them much more disposed to vex and
oppress each other, than to co-operate for their common good. So strong is this
propensity of mankind to fall into mutual animosities, that where no substantial
occasion presents itself, the most frivolous and fanciful distinctions have been
sufficient to kindle their unfriendly passions, and excite their most violent con-
70   flicts. But the most common and durable source of factions, has been the various
and unequal distribution of property. Those who hold, and those who are without property, have ever formed distinct interests in society. Those who are creditors, and those who are debtors, fall under a like discrimination. A landed
interest, a manufacturing interest, a mercantile interest, a monied interest, with
75   many lesser interests, grow up of necessity in civilized nations, and divide them
into different classes, actuated by different sentiments and views. The regulation
of these various and interfering interests forms the principal task of modern legislation, and involves the spirit of party and faction in the necessary and ordinary
operations of government.
80   No man is allowed to be a judge in his own cause; because his interest would
certainly bias his judgment, and, not improbably, corrupt his integrity. With
equal, nay with greater reason, a body of men, are unfit to be both judges and
parties, at the same time; yet, what are many of the most important acts of legislation, but so many judicial determinations, not indeed concerning the rights of
85   single persons, but concerning the rights of large bodies of citizens; and what are
the different classes of legislators, but advocates and parties to the causes which
they determine? Is a law proposed concerning private debts? It is a question to
which the creditors are parties on one side, and the debtors on the other. Justice
ought to hold the balance between them. Yet the parties are and must be them-

---

Lines 71–79 This description of the "interests" which make up a "civilized" nation
derives ultimately from Edmund Burke's celebrated essay, *Thoughts on the Cause of
the Present Discontents* (1770), which introduced the concept of interest representation into political discourse.

Much of the analysis of the sources of social discord, and of the concept of "interests" in political society in this essay, had been anticipated by Madison in a long
speech in the preceding summer's Federal Convention on June 6.

In Burke's view, famously propounded in his *Letter to the Electors of Bristol*
(1774), in which he refused to accept instructions from them, a member of Parliament, once elected, was a member for the whole nation. This doctrine, which reflected the British feeling for the unity of the nation, and helped to give a certain
cohesive force to parliamentary government (though it did not prevent party divisions) was not available to Madison, who was faced to a much greater degree with
the politics of special interests, whether local, economic, or religious. Congress has
always derived its claim to political legitimacy from its ability to represent the aggregation of local interests.

selves the judges; and the most numerous party, or, in other words, the most 90
powerful faction must be expected to prevail. Shall domestic manufactures be
encouraged, and in what degree, by restrictions on foreign manufactures? are
questions which would be differently decided by the landed and the manufacturing classes; and probably by neither, with a sole regard to justice and the public
good. The apportionment of taxes on the various descriptions of property, is an 95
act which seems to require the most exact impartiality; yet, there is perhaps no
legislative act in which greater opportunity and temptation are given to a predominant party, to trample on the rules of justice. Every shilling with which they
over-burden the inferior number, is a shilling saved to their own pockets.

It is in vain to say, that enlightened statesmen will be able to adjust these 100
clashing interests, and render them all subservient to the public good. Enlightened statesmen will not always be at the helm: Nor, in many cases, can such an
adjustment be made at all, without taking into view indirect and remote considerations, which will rarely prevail over the immediate interest which one party
may find in disregarding the rights of another, or the good of the whole. 105

The inference to which we are brought, is, that the *causes* of faction cannot be
removed; and that relief is only to be sought in the means of controling its *effects*.

If a faction consists of less than a majority, relief is supplied by the republican
principle, which enables the majority to defeat its sinister views by regular vote: It
may clog the administration, it may convulse the society; but it will be unable to 110
execute and mask its violence under the forms of the constitution. When a majority is included in a faction, the form of popular government on the other hand
enables it to sacrifice to its ruling passion or interest, both the public good and
the rights of other citizens. To secure the public good, and private rights against
the danger of such a faction, and at the same time to preserve the spirit and the 115
form of popular government, is then the great object to which our enquiries are
directed. Let me add that it is the great desideratum, by which alone this form of
government can be rescued from the opprobrium under which it has so long labored, and be recommended to the esteem and adoption of mankind.

By what means is this object attainable? Evidently by one of two only. Either 120
the existence of the same passion or interest in a majority at the same time must
be prevented; or the majority, having such co-existent passion or interest, must
be rendered, by their number and local situation, unable to concert and carry
into effect schemes of oppression. If the impulse and the opportunity be suffered
to coincide, we well know that neither moral nor religious motives can be relied 125
on as an adequate control. They are not found to be such on the injustice and violence of individuals, and lose their efficacy in proportion to the number combined together; that is, in proportion as their efficacy becomes needful.

From this view of the subject, it may be concluded, that a pure democracy, by
which I mean a society consisting of a small number of citizens, who assemble 130
and administer the government in person, can admit of no cure for the mischiefs
of faction. A common passion or interest will, in almost every case, be felt by a
majority of the whole; a communication and concert results from the form of

government itself; and there is nothing to check the inducements to sacrifice the
weaker party, or an obnoxious individual. Hence it is, that such democracies
have ever been spectacles of turbulence and contention; have ever been found
incompatible with personal security or the rights of property; and have in general
been as short in their lives, as they have been violent in their deaths. Theoretic
politicians, who have patronized this species of government, have erroneously
supposed, that by reducing mankind to a perfect equality in their political rights,
they would, at the same time, be perfectly equalized and assimilated in their possessions, their opinions, and their passions.

A republic, by which I mean a government in which the scheme of representation takes place, opens a different prospect, and promises the cure for which we
are seeking. Let us examine the points in which it varies from pure democracy,
and we shall comprehend both the nature of the cure, and the efficacy which it
must derive from the union.

The two great points of difference between a democracy and a republic are,
first, the delegation of the government, in the latter, to a small number of citizens
elected by the rest: secondly, the greater number of citizens and greater sphere of
country, over which the latter may be extended.

The effect of the first difference is, on the one hand to refine and enlarge the
public views, by passing them through the medium of a chosen body of citizens,
whose wisdom may best discern the true interest of their country, and whose patriotism and love of justice, will be least likely to sacrifice it to temporary or partial considerations. Under such a regulation, it may well happen that the public
voice pronounced by the representatives of the people, will be more consonant
to the public good, than if pronounced by the people themselves convened for
the purpose. On the other hand, the effect may be inverted. Men of factious
tempers, of local prejudices, or of sinister designs, may by intrigue, by corruption
or by other means, first obtain the suffrages, and then betray the interests of the
people. The question resulting is, whether small or extensive republics are most
favorable to the election of proper guardians of the public weal: and it is clearly
decided in favor of the latter by two obvious considerations.

In the first place it is to be remarked that however small the republic may be,
the representatives must be raised to a certain number, in order to guard against
the cabals of a few; and that however large it may be, they must be limited to a
certain number, in order to guard against the confusion of a multitude. Hence
the number of representatives in the two cases, not being in proportion to that of
the constituents, and being proportionally greatest in the small republic, it fol-

---

Lines 138–39 Foremost among the "theoretic politicians" Madison has in mind is
no doubt Jean-Jacques Rousseau, whose *Social Contract (Du Contrat Sociale)* (1762)
argued for the equality of citizens and subordination of individuals to the general
will. But Rousseau, although known to the *cognoscenti,* or those we would now call
"intellectuals," failed to make much impact on American thought.

lows, that if the proportion of fit characters, be not less, in the large than in the small republic, the former will present a greater option, and consequently a greater probability of a fit choice.

In the next place, as each representative will be chosen by a greater number of citizens in the large than in the small republic, it will be more difficult for un- *175* worthy candidates to practise with success the vicious arts, by which elections are too often carried; and the suffrages of the people being more free, will be more likely to centre on men who possess the most attractive merit, and the most diffusive and established characters.

It must be confessed, that in this, as in most other cases, there is a mean, on *180* both sides of which inconveniencies will be found to lie. By enlarging too much the number of electors, you render the representative too little acquainted with all their local circumstances and lesser interests; as by reducing it too much, you render him unduly attached to these, and too little fit to comprehend and pursue great and national objects. The federal constitution forms a happy combination *185* in this respect; the great and aggregate interests being referred to the national, the local and particular, to the state legislatures.

The other point of difference is, the greater number of citizens and extent of territory which may be brought within the compass of republican, than of democratic government; and it is this circumstance principally which renders factious *190* combinations less to be dreaded in the former, than in the latter. The smaller the society, the fewer probably will be the distinct parties and interests composing it, the fewer the distinct parties and interests, the more frequently will a majority be found of the same party; and the smaller the number of individuals composing a majority, and the smaller the compass within which they are placed, the more *195* easily will they concert and execute their plans of oppression. Extend the sphere, and you take in a greater variety of parties and interests; you make it less probable that a majority of the whole will have a common motive to invade the rights of other citizens; or if such a common motive exists, it will be more difficult for all who feel it to discover their own strength, and to act in unison with each other. *200* Besides other impediments, it may be remarked, that where there is a consciousness of unjust or dishonorable purposes, communication is always checked by distrust, in proportion to the number whose concurrence is necessary.

Hence it clearly appears, that the same advantage, which a republic has over a democracy, in controling the effects of faction, is enjoyed by a large over a *205* small republic—is enjoyed by the union over the states composing it. Does this advantage consist in the substitution of representatives, whose enlightened views and virtuous sentiments render them superior to local prejudices, and to schemes of injustice? It will not be denied, that the representation of the union

---

Lines 188–203 This answers the objection to republican government over large territories from Montesquieu, for which see No. 9, lines 53–55 (and comment) and lines 59–74.

210   will be most likely to possess these requisite endowments. Does it consist in the greater security afforded by a greater variety of parties, against the event of any one party being able to outnumber and oppress the rest? In an equal degree does the encreased variety of parties, comprised within the union, encrease this security. Does it, in fine, consist in the greater obstacles opposed to the concert and

215   accomplishment of the secret wishes of an unjust and interested majority? Here, again, the extent of the union gives it the most palpable advantage.

    The influence of factious leaders may kindle a flame within their particular states, but will be unable to spread a general conflagration through the other states: A religious sect, may degenerate into a political faction in a part of the

220   confederacy; but the variety of sects dispersed over the entire face of it, must secure the national councils against any danger from that source: A rage for paper money, for an abolition of debts, for an equal division of property, or for any other improper or wicked project, will be less apt to pervade the whole body of the union, than a particular member of it; in the same proportion as such a malady

225   is more likely to taint a particular county or district, than an entire state.

    In the extent and proper structure of the union, therefore, we behold a republican remedy for the diseases most incident to republican government. And according to the degree of pleasure and pride, we feel in being republicans, ought to be our zeal in cherishing the spirit, and supporting the character of federalists.

PUBLIUS.

Lines 226–29 This summarizing paragraph, with its emphasis that the Constitution offers Americans a *republican* remedy for the problems of republican government, may be considered the keynote of *The Federalist* enterprise. The Americans have shaken off the coils of monarchy and must now confront human nature in its own form.

ELEVEN

ALEXANDER HAMILTON
November 24, 1787
The Utility of the Union in Respect to Commerce and a Navy

To the People of the State of New York.

The importance of the union, in a commercial light, is one of those points, about which there is least room to entertain a difference of opinion, and which has in fact commanded the most general assent of men, who have any acquaintance with the subject. This applies as well to our intercourse with foreign countries, as with each other.   5

    There are appearances to authorise a supposition, that the adventurous spirit, which distinguishes the commercial character of America, has already excited uneasy sensations in several of the maritime powers of Europe. They seem to be apprehensive of our too great interference in that carrying trade, which is the support of their navigation and the foundation of their naval strength. Those of   10
them, which have colonies in America, look forward, to what this country is capable of becoming, with painful solicitude. They foresee the dangers, that may threaten their American dominions from the neighbourhood of states, which have all the dispositions, and would possess all the means, requisite to the creation of a powerful marine. Impressions of this kind will naturally indicate the   15
policy of fostering divisions among us, and of depriving us as far as possible of an ACTIVE COMMERCE in our own bottoms. This would answer the threefold purpose of preventing our interference in their navigation, of monopolising the profits of our trade, and of clipping the wings, by which we might soar to a dangerous greatness. Did not prudence forbid the detail, it would not be difficult to   20
trace by facts the workings of this policy to the cabinets of ministers.

Lines 6–21 Hamilton's view of American prospects is enthusiastic but in existing circumstances, overly optimistic. In Britain, Parliament had rejected the plan put forward by the Prime Minister, William Pitt the younger—his father was the famous William Pitt, Earl of Chatham—for a favorable trade treaty with the newly recognized United States. The opposition, led by the Earl of Sheffield, argued that the British trading position was strong and that Britain did not need to do favors to her ex-colonies. In 1783, as the War of Independence ended, the British government had issued orders in council banning United States merchant shipping from ports in the British West Indies. This move, which of course was entirely contrary to the concept of free trade advocated by Adam Smith, gave Americans such as John Adams a severe shock.

If we continue united, we may counteract a policy so unfriendly to our prosperity in a variety of ways. By prohibitory regulations, extending at the same time throughout the states, we may oblige foreign countries to bid against each other, for the privileges of our markets. This assertion will not appear chimerical to those who are able to appreciate the importance to any manufacturing nation of the markets of three millions of people—increasing in rapid progression, for the most part exclusively addicted to agriculture, and likely from local circumstances to remain in this disposition and the immense difference there would be to the trade and navigation of such a nation, between a direct communication in its own ships, and an indirect conveyance of its products and returns, to and from America, in the ships of another country. Suppose, for instance, we had a government in America, capable of excluding Great-Britain (with whom we have at present no treaty of commerce) from all our ports, what would be the probable operation of this step upon her politics? Would it not enable us to negotiate with the fairest prospect of success for commercial privileges of the most valuable and extensive kind in the dominions of that kingdom? When these questions have been asked, upon other occasions, they have received a plausible but not a solid or satisfactory answer. It has been said, that prohibitions on our part would produce no change in the system of Britain; because she could prosecute her trade with us, through the medium of the Dutch, who would be her immediate customers and paymasters for those articles which were wanted for the supply of our markets. But would not her navigation be materially injured, by the loss of the important advantage of being her own carrier in that trade? Would not the principal part of its profits be intercepted by the Dutch, as a compensation for their agency and risk? Would not the mere circumstance of freight occasion a considerable deduction? Would not so circuitous an intercourse facilitate the competitions of other nations, by enhancing the price of British commodities in our markets, and by transferring to other hands the management of this interesting branch of the British commerce?

A mature consideration of the objects, suggested by these questions, will justify a belief, that the real disadvantages to Great-Britain from such a state of things, conspiring with the prepossessions of a great part of the nation in favour of the American trade, and with the importunities of the West-India islands, would produce a relaxation in her present system, and would let us into the enjoyment of privileges in the markets of those islands and elsewhere, from which our trade would derive the most substantial benefits. Such a point gained from the British government, and which could not be expected without an equivalent in exemptions and immunities in our markets, would be likely to have a corre-

---

Lines 22–50 About 80 percent of Americans lived by agriculture. It is significant that Hamilton, whose name is associated with the promotion of government finance, commerce, and industry, believed that agriculture would continue to be the predominant feature of the American economy.

spondent effect on the conduct of other nations, who would not be inclined to   *60*
see themselves, altogether supplanted in our trade.

A further resource for influencing the conduct of European nations towards
us, in this respect would arise from the establishment of a federal navy. There
can be no doubt, that the continuance of the union, under an efficient government, would put it in our power, at a period not very distant, to create a navy,   *65*
which, if it could not vie with those of the great maritime powers, would at least
be of respectable weight, if thrown into the scale of either of two contending parties. This would be more particularly the case in relation to operations in the
West-Indies. A few ships of the line sent opportunely to the reinforcement of
either side, would often be sufficient to decide the fate of a campaign, on the event   *70*
of which interests of the greatest magnitude were suspended. Our position is in
this respect a very commanding one. And if to this consideration we add that of
the usefulness of supplies from this country, in the prosecution of military operations in the West-Indies, it will readily be perceived, that a situation so favourable
would enable us to bargain with great advantage for commercial privileges. A   *75*
price would be set not only upon our friendship, but upon our neutrality. By a
steady adherance to the union we may hope ere long to become the arbiter of
Europe in America; and to be able to incline the balance of European competitions in this part of the world as our interest may dictate.

But in the reverse of this eligible situation we shall discover, that the rivalships   *80*
of the parts would make them checks upon each other, and would frustrate all
the tempting advantages, which nature has kindly placed within our reach. In a
state so insignificant, our commerce would be a prey to the wanton intermed-
dlings of all nations at war with each other; who, having nothing to fear from us,
would with little scruple or remorse supply their wants by depredations on our   *85*
property, as often as it fell in their way. The rights of neutrality will only be respected, when they are defended by an adequate power. A nation, despicable by
its weakness, forfeits even the privilege of being neutral.

Under a vigorous national government, the natural strength and resources of
the country, directed to a common interest, would baffle all the combinations of   *90*
European jealousy to restrain our growth. This situation would even take away
the motive to such combinations, by inducing an impracticability of success. An
active commerce, an extensive navigation, a flourishing marine would then be
the inevitable offspring of moral and physical necessity. We might defy the little
arts of little politicians to controul, or vary, the irresistible and unchangeable   *95*
course of nature.

But in a state of disunion these combinations might exist, and might operate
with success. It would be in the power of the maritime nations, availing themselves

---

Line 80 "Eligible" here means *desirable*—something one would elect.

Lines 89–96 Hamilton rhetorically invokes nature in alliance with *moral* as well as
physical necessity. Nature becomes a moral force.

of our universal impotence, to prescribe the conditions of our political existence;
and as they have a common interest in being our carriers, and still more in preventing our being theirs, they would in all probability combine to embarrass our navigation in such a manner, as would in effect destroy it, and confine us to a PASSIVE COMMERCE. We should thus be compelled to content ourselves with the first price of our commodities, and to see the profits of our trade snatched from us to enrich our enemies and persecutors. That unequalled spirit of enterprise, which signalises the genius of the American Merchants and Navigators, and which is in itself an inexhaustible mine of national wealth, would be stifled and lost; and poverty and disgrace would overspread a country, which with wisdom might make herself the admiration and envy of the world.

There are rights of great moment to the trade of America, which are rights of the union. — I allude to the fisheries, to the navigation of the lakes, and to that of the Mississippi. The dissolution of the confederacy would give room for delicate questions, concerning the future existence of these rights; which the interest of more powerful partners would hardly fail to solve to our disadvantage. The disposition of Spain with regard to the Mississippi needs no comment. France and Britain are concerned with us in the fisheries; and view them as of the utmost moment to their navigation. They, of course, would hardly remain long indifferent to that decided mastery of which experience has shown us to be possessed in this valuable branch of traffic; and by which we are able to undersell those nations in their own markets. What more natural, than that they should be disposed to exclude, from the lists, such dangerous competitors?

This branch of trade ought not to be considered as a partial benefit. All the navigating states may in different degrees advantageously participate in it and under circumstances of a greater extension of mercantile capital would not be unlikely to do it. As a nursery of seamen it now is, or when time shall have more nearly assimilated the principles of navigation in the several states, will become an universal resource. To the establishment of a navy it must be indispensible.

To this great national object a NAVY, union will contribute in various ways. Every institution will grow and flourish in proportion to the quantity and extent of the means concentered towards its formation and support. A navy of the

---

Lines 114–21 Spain, which owned the enormous Louisiana territory (including all of what is now Texas and California), had closed the Mississippi to American traffic in 1784. During subsequent negotiations with the Spanish foreign minister Gardoqui, John Jay, representing the Continental Congress, had provisionally agreed to this closure for twenty-five years in return for commercial privileges on the Spanish mainland. These terms caused an outcry. Jay, from New York (and later, of course, one of the authors of *The Federalist*), was denounced for selling out the Southern states' interests in the development prospects of the Southwest; the issue was one of the first to raise the specter of great sectional divisions based on geo-economic interests. The proposed treaty was rejected by the Congress. But the feeble power of the United States could do nothing to coerce Spain. See also No. 15, lines 34–68.

United States, as it would embrace the resources of all, is an object far less re- *135*
mote than a navy of any single state, or partial confederacy, which would only
embrace the resources of a part. It happens indeed that different portions of confederated America possess each some peculiar advantage for this essential establishment. The more Southern states furnish in greater abundance certain kinds
of naval stores—tar, pitch and turpentine. Their wood for the construction of
ships is also of a more solid and lasting texture. The difference in the duration of
the ships of which the navy might be composed, if chiefly constructed of Southern wood would be of signal importance either in the view of naval strength or of
national economy. Some of the Southern and of the middle states yield a greater *140*
plenty of iron and of better quality. Seamen must chiefly be drawn from the
Northern hive. The necessity of naval protection to external or maritime commerce, and the conduciveness of that species of commerce to the prosperity of a
navy, are points too manifest to require a particular elucidation. They, by a kind
of reaction, mutually beneficial, promote each other. *145*

An unrestrained intercourse between the states themselves will advance the
trade of each, by an interchange of their respective productions, not only for the
supply of reciprocal wants at home, but for exportation to foreign markets. The
veins of commerce in every part will be replenished, and will acquire additional
motion and vigour from a free circulation of the commodities of every part. *150*
Commercial enterprise will have much greater scope, from the diversity in the
productions of different states. When the staple of one fails, from a bad harvest or
unproductive crop, it can call to its aid the staple of another. The variety not less
than the value of products for exportation, contributes to the activity of foreign
commerce. It can be conducted upon much better terms, with a large number of *155*
materials of a given value, than with a small number of materials of the same
value; arising from the competitions of trade and from the fluctuations of markets. Particular articles may be in great demand, at certain periods, and un-
saleable at others; but if there be a variety of articles it can scarcely happen that
they should all be at one time in the latter predicament; and on this account the *160*
operations of the merchant would be less liable to any considerable obstruction,
or stagnation. The speculative trader will at once perceive the force of these observations; and will acknowledge that the aggregate ballance of the commerce of
the United States would bid fair to be much more favorable, than that of the thirteen states, without union, or with partial unions. *165*

It may perhaps be replied to this, that whether the states are united, or disunited, there would still be an intimate intercourse between them which would
answer the same ends: But this intercourse would be fettered, interrupted and
narrowed by a multiplicity of causes; which in the course of these papers have
been amply detailed. An unity of commercial, as well as political interests, can *170*
only result from an unity of government.

Line 162 "Speculative" here means *intelligent*—one who thinks.

There are other points of view, in which this subject might be placed, of a striking and animating kind. But they would lead us too far into the regions of futurity, and would involve topics not proper for a Newspaper discussion. I shall
175 briefly observe, that our situation invites, and our interests prompt us, to aim at an ascendant in the system of American affairs. The world may politically, as well as geographically, be divided into four parts, each having a distinct set of interests. Unhappily for the other three, Europe by her arms and by her negociations, by force and by fraud, has, in different degrees, extended her dominion over
180 them all. Africa, Asia, and America have successively felt her domination. The superiority, she has long maintained, has tempted her to plume herself as the Mistress of the World, and to consider the rest of mankind as created for her benefit. Men admired as profound philosophers have, in direct terms, attributed to her inhabitants a physical superiority; and have gravely asserted that all ani-
185 mals, and with them the human species, degenerate in America—that even dogs cease to bark after having breathed a while in our atmosphere.* Facts have too long supported these arrogant pretensions of the European. It belongs to us to vindicate the honor of the human race, and to teach that assuming brother moderation. Union will enable us to do it. Disunion will add another victim to his tri-
190 umphs. Let Americans disdain to be the instruments of European greatness! Let the thirteen states, bound together in a strict and indissoluble union, concur in erecting one great American system, superior to the controul of all trans-atlantic force or influence, and able to dictate the terms of the connection between the old and the new world!

PUBLIUS.

*Recherches philosophiques sur les Americains.

Line 177 The "four parts" were Europe, Africa, Asia, and the American hemisphere.

Line 183 "Men admired as profound philosophers" replies to the views of the respected French naturalist George Louis Leclerc Comte de Buffon (1707–1788). Many passages in Thomas Jefferson's recently published *Notes on the State of Virginia* were designed to refute Buffon's disparaging assessments of American natural history.

Lines 187–88 Hamilton's statement that it belonged to Americans "to vindicate the honor of the human race" is a very rare piece of rhetoric in which he invokes honor as a *motive* for human action. Although Publius did recognize the need for *virtue* in republican citizens, the political science of *The Federalist* is based on the motivating force of self-interest; there is very little in any of the creators of Publius's persona to suggest that they really believed that human nature in America was any different.

Line 192 The phrase "American system" would be used some thirty years later by Henry Clay to designate his plan to capitalize on the mutual interests of the nation's great geo-economic sections. In Hamilton's argument, only union could promote these ambitions; toward the end of Clay's life it became his primary object to avert the threatening disunion.

TWELVE

ALEXANDER HAMILTON
November 27, 1787
The Utility of the Union in Respect to Revenue

To the People of the State of New York.

The effects of union upon the commercial prosperity of the states have been sufficiently delineated. Its tendency to promote the interests of revenue will be the subject of our present enquiry.

The prosperity of commerce is now perceived and acknowledged, by all enlightened statesmen, to be the most useful as well as the most productive source of national wealth; and has accordingly become a primary object of their political cares. By multiplying the means of gratification, by promoting the introduction and circulation of the precious metals, those darling objects of human avarice and enterprise, it serves to vivify and invigorate all the channels of industry, and to make them flow with greater activity and copiousness. The assiduous merchant, the laborious husbandman, the active mechanic, and the industrious manufacturer, all orders of men look forward with eager expectation and growing alacrity to this pleasing reward of their toils. The often-agitated question, between agriculture and commerce, has from indubitable experience received a decision, which has silenced the rivalships, that once subsisted between them, and has proved to the entire satisfaction of their friends, that their interests are intimately blended and interwoven. It has been found, in various countries, that in proportion as commerce has flourished, land has risen in value. And how could it have happened otherwise? Could that which procures a freer vent for the products of the earth—which furnishes new incitements to the cultivators of land—which is the most powerful instrument in encreasing the quantity of money in a state—could that, in fine, which is the faithful handmaid of labor and industry in every shape, fail to augment the value of that article,

---

Lines 4–28 The argument of this paragraph may seem inconsistent with the emphasis on the predominance of agriculture in No. 11. But the plan of *The Federalist* now calls for attention to commerce, which, if not providing America with its subsistence, gives the leading edge to economic activity by "multiplying the means of gratification" (line 7).

Notice the choice of adjectives and nouns, reflecting appropriate expressions of approval: "Assiduous" (line 11) is defined by Johnson's *Dictionary* as "constant in application." "Laborious" means hardworking, and a "husbandman" is a farmer, or "one who works in tillage."

Line 12 A "manufacturer" was originally one who produced by the work of his hands—we might say a craftsperson, artisan, or small-scale producer.

which is the prolific parent of far the greatest part of the objects upon which they
are exerted? It is astonishing, that so simple a truth should ever have had an adversary; and it is one among a multitude of proofs, how apt a spirit of ill-informed
jealousy, or of too great abstraction and refinement is to lead men astray from the
plainest paths of reason and conviction.

The ability of a country to pay taxes must always be proportioned, in a great
degree, to the quantity of money in circulation, and to the celerity with which it
circulates. Commerce, contributing to both these objects, must of necessity
render the payment of taxes easier, and facilitate the requisite supplies to the
treasury. The hereditary dominions of the emperor of Germany, contain a great
extent of fertile, cultivated and populous territory, a large proportion of which is
situated in mild and luxuriant climates. In some parts of this territory are to be
found the best gold and silver mines in Europe. And yet, from the want of the fostering influence of commerce, that monarch can boast but slender revenues. He
has several times been compelled to owe obligations to the pecuniary succours of
other nations, for the preservation of his essential interests; and is unable, upon
the strength of his own resources, to sustain a long or continued war.

But it is not in this aspect of the subject alone, that union will be seen to conduce to the purposes of revenue. There are other points of view, in which its influence will appear more immediate and decisive. It is evident from the state of
the country, from the habits of the people, from the experience we have had on
the point itself, that it is impracticable to raise any very considerable sums by direct taxation. Tax laws have in vain been multiplied—new methods to enforce
the collection have in vain been tried—the public expectation has been uniformly disappointed, and the treasuries of the states have remained empty. The
popular system of administration, inherent in the nature of popular government,
coinciding with the real scarcity of money, incident to a languid and mutilated
state of trade, has hitherto defeated every experiment for extensive collections,
and has at length taught the different legislatures the folly of attempting them.

No person, acquainted with what happens in other countries, will be surprised
at this circumstance. In so opulent a nation as that of Britain, where direct taxes
from superior wealth, must be much more tolerable, and from the vigor of the
government, much more practicable, than in America, far the greatest part of the
national revenue is derived from taxes of the indirect kind; from imposts and from
excises. Duties on imported articles form a large branch of this latter description.

Line 33 The reference to the "emperor of Germany" is to the Hapsburg titular head of
the Holy Roman Empire, to whom all German rulers were theoretically subordinate.

Lines 41–52 It is significant that the experience of popular hostility to direct taxation
within the existing states convinces Hamilton that this will never be an adequate
source of public revenue. The passage is a realistic enough reflection on what is and
will be politically possible in a "popular government."

In America it is evident, that we must a long time depend, for the means of revenue, chiefly on such duties. In most parts of it, excises must be confined within a narrow compass. The genius of the people will ill brook the inquisitive and peremptory spirit of excise laws. The pockets of the farmers, on the other hand, will reluctantly yield but scanty supplies in the unwelcome shape of impositions on their houses and lands—and personal property is too precarious and invisible a fund to be laid hold of in any other way, than by the imperceptible agency of taxes on consumption.

If these remarks have any foundation, that state of things, which will best enable us to improve and extend so valuable a resource, must be the best adapted to our political welfare. And it cannot admit of a serious doubt, that this state of things must rest on the basis of a general union. As far as this would be conducive to the interests of commerce, so far it must tend to the extension of the revenue to be drawn from that source. As far as it would contribute to rendering regulations for the collection of the duties more simple and efficacious, so far it must serve to answer the purposes of making the same rate of duties more productive, and of putting it into the power of the government to increase the rate, without prejudice to trade.

The relative situation of these states, the number of rivers, with which they are intersected, and of bays that wash their shores, the facility of communication in every direction, the affinity of language, and manners, the familiar habits of intercourse; all these are circumstances, that would conspire to render an illicit trade between them, a matter of little difficulty, and would insure frequent evasions of the commercial regulations of each other. The separate states, or confederacies would be necessitated by mutual jealousy to avoid the temptations to that kind of trade, by the lowness of their duties. The temper of our governments, for a long time to come, would not permit those rigorous precautions, by which the European nations guard the avenues into their respective countries, as well by land as by water; and which even there are found insufficient obstacles to the adventurous stratagems of avarice.

In France there is an army of patrols (as they are called) constantly employed to secure her fiscal regulations against the inroads of the dealers in contraband. Mr. *Neckar* computes the number of these patrols at upwards of twenty thousand. This proves the immense difficulty in preventing that species of traffic,

---

Line 91 Jacques Neckar, usually spelled "Necker" (1732–1804), was a Swiss banker, appointed French finance minister in 1777 by Louis XVI. By the time of *The Federalist*, he had been replaced, but his economic competence and attempted reforms of the French financial system had earned great respect in Europe. Jefferson, in Paris, purchased for Madison a three-volume work by Necker on *The Administration of the Finances of France* (in French) in September 1784. Madison probably lent it to Hamilton, who had no similar source in Europe, though he may have ordered his own copy.

where there is an inland communication, and shews in a strong light the disadvantages with which the collection of duties in this country would be incum-
95 bered, if by disunion the states should be placed in a situation, with respect to each other, resembling that of France with respect to her neighbours. The arbitrary and vexatious powers with which the patrols are necessarily armed would be intolerable in a free country.

If on the contrary, there be but one government pervading all the states, there
100 will be as to the principal part of our commerce but ONE SIDE to guard, the ATLANTIC COAST. Vessels arriving directly from foreign countries, laden with valuable cargoes, would rarely choose to hazard themselves to the complicated and critical perils, which would attend attempts to unlade prior to their coming into port. They would have to dread both the dangers of the coast, and of detec-
105 tion as well after as before their arrival at the places of their final destination. An ordinary degree of vigilance would be competent to the prevention of any material infractions upon the rights of the revenue. A few armed vessels, judiciously stationed at the entrances of our ports, might at small expence be made useful sentinels of the laws. And the government having the same interests to provide
110 against violations every where, the co-operation of its measures in each state would have a powerful tendency to render them effectual. Here also we should preserve by union an advantage which nature holds out to us, and which would be relinquished by separation. The United States lie at a great distance from Europe, and at a considerable distance from all other places with which they would
115 have extensive connections of foreign trade. The passage from them to us, in a few hours, or in a single night, as between the coasts of France and Britain, and of other neighbouring nations, would be impracticable. This is a prodigious security against a direct contraband with foreign countries; but a circuitous contraband to one state, through the medium of another, would be both easy and safe.
120 The difference between a direct importation from abroad and an indirect importation, through the channel of a neighbouring state, in small parcels, according to time and opportunity, with the additional facilities of inland communication, must be palpable to every man of discernment.

It is therefore, evident, that one national government would be able, at much
125 less expence, to extend the duties on imports, beyond comparison further, than would be practicable to the states separately, or to any partial confederacies: Hitherto I believe it may safely be asserted, that these duties have not upon an average exceeded in any state three per cent. In France they are estimated at about fifteen per cent. and in Britain the proportion is still greater. There seems
130 to be nothing to hinder their being increased in this country, to at least treble their present amount. The single article of ardent spirits, under federal regulation, might be made to furnish a considerable revenue. Upon a ratio to the importation into this state, the whole quantity imported into the United States at a low computation may be estimated at four millions of Gallons; which at a
135 shilling per gallon would produce two hundred thousand pounds. That article would well bear this rate of duty: and if it should tend to diminish the con-

sumption of it, such an effect would be equally favorable to the agriculture, to the economy, to the morals and to the health of the society. There is perhaps nothing, so much a subject of national extravagance, as this very article.

What will be the consequence, if we are not able to avail ourselves of the re- *140* source in question in its full extent? A nation cannot long exist without revenue. Destitute of this essential support, it must resign its independence and sink into the degraded condition of a province. This is an extremity to which no government will of choice accede. Revenue therefore must be had at all events. In this country, if the principal part be not drawn from commerce, it must fall with op- *145* pressive weight upon land. It has been already intimated, that excises in their true signification are too little in unison with the feelings of the people, to admit of great use being made of that mode of taxation, nor indeed, in the states where almost the sole employment is agriculture, are the objects, proper for excise sufficiently numerous to permit very ample collections in that way. Personal estate, *150* (as has been before remarked) from the difficulty of tracing it cannot be subjected to large contributions, by any other means, than by taxes on consumption. In populous cities, it may be enough the subject of conjecture, to occasion the oppression of individuals, without much aggregate benefit to the state; but beyond these circles it must in a great measure escape the eye and the hand of the *155* tax-gatherer. As the necessities of the state, nevertheless, must be satisfied, in some mode or other, the defect of other resources must throw the principal weight of the public burthens on the possessors of land. And as, on the other hand, the wants of the government can never obtain an adequate supply, unless all the sources of revenue are open to its demands, the finances of the commu- *160* nity under such embarrassments, cannot be put into a situation consistent with its respectability, or its security. Thus we shall not even have the consolations of a full treasury to atone for the oppression of that valuable class of the citizens, who are employed in the cultivation of the soil. But public and private distress will keep pace with each other in gloomy concert; and unite in deploring the in- *165* fatuation of those councils, which led to disunion.

PUBLIUS.

Line 146 Excises are internal taxes on goods produced or sold within a country; "a hateful tax on commodities" (Johnson's *Dictionary*).

THIRTEEN

ALEXANDER HAMILTON
November 28, 1787
The Same Subject Continued with a View to Economy

To the People of the State of New York.

As connected with the subject of revenue, we may with propriety consider that of economy. The money saved from one object may be usefully applied to another; and there will be so much the less to be drawn from the pockets of the people. If the states are united under one government, there will be but one national civil
5 list to support; if they are divided into several confederacies, there will be as many different national civil lists to be provided for; and each of them, as to the principal departments coextensive with that which would be necessary for a government of the whole. The entire separation of the states into thirteen unconnected sovereignties is a project too extravagant and too replete with danger to
10 have many advocates. The ideas of men who speculate upon the dismemberment of the empire, seem generally turned towards three confederacies; one consisting of the four Northern, another of the four Middle, and a third of the five Southern states. There is little probability that there would be a greater number. According to this distribution each confederacy would comprise an extent of
15 territory larger than that of the kingdom of Great-Britain. No well informed man will suppose that the affairs of such a confederacy can be properly regulated by a government, less comprehensive in its organs or institutions, than that, which has been proposed by the convention. When the dimensions of a state attain to a certain magnitude, it requires the same energy of government and the same
20 forms of administration; which are requisite in one of much greater extent. This idea admits not of precise demonstration, because there is no rule by which we can measure the momentum of civil power, necessary to the government of any given number of individuals; but when we consider that the island of Britain, nearly commensurate with each of the supposed confederacies, contains about
25 eight millions of people, and when we reflect upon the degree of authority required to direct the passions of so large a society to the public good, we shall see no reason to doubt that the like portion of power would be sufficient to perform

---

Line 11 The "empire" here is simply the Union, as far as it went, of the states under the Confederation.

Line 18 This thesis continues by implication the response to Montesquieu, as noted in Nos. 9 and 10.

the same task in a society far more numerous. Civil power properly organised and exerted is capable of diffusing its force to a very great extent; and can in a manner reproduce itself in every part of a great empire by a judicious arrange- *30* ment of subordinate institutions.

The supposition, that each confederacy into which the states would be likely to be divided, would require a government not less comprehensive, than the one proposed, will be strengthened by another supposition, more probable than that which presents us with three confederacies as the alternative to a general union. *35* If we attend carefully to geographical and commercial considerations, in con- junction with the habits and prejudices of the different states, we shall be led to conclude, that in case of disunion they will most naturally league themselves under two governments. The four eastern states, from all the causes that form the links of national sympathy and connection, may with certainty be expected to *40* unite. New-York, situated as she is, would never be unwise enough to oppose a feeble and unsupported flank to the weight of that confederacy. There are obvi- ous reasons, that would facilitate her accession to it. New-Jersey is too small a state to think of being a frontier, in opposition to this still more powerful combi- nation; nor do there appear to be any obstacles to her admission into it. Even *45* Pennsylvania would have strong inducements to join the Northern league. An active foreign commerce on the basis of her own navigation is her true policy, and coincides with the opinions and dispositions of her citizens. The more Southern states, from various circumstances, may not think themselves much in- terested in the encouragement of navigation. They may prefer a system, which *50* would give unlimited scope to all nations, to be the carriers as well as the pur- chasers of their commodities. Pennsylvania may not choose to confound her in- terests in a connection so adverse to her policy. As she must at all events be a frontier, she may deem it most consistent with her safety to have her exposed side turned towards the weaker power of the Southern, rather than towards the *55* stronger power of the Northern confederacy. This would give her the fairest chance to avoid being the FLANDERS of America. Whatever may be the deter- mination of Pennsylvania, if the northern confederacy includes New-Jersey, there is no likelihood of more than one confederacy to the south of that state.

Nothing can be more evident than that the thirteen states will be able to sup- *60* port a national government, better than one half, or one third, or any number less than the whole. This reflection must have great weight in obviating that ob- jection to the proposed plan, which is founded on the principle of expence; an objection however, which, when we come to take a nearer view of it, will appear in every light to stand on mistaken ground. *65*

If in addition to the consideration of a plurality of civil lists, we take into view the number of persons who must necessarily be employed to guard the inland

---

Line 57 "[T]he Flanders of America" refers to battles fought in Flanders—now Belgium—during the War of Spanish Succession. See notes to No. 6.

communication, between the different confederacies, against illicit trade, and who in time will infallibly spring up out of the necessities of revenue; and if we also take into view the military establishments, which it has been shewn would unavoidably result from the jealousies and conflicts of the several nations, into which the states would be divided, we shall clearly discover, that a separation would be not less injurious to the economy than to the tranquillity, commerce, revenue and liberty of every part.

PUBLIUS.

FOURTEEN

JAMES MADISON
November 30, 1787
An Objection Drawn from the Extent of Country Answered

To the People of the State of New York.

We have seen the necessity of the union as our bulwark against foreign danger, as the conservator of peace among ourselves, as the guardian of our commerce and other common interests, as the only substitute for those military establishments which have subverted the liberties of the old world; and as the proper antidote for the diseases of faction, which have proved fatal to other popular governments, and of which alarming symptoms have been betrayed by our own. All that remains, within this branch of our enquiries, is to take notice of an objection, that may be drawn from the great extent of country which the union embraces. A few observations on this subject will be the more proper, as it is perceived that the adversaries of the new constitution are availing themselves of a prevailing prejudice, with regard to the practicable sphere of republican administration, in order to supply by imaginary difficulties, the want of those solid objections, which they endeavor in vain to find.

The error which limits republican government to a narrow district, has been unfolded and refuted in preceding papers. I remark here only, that it seems to owe its rise and prevalence, chiefly to the confounding of a republic with a democracy: And applying to the former reasonings drawn from the nature of the latter. The true distinction between these forms was also adverted to on a former occasion. It is, that in a democracy, the people meet and exercise the government in person; in a republic they assemble and administer it by their representatives and agents. A democracy consequently must be confined to a small spot. A republic may be extended over a large region.

To this accidental source of the error may be added the artifice of some celebrated authors, whose writings have had a great share in forming the modern standard of political opinions. Being subjects either of an absolute, or limited monarchy, they have endeavored to heighten the advantages or palliate the evils of those forms; by placing in comparison with them, the vices and defects of the republican, and by citing as specimens of the latter, the turbulent democracies of

---

Lines 23–32 The reply to Montesquieu continues. Note the tribute to his influence in forming modern political ideas.

Lines 28–29 The "turbulent democracies of ancient Greece" are primarily Athens and Sparta. Those of "modern Italy" appear to be a rhetorical invention by Madison,

ancient Greece, and modern Italy. Under the confusion of names, it has been an
easy task to transfer to a republic, observations applicable to a democracy only,
and among others, the observation that it can never be established but among a
small number of people, living within a small compass of territory.

Such a fallacy may have been the less perceived as most of the popular
governments of antiquity were of the democratic species; and even in modern
Europe, to which we owe the great principle of representation, no example is
seen of a government wholly popular, and founded at the same time wholly on
that principle. If Europe has the merit of discovering this great mechanical
power in government, by the simple agency of which, the will of the largest political body may be concentred, and its force directed to any object, which the
public good requires; America can claim the merit of making the discovery the
basis of unmixed and extensive republics. It is only to be lamented, that any of
her citizens should wish to deprive her of the additional merit of displaying its
full efficacy in the establishment of the comprehensive system now under her
consideration.

As the natural limit of a democracy is that distance from the central point,
which will just permit the most remote citizens to assemble as often as their public functions demand; and will include no greater number than can join in those
functions; so the natural limit of a republic is that distance from the center,
which will barely allow the representatives of the people to meet as often as may
be necessary for the administration of public affairs. Can it be said, that the limits of the United States exceed this distance? It will not be said by those who recollect that the Atlantic coast is the longest side of the union; that during the term
of thirteen years, the representatives of the states have been almost continually
assembled; and that the members from the most distant states are not chargeable
with greater intermissions of attendance, than those from the states in the neighbourhood of congress.

---

who might himself be accused of linguistic manipulation; none of the Italian states
was a democracy; such republics as existed in Italy (Venice, Genoa, Lucca) were
controlled by tight oligarchies.

Lines 40–56 An "unmixed" republic stood in contrast to a "mixed monarchy," that
of Britain being the prime example. The mixed elements were the estates—ecclesiastical, aristocratic, and common, while political authority was represented in the
mixture of the king, the lords, and the commons. In America's "unmixed" republic,
social privilege might exist, but neither hereditary nor privileged classes had constitutional standing or rights. Madison here claims for America the discovery that a republic could be both extensive and unmixed: under representative institutions, the
natural limit (to the geographical size) of a republic is the maximum distance that
can separate representatives from the center (or representative assembly) without
inhibiting the operation of the representative institutions. This claim requires the
acknowledgment that an extended republic is a novel concept.

That we may form a juster estimate with regard to this interesting subject, let us resort to the actual dimensions of the union. The limits as fixed by the treaty of peace are on the east the Atlantic, on the south the latitude of thirty-one degrees, on the west the Mississippi, and on the north an irregular line running in some instances beyond the forty-fifth degree, in others falling as low as the forty-second. The southern shore of Lake Erie lies below that latitude. Computing the distance between the thirty-first and forty-fifth degrees, it amounts to nine hundred and seventy-three common miles; computing it from thirty-one to forty-two degrees to seven hundred, sixty four miles and an half. Taking the mean for the distance, the amount will be eight hundred, sixty-eight miles and three fourths. The mean distance from the Atlantic to the Mississippi does not probably exceed seven hundred and fifty miles. On a comparison of this extent, with that of several countries in Europe, the practicability of rendering our system commensurate to it, appears to be demonstrable. It is not a great deal larger than Germany, where a diet, representing the whole empire is continually assembled; or than Poland before the late dismemberment, where another national Diet was the depository of the supreme power. Passing by France and Spain, we find that in Great Britain, inferior as it may be in size, the representatives of the northern extremity of the island, have as far to travel to the national council, as will be required of those of the most remote parts of the union.

Favorable as this view of the subject may be, some observations remain which will place it in a light still more satisfactory.

In the first place it is to be remembered, that the general government is not to be charged with the whole power of making and administering laws. Its jurisdiction is limited to certain enumerated objects, which concern all the members of the republic, but which are not to be attained by the separate provisions of any. The subordinate governments which can extend their care to all those other objects, which can be separately provided for, will retain their due authority and activity. Were it proposed by the plan of the convention to abolish the governments of the particular states, its adversaries would have some ground for their objection, though it would not be difficult to shew that if they were abolished, the general government would be compelled by the principle of self-preservation, to reinstate them in their proper jurisdiction.

A second observation to be made is, that the immediate object of the federal constitution is to secure the union of the Thirteen Primitive states, which we

---

Line 72 Poland had been subjected to a partial partition in 1771 among its more powerful neighbors, Prussia, Russia, and Austria.

Publius was not to know, but would not have been surprised, that the process would be resumed in the Second Partition of 1793 and completed by the Third Partition, or extinction, of 1795. (Poland's national identity was restored in 1919 by the Treaty of Versailles.)

Line 91 "Primitive" here means "original"—a good example of change in word meaning.

know to be practicable; and to add to them such other states, as may arise in their own bosoms or in their neighbourhoods, which we cannot doubt to be equally practicable. The arrangements that may be necessary for those angles and frac-
95 tions of our territory, which lie on our north western frontier, must be left to those whom further discoveries and experience will render more equal to the task.

Let it be remarked in the third place, that the intercourse throughout the union will be daily facilitated by new improvements. Roads will every where be shortened, and kept in better order; accommodations for travellers will be multi-
100 plied and meliorated; an interior navigation on our eastern side will be opened throughout, or nearly throughout the whole extent of the Thirteen states. The communication between the western and Atlantic districts, and between differ-ent parts of each, will be rendered more and more easy by those numerous canals with which the beneficence of nature has intersected our country, and which art
105 finds it so little difficult to connect and complete.

A fourth and still more important consideration is, that as almost every state will on one side or other, be a frontier, and will thus find in a regard to its safety, an inducement to make some sacrifices for the sake of the general protection; so the states which lie at the greatest distance from the heart of the union, and
110 which of course may partake least of the ordinary circulation of its benefits, will be at the same time immediately contiguous to foreign nations, and will conse-quently stand on particular occasions, in greatest need of its strength and re-sources. It may be inconvenient for Georgia or the states forming our western or North Eastern borders to send their representatives to the seat of government,
115 but they would find it more so to struggle alone against an invading enemy, or even to support alone the whole expence of those precautions, which may be dictated by the neighbourhood of continual danger. If they should derive less benefit therefore from the union in some respects, than the less distant states, they will derive greater benefit from it in other respects, and thus the proper
120 equilibrium will be maintained throughout.

I submit to you my fellow citizens, these considerations, in full confidence that the good sense which has so often marked your decisions, will allow them their due weight and effect; and that you will never suffer difficulties, however formidable in appearance or however fashionable the error on which they may
125 be founded, to drive you into the gloomy and perilous scene into which the ad-vocates for disunion would conduct you. Hearken not to the unnatural voice which tells you that the people of America, knit together as they are by so many chords of affection, can no longer live together as members of the same family; can no longer continue the mutual guardians of their mutual happiness; can no

---

Line 103 From the context, "canals" is an expression for natural channels of com-munication. Artificial canals were being dug in this period in England and France.

longer be fellow citizens of one great respectable and flourishing empire. Hear- *130*
ken not to the voice which petulantly tells you that the form of government recommended for your adoption is a novelty in the political world; that it has never
yet had a place in the theories of the wildest projectors; that it rashly attempts
what it is impossible to accomplish. No my countrymen, shut your ears against
this unhallowed language. Shut your hearts against the poison which it conveys; *135*
the kindred blood which flows in the veins of American citizens, the mingled
blood which they have shed in defence of their sacred rights, consecrate their
union, and excite horror at the idea of their becoming aliens, rivals, enemies.
And if novelties are to be shunned, believe me the most alarming of all novelties,
the most wild of all projects, the most rash of all attempts, is that of rending us in *140*
pieces, in order to preserve our liberties and promote our happiness. But why is
the experiment of an extended republic to be rejected merely because it may
comprise what is new? Is it not the glory of the people of America, that whilst
they have paid a decent regard to the opinions of former times and other nations,
they have not suffered a blind veneration for antiquity, for custom, or for names, *145*
to overrule the suggestions of their own good sense, the knowledge of their own
situation, and the lessons of their own experience? To this manly spirit, posterity
will be indebted for the possession, and the world for the example of the numerous innovations displayed on the American theatre, in favor of private rights and
public happiness. Had no important step been taken by the leaders of the revo- *150*
lution for which a precedent could not be discovered, no government established of which an exact model did not present itself, the people of the United
States might, at this moment, have been numbered among the melancholy vic-
tims of misguided councils, must at best have been labouring under the weight of
some of those forms which have crushed the liberties of the rest of mankind. *155*
Happily for America, happily we trust for the whole human race, they pursued a
new and more noble course. They accomplished a revolution which has no parallel in the annals of human society: They reared the fabrics of governments
which have no model on the face of the globe. They formed the design of a great
confederacy, which it is incumbent on their successors to improve and perpetu- *160*
ate. If their works betray imperfections, we wonder at the fewness of them. If they
erred most in the structure of the union; this was the work most difficult to be
executed; this is the work which has been new modelled by the act of your convention, and it is that act on which you are now to deliberate and to decide.

PUBLIUS.

FIFTEEN

ALEXANDER HAMILTON
December 1, 1787
Concerning the Defects of the Present Confederation in Relation to the
Principle of Legislation for the States in Their Collective Capacities

To the People of the State of New York.

In the course of the preceding papers, I have endeavoured, my fellow citizens, to place before you in a clear and convincing light, the importance of union to your political safety and happiness. I have unfolded to you a complication of dangers to which you would be exposed should you permit that sacred knot which binds
5   the people of America together to be severed or dissolved by ambition or by avarice, by jealousy or by misrepresentation. In the sequel of the inquiry, through which I propose to accompany you, the truths intended to be inculcated will receive further confirmation from facts and arguments hitherto unnoticed. If the road, over which you will still have to pass, should in some places appear to you
10   tedious or irksome, you will recollect, that you are in quest of information on a subject the most momentous which can engage the attention of a free people: that the field through which you have to travel is in itself spacious, and that the difficulties of the journey have been unnecessarily increased by the mazes with which sophistry has beset the way. It will be my aim to remove the obstacles to
15   your progress in as compendious a manner, as it can be done, without sacrificing utility to dispatch.

    In pursuance of the plan, which I have laid down, for the discussion of the subject, the point next in order to be examined is the "insufficiency of the present confederation to the preservation of the union." It may perhaps be asked,
20   what need is there of reasoning or proof to illustrate a position, which is not either controverted or doubted; to which the understandings and feelings of all classes of men assent; and which in substance is admitted by the opponents as well as by the friends of the new constitution?—It must in truth be acknowledged that however these may differ in other respects, they in general appear to har-
25   monise in this sentiment at least, that there are material imperfections in our national system, and that something is necessary to be done to rescue us from

---

Lines 25–26 "[T]here are material imperfections in our national system. . . . " This language subtly preempts the concept of "nation," implying that the Confederation *already* constitutes a nation. But observe that in the same paragraph, "the scheme of our federal government" (lines 31–32) actually refers to the existing, *Confederation*

impending anarchy. The facts that support this opinion are no longer objects of speculation. They have forced themselves upon the sensibility of the people at large, and have at length extorted from those, whose mistaken policy has had the principal share in precipitating the extremity, at which we are arrived, a reluctant confession of the reality of those defects in the scheme of our federal government, which have been long pointed out and regretted by the intelligent friends of the union.

We may indeed with propriety be said to have reached almost the last stage of national humiliation. There is scarcely any thing that can wound the pride, or degrade the character of an independent nation, which we do not experience. Are there engagements to the performance of which we are held by every tie respectable among men? These are the subjects of constant and unblushing violation. Do we owe debts to foreigners and to our own citizens contracted in a time of imminent peril, for the preservation of our political existence? These remain without any proper or satisfactory provision for their discharge. Have we valuable territories and important posts in the possession of a foreign power, which by express stipulations ought long since to have been surrendered? These are still retained, to the prejudice of our interests not less than of our rights. Are we in a condition to resent, or to repel the aggression? We have neither troops nor treasury nor government.⊛ Are we even in a condition to remonstrate with dignity? The just imputations on our own faith, in respect to the same treaty, ought first to be removed. Are we entitled by nature and compact to a free participation in the navigation of the Mississippi? Spain excludes us from it. Is public credit an indispensable resource in time of public danger? We seem to have abandoned its cause as desperate and irretrievable. Is commerce of importance to national wealth? Ours is at the lowest point of declension. Is respectability in the eyes of foreign powers a safeguard against foreign encroachments? The imbecility of our government even forbids them to treat with us: Our ambassadors abroad are the mere pageants of mimic sovereignty. Is a violent and unnatural decrease in the

⊛I mean for the union.

---

government. By calling his own publication *The Federalist*, Publius makes the rhetorically significant claim that the *new* form of government will retain a federalist form, rather than the consolidated system that is at the very center of the Anti-Federalists' fears and accusations. The strategy is implicit in the title, but this is its first indication in the actual text of *The Federalist*.

Line 49 "Spain excludes us from [the Mississippi]." See note to No. 11, lines 114–21.

Line 54 "Our ambassadors abroad . . . ," while intended as a criticism of the feeble pretensions of the Congress on the international scene, hardly seems calculated to flatter such emissaries as John Adams in London or Thomas Jefferson in Paris!

value of land a symptom of national distress? The price of improved land in most parts of the country is much lower than can be accounted for by the quantity of waste land at market, and can only be fully explained by that want of private and public confidence, which are so alarmingly prevalent among all ranks and which

60 have a direct tendency to depreciate property of every kind. Is private credit the friend and patron of industry? That most useful kind which relates to borrowing and lending is reduced within the narrowest limits, and this still more from an opinion of insecurity than from a scarcity of money. To shorten an enumeration of particulars which can afford neither pleasure nor instruction it may in general

65 be demanded, what indication is there of national disorder, poverty and insignificance that could befal a community so peculiarly blessed with natural advantages as we are, which does not form a part of the dark catalogue of our public misfortunes?

This is the melancholy situation, to which we have been brought by those

70 very maxims and councils, which would now deter us from adopting the proposed constitution; and which not content with having conducted us to the brink of a precipice, seem resolved to plunge us into the abyss, that awaits us below. Here, my countrymen, impelled by every motive that ought to influence an enlightened people, let us make a firm stand for our safety, our tranquillity, our dig-

75 nity, our reputation. Let us at last break the fatal charm which has too long seduced us from the paths of felicity and prosperity.

It is true, as has been before observed, that facts too stubborn to be resisted have produced a species of general assent to the abstract proposition that there exist material defects in our national system; but the usefulness of the conces-

80 sion, on the part of the old adversaries of federal measures, is destroyed by a strenuous opposition to a remedy, upon the only principles, that can give it a chance of success. While they admit that the government of the United States is destitute of energy; they contend against conferring upon it those powers which are requisite to supply that energy: They seem still to aim at things repugnant

---

Lines 56–57 The reference to the price of improved land "in most parts of the country" is difficult to locate. "The country" could have meant New York State, but probably meant the United States as a whole; when Americans referred to their own states as "countries," they generally said "this" or, as with Jefferson, "my" country. Hamilton is making a political point, but his inference about land values is probably correct.

Lines 77–92 This paragraph contains a forceful statement of the conventional view that sovereignty cannot be divided. State authority must diminish if federal power is to be increased; this is seen, of course, as being in the states' own long-term interests. An *imperium in imperio*—a sovereignty within a sovereignty, in modern language— is a "political monster" (lines 87–88). Those who believe in it are deluding themselves. In fact, this article, while reasserting states' sovereignty, begins the process of erosion by stating that certain "sovereign" powers are expressly delegated. We shall see modifications in this concept as the argument goes on. See No. 9, lines 141–46.

and irreconcilable—at an augmentation of federal authority without a diminution of state authority—at sovereignty in the union and complete independence in the members. They still in fine seem to cherish with blind devotion the political monster of an *imperium in imperio*. This renders a full display of the principal defects of the confederation necessary, in order to shew, that the evils we experience do not proceed from minute or partial imperfections, but from fundamental errors in the structure of the building which cannot be amended otherwise than by an alteration in the first principles and main pillars of the fabric.

The great and radical vice in the construction of the existing confederation is in the principle of LEGISLATION for STATES or GOVERNMENTS, in their CORPORATE or COLLECTIVE CAPACITIES and as contradistinguished from the INDIVIDUALS of whom they consist. Though this principle does not run through all the powers delegated to the union; yet it pervades and governs those, on which the efficacy of the rest depends. Except as to the rule of apportionment, the United States have an indefinite discretion to make requisitions for men and money; but they have no authority to raise either by regulations extending to the individual citizens of America. The consequence of this is, that though in theory their resolutions concerning those objects are laws, constitutionally binding on the members of the union, yet in practice they are mere recommendations, which the states observe or disregard at their option.

It is a singular instance of the capriciousness of the human mind, that after all the admonitions we have had from experience on this head, there should still be found men, who object to the new constitution for deviating from a principle which has been found the bane of the old; and which is in itself evidently incompatible with the idea of GOVERNMENT; a principle in short which if it is to be executed at all must substitute the violent and sanguinary agency of the sword to the mild influence of the magistracy.

There is nothing absurd or impracticable in the idea of a league or alliance between independent nations, for certain defined purposes precisely stated in a treaty; regulating all the details of time, place, circumstance and quantity; leaving nothing to future discretion; and depending for its execution on the good faith of the parties. Compacts of this kind exist among all civilized nations subject to the usual vicissitudes of peace and war, of observance and non observance, as the interests or passions of the contracting powers dictate. In the early part of the present century, there was an epidemical rage in Europe for this species of compacts; from which the politicians of the times fondly hoped for benefits which were never realized. With a view to establishing the equilibrium of power and the peace of that part of the world, all the resources of negotiation were exhausted, and triple and quadruple alliances were formed; but they were scarcely formed before they were broken, giving an instructive but afflicting lesson to mankind how little dependence is to be placed on treaties which have no other sanction than the obligations of good faith; and which oppose general considerations of peace and justice to the impulse of any immediate interest or passion.

If the particular states in this country are disposed to stand in a similar relation
to each other, and to drop the project of a general DISCRETIONARY SUPER-
INTENDENCE, the scheme would indeed be pernicious, and would entail
upon us all the mischiefs that have been enumerated under the first head; but it
would have the merit of being at least consistent and practicable. Abandoning all
views towards a confederate government, this would bring us to a simple alliance
offensive and defensive; and would place us in a situation to be alternately
friends and enemies of each other as our mutual jealousies and rivalships nourished by the intrigues of foreign nations should prescribe to us.

But if we are unwilling to be placed in this perilous situation; if we will still
adhere to the design of a national government, or which is the same thing of a superintending power under the direction of a common council, we must resolve
to incorporate into our plan those ingredients which may be considered as forming the characteristic difference between a league and a government; we must
extend the authority of the union to the persons of the citizens,—the only proper
objects of government.

Government implies the power of making laws. It is essential to the idea of a
law, that it be attended with a sanction; or, in other words, a penalty or punishment for disobedience. If there be no penalty annexed to disobedience, the resolutions or commands which pretend to be laws will in fact amount to nothing
more than advice or recommendation. This penalty, whatever it may be, can only
be inflicted in two ways; by the agency of the courts and ministers of Justice, or by
military force; by the COERTION of the magistracy, or by the COERTION of
arms. The first kind can evidently apply only to men—the last kind must of necessity be employed against bodies politic, or communities or states. It is evident,
that there is no process of a court by which their observance of the laws can in
the last resort be enforced. Sentences may be denounced against them for violations of their duty; but these sentences can only be carried into execution by the
sword. In an association where the general authority is confined to the collective
bodies of the communities that compose it, every breach of the laws must involve
a state of war, and military execution must become the only instrument of civil
obedience. Such a state of things can certainly not deserve the name of government, nor would any prudent man choose to commit his happiness to it.

There was a time when we were told that breaches, by the states, of the regulations of the federal authority were not to be expected—that a sense of common
interest would preside over the conduct of the respective members, and would
beget a full compliance with all the constitutional requisitions of the union. This
language at the present day would appear as wild as a great part of what we now

---

Lines 162–80 Human nature is subject to immediate, shortsighted self-interest, so
that—an argument that anticipates Madison in No. 51—an enlightened view of
long-term self-interest dictates the need for government.

hear from the same quarter will be thought, when we shall have received further lessons from that best oracle of wisdom, experience. It at all times betrayed an ignorance of the true springs by which human conduct is actuated, and belied the original inducements to the establishment of civil power. Why has government *170* been instituted at all? Because the passions of men will not conform to the dictates of reason and justice, without constraint. Has it been found that bodies of men act with more rectitude or greater disinterestedness than individuals? The contrary of this has been inferred by all accurate observers of the conduct of mankind; and the inference is founded upon obvious reasons. Regard to reputa- *175* tion has a less active influence, when the infamy of a bad action is to be divided among a number, than when it is to fall singly upon one. A spirit of faction which is apt to mingle its poison in the deliberations of all bodies of men, will often hurry the persons of whom they are composed into improprieties and excesses, for which they would blush in a private capacity. *180*

In addition to all this, there is in the nature of sovereign power an impatience of controul, that disposes those who are invested with the exercise of it, to look with an evil eye upon all external attempts to restrain or direct its operations. From this spirit it happens that in every political association which is formed upon the principle of uniting in a common interest a number of lesser sover- *185* eignties, there will be found a kind of excentric tendency in the subordinate or inferior orbs, by the operation of which there will be a perpetual effort in each to fly off from the common center. This tendency is not difficult to be accounted for. It has its origin in the love of power. Power controuled or abridged is almost always the rival and enemy of that power by which it is controuled or abriged. *190* This simple proposition will teach us how little reason there is to expect, that the persons, entrusted with the administration of the affairs of the particular members of a confederacy, will at all times be ready, with perfect good humour, and an unbiassed regard to the public weal, to execute the resolutions or decrees of the general authority. The reverse of this results from the constitution of man. *195*

If therefore the measures of the confederacy cannot be executed, without the intervention of the particular administrations, there will be little prospect of their being executed at all. The rulers of the respective members, whether they have a

---

Lines 181–95 Those who exercise sovereign power have a disposition to extend it that makes them impatient of restraint. This argument deduces the need for a carefully articulated structure of government from human nature itself.

Lines 196–215 The popular assemblies in this passage are the state assemblies, which exercised virtually unrestrained legislative power from which there was no appeal to higher authority—except in the very rare cases in which the courts were willing to overrule a statute (see note to No. 78). Hamilton, Madison, and Jay's perception of the reckless irresponsibility of state governments, particularly with regard to paper money, stay laws, and other populistic measures, went far to convince them of the need for built-in restraints and the importance of the separation of powers.

constitutional right to do it or not, will undertake to judge of the propriety of the
200   measures themselves. They will consider the conformity of the thing proposed or
required to their immediate interests or aims, the momentary conveniences or
inconveniences that would attend its adoption. All this will be done, and in a
spirit of interested and suspicious scrutiny, without that knowledge of national
circumstances and reasons of state, which is essential to a right judgment, and
205   with that strong predilection in favour of local objects, which can hardly fail to
mislead the decision. The same process must be repeated in every member of
which the body is constituted; and the execution of the plans, framed by the
councils of the whole, will always fluctuate on the discretion of the ill-informed
and prejudiced opinion of every part. Those who have been conversant in the
210   proceedings of popular assemblies; who have seen how difficult it often is, when
there is no exterior pressure of circumstances, to bring them to harmonious resolutions on important points, will readily conceive how impossible it must be to
induce a number of such assemblies, deliberating at a distance from each other,
at different times, and under different impressions, long to cooperate in the same
215   views and pursuits.

In our case, the concurrence of thirteen distinct sovereign wills is requisite
under the confederation to the complete execution of every important measure,
that proceeds from the union. It has happened as was to have been foreseen. The
measures of the union have not been executed; and the delinquencies of the
220   states have step by step matured themselves to an extreme; which has at length
arrested all the wheels of the national government, and brought them to an awful
stand. Congress at this time scarcely possess the means of keeping up the forms
of administration; till the states can have time to agree upon a more substantial
substitute for the present shadow of a federal government. Things did not come
225   to this desperate extremity at once. The causes which have been specified produced at first only unequal and disproportionate degrees of compliance with the
requisitions of the union. The greater deficiencies of some states furnished the
pretext of example and the temptation of interest to the complying, or to the least
delinquent states. Why should we do more in proportion than those who are em-
230   barked with us in the same political voyage? Why should we consent to bear

---

Lines 216–36 This paragraph reviews in broad terms the delinquencies of the states
and the deficiencies of the Confederation. Congress has made requisitions with
which many states have notoriously and persistently failed to comply, causing gross
shortages in congressional finances; Congress has signed a treaty of peace with
Britain under which outstanding pre-war debts owing to British merchants are valid,
but state courts have refused to enforce them; states have set up customs barriers
against one another; and so on. The powerlessness of Congress to enforce its own
treaties was particularly serious in international relations. In retaliation for American
default on debts, Britain refused to withdraw troops from certain frontier posts admitted to be in United States territory.

more than our proper share of the common burthen? These were suggestions which human selfishness could not withstand, and which even speculative men, who looked forward to remote consequences, could not, without hesitation, combat. Each state yielding to the persuasive voice of immediate interest or convenience has successively withdrawn its support, till the frail and tottering edifice seems ready to fall upon our heads and to crush us beneath its ruins. *235*

PUBLIUS.

SIXTEEN

ALEXANDER HAMILTON
December 4, 1787
The Same Subject Continued in Relation to the Same Principles

To the People of the State of New York.

The tendency of the principle of legislation for states, or communities, in their political capacities, as it has been exemplified by the experiment we have made of it, is equally attested by the events which have befallen all other governments of the confederate kind, of which we have any account, in exact proportion to its
5   prevalence in those systems. The confirmations of this fact will be worthy of a distinct and particular examination. I shall content myself with barely observing here, that of all the confederacies of antiquity, which history has handed down to us, the Lycian and Achaean leagues, as far as there remain vestiges of them, appear to have been most free from the fetters of that mistaken principle, and were
10   accordingly those which have best deserved, and have most liberally received the applauding suffrages of political writers.

This exceptionable principle may as truly as emphatically be stiled the parent of anarchy: It has been seen that delinquencies in the members of the union are its natural and necessary offspring; and that whenever they happen, the only con-
15   stitutional remedy is force, and the immediate effect of the use of it, civil war.

It remains to enquire how far so odious an engine of government, in its application to us, would even be capable of answering its end. If there should not be a

---

Lines 1–9 The "mistaken principle" (line 9) of "legislation for states" (line 1) must mean by states in their own self-interest. "All other governments of the confederate kind" (lines 3–4) must be considered rather sweeping; the Netherlands, the Hanseatic League, and the Swiss cantons represented various forms of viable confederation. This appears to reassert the argument of No. 15, which calls for the power of central government to legislate for individuals rather than state.

Line 8 On the Lycian League, see No. 9, lines 147–48 (and comment). The Achaean League was formed for their own protection, by twelve cities of Achaea in the northern Peloponnese in or by the 4th century B.C.

Rome dissolved the league in 146 B.C., but a smaller league survived or was reformed. Under the league's constitution, a central board determined matters of foreign policy, federal taxes, and war; in all other matters, the city-states enjoyed a great measure of autonomy. Hamilton, however, is not stressing the autonomy as an end in itself so much as the willingness of the components to subscribe to the common interest. (Hamilton may have believed there was more central control than modern scholars believe to have been the case.)

large army, constantly at the disposal of the national government, it would either
not be able to employ force at all, or when this could be done, it would amount
to a war between different parts of the confederacy, concerning the infractions of
a league; in which the strongest combination would be most likely to prevail,
whether it consisted of those who supported, or of those who resisted the general
authority. It would rarely happen that the delinquency to be redressed would be
confined to a single member, and if there were more than one, who had neglected their duty, similarity of situation would induce them to unite for common
defence. Independent of this motive of sympathy, if a large and influential state
should happen to be the aggressing member, it would commonly have weight
enough with its neighbours, to win over some of them as associates to its cause.
Specious arguments of danger to the general liberty could easily be contrived;
plausible excuses for the deficiencies of the party, could, without difficulty be invented, to alarm the apprehensions, inflame the passions, and conciliate the
good will even of those states which were not chargeable with any violation, or
omission of duty. This would be the more likely to take place, as the delinquencies of the larger members might be expected sometimes to proceed from an ambitious premeditation in their rulers, with a view to getting rid of all external
controul upon their designs of personal aggrandizement; the better to effect
which, it is presumable they would tamper beforehand with leading individuals
in the adjacent states. If associates could not be found at home, recourse would
be had to the aid of foreign powers, who would seldom be disinclined to encour-
aging the dissentions of a confederacy, from the firm union of which they had so
much to fear. When the sword is once drawn, the passions of men observe no
bounds of moderation. The suggestions of wounded pride, the instigations of irritated resentment, would be apt to carry the states, against which the arms of the
union were exerted to any extremes necessary to avenge the affront, or to avoid
the disgrace of submission. The first war of this kind would probably terminate in
a dissolution of the union.

This may be considered as the violent death of the confederacy. Its more natural death is what we now seem to be on the point of experiencing, if the federal
system be not speedily renovated in a more substantial form. It is not probable,
considering the genius of this country, that the complying states would often be
inclined to support the authority of the union by engaging in a war against the
non-complying states. They would always be more ready to pursue the milder
course of putting themselves upon an equal footing with the delinquent members, by an imitation of their example. And the guilt of all would thus become
the security of all. Our past experience has exhibited the operation of this spirit
in its full light. There would in fact be an insuperable difficulty in ascertaining
when force could with propriety be employed. In the article of pecuniary contribution, which would be the most usual source of delinquency, it would often be
impossible to decide whether it had proceeded from disinclination, or inability.
The pretence of the latter would always be at hand. And the case must be very
flagrant in which its fallacy could be detected with sufficient certainty to justify

the harsh expedient of compulsion. It is easy to see that this problem alone, as often as it should occur, would open a wide field to the majority that happened to prevail in the national council, for the exercise of factious views, of partiality and of oppression.

It seems to require no pains to prove that the states ought not to prefer a national constitution, which could only be kept in motion by the instrumentality of a large army, continually on foot to execute the ordinary requisitions or decrees of the government. And yet this is the plain alternative involved by those who wish to deny it the power of extending its operations to individuals. Such a scheme, if practicable at all, would instantly degenerate into a military despotism; but it will be found in every light impracticable. The resources of the union would not be equal to the maintenance of an army considerable enough to confine the larger states within the limits of their duty; nor would the means ever be furnished of forming such an army in the first instance. Whoever considers the populousness and strength of several of these states singly at the present juncture, and looks forward to what they will become, even at the distance of half a century, will at once dismiss as idle and visionary any scheme, which aims at regulating their movements by laws, to operate upon them in their collective capacities, and to be executed by a coertion applicable to them in the same capacities. A project of this kind is little less romantic than the monster-taming spirit, attributed to the fabulous heroes and demi-gods of antiquity.

Even in those confederacies, which have been composed of members smaller than many of our counties, the principle of legislation for sovereign states, supported by military coertion, has never been found effectual. It has rarely been attempted to be employed, but against the weaker members: And in most instances attempts to coerce the refractory and disobedient, have been the signals of bloody wars; in which one half of the confederacy has displayed its banners against the other half.

The result of these observations to an intelligent mind must be clearly this, that if it be possible at any rate to construct a federal government capable of regulating the common concerns and preserving the general tranquility, it must be founded, as to the objects committed to its care, upon the reverse of the principle contended for by the opponents of the proposed constitution. It must carry its agency to the persons of the citizens. It must stand in need of no intermediate legislations; but must itself be empowered to employ the arm of the ordinary magistrate to execute its own resolutions. The majesty of the national authority

---

Line 97 "The majesty of the national authority" is a rhetorically decorative expression for sovereignty. The word "national" is used to redefine the character of the union—a device at which Publius was adept. The Confederation, as we have seen, was conspicuously deficient in powers of legal enforcement. The proposed Constitution radically reformed this defect by instituting a judicial branch of government. The theme is developed in No. 78.

must be manifested through the medium of the courts of Justice. The government of the union, like that of each state, must be able to address itself immediately to the hopes and fears of individuals; and to attract to its support, those passions, which have the strongest influence upon the human heart. It must in short, possess all the means and have a right to resort to all the methods of executing the powers, with which it is entrusted, that are possessed and exercised by the governments of the particular states.

To this reasoning it may perhaps be objected, that if any state should be disaffected to the authority of the union, it could at any time obstruct the execution of its laws, and bring the matter to the same issue of force, with the necessity of which the opposite scheme is reproached.

The plausibility of this objection will vanish the moment we advert to the essential difference between a mere NON COMPLIANCE and a DIRECT and ACTIVE RESISTANCE. If the interposition of the state-legislatures be necessary to give effect to a measure of the union, they have only NOT TO ACT or TO ACT EVASIVELY, and the measure is defeated. This neglect of duty may be disguised under affected but unsubstantial provisions, so as not to appear, and of course not to excite any alarm in the people for the safety of the constitution. The state leaders may even make a merit of their surreptitious invasions of it, on the ground of some temporary convenience, exemption, or advantage.

But if the execution of the laws of the national government, should not require the intervention of the state legislatures; if they were to pass into immediate operation upon the citizens themselves, the particular governments could not interrupt their progress without an open and violent exertion of an unconstitutional power. No omissions, nor evasions would answer the end. They would be obliged to act, and in such a manner, as would leave no doubt that they had encroached on the national rights. An experiment of this nature would always be hazardous in the face of a constitution in any degree competent to its own defence, and of a people enlightened enough to distinguish between a legal exercise and an illegal usurpation of authority. The success of it would require not merely a factious majority in the legislature, but the concurrence of the courts of justice, and of the body of the people. If the judges were not embarked in a conspiracy with the legislature they would pronounce the resolutions of such a majority to be contrary to the supreme law of the land, unconstitutional and void. If the people were not tainted with the spirit of their state representatives, they, as the natural guardians of the constitution, would throw their weight into

---

Lines 118–37 The laws will operate immediately—without an intermediary—on individual citizens. This paragraph introduces the concept later to be known as *judicial review* (for which, see No. 78, but also touched on by Madison in No. 39). At this point, however, the discussion is confined to review by the federal judiciary of *state* legislation.

the national scale, and give it a decided preponderancy in the contest. Attempts
135   of this kind would not often be made with levity or rashness; because they could
seldom be made without danger to the authors; unless in cases of a tyrannical
exercise of the federal authority.

If opposition to the national government should arise from the disorderly conduct of refractory, or seditious individuals, it could be overcome by the same
140   means which are daily employed against the same evil, under the state governments. The magistracy, being equally the ministers of the law of the land, from
whatever source it might emanate, would doubtless be as ready to guard the national as the local regulations from the inroads of private licentiousness. As to
those partial commotions and insurrections which sometimes disquiet society,
145   from the intrigues of an inconsiderable faction, or from sudden or occasional ill
humours that do not infect the great body of the community, the general government could command more extensive resources for the suppression of disturbances of that kind, than would be in the power of any single member. And as to
those mortal feuds, which in certain conjunctures spread a conflagration
150   through a whole nation, or through a very large proportion of it, proceeding
either from weighty causes of discontent given by the government, or from the
contagion of some violent popular paroxism, they do not fall within any ordinary
rules of calculation. When they happen, they commonly amount to revolutions
and dismemberments of empire. No form of government can always either avoid
155   or controul them. It is in vain to hope to guard against events too mighty for
human foresight or precaution, and it would be idle to object to a government
because it could not perform impossibilities.

PUBLIUS.

Lines 138–57 This gloomy prognostication was made some nineteen months before
the outbreak of the French Revolution!

SEVENTEEN

ALEXANDER HAMILTON
December 5, 1787
The Subject Continued, and Illustrated By Examples to Show the Tendency of Federal Governments, Rather to Anarchy Among the Members Than Tyranny in the Head

To the People of the State of New York.

An objection of a nature different from that which has been stated and answered, in my last address, may perhaps be likewise urged against the principle of legislation for the individual citizens of America. It may be said, that it would tend to render the government of the union too powerful, and to enable it to absorb in itself those residuary authorities, which it might be judged proper to leave with the states for local purposes. Allowing the utmost latitude to the love of power, which any reasonable man can require, I confess I am at a loss to discover what temptation the persons entrusted with the administration of the general government could ever feel to divest the states of the authorities of that description. The regulation of the mere domestic police of a state appears to me to hold out slender allurements to ambition. Commerce, finance, negociation and war seem to comprehend all the objects, which have charms for minds governed by that passion; and all the powers necessary to these objects ought in the first instance to be lodged in the national depository. The administration of private justice between the citizens of the same state, the supervision of agriculture and of other concerns of a similar nature, all those things in short which are proper to be provided for by local legislation, can never be desirable cares of a general jurisdiction. It is therefore improbable that there should exist a disposition in the federal councils to usurp the powers with which they are connected; because the attempt to exercise those powers would be as troublesome as it would be nugatory; and the possession of them, for that reason, would contribute nothing to the dignity, to the importance, or to the splendor of the national government.

But let it be admitted for argument sake, that mere wantonness and lust of domination would be sufficient to beget that disposition, still it may be safely affirmed, that the sense of the constituent body of the national representatives, or in other words of the people of the several states would controul the indulgence of so extravagant an appetite. It will always be far more easy for the state

---

Lines 1–11 The suggestion here is that federal legislation governing individuals as in, e.g., the 5th Amendment, poses no inherent threat of usurpation of the power of the states by the federal government.

governments to encroach upon the national authorities, than for the national government to encroach upon the state authorities. The proof of this proposition
30 turns upon the greater degree of influence, which the state governments, if they
administer their affairs with uprightness and prudence, will generally possess
over the people; a circumstance which at the same time teaches us, that there is
an inherent and intrinsic weakness in all federal constitutions; and that too much
pains cannot be taken in their organization, to give them all the force which is
35 compatible with the principles of liberty.

The superiority of influence in favour of the particular governments would result partly from the diffusive construction of the national government; but chiefly
from the nature of the objects to which the attention of the state administrations
would be directed.

40 It is a known fact in human nature that its affections are commonly weak in
proportion to the distance or diffusiveness of the object. Upon the same principle
that a man is more attached to his family than to his neighbourhood, to his
neighbourhood than to the community at large, the people of each state would
be apt to feel a stronger byass towards their local governments than towards the
45 government of the union; unless the force of that principle should be destroyed
by a much better administration of the latter.

This strong propensity of the human heart would find powerful auxiliaries in
the objects of state regulation.

The variety of more minute interests, which will necessarily fall under the su-
50 perintendence of the local administrations, and which will form so many rivulets
of influence running through every part of the society, cannot be particularised
without involving a detail too tedious and uninteresting to compensate for the instruction it might afford.

There is one transcendent advantage belonging to the province of the state
55 governments which alone suffices to place the matter in a clear and satisfactory
light.—I mean the ordinary administration of criminal and civil justice. This of
all others is the most powerful, most universal and most attractive source of popular obedience and attachment. It is this which—being the immediate and
visible guardian of life and property—having its benefits and its terrors in con-
60 stant activity before the public eye—regulating all those personal interests and
familiar concerns to which the sensibility of individuals is more immediately
awake—contributes more than any other circumstance to impressing upon the
minds of the people affection, esteem and reverence towards the government.
This great cement of society which will diffuse itself almost wholly through the
65 channels of the particular governments, independent of all other causes of influ-

---

Lines 40–46 Note the renewed invocation of human nature. A better administration
of the government of the Union might alter the natural force of attachment to local
government, however; it seems that reason is here brought in to balance the inclinations of nature.

ence, would ensure them so decided an empire over their respective citizens, as to render them at all times a complete counterpoise and not unfrequently dangerous rivals to the power of the union.

The operations of the national government on the other hand falling less immediately under the observation of the mass of the citizens the benefits derived from it will chiefly be perceived and attended to by speculative men. Relating to more general interests, they will be less apt to come home to the feelings of the people; and, in proportion, less likely to inspire a habitual sense of obligation and an active sentiment of attachment.

The reasoning on this head has been abundantly exemplified by the experience of all federal constitutions, with which we are acquainted, and of all others, which have borne the least analogy to them.

Though the ancient feudal systems were not strictly speaking confederacies, yet they partook of the nature of that species of association. There was a common head, chieftain, or sovereign, whose authority extended over the whole nation; and a number of subordinate vassals; or feudatories, who had large portions of land allotted to them and numerous trains of *inferior* vassals or retainers, who occupied and cultivated that land upon the tenure of fealty or obedience to the persons of whom they held it. Each principal vassal was a kind of sovereign within his particular demesnes. The consequences of this situation were a continual opposition to the authority of the sovereign, and frequent wars between the great barons, or chief feudatories themselves. The power of the head of the nation was commonly too weak either to preserve the public peace or to protect the people against the oppressions of their immediate lords. This period of European affairs is emphatically stiled by historians the times of feudal anarchy.

When the sovereign happened to be a man of vigorous and warlike temper and of superior abilities, he would acquire a personal weight and influence, which answered for the time the purposes of a more regular authority. But in

---

Lines 69–74 The note accompanying lines 40–46 is supported here; "speculative men" are not in the modern sense speculators, but men who do their own thinking.

Lines 78–90 The periods of English history to which this alludes are those known to modern historians as "the anarchy of Stephen's reign" (1135–1154), and the Wars of the Roses (1455 intermittently to 1485). King Stephen, however, was followed by the strong and innovative Henry II, who institutionalized the common law; Henry VII, who put an end to the Wars of the Roses, between the houses of Lancaster (the red rose) and York (the white rose) and who succeeded Richard III in 1485, was the first of the formidable Tudor dynasty.

Lines 91–105 This paragraph may have a good measure of general truth, but rather curiously makes no mention of the Magna Carta, wrested from King John by strong barons and clergy in 1215. But the intention seems to be to refer to the weakening of the powers of the holy Roman emperors in Europe, leading to the emergence of independent states in early modern Europe.

general the power of the barons triumphed over that of the prince; and in many
95   instances his dominion was entirely thrown off, and the great fiefs were erected
into independent principalities or states. In those instances in which the
monarch finally prevailed over his vassals, his success was chiefly owing to the
tyranny of those vassals over their dependents. The barons, or nobles equally the
enemies of the sovereign and the oppressors of the common people were
100 dreaded and detested by both; till mutual danger and mutual interest effected an
union between them fatal to the power of the aristocracy. Had the nobles, by a
conduct of clemency and justice, preserved the fidelity and devotion of their retainers and followers, the contests between them and the prince must almost always have ended in their favour and in the abridgement or subversion of the
105 royal authority.

This is not an assertion founded merely in speculation or conjecture. Among
other illustrations of its truth which might be cited Scotland will furnish a cogent
example. The spirit of clanship which was at an early day introduced into that
kingdom, uniting the nobles and their dependents by ties equivalent to those of
110 kindred, rendered the aristocracy a constant overmatch for the power of the
monarch; till the incorporation with England subdued its fierce and ungovernable spirit, and reduced it within those rules of subordination, which a more rational and a more energetic system of civil polity had previously established in
the latter kingdom.

115 The separate governments in a confederacy may aptly be compared with the
feudal baronies; with this advantage in their favour, that from the reasons already
explained, they will generally possess the confidence and good will of the people;
and with so important a support will be able effectually to oppose all incroachments of the national government. It will be well if they are not able to counter-
120 act its legitimate and necessary authority. The points of similitude consist in the

---

Lines 106–14 The lesson drawn here once again is that peace, order, and stability require not only good government but government strong enough to subdue and contain internal forces of disaffection. The reference to "the incorporation with England" (line 111) is to the accession of James VI of Scotland as James I of England, in succession to Elizabeth I, in 1603. His new position did give him a stronger hand in dealing with turbulent Scottish chiefs. But the united monarchy did not amount to full incorporation, and the process was formally completed in 1707 with the Act of Union, after which Scotland was represented in and ruled by the Parliament of Westminster. (But it retained its own legal system and established church.) In 1999, by an Act of Parliament at Westminster, Scotland regained a Parliament of its own.

Lines 115–24 The argument of this essay is rounded off with the comparison of the American states with feudal baronies. This comparison is not expected to appeal to enlightened Americans, who, with their British contemporaries, regard feudal institutions as barbarous. It is arguable, however, that feudal traces have survived in the locally-based political power and privileges of United States senators.

rivalship of power, applicable to both, and in the CONCENTRATION of large portions of the strength of the community into particular DEPOSITORIES, in one case at the disposal of individuals, in the other case at the disposal of political bodies.

A concise review of the events that have attended confederate governments *125* will further illustrate this important doctrine; an inattention to which has been the great source of our political mistakes, and has given our jealousy a direction to the wrong side. This review shall form the subject of some ensuing papers.

PUBLIUS.

EIGHTEEN

JAMES MADISON (WITH THE ASSISTANCE
OF ALEXANDER HAMILTON)
December 7, 1787
The Subject Continued, with Farther Examples

To the People of the State of New York.

Among the confederacies of antiquity, the most considerable was that of the Grecian republics associated under the Amphyctionic council. From the best accounts transmitted of this celebrated institution, it bore a very instructive analogy to the present confederation of the American states.

5   The members retained the character of independent and sovereign states, and had equal votes in the federal council. This council had a general authority to propose and resolve whatever it judged necessary for the common welfare of Greece—to declare and carry on war—to decide in the last resort all controversies between the members—to fine the aggressing party—to employ the whole
10 force of the confederacy against the disobedient—to admit new members. The Amphyctions were the guardians of religion, and of the immense riches belonging to the temple of Delphos, where they had the right of jurisdiction in controversies between the inhabitants and those who came to consult the oracle. As a further provision for the efficacy of the federal powers, they took an oath mutu-
15 ally to defend and protect the united cities, to punish the violators of this oath, and to inflict vengeance on sacrilegious despoilers of the temple.

Lines 1–4 ff Hamilton and Madison had prepared themselves for the previous summer's debates by a great deal of reading. It is doubtful that Madison, who had received a parcel of books from Jefferson in Paris, had much need of the assistance attributed to Hamilton by Jacob E. Cooke. On June 19, 1787 Madison had made a long and carefully prepared speech containing comparisons and parallels from the ancient world; reviewing the histories of the Amphyctionic and Achaean confederacies as well as the "Helvetic, Germanic and Belgic among the moderns," arguing that the tendency of particular members to usurp power brought "confusion & ruin on the whole." His account of various forms of ancient leagues and confederations is a highly pragmatic instance of history applied to present circumstance. This essay drew heavily on the notes he had used for this speech.

The various leagues of the ancient Aegean were associations of neighboring states formed around a religious center; the term *Amphyctionic* was generic for "neighbors," but the most important, known as the Amphyctionic League, was originally composed of twelve tribes inhabiting the area around Thermopylae. In the 4th century B.C. the league rebuilt the Delphic temple. Each state sent two deputies to

In theory and upon paper, this apparatus of powers, seems amply sufficient for all general purposes. In several material instances, they exceed the powers enumerated in the articles of confederation. The Amphyctions had in their hands the superstition of the times, one of the principal engines by which government was then maintained; they had declared authority to use coertion against refractory cities, and were bound by oath to exert this authority on the necessary occasions. 20

Very different nevertheless was the experiment from the theory. The powers, like those of the present congress, were administered by deputies appointed wholly by the cities in their political capacities; and exercised over them in the same capacities. Hence the weakness, the disorders, and finally the destruction of the confederacy. The more powerful members instead of being kept in awe and subordination, tyrannized successively over all the rest. Athens, as we learn from Demosthenes, was the arbiter of Greece seventy-three years. The Lacedemonians next governed it twenty-nine years; at a subsequent period, after the battle of Leuctra, the Thebans had their turn of domination. 25 30

It happened but too often, according to Plutarch, that the deputies of the strongest cities, awed and corrupted those of the weaker, and that judgment went in favor of the most powerful party.

Even in the midst of defensive and dangerous wars with Persia and Macedon, the members never acted in concert, and were more or fewer of them, eternally the dupes, or the hirelings of the common enemy. The intervals of foreign war, were filled up by domestic vicissitudes, convulsions and carnage. 35

After the conclusion of the war with Xerxes, it appears that the Lacedemonians, required that a number of the cities should be turned out of the confederacy for the unfaithful part they had acted. The Athenians finding that the Lacedemonians would lose fewer partizans by such a measure than themselves; and would become masters of the public deliberations, vigorously opposed and defeated the attempt. This piece of history proves at once the inefficiency of the union; the ambition and jealousy of its most powerful members, and the dependent and degraded condition of the rest. The smaller members, though entitled by the theory 40 45

---

meet twice a year in a council, which exercised a variety of temporal powers and conducted the Pythian Games. The central institutions were too weak to prevent the strongest tribes from abusing their powers—a conclusion drawn from Plutarch (see lines 32–34). Lines 111–14 credit Abbé Mably (Gabriel Bonnot de Mably, 1709–1785) as another source of information. Mably, who wrote books on the Greeks and the Romans, was an advocate of applying historical lessons to the present. Publius is indulging in exactly the same exercise with regard to the Confederation. On September 1, 1784, Jefferson, in Paris, informed Madison of a long list of books he had bought for him, including Mably on a variety of subjects in history, philosophy, and law, about France, the American Constitution (no doubt meaning the Articles), the Romans, the Greeks, and Poland. Madison had every opportunity of instructing his colleagues in the lessons of ancient history.

of their system, to revolve in equal pride and majesty around the common center, had become in fact, satellites of the orbs of primary magnitude.

Had the Greeks, says the Abbe Milot, been as wise as they were courageous, they would have been admonished by experience of the necessity of a closer union, and would have availed themselves of the peace which followed their success against the Persian arms, to establish such a reformation. Instead of this obvious policy, Athens and Sparta, inflated with the victories and the glory they had acquired, became first rivals and then enemies; and did each other infinitely more mischief, than they had suffered from Xerxes. Their mutual jealousies, fears, hatreds and injuries ended in the celebrated Peloponnesian war; which itself ended in the ruin and slavery of the Athenians, who had begun it.

As a weak government, when not at war, is ever agitated by internal dissentions; so these never fail to bring on fresh calamities from abroad. The Phocians having ploughed up some consecrated ground belonging to the temple of Apollo; the Amphyctionic council, according to the superstition of the age, imposed a fine on the sacrilegious offenders. The Phocians being abetted by Athens and Sparta, refused to submit to the decree. The Thebans, with others of the cities, undertook to maintain the authority of the Amphyctions, and to avenge the violated god. The latter being the weaker party, invited the assistance of Philip of Macedon, who had secretly fostered the contest. Philip gladly seized the opportunity of executing the designs he had long planned against the liberties of Greece. By his intrigues and bribes he won over to his interests the popular leaders of several cities; by their influence and votes, gained admission into the Amphyctionic council; and by his arts and his arms, made himself master of the confederacy.

Such were the consequences of the fallacious principle, on which this interesting establishment was founded. Had Greece, says a judicious observer on her fate, been united by a stricter confederation, and persevered in her union, she would never have worn the chains of Macedon; and might have proved a barrier to the vast projects of Rome.

The Achaean league, as it is called, was another society of Grecian republics, which supplies us with valuable instruction.

The union here was far more intimate, and its organization much wiser, than in the preceding instance. It will accordingly appear, that though not exempt from a similar catastrophe, it by no means equally deserved it.

The cities composing this league, retained their municipal jurisdiction, appointed their own officers, and enjoyed a perfect equality. The senate in which they were represented, had the sole and exclusive right of peace and war, of send-

---

Line 49 Charles François Xavier Millot [sic], *Éléments d'histoire générale* (continués par Delisle de Sales), 11 volumes, Paris, 1772–1811.

Line 73 Unfortunately, Publius does not favor the reader with the *identity* of the "judicious observer" on the fate of Greece.

ing and receiving ambassadors—of entering into treaties and alliances—of ap- *85*
pointing a chief magistrate or praetor, as he was called, who commanded their
armies; and who with the advice and consent of ten of the senators, not only administered the government in the recess of the senate, but had a great share in its
deliberation, when assembled. According to the primitive constitution, there
were two praetors associated in the administration; but on trial, a single one was *90*
preferred.

It appears that the cities had all the same laws and customs, the same weights
and measures, and the same money. But how far this effect proceeded from the
authority of the federal council, is left in uncertainty. It is said only, that the cities
were in a manner compelled to receive the same laws and usages. When Lacede- *95*
mon was brought into the league by Philopoemen, it was attended with an abolition of the institutions and laws of Lycurgus, and an adoption of those of the
Achaeans. The Amphyctionic confederacies of which she had been a member,
left her in the full exercise of her government and her legislation. This circumstance alone proves a very material difference in the genius of the two systems. *100*

It is much to be regretted that such imperfect monuments remain of this curious political fabric. Could its interior structure and regular operation be ascertained, it is probable that more light would be thrown by it on the science of
federal government, than by any of the like experiments with which we are
acquainted. *105*

One important fact seems to be witnessed by all the historians who take notice of Achaean affairs. It is, that as well after the renovation of the league by
Aratus, as before its dissolution by the arts of Macedon, there was infinitely more
of moderation and justice in the administration of its government, and less of

---

Lines 95–100 Lycurgus (7th century B.C.?) is the legendary lawgiver whom many
generations of Greeks credited with the laws that made Sparta uniquely egalitarian,
communitarian, and militaristic. (In Hamilton's opinion, it was "little better than a
well regulated camp" [see No. 6, line 98].) Even these superior institutions could not
make the Achaeans invulnerable to foreign enemies. The implications are obvious:
both to avert the distractions of internal disorder, and for external defense, Americans need an even higher level of unity enforced by a central government.

Line 96 Philopoemen (ca. 252–152 B.C.) was a general noted for restoring military
efficiency to the Achaean League. Lacedaemonia is a name historically interchangeable with Sparta. The point of these paragraphs is that the Achaean League was far
more closely integrated, and therefore far more efficient, than those of the loosely
knit Amphyctions, and that although the Achaean cities enjoyed "perfect equality,"
they had advantages in a monetary union, similar trading laws, and the same laws
and customs; also in that their senate controlled a joint foreign policy.

Lines 106–14 As we see here, the Achaeans' superior institutions served to keep
local popular disturbances under control. Shays's rebellion is just around the corner
in these historical reflections.

110 violence and sedition in the people, than were to be found in any of the cities exercising *singly* all the prerogatives of sovereignty. The Abbe Mably, in his observations on Greece, says that the popular government, which was so tempestuous elsewhere, caused no disorders in the members of the Achaean republic, *because it was there tempered by the general authority and laws of the confederacy.*

115 We are not to conclude too hastily, however, that faction did not in a certain degree agitate the particular cities; much less, that a due subordination and harmony reigned in the general system. The contrary is sufficiently displayed in the vicissitudes and fate of the republic.

Whilst the Amphyctionic confederacy remained, that of the Achaeans, which *120* comprehended the less important cities only, made little figure on the theatre of Greece. When the former became a victim to Macedon, the latter was spared by the policy of Philip and Alexander. Under the successors of these princes, however, a different policy prevailed. The arts of division were practised among the Achaeans: Each city was seduced into a separate interest; the union was dis- *125* solved. Some of the cities fell under the tyranny of Macedonian garrisons; others under that of usurpers springing out of their own confusions. Shame and oppression ere long awakened their love of liberty. A few cities re-united. Their example was followed by others, as opportunities were found of cutting off their tyrants. The league soon embraced almost the whole Peloponnesus. Macedon saw its *130* progress; but was hindered by internal dissentions from stopping it. All Greece caught the enthusiasm, and seemed ready to unite in one confederacy; when the jealousy and envy in Sparta and Athens, of the rising glory of the Achaeans, threw a fatal damp on the enterprize. The dread of the Macedonian power induced the league to court the alliance of the kings of Egypt and Syria; who, as *135* successors of Alexander, were rivals of the king of Macedon. This policy was defeated by Cleomenes, king of Sparta, who was led by his ambition to make an unprovoked attack on his neighbours the Achaeans; and who as an enemy to Macedon, had interest enough with the Egyptian and Syrian princes, to effect a breach of their engagements with the league. The Achaeans were now reduced *140* to the dilemma of submitting to Cleomenes, or of supplicating the aid of Macedon, its former oppressor. The latter expedient was adopted. The contests of the Greeks always afforded a pleasing opportunity to that powerful neighbour, of intermeddling in their affairs. A Macedonian army quickly appeared: Cleomenes was vanquished. The Achaeans soon experienced, as often happens, that

---

Lines 111–14 See discussion of Mably at p. 93, note.

Lines 119–66 The Amphyctionic confederation came under the influence of Philip II of Macedon (reigned 359–336 B.C.) after he had been admitted to its councils. Philip, not himself Greek, consolidated Macedonian power in ancient Greece, and on the whole maintained good relations with Athens. He created the finest army yet seen, but was assassinated before he could use it to extend his power in the east. This task fell to his son, Alexander the Great.

a victorious and powerful ally, is but another name for a master. All that their *145* most abject compliances could obtain from him, was a toleration of the exercise of their laws. Philip, who was now on the throne of Macedon, soon provoked, by his tyrannies, fresh combinations among the Greeks. The Achaeans, though weakened by internal dissentions, and by the revolt of Messene one of its members, being joined by the Etolians and Athenians, erected the standard of opposi- *150* tion. Finding themselves, though thus supported, unequal to the undertaking, they once more had recourse to the dangerous expedient of introducing the succour of foreign arms. The Romans to whom the invitation was made, eagerly embraced it. Philip was conquered: Macedon subdued. A new crisis ensued to the league. Dissentions broke out among its members. These the Romans fostered. *155* Callicrates and other popular leaders, became mercenary instruments for inveigling their countrymen. The more effectually to nourish discord and disorder, the Romans had, to the astonishment of those who confided in their sincerity, already proclaimed universal liberty* throughout Greece. With the same insidious views, they now seduced the members from the league, by representing to their *160* pride, the violation it committed on their sovereignty. By these arts, this union, the last hope of Greece, the last hope of antient liberty, was torn into pieces; and such imbecility and distraction introduced, that the arms of Rome found little difficulty in compleating the ruin which their arts had commenced. The Achaeans were cut to pieces; and Achaia loaded with chains, under which it is *165* groaning at this hour.

I have thought it not superfluous to give the outlines of this important portion of history; both because it teaches more than one lesson and because, as a supplement to the outlines of the Achaean constitution, it emphatically illustrates the tendency of federal bodies, rather to anarchy among the members, than to *170* tyranny in the head.

PUBLIUS.

---

* This was but another name more specious for the independence of the members on the federal head.

Lines 167–71 The purpose of this extended essay in ancient history is to inculcate the dangers of disorder and defeat by foreign enemies inherent in federal forms of government.

NINETEEN

JAMES MADISON (WITH THE ASSISTANCE OF
ALEXANDER HAMILTON)
December 8, 1787
The Subject Continued, with Farther Examples

To the People of the State of New York.

The examples of antient confederacies, cited in my last paper, have not exhausted the source of experimental instruction on this subject. There are existing institutions, founded on a similar principle, which merit particular consideration. The first which presents itself is the Germanic body.

5   In the early ages of Christianity Germany was occupied by seven distinct nations, who had no common chief. The Franks, one of the number, having conquered the Gauls, established the kingdom which has taken its name from them. In the ninth century, Charlemagne, its warlike monarch, carried his victorious arms in every direction; and Germany became a part of his vast dominions.

10 On the dismemberment, which took place under his sons, this part was erected into a separate and independent empire. Charlemagne and his immediate descendants possessed the reality, as well as the ensigns and dignity of imperial power. But the principal vassals, whose fiefs had become hereditary, and who composed the national diets which Charlemagne had not abolished, gradually

15 threw off the yoke, and advanced to sovereign jurisdiction and independence. The force of imperial sovereignty was insufficient to restrain such powerful dependents; or to preserve the unity and tranquility of the empire. The most furious private wars, accompanied with every species of calamity, were carried on between the different princes and states. The imperial authority, unable to main-

20 tain the public order, declined by degrees, till it was almost extinct in the anarchy, which agitated the long interval between the death of the last emperor of the Suabian, and the accession of the first emperor of the Austrian lines. In the eleventh century, the emperors enjoyed full sovereignty: In the fifteenth they had little more than the symbols and decorations of power.

Lines 5–24 Charlemagne (Charles the Great) (ca. 742–814) reigned over the Franks from 768 to 814, extending Frankish rule to establish the greatest empire in the West since the greatness of Rome. He supported the Church, which he effectively brought under his aegis, having the Pope crown him emperor on Christmas Day 800. The word "sovereignty" was not used in this period, and in that sense its use is anachronistic; but in practical terms, the exercise of power by Charlemagne was as extensive as that claimed by early modern monarchies as they emerged from their contests with feudal barons. The structure began to disintegrate soon after his death, however.

Out of this feudal system, which has itself many of the important features of a confederacy, has grown the federal system, which constitutes the Germanic empire. Its powers are vested in a diet representing the component members of the confederacy; in the emperor who is the executive magistrate, with a negative on the decrees of the diet; and in the imperial chamber and aulic council, two judiciary tribunals having supreme jurisdiction in controversies which concern the empire, or which happen among its members.

The diet possesses the general power of legislating for the empire—of making war and peace—contracting alliances—assessing quotas of troops and money—constructing fortresses—regulating coin—admitting new members, and subjecting disobedient members to the ban of the empire, by which the party is degraded from his sovereign rights, and his possessions forfeited. The members of the confederacy are expressly restricted from entering into compacts, prejudicial to the empire, from imposing tolls and duties on their mutual intercourse, without the consent of the emperor and diet; from altering the value of money; from doing injustice to one another; or from affording assistance or retreat to disturbers of the public peace. And the ban is denounced against such as shall violate any of these restrictions. The members of the diet, as such, are subject in all cases to be judged by the emperor and diet, and in their private capacities, by the aulic council and imperial chamber.

The prerogatives of the emperor are numerous. The most important of them are, his exclusive right to make propositions to the diet—to negative its resolutions—to name ambassadors—to confer dignities and titles—to fill vacant electorates—to found universities—to grant privileges not injurious to the states of the empire—to receive and apply the public revenues—and generally to watch over the public safety. In certain cases, the electors form a council to him. In quality of emperor he possesses no territory within the empire; nor receives any revenue for his support. But his revenue and dominions, in other qualities, constitute him one of the most powerful princes in Europe.

Line 29 "Aulic" means pertaining to a court; the aulic council was still, at that time, the German emperor's personal council.

Line 52 The estimate of the German emperor as "one of the most powerful princes in Europe" prepares the way for an ironic contrast between his potentialities and his pretensions. The concept of German nationality implied in the incongruous title "The Holy Roman Empire of the German nation" had to comprehend a multitude of diminutive principalities, dukedoms, electorates, and other denominations of statehood, all with their own jurisdictions and currencies, levying their own customs duties, and often going to war against each other and in defiance of the empire. Voltaire famously quipped that it was neither holy nor Roman nor an empire. The fragmentation and the helplessness of the empire itself permitted the emergence from the mid-18th century of the dual power structure of Prussia and Austria. But Prussia was brushed aside by Napoleon in 1806.

From such a parade of constitutional powers, in the representatives and head of this confederacy, the natural supposition would be, that it must form an ex-
55 ception to the general character which belongs to its kindred systems. Nothing would be farther from the reality. The fundamental principle, on which it rests, that the empire is a community of sovereigns; that the diet is a representation of sovereigns; and that the laws are addressed to sovereigns; render the empire a nerveless body; incapable of regulating its own members; insecure against exter-
60 nal dangers; and agitated with unceasing fermentations in its own bowels.

The history of Germany is a history of wars between the emperor and the princes and states; of wars among the princes and states themselves; of the licentiousness of the strong, and the oppression of the weak; of foreign intrusions, and foreign intrigues; of requisitions of men and money, disregarded, or partially
65 complied with; of attempts to enforce them, altogether abortive, or attended with slaughter and desolation, involving the innocent with the guilty; of general imbecility, confusion and misery.

In the sixteenth century, the emperor with one part of the empire on his side, was seen engaged against the other princes and states. In one of the conflicts, the
70 emperor himself was put to flight, and very near being made prisoner by the Elector of Saxony. The late king of Prussia was more than once pitted against his imperial sovereign; and commonly proved an overmatch for him. Controversies and wars among the members themselves have been so common, that the German annals are crowded with the bloody pages which describe them. Previous to
75 the peace of Westphalia, Germany was desolated by a war of thirty years, in which the emperor, with one half of the empire was on one side; and Sweden with the other half on the opposite side. Peace was at length negociated and dictated by foreign powers; and the articles of it, to which foreign powers are parties, made a fundamental part of the Germanic constitution.

Lines 53–60 This paragraph comes to the point by exposing the structural weakness of the empire behind its parade of pomp and dignity. A "community of sovereigns" is politically ineffective because it cannot act with unity (line 57).

Lines 68–79 The Thirty Years' War, which began in Bohemia in 1618, was concluded by the general European settlement of the Peace of Westphalia in 1648. It was a conflict of extreme complexity, ultimately involving most of central, northern, and northwestern Europe, often savagely prosecuted, in which pretensions to religious motivation were cast aside when Catholic France formed an alliance with Lutheran Sweden. Berthold Brecht's famous play *Mother Courage and Her Children* is set in the Thirty Years' War.

If the nation happens, on any emergency, to be more united by the necessity 80
of self defence; its situation is still deplorable. Military preparations must be pre-
ceded by so many tedious discussions, arising from the jealousies, pride, separate
views, and clashing pretensions, of sovereign bodies; that before the diet can settle the arrangements, the enemy are in the field; and before the federal troops are
ready to take it, are retiring into winter quarters. 85

The small body of national troops which has been judged necessary in time of
peace, is defectively kept up, badly paid, infected with local prejudices, and supported by irregular and disproportionate contributions to the treasury.

The impossibility of maintaining order, and dispensing justice among these sovereign subjects, produced the experiment of dividing the Empire into nine or ten 90
circles or districts; of giving them an interior organization; and of charging them
with the military execution of the laws against delinquent and contumacious members. This experiment has only served to demonstrate more fully, the radical vice of
the constitution. Each circle is the miniature picture of the deformities of this political monster. They either fail to execute their commissions, or they do it with all 95
the devastation and carnage of civil war. Sometimes whole circles are defaulters,
and then they increase the mischief which they were instituted to remedy.

We may form some judgment of this scheme of military coertion, from a
sample given by Thuanus. In Donawerth, a free and imperial city, of the circle of
Suabia, the Abbe de St. Croix enjoyed certain immunities which had been re- 100
served to him. In the exercise of these, on some public occasion, outrages were
committed on him, by the people of the city. The consequence was, that the city
was put under the ban of the empire; and the Duke of Bavaria, though director
of another circle, obtained an appointment to enforce it. He soon appeared before the city, with a corps of ten thousand troops and finding it a fit occasion, as 105
he had secretly intended from the beginning, to revive an antiquated claim, on
the pretext that his ancestors had suffered the place to be dismembered from his

---

Lines 89–97 The ten so-called Circles (kreise) of the German Empire were not circles but large districts, organized for administrative purposes in the 15th century. By
the 18th century, they were increasingly defunct; the best organized was the
Swabian Circle, which held an annual parliament, or Kreistag, which dealt mainly
with roads, coinage, and keeping checks on the imperial ambassador at the Kreistag.
Minor estates such as those of the knights and the towns felt able to protect their interests through the system.

Line 99 Thuanus is Jacques-Auguste de Thou, author of a multivolume *Histoire Uni-
verselle* of which an edition published in Basle in 1742 is the likely source according to Jacob E. Cooke.

territory;* he took possession of it, in his own name; disarmed and punished the inhabitants, and re-annexed the city to his domains.

110 It may be asked perhaps what has so long kept this disjointed machine from falling entirely to pieces? The answer is obvious. The weakness of most of the members, who are unwilling to expose themselves to the mercy of foreign powers; the weakness of most of the principal members; compared with the formidable powers all around them; the vast weight and influence which the emperor

115 derives from his separate and hereditary dominions; and the interest he feels in preserving a system, with which his family pride is connected, and which constitutes him the first prince in Europe; these causes support a feeble and precarious union; whilst the repellent quality, incident to the nature of sovereignty, and which time continually strengthens, prevents any reform whatever, founded on a

120 proper consolidation. Nor is it to be imagined, if this obstacle could be surmounted, that the neighbouring powers would suffer a revolution to take place, which would give to the Empire the force and pre-eminence to which it is entitled. Foreign nations have long considered themselves as interested in the changes made by events in this constitution; and have, on various occasions, be-

125 trayed their policy of perpetuating its anarchy and weakness.

If more direct examples were wanting, Poland as a government over local sovereigns, might not improperly be taken notice of. Nor could any proof more striking, be given of the calamities flowing from such institutions. Equally unfit for self-government, and self-defence, it has long been at the mercy of its power-

130 ful neighbours; who have lately had the mercy to disburden it of one third of its people and territories.

* Pfeffel, Nouvel abreg. chronol. de l'hist. &c. d'Allemagne, says the pretext was to indemnify himself for the expence of the expedition.

Line 110 Much is said in this essay to the disparagement of the power structure of the German nation—an aggregation for which the word "nation" was plainly anomalous. Publius is interested in politics, and particularly in the politics of power. It is worth observing that several of these dukes, margraves, electors (of the emperor), archbishops and other minor potentates were notable patrons of art and music, and that some of the world's most distinguished philosophy, music, and literature were created and fostered in this ramshackle empire. (Mozart's first patron—though not his most appreciative—was the Archbishop of Salzburg.) A sense of German nationality was also beginning to emerge. These matters, of course, lie beyond the brief that Publius has set himself.

Lines 126–31 The *liberum veto,* or power of veto, exercised individually by each of the Polish nobility, paralyzed government, and was often cited as a notorious example of political imbecility. For the partitions of Poland see No. 14, line 72.

Madison's footnote Pfeffel is Christien Fredrich Pfeffel von Kriegelstein, author of a history of Germany published in French in Paris in 1776 (Cooke).

The connection among the Swiss cantons scarcely amounts to a confederacy: Though it is sometimes cited as an instance of the stability of such institutions.

They have no common treasury—no common troops even in war—no common coin—no common judicatory, nor any other common mark of sovereignty. 135

They are kept together by the peculiarity of their topographical position, by their individual weakness and insignificancy; by the fear of powerful neighbours, to one of which they were formerly subject; by the few sources of contention among a people of such simple and homogeneous manners; by their joint interest in their dependent possessions; by the mutual aid they stand in need of, for 140 suppressing insurrections and rebellions; an aid expressly stipulated, and often required and afforded; and by the necessity of some regular and permanent provision for accommodating disputes among the cantons. The provision is, that the parties at variance shall each choose four judges out of the neutral cantons, who in case of disagreement, chuse an umpire. This tribunal, under an oath of impartiality, pronounces definitive sentence: which all the cantons are bound to enforce. The competency of this regulation may be estimated, by a clause in their treaty of 1683, with Victor Amadeus of Savoy; in which he obliges himself to interpose as mediator in disputes between the cantons; and to employ force, if necessary, against the contumacious party. 150

So far as the peculiarity of their case will admit of comparison with that of the United States, it serves to confirm the principle intended to be established. Whatever efficacy the union may have had in ordinary cases, it appears that the moment a cause of difference sprang up, capable of trying its strength, it failed. The controversies on the subject of religion, which in three instances have 155 kindled violent and bloody contests, may be said in fact to have severed the

---

Line 132–63 The Swiss confederation gained recognition from the empire in 1648. Its structure was complex but, as Publius says, its internal connections were weak. Though often cited as an example of liberty, the Swiss system really only meant liberty from external domination; rural landowners and city magnates ruled the cantons as privileged oligarchies.

Line 148 Victor Amadeus II, 1666–1732.

Lines 151–59 The comparison with the United States, as Publius implicitly admits, is thin. But the separation of Protestant and Catholic cantons, while setting an example of mutual religious toleration, represents a form of religious establishment within each canton. Madison, who had steered Jefferson's Statute for Religious Freedom through the Virginia legislature in 1786, disapproved of all religious establishments. In the first Congress under the Constitution, he was to chair the committee that drafted the 1st Amendment. As president, he would veto legislation in 1811 providing for land reserved for churches.

league. The Protestant and Catholic cantons have since had their separate diets; where all the most important concerns are adjusted, and which have left the general diet little other business than to take care of the common bailages.

160   That separation had another consequence which merits attention. It produced opposite alliances with foreign powers; at Berne at the head of the Protestant association, with the United Provinces; and of Luzerne, as the head of the Catholic association, with France.

PUBLIUS.

Lines 160–63 These separate alliances were supreme examples of political weakness at the center. The survival of the Swiss confederation was possible not on account of its internal freedom but more simply because powerful neighbors did not have designs on Swiss territory. Publius does not, however, mention that as far as any analogy with the American situation was concerned, such separate alliances would already be banned under Article VI of the Articles of Confederation.

TWENTY

JAMES MADISON (WITH THE ASSISTANCE
OF ALEXANDER HAMILTON)
December 11, 1787
The Subject Continued, with Farther Examples

To the People of the State of New York.

The United Netherlands are a confederacy of republics, or rather of aristocracies, of a very remarkable texture; yet confirming all the lessons derived from those which we have already reviewed.

The union is composed of seven co-equal and sovereign states, and each state or province is a composition of equal and independent cities. In all important cases not only the provinces, but the cities must be unanimous.

The sovereignty of the union is represented by the states general, consisting usually of about fifty deputies appointed by the provinces. They hold their seats, some for life, some for six, three and one years. From two provinces they continue in appointment during pleasure.

The states general have authority to enter into treaties and alliances—to make war and peace—to raise armies and equip fleets—to ascertain quotas and demand contributions. In all these cases however, unanimity and the sanction of their constituents are requisite. They have authority to appoint and receive ambassadors—to execute treaties and alliances already formed—to provide for the collection of duties on imports and exports—to regulate the mint, with a saving to the provincial rights—to govern as sovereigns the dependent territories. The provinces are restrained, unless with the general consent, from entering into foreign treaties—from establishing imposts injurious to others, or charging their

---

Lines 1–6 Under the settlement of 1648, the seven northern, and predominantly Protestant, provinces of Holland, Zeeland, Utrecht, Gelderland, Friesland, Gröningen-Drente, and Overijssel constituted the United Provinces of the Dutch Republic. This establishment represented the formal conclusion of the struggle for Dutch independence from Spanish domination, begun in 1568, and continued through intermittent wars and truces. The settlement left the predominantly Catholic southern provinces under imperial (actually now Austrian Hapsburg) control. (These southern provinces eventually became the independent kingdom of Belgium in 1831.) The Dutch story had particular resonance for Americans: the Dutch were the first to achieve independence from the rule of an empire, they were mainly Protestant, and, of course, their forebears had colonized New York, leaving strong traces in the population, religion, and language of the city and parts of the state. New York still has its Harlem, Amsterdam Avenue, and other Dutch place and street names.

20   neighbours with higher duties than their own subjects. A council of state, a chamber of accounts, with five colleges of admiralty, aid and fortify the federal administration.

The executive magistrate of the union is the stadtholder, who is now a hereditary prince. His principal weight and influence in the republic are derived from *25*   his independent title; from his great patrimonial estates; from his family connections with some of the chief potentates of Europe; and more than all, perhaps, from his being stadtholder in the several provinces, as well as for the union, in which provincial quality, he has the appointment of town magistrates under certain regulations, executes provincial decrees, presides when he pleases in the *30*   provincial tribunals; and has throughout the power of pardon.

As stadtholder of the union, he has however considerable prerogatives.

In his political capacity he has authority to settle disputes between the provinces, when other methods fail—to assist at the deliberations of the states general, and at their particular conferences—to give audiences to foreign ambas-*35*   sadors, and to keep agents for his particular affairs at foreign courts.

In his military capacity, he commands the federal troops—provides for garrisons, and in general regulates military affairs—disposes of all appointments from Colonels to Ensigns, and of the governments and posts of fortified towns.

In his marine capacity, he is admiral general, and superintends and directs *40*   every thing relative to naval forces, and other naval affairs—presides in the admiralties in person or by proxy—appoints lieutenant admirals and other officers— and establishes councils of war, whose sentences are not executed till he approves them.

His revenue, exclusive of his private income, amounts to 300,000 florins. The *45*   standing army which he commands consists of about 40,000 men.

Such is the nature of the celebrated Belgic confederacy, as delineated on parchment. What are the characters which practice has stampt upon it? Imbecility in the government; discord among the provinces; foreign influence and indignities; a precarious existence in peace, and peculiar calamities from war.

50   It was long ago remarked by Grotius, that nothing but the hatred of his countrymen to the house of Austria, kept them from being ruined by the vices of their constitution.

Line 49 Netherlands history was intimately linked to problems of survival, and the Dutch Republic had always been involved in complex and often precarious relationships with its physically more powerful neighbors, principally France, but also Prussia. These conditions were far closer and posed far more immediate and serious threats than those that bore on the United States; nevertheless, America had powerful potential continental rivals in Britain and Spain, not to mention its often formidable Native American populations. Publius now makes his own explicit appeal to Americans to learn the vital importance of internal unity from the lessons of history.

Line 50 Hugo Grotius (1583–1645) was a Dutch scholar and juristic thinker whose masterpiece, *On the Law of War and Peace* (1625), was the greatest early contribution to the concept of international law.

The union of Utrecht, says another respectable writer, reposes an authority in the states general seemingly sufficient to secure harmony, but the jealousy in each province renders the practice very different from the theory. *55*

The same instrument says another, obliges each province to levy certain contributions; but this article never could and probably never will be executed; because the inland provinces who have little commerce cannot pay an equal quota.

In matters of contribution, it is the practice to wave the articles of the constitution. The danger of delay obliges the consenting provinces to furnish their *60* quotas, without waiting for the others; and then to obtain reimbursement from the others, by deputations, which are frequent, or otherwise as they can. The great wealth and influence of the province of Holland, enable her to effect both these purposes.

It has more than once happened that the deficiencies have been ultimately to *65* be collected at the point of the bayonet; a thing practicable, though dreadful, in a confederacy, where one of the members, exceeds in force all the rest; and where several of them are too small to meditate resistance: but utterly impracticable in one composed of members, several of which are equal to each other in strength and resources, and equal singly to a vigorous and persevering defence. *70*

Foreign ministers, says Sir William Temple, who was himself a foreign minister, elude matters taken ad referendum, by tampering with the provinces and cities. In 1726, the treaty of Hanover was delayed by these means a whole year. Instances of a like nature are numerous and notorious.

In critical emergencies, the states general are often compelled to overleap *75* their constitutional bounds. In 1688, they concluded a treaty of themselves at the risk of their heads. The treaty of Westphalia in 1648, by which their independence was formally and finally recognized, was concluded without the consent of Zeland. Even as recently as the last treaty of peace with Great Britain, the constitutional principle of unanimity was departed from. A weak constitution must *80*

Lines 62–64 Holland was the one province that exceeded all the rest in force (and wealth). No one American state could exert this kind of power over the others.

Lines 71–74 Sir William Temple (1628–1699) served Charles II with great skill as ambassador at The Hague, but eventually proved too sympathetic to the Dutch for his increasingly pro-French master. Temple's book, *Observations upon the United Provinces* (1673) is regarded today as a pioneering essay in the interpretation of one people to another. The point of the rather obscure language of this citation seems to be that decisions taken by referendum in individual provinces can be circumvented by diplomacy.

Line 73 The mutually defensive Treaty of Hanover between Britain and Prussia was signed in 1725, but another year was spent in bringing in the Dutch Republic in 1726.

Lines 76–77 The reference is to a treaty between the United Provinces and England. The risk presumably came from Louis XIV, against whom the alliance was directed.

necessarily terminate in dissolution, for want of proper powers, or the usurpation of powers requisite for the public safety. Whether the usurpation, when once begun, will stop at the salutary point, or go forward to the dangerous extreme, must depend on the contingencies of the moment. Tyranny has perhaps oftener
85 grown out of the assumptions of power, called for, on pressing exigencies, by a defective constitution, than out of the full exercise of the largest constitutional authorities.

Notwithstanding the calamities produced by the stadtholdership, it has been supposed, that without his influence in the individual provinces, the causes of
90 anarchy manifest in the confederacy, would long ago have dissolved it. "Under such a government, says the Abbe Mably, "the union could never have subsisted, if the provinces had not a spring within themselves, capable of quickening their tardiness, and compelling them to the same way of thinking. This spring is the stadtholder." It is remarked by Sir William Temple, "that in the intermissions of
95 the stadtholdership, Holland by her riches and her authority, which drew the others into a sort of dependence, supplied the place."

These are not the only circumstances which have controuled the tendency to anarchy and dissolution. The surrounding powers impose an absolute necessity of union to a certain degree, at the same time, that they nourish by their in-
100 trigues, the constitutional vices, which keep the republic in some degree always at their mercy.

The true patriots have long bewailed the fatal tendency of these vices, and have made no less than four regular experiments, by *extraordinary assemblies*, convened for the special purpose, to apply a remedy: As many times, has their
105 laudable zeal found it impossible to *unite the public councils* in reforming the known, the acknowledged, the fatal evils of the existing constitution. Let us pause my fellow citizens, for one moment, over this melancholy and monitory lesson of history; and with the tear that drops for the calamities brought on mankind by their adverse opinions and selfish passions; let our gratitude mingle
110 an ejaculation to Heaven, for the propitious concord which has distinguished the consultations for our political happiness.

A design was also conceived of establishing a general tax to be administered by the federal authority. This also had its adversaries and failed.

This unhappy people seem to be now suffering from popular convulsions,
115 from dissentions among the states, and from the actual invasion of foreign arms,

---

Line 91 Regarding Mably, see p. 93, note.

Line 114 "This unhappy people" is still the Dutch. In 1786 a group calling themselves the Patriot Regents, some of them out of anti-Orange animosity but others from more democratic leanings, had seized power in Holland, Gröningen, and Overijssel and had deposed the Stadtholder William V. He was restored in 1787 by the intervention of the king of Prussia. In deploring the instability of Dutch institutions, Publius completely misses the irony that the origins of the internal reform

the crisis of their destiny. All nations have their eyes fixed on the awful spectacle. The first wish prompted by humanity is, that this severe trial may issue in such a revolution of their government, as will establish their union, and render it the parent of tranquility, freedom and happiness: The next, that the asylum under which, we trust, the enjoyment of these blessings, will speedily be secured in this *120* country, may receive and console them for the catastrophe of their own.

I make no apology for having dwelt so long on the contemplation of these federal precedents. Experience is the oracle of truth; and where its responses, are unequivocal, they ought to be conclusive and sacred. The important truth, which it unequivocally pronounces in the present case, is, that a sovereignty over *125* sovereigns, a government over governments, a legislation for communities, as contradistinguished from individuals; as it is a solecism in theory; so in practice, it is subversive of the order and ends of civil polity, by substituting *violence* in place of *law,* or the destructive *coertion* of the *sword,* in place of the mild and salutary *coertion* of the *magistracy.* *130*

PUBLIUS.

---

movement were inspired, at least in part, by the success of the American Revolution. Dutch loans, negotiated by John Adams, had played an important part in financing the War of Independence.

Lines 122–30 Compare this conclusion with Madison's paper on "Vices of the Political System of the United States," written in preparation for the Convention. See also Hamilton's comments on the principles of sovereignty, No. 9, lines 120–46. Publius's strong language is consistent with the whole argument of these essays and the lessons drawn from history ancient and modern. Mixed or divided sovereignty is still "a solecism."

TWENTY-ONE

ALEXANDER HAMILTON
December 12, 1787
Further Defects of the Present Constitution

To the People of the State of New York.

Having in the three last numbers taken a summary review of the principal circumstances and events, which depict the genius and fate of other confederate
governments; I shall now proceed in the enumeration of the most important of
those defects, which have hitherto disappointed our hopes from the system es-
5   tablished among ourselves. To form a safe and satisfactory judgment of the
proper remedy, it is absolutely necessary that we should be well acquainted with
the extent and malignity of the disease.

   The next most palpable defect of the existing confederation is the total want
of a SANCTION to its laws. The United States as now composed, have no power
10   to exact obedience, or punish disobedience to their resolutions, either by
pecuniary mulcts by a suspension or divestiture of privileges, or by any other
constitutional means. There is no express delegation of authority to them to use
force against delinquent members; and if such a right should be ascribed to the
federal head, as resulting from the nature of the social compact between the
15   states, it must be by inference and construction, in the face of that part of
the second article, by which it is declared, "that each state shall retain every
power, jurisdiction and right, not *expressly* delegated to the United States in congress assembled." The want of such a right involves no doubt a striking absurdity;
but we are reduced to the dilemma either of supposing that deficiency, prepos-
20   terous as it may seem, or of contravening or explaining away a provision, which
has been of late a repeated theme of the eulogies of those, who oppose the new
constitution; and the omission of which in that plan, has been the subject of
much plausible animadaversion and severe criticism. If we are unwilling to impair the force of this applauded provision, we shall be obliged to conclude, that
25   the United States afford the extraordinary spectacle of a government, destitute
even of the shadow of constitutional power to enforce the execution of its own

---

Lines 8–30 The form is plural: "The United States as now composed, have no
power. . . . " This lack of precision as to the official designation of the Confederation
accurately reflected the country's lack of unity and self-definition.

   Consolidation, with its threat of centralized powers of enforcement, was the principal theme of Anti-Federalist opposition, appearing in numerous pamphlets; this
passage opens the reply to these charges.

laws. It will appear from the specimens which have been cited, that the American confederacy in this particular, stands discriminated from every other institution of a similar kind, and exhibits a new and unexampled phenomenon in the political world.

The want of a mutual guarantee of the state governments is another capital imperfection in the federal plan. There is nothing of this kind declared in the articles that compose it; and to imply a tacit guarantee from considerations of utility, would be a still more flagrant departure from the clause which has been mentioned, than to imply a tacit power of coertion, from the like considerations. The want of a guarantee, though it might in its consequences endanger the union, does not so immediately attack its existence as the want of a constitutional sanction to its laws.

Without a guarantee, the assistance to be derived from the union in repelling those domestic dangers, which may sometimes threaten the existence of the state constitutions, must be renounced. Usurpation may rear its crest in each state, and trample upon the liberties of the people; while the national government could legally do nothing more than behold its encroachments with indignation and regret. A successful faction may erect a tyranny on the ruins of order and law, while no succour could constitutionally be afforded by the union to the friends and supporters of the government. The tempestuous situation, from which Massachusetts has scarcely emerged, evinces that dangers of this kind are not merely speculative. Who can determine what might have been the issue of her late convulsions, if the mal-contents had been headed by a Caesar or by a Cromwell? Who can predict what effect a despotism established in Massachusetts, would have upon the liberties of New-Hampshire or Rhode-Island; of Connecticut or New-York?

The inordinate pride of state importance has suggested to some minds an objection to the principle of a guarantee in the federal government; as involving an officious interference in the domestic concerns of the members. A scruple of this kind would deprive us of one of the principal advantages to be expected from union; and can only flow from a misapprehension of the nature of the provision itself. It could be no impediment to reforms of the state constitutions by a majority of the people in a legal and peaceable mode. This right would remain undiminished. The guarantee could only operate against changes to be effected by violence. Towards the prevention of calamities of this kind too many checks cannot be provided. The peace of society, and the stability of government, depend absolutely on the efficacy of the precautions adopted on this head. Where the

---

Line 46 The "tempestuous situation," of course, was Shays's rebellion. Publius again misrepresents the character and aims of the rebels when he invokes the threat of "despotism" (line 50) with reference to Julius Caesar or Oliver Cromwell, whose regime in England culminated in his assuming the title of Lord Protector, to which his son was designated to succeed. Notwithstanding this dictatorial tendency, many New England Puritans could feel some sense of identification with Cromwell's aims.

whole power of the government is in the hands of the people, there is the less
pretence for the use of violent remedies, in partial or occasional distempers of the
65 state. The natural cure for an ill administration, in a popular or representative
constitution, is a change of men. A guarantee by the national authority would be
as much directed against the usurpations of rulers, as against the ferments and
outrages of faction and sedition in the community.

The principle of regulating the contributions of the states to the common
70 treasury by QUOTAS is another fundamental error in the confederation. Its
repugnancy to an adequate supply of the national exigencies has been already
pointed out, and has sufficiently appeared from the trial which has been made of
it. I speak of it now solely with a view to equality among the states. Those who
have been accustomed to contemplate the circumstances, which produce and
75 constitute natural wealth, must be satisfied that there is no common standard, or
barometer, by which the degrees of it can be ascertained. Neither the value of
lands nor the numbers of the people, which have been successively proposed as
the rule of state contributions, has any pretension to being a just representative.
If we compare the wealth of the United Netherlands with that of Russia or Ger-
80 many or even of France; and if we at the same time compare the total value of
the lands, and the aggregate population of the contracted territory of that republic with the total value of the lands, and the aggregate population of the immense
regions of either of the those kingdoms, we shall at once discover that there is no
comparison between the proportion of either of these two objects and that of the
85 relative wealth of those nations. If the like parallel were to be run between several of the American states; it would furnish a like result. Let Virginia be contrasted with North-Carolina, Pennsylvania with Connecticut, or Maryland with
New-Jersey, and we shall be convinced that the respective abilities of those states,
in relation to revenue, bear little or no analogy to their comparative stock in
90 lands or to their comparative population. The position may be equally illustrated
by a similar process between the counties of the same state. No man acquainted
with the state of New-York will doubt, that the active wealth of Kings County
bears a much greater proportion to that of Montgomery, than it would appear to
do, if we should take either the total value of the lands or the total numbers of the
95 people as a criterion!

The wealth of nations depends upon an infinite variety of causes. Situation,
soil, climate, the nature of the productions, the nature of the government, the genius of the citizens—the degree of information they possess—the state of commerce, of arts, of industry—these circumstances and many more too complex,
100 minute, or adventitious, to admit of a particular specification, occasion differences hardly conceivable in the relative opulence and riches of different countries. The consequence clearly is, that there can be no common measure of
national wealth; and of course, no general or stationary rule, by which the ability
of a state to pay taxes can be determined. The attempt therefore to regulate the
105 contributions of the members of a confederacy, by any such rule, cannot fail to
be productive of glaring inequality and extreme oppression.

This inequality would of itself be sufficient in America to work the eventual destruction of the union, if any mode of inforcing a compliance with its requisitions could be devised. The suffering states would not long consent to remain associated upon a principle which distributed the public burthens with so unequal a hand; and which was calculated to impoverish and oppress the citizens of some states, while those of others would scarcely be conscious of the small proportion of the weight they were required to sustain. This however is an evil inseparable from the principle of quotas and requisitions.

There is no method of steering clear of this inconvenience but by authorising the national government to raise its own revenues in its own way. Imposts, excises and in general all duties upon articles of consumption may be compared to a fluid, which will in time find its level with the means of paying them. The amount to be contributed by each citizen will in a degree be at his own option, and can be regulated by an attention to his resources. The rich may be extravagant, the poor can be frugal. And private oppression may always be avoided by a judicious selection of objects proper for such impositions. If inequalities should arise in some states from duties on particular objects, these will in all probability be counterballanced by proportional inequalities in other states from the duties on other objects. In the course of time and things, an equilibrium, as far as it is attainable, in so complicated a subject, will be established every where. Or if inequalities should still exist they would neither be so great in their degree, so uniform in their operation, nor so odious in their appearance, as those which would necessarily spring from quotas upon any scale, that can possibly be devised.

It is a signal advantage of taxes on articles of consumption, that they contain in their own nature a security against excess. They prescribe their own limit; which cannot be exceeded without defeating the end proposed—that is an extension of the revenue. When applied to this object, the saying is as just as it is witty, that "in political arithmetic, two and two do not always make four." If duties are too high they lessen the consumption—the collection is eluded; and the product to the treasury is not so great as when they are confined within proper and moderate bounds. This forms a complete barrier against any material oppression of the citizens, by taxes of this class, and is itself a natural limitation of the power of imposing them.

Impositions of this kind usually fall under the denomination of indirect taxes, and must for a long time constitute the chief part of the revenue raised in this country. Those of the direct kind, which principally relate to lands and buildings, may admit of a rule of apportionment. Either the value of land, or the number of the people may serve as a standard. The state of agriculture, and the populousness of a country are considered as having a near relation with each other. And as a rule for the purpose intended, numbers in the view of simplicity and certainty, are entitled to a preference. In every country it is an Herculean task to obtain a valuation of the land; in a country imperfectly settled and progressive in improvement, the difficulties are increased almost to impracticability. The expence of an accurate valuation is in all situations a formidable objection. In a branch of taxation where no limits to the discretion of the government are to be found in the nature of the thing, the establishment of a fixed rule, not incompatible with the end, may be attended with fewer inconveniencies than to leave that discretion altogether at large.

PUBLIUS.

TWENTY-TWO

ALEXANDER HAMILTON
December 14, 1787
The Same Subject Continued and Concluded

To the People of the State of New York.

In addition to the defects already enumerated in the existing federal system, there are others of not less importance, which concur in rendering it altogether unfit for the administration of the affairs of the union.

The want of a power to regulate commerce is by all parties allowed to be of the number. The utility of such a power has been anticipated under the first head of our inquiries; and for this reason as well as from the universal conviction entertained upon the subject, little need be added in this place. It is indeed evident, on the most superficial view, that there is no object, either as it respects the interests of trade or finance that more strongly demands a federal superintendence. The want of it has already operated as a bar to the formation of beneficial treaties with foreign powers; and has given occasions of dissatisfaction between the states. No nation acquainted with the nature of our political association would be unwise enough to enter into stipulations with the United States, conceding on their part privileges of importance, while they were apprised that the engagements on the part of the union, might at any moment be violated by its members; and while they found from experience that they might enjoy every advantage they desired in our markets, without granting us any return, but such as their momentary convenience might suggest. It is not therefore to be wondered at, that Mr. Jenkinson in ushering into the house of commons a bill for regulating the temporary intercourse between the two countries, should preface its

---

Lines 18–24 Hamilton presumably refers to an "Act for the further Increase and Encouragement of Shipping and Navigation," introduced by Charles Jenkinson in the Commons in 1786. Jenkinson (1727–1808), a prominent political figure, credited with great influence in the 1770s and 1780s, was soon to be Lord Hawkesbury and then first Earl of Liverpool. There is an important point to note here: Hamilton had this information because he could read the *Parliamentary History*, a running record of debates in Parliament later taken over by T. C. Hansard (under whose name the parliamentary debates are still published). No American assembly debates were ever published until 1785, when the recently arrived Irish immigrant Mathew Carey opened the pages of his newspaper, *The Pennsylvania Evening Herald*, to the debates in the Pennsylvania assembly. (He took the notes himself, gaining permission to occupy an advantageous seat.) The Constitutional Convention had met behind

introduction by a declaration that similar provisions in former bills had been found to answer every purpose to the commerce of Great Britain, and that it would be prudent to persist in the plan until it should appear whether the American government was likely or not to acquire greater consistency.[*]

25 Several states have endeavoured by separate prohibitions, restrictions and exclusions, to influence the conduct of that kingdom in this particular; but the want of concert, arising from the want of a general authority, and from clashing, and dissimilar views in the states, has hitherto frustrated every experiment of the kind; and will continue to do so as long as the same obstacles to an uniformity of

30 measures continue to exist.

The interfering and unneighbourly regulations of some states contrary to the true spirit of the union, have in different instances given just cause of umbrage and complaint to others; and it is to be feared that examples of this nature, if not restrained by a national controul, would be multiplied and extended till they be-

35 came not less serious sources of animosity and discord, than injurious impediments to the intercourse between the different parts of the confederacy. "The commerce of the German empire[†] is in continual trammels from the multiplic-

---

[*] This, as nearly as I can recollect, was the sense of this speech in introducing the last bill.

[†] *Encyclopedia*, article *Empire*.

---

closed doors, under a strict self-imposed prohibition against divulging the proceedings. Until press freedom to report parliamentary debates was effectively gained in Britain in 1771 (officially only in 1803, when the speaker set aside space for the press in the gallery), any reporting of what passed in either house of Parliament without the speaker's permission (or the Lord Chancellor's, for the Lords) was a breach of privilege. This privacy had originally been a protection against intrusion by the crown; later, it served to insulate Parliament from the people. American colonial assemblies, imitating the House of Commons, adopted the same principle. Colonial assemblies only authorized a designated printer to publish their journals—a record of formal proceedings, resolutions, and acts, which did not include debates—at the end of each session. State constitutions of the revolutionary era generally required assemblies to open their doors to the public and to publish their journals—but this still did not mean publishing debates or roll calls.

The British order-in-council of 1783 closing the British West Indies to American commerce had badly hit the New England carrying trade; the policy of trying to pressure the British into reversing this policy by countervailing restrictions was adopted, without effect, by Massachusetts in 1786. There was much talk of similar policies in other New England states. The obvious conclusion was that Americans needed a strong, unified commercial authority, which only the Constitution would provide.

Lines 31–41 Several states had erected their own customs barriers against each other, which, as sovereign states, the Articles permitted them to do. The quotation on the German empire is from the article on "Empire" from Diderot and d'Alembert's Encyclopédie.

ity of the duties which the several princes and states exact upon the merchandizes passing through their territories; by means of which the fine streams and navigable rivers with which Germany is so happily watered, are rendered almost useless." Though the genius of the people of this country might never permit this description to be strictly applicable to us, yet we may reasonably expect, from the gradual conflicts of state regulations, that the citizens of each, would at length come to be considered and treated by the others in no better light than that of foreigners and aliens.

The power of raising armies, by the most obvious construction of the articles of the confederation, is merely a power of making requisitions upon the states for quotas of men. This practice, in the course of the late war, was found replete with obstructions to a vigorous and to an economical system of defence. It gave birth to a competition between the states, which created a kind of auction for men. In order to furnish the quotas required of them, they outbid each other, till bounties grew to an enormous and insupportable size. The hope of a still further increase afforded an inducement to those who were disposed to serve to procrastinate their inlistment; and disinclined them to engaging for any considerable periods. Hence slow and scanty levies of men in the most critical emergencies of our affairs—short inlistments at an unparalleled expence—continual fluctuations in the troops, ruinous to their discipline, and subjecting the public safety frequently to the perilous crisis of a disbanded army. Hence also those oppressive expedients for raising men which were upon several occasions practised, and which nothing but the enthusiasm of liberty would have induced the people to endure.

This method of raising troops is not more unfriendly to economy and vigor, than it is to an equal distribution of the burthen. The states near the seat of war, influenced by motives of self preservation, made efforts to furnish their quotas, which even exceeded their abilities, while those at a distance from danger were for the most part as remiss as the others were diligent in their exertions. The immediate pressure of this inequality was not in this case, as in that of the contributions of money, alleviated by the hope of a final liquidation. The states which did not pay their proportions of money, might at least be charged with their deficiencies; but no account could be formed of the deficiencies in the supplies of men. We shall not, however, see much reason to regret the want of this hope, when we consider how little prospect there is, that the most delinquent states will ever be able to make compensation for their pecuniary failures. The system of quotas and requisitions, whether it be applied to men or money, is in every view a system of imbecility in the union, and of inequality and injustice among the members.

Line 58 The "oppressive expedients" in the form of draft measures resorted to in Virginia had provoked resistance ranging from absenteeism to armed revolts. Too many of the people did not in fact willingly "endure" (line 60) these impositions. This side of the history of the War of Independence has not received much attention.

75   The right of equal suffrage among the states is another exceptionable part of the confederation. Every idea of proportion, and every rule of fair representation conspire to condemn a principle, which gives to Rhode-Island an equal weight in the scale of power with Massachusetts, or Connecticut, or New-York; and to Delaware, an equal voice in the national deliberations with Pennsylvania or Vir-
80   ginia, or North-Carolina. Its operation contradicts that fundamental maxim of republican government, which requires that the sense of the majority should prevail. Sophistry may reply, that sovereigns are equal, and that a majority of the votes of the states will be a majority of confederated America. But this kind of logical legerdemain will never counteract the plain suggestions of justice and
85   common sense. It may happen that this majority of states is a small minority of the people of America,⊗ and two thirds of the people of America, could not long be persuaded, upon the credit of artificial distinctions and syllogistic subtleties, to submit their interests to the management and disposal of one third. The larger states would after a while revolt from the idea of receiving the law from the
90   smaller. To acquiesce in such a privation of their due importance in the political scale, would be not merely to be insensible to the love of power, but even to sacrifice the desire of equality. It is neither rational to expect the first, nor just to require the last—the smaller states considering how peculiarly their safety and welfare depend on union, ought readily to renounce a pretension; which, if not
95   relinquished would prove fatal to its duration.

⊗New-Hampshire, Rhode-Island, New-Jersey, Delaware, Georgia, South-Carolina and Maryland, are a majority of the whole number of the states, but they do not contain one third of the people.

Lines 80–82 This "fundamental maxim of republican government" can be traced to John Locke's *Second Treatise*, chapter 8, section 95. It is not, however, the only principle (as Publius has already insisted in No. 10, lines 111–17) that envisages the possibility that a majority might constitute a "faction." Other forms of republic, moreover, as imagined in James Harrington's *Oceana* (1656), or as actually existed in Venice, the Swiss cantons or the United Provinces, protected powerful vested interests without submitting to majority rule. The point is of some importance for political science, because Publius is constructing an Anglo-American style of republican principles, and applying it to the government of the continent. The Constitution still provided for a republic of individual states, and though it is not part of his strategy to emphasise the point, the large states that were already preponderant in numbers and wealth would have most to gain and least to lose if the continent adopted the majority principle. France—influenced by Rousseau more than the Americans had been—would adopt, but would also modify, the majority principle in the early years of the Revolution.

The essential majority principle underlying the American Constitution was reaffirmed by the Supreme Court in *Baker v. Carr* 369 U.S. 186 (1962) and subsequent reapportionment cases.

It may be objected to this, that not seven but nine states, or two thirds of the whole number must consent to the most important resolutions; and it may be thence inferred, that nine states would always comprehend a majority of the inhabitants of the union. But this does not obviate the impropriety of an equal vote between states of the most unequal dimensions and populousness; nor is the inference accurate in point of fact; for we can enumerate nine states which contain less than a majority of the people,* and it is constitutionally possible, that these nine may give the vote. Besides there are matters of considerable moment determinable by a bare majority; and there are others, concerning which doubts have been entertained, which if interpreted in favor of the sufficiency of a vote of seven states, would extend its operation to interests of the first magnitude. In addition to this, it is to be observed, that there is a probability of an increase in the number of states, and no provision for a proportional augmentation of the ratio of votes.

But this is not all; what at first sight may seem a remedy, is in reality a poison. To give a minority a negative upon the majority (which is always the case where more than a majority is requisite to a decision) is in its tendency to subject the sense of the greater number to that of the lesser number. Congress from the non-attendance of a few states have been frequently in the situation of a Polish diet, where a single veto has been sufficient to put a stop to all their movements. A sixtieth part of the union, which is about the proportion of Delaware and Rhode-Island, has several times been able to oppose an intire bar to its operations. This is one of those refinements which in practice has an effect, the reverse of what is expected from it in theory. The necessity of unanimity in public bodies, or of something approaching towards it, has been founded upon a supposition that it would contribute to security. But its real operation is to embarrass the administration, to destroy the energy of government, and to substitute the pleasure, caprice or artifices of an insignificant, turbulent or corrupt junto, to the regular deliberations and decisions of a respectable majority. In those emergencies of a nation, in which the goodness or badness, the weakness or strength of its government, is of the greatest importance, there is commonly a necessity for action. The public business must in some way or other go forward. If a pertinacious minority can controul the opinion of a majority respecting the best mode of conducting it; the majority in order that something may be done, must conform to the views of the minority; and thus the sense of the smaller number will over-rule

*Add New-York and Connecticut, to the foregoing seven, and they will still be less than a majority.

Lines 114–16 The specific reference here is to Rhode Island's blocking of the Impost Plan in 1782. Under this plan, Congress would have been empowered to raise a 5 percent impost to relieve its debt burden. The setback helped to convince nascent nationalists of the necessity for a stronger central government.

130 that of the greater, and give a tone to the national proceedings. Hence tedious delays—continual negotiation and intrigue—contemptible compromises of the public good. And yet in such a system, it is even happy when such compromises can take place: For upon some occasions, things will not admit of accommodation; and then the measures of government must be injuriously suspended or fa-

135 tally defeated. It is often, by the impracticability of obtaining the concurrence of the necessary number of votes, kept in a state of inaction. Its situation must always savour of weakness—sometimes border upon anarchy.

It is not difficult to discover that a principle of this kind gives greater scope to foreign corruption as well as to domestic faction, than that which permits the

140 sense of the majority to decide; though the contrary of this has been presumed. The mistake has proceeded from not attending with due care to the mischiefs that may be occasioned by obstructing the progress of government at certain critical seasons. When the concurrence of a large number is required by the constitution to the doing of any national act, we are apt to rest satisfied that all is safe, because

145 nothing improper will be likely *to be done*; but we forget how much good may be prevented, and how much ill may be produced, by the power of hindering that which is necessary from being done, and of keeping affairs in the same unfavorable posture in which they may happen to stand at particular periods.

Suppose for instance we were engaged in a war, in conjunction with one for-

150 eign nation against another. Suppose the necessity of our situation demanded peace, and the interest or ambition of our ally led him to seek the prosecution of the war, with views that might justify us in making separate terms. In such a state of things, this ally of ours would evidently find it much easier by his bribes and intrigues to tie up the hands of government from making peace, where two thirds

155 of all the votes were requisite to that object, than where a simple majority would suffice. In the first case he would have to corrupt a smaller number; in the last a greater number. Upon the same principle it would be much easier for a foreign power with which we were at war, to perplex our councils and embarrass our exertions. And in a commercial view we may be subjected to similar inconven-

160 iences. A nation, with which we might have a treaty of commerce, could with much greater facility prevent our forming a connection with her competitor in trade; though such a connection should be ever so beneficial to ourselves.

Evils of this description ought not to be regarded as imaginary. One of the weak sides of republics, among their numerous advantages, is that they afford too

165 easy an inlet to foreign corruption. An hereditary monarch, though often disposed to sacrifice his subjects to his ambition, has so great a personal interest in the government, and in the external glory of the nation, that it is not easy for a foreign power to give him an equivalent for what he would sacrifice by treachery to the state. The world has accordingly been witness to few examples of this

170 species of royal prostitution, though there have been abundant specimens of every other kind.

In republics, persons elevated from the mass of the community, by the suffrages of their fellow-citizens, to stations of great pre-eminence and power, may find compensations for betraying their trust, which to any but minds actuated by superior virtue, may appear to exceed the proportion of interest they have in the common stock, and to over-balance the obligations of duty. Hence it is that history furnishes us with so many mortifying examples of the prevalency of foreign corruption in republican governments. How much this contributed to the ruin of the ancient commonwealths has been already disclosed. It is well known that the deputies of the United Provinces have, in various instances been purchased by the emissaries of the neighbouring kingdoms. The Earl of Chesterfield (if my memory serves me right) in a letter to his court, intimates that his success in an important negotiation, must depend on his obtaining a Major's commission for one of those deputies. And in Sweden, the parties were alternately bought by France and England, in so barefaced and notorious a manner that it excited universal disgust in the nation; and was a principal cause that the most limited monarch in Europe, in a single day, without tumult, violence, or opposition, became one of the most absolute and uncontrouled.

A circumstance, which crowns the defects of the confederation, remains yet to be mentioned—the want of a judiciary power. Laws are a dead letter without courts to expound and define their true meaning and operation. The treaties of the United States to have any force at all, must be considered as part of the law of the land. Their true import as far as respects individuals, must, like all other laws, be ascertained by judicial determinations. To produce uniformity in these determinations, they ought to be submitted in the last resort, to one SUPREME TRIBUNAL. And this tribunal ought to be instituted under the same authority which forms the treaties themselves. These ingredients are both indispensable. If there is in each state, a court of final jurisdiction, there may be as many different final determinations on the same point, as there are courts. There are endless diversities in the opinions of men. We often see not only different courts, but the judges of the same court differing from each other. To avoid the confusion which would unavoidably result from the contradictory decisions of a number of independent judicatories, all nations have found it necessary to establish one court paramount to the rest—possessing a general superintendance, and authorised to settle and declare in the last resort an uniform rule of civil justice.

Line 181 Philip Dormer Stanhope, Earl of Chesterfield (1694–1773), English statesman, diplomatist, and man of letters, famous for his *Letters to His Son*. Ambassador to The Hague, 1728–1732.

Lines 184–88 Hamilton's reference to Sweden is unclear; he seems to be offering a simple explanation for a complex period of party warfare in the 1750s and 1760s, which was followed by the absolutist government of Gustav III, who acceded in 1771 and was still on the throne. But it was Russia rather than England or France that bought political influence in one of the parties—the Nightcaps or "Caps." Sweden had a turbulent history, not clarified by Hamilton's extreme language, and he may have had an earlier period in mind.

This is the more necessary where the frame of the government is so compounded, that the laws of the whole are in danger of being contravened by the
laws of the parts. In this case if the particular tribunals are invested with a right of
ultimate jurisdiction, besides the contradictions to be expected from difference
of opinion, there will be much to fear from the bias of local views and prejudices,
and from the interference of local regulations. As often as such an interference
was to happen, there would be reason to apprehend, that the provisions of the
particular laws might be preferred to those of the general laws; from the deference with which men in office naturally look up to that authority to which they
owe their official existence.

The treaties of the United States, under the present constitution, are liable to
the infractions of thirteen different legislatures, and as many different courts of
final jurisdiction, acting under the authority of those legislatures. The faith, the
reputation, the peace of the whole union, are thus continually at the mercy of
the prejudices, the passions, and the interests of every member of which it is
composed. Is it possible that foreign nations can either respect or confide in such
a government? Is it possible that the people of America will longer consent to
trust their honor, their happiness, their safety, on so precarious a foundation?

In this review of the confederation, I have confined myself to the exhibition of
its most material defects; passing over those imperfections in its details, by which
even a considerable part of the power intended to be conferred upon it has been
in a great measure rendered abortive. It must be by this time evident to all
men of reflection, who are either free from erroneous prepossessions, or can
divest themselves of them, that it is a system so radically vicious and unsound, as
to admit not of amendment but by an entire change in its leading features and
characters.

The organization of congress, is itself utterly improper for the exercise of those
powers which are necessary to be deposited in the union. A single assembly may
be a proper receptacle of those slender, or rather fettered authorities, which have
been heretofore delegated to the federal head; but it would be inconsistent with
all the principles of good government, to intrust it with those additional powers
which even the moderate and more rational adversaries of the proposed constitution admit ought to reside in the United States. If that plan should not be
adopted; and if the necessity of union should be able to withstand the ambitious
aims of those men, who may indulge magnificent schemes of personal aggrandizement from its dissolution; the probability would be, that we should run into
the project of conferring supplementary powers upon congress as they are now

---

Lines 227–31 A further reference to state sovereignty. There is a hinted implication
that a government may possess some but not all of its prerogatives—but is ineffective
if they are not the most important ones.

constituted; and either the machine, from the intrinsic feebleness of its structure, will moulder into pieces in spite of our ill-judged efforts to prop it; or by successive augmentations of its force and energy, as necessity might prompt, we shall finally accumulate in a single body, all the most important prerogatives of sovereignty; and thus entail upon our posterity, one of the most execrable forms of government that human infatuation ever contrived. Thus we should create in reality that very tyranny, which the adversaries of the new constitution either are, or affect to be solicitous to avert. 245

250

It has not a little contributed to the infirmities of the existing federal system, that it never had a ratification by the PEOPLE. Resting on no better foundation than the consent of the several legislatures; it has been exposed to frequent and intricate questions concerning the validity of its powers; and has in some instances given birth to the enormous doctrine of a right of legislative repeal. 255 Owing its ratification to the law of a state, it has been contended, that the same authority might repeal the law by which it was ratified. However gross a heresy it may be, to maintain that *a party* to *a compact* has a right to revoke that *compact,* the doctrine itself has had respectable advocates. The possibility of a question of this nature, proves the necessity of laying the foundations of our national govern- 260 ment deeper than in the mere sanction of delegated authority. The fabric of American Empire ought to rest on the solid basis of THE CONSENT OF THE PEOPLE. The streams of national power ought to flow immediately from that pure original fountain of all legitimate authority.

PUBLIUS.

Lines 251–64 It is difficult to locate the contention that individual states might repeal their assent to the Articles. As sovereign states, they could argue that they were free to do so—though that would have made nonsense of the designation, "Articles of Confederation and Perpetual Union. . . . "

Note the grand strategy emerging in the conclusion. *The Federalist* here preempts the populist and democratic thesis that all government ought to rest on "the consent of the people" (lines 262–63)—"that pure original fountain of all legitimate authority" (lines 263–64). This was hardly the sort of expression to be expected of such stringent critics of the behavior of popular legislatures! However, it dextrously takes the popular ground away from the Anti-Federalists. Moreover, *the people* can only be the people of the Union considered as a whole, which leaves the states only as guardians of particular, local interests.

TWENTY-THREE

ALEXANDER HAMILTON
December 18, 1787
The Necessity of a Government, at Least Equally
Energetic with the One Proposed

To the People of the State of New York.

The necessity of a constitution, at least equally energetic with the one proposed, to the preservation of the union, is the point, at the examination of which we are now arrived.

5   This enquiry will naturally divide itself into three branches—the objects to be provided for by a federal government—the quantity of power necessary to the accomplishment of those objects—the persons upon whom that power ought to operate. Its distribution and organization will more properly claim our attention under the succeeding head.

    The principal purposes to be answered by union are these—The common de-
10 fence of the members—the preservation of the public peace as well against internal convulsions as external attacks—the regulation of commerce with other nations and between the states—the superintendence of our intercourse, political and commercial, with foreign countries.

    The authorities essential to the care of the common defence are these—to
15 raise armies—to build and equip fleets—to prescribe rules for the government of both—to direct their operations—to provide for their support. These powers ought to exist without limitation: *Because it is impossible to foresee or to define the extent and variety of national exigencies, and the correspondent extent and variety of the means which may be necessary to satisfy them.* The circumstances that
20 endanger the safety of nations are infinite; and for this reason no constitutional shackles can wisely be imposed on the power to which the care of it is committed. This power ought to be co-extensive with all the possible combinations of such circumstances; and ought to be under the direction of the same councils, which are appointed to preside over the common defence.

25   This is one of those truths, which to a correct and unprejudiced mind, carries its own evidence along with it; and may be obscured, but cannot be made plainer by argument or reasoning. It rests upon axioms as simple as they are uni-

---

Lines 9–13 How far the "principal purposes to be answered by union" have changed since *The Federalist* was written, can be seen from the silence of this paragraph on the entire field covered in the 20th century by fiscal policy, the FBI, health, education, welfare, national transport, and civil rights.

versal. The *means* ought to be proportioned to the *end*; the persons, from whose agency the attainment of any *end* is expected, ought to possess the *means* by which it is to be attained.

Whether there ought to be a federal government intrusted with the care of the common defence, is a question in the first instance open to discussion; but the moment it is decided in the affirmative, it will follow, that that government ought to be cloathed with all the powers requisite to the complete execution of its trust. And unless it can be shewn, that the circumstances which may affect the public safety are reducible within certain determinate limits; unless the contrary of this position can be fairly and rationally disputed, it must be admitted, as a necessary consequence, that there can be no limitation of that authority, which is to provide for the defence and protection of the community, in any matter essential to its efficacy; that is, in any matter essential to the *formation, direction* or *support* of the NATIONAL FORCES.

Defective as the present confederation has been proved to be, this principle appears to have been fully recognized by the framers of it; though they have not made proper or adequate provision for its exercise. Congress have an unlimited discretion to make requisitions of men and money—to govern the army and navy—to direct their operations. As their requisitions are made constitutionally binding upon the states, who are in fact under the most solemn obligations to furnish the supplies required of them, the intention evidently was, that the United States should command whatever resources were by them judged requisite to the "common defence and general welfare." It was presumed that a sense of their true interests, and a regard to the dictates of good faith, would be found sufficient pledges for the punctual performance of the duty of the members to the federal head.

The experiment has, however demonstrated, that this expectation was ill founded and illusory; and the observations made under the last head, will, I imagine, have sufficed to convince the impartial and discerning, that there is an absolute necessity for an entire change in the first principles of the system: That if we are in earnest about giving the union energy and duration, we must abandon the vain project of legislating upon the states in their collective capacities: We must extend the laws of the federal government to the individual citizens of America: We must discard the fallacious scheme of quotas and requisitions, as equally impracticable and unjust. The result from all this is, that the union ought to be invested with full power to levy troops; to build and equip fleets, and to raise the revenues, which will be required for the formation and support of an army and navy, in the customary and ordinary modes practiced in other governments.

If the circumstances of our country are such, as to demand a compound instead of a simple, a confederate instead of a sole government, the essential point which will remain to be adjusted, will be to discriminate the OBJECTS, as far as it can be done, which shall appertain to the different provinces or departments of power; allowing to each the most ample authority for fulfilling the objects committed to its charge. Shall the union be constituted the guardian of the common safety? Are fleets and armies and revenues necessary to this purpose? The government of the union must be empowered to pass all laws, and to make all regulations which have relation to them. The same must be the case, in respect to commerce, and to every other matter to which its jurisdiction is permitted to extend. Is the administration of justice between the citizens of the same state, the proper department of the local governments? These must possess all the authorities which are connected with this object, and with every other that may be allotted to their particular cognizance and direction. Not to confer in each case a degree of power, commensurate to the end, would be to violate the most obvious rules of prudence and propriety, and improvidently to trust the great interests of the nation to hands, which are disabled from managing them with vigour and success.

Who so likely to make suitable provisions for the public defence, as that body to which the guardianship of the public safety is confided—which, as the center of information, will best understand the extent and urgency of the dangers that threaten—as the representative of the WHOLE will feel itself most deeply interested in the preservation of every part—which, from the responsibility implied in the duty assigned to it, will be most sensibly impressed with the necessity of proper exertions—and which, by the extension of its authority throughout the states, can alone establish uniformity and concert in the plans and measures, by which the common safety is to be secured? Is there not a manifest inconsistency in devolving upon the federal government the care of the general defence, and leaving in the state governments the *effective* powers, by which it is to be provided for? Is not a want of co-operation the infallible consequence of such a system? And will not weakness, disorder, an undue distribution of the burthens and calamities of war, an unnecessary and intolerable increase of expence, be its natural and inevitable concomitants? Have we not had unequivocal experience of its effects in the course of the revolution, which we have just achieved?

Every view we may take of the subject, as candid enquirers after truth, will serve to convince us, that it is both unwise and dangerous to deny the federal government an unconfined authority in respect to all those objects which are intrusted to its management. It will indeed deserve the most vigilant and careful attention of the people, to see that it be modelled in such a manner, as to admit of its being safely vested with the requisite powers. If any plan which has been, or may be offered to our consideration, should not, upon a dispassionate inspection, be found to answer this description, it ought to be rejected. A government, the constitution of which renders it unfit to be trusted with all the powers, which a free people *ought to delegate to any government*, would be an unsafe and improper depository of the NATIONAL INTERESTS, wherever THESE can with propriety be confided, the co-incident powers may safely accompany them. This is the true result of all just reasoning upon the subject. And the adversaries of the plan, promulgated by the convention would have given a better impression of their candor if they had confined themselves to showing that the internal structure of the proposed government, was such as to render it unworthy of the confidence of the people. They ought not to have wandered into inflammatory

126

declamations, and unmeaning cavils about the extent of the powers. The POW-ERS are not too extensive for the OBJECTS of federal administration, or in other words, for the management of our NATIONAL INTERESTS; nor can any satisfactory argument be framed to shew that they are chargeable with such an excess. If it be true, as has been insinuated by some of the writers on the other side, that the difficulty arises from the nature of the thing, and that the extent of the country will not permit us to form a government, in which such ample powers can safely be reposed, it would prove that we ought to contract our views, and resort to the expedient of separate confederacies, which will move within more practicable spheres. For the absurdity must continually stare us in the face of confiding to a government, the direction of the most essential national inter-ests, without daring to trust it with the authorities which are indispensable to their proper and efficient management. Let us not attempt to reconcile contra-dictions, but firmly embrace a rational alternative.

I trust, however, that the impracticability of one general system cannot be shewn. I am greatly mistaken, if any thing of weight, has yet been advanced of this tendency; and I flatter myself, that the observations which have been made in the course of these papers, have served to place the reverse of that position in as clear a light as any matter still in the womb of time and experience can be sus-ceptible of. This at all events must be evident, that the very difficulty itself drawn from the extent of the country, is the strongest argument in favor of an energetic government; for any other can certainly never preserve the union of so large an empire. If we embrace the tenets of those, who oppose the adoption of the pro-posed constitution, as the standard of our political creed, we cannot fail to verify the gloomy doctrines, which predict the impracticability of a national system, pervading the entire limits of the present confederacy.

PUBLIUS.

Lines 120–21 An allusive reference once again to Montesquieu.

Line 134 The expression "the womb of time" is from Shakespeare, *Othello*, 1.3.377.

TWENTY-FOUR

ALEXANDER HAMILTON
December 19, 1787
**The Subject Continued, with an Answer to an
Objection Concerning Standing Armies**

To the People of the State of New York.

To the powers proposed to be conferred upon the federal government in respect
to the creation and direction of the national forces,—I have met with but one
specific objection; which if I understand it rightly is this—that proper provision
has not been made against the existence of standing armies in time of peace; an
objection which I shall now endeavour to shew rests on weak and unsubstantial
foundations.

It has indeed been brought forward in the most vague and general form, supported only by bold assertions—without the appearance of argument—without
even the sanction of theoretical opinions, in contradiction to the practice of
other free nations, and to the general sense of America, as expressed in most of
the existing constitutions. The propriety of this remark will appear the moment it
is recollected that the objection under consideration turns upon a supposed necessity of restraining the LEGISLATIVE authority of the nation, in the article of
military establishments; a principle unheard of except in one or two of our state
constitutions, and rejected in all the rest.

A stranger to our politics, who was to read our newspapers, at the present juncture, without having previously inspected the plan reported by the convention,
would be naturally led to one of two conclusions: either that it contained a positive injunction and standing armies should be kept up in time of peace, or that it
vested in the EXECUTIVE the whole power of levying troops, without subjecting his discretion in any shape to the controul of the legislature.

If he came afterwards to peruse the plan itself, he would be surprised to discover that neither the one nor the other was the case—that the whole power of
raising armies was lodged in the *legislature*, not in the *executive*; that this legislature was to be a popular body, consisting of the representatives of the people,
periodically elected; and that, instead of the provision he had supposed in favour
of standing armies, there was to be found, in respect to this object, an important
qualification even of the legislative discretion, in that clause which forbids the

---

Lines 11–15 The two states are Pennsylvania and North Carolina; for the provisions
of their constitutions, see Francis Newton Thorpe, *American Charters, Constitutions
and Organic Laws, 1402–1908* (Washington, D.C., 1909), V, 2789 and VI, 3083.

appropriation of money for the support of an army for any longer period than two
years: a precaution, which, upon a nearer view of it, will appear to be a great and
real security against military establishments without evident necessity. 30

Disappointed in his first surmise, the person I have supposed would be apt to
pursue his conjectures a little further. He would naturally say to himself, it is impossible that all this vehement and pathetic declamation can be without some
colorable pretext. It must needs be, that this people so jealous of their liberties, 35
have in all the preceding models of the constitutions, which they have established, inserted the most precise and rigid precautions on this point, the omission
of which in the new plan has given birth to all this apprehension and clamour.

If under this impression he proceeded to pass in review the several state constitutions, how great would be his disappointment to find that *two* only of them 40
contained an interdiction of standing armies in time of peace; that the other
eleven had either observed a profound silence on the subject, or had in express
terms admitted the right of the legislature to authorise their existence.

Still however he would be persuaded that there must be some plausible foundation for the cry raised on this head. He would never be able to imagine, while 45
any source of information remained unexplored, that it was nothing more than
an experiment upon the public credulity, dictated either by a deliberate intention to deceive or by the overflowings of a zeal too intemperate to be ingenuous.
It would probably occur to him that he would be likely to find the precautions he
was in search of in the primitive compact between the states. Here, at length, he 50
would expect to meet with a solution of the enigma. No doubt he would observe
to himself the existing confederation must contain the most explicit provisions
against military establishments in time of peace; and a departure from this model
in a favourite point has occasioned the discontent which appears to influence
these political champions. 55

If he should now apply himself to a careful and critical survey of the articles of
confederation, his astonishment would not only be increased but would acquire
a mixture of indignation at the unexpected discovery that these articles instead of

---

*This statement of the matter is taken from the printed collections of state consti-
tutions—Pennsylvania and North-Carolina are the two which contain the interdiction in these words—"as standing armies in time of peace are dangerous to liberty,
THEY OUGHT NOT to be kept up." This is, in truth, rather a CAUTION than a
PROHIBITION. New-Hampshire, Massachusetts, Delaware, and Maryland, have
in each of their bills of rights a clause to this effect—"standing armies are dangerous to liberty, and ought not to be raised or kept up *without the consent of the legislature*"; which is a formal admission of the authority of the legislature. NEW-YORK
has no bill of her rights and her constitution says not a word about the matter. NO
bills of rights appear annexed to the constitutions of the other states, except the
foregoing, and their constitutions are equally silent. I am told, however, that one or
two states have bills of rights which do not appear in this collection, but that those
also recognize the right of the legislative authority in this respect.

containing the prohibition he looked for, and though they had with a jealous cir-
60 cumspection restricted the authority of the state Legislatures in this particular,
had not imposed a single restraint on that of the United States. If he happened to
be a man of quick sensibility or ardent temper, he could now no longer refrain
from pronouncing these clamors to be the dishonest artifices of a sinister and un-
principled opposition to a plan which ought at least to receive a fair and candid
65 examination from all sincere lovers of their country! How else, he would say,
could the authors of them have been tempted to vent such loud censures upon
that plan, about a point, in which it seems to have conformed itself to the general
sense of America as declared in its different forms of government, and in which
it has even superadded a new and powerful guard unknown to any of them? If on
70 the contrary he happened to be a man of calm and dispassionate feelings—he
would indulge a sigh for the frailty of human nature; and would lament that in a
matter so interesting to the happiness of millions the true merits of the question
should be perplexed and obscured by expedients so unfriendly to an impartial
and right determination. Even such a man could hardly forbear remarking that a
75 conduct of this kind has too much the appearance of an intention to mislead the
people by alarming their passions rather than to convince them by arguments addressed to their understandings.

But however little this objection may be countenanced even by precedents
among ourselves, it may be satisfactory to take a nearer view of its intrinsic
80 merits. From a close examination it will appear that restraints upon the discretion of the legislature in respect to military establishments would be improper
to be imposed, and if imposed, from the necessities of society would be unlikely
to be observed.

Though a wide ocean separates the United States from Europe; yet there are
85 various considerations that warn us against an excess of confidence or security.
On one side of us and stretching far into our rear are growing settlements subject
to the dominion of Britain. On the other side and extending to meet the British
settlements are colonies and establishments subject to the dominion of Spain.

Lines 84–102 The British possessions in Canada, to the north, are not usually
thought of as being in the "rear" (line 86) of the United States, but they extended to
the frontiers of New Spain, which comprised the vast Louisiana territory, west of the
Mississippi; a global map shows that the United States claimed much the smallest
section of North America, and from either an expansionist or a defensive point of
view, could be seen as boxed into a corner. Spain's closure of the Mississippi had recently revealed the limits of American power.

France and Spain were both under Bourbon monarchs, and in the early years of
the century, this "family compact" (line 98) had been a factor in Louis XIV's determination to force Europe back into war. The allies, principally Austria, the Netherlands,
and Britain, prolonged the war to destroy French power. The War of the Spanish Succession lasted until the Peace of Utrecht, 1713.

This situation and the vicinity of the West-India islands belonging to these two powers create between them, in respect to their American possessions, and in relation to us, a common interest. The savage tribes on our western frontier ought to be regarded as our natural enemies their natural allies; because they have most to fear from us and most to hope from them. The improvements in the art of navigation have, as to the facility of communication, rendered distant nations in a great measure neighbours. Britain and Spain are among the principal maritime powers of Europe. A future concert of views between these nations ought not to be regarded as improbable. The increasing remoteness of consanguinity is every day diminishing the force of the family compact between France and Spain. And politicians have ever with great reason considered the ties of blood as feeble and precarious links of political connection. These circumstances combined admonish us not to be too sanguine in considering ourselves as entirely out of the reach of danger.

Previous to the revolution, and ever since the peace, there has been a constant necessity for keeping small garrisons on our western frontier. No person can doubt that these will continue to be indispensible, if it should only be against the ravages and depredations of the Indians. These garrisons must either be furnished by occasional detachments from the militia, or by permanent corps in the pay of government. The first is impracticable; and if practicable, would be pernicious. The militia would not long, if at all, submit to be dragged from their occupations and families to perform that most disagreeable duty in times of profound peace. And if they could be prevailed upon, or compelled to do it, the increased expence of a frequent rotation of service and the loss of labor, and disconcertion of the industrious pursuits of individuals, would form conclusive objections to the scheme. It would be as burthensome and injurious to the public, as ruinous to private citizens. The latter resource of permanent corps in the pay of government amounts to a standing army in time of peace; a small one indeed, but not the less real for being small. Here is a simple view of the subject that shows us at once the impropriety of a constitutional interdiction of such establishments, and the necessity of leaving the matter to the discretion and prudence of the legislature.

In proportion to our increase in strength, it is probable, nay it may be said certain, that Britain and Spain would augment their military establishments in our neighbourhood. If we should not be willing to be exposed in a naked and defenceless condition to their insults or encroachments, we should find it expedient to increase our frontier garrisons in some ratio to the force by which our western settlements might be annoyed. There are and will be particular posts the possession of which will include the command of large districts of territory and facilitate future invasions of the remainder. It may be added that some of those posts will be keys to the trade with the Indian nations. Can any man think it would be wise to leave such posts in a situation to be at any instant seized by one or the other of two neighbouring and formidable powers? To act this part would be to desert all the usual maxims of prudence and policy.

If we mean to be a commercial people or even to be secure on our Atlantic side, we must endeavour as soon as possible to have a navy. To this purpose there must be dock-yards and arsenals, and, for the defence of these, fortifications and probably garrisons. When a nation has become so powerful by sea, that it can protect its dock-yards by its fleets, this supersedes the necessity of garrisons for that purpose; but where naval establishments are in their infancy, moderate garrisons will in all likelihood be found an indispensible security against descents for the destruction of the arsenals and dock-yards, and sometimes of the fleet itself.

PUBLIUS.

TWENTY-FIVE

ALEXANDER HAMILTON
December 21, 1787
The Subject Continued with the Same View

To the People of the State of New York.

It may perhaps be urged, that the objects enumerated in the preceding number ought to be provided for by the state governments, under the direction of the union. But this would be in reality an inversion of the primary principle of our political association; as it would in practice transfer the care of the common defence from the federal head to the individual members: A project oppressive to some states, dangerous to all, and baneful to the confederacy. 5

The territories of Britain, Spain and of the Indian nations in our neighbourhood, do not border on particular states; but incircle the union from MAINE to GEORGIA. The danger, though in different degrees, is therefore common. And the means of guarding against it ought in like manner to be the objects of common councils and of a common treasury. It happens that some states, from local situation, are more directly exposed. NEW-YORK is of this class. Upon the plan of separate provisions, New-York would have to sustain the whole weight of the establishments requisite to her immediate safety, and to the mediate or ultimate protection of her neighbours. This would neither be equitable as it respected New-York, nor safe as it respected the other states. Various inconveniences would attend such a system. The states, to whose lot it might fall to support the necessary establishments, would be as little able as willing, for a considerable time to come, to bear the burthen of competent provisions. The security of all would thus be subjected to the parsimony, improvidence or inability of a part. If the resources of such part becoming more abundant and extensive, its provisions should be proportionally enlarged, the other states would quickly take the alarm at seeing the whole military force of the union in the hands of two or three of its members; and those probably amongst the most powerful. They would each choose to have some counterpoise; and pretences could easily be contrived. In this situation, military establishments, nourished by mutual jealousy, would be apt to swell beyond their natural or proper size; and being at the separate disposal of the members, they would be engines for the abridgment, or demolition of the national authority. 10 15 20 25

Line 12 "NEW-YORK is of this class"—of states which are "more directly exposed." And, of course, these essays are primarily directed to New Yorkers.

30   Reasons have been already given to induce a supposition, that the state governments will too naturally be prone to a rivalship with that of the union, the
foundation of which will be the love of power; and that in any contest between
the federal head and one of its members, the people will be most apt to unite
with their local government: If in addition to this immense advantage, the ambi-
35   tion of the members should be stimulated by the separate and independent possession of military forces, it would afford too strong a temptation, and too great
facility to them to make enterprises upon, and finally to subvert the constitutional authority of the union. On the other hand, the liberty of the people would
be less safe in this state of things, than in that which left the national forces in the
40   hands of the national government. As far as an army may be considered as a dangerous weapon of power, it had better be in those hands, of which the people are
most likely to be jealous, than in those of which they are least likely to be jealous.
For it is a truth which the experience of all ages has attested, that the people are
commonly most in danger, when the means of injuring their rights are in the
45   possession of those of whom they entertain the least suspicion.

      The framers of the existing confederation, fully aware of the danger to the
union from the separate possession of military forces by the states, have in express
terms, prohibited them from having either ships or troops, unless with the consent of congress. The truth is, that the existence of a federal government and mil-
50   itary establishments, under state authority, are not less at variance with each
other, than a due supply of the federal treasury and the system of quotas and
requisitions.

      There are other lights besides those already taken notice of, in which the im-
propriety of restraints on the discretion of the national legislature will be equally
55   manifest. The design of the objection, which has been mentioned, is to preclude
standing armies in time of peace; though we have never been informed how far
it is desired the prohibition should extend; whether to raising armies as well as to
keeping them up in a season of tranquility or not. If it be confined to the latter, it
will have no precise signification, and it will be ineffectual for the purpose in-
60   tended. When armies are once raised, what shall be denominated "keeping them
up," contrary to the sense of the constitution? What time shall be requisite to ascertain the violation? Shall it be a week, a month, or a year? Or shall we say, they
may be continued as long as the danger which occasioned their being raised continues? This would be to admit that they might be kept up *in time of peace*
65   against threatening, or impending danger; which would be at once to deviate
from the literal meaning of the prohibition, and to introduce an extensive latitude of construction. Who shall judge of the continuance of the danger? This
must undoubtedly be submitted to the national government—and the matter
would then be brought to this issue, that the national government, to provide

---

Lines 46–49 Article VI of the Articles of Confederation.

against apprehended danger, might, in the first instance, raise troops, and might afterwards keep them on foot, as long as they supposed the peace or safety of the community was in any degree of jeopardy. It is easy to perceive, that a discretion so latitudinary as this, would afford ample room for eluding the force of the provision.

The supposed utility of a provision of this kind, must be founded upon a supposed probability, or at least possibility, of a combination between the executive and the legislative in some scheme of usurpation. Should this at any time happen, how easy would it be to fabricate pretences of approaching danger? Indian hostilities instigated by Spain or Britain, would always be at hand. Provocations to produce the desired appearances, might even be given to some foreign power, and appeased again by timely concessions. If we can reasonably presume such a combination to have been formed, and that the enterprize is warranted by a sufficient prospect of success; the army when once raised, from whatever cause, or on whatever pretext, may be applied to the execution of the project.

If to obviate this consequence, it should be resolved to extend the prohibition to the *raising* of armies in time of peace, the United States would then exhibit the most extraordinary spectacle, which the world has yet seen—that of a nation incapacitated by its constitution to prepare for defence, before it was actually invaded. As the ceremony of a formal denunciation of war has of late fallen into disuse, the presence of an enemy within our territories must be waited for as the legal warrant to the government to begin its levies of men for the protection of the state. We must receive the blow before we could even prepare to return it. All that kind of policy by which nations anticipate distant danger, and meet the gathering storm, must be abstained from, as contrary to the genuine maxims of a free government. We must expose our property and liberty to the mercy of foreign invaders, and invite them, by our weakness, to seize the naked and defenceless prey, because we are afraid that rulers, created by our choice—dependent on our will—might endanger that liberty, by an abuse of the means necessary to its preservation.

Here I expect we shall be told, that the Militia of the country is its natural bulwark, and would be at all times equal to the national defence. This doctrine in substance had like to have lost us our independence. It cost millions to the United States, that might have been saved. The facts, which from our own experience forbid a reliance of this kind, are too recent to permit us to be the dupes of such a suggestion. The steady operations of war against a regular and disciplined army, can only be successfully conducted by a force of the same kind. Considerations of economy, not less than of stability and vigor, confirm this position. The American Militia, in the course of the late war, have by their valour on numerous occasions, erected eternal monuments to their fame; but the bravest of them feel

---

Line 89 "Denunciation" was already old-fashioned; we now say "declaration"—as does the Constitution.

110 and know, that the liberty of their country could not have been established by
their efforts alone, however great and valuable they were. War, like most other
things, is a science to be acquired and perfected by diligence, by perseverance,
by time, and by practice.

All violent policy, contrary to the natural and experienced course of human
115 affairs, defeats itself. Pennsylvania at this instant affords an example of the truth
of this remark. The bill of rights of that state declares, that standing armies are
dangerous to liberty, and ought not to be kept up in time of peace. Pennsylvania,
nevertheless, in a time of profound peace, from the existence of partial disorders
in one or two of her counties, has resolved to raise a body of troops; and in all
120 probability, will keep them up as long as there is an appearance of danger to the
public peace. The conduct of Massachusetts affords a lesson on the same subject, though on different ground. That state (without waiting for the sanction of
congress as the articles of the confederation require) was compelled to raise
troops to quell a domestic insurrection, and still keeps a corps in pay to prevent a
125 revival of the spirit of revolt. The particular constitution of Massachusetts opposed no obstacle to the measure; but the instance is still of use to instruct us,
that cases are likely to occur under our governments, as well as under those of
other nations, which will sometimes render a military force in time of peace essential to the security of the society; and that it is therefore improper, in this re-
130 spect, to controul the legislative discretion. It also teaches us, in its application to
the United States, how little the rights of a feeble government are likely to be respected, even by its own constituents. And it teaches us, in addition to the rest,
how unequal parchment provisions are to a struggle with public necessity.

It was a fundamental maxim of the Lacedemonian commonwealth, that the
135 post of admiral should not be conferred twice on the same person. The Pelopponesian confederates, having suffered a severe defeat at sea from the Athenians,
demanded Lysander, who had before served with success in that capacity, to
command the combined fleets. The Lacedemonians, to gratify their allies, and
yet preserve the semblance of an adherence to their ancient institutions, had re-
140 course to the flimsy subterfuge of investing Lysander with the real power of admiral, under the nominal title of vice-admiral. This instance is selected from
among a multitude that might be cited to confirm the truth already advanced
and illustrated by domestic examples; which is, that nations pay little regard to
rules and maxims calculated in their very nature to run counter to the necessities

---

Lines 114–21 See Thorpe, *American Charters*, VI, 3083. This passage refers to
Pennsylvania's troubles with would-be settlers from Connecticut in the western
Wyoming Valley. See notes for No. 6, line 60, and No. 7, lines 419–60.

Lines 134–38 "Lacedaemonia," see No. 18, lines 28–29; "Lacedaemon" is another
name for Sparta. The "Peloponnesian confederates" are the alliance led by Sparta
against Athens in the Peloponnesian War.

of society. Wise politicians will be cautious about fettering the government with   *145*
restrictions, that cannot be observed; because they know that every breach of the
fundamental laws, though dictated by necessity, impairs that sacred reverence,
which ought to be maintained in the breast of rulers towards the constitution of
a country, and forms a precedent for other breaches, where the same plea of necessity does not exist at all, or is less urgent and palpable.   *150*

PUBLIUS.

TWENTY-SIX

ALEXANDER HAMILTON
December 22, 1787

The Subject Continued with the Same View

To the People of the State of New York.

It was a thing hardly to be expected, that in a popular revolution the minds of men should stop at that happy mean, which marks the salutary boundary between POWER and PRIVILEGE, and combines the energy of government with the security of private rights. A failure in this delicate and important point is the
5 great source of the inconveniences we experience; and if we are not cautious to avoid a repetition of the error, in our future attempts to rectify and ameliorate our system, we may travel from one chimerical project to another; we may try change after change; but we shall never be likely to make any material change for the better.

10   The idea of restraining the legislative authority, in the means of providing for the national defence, is one of those refinements, which owe their origin to a zeal for liberty more ardent than enlightened. We have seen however that it has not had thus far an extensive prevalency: That even in this country, where it has made its first appearance, Pennsylvania and North-Carolina are the only two
15 states by which it has been in any degree patronised: And that all the others have refused to give it the least countenance; wisely judging that confidence must be placed some where; that the necessity of doing it is implied in the very act of delegating power; and that it is better to hazard the abuse of that confidence, than to embarrass the government and endanger the public safety, by impolitic restric-
20 tions on the legislative authority. The opponents of the proposed constitution combat in this respect the general decision of America; and instead of being taught by experience the propriety of correcting any extremes, into which we may have heretofore run, they appear disposed to conduct us into others still more dangerous and more extravagant. As if the tone of government had been
25 found too high, or too rigid, the doctrines they teach are calculated to induce us to depress, or to relax it, by expedients which upon other occasions have been condemned or forborn. It may be affirmed without the imputation of invective, that if the principles they inculcate on various points could so far obtain as to become the popular creed, they would utterly unfit the people of this country for
30 any species of government whatever. But a danger of this kind is not to be apprehended. The citizens of America have too much discernment to be argued into anarchy. And I am much mistaken if experience has not wrought a deep and solemn conviction in the public mind, that greater energy of government is essential to the welfare and prosperity of the community.

It may not be amiss in this place concisely to remark the origin and progress of   *35*
the idea which aims at the exclusion of military establishments in time of peace.
Though in speculative minds it may arise from a contemplation of the nature
and tendency of such institutions fortified by the events that have happened in
other ages and countries; yet as a national sentiment it must be traced to those
habits of thinking, which we derive from the nation from whom the inhabitants   *40*
of these states have in general sprung.

In England for a long time after the Norman conquest the authority of the
monarch was almost unlimited. Inroads were gradually made upon the prerogative, in favour of liberty, first by the Barons and afterwards by the people, till the
greatest part of its most formidable pretensions became extinct. But it was not till   *45*
the revolution in 1688, which elevated the prince of Orange to the throne of
Great Britain, that English liberty was completely triumphant. As incident to the
undefined power of making war, an acknowledged prerogative of the crown,
Charles II had by his own authority kept on foot in time of peace a body of 5,000
regular troops. And this number James IId. increased to 30,000; which were paid   *50*
out of his civil list. At the revolution, to abolish the exercise of so dangerous an
authority, it became an article of the bill of rights then framed, that "raising or
keeping a standing army within the kingdom in time of peace, *unless with the
consent of Parliament*, was against law."

In that kingdom, when the pulse of liberty was at its highest pitch, no security   *55*
against the danger of standing armies was thought requisite, beyond a prohibition
of their being raised or kept up by the mere authority of the executive magistrate.
The patriots, who effected that memorable revolution, were too temperate and
too well informed, to think of any restraint on the legislative discretion. They

---

Lines 42–65 A somewhat hasty overview of English medieval history, designed for political use. To describe the authority of the monarch as "almost unlimited" is a decided
simplification. During the anarchy of Stephen's reign, in the early to mid-12th century,
the monarch had to struggle to assert any authority at all. Between kings and barons
there were frequent struggles, if not for power, then over territorial influence. "Inroads"
presumably refers to the Magna Carta, forced from a reluctant King John in 1215.

The Declaration of Rights, usually called The Bill of Rights (1 Will. and Mary sess.
2 ch. 2, 1689), was adopted by Parliament as a correction of the errors and illegali-
ties of the rule of James II, who was deemed to have abdicated, and as a set of conditions pertaining to the accession of William and Mary. The Bill lists the crimes that
have rendered James unfit to be king, including: "by raising and keeping a Standing
Army within this Kingdome in time of Peace without the consent of Parliament and
Quartering Soldiers contrary to Law." The Bill goes on to prohibit these actions *by
the monarch*, without parliamentary agreement. This enacts the Whig doctrine on
standing armies (see No. 8 lines 43–57 and comment), which Pennsylvania and
North Carolina are here reported to have implicitly translated into admonitions to
their own legislatures. (See No. 24, lines 39–43 and Hamilton's note to line 40; the
arguments continue at lines 103–20 and lines 133–40.) For more on standing armies
in the United States, see lines 66 ff of the present essay.

60 were aware that a certain number of troops for guards and garrisons were indispensable, that no precise bounds could be set to the national exigencies; that a power equal to every possible contingency must exist somewhere in the government; and that when they referred the exercise of that power to the judgement of the legislature, they had arrived at the ultimate point of precaution, which was
65 reconciliable with the safety of the community.

From the same source, the people of America may be said to have derived a hereditary impression of danger to liberty from standing armies in time of peace. The circumstances of a revolution quickened the public sensibility on every point connected with the security of popular rights; and in some instances raised
70 the warmth of our zeal beyond the degree which consisted with the due temperature of the body politic. The attempts of two of the states to restrict the authority of the legislature in the article of military establishments are of the number of these instances. The principles, which had taught us to be jealous of the power of an hereditary monarch, were by an injudicious excess extended to the repre-
75 sentatives of the people in their popular assemblies. Even in some of the states, where this error was not adopted, we find unnecessary declarations, that standing armies ought not to be kept up, in time of peace WITHOUT THE CONSENT OF THE LEGISLATURE—I call them unnecessary, because the reason, which had introduced a similar provision into the English bill of rights, is not applica-
80 ble to any of the state constitutions. The power of raising armies at all, under those constitutions, can by no construction be deemed to reside any where else, than in the legislatures themselves; and it was superfluous, if not absurd, to declare that a matter should not be done without the consent of a body, which alone had the power of doing it. Accordingly in some of those constitutions, and
85 among others in that of the state of New-York; which has been justly celebrated both in Europe and in America as one of the best of the forms of government established in this country, there is a total silence upon the subject.

It is remarkable, that even in the two states, which seem to have meditated an interdiction of military establishments in time of peace, the mode of expression
90 made use of is rather monitory than prohibitory. It is not said, that standing armies *shall not be* kept up, but that they *ought not* to be kept up in time of peace. This ambiguity of terms appears to have been the result of a conflict between jealousy and conviction, between the desire of excluding such establishments at all events, and the persuasion that an absolute exclusion would be
95 unwise and unsafe.

Lines 66–101 Wherever standing armies appear to have been permitted in time of peace, they were always subordinated to civil authority, with slight differences of language. See No. 24, lines 39–43 and Hamilton's note to line 40. See also Thorpe, *American Charters,* regarding New Hampshire, IV, 2456; Massachusetts, III, 1902; Pennsylvania, VI, 3083; Maryland, III, 1688; Virginia, VII, 3814; North Carolina, V, 2788; South Carolina, VI, 3246; Georgia, II, 782.

Can it be doubted that such a provision, whenever the situation of public affairs was understood to require a departure from it, would be interpreted by the legislature into a mere admonition and would be made to yield to the necessities or supposed necessities of the state? Let the fact already mentioned with respect to Pennsylvania decide. What then (it may be asked) is the use of such a provision, *100* if it cease to operate, the moment there is an inclination to disregard it?

Let us examine whether there be any comparison, in point of efficacy, between the provision alluded to and that which is contained in the new constitution, for restraining the appropriations of money for military purposes to the period of two years. The former by aiming at too much is calculated to effect *105* nothing; the latter, by steering clear of an imprudent extreme, and by being perfectly compatible with a proper provision for the exigencies of the nation, will have a salutary and powerful operation.

The legislature of the United States will be *obliged* by this provision, once at least in every two years, to deliberate upon the propriety of keeping a military *110* force on foot; to come to a new resolution on the point; and to declare their sense of the matter, by a formal vote in the face of their constituents. They are not *at liberty* to vest in the executive department permanent funds for the support of an army; if they were even incautious enough to be willing to repose in it so improper a confidence. As the spirit of party, in different degrees, must be expected *115* to infect all political bodies, there will be no doubt persons in the national legislature willing enough to arraign the measures and criminate the views of the majority. The provision for the support of a military force will always be a favourable topic for declamation. As often as the question comes forward, the public attention will be roused and attracted to the subject, by the party in opposition: And if *120* the majority should be really disposed to exceed the proper limits the community will be warned of the danger and will have an opportunity of taking measures to guard against it. Independent of parties in the national legislature itself, as often as the period of discussion arrived, the state legislatures, who will always be not only vigilant but suspicious and jealous guardians of the rights of the citizens, *125* against incroachments from the federal government, will constantly have their attention awake to the conduct of the national rulers and will be ready enough, if any thing improper appears, to sound the alarm to the people and not only to be the VOICE but if necessary the ARM of their discontent.

Schemes to subvert the liberties of a great community *require time* to mature *130* them for execution. An army so large as seriously to menace those liberties could only be formed by progressive augmentations; which would suppose, not merely a temporary combination between the legislature and executive, but a continued conspiracy for a series of time. Is it probable that such a combination would exist at all? Is it probable that it would be persevered in and transmitted along, *135* through all the successive variations in the representative body, which biennial elections would naturally produce in both houses? Is it presumable, that every man, the instant he took his seat in the national senate, or house of representatives, would commence a traitor to his constituents and to his country? Can it be

140 supposed, that there would not be found one man, discerning enough to detect so atrocious a conspiracy, or bold or honest enough to apprise his constituents of their danger? If such presumptions can fairly be made, there ought to be at once an end of all delegated authority. The people should resolve to recall all the powers they have heretofore parted with out of their own hands; and to divide them-

145 selves into as many states as there are counties, in order that they may be able to manage their own concerns in person.

If such suppositions could even be reasonably made, still the concealment of the design, for any duration, would be impracticable. It would be announced by the very circumstance of augmenting the army to so great an extent in time of

150 profound peace. What colorable reason could be assigned in a country so situated, for such vast augmentations of the military force? It is impossible that the people could be long deceived; and the destruction of the project and of the projectors would quickly follow the discovery.

It has been said that the provision, which limits the appropriation of money

155 for the support of an army to the period of two years would be unavailing; because the executive, when once possessed of a force large enough to awe the people into submission, would find resources in that very force sufficient to enable him to dispense with supplies from the votes of the legislature. But the question again recurs: Upon what pretence could he be put in possession of a force of

160 that magnitude in time of peace? If we suppose it to have been created in consequence of some domestic insurrection, or foreign war, then it becomes a case not within the principle of the objection; for this is levelled against the power of keeping up troops in time of peace. Few persons will be so visionary, as seriously to contend, that military forces ought not to be raised to quell a rebellion, or re-

165 sist an invasion; and if the defence of the community, under such circumstances, should make it necessary to have an army, so numerous as to hazard its liberty, this is one of those calamities for which there is neither preventative nor cure. It cannot be provided against by any possible form of government: It might even result from a simple league offensive and defensive; if it should ever be necessary

170 for the confederates or allies to form an army for common defence.

But it is an evil infinitely less likely to attend us in an united than in a disunited state; nay it may be safely asserted that it is an evil altogether unlikely to attend us in the latter situation. It is not easy to conceive a possibility, that dangers so

---

Lines 147–48 Consider, however, the formation of highly armed private "militia" groups in the 1990s.

Lines 154–70 For Anti-Federalist arguments against standing armies (which essentially replicate standard Whig doctrine) see Essays of Brutus, *The New York Journal*, Essay VIII, January 10, 1788, and Essay IX, January 17, 1788 (Brutus's identity has not been satisfactorily established); and Agrippa (probably James Winthrop, a former librarian of Harvard), *Massachusetts Gazette*, December 11, 1787. (These can be found in Herbert J. Storing, ed., *The Anti-Federalist*, selected by Murray Dry

formidable can assail the whole union, as to demand a force considerable enough to place our liberties in the least jeopardy; especially if we take into view *175* the aid to be derived from the militia, which ought always to be counted upon, as a valuable and powerful auxiliary. But in a state of disunion (as has been fully shewn in another place) the contrary of this supposition would become not only probable but almost unavoidable.

PUBLIUS.

[Chicago, University of Chicago Press, 1985], to which acknowledgment is hereby made.) A running dialogue between Publius and these Anti-Federalist authors can be traced through these essays, though it would be more difficult to be sure that they deflected Hamilton from his original plan. The authors of *The Federalist* were familiar with the arguments; but they did need to reply to warnings of the dangers of standing armies as raised by their opponents; state constitutions had already raised them. In brushing off the provisions of state constitutions against military establishments, however, Hamilton was careless of the facts: the constitutions of seven states (Virginia, Pennsylvania, North Carolina, Maryland, New York, Massachusetts, and New Hampshire) had such provisions on the militia; the constitutions of North Carolina, Virginia, and Pennsylvania "advised" their states to avoid standing armies "in time of peace"; those of Massachusetts, Maryland, and New Hampshire permitted standing armies but only with the consent of the legislature. All these provisions are in No. 24, lines 22–31, note 1.

Lines 176–77 This sentence seems to be a hasty and imprecise reference to Nos. 16 and 17, though the argument is scattered through subsequent numbers.

TWENTY-SEVEN

ALEXANDER HAMILTON
December 25, 1787
The Subject Continued with the Same View

To the People of the State of New York.

It has been urged in different shapes that a constitution of the kind proposed by the convention, cannot operate without the aid of a military force to execute its laws. This however, like most other things that have been alledged on that side, rests on mere general assertion; unsupported by any precise or intelligible desig-
5 nation of the reasons upon which it is founded. As far as I have been able to divine the latent meaning of the objectors, it seems to originate in a pre-supposition that the people will be disinclined to the exercise of federal authority in any matter of an internal nature. Waving any exception that might be taken to the inaccuracy or inexplicitness of the distinction between internal and external, let us enquire
10 what ground there is to presuppose that disinclination in the people. Unless we presume, at the same time, that the powers of the general government will be worse administered than those of the state governments, there seems to be no room for the presumption of ill-will, disaffection or opposition in the people. I believe it may be laid down as a general rule, that their confidence in and obedi-
15 ence to a government, will commonly be proportioned to the goodness or bad-ness of its administration. It must be admitted that there are exceptions to this rule; but these exceptions depend so entirely on accidental causes, that they can-not be considered as having any relation to the intrinsic merits or demerits of a constitution. These can only be judged of by general principles and maxims.
20 Various reasons have been suggested in the course of these papers, to induce a probability that the general government will be better administered than the particular governments: The principal of which are that the extension of the spheres of election will present a greater option, or latitude of choice to the people, that through the medium of the state legislatures, — who are select bodies of

---

Lines 1–3 In one or another form, a common Anti-Federalist anxiety. Examples: The Federal Farmer (who has been identified, but on only one piece of uncorroborated evidence, as Richard Henry Lee), October 9, 1787; Cato (attributed to George Clinton, governor of New York), III; Pennsylvania Convention Minority 3.11.50.

Lines 13–16 The remark about the goodness or badness of a government's adminis-tration would evoke a familiar passage, known to all educated Americans, from Alexander Pope's *Essay on Man* (1733): "For forms of government let fools con-test/That which is best administered is best" (Epistle III, lines 303–304).

men, and who are to appoint the members of the national senate,—there is reason 25
to expect that this branch will generally be composed with peculiar care and
judgment: That these circumstances promise greater knowledge and more comprehensive information in the national councils: And that on account of the extent of the country from which those, to whose direction they will be committed,
will be drawn, they will be less apt to be tainted by the spirit of faction, and more 30
out of the reach of those occasional ill humors or temporary prejudices and
propensities, which in smaller societies frequently contaminate the public deliberations, beget injustice and oppression of a part of the community, and engen-
der schemes, which though they gratify a momentary inclination or desire,
terminate in general distress, dissatisfaction and disgust. Several additional rea- 35
sons of considerable force, to fortify that probability, will occur when we come to
survey with a more critic eye, the interior structure of the edifice, which we are
invited to erect. It will be sufficient here to remark, that until satisfactory reasons
can be assigned to justify an opinion, that the federal government is likely to be
administered in such a manner as to render it odious or contemptible to the 40
people, there can be no reasonable foundation for the supposition, that the laws
of the union will meet with any greater obstruction from them, or will stand in
need of any other methods to enforce their execution, than the laws of the particular members.

The hope of impunity is a strong incitement to sedition—the dread of 45
punishment—a proportionately strong discouragement to it. Will not the government of the union, which, if possessed of a due degree of power, can call to its aid
the collective resources of the whole confederacy, be more likely to repress the
former sentiment, and to inspire the *latter*, than that of a single state, which can
only command the resources within itself? A turbulent faction in a state may eas- 50
ily suppose itself able to contend with the friends to the government in that state;
but it can hardly be so infatuated as to imagine itself a match for the combined
efforts of the union. If this reflection be just, there is less danger of resistance
from irregular combinations of individuals, to the authority of the confederacy,
than to that of a single member. 55

I will in this place hazard an observation which will not be the less just, because to some it may appear new; which is, that the more the operations of the
national authority are intermingled in the ordinary exercise of government; the
more the citizens are accustomed to meet with it in the common occurrences of

---

Lines 45–55 The reference is once more a generalization from the recent example
of Shays's Rebellion. What Hamilton could not yet know was that even the new federal government would face rebellion in western Pennsylvania over the excise on
whiskey (1792), and that a land tax revolt would break out under Jacob Fries, also in
Pennsylvania, in 1798.

The other side of this coin, not mentioned by Hamilton, is the hostility attracted
to the government by taxation!

60 their political life; the more it is familiarised to their sight and to their feelings; the further it enters into those objects which touch the most sensible cords, and put in motion the most active springs of the human heart; the greater will be the probability that it will conciliate the respect and attachment of the community. Man is very much a creature of habit. A thing that rarely strikes his senses will
65 generally have but transient influence upon his mind. A government continually at a distance and out of sight, can hardly be expected to interest the sensations of the people. The inference is, that the authority of the union, and the affections of the citizens towards it, will be strengthened rather than weakened by its exten- sion to what are called matters of internal concern; and that it will have less oc-
70 casion to recur to force in proportion to the familiarity and comprehensiveness of its agency. The more it circulates through those channels and currents, in which the passions of mankind naturally flow, the less will it require the aid of the vio- lent and perilous expedients of compulsion.

One thing at all events, must be evident, that a government like that proposed
75 would bid much fairer to avoid the necessity of using force, than the species of league contended for by most of its opponents; the authority of which should only operate upon the states in their political or collective capacities. It has been shewn, that in such a confederacy, there can be no sanction for the laws but force; that frequent delinquencies in the members, are the natural offspring of
80 the very frame of the government; and that as often as these happen they can only be redressed, if at all, by war and violence.

The plan reported by the convention, by extending the authority of the fed- eral head to the individual citizens of the several states, will enable the govern- ment to employ the ordinary magistracy of each in the execution of its laws. It is
85 easy to perceive that this will tend to destroy, in the common apprehension, all distinction between the sources from which they might proceed; and will give the federal government the same advantage for securing a due obedience to its authority, which is enjoyed by the government of each state; in addition to the influence on public opinion, which will result from the important consideration
90 of its having power to call to its assistance and support the resources of the whole union. It merits particular attention in this place, that the laws of the confeder- acy, as to the *enumerated* and *legitimate* objects of its jurisdiction, will become the SUPREME LAW of the land; to the observance of which, all officers legisla- tive, executive and judicial in each state, will be bound by the sanctity of an oath.
95 Thus the legislatures, courts and magistrates of the respective members will be incorporated into the operations of the national government, *as far as its just and constitutional authority extends*; and will be rendered auxiliary to the enforce- ment of its laws.✪ Any man, who will pursue by his own reflections the conse- quences of this situation, will perceive that there is good ground to calculate

✪ The sophistry which has been employed to show that this will tend to the de- struction of the state governments will, in its proper place, be fully detected.

upon a regular and peaceable execution of the laws of the union; if its powers are   *100*
administered with a common share of prudence. If we will arbitrarily suppose
the contrary, we may deduce any inferences we please from the supposition; for
it is certainly possible, by an injudicious exercise of the authorities of the best
government, that ever was or ever can be instituted, to provoke and precipitate
the people into the wildest excesses. But though the adversaries of the proposed   *105*
constitution should presume that the national rulers would be insensible to the
motives of public good, or to the obligations of duty; I would still ask them, how
the interests of ambition, or the views of encroachment, can be promoted by
such a conduct?

PUBLIUS.

Hamilton's footnote (on page 146) The alleged danger to state governments is dealt
with, by Madison, in No. 45—showing how carefully the arguments had been
planned. Plans at this stage probably did not yet include Hamilton's explanation of
the role of the Supreme Court in No. 78. In replying on an ad hoc basis to Anti-Federalist criticisms on these issues, the joint authors of *The Federalist* are not obliged to
depart far from either their original design or their allocation of responsibilities
among themselves.

TWENTY-EIGHT

ALEXANDER HAMILTON
December 26, 1787
The Same Subject Continued

To the People of the State of New York.

That there may happen cases, in which the national government may be necessitated to resort to force, cannot be denied. Our own experience has corroborated the lessons taught by the examples of other nations; that emergencies of this sort will sometimes exist in all societies, however constituted; that seditions and
5 insurrections are unhappily maladies as inseparable from the body politic, as tumours and eruptions from the natural body; that the idea of governing at all times by the simple force of law (which we have been told is the only admissible principle of republican government) has no place but in the reveries of those political doctors, whose sagacity disdains the admonitions of experimental instruction.

10 Should such emergencies at any time happen under the national government, there could be no remedy but force. The means to be employed must be proportioned to the extent of the mischief. If it should be a slight commotion in a small part of a state, the militia of the residue would be adequate to its suppression: and the natural presumption is, that they would be ready to do their duty. An insur-
15 rection, whatever may be its immediate cause, eventually endangers all government: Regard to the public peace, if not to the rights of the union, would engage the citizens, to whom the contagion had not communicated itself, to oppose the insurgents: And if the general government should be found in practice con-

---

Lines 2–9 The disorders that had broken out even under American republican governments were proof of this point (lines 1–2). It is not quite clear by whom they had "been told" that force was "the only admissible principle of republican government" (lines 7–8), but the allusion may be to Hobbes's *Leviathan* (1651).

Lines 15–16 Hamilton's comment that insurrection "eventually endangers all government" deserves to be contrasted with Jefferson's observations, written from Paris, on Shays's rebellion: "I hold it that a little rebellion now and then is a good thing, and as necessary in the political world as storms in the physical . . . " (to Madison, January 30, 1787); and "The tree of liberty must be refreshed from time to time with the blood of tyrants. It is its natural manure" (to Col. William S. Smith, November 13, 1787). To imply that armed rebellion against the legislators of Massachusetts, freely elected on a basis of a constitution adopted only six years previously by the people in their towns, was a legitimate form of protest, must have struck Madison as the height of irresponsibility, and he avoided the subject in his own subsequent letters to Jefferson.

ducive to the prosperity and felicity of the people, it were irrational to believe that they would be disinclined to its support. *20*

If on the contrary the insurrection should pervade a whole state, or a principal part of it, the employment of a different kind of force might become unavoidable. It appears that Massachusetts found it necessary to raise troops for suppressing the disorders within that state; that Pennsylvania, from the mere apprehension of commotions among a part of her citizens, has thought proper to have recourse to *25* the same measure. Suppose the state of New-York had been inclined to re-establish her lost jurisdiction over the inhabitants of Vermont; could she have hoped for success in such an enterprise from the efforts of the militia alone? Would she not have been compelled to raise and to maintain a more regular force for the execution of her design? If it must then be admitted that the neces- *30* sity of recurring to a force different from the militia in cases of this extraordinary nature, is applicable to the state governments themselves, why should the possi-bility that the national government might be under a like necessity in similar ex-tremities, be made an objection to its existence? Is it not surprising that men, who declare an attachment to the union in the abstract, should urge, as an ob- *35* jection to the proposed constitution, what applies with tenfold weight to the plan for which they contend; and what as far as it has any foundation in truth is an in-evitable consequence of civil society upon an enlarged scale? Who would not prefer that possibility to the unceasing agitations and frequent revolutions which are the continual scourges of petty republics? *40*

Let us pursue this examination in another light. Suppose, in lieu of one gen-eral system, two or three or even four confederacies were to be formed, would not the same difficulty oppose itself to the operations of either of these confed-eracies? Would not each of them be exposed to the same casualties; and, when these happened, be obliged to have recourse to the same expedients for uphold- *45* ing its authority, which are objected to a government for all the states? Would the militia in this supposition be more ready or more able to support the federal au-thority than in the case of a general union? All candid and intelligent men must upon due consideration acknowledge that the principle of the objection is equally applicable to either of the two cases; and that whether we have one *50* government for all the states, or different governments for different parcels of them, or as many unconnected governments as there are states, there might sometimes be a necessity to make use of a force constituted differently from the militia to preserve the peace of the community, and to maintain the just author-ity of the laws against those violent invasions of them which amount to insurrec- *55* tions and rebellions.

Lines 21–28 Yet another reference to Shays in Massachusetts; the "commotions" in Pennsylvania's Wyoming Valley have also been noted. The Vermonters were led by Ethan Allen (1738–1789). Taken up in No. 46.

Independent of all other reasonings upon the subject, it is a full answer to those who require a more peremptory provision against military establishments in time of peace, to say that the whole power of the proposed government is to be in the hands of the representatives of the people. This is the essential, and after all the only efficacious security for the rights and privileges of the people which is attainable in civil society.*

If the representatives of the people betray their constituents, there is then no resource left but in the exertion of that original right of self-defence, which is paramount to all positive forms of government; and which, against the usurpations of the national rulers, may be exerted with infinitely better prospect of success, than against those of the rulers of an individual state. In a single state, if the persons entrusted with supreme power become usurpers, the different parcels, subdivisions or districts, of which it consists, having no distinct government in each, can take no regular measures for defence. The citizens must rush tumultuously to arms, without concert, without system, without resource; except in their courage and despair. The usurpers, cloathed with the forms of legal authority, can too often crush the opposition in embryo. The smaller the extent of territory, the more difficult will it be for the people to form a regular or systematic plan of opposition; and the more easy will it be to defeat their early efforts. Intelligence can be more speedily obtained of their preparations and movements; and the military force in the possession of the usurpers, can be more rapidly directed against the part where the opposition has begun. In this situation, there must be a peculiar coincidence of circumstances to ensure success to the popular resistance.

The obstacles to usurpation and the facilities of resistance increase with the increased extent of the state; provided the citizens understand their rights and are disposed to defend them. The natural strength of the people in a large community, in proportion to the artificial strength of the government, is greater than in a small; and of course more competent to a struggle with the attempts of the government to establish a tyranny. But in a confederacy the people, without exaggeration, may be said to be entirely the masters of their own fate. Power being almost always the rival of power; the general government will at all times stand ready to check the usurpations of the state governments; and these will have the same disposition towards the general government. The people, by throwing themselves into either scale, will infallibly make it preponderate. If their rights are invaded by either, they can make use of the other, as the instrument of redress. How wise will it be in them by cherishing the union to preserve to themselves an advantage which can never be too highly prised!

It may safely be received as an axiom in our political system, that the state governments will in all possible contingencies afford complete security against invasions of the public liberty by the national authority. Projects of usurpation cannot be masked under pretences so likely to escape the penetration of select bodies of

---

* Its full efficacy will be examined hereafter.

men as of the people at large. The legislatures will have better means of information. They can discover the danger at a distance; and possessing all the organs of civil power and the confidence of the people, they can at once adopt a regular *100* plan of opposition, in which they can combine all the resources of the community. They can readily communicate with each other in the different states; and unite their common forces for the protection of their common liberty.

The great extent of the country is a further security. We have already experienced its utility against the attacks of a foreign power. And it would have pre- *105* cisely the same effect against the enterprises of ambitious rulers in the national councils. If the federal army should be able to quell the resistance of one state, the distant states would be able to make head with fresh forces. The advantages obtained in one place must be abandoned to subdue the opposition in others; and the moment the part which had been reduced to submission was left to itself *110* its efforts would be renewed and its resistance revive.

We should recollect that the extent of the military force must at all events be regulated by the resources of the country. For a long time to come, it will not be possible to maintain a large army: and as the means of doing this increase, the population and natural strength of the community will proportionably increase. *115* When will the time arrive, that the federal government can raise and maintain an army capable of erecting a despotism over the great body of the people of an immense empire; who are in a situation, through the medium of their state governments, to take measures for their own defence with all the celerity, regularity and system of independent nations? The apprehension may be considered *120* as a disease, for which there can be found no cure in the resources of argument and reasoning.

PUBLIUS.

Lines 112–22 There is an implied response here to Montesquieu's views on power. Hamilton responded directly to Anti-Federalist proponents of Montesquieu's views in No. 9.

TWENTY-NINE
{NO. 35 IN NEWSPAPERS}

ALEXANDER HAMILTON
January 9, 1788
Concerning the Militia

To the People of the State of New York.

The power of regulating the militia and of commanding its services in times of insurrection and invasion are natural incidents to the duties of superintending the common defence, and of watching over the internal peace of the confederacy.

5   It requires no skill in the science of war to discern that uniformity in the organization and discipline of the militia would be attended with the most beneficial effects, whenever they were called into service for the public defence. It

---

Lines 1–3 ff The militia was an ancient English institution of local defense, which was naturally adopted by colonial Americans. Militia training duties normally fell on all males from fifteen or sixteen to sixty. Under English rules, members of the aristocracy, clergymen, and the infirm were exempt. The militia was always a force in the king's service, acting through his county lord lieutenants; but it was also a local, defensive force, and could not be ordered to serve out of the kingdom—indeed militiamen often claimed a right not to serve outside their own counties. Though normally under the command of social superiors, they often had strong local and democratic sentiments, and could not always be relied on to suppress riots with which they sympathized. And although the county militia was in the king's service and under his authority, its democratic proclivities also acted as a counterweight in the debate about standing armies. In America, the militia in many respects replicated the English forms, but was less well disciplined or trained. The officers were usually well-to-do farmers, lawyers, and respected members of society. Upper-class young men could sometimes purchase substitutes—a practice to be repeated in the purchase of draft substitutes in the Civil War. The militia reflected social structures: servants, apprentices, and African-Americans were not included, though free black men were sometimes pressed into service in military emergencies, usually for their labor. The great advantage of the militia was that it could assemble from the farms, often at short notice, the members bringing their own arms with them. This and their knowledge of local terrain did much to compensate for their rough-and-ready style of drill and the often crude nature of their training—about which Washington more than once made scathing remarks. Potentially the militias of different states in which fighting took place could amount to large-scale reinforcements to the Continental army, sometimes fighting alongside it. The state or local government was thus not under the burden of supplying arms for these forces. This connects the militia with the issue of whether there was a legally protected right to bear arms—linked in a

would enable them to discharge the duties of the camp and of the field with mutual intelligence and concert; an advantage of peculiar moment in the operations of an army: And it would fit them much sooner to acquire the degree of proficiency in military functions, which would be essential to their usefulness. *10* This desirable uniformity can only be accomplished by confiding the regulation of the militia to the direction of the national authority. It is therefore with the

---

single sentence in the 2nd Amendment. The history of arms ownership in America from the colonial to the early national periods was in a sense the history of an extension of existing English rights. In 1671, Parliament enacted the notorious Game Act, which, under the guise of protecting the game on lands owned by the aristocracy from poaching, effectively disarmed a large proportion of the country population, transferred power of the control of arms ownership to the gentry, and gave the Protestant gentry power to disarm Catholics. The Bill of Rights (1689) restored the right to own personal arms to Protestants, nominally for their own defense, but continued to disarm Catholics. Even Catholics, however, were permitted in certain cases to own personal firearms for the protection of their households. In the colonies, where wildlife was abundant and land widely owned, game laws had no place, and class legislation either to protect the landed gentry's property or to disarm the populace was not called for—and could not have been enacted or enforced. Colonial governments actually insisted on the private ownership of arms for personal, family, and local protection. There was no significant Catholic or otherwise potentially dissident population to be feared. Significantly, where colonial governments did impose restrictions, they were on African and Native Americans. The militia had, as we have seen, played an important part in the War of Independence, and since both the Congress and the state legislatures were able to rely on such persons as large and small farmers to bring their own firearms, normally used mainly for hunting and for defense against marauders—or against Native Americans in exposed areas—it follows that almost every competent adult male may have been expected, or at least entitled, to bear his own arms. How many actually did has become a question of unresolved controversy. The italicized passage in the text (lines 16–17) constitutes an important but little recognized element in the background for what later became the 2nd Amendment. Although this was obviously not on Publius's own agenda, Madison, as a member of the first House of Representatives, chaired the committee that wrote that and the other original amendments. Recent disorders and even rebellions had shown that an armed and turbulent citizenry could present serious dangers even to republican governments. While nothing is done to disarm the citizenry, Article I, Section 8 of the Constitution provides for militia forces whose discipline is prescribed by Congress, and which is solely at Congress's disposal. In the terms of the (subsequently adopted) 2nd Amendment, Article 1, Section 8 defines the needs or rights of the citizen "to keep and bear arms" in strict connection with the state's need for "a well-regulated militia" to protect freedom. The needs or rights of the citizen may, arguably, be implied, but are not specified in this carefully worded clause. It has been plausibly argued that, since the individual right as defined in the 2nd Amendment is grammatically connected with the need for a militia, the disappearance of the militia in the early nineteenth century left the right without constitutional standing.

most evident propriety that the plan of the convention proposes to empower the union "to provide for organizing, arming and disciplining the militia, and for governing such part of them as may be employed in the service of the United States, *reserving to the states respectively the appointment of the officers and the authority of training the militia according to the discipline prescribed by congress.*"

Of the different grounds which have been taken in opposition to this plan, there is none that was so little to have been expected, or is so untenable in itself, as the one from which this particular provision has been attacked. If a well regulated militia be the most natural defence of a free country, it ought certainly to be under the regulation and at the disposal of that body which is constituted the guardian of the national security. If standing armies are dangerous to liberty, an efficacious power over the militia, in the same body, ought as far as possible to take away the inducement and the pretext to such unfriendly institutions. If the federal government can command the aid of the militia in those emergencies which call for the military arm in support of the civil magistrate, it can the better dispense with the employment of a different kind of force. If it cannot avail itself of the former, it will be obliged to recur to the latter. To render an army unnecessary will be a more certain method of preventing its existence than a thousand prohibitions upon paper.

In order to cast an odium upon the power of calling forth the militia to execute the Laws of the union, it has been remarked that there is no where any provision in the proposed constitution for requiring the aid of the POSSE COMITATUS to assist the magistrate in the execution of his duty; whence it has been inferred that military force was intended to be his only auxiliary. There is a

---

Lines 20–21 Note the phraseology's similarity to what was to appear in the 2nd Amendment. This is interesting, bearing in mind that Hamilton wrote this essay, while Madison chaired the committee. Very probably, Madison looked up what they had said in their joint production, *The Federalist*, and made the language of the amendment conform to it.

Lines 34–35 "Posse comitatus" is medieval Latin for "force of the county," and meant the body of men who later became the militia—age fifteen and upwards, excluding the clergy, the aristocracy, and the infirm (see note on lines 1–3 ff), whom the sheriff—a county officer—could summon to suppress disorders. Hamilton is applying the English usage and institution to the American militia—possibly a tendentious application, since English usages can't always be adapted for American conditions. The powers of Congress over the militia, it may be noted, distinctly resemble those of the king in 17th century England before the Bill of Rights. The reference to Anti-Federalist objections that the Congress will not have power to summon the *posse comitatus* appears to catch them in a contradiction; the very much more serious objection was that the Constitution would give Congress—or, when it was not sitting, the president—powers to enforce its will and even to march militias from state to state. This fear was far from being as fantastic as Publius pretends: the point was that Congress might use the militias of other states to suppress outbreaks like Shays's

striking incoherence in the objections which have appeared, and sometimes even from the same quarter, not much calculated to inspire a very favourable opinion of the sincerity or fair dealing of their authors. The same persons who tell us in one breath that the powers of the federal government will be despotic and unlimited, inform us in the next that it has not authority sufficient even to call out the POSSE COMITATUS. The latter fortunately is as much short of the truth as the former exceeds it. It would be as absurd to doubt that a right to pass all laws *necessary* and *proper* to execute its declared powers would include that of requiring the assistance of the citizens to the officers who may be entrusted with the execution of those laws; as it would be to believe that a right to enact laws necessary and proper for the imposition and collection of taxes would involve that of varying the rules of descent and of the alienation of landed property or of abolishing the trial by jury in cases relating to it. It being therefore evident that the supposition of a want of power to require the aid of the POSSE COMITATUS is entirely destitute of colour, it will follow that the conclusion which has been drawn from it, in its application to the authority of the federal government over the militia is as uncandid as it is illogical. What reason could there be to infer that force was intended to be the sole instrument of authority merely because there is a power to make use of it when necessary? What shall we think of the motives which could induce men of sense to reason in this extraordinary manner? How shall we prevent a conflict between charity and judgment?

By a curious refinement upon the spirit of republican jealousy, we are even taught to apprehend danger from the militia itself in the hands of the federal government. It is observed that select corps may be formed, composed of the young and the ardent, who may be rendered subservient to the views of arbitrary power. What plan for the regulation of the militia may be pursued by the national government is impossible to be foreseen. But so far from viewing the matter in the same light with those who object to select corps as dangerous, were the constitution ratified, and were I to deliver my sentiments to a member of the federal legislature on the subject of a militia establishment, I should hold to him in substance the following discourse:

"The project of disciplining all the militia of the United States is as futile as it would be injurious, if it were capable of being carried into execution. A tolerable

40

45

50

55

60

65

Rebellion. These Anti-Federalist objections appear in *Letters of Centinel* (George Bryan) in *The Independent Gazetteer* (Philadelphia), November 8, 1787, Letter III; *The Address and Reasons of . . . the Minority of the Convention of Pennsylvania,* printed in Pennsylvania newspapers in December 1787—which makes the observation that the Congress will lack the requisite power, as noted above; "The Letter of 'Montezuma'" (not identified) in *The Independent Gazetteer,* October 17, 1787; in Richard Henry Lee's *Letters from the Federal Farmer,* Letter III, October 10, 1787. The tyranny argument would later be renewed with great eloquence by Patrick Henry in the Virginia Convention in June 1788.

70   expertness in military movements is a business that requires time and practice. It is not a day, nor a week, nor even a month that will suffice for the attainment of it. To oblige the great body of the yeomanry and of the other classes of the citizens to be under arms for the purpose of going through military exercises and evolutions as often as might be necessary, to acquire the degree of perfection which would
75   intitle them to the character of a well regulated militia, would be a real grievance to the people, and a serious public inconvenience and loss. It would form an annual deduction from the productive labour of the country to an amount which, calculating upon the present numbers of the people, would not fall far short of a million pounds. To attempt a thing which would abridge the mass of labour and
80   industry to so considerable an extent would be unwise; and the experiment, if made, could not succeed, because it would not long be endured. Little more can reasonably be aimed at with respect to the people at large than to have them properly armed and equipped; and in order to see that this be not neglected, it will be necessary to assemble them once or twice in the course of a year.
85   "But though the scheme of disciplining the whole nation must be abandoned as mischievous or impracticable; yet it is a matter of the utmost importance that a well digested plan should as soon as possible be adopted for the proper establishment of the militia. The attention of the government ought particularly to be directed to the formation of a select corps of moderate size upon such principles
90   as will really fit it for service in case of need. By thus circumscribing the plan it will be possible to have an excellent body of well trained militia ready to take the field whenever the defence of the state shall require it. This will not only lessen the call for military establishments; but if circumstances should at any time oblige the government to form an army of any magnitude, that army can never
95   be formidable to the liberties of the people, while there is a large body of citizens little if at all inferior to them in discipline and the use of arms, who stand ready to defend their own rights and those of their fellow citizens. This appears to me the only substitute that can be devised for a standing army; and the best possible security against it, if it should exist."
100   Thus differently from the adversaries of the proposed constitution should I reason on the same subject; deducing arguments of safety from the very sources which they represent as fraught with danger and perdition. But how the national legislature may reason on the point is a thing which neither they nor I can foresee.
      There is something so far fetched and so extravagant in the idea of danger to
105   liberty from the militia, that one is at a loss whether to treat it with gravity or with raillery; whether to consider it as a mere trial of skill, like the paradoxes of rhetoricians, as a disingenuous artifice to instill prejudices at any price or as the serious offspring of political fanaticism. Where in the name of common sense are our fears to end if we may not trust our sons, our brothers, our neighbours,
110   our fellow-citizens? What shadow of danger can there be from men who are daily mingling with the rest of their countrymen; and who participate with them in the same feelings, sentiments, habits and interests? What reasonable cause of apprehension can be inferred from a power in the union to prescribe regulations for

the militia and to command its services when necessary; while the particular states are to have the *sole and exclusive appointment of the officers?* If it were possible seriously to indulge a jealousy of the militia upon any conceivable establishment under the federal government, the circumstance of the officers being in the appointment of the states ought at once to extinguish it. There can be no doubt that this circumstance will always secure to them a preponderating influence over the militia. 120

In reading many of the publications against the constitution, a man is apt to imagine that he is perusing some ill written tale or romance; which instead of natural and agreeable images exhibits to the mind nothing but frightful and distorted shapes—Gorgons, Hydras and Chimeras dire—discoloring and disfiguring whatever it represents and transforming every thing it touches into a monster. 125

A sample of this is to be observed in the exaggerated and improbable suggestions which have taken place respecting the power of calling for the services of the militia. That of New-Hampshire is to be marched to Georgia, of Georgia to New-Hampshire, of New-York to Kentuke and of Kentuke to Lake Champlain. Nay the debts due to the French and Dutch are to be paid in militia-men instead of Louis 130 d'ors and ducats. At one moment there is to be a large army to lay prostrate the liberties of the people; at another moment the militia of Virginia are to be dragged from their homes five or six hundred miles to tame the republican contumacy of Massachusetts; and that of Massachusetts is to be transported an equal distance to subdue the refractory haughtiness of the aristocratic Virginians. Do the persons, 135 who rave at this rate, imagine, that their art or their eloquence can impose any conceits or absurdities upon the people of America for infallible truths?

If there should be an army to be made use of as the engine of despotism what need of the militia? If there should be no army, whither would the militia, irritated at being required to undertake a distant and distressing expedition for the 140 purpose of rivetting the chains of slavery upon a part of their countrymen direct their course, but to the seat of the tyrants, who had meditated so foolish as well as so wicked a project; to crush them in their imagined intrenchments of power and to make them an example of the just vengeance of an abused and incensed people? Is this the way in which usurpers stride to dominion over a numerous and 145 enlightened nation? Do they begin by exciting the detestation of the very instruments of their intended usurpations? Do they usually commence their career by wanton and disgustful acts of power calculated to answer no end, but to draw upon themselves universal hatred and execration? Are suppositions of this sort the sober admonitions of discerning patriots to a discerning people? Or are they 150

Lines 112–15 Article 1, Section 8 of the Constitution gives the states the power to appoint militia officers.

Lines 126–28 For these alarms, see references in note on lines 34–35.

the inflammatory ravings of chagrined incendiaries or distempered enthusiasts? If we were even to suppose the national rulers actuated by the most ungovernable ambition, it is impossible to believe that they would employ such preposterous means to accomplish their designs.

In times of insurrection or invasion it would be natural and proper that the militia of a neighbouring state should be marched into another to resist a common enemy or to guard the republic against the violences of faction or sedition. This was frequently the case in respect to the first object in the course of the late war; and this mutual succour is indeed a principal end of our political association. If the power of affording it be placed under the direction of the union, there will be no danger of a supine and listless inattention to the dangers of a neighbour, till its near approach had superadded the incitements of self preservation to the too feeble impulses of duty and sympathy.

PUBLIUS.

Line 151 "Distempered," now archaic, means out of their minds.

THIRTY
{NO. 29 IN NEWSPAPERS}

ALEXANDER HAMILTON
December 28, 1787
Concerning Taxation

To the People of the State of New York.

It has been already observed, that the federal government ought to possess the power of providing for the support of the national forces; in which proposition was intended to be included the expence of raising troops, of building and equipping fleets, and all other expences in any wise connected with military arrangements and operations. But these are not the only objects to which the 5
jurisdiction of the union, in respect to revenue, must necessarily be empowered to extend—It must embrace a provision for the support of the national civil list— for the payment of the national debts contracted, or that may be contracted—and in general for all those matters which will call for disbursements out of the national treasury. The conclusion is, that there must be interwoven in the frame of 10
the government, a general power of taxation in one shape or another.

Money is with propriety considered as the vital principle of the body politic; as that which sustains its life and motion, and enables it to perform its most essential functions. A complete power therefore to procure a regular and adequate supply of revenue, as far as the resources of the community will permit, may be regarded as an 15
indispensable ingredient in every constitution. From a deficiency in this particular, one of two evils must ensue; either the people must be subjected to continual plunder as a substitute for a more eligible mode of supplying the public wants, or the government must sink into a fatal atrophy, and in a short course of time perish.

In the Ottoman or Turkish empire, the sovereign, though in other respects absolute master of the lives and fortunes of his subjects, has no right to impose a 20

Lines 1–11 See No. 16. The latter part of this paragraph anticipates Hamilton's policy of funding public debts.

Lines 20–29 At the height of its power, the Ottoman (from Uthman) Empire extended from its base in Anatolia over all of the ancient Middle East, and over the Balkans to the gates of Vienna; it was a constant threat to Europe, until it was repelled in the late 17th century. Notwithstanding the despotic powers always attributed to the sultans by Europeans, the administrative arrangements of the empire had for centuries effectively leased out the taxing power to local notables, and associated each senior administrative officer with a power to collect his own salary. The Ottoman Empire's slow decline was already evident by the time of *The Federalist*.

new tax. The consequence is, that he permits the bashaws or governors of provinces to pillage the people at discretion; and in turn squeezes out of them the sums of which he stands in need to satisfy his own exigencies and those of the
25 state. In America, from a like cause, the government of the union has gradually dwindled into a state of decay, approaching nearly to annihilation. Who can doubt that the happiness of the people in both countries would be promoted by competent authorities in the proper hands, to provide the revenues which the necessities of the public might require?

30 The present confederation, feeble as it is, intended to repose in the United States, an unlimited power of providing for the pecuniary wants of the union. But proceeding upon an erroneous principle, it has been done in such a manner as entirely to have frustrated the intention. Congress by the articles which compose that compact (as has already been stated) are authorised to ascertain and call for
35 any sums of money necessary, in their judgment, to the service of the United States; and their requisitions, if conformable to the rule of apportionment, are in every constitutional sense obligatory upon the states. These have no right to question the propriety of the demand—no discretion beyond that of devising the ways and means of furnishing the sums demanded. But though this be strictly and truly
40 the case; though the assumption of such a right would be an infringement of the articles of union; though it may seldom or never have been avowedly claimed; yet in practice it has been constantly exercised; and would continue to be so, as long as the revenues of the confederacy should remain dependent on the intermediate agency of its members. What the consequences of this system have been, is within
45 the knowledge of every man, the least conversant in our public affairs, and has been abundantly unfolded in different parts of these inquiries. It is this which has chiefly contributed to reduce us to a situation which affords ample cause, of mortification to ourselves, and of triumph to our enemies.

What remedy can there be for this situation but, in a change of the system, which has produced it? In a change of the fallacious and delusive system of quo-
50 tas and requisitions? What substitute can there be imagined for this *ignis fatuus* in finance, but that of permitting the national government to raise its own revenues by the ordinary methods of taxation, authorised in every well ordered constitution of civil government? Ingenious men may declaim with plausibility on
55 any subject; but no human ingenuity can point out any other expedient to rescue us from the inconveniences and embarrassments, naturally resulting from defective supplies of the public treasury.

The more intelligent adversaries of the new constitution admit the force of this reasoning; but they qualify their admission by a distinction between what
60 they call *internal* and *external* taxation. The former they would reserve to the state governments; the latter, which they explain into commercial imposts, or

---

Lines 58–63 The distinction drawn here between internal and external taxes would have recalled to many minds the same distinction relied on by Britain's chancellor of

rather duties on imported articles, they declare themselves willing to concede to the federal head. This distinction, however, would violate that fundamental maxim of good sense and sound policy, which dictates that every POWER ought to be proportionate to its OBJECT; and would still leave the general government in a kind of tutelage to the state governments, inconsistent with every idea of vigor or efficiency. Who can pretend that commercial imposts are or would be alone equal to the present and future exigencies of the union? Taking into the account the existing debt, foreign and domestic, upon any plan of extinguishment, which a man moderately impressed with the importance of public justice and public credit could approve, in addition to the establishments, which all parties will acknowledge to be necessary, we could not reasonably flatter ourselves, that this resource alone, upon the most improved scale, would even suffice for its present necessities. Its future necessities admit not of calculation or limitation; and upon the principle, more than once adverted to, the power of making provision for them as they arise, ought to be equally unconfined. I believe it may be regarded as a position, warranted by the history of mankind, that *in the usual progress of things, the necessities of a nation in every stage of its existence will be found at least equal to its resources.*

To say that deficiencies may be provided for by requisitions upon the states, is on the one hand, to acknowledge that this system cannot be depended upon; and on the other hand, to depend upon it for every thing beyond a certain limit. Those who have carefully attended to its vices and deformities as they have been exhibited by experience, or delineated in the course of these papers, must feel an invincible repugnancy to trusting the national interests, in any degree, to its operation. Its inevitable tendency, whenever it is brought into activity, must be to enfeeble the union and sow the seeds of discord and contention between the federal head and its members, and between the members themselves. Can it be expected that the deficiencies would be better supplied in this mode, than the total wants of the union have heretofore been supplied, in the same mode? It ought to be recollected, that if less will be required from the states, they will have proportionably less means to answer the demand. If the opinions of those who contend for the distinction which has been mentioned, were to be received as evidence of truth, one would be led to conclude that there was some known point in the economy of national affairs, at which it would be safe to stop, and to say, thus far the ends of public happiness will be promoted by supplying the wants of government, and all beyond this is unworthy of our care or anxiety. How is it

65

70

75

80

85

90

95

---

the exchequer, Charles Townshend, when he imposed his system of taxes on the colonies in 1767.

Lines 77–79 The italicized phrase seems to be the wrong way round. Would it not have seemed more plausible to have made the resources equal to the necessities? The observation, whatever its merits, deserves note for its implied belief in progressive stages of historical development.

possible that a government half supplied and always necessitous, can fulfil the purposes of its institution—can provide for the security,—advance the
100 prosperity—or support the reputation of the commonwealth? How can it ever possess either energy or stability, dignity or credit, confidence at home or respectability abroad? How can its administration be any thing else than a succession of expedients temporising, impotent, disgraceful? How will it be able to avoid a frequent sacrifice of its engagements to immediate necessity? How can it
105 undertake or execute any liberal or enlarged plans of public good?

Let us attend to what would be the effects of this situation in the very first war in which we should happen to be engaged. We will presume for argument sake, that the revenue arising from the import duties answers the purposes of a provision for the public debt, and of a peace establishment for the union. Thus cir-
110 cumstanced, a war breaks out. What would be the probable conduct of the government in such an emergency? Taught by experience that proper dependence could not be placed on the success of requisitions: unable by its own authority to lay hold of fresh resources, and urged by considerations of national danger, would it not be driven to the expedient of diverting the funds already ap-
115 propriated from their proper objects to the defence of the state? It is not easy to see how a step of this kind could be avoided; and if it should be taken, it is evident that it would prove the destruction of public credit at the very moment that it was become essential to the public safety. To imagine that at such a crisis credit might be dispensed with, would be the extreme of infatuation. In the modern sys-
120 tem of war, nations the most wealthy are obliged to have recourse to large loans. A country so little opulent as ours, must feel this necessity in a much stronger degree. But who would lend to a government that prefaced its overtures for borrowing, by an act which demonstrated that no reliance could be placed on the steadiness of its measures for paying? The loans it might be able to procure, would
125 be as limited in their extent as burthensome in their conditions. They would be made upon the same principles that usurers commonly lend to bankrupt and fraudulent debtors; with a sparing hand, and at enormous premiums.

It may perhaps be imagined, that from the scantiness of the resources of the country, the necessity of diverting the established funds in the case supposed,
130 would exist; though the national government should possess an unrestrained power of taxation. But two considerations will serve to quiet all apprehension on this head; one is, that we are sure the resources of the community in their full extent, will be brought into activity for the benefit of the union; the other is, that whatever deficiencies there may be, can without difficulty be supplied by loans.
135 The power of creating new funds upon new objects of taxation by its own authority, would enable the national government to borrow, as far as its necessities might require. Foreigners as well as the citizens of America, could then reason-

---

Lines 137–43 See Article 8 of the Articles of Confederation.

Under internal pressure from those of their citizens who were creditors of the national (i.e., congressional) debt, some of the states had begun to assume responsibil-

ably repose confidence in its engagements; but to depend upon a government, that must itself depend upon thirteen other governments for the means of fulfilling its contracts, when once its situation is clearly understood, would require a *140* degree of credulity, not often to be met with in the pecuniary transactions of mankind, and little reconcileable with the usual sharp-sightedness of avarice.

Reflections of this kind, may have trifling weight with men, who hope to see realized in America, the halcyon scenes of the poetic or fabulous age; but to those who believe we are likely to experience a common portion of the vicissi- *145* tudes and calamities, which have fallen to the lot of other nations, they must appear entitled to serious attention. Such men must behold the actual situation of their country with painful solicitude, and deprecate the evils which ambition or revenge might, with too much facility, inflict upon it.

PUBLIUS.

---

ity for discharging these debts. Maryland began to do so before the end of 1782, New Jersey in 1784, and Pennsylvania in 1785. The obvious effect was to weaken the authority of the Congress over the citizens of those states.

THIRTY-ONE
{NO. 30 IN NEWSPAPERS}

ALEXANDER HAMILTON
January 1, 1788
The Same Subject Continued

To the People of the State of New York.

In disquisitions of every kind there are certain primary truths or first principles upon which all subsequent reasonings must depend. These contain an internal evidence, which antecedent to all reflection or combination commands the assent of the mind. Where it produces not this effect, it must proceed either from
5   some disorder in the organs of perception, or from the influence of some strong interest, or passion, or prejudice. Of this nature are the maxims in geometry, that the whole is greater than its part; that things equal to the same are equal to one another; that two straight lines cannot inclose a space; and that all right angles are equal to each other. Of the same nature are these other maxims in ethics and
10 politics, that there cannot be an effect without a cause; that the means ought to be proportioned to the end; that every power ought to be commensurate with its object; that there ought to be no limitation of a power destined to effect a purpose, which is itself incapable of limitation. And there are other truths in the two latter sciences, which if they cannot pretend to rank in the class of axioms, are yet
15 such direct inferences from them, and so obvious in themselves, and so agreeable to the natural and unsophisticated dictates of common sense, that they challenge the assent of a sound and unbiassed mind, with a degree of force and conviction almost equally irresistable.

    The objects of geometrical enquiry are so entirely abstracted from those pur-
20 suits which stir up and put in motion the unruly passions of the human heart, that mankind without difficulty adopt not only the more simple theorems of the science, but even those abstruse paradoxes, which however they may appear susceptible of demonstration, are at variance with the natural conceptions which the mind, without the aid of philosophy, would be led to entertain upon the sub-

---

Lines 1–6 This is Hamilton's definition of a self-evident truth, which, of course, appeared in Jefferson's draft of the Declaration of Independence in circumstances that did not call for such a philosophical explanation.

Lines 6–13 Note the transition from maxims in *logic* to maxims in *ethics* (i.e., from "is" to "ought") with the implication that they are of the same order of certainty. Maxims also support much of common law reasoning, particularly in Sir Edward Coke's *Institutes*, familiar to American legal practitioners.

ject. The INFINITE DIVISIBILITY of matter, or in other words, the INFINITE _25_
divisibility of a FINITE thing, extending even to the minutest atom, is a point
agreed among geometricians; though not less incomprehensible to common
sense, than any of those mysteries in religion, against which the batteries of infi-
delity have been so industriously levelled.

But in the sciences of morals and politics men are found far less tractable. To _30_
a certain degree it is right and useful, that this should be the case. Caution and
investigation are a necessary armour against error and imposition. But this un-
tractableness may be carried too far, and may degenerate into obstinacy, perverseness or disingenuity. Though it cannot be pretended that the principles of
moral and political knowledge have in general the same degree of certainty with _35_
those of the mathematics; yet they have much better claims in this respect, than
to judge from the conduct of men in particular situations, we should be disposed
to allow them. The obscurity is much oftener in the passions and prejudices of
the reasoner than in the subject. Men upon too many occasions do not give their
own understandings fair play; but yielding to some untoward bias they entangle _40_
themselves in words and confound themselves in subtleties.

How else could it happen (if we admit the objectors to be sincere in their opposition) that positions so clear as those which manifest the necessity of a general
power of taxation in the government of the union, should have to encounter any
adversaries among men of discernment? Though these positions have been else- _45_
where fully stated, they will perhaps not be improperly recapitulated in this
place, as introductory to an examination of what may have been offered by way of
objection to them. They are in substance as follow: —

A government ought to contain in itself every power requisite to the full accomplishment of the objects committed to its care, and to the complete execu- _50_
tion of the trusts for which it is responsible; free from every other control, but a
regard to the public good and to the sense of the people.

As the duties of superintending the national defence and of securing the public peace against foreign or domestic violence, involve a provision for casualties
and dangers, to which no possible limits can be assigned, the power of making _55_
that provision ought to know no other bounds than the exigencies of the nation
and the resources of the community.

As revenue is the essential engine by which the means of answering the national
exigencies must be procured, the power of procuring that article in its full extent,
must necessarily be comprehended in that of providing for those exigencies. _60_

As theory and practice conspire to prove that the power of procuring revenue
is unavailing, when exercised over the states in their collective capacities, the

---

Lines 42–48 No. 12 actually discounts taxation as a major source of national revenue. The reference in lines 45–46 is presumably to Nos. 21 and 30.

Lines 53–57 From the 20th- or 21st-century perspective, this paragraph must appear farsighted!

federal government must of necessity be invested with an unqualified power of taxation in the ordinary modes.

65 Did not experience evince the contrary, it would be natural to conclude that the propriety of a general power of taxation in the national government might safely be permitted to rest on the evidence of these propositions, unassisted by any additional arguments or illustrations. But we find in fact, that the antagonists of the proposed constitution, so far from acquiescing in their justness or truth, seem

70 to make their principal and most zealous effort against this part of the plan. It may therefore be satisfactory to analize the arguments with which they combat it.

Those of them, which have been most labored with that view, seem in substance to amount to this: "It is not true, because the exigencies of the union may not be susceptible of limitation, that its power of laying taxes ought to be uncon-

75 fined. Revenue is as requisite to the purposes of the local administrations as to those of the union; and the former are at least of equal importance with the latter to the happiness of the people. It is therefore as necessary, that the state governments should be able to command the means of supplying their wants, as, that the national government should possess the like faculty, in respect to the wants of

80 the union. But an indefinite power of taxation in the *latter* might, and probably would in time deprive the former of the means of providing for their own necessities; and would subject them entirely to the mercy of the national legislature. As the laws of the union are to become the supreme law of the land; as it is to have power to pass all laws that may be NECESSARY for carrying into execu-

85 tion, the authorities with which it is proposed to vest it; the national government might at any time abolish the taxes imposed for state objects, upon the pretence of an interference with its own. It might alledge a necessity of doing this, in order to give efficacy to the national revenues: And thus all the resources of taxation might by degrees, become the subjects of federal monopoly, to the intire exclu-

90 sion and destruction of the state governments."

This mode of reasoning appears sometimes to turn upon the supposition of usurpation in the national government; at other times it seems to be designed only as a deduction from the constitutional operation of its intended powers. It is only in the latter light, that it can be admitted to have any pretensions to fairness.

95 The moment we launch into conjectures about the usurpations of the federal government, we get into an unfathomable abyss, and fairly put ourselves out of the reach of all reasoning. Imagination may range at pleasure till it gets bewildered amidst the labyrinths of an enchanted castle, and knows not on which side to turn to escape from the apparitions which itself has raised. Whatever may be

---

Lines 72–90 This paragraph homogenizes a mass of Anti-Federalist arguments on the relation of taxation to political power, which Publius intends to answer. Americans had every reason for a high sense of political awareness on this issue: "No taxation without representation" had been the early rallying cry of opposition to parliamentary taxation, deriving from the fundamental English historical right to one's own property.

the limits or modifications of the powers of the union, it is easy to imagine an   *100*
endless train of possible dangers; and by indulging an excess of jealousy and
timidity, we may bring ourselves to a state of absolute scepticism and irresolution. I repeat here what I have observed in substance in another place that all observations founded upon the danger of usurpation, ought to be referred to the
composition and structure of the government, not to the nature or extent of its   *105*
powers. The state governments, by their original constitutions, are invested with
complete sovereignty. In what does our security consist against usurpations from
that quarter? Doubtless in the manner of their formation, and in a due dependence of those who are to administer them upon the people. If the proposed construction of the federal government, be found upon an impartial examination of   *110*
it, to be such as to afford, to a proper extent, the same species of security, all apprehensions on the score of usurpation ought to be discarded.

It should not be forgotten, that a disposition in the state governments to encroach upon the rights of the union, is quite as probable, as a disposition in the
union to encroach upon the rights of the state governments. What side would be   *115*
likely to prevail in such a conflict, must depend on the means which the contending parties could employ towards ensuring success. As in republics, strength
is always on the side of the people; and as there are weighty reasons to induce a
belief, that the state governments will commonly possess most influence over
them, the natural conclusion is, that such contests will be most apt to end to the   *120*
disadvantage of the union; and that there is greater probability of encroachments
by the members upon the federal head, than by the federal head upon the members. But it is evident, that all conjectures of this kind, must be extremely vague
and fallible, and that it is by far the safest course to lay them altogether aside; and
to confine our attention wholly to the nature and extent of the powers as they are   *125*
delineated in the constitution. Every thing beyond this, must be left to the prudence and firmness of the people; who, as they will hold the scales in their own
hands, it is to be hoped, will always take care to preserve the constitutional equilibrium between the general and the state governments. Upon this ground,
which is evidently the true one, it will not be difficult to obviate the objections   *130*
which have been made to an indefinite power of taxation in the United States.

PUBLIUS.

THIRTY-TWO
{NO. 31 IN NEWSPAPERS}

ALEXANDER HAMILTON
January 2, 1788
The Same Subject Continued

To the People of the State of New York.

Although I am of opinion that there would be no real danger of the consequences, which seem to be apprehended to the state governments, from a power
in the union to controul them in the levies of money; because I am persuaded
that the sense of the people, the extreme hazard of provoking the resentments of
5 the state governments, and a conviction of the utility and necessity of local administrations, for local purposes, would be a complete barrier against the oppressive use of such a power: Yet I am willing here to allow in its full extent the
justness of the reasoning, which requires that the individual states should possess
an independent and uncontrolable authority to raise their own revenues for the
10 supply of their own wants. And making this concession I affirm that (with the
sole exception of duties on imports and exports) they would under the plan of the
convention retain that authority in the most absolute and unqualified sense; and
that an attempt on the part of the national government to abridge them in the exercise of it would be a violent assumption of power unwarranted by any article or
15 clause of its constitution.

An intire consolidation of the states into one complete national sovereignty
would imply an intire subordination of the parts; and whatever powers might remain in them would be altogether dependent on the general will. But as the plan

---

Lines 16–49 The "general will" (line 18)—an expression recalling Jean-Jacques
Rousseau's (1712–1778) *Social Contract* (1762)—is here the will of the people of the
United States considered collectively, not as citizens of individuated states.

This paragraph marks the beginning of an important semantic transition in the
concept of sovereignty. In No. 15, lines 87–88, dated December 1, 1787 by Hamilton, an "*imperium in imperio*" is a self-contradiction, "a political monster." If federal
authority is to be augmented, the power of the states *must* correspondingly diminish;
for we know as a matter of theoretical principle that *sovereignty* is a power that
knows no superior. So what is left to the states cannot properly be called "sovereignty." In No. 20, lines 124–30, dated December 11, 1787 by Hamilton and Madison jointly, the concept of sovereignty over sovereigns is, again, "a political
monster." (Hamilton must have liked the expression.) Now, in No. 32, on January 2,
1788 by Hamilton, certain "rights" pertaining to sovereignty remain with the states.

of the convention aims only at a partial union or consolidation, the state governments would clearly retain all the rights of sovereignty which they before had and which were not by that act *exclusively* delegated to the United States. This exclusive delegation or rather this alienation of state sovereignty would only exist in three cases; where the constitution in express terms granted an exclusive authority to the union; where it granted in one instance an authority to the union and in another prohibited the states from exercising the like authority; and where it granted an authority to the union, to which a similar authority in the states would be absolutely and totally *contradictory* and *repugnant.* I use these terms to distinguish this last case from another which might appear to resemble it; but which would in fact be essentially different; I mean where the exercise of a concurrent jurisdiction might be productive of occasional interferences in the *policy* of any branch of administration, but would not imply any direct contradiction or repugnancy in point of constitutional authority. These three cases of exclusive jurisdiction in the federal government may be exemplified by the following instances: The last clause but one in the eighth section of the first article provides expressly that congress shall exercise *"exclusive legislation"* over the district to be appropriated as the seat of government. This answers to the first case. The first clause of the same section impowers congress *"to lay and collect taxes, duties, imposts and excises"* and the second clause of the tenth section of the same article declares that *"no state shall* without the consent of congress, *lay any imposts or duties on imports or exports* except for the purpose of executing its inspection laws." Hence would result an exclusive power in the union to lay duties on imports and exports with the particular exception mentioned; but this power is abriged by another clause which declares that no tax or duty shall be laid on articles exported from any state; in consequence of which qualification it now only extends to the *duties on imports.* This answers to the second case. The third will be found in that clause, which declares that congress shall have power "to establish an UNIFORM RULE of naturalization throughout the United States." This must necessarily be exclusive; because if each state had power to prescribe a DISTINCT RULE there could be no UNIFORM RULE.

A case which may perhaps be thought to resemble the latter, but which is in fact widely different, affects the question immediately under consideration. I mean the power of imposing taxes on all articles other than exports and imports. This, I contend, is manifestly a concurrent and coequal authority in the United

20

25

30

35

40

45

50

But he is careful to reaffirm that conflicting "sovereign" powers would be "totally *contradictory* and *repugnant"*—obviously still a "solecism." What is being offered by way of compromise is the argument that the formal *separation* of federal and state functions, under which the states can be reassured that they will retain such "rights" of sovereignty as have not been surrendered to the federal government, remains consistent with the hitherto prevailing concept of sovereignty adhering to the states. This use of sovereignty must be considered either a piece of semantic tactics, or a subtle but significant dilution of the concept itself. For further comment, see No. 39.

States and in the individual states. There is plainly no expression in the granting
55 clause which makes that power *exclusive* in the union. There is no independent
clause or sentence which prohibits the states from exercising it. So far is this from
being the case, that a plain and conclusive argument to the contrary is to be deducible from the restraint laid upon the states in relation to duties on imports
and exports. This restriction implies an admission, that if it were not inserted the
60 states would possess the power it excludes, and it implies a further admission,
that as to all other taxes the authority of the states remains undiminished. In any
other view it would be both unnecessary and dangerous; it would be unnecessary
because if the grant to the union of the power of laying such duties implied the
exclusion of the states, or even their subordination in this particular there could
65 be no need of such a restriction; it would be dangerous because the introduction
of it leads directly to the conclusion which has been mentioned and which if the
reasoning of the objectors be just, could not have been intended; I mean that the
states in all cases to which the restriction did not apply would have a concurrent
power of taxation with the union. The restriction in question amounts to what
70 lawyers call a NEGATIVE PREGNANT; that is a *negation* of one thing and an
affirmance of another; a negation of the authority of the states to impose taxes on
imports and exports, and an affirmance of their authority to impose them on all
other articles. It would be mere sophistry to argue that it was meant to exclude
them *absolutely* from the imposition of taxes of the former kind, and to leave
75 them at liberty to lay others *subject to the controul* of the national legislature. The
restraining or prohibitory clause only says, that they shall not *without the consent
of congress* lay such duties; and if we are to understand this in the sense last mentioned, the constitution would then be made to introduce a formal provision for
the sake of a very absurd conclusion; which is that the states *with the consent* of
80 the national legislature might tax imports and exports; and that they might tax
every other article *unless controuled* by the same body. If this was the intention,
why was it not left in the first instance to what is alleged to be the natural operation of the original clause conferring a general power of taxation upon the
union? It is evident that this could not have been the intention and that it will
85 not bear a construction of the kind.

As to a supposition of repugnancy between the power of taxation in the states
and in the union, it cannot be supported in that sense which would be requisite
to work an exclusion of the states. It is indeed possible that a tax might be laid on
a particular article by a state which might render it *inexpedient* that a further tax
90 should be laid on the same article by the union; but it would not imply a constitutional inability to impose a further tax. The quantity of the imposition, the

---

Lines 86–98 Hamilton and Madison are aware of the need to justify their argument.
The concept of "an immediate constitutional repugnancy" is a necessary reminder
that the states cannot contravene the federal Constitution—whose interpretation, of
course, will be in the hands of the new *federal* Supreme Court.
On the Court, see No. 78.

expediency or inexpediency of an increase on either side, would be mutually questions of prudence; but there would be involved no direct contradiction of power. The particular policy of the national and of the state systems of finance might now and then not exactly coincide, and might require reciprocal forbear- *95* ances. It is not however a mere possibility of inconvenience in the exercise of powers, but an immediate constitutional repugnancy, that can by implication alienate and extinguish a pre-existing right of sovereignty.

The necessity of a concurrent jurisdiction in certain cases results from the di- vision of the sovereign power; and the rule that all authorities of which the states *100* are not explicitly divested in favour of the union remain with them in full vigour, is not only a theoretical consequence of that division, but is clearly admitted by the whole tenor of the instrument which contains the articles of the proposed constitution. We there find that notwithstanding the affirmative grants of general authorities, there has been the most pointed care in those cases where it was *105* deemed improper that the like authorities should reside in the states, to insert negative clauses prohibiting the exercise of them by the states. The tenth section of the first article consists altogether of such provisions. This circumstance is a clear indication of the sense of the convention, and furnishes a rule of interpre- tation out of the body of the act which justifies the position I have advanced, and *110* refutes every hypothesis to the contrary.

PUBLIUS.

THIRTY-THREE
{NO. 31 IN NEWSPAPERS}

ALEXANDER HAMILTON
January 2, 1788
The Same Subject Continued

To the People of the State of New York.

The residue of the argument against the provisions in the constitution, in respect to taxation, is ingrafted upon the following clauses; the last clause of the eighth section of the first article, authorises the national legislature "to make all laws which shall be *necessary* and *proper*, for carrying into execution *the powers* by
5 that constitution vested in the government of the United States, or in any department or officer thereof"; and the second clause of the sixth article declares, that "the constitution and the Laws of the United States made *in pursuance thereof*, and the treaties made by their authority shall be the *supreme law* of the land; any thing in the constitution or laws of any state to the contrary notwithstanding."
10 These two clauses have been the sources of much virulent invective and petulant declamation against the proposed constitution, they have been held up to the people, in all the exaggerated colours of misrepresentation, as the pernicious engines by which their local governments were to be destroyed and their liberties exterminated—as the hideous monster whose devouring jaws would spare neither
15 sex nor age, nor high nor low, nor sacred nor profane; and yet strange as it may appear, after all this clamour, to those who may not have happened to contemplate them in the same light, it may be affirmed with perfect confidence, that the constitutional operation of the intended government would be precisely the same, if these clauses were entirely obliterated, as if they were repeated in every
20 article. They are only declaratory of a truth, which would have resulted by necessary and unavoidable implication from the very act of constituting a federal government, and vesting it with certain specified powers. This is so clear a proposition, that moderation itself can scarcely listen to the railings which have been so copiously vented against this part of the plan, without emotions that disturb its
25 equanimity.

Line 14 Another monster. The frequent appearance of these beasts suggests that the authors may have had in their minds Alexander Pope's satirical lines: "Vice is a monster of so frightful mien, / As, to be hated, needs but to be seen; / Yet, seen too oft, familiar with her face / We first endure, then pity, then embrace" (*Essay on Man*, 1.217).

What is a power, but the ability or faculty of doing a thing? What is the ability to do a thing but the power of employing the *means* necessary to its execution? What is a LEGISLATIVE power but a power of making LAWS? What are the *means* to execute a LEGISLATIVE power but LAWS? What is the power of laying and collecting taxes but a *legislative power,* or a power of *making laws,* to lay and collect taxes? What are the proper means of executing such a power but *necessary* and *proper* laws?

This simple train of enquiry furnishes us at once with a test of the true nature of the clause complained of. It conducts us to this palpable truth, that a power to lay and collect taxes must be a power to pass all laws *necessary* and *proper* for the execution of that power; and what does the unfortunate and calumniated provision in question do more than declare the same truth; to wit, that the national legislature to whom the power of laying and collecting taxes had been previously given, might in the execution of that power pass all laws *necessary* and *proper* to carry it into effect? I have applied these observations thus particularly to the power of taxation, because it is the immediate subject under consideration, and because it is the most important of the authorities proposed to be conferred upon the union. But the same process will lead to the same result in relation to all other powers declared in the constitution. And it is *expressly* to execute these powers, that the sweeping clause, as it has been affectedly called, authorises the national legislature to pass all *necessary* and *proper* laws. If there be anything exceptionable, it must be sought for in the specific powers, upon which this general declaration is predicated. The declaration itself, though it may be chargeable with tautology or redundancy, is at least perfectly harmless.

But SUSPICION may ask why then was it introduced? The answer is, that it could only have been done for greater caution, and to guard against all cavilling refinements in those who might hereafter feel a disposition to curtail and evade the legitimate authorities of the union. The convention probably foresaw what it has been a principal aim of these papers to inculcate that the danger which most threatens our political welfare, is, that the state governments will finally sap the foundations of the union; and might therefore think it necessary, in so cardinal a point, to leave nothing to construction. Whatever may have been the inducement to it, the wisdom of the precaution is evident from the cry which has been raised against it; as that very cry betrays a disposition to question the great and essential truth which it is manifestly the object of that provision to declare.

But it may be again asked, who is to judge of the *necessity* and *propriety* of the laws to be passed for executing the powers of the union? I answer first that this question arises as well and as fully upon the simple grant of those powers, as

---

Lines 53–57 Hamilton and Madison had every reason to know what "the convention probably foresaw. . . . " The Virginia Plan, introduced early in the proceedings on May 29, which effectively became the Convention's agenda, was designed to overcome the danger.

upon the declaratory clause: And I answer in the second place, that the national
65 government, like every other, must judge in the first instance of the proper exercise of its powers; and its constituents in the last. If the federal government
should overpass the just bounds of its authority, and make a tyrannical use of its
powers; the people whose creature it is must appeal to the standard they have
formed, and take such measures to redress the injury done to the constitution, as
70 the exigency may suggest and prudence justify. The propriety of a law in a constitutional light, must always be determined by the nature of the powers upon
which it is founded. Suppose by some forced constructions of its authority
(which indeed cannot easily be imagined) the federal legislature should attempt
to vary the law of descent in any state; would it not be evident that in making
75 such an attempt it had exceeded its jurisdiction and infringed upon that of the
state? Suppose again that upon the pretence of an interference with its revenues,
it should undertake to abrogate a land tax imposed by the authority of a state,
would it not be equally evident that this was an invasion of that concurrent jurisdiction in respect to this species of tax which its constitution plainly supposes to
80 exist in the state governments? If there ever should be a doubt on this head the
credit of it will be entirely due to those reasoners, who, in the imprudent zeal of
their animosity to the plan of the convention, have laboured to invelope it in a
cloud calculated to obscure the plainest and simplest truths.

But it is said, that the laws of the union are to be the *supreme law* of the land.
85 What inference can be drawn from this or what would they amount to, if they
were not to be supreme? It is evident they would amount to nothing. A LAW by
the very meaning of the term includes supremacy. It is a rule which those to
whom it is prescribed are bound to observe. This results from every political association. If individuals enter into a state of society the laws of that society must
90 be the supreme regulator of their conduct. If a number of political societies enter
into a larger political society, the laws which the latter may enact, pursuant to the
powers entrusted to it by its constitution, must necessarily be supreme over those
societies, and the individuals of whom they are composed. It would otherwise be
a mere treaty, dependent on the good faith of the parties, and not a government;
95 which is only another word for POLITICAL POWER AND SUPREMACY. But
it will not follow from this doctrine that acts of the larger society which are *not
pursuant* to its constitutional powers but which are invasions of the residuary authorities of the smaller societies will become the supreme law of the land. These
will be merely acts of usurpation and will deserve to be treated as such. Hence

---

Lines 84–124 These paragraphs introduce discussion of the Constitution as the
"*supreme law* of the land"—an expression that recalls the Magna Carta of 1215. But
how and by whom is the supreme law to be enforced? The full exposition of the
powers of the federal judiciary has to wait for No. 78, but, unusually, we are given
no forward reference, which raises the possibility that the authors had not yet
thought forward to that stage of the project.

we perceive that the clause which declares the supremacy of the laws of the *100* union, like the one we have just before considered, only declares a truth, which flows immediately and necessarily from the institution of a federal government. It will not, I presume, have escaped observation that it *expressly* confines this supremacy to laws made *pursuant to the constitution*; which I mention merely as an instance of caution in the convention; since that limitation would have been *105* to be understood though it had not been expressed.

Though a law therefore for laying a tax for the use of the United States would be supreme in its nature, and could not legally be opposed or controuled, yet a law for abrogating or preventing the collection of a tax laid by the authority of a state (unless upon imports and exports) would not be the supreme law of the *110* land, but an usurpation of power not granted by the constitution. As far as an improper accumulation of taxes on the same object might tend to render the collection difficult or precarious, this would be a mutual inconvenience not arising from a superiority or defect of power on either side, but from an injudicious exercise of power by one or the other, in a manner equally disadvantageous to both. *115* It is to be hoped and presumed however that mutual interest would dictate a concert in this respect which would avoid any material inconvenience. The inference from the whole is—that the individual states would, under the proposed constitution, retain an independent and uncontroulable authority to raise revenue to any extent of which they may stand in need by every kind of taxation ex- *120* cept duties on imports and exports. It will be shewn in the next paper that this concurrent jurisdiction in the article of taxation was the only admissible substitute for an intire subordination, in respect to this branch of power, of state authority to that of the union.

PUBLIUS.

THIRTY-FOUR
{NO. 32 IN NEWSPAPERS}

ALEXANDER HAMILTON
January 5, 1788
The Same Subject Continued

To the People of the State of New York.

I flatter myself it has been clearly shewn in my last number, that the particular states, under the proposed constitution, would have CO-EQUAL authority with the union in the article of revenue, except as to duties on imports. As this leaves open to the states far the greatest part of the resources of the community, there
5 can be no color for the assertion, that they would not possess means, as abundant as could be desired, for the supply of their own wants, independent of all external control. That the field is sufficiently wide, will more fully appear, when we come to develope the inconsiderable share of the public expences, for which, it will fall to the lot of the state governments to provide.
10   To argue upon abstract principles, that this co-ordinate authority cannot exist, would be to set up theory and supposition, against fact and reality. However proper such reasonings might be, to show that a thing *ought not to exist*, they are wholly to be rejected, when they are made use of to prove that it does not exist, contrary to the evidence of the fact itself. It is well known, that in the Roman re-
15 public, the legislative authority in the last resort, resided for ages in two different political bodies; not as branches of the same legislature, but as distinct and inde-

---

Lines 14–18 "It is well known . . . " allows for a variety of possible sources. Thomas Bever's *The History of the Legal Polity of the Roman State* had appeared in London, published by the publishers of Gibbon's *Decline and Fall of the Roman Empire*, as recently as 1781. Among well-known ancient historians, Polybius (ca. 200–120 B.C.), the celebrated Greek historian of Rome's struggles with Carthage, is often credited with the first exposition of the principle of separating the different elements of society into separate political institutions, a system also known as "checks and balances." This is sometimes seen as a prototype for the Senate and House of Representatives. But the American plan actually descends more immediately, though with different objectives, not from theories held in the ancient world but from the British principle by which different "estates" were held to be present in the two houses of Parliament. This is not to be confused with the "separation of powers," by which different branches or activities of government—executive, legislative, judicial—are given separate formal institutions. A marked preference for Rome over Greece emerges in the last sentence of the paragraph. Compare Hamilton on Greece in No. 6!

pendent legislatures, in each of which an opposite interest prevailed; in one, the Patrician—in the other, the Plebeian. Many arguments might have been adduced to prove the unfitness of two such seemingly contradictory authorities, each having power to *annul* or *repeal* the acts of the other. But a man would have been regarded as frantic, who should have attempted at Rome, to disprove their existence. It will readily be understood, that I allude to the COMITIA CENTURIATA, *and* COMITIA TRIBUTA. The former, in which the people voted by Centuries, was so arranged as to give a superiority to the Patrician interest: in the latter, in which numbers prevailed, the Plebeian interest had an entire predominancy. And yet these two legislatures co-existed for ages, and the Roman republic attained to the pinnacle of human greatness.

In the case particularly under consideration, there is no such contradiction as appears in the example cited, there is no power on either side to annul the acts of the other. And in practice, there is little reason to apprehend any inconvenience; because, in a short course of time, the wants of the states will naturally reduce themselves within *a very narrow compass;* and in the interim, the United States will, in all probability, find it convenient to abstain wholly from those objects, to which the particular states would be inclined to resort.

To form a more precise judgment of the true merits of this question, it will be well to advert to the proportion between the objects that will require a federal provision in respect to revenue; and those which will require a state provision. We shall discover that the former are altogether unlimited; and, that the latter are circumscribed within very moderate bounds. In pursuing this enquiry, we must bear in mind, that we are not to confine our view to the present period, but to look forward to remote futurity. Constitutions of civil government are not to be framed upon a calculation of existing exigencies; but upon a combination of these, with the probable exigencies of ages, according to the natural and tried course of human affairs. Nothing therefore can be more fallacious, than to infer the extent of any power, proper to be lodged in the national government, from an estimate of its immediate necessities. There ought to be a CAPACITY to provide for future contingencies, as they may happen; and, as these are illimitable in their nature, so it is impossible safely to limit that capacity. It is true, perhaps, that a computation might be made, with sufficient accuracy to answer the purpose of the quantity of revenue, requisite to discharge the subsisting engagements of the union, and to maintain those establishments, which for some time to come, would suffice in time of peace. But would it be wise, or would it not rather be the extreme of folly, to stop at this point, and to leave the government entrusted with the care of the national defence, in a state of absolute incapacity to provide for the protection of the community, against future invasions of the public peace, by foreign war, or domestic convulsions? If we must be obliged to exceed this point, where can we stop, short of an indefinite power of providing for emergencies as they may arise? Though it be easy to assert, in general terms, the possibility of forming a rational judgment of a due provision against probable dangers; yet we may safely challenge those who make the assertion, to bring forward their data, and may affirm, that they would be found as vague and uncertain, as any that could be produced to establish the probable duration of the world. Observations, confined to the mere prospects of internal attacks, can deserve no weight, though even these will admit of no satisfactory calculation: But if we mean to be a commercial people, 65 it must form a part of our policy, to be able one day to defend that commerce. The support of a navy, and of naval wars would involve contingencies that must baffle all the efforts of political arithmetic.

Admitting that we ought to try the novel and absurd experiment in politics, of tying up the hands of government from offensive war, founded upon reasons of 70 state: Yet, certainly we ought not to disable it from guarding the community against the ambition or enmity of other Nations. A cloud has been for some time hanging over the European world. If it should break forth into a storm, who can insure us, that in its progress, a part of its fury would not be spent upon us? No reasonable man would hastily pronounce that we are entirely out of its reach. Or 75 if the combustible materials that now seem to be collecting, should be dissipated without coming to maturity; or, if a flame should be kindled, without extending to us, what security can we have, that our tranquility will long remain undisturbed from some other cause, or from some other quarter? Let us recollect, that peace or war, will not always be left to our option; that however moderate or un-80 ambitious we may be, we cannot count upon the moderation, or hope to extinguish the ambition of others. Who could have imagined, at the conclusion of the last war, that France and Britain, wearied and exhausted as they both were, would so soon have looked with so hostile an aspect upon each other? To judge from the history of mankind, we shall be compelled to conclude, that the fiery 85 and destructive passions of war, reign in the human breast, with much more powerful sway, than the mild and beneficent sentiments of peace; and, that to model our political systems upon speculations of lasting tranquillity, would be to calculate on the weaker springs of the human character.

What are the chief sources of expence in every government? What has occa-90 sioned that enormous accumulation of debts with which several of the European Nations are oppressed? The answer, plainly is, wars and rebellions—the support of those institutions which are necessary to guard the body politic, against these two most mortal diseases of society. The expences arising from those institutions, which are relative to the mere domestic police of a state—to the support of its 95 legislative, executive and judiciary departments, with their different appendages,

---

Lines 68–88 These remarks, made early in 1788, reflect a sense of foreboding; Hamilton evidently studied European news closely. On August 2, 1787, Jefferson had written to Madison from Paris anticipating an "explosion" in France. Hamilton's gloomy views of human nature also make a renewed appearance.

Lines 89–98 Hamilton is shrewd in his estimate of the costs of war and preparations for war. The side that lost a prolonged war was not so much the side that lost a decisive battle, but the one that was the first to exhaust its treasury.

and to the encouragement of agriculture and manufactures, (which will comprehend almost all the objects of state expenditure) are insignificant in comparison with those which relate to the national defence.

In the kingdom of Great-Britain, where all the ostentatious apparatus of monarchy is to be provided for, not above a fifteenth part of the annual income _100_ of the nation is appropriated to the class of expences last mentioned; the other fourteen fifteenths are absorbed in the payment of the interest of debts, contracted for carrying on the wars in which that country has been engaged, and in the maintenance of fleets and armies. If on the one hand it should be observed, that the expences incurred in the prosecution of the ambitious enterprizes and _105_ vainglorious pursuits of a monarchy, are not a proper standard by which to judge of those which might be necessary in a republic; it ought on the other hand to be remarked, that there should be as great a disproportion, between the profusion and extravagance of a wealthy kingdom in its domestic administration, and the frugality and economy, which, in that particular, become the modest simplicity _110_ of republican government. If we balance a proper deduction from one side against that which it is supposed ought to be made from the other, the proportion may still be considered as holding good.

But let us take a view of the large debt which we have ourselves contracted in a single war, and let us only calculate on a common share of the events which _115_ disturb the peace of nations, and we shall instantly perceive without the aid of any elaborate illustration, that there must always be an immense disproportion between the objects of federal and state expenditure. It is true that several of the states separately are incumbered with considerable debts, which are an excrescence of the late war. But this cannot happen again, if the proposed system be _120_ adopted; and when these debts are discharged, the only call for revenue of any consequence, which the state governments will continue to experience, will be for the mere support of their respective civil lists; to which, if we add all contingencies, the total amount in every state, ought not to exceed two hundred thousand pounds. _125_

If it cannot be denied to be a just principle, that in framing a constitution of government for a nation, we ought in those provisions which are designed to be permanent, to calculate not on temporary, but on permanent causes of expence; our attention would be directed to a provision in favor of the state governments for an annual sum of about 200,000 pounds; while the exigencies of the union _130_ could be susceptible of no limits, even in imagination. In this view of the subject by what logic can it be maintained, that the local governments ought to command in perpetuity, an EXCLUSIVE source of revenue for any sum beyond the

---

Lines 99–104 The British civil list was authorized by Parliament, whose votes were published.

Lines 120–25 Hamilton must have studied the states' civil lists, published in the legislative journals or in their official _Votes and Proceedings_.

extent of 200,000 pounds? To extend its power further, in *exclusion* of the authority of the union, would be to take the resources of the community out of those hands which stood in need of them for the public welfare, in order to put them into other hands, which could have no just or proper occasion for them.

Suppose then the convention had been inclined to proceed upon the principle of a repartition of the objects of revenue between the union and its members, in *proportion* to their comparative necessities; what particular fund could have been selected for the use of the states, that would not either have been too much or too little; too little for their present, too much for their future wants? As to the line of separation between external and internal taxes, this would leave to the states at a rough computation, the command of two thirds of the resources of the community, to defray from a tenth to a twentieth of its expences, and to the union, one third of the resources of the community, to defray from nine tenths to nineteen twentieths of its expences. If we desert this boundary, and content ourselves with leaving to the states an exclusive power of taxing houses and lands, there would still be a great disproportion between the *means* and the *end*; the possession of one third of the resources of the community, to supply at most one tenth of its wants. If any fund could have been selected and appropriated equal to and not greater than the object, it would have been inadequate to the discharge of the existing debts of the particular states, and would have left them dependent on the union for a provision for this purpose.

The preceding train of observations will justify the position which has been elsewhere laid down, that "A CONCURRENT JURISDICTION in the article of taxation, was the only admissible substitute for an entire subordination, in respect to this branch of power, of state authority to that of the union." Any separation of the objects of revenue, that could have been fallen upon, would have amounted to a sacrifice of the great INTERESTS of the union to the POWER of the individual states. The convention thought the concurrent jurisdiction preferable to that subordination; and it is evident that it has at least the merit of reconciling an indefinite constitutional power of taxation in the federal government, with an adequate and independent power in the states to provide for their own necessities. There remain a few other lights, in which this important subject of taxation will claim a further consideration.

PUBLIUS.

THIRTY-FIVE
{NO. 33 IN NEWSPAPERS}

ALEXANDER HAMILTON
January 5, 1788
The Same Subject Continued

To the People of the State of New York.

Before we proceed to examine any other objections to an indefinite power of taxation in the union, I shall make one general remark; which is, that if the jurisdiction of the national government in the article of revenue should be restricted to particular objects, it would naturally occasion an undue proportion of the public burthens to fall upon those objects. Two evils would spring from this source, the oppression of particular branches of industry, and an unequal distribution of the taxes, as well among the several states as among the citizens of the same state.

Suppose, as has been contended for, the federal power of taxation were to be confined to duties on imports, it is evident that the government, for want of being able to command other resources, would frequently be tempted to extend these duties to an injurious excess. There are persons who imagine that it can never be the case; since the higher they are, the more it is alleged they will tend to discourage an extravagant consumption, to produce a favourable balance of trade, and to promote domestic manufactures. But all extremes are pernicious in various ways. Exorbitant duties on imported articles serve to beget a general spirit of smuggling; which is always prejudicial to the fair trader, and eventually to the revenue itself: They tend to render other classes of the community tributary in an improper degree to the manufacturing classes to whom they give a premature monopoly of the markets: They sometimes force industry out of its more natural channels into others in which it flows with less advantage. And in the last place they oppress the merchant, who is often obliged to pay them himself without any retribution from the consumer. When the demand is equal to the quantity of goods at market, the consumer generally pays the duty; but when the markets happen to be overstocked, a great proportion falls upon the merchant, and sometimes not only exhausts his profits, but breaks in upon his capital. I am apt to think that a division of the duty between the seller and the buyer more often happens than is commonly imagined. It is not always possible to raise the price of a commodity, in exact proportion to every additional imposition laid upon it. The merchant especially, in a country of small commercial capital, is often under a necessity of keeping prices down, in order to a more expeditious sale.

The maxim that the consumer is the payer, is so much oftener true than the reverse of the proposition, that it is far more equitable the duties on imports
35 should go into a common stock, than that they should redound to the exclusive benefit of the importing states. But it is not so generally true as to render it equitable that those duties should form the only national fund. When they are paid by the merchant, they operate as an additional tax upon the importing state; whose citizens pay their proportion of them in the character of consumers. In
40 this view they are productive of inequality among the states; which inequality would be encreased with the encreased extent of the duties. The confinement of the national revenues to this species of imposts, would be attended with inequality, from a different cause between the manufacturing and the non-manufacturing states. The states which can go furthest towards the supply of their own wants, by
45 their own manufactures, will not, according to their numbers or wealth, consume so great a proportion of imported articles, as those states which are not in the same favourable situation; they would not therefore in this mode alone contribute to the public treasury in a ratio to their abilities. To make them do this, it is necessary that recourse be had to excises; the proper objects of which are par-
50 ticular kinds of manufactures. New-York is more deeply interested in these considerations than such of her citizens as contend for limiting the power of the union to external taxation may be aware of—New-York is an importing state, and from a greater disproportion between her population and territory, is less likely, than some other states, speedily to become in any considerable degree a manu-
55 facturing state. She would of course suffer in a double light from restraining the jurisdiction of the union to commercial imposts.

So far as these observations tend to inculcate a danger of the import duties being extended to an injurious extreme it may be observed, conformably to a remark made in another part of these papers, that the interest of the revenue itself
60 would be a sufficient guard against such an extreme. I readily admit that this would be the case as long as other resources were open; but if the avenues to them were closed HOPE stimulated by necessity might beget experiments fortified by rigorous precautions and additional penalties; which for a time might have the intended effect, till there had been leisure to contrive expedients to elude these

---

Lines 33–56 Hamilton here tactically addresses fears of inequality among states, playing on an Anti-Federalist sentiment that he can hardly be said to share. The equal representation of the states in the Senate regardless of population produces a system of representation that Hamilton and Madison actually regarded as a gross *inequality*. Their own views of a desirable representation are reflected in the numerical arrangements for the House of Representatives. Virginia voted "no" to this compromise, reached on July 16, 1787, which was for Madison a disastrous defeat. (New York is not on the record; Hamilton and his colleagues do not appear to have been present that day.)

See Max Farrand, *Records of the Federal Convention of 1787*, 4 vols. (New Haven, 1937) II, 15–20.

new precautions. The first success would be apt to inspire false opinions; which it might require a long course of subsequent experience to correct. Necessity, especially in politics, often occasions false hopes, false reasonings and a system of measures, correspondently erroneous. But even if this supposed excess should not be a consequence of the limitation of the federal power of taxation the inequalities spoken of would still ensue, though not in the same degree, from the other causes that have been noticed. Let us now return to the examination of objections— 70

One, which if we may judge from the frequency of its repetition seems most to be relied on, is that the house of representatives is not sufficiently numerous for the reception of all the different classes of citizens; in order to combine the interests and feelings of every part of the community, and to produce a true 75 sympathy between the representative body and its constituents. This argument presents itself under a very specious and seducing form; and is well calculated to lay hold of the prejudices of those to whom it is addressed. But when we come to dissect it with attention it will appear to be made up of nothing but fair sounding words. The object it seems to aim at is in the first place impracticable, and in the 80 sense in which it is contended for is unnecessary. I reserve for another place the discussion of the question which relates to the sufficiency of the representative body in respect to numbers; and shall content myself with examining here the particular use which has been made of a contrary supposition in reference to the immediate subject of our inquiries. 85

The idea of an actual representation of all classes of the people by persons of each class is altogether visionary. Unless it were expressly provided in the constitution that each different occupation should send one or more members the thing would never take place in practice. Mechanics and manufacturers will always be inclined with few exceptions to give their votes to merchants in prefer- 90 ence to persons of their own professions or trades. Those discerning citizens are well aware that the mechanic and manufacturing arts furnish the materials of mercantile enterprise and industry. Many of them indeed are immediately connected with the operations of commerce. They know that the merchant is their

---

Lines 81–85 Discussion of "the sufficiency of the representative body in respect to numbers" is in No. 55.

Line 87 Here "visionary" means fanciful.

Lines 89–128 This passage expounds a view of social relations in which occupational groups are maintained in a stable relationship to each other, not by coercion or fear but by factors of deference and mutual interest. Hamilton's discussion of methods of attaining a valid form of representation is based on a concept of interest representation in which each of what we would now call "economic" interests is more unified than divided. Hamilton's glowing vision of the community of the landed interests overlooks the history of land riots in New York in the mid-1760s and ignores differences between landlords and their tenants in New York and New Jersey. He is right, however, in observing that moderate proprietors of land prevailed in both upper and lower houses by the time of writing.

95 natural patron and friend; and they are aware that however great the confidence they may justly feel in their own good sense, their interests can be more effectually promoted by the merchant than by themselves. They are sensible that their habits in life have not been such as to give them those acquired endowments, without which in a deliberative assembly the greatest natural abilities are for the 100 most part useless; and that the influence and weight and superior acquirements of the merchants render them more equal to a contest with any spirit which might happen to infuse itself into the public councils unfriendly to the manufacturing and trading interests. These considerations and many others that might be mentioned prove, and experience confirms it, that artisans and manufacturers 105 will commonly be disposed to bestow their votes upon merchants and those whom they recommend. We must therefore consider merchants as the natural representatives of all these classes of the community.

With regard to the learned professions, little need be observed; they truly form no distinct interest in society; and according to their situation and talents will be 110 indiscriminately the objects of the confidence and choice of each other and of other parts of the community.

Nothing remains but the landed interest; and this in a political view and particularly in relation to taxes I take to be perfectly united from the wealthiest landlord to the poorest tenant. No tax can be laid on land which will not affect the 115 proprietor of millions of acres as well as the proprietor of a single acre. Every land-holder will therefore have a common interest to keep the taxes on land as low as possible; and common interest may always be reckoned upon as the surest bond of sympathy. But if we even could suppose a distinction of interest between the opulent land-holder and the middling farmer, what reason is there to con- 120 clude that the first would stand a better chance of being deputed to the national legislature than the last? If we take fact as our guide and look into our own senate and assembly we shall find that moderate proprietors of land prevail in both; nor is this less the case in the senate which consists of a smaller number than in the assembly, which is composed of a greater number. Where the qualifications of 125 the electors are the same, whether they have to choose a small or a large number their votes will fall upon those in whom they have most confidence; whether these happen to be men of large fortunes or of moderate property or of no property at all.

It is said to be necessary that all classes of citizens should have some of their 130 own number in the representative body, in order that their feelings and interests may be the better understood and attended to. But we have seen that this will never happen under any arrangement that leaves the votes of the people free.

Lines 129–46 This account of the "interests" of landed property continues to assume an ideal unity between landlord and tenant in which the tenants' interests can be safely reposed in the care of their landlords.

For the promise of general economic improvement and national income, see No. 12.

Where this is the case, the representative body, with too few exceptions to have any influence on the spirit of the government, will be composed of land-holders, merchants, and men of the learned professions. But where is the danger that the interests and feelings of the different classes of citizens will not be understood or attended to by these three descriptions of men? Will not the land-holder know and feel whatever will promote or injure the interests of landed property? and will he not from his own interest in that species of property be sufficiently prone to resist every attempt to prejudice or incumber it? Will not the merchant understand and be disposed to cultivate as far as may be proper the interests of the mechanic and manufacturing arts to which his commerce is so nearly allied? Will not the man of the learned profession, who will feel a neutrality to the rival-ships between the different branches of industry, be likely to prove an impartial arbiter between them, ready to promote either, so far as it shall appear to him conducive to the general interests of the society?

If we take into the account the momentary humors or dispositions which may happen to prevail in particular parts of the society, and to which a wise administration will never be inattentive, is the man whose situation leads to extensive inquiry and information less likely to be a competent judge of their nature, extent and foundation than one whose observation does not travel beyond the circle of his neighbours and acquaintances? Is it not natural that a man who is a candidate for the favour of the people and who is dependent on the suffrages of his fellow-citizens for the continuance of his public honors should take care to inform himself of their dispositions and inclinations and should be willing to allow them their proper degree of influence upon his conduct? This dependence, and the necessity of being bound himself and his posterity by the laws to which he gives his assent are the true, and they are the strong chords of sympathy between the representative and the constituent.

There is no part of the administration of government that requires extensive information and a thorough knowledge of the principles of political economy so much as the business of taxation. The man who understands those principles best will be least likely to resort to oppressive expedients, or to sacrifice any particular class of citizens to the procurement of revenue. It might be demonstrated that the most productive system of finance will always be the least burthensome. There can be no doubt that in order to a judicious exercise of the power of taxation it is necessary that the person in whose hands it is should be acquainted with the general genius, habits and modes of thinking of the people at large and with the resources of the country. And this is all that can be reasonably meant by a knowledge of the interests and feelings of the people. In any other sense the proposition has either no meaning, or an absurd one. And in that sense let every considerate citizen judge for himself where the requisite qualification is most likely to be found.

PUBLIUS.

THIRTY-SIX
{NO. 34 IN NEWSPAPERS}

ALEXANDER HAMILTON
January 8, 1788
The Same Subject Continued

To the People of the State of New York.

We have seen that the result of the observations, to which the foregoing number has been principally devoted, is that from the natural operation of the different interests and views of the various classes of the community, whether the representation of the people be more or less numerous, it will consist almost entirely
5   of proprietors of land, of merchants and of members of the learned professions, who will truly represent all those different interests and views. If it should be objected that we have seen other descriptions of men in the local legislatures; I answer, that it is admitted there are exceptions to the rule, but not in sufficient number to influence the general complexion or character of the government.
10   There are strong minds in every walk of life that will rise superior to the disadvantages of situation, and will command the tribute due to their merit, not only from the classes to which they particularly belong, but from the society in general. The door ought to be equally open to all; and I trust, for the credit of human nature, that we shall see examples of such vigorous plants flourishing in the soil of federal,
15   as well as of state legislation; but occasional instances of this sort, will not render the reasoning founded upon the general course of things less conclusive.

The subject might be placed in several other lights that would lead all to the same result; and in particular it might be asked, what greater affinity or relation of interest can be conceived between the carpenter and blacksmith, and the
20   linen manufacturer or stocking weaver, than between the merchant and either of them? It is notorious, that there are often as great rivalships between different branches of the mechanic or manufacturing arts, as there are between any of the departments of labor and industry; so that unless the representative body were to

---

Lines 12–13 "The door ought to be equally open to all." Hamilton's commitment to equality of opportunity, expressed in this powerful passage, has too frequently been overlooked by historians. Hamilton, born out of wedlock on the West Indian island of Nevis, had every reason for this commitment.

Lines 17–26 Some twenty years on from this time of writing, labor relations had falsified this glowing view. In New York, the cordwainers (i.e., shoemakers) were tried and convicted on charges under the common law crime of conspiracy for combining to withdraw their labor in support of wage claims.

be far more numerous than would be consistent with any idea of regularity or wisdom in its deliberations, it is impossible that what seems to be the spirit of the objection we have been considering, should ever be realised in practice. But I forbear to dwell longer on a matter, which has hitherto worn too loose a garb to admit even of an accurate inspection of its real shape or tendency. *25*

There is another objection of a somewhat more precise nature which claims our attention. It has been asserted that a power of internal taxation in the national legislature could never be exercised with advantage, as well from the want of a sufficient knowledge of local circumstances as from an interference between the revenue laws of the union and of the particular states. The supposition of a want of proper knowledge, seems to be entirely destitute of foundation. If any question is depending in a state legislature respecting one of the counties which demands a knowledge of local details, how is it acquired? No doubt from the information of the members of the county. Cannot the like knowledge be obtained in the national legislature from the representatives of each state. And is it not to be presumed that the men who will generally be sent there, will be possessed of the necessary degree of intelligence, to be able to communicate that information? Is the knowledge of local circumstances, as applied to taxation, a minute topographical acquaintance with all the mountains, rivers, streams, highways and bye-paths in each state, or is it a general acquaintance with its situation and resources—with the state of its agriculture, commerce, manufactures—with the nature of its products and consumptions—with the different degrees and kinds of its wealth, property and industry? *30* *35* *40* *45*

Nations in general, even under governments of the more popular kind, usually commit the administration of their finances to single men or to boards composed of a few individuals, who digest and prepare, in the first instance, the plans of taxation, which are afterwards passed into laws by the authority of the sovereign or legislature. *50*

Inquisitive and enlightened statesmen are every where deemed best qualified to make a judicious selection of the objects proper for revenue; which is a clear indication, as far as the sense of mankind can have weight in the question, of the species of knowledge of local circumstances requisite to the purposes of taxation. *55*

The taxes intended to be comprised under the general denomination of internal taxes, may be subdivided into those of the *direct* and those of the *indirect* kind. Though the objection be made to both, yet the reasoning upon it seems to be confined to the former branch. And indeed, as to the latter, by which must be understood duties and excises on articles of consumption, one is at a loss to conceive what can be the nature of the difficulties apprehended. The knowledge relating to them, must evidently be of a kind that will either be suggested by the nature of the article itself, or can easily be procured from any well informed *60*

Lines 29–46 There are many discussions of conflicting powers of taxation. Examples are Federal Farmer, Letter III (October 10, 1787); Brutus I (October 18, 1787).

man, especially of the mercantile class. The circumstances that may distinguish
its situation in one state from its situation in another must be few, simple, and
easy to be comprehended. The principal thing to be attended to would be to
avoid those articles which had been previously appropriated to the use of a particular state; and there could be no difficulty in ascertaining the revenue system
of each. This could always be known from the respective codes of laws, as well as
from the information of the members of the several states.

The objection when applied to real property, or to houses and lands, appears
to have, at first sight, more foundation; but even in this view, it will not bear a
close examination. Land taxes are commonly laid in one of two modes, either by
actual valuations permanent or periodical, or by occasional assessments, at the
discretion or according to the best judgment of certain officers, whose duty it is
to make them. In either case the EXECUTION of the business, which alone requires the knowledge of local details, must be devolved upon discreet persons in
the character of commissioners or assessors, elected by the people or appointed
by the government for the purpose. All that the law can do must be to name the
persons or to prescribe the manner of their election or appointment, to fix their
numbers and qualifications; and to draw the general outlines of their powers and
duties. And what is there in all this, that cannot as well be performed by the national legislature as by a state legislature? The attention of either can only reach
to general principles; local details, as already observed, must be referred to those
who are to execute the plan.

But there is a simple point of view in which this matter may be placed, that
must be altogether satisfactory. The national legislature can make use of the *system of each state within that state*. The method of laying and collecting this
species of taxes in each state, can, in all its parts, be adopted and employed by the
federal government.

Let it be recollected, that the proportion of these taxes is not to be left to the
discretion of the national legislature: but is to be determined by the numbers of
each state as described in the second section of the first article. An actual census
or enumeration of the people must furnish the rule; a circumstance which effectually shuts the door to partiality or oppression. The abuse of this power of taxation seems to have been provided against with guarded circumspection. In
addition to the precaution just mentioned, there is a provision that "all duties,
imposts and excises, shall be UNIFORM throughout the United States."

It has been very properly observed by different speakers and writers on the side
of the constitution, that if the exercise of the power of internal taxation by the
union, should be judged beforehand upon mature consideration, or be discov-

---

Lines 99–112 The argument appears to reply to Federal Farmer III; in the same connection, see also Brutus III, which had appeared on January 3—and was itself a reply
to No. 23—examples of the flexibility of the plan of *The Federalist*, which could be
adapted to the development of the debate.

ered on experiment, to be really inconvenient, the federal government may forbear the use of it and have recourse to requisitions in its stead. By way of answer
to this, it has been triumphantly asked, why not in the first instance omit that ambiguous power and rely upon the latter resource? Two solid answers may be   105
given; the first is, that the actual exercise of the power, may be found both convenient and necessary; for it is impossible to prove in theory or otherwise than by
the experiment that it cannot be advantageously exercised. The contrary indeed
appears most probable. The second answer is, that the existence of such a power
in the constitution, will have a strong influence in giving efficacy to requisitions.   110
When the states know that the union can supply itself without their agency, it
will be a powerful motive for exertion on their part.

As to the interference of the revenue laws of the union, and of its members; we
have already seen that there can be no clashing or repugnancy of authority. The
laws cannot therefore in a legal sense, interfere with each other; and it is far from   115
impossible to avoid an interference even in the policy of their different systems.
An effectual expedient for this purpose will be mutually to abstain from those objects, which either side may have first had recourse to. As neither can *controul*
the other, each will have an obvious and sensible interest in this reciprocal forbearance. And where there is an *immediate* common interest, we may safely   120
count upon its operation. When the particular debts of the states are done away,
and their expences come to be limited within their natural compass, the possibility almost of interference will vanish. A small land tax will answer the purposes of
the states, and will be their most simple and most fit resource.

Many spectres have been raised out of this power of internal taxation to excite   125
the apprehensions of the people—double sets of revenue officers—a duplication
of their burthens by double taxations, and the frightful forms of odious and oppressive poll taxes, have been played off with all the ingenious dexterity of political legerdemain.

As to the first point, there are two cases, in which there can be no room for   130
double sets of officers; one where the right of imposing the tax is exclusively
vested in the union, which applies to the duties on imports; the other, where the
object has not fallen under any state regulation or provision, which may be applicable to a variety of objects. In other cases, the probability is, that the United
States will either wholly abstain from the objects pre-occupied for local pur-   135
poses, or will make use of the state officers and state regulations, for collecting
the additional imposition. This will best answer the views of revenue, because it
will save expence in the collection, and will best avoid any occasion of disgust to
the state governments and to the people. At all events, here is a practicable expedient for avoiding such an inconvenience; and nothing more can be required   140
than to show that evils predicted do not necessarily result from the plan.

Lines 125–95 See previous citations from the Federal Farmer for double sets of revenue officers, etc.

As to any argument derived from a supposed system of influence, it is a sufficient answer to say, that it ought not to be presumed; but the supposition is susceptible of a more precise answer. If such a spirit should infest the councils of the union, the most certain road to the accomplishment of its aim would be to employ the state officers as much as possible, and to attach them to the union by an accumulation of their emoluments. This would serve to turn the tide of state influence into the channels of the national government, instead of making federal influence flow in an opposite and adverse current. But all suppositions of this kind are invidious, and ought to be banished from the consideration of the great question before the people. They can answer no other end than to cast a mist over the truth.

As to the suggestion of double taxation, the answer is plain. The wants of the union are to be supplied in one way or another; if to be done by the authority of the federal government, it will not be to be done by that of the state governments. The quantity of taxes to be paid by the community, must be the same in either case; with this advantage, if the provision is to be made by the union, that the capital resource of commercial imposts, which is the most convenient branch of revenue, can be prudently improved to a much greater extent under federal than under state regulation, and of course will render it less necessary to recur to more inconvenient methods; and with this further advantage, that as far as there may be any real difficulty in the exercise of the power of internal taxation, it will impose a disposition to greater care in the choice and arrangement of the means; and must naturally tend to make it a fixed point of policy in the national administration to go as far as may be practicable in making the luxury of the rich tributary to the public treasury, in order to diminish the necessity of those impositions, which might create dissatisfaction in the poorer and most numerous classes of the society. Happy it is when the interest which the government has in the preservation of its own power, coincides with a proper distribution of the public burthens, and tends to guard the least wealthy part of the community from oppression!

As to poll taxes, I, without scruple, confess my disapprobation of them; and though they have prevailed from an early period in those states* which have uniformly been the most tenacious of their rights, I should lament to see them introduced into practice under the national government. But does it follow because there is a power to lay them, that they will actually be laid? Every state in the union has power to impose taxes of this kind; and yet in several of them they are unknown in practice. Are the state governments to be stigmatised as tyrannies because they possess this power? If they are not, with what propriety can the like power justify such a charge against the national government, or even be urged as an obstacle to its adoption? As little friendly as I am to the species of imposition, I still feel a thorough conviction, that the power of having recourse to

* The New-England states.

190

it ought to exist in the federal government. There are certain emergencies of na- tions, in which expedients that in the ordinary state of things ought to be fore- born, become essential to the public weal. And the government from the   *185* possibility of such emergencies ought ever to have the option of making use of them. The real scarcity of objects in this country, which may be considered as productive sources of revenue, is a reason peculiar to itself, for not abridging the discretion of the national councils in this respect. There may exist certain critical and tempestuous conjunctures of the state, in which a poll tax may become an   *190* inestimable resource. And as I know nothing to exempt this portion of the globe from the common calamities that have befallen other parts of it, I acknowledge my aversion to every project that is calculated to disarm the government of a sin- gle weapon, which in any possible contingency might be usefully employed for the general defence and security.   *195*

I have now gone through the examination of those powers proposed to be con- ferred upon the federal government; which relate more peculiarly to its energy, and to its efficiency for answering the great and primary objects of union. There are others, which though omitted here, will in order to render the view of the subject more complete, be taken notice of under the next head of our enquiries.   *200* I flatter myself the progress already made will have sufficed to satisfy the candid and judicious part of the community, that some of the objections which have been most strenuously urged against the constitution, and which were most for- midable in their first appearance, are not only destitute of substance, but if they had operated in the formation of the plan, would have rendered it incompetent   *205* to the great ends of public happiness and national prosperity. I equally flatter my- self that a further and more critical investigation of the system will serve to recommend it still more to every sincere and disinterested advocate for good gov- ernment; and will leave no doubt with men of this character of the propriety and expediency of adopting it. Happy will it be for ourselves, and most honorable for   *210* human nature, if we have wisdom and virtue enough, to set so glorious an example to mankind!

PUBLIUS.

Line 197 First use of the concept of "energy" as a necessary attribute of the new government.

THIRTY-SEVEN
{NO. 36 IN NEWSPAPERS}

JAMES MADISON
January 11, 1788
**Concerning the Difficulties Which the Convention
Must Have Experienced in the Formation of a Proper Plan**

To the People of the State of New York.

In reviewing the defects of the existing confederation, and shewing that they
cannot be supplied by a government of less energy than that before the public,
several of the most important principles of the latter fell of course under consideration. But as the ultimate object of these papers is to determine clearly and
5   fully the merits of this constitution, and the expediency of adopting it, our plan
cannot be compleated without taking a more critical and thorough survey of the
work of the convention; without examining it on all its sides; comparing it in all
its parts, and calculating its probable effects. That this remaining task may be executed under impressions conducive to a just and fair result, some reflections
10   must in this place be indulged, which candor previously suggests.

It is a misfortune, inseparable from human affairs, that public measures are
rarely investigated with that spirit of moderation which is essential to a just estimate of their real tendency to advance or obstruct the public good; and that this
spirit is more apt to be diminished than promoted, by those occasions which
15   require an unusual exercise of it. To those who have been led by experience to attend to this consideration, it could not appear surprising, that the act of the convention which recommends so many important changes and innovations, which
may be viewed in so many lights and relations, and which touches the springs of
so many passions and interests, should find or excite dispositions unfriendly both
20   on one side, and on the other, to a fair discussion and accurate judgment of its
merits. In some, it has been too evident from their own publications, that they
have scanned the proposed constitution, not only with a predisposition to censure; but with a predetermination to condemn: as the language held by others
betrays an opposite predetermination or bias, which must render their opinions
25   also of little moment in the question. In placing however, these different characters on a level, with respect to the weight of their opinions, I wish not to insinuate
that there may not be a material difference in the purity of their intentions. It is
but just to remark in favor of the latter description, that as our situation is universally admitted to be peculiarly critical, and to require indispensibly, that some-
30   thing should be done for our relief, the predetermined patron of what has been
actually done, may have taken his bias from the weight of these considerations,

as well as from considerations of a sinister nature. The predetermined adversary on the other hand, can have been governed by no venial motive whatever. The intentions of the first may be upright, as they may on the contrary be culpable. The views of the last cannot be upright, and must be culpable. But the truth is, that these papers are not addressed to persons falling under either of these characters. They solicit the attention of those only, who add to a sincere zeal for the happiness of their country, a temper favorable to a just estimate of the means of promoting it.

Persons of this character will proceed to an examination of the plan submitted by the convention, not only without a disposition to find or to magnify faults; but will see the propriety of reflecting that a faultless plan was not to be expected. Nor will they barely make allowances for the errors which may be chargeable on the fallibility to which the convention, as a body of men, were liable; but will keep in mind that they themselves also are but men, and ought not to assume an infallibility in rejudging the fallible opinions of others.

With equal readiness will it be perceived, that besides these inducements to candor, many allowances ought to be made for the difficulties inherent in the very nature of the undertaking referred to the convention.

The novelty of the undertaking immediately strikes us. It has been shewn in the course of these papers, that the existing confederation is founded on principles which are fallacious; that we must consequently change this first foundation, and with it, the superstructure resting upon it. It has been shewn, that the other confederacies which could be consulted as precedents, have been viciated by the same erroneous principles, and can therefore furnish no other light than that of beacons, which give warning of the course to be shunned, without pointing out that which ought to be pursued. The most that the convention could do in such a situation, was to avoid the errors suggested by the past experience of other countries, as well as of our own; and to provide a convenient mode of rectifying their own errors, as future experience may unfold them.

Among the difficulties encountered by the convention, a very important one must have lain, in combining the requisite stability and energy in government, with the inviolable attention due to liberty, and to the republican form. Without substantially accomplishing this part of their undertaking, they would have very imperfectly fulfilled the object of their appointment, or the expectation of the public: Yet, that it could not be easily accomplished, will be denied by no one, who is unwilling to betray his ignorance of the subject. Energy in government is essential to that security against external and internal danger, and to that prompt and salutary execution of the laws, which enter into the very definition of good

---

Lines 50–60 Refer to Nos. 18, 19, and 20.

Line 62 The word "energy" as needed by government appears now for the second time in this essay.

70　government. Stability in government, is essential to national character, and to the advantages annexed to it, as well as to that repose and confidence in the minds of the people, which are among the chief blessings of civil society. An irregular and mutable legislation, is not more an evil in itself, than it is odious to the people; and it may be pronounced with assurance, that the people of this 75　country, enlightened as they are, with regard to the nature, and interested, as the great body of them are, in the effects of good government, will never be satisfied, till some remedy be applied to the vicissitudes and uncertainties, which characterize the state administrations. On comparing, however, these valuable ingredients with the vital principles of liberty, we must perceive at once, the difficulty of 80　mingling them together in their due proportions. The genius of republican liberty, seems to demand on one side, not only that all power should be derived from the people; but, that those entrusted with it should be kept in dependence on the people, by a short duration of their appointments; and, that, even during this short period, the trust should be placed not in a few, but in a number of 85　hands. Stability, on the contrary, requires, that the hands, in which power is lodged, should continue for a length of time, the same. A frequent change of men will result from a frequent return of electors, and a frequent change of measures, from a frequent change of men: whilst energy in government requires not only a certain duration of power, but the execution of it by a single hand.

90　　How far the convention may have succeeded in this part of their work, will better appear on a more accurate view of it. From the cursory view, here taken, it must clearly appear to have been an arduous part.

　　Not less arduous must have been the task of marking the proper line of partition, between the authority of the general, and that of the state governments. 95　Every man will be sensible of this difficulty, in proportion, as he has been accustomed to contemplate and discriminate objects, extensive and complicated in their nature. The faculties of the mind itself have never yet been distinguished and defined, with satisfactory precision, by all the efforts of the most acute and metaphysical Philosophers. Sense, perception, judgment, desire, volition, mem-100　ory, imagination, are found to be separated by such delicate shades, and minute gradations, that their boundaries have eluded the most subtle investigations, and remain a pregnant source of ingenious disquisition and controversy. The boundaries between the great kingdoms of nature, and still more, between the various

---

Lines 82–83 "[I]n dependence on the people. . . . " The point here is that republican government draws its authority from the people but must be independent of their day-to-day shifts of opinion. Opinion polls have done much to alter this view of government.

Lines 93–111 This paragraph adopts the formalistic psychology that viewed the mind as constituted of distinct "faculties"; this typology was deeply engrained in the Western philosophical tradition, having been inherited from the ancient world through medieval philosophy.

provinces, and lesser portions, into which they are subdivided, afford another illustration of the same important truth. The most sagacious and laborious natu-
ralists have never yet succeeded, in tracing with certainty, the line which
separates the district of vegetable life from the neighboring region of unorgan-
ized matter, or which marks the termination of the former and the commencement of the animal empire. A still greater obscurity lies in the distinctive
characters, by which the objects in each of these great departments of nature,
have been arranged and assorted.

When we pass from the works of nature, in which all the delineations are perfectly accurate, and appear to be otherwise only from the imperfection of the eye
which surveys them, to the institutions of man, in which the obscurity arises as
well from the object itself, as from the organ by which it is contemplated; we must
perceive the necessity of moderating still farther our expectations and hopes from
the efforts of human sagacity. Experience has instructed us that no skill in the science of government has yet been able to discriminate and define, with sufficient
certainty, its three great provinces, the legislative, executive and judiciary; or even
the privileges and powers of the different legislative branches. Questions daily
occur in the course of practice, which prove the obscurity which reigns in these
subjects, and which puzzles the greatest adepts in political science.

The experience of ages, with the continued and combined labors of the most
enlightened legislators and jurists, have been equally unsuccessful in delineating
the several objects and limits of different codes of laws and different tribunals of
justice. The precise extent of the common law, the statute law, the maritime law,
the ecclesiastical law, the law of corporations and other local laws and customs,
remain still to be clearly and finally established in Great-Britain, where accuracy

105

110

115

120

125

Lines 123–51 By the time of the founding of the American colonies, common law
had established a considerable measure of precedence over other forms of jurisprudence. There was a certain rivalry between common law and equity or chancery
courts. The notorious prerogative courts, notably the Court of Star Chamber, were
abolished in 1641 by the parliament that became the Long Parliament. Madison is
right in saying that the boundaries were uncertain and subject to fluctuation. In general, ecclesiastical law as a separate branch of jurisprudence did not cross the ocean,
and neither did the law, or laws, of corporations (an example of which would be the
medieval corporate status of the City of London; city corporations such as that of New
York exercised much more limited powers). The colonial situation was simpler, and
common law in the colonies tended to subsume other types of jurisdiction. Some
colonies, notably Pennsylvania, had had no chancery division since the 1730s.

This paragraph contains Madison's reflection on the imperfections of language as
a medium for communication of thought, an observation that has attracted attention
from scholars interested in the "linguistic turn" in the interpretation of political discourse. Although the remark about "the Almighty" (line 149) may appear to the p. 196
skeptical mind as tinged with irony, Madison, a devout Christian, was not in the habit
of introducing ironic humor into his writings, least of all about the Deity, and must

in such subjects has been more industriously pursued than in any other part of
130 the world. The jurisdiction of her several courts, general and local, of law, of equity, of admiralty, &c. is not less a source of frequent and intricate discussions,
sufficiently denoting the indeterminate limits by which they are respectively circumscribed. All new laws, though penned with the greatest technical skill, and
passed on the fullest and most mature deliberation, are considered as more or
135 less obscure and equivocal, until their meaning be liquidated and ascertained by
a series of particular discussions and adjudications. Besides the obscurity arising
from the complexity of objects, and the imperfection of the human faculties, the
medium through which the conceptions of men are conveyed to each other,
adds a fresh embarrassment. The use of words is to express ideas. Perspicuity
140 therefore requires not only that the ideas should be distinctly formed, but that
they should be expressed by words distinctly and exclusively appropriated to
them. But no language is so copious as to supply words and phrases for every
complex idea, or so correct as not to include many equivocally denoting different
ideas. Hence, it must happen, that however accurately objects may be discrimi-
145 nated in themselves, and however accurately the discrimination may be considered, the definition of them may be rendered inaccurate by the inaccuracy of the
terms in which it is delivered. And this unavoidable inaccuracy must be greater
or less, according to the complexity and novelty of the objects defined. When the
Almighty himself condescends to address mankind in their own language, his
150 meaning, luminous as it must be, is rendered dim and doubtful, by the cloudy
medium through which it is communicated.

Here then are three sources of vague and incorrect definitions; indistinctness
of the object, imperfection of the organ of conception, inadequateness of the ve-
hicle of ideas. Any one of these must produce a certain degree of obscurity. The
155 convention, in delineating the boundary between the federal and state jurisdictions, must have experienced the full effect of them all.

To the difficulties already mentioned, may be added the interfering pretensions of the larger and smaller states. We cannot err in supposing that the former
would contend for a participation in the government, fully proportioned to their
160 superior wealth and importance; and that the latter would not be less tenacious
of the equality at present enjoyed by them. We may well suppose that neither
side would entirely yield to the other, and consequently that the struggle could

---

be taken at face value. In view, however, of his own recent struggles in the cause of
religious freedom and his condemnation of dogmatism in Virginia, he was clearly
making the point that no one can be certain of possessing exclusive understanding of
the meaning and intention of Scripture.

Lines 158–61 We observe that superior wealth confers superior importance. Madison, of course, speaks from immediate knowledge of the struggles in the convention,
resulting in several major compromises. He had not himself approved of the compromise over the Senate. See Brief Chronology, p. xl: "Connecticut Compromise."

be terminated only by compromise. It is extremely probable also, that after the ratio of representation had been adjusted, this very compromise must have produced a fresh struggle between the same parties, to give such a turn to the organization of the government, and to the distribution of its powers, as would encrease the importance of the branches, in forming which they had respectively obtained the greatest share of influence. There are features in the constitution which warrant each of these suppositions; and as far as either of them is well founded, it shews that the convention must have been compelled to sacrifice theoretical propriety to the force of extraneous considerations.

Nor could it have been the large and small states only which would marshal themselves in opposition to each other on various points. Other combinations, resulting from a difference of local position and policy, must have created additional difficulties. As every state may be divided into different districts, and its citizens into different classes, which give birth to contending interests and local jealousies; so the different parts of the United States are distinguished from each other, by a variety of circumstances, which produce a like effect on a larger scale. And although this variety of interests, for reasons sufficiently explained in a former paper, may have a salutary influence on the administration of the government when formed; yet every one must be sensible of the contrary influence which must have been experienced in the task of forming it.

Would it be wonderful if under the pressure of all these difficulties, the convention should have been forced into some deviations from that artificial structure and regular symmetry, which an abstract view of the subject might lead an ingenious theorist to bestow on a constitution planned in his closet or in his imagination? The real wonder is, that so many difficulties should have been surmounted; and surmounted with a unanimity almost as unprecedented as it must have been unexpected. It is impossible for any man of candor to reflect on this circumstance, without partaking of the astonishment. It is impossible for the man of pious reflection not to perceive in it, a finger of that Almighty hand which has been so frequently and signally extended to our relief in the critical stages of the revolution.

We had occasion in a former paper, to take notice of the repeated trials which have been unsuccessfully made in the United Netherlands, for reforming the baneful and notorious vices of their constitution. The history of almost all the great councils and consultations, held among mankind for reconciling their discordant opinions, assuaging their mutual jealousies, and adjusting their respective interests, is a history of factions, contentions, and disappointments; and may be

---

Lines 179–82 The former paper referred to appears to be No. 10.

Lines 196–213 Madison's skeptical appraisal of human nature seems to converge with Hamilton's, but Madison emerges with hopes for as much virtue as republican government needs.

200 classed among the most dark and degrading pictures which display the infirmities and depravities of the human character. If, in a few scattered instances, a brighter aspect is presented, they serve only as exceptions to admonish us of the general truth; and by their lustre to darken the gloom of the adverse prospect to which they are contrasted. In revolving the causes from which these exceptions

205 result, and applying them to the particular instance before us, we are necessarily led to two important conclusions. The first is, that the convention must have enjoyed in a very singular degree, an exemption from the pestilential influence of party animosities; the diseases most incident to deliberative bodies, and most apt to contaminate their proceedings. The second conclusion is, that all the deputa-

210 tions composing the convention, were either satisfactorily accommodated by the final act; or were induced to accede to it, by a deep conviction of the necessity of sacrificing private opinions and partial interests to the public good, and by a despair of seeing this necessity diminished by delays or by new experiments.

PUBLIUS.

Line 204 Here "revolving" means considering, i.e., turning over in our minds.

Lines 209–13 This conclusion suppresses the fact that although "all the deputations" may have acceded to the final draft, several members of the Convention had declined to sign it.

THIRTY-EIGHT
{NO. 37 IN NEWSPAPERS}

JAMES MADISON

January 12, 1788

The Subject Continued, and the Incoherence of the
Objections to the Plan Exposed

To the People of the State of New York.

It is not a little remarkable that in every case reported by antient history, in which government has been established with deliberation and consent, the task of framing it has not been committed to an assembly of men; but has been performed by some individual citizen of pre-eminent wisdom and approved integrity.

Minos, we learn, was the primitive founder of the government of Crete; as Zaleucus was of that of the Locrians. Theseus first, and after him Draco and Solon, instituted the government of Athens. Lycurgus was the Lawgiver of Sparta. The foundation of the original government of Rome was laid by Romulus; and the work compleated by two of his elective successors, Numa, and Tullus Hostilius. On the abolition of Royalty, the consular administration was substituted by Brutus, who stepped forward with a project for such a reform, which he alledged had been prepared by Servius Tullius, and to which his address obtained the assent and ratification of the senate and people. This remark is applicable to confederate governments also. Amphyction, we are told, was the author of that which bore his name. The Achaean League received its first birth from Achaeus and its second from Aratus.

What degree of agency these reputed Lawgivers might have in their respective establishments, or how far they might be cloathed with the legitimate authority of the people, cannot in every instance be ascertained. In some, however, the

---

Lines 5–16 Madison appears to take literally the legend of the founding of Rome—which Plutarch had viewed as mythological. The attributions listed in this paragraph are in the province of legend (as suggested by "we learn" and "we are told"), but serve Madison's purpose, which is to argue that it is appropriate for a citizen "of pre-eminent wisdom and approved integrity" (in the present case represented by the Constitutional Convention) to draft laws for the approval of the people at large. Draco (ca. 7th century B.C.) was the Athenian lawgiver whose laws were so severe that we still use the adjective "draconian."

Plutarch records of Solon (638 B.C.–539 B.C.) that he said he was giving not the best laws, but the best that the people would receive—a remark repeated in adapted form by Madison in this essay.

20 proceeding was strictly regular. Draco appears to have been entrusted by the people of Athens, with indefinite powers to reform its government and laws. And Solon, according to Plutarch, was in a manner compelled by the universal suffrage of his fellow citizens, to take upon him the sole and absolute power of new modelling the constitution. The proceedings under Lycurgus were less regular;

25 but as far as the advocates for a regular reform could prevail, they all turned their eyes towards the single efforts of that celebrated patriot and sage, instead of seeking to bring about a revolution, by the intervention of a deliberative body of citizens.

Whence could it have proceeded that a people jealous as the Greeks were of

30 their liberty, should so far abandon the rules of caution, as to place their destiny in the hands of a single citizen? Whence could it have proceeded, that the Atheniens, a people who would not suffer an army to be commanded by fewer than ten generals, and who required no other proof of danger to their liberties than the illustrious merit of a fellow citizen should consider one illustrious citizen as

35 a more eligible depository of the fortunes of themselves and their posterity, than a select body of citizens, from whose common deliberations more wisdom, as well as more safety, might have been expected? These questions cannot be fully answered without supposing that the fears of discord and disunion among a number of Counsellors, exceeded the apprehension of treachery or incapacity in a

40 single individual. History informs us likewise of the difficulties with which these celebrated reformers had to contend; as well as of the expedients which they were obliged to employ, in order to carry their reforms into effect. Solon, who seems to have indulged a more temporising policy, confessed that he had not given to his countrymen the government best suited to their happiness, but most

45 tolerable to their prejudices. And Lycurgus, more true to his object, was under the necessity of mixing a portion of violence with the authority of superstition; and of securing his final success, by a voluntary renunciation, first of his country, and then of his life. If these lessons teach us, on one hand, to admire the improvement made by America on the ancient mode of preparing and establishing

50 regular plans of government; they serve not less on the other, to admonish us of the hazards and difficulties incident to such experiments, and of the great imprudence of unnecessarily multiplying them.

Is it an unreasonable conjecture that the errors which may be contained in the plan of the convention are such as have resulted rather from the defect of an-

55 tecedent experience on this complicated and difficult subject, than from a want of accuracy or care in the investigation of it; and consequently such as will not be

---

Lines 53–75 Madison himself here comes close to admitting that the Constitution contains errors. When his own notes of the debates were published after his death in 1836, it became known that he had opposed the compromise that gave the states equal voting rights in the Senate. The reference to New Jersey's position shows that some of what had passed in the Convention had already leaked.

ascertained until an actual trial shall have pointed them out? This conjecture is rendered probable not only by many considerations of a general nature, but by the particular case of the articles of confederation. It is observable that among the numerous objections and amendments suggested by the several states, when these articles were submitted for their ratification, not one is found which alludes to the great and radical error, which on actual trial has discovered itself. And if we except the observations which New-Jersey was led to make rather by her local situation than by her peculiar foresight, it may be questioned whether a single suggestion was of sufficient moment to justify a revision of the system. There is abundant reason nevertheless to suppose that immaterial as these objections were they would have been adhered to with a very dangerous inflexibility in some states, had not a zeal for their opinions and supposed interests, been stifled by the more powerful sentiment of self-preservation. One state, we may remember, persisted for several years in refusing her concurrence, although the enemy remained the whole period at our gates, or rather in the very bowels of our country. Nor was her pliancy in the end effected by a less motive than the fear of being chargeable with protracting the public calamities, and endangering the event of the contest. Every candid reader will make the proper reflections on these important facts.

A patient who finds his disorder daily growing worse; and that an efficacious remedy can no longer be delayed without extreme danger; after cooly revolving his situation, and the characters of different physicians, selects and calls in such of them as he judges most capable of administering relief, and best entitled to his confidence. The physicians attend: The case of the patient is carefully examined: a consultation is held. They are unanimously agreed that the symptoms are critical, but that the case, with proper and timely relief, is so far from being desperate, that it may be made to issue in an improvement of his constitution. They are equally equanimous in prescribing the remedy by which this happy effect is to be produced. The prescription is no sooner made known however, than a number of persons interpose, and without denying the reality or danger of the disorder, assure the patient that the prescription will be poison to his constitution, and forbid him under pain of certain death to make use of it. Might not the patient reasonably demand before he ventured to follow this advice, that the authors of it should at least agree among themselves, on some other remedy to be substituted? and if he found them differing as much from one another, as from his first counsellors, would he not act prudently, in trying the experiment unanimously recommended by the latter, rather than in hearkening to those who could neither deny the necessity of a speedy remedy, nor agree in proposing one?

The "one state" that had refused concurrence to the Articles (until 1781) was Maryland.

Line 92 The "unanimously" in the final sentence of this paragraph is tendentious, in view of the withdrawals from the Convention before its conclusion.

95   Such a patient, and in such a situation is America at this moment. She has been sensible of her malady. She has obtained a regular and unanimous advice from men of her own deliberate choice. And she is warned by others against following this advice, under pain of the most fatal consequences. Do the monitors deny the reality of her danger? No. Do they deny the necessity of some speedy

100 and powerful remedy? No. Are they agreed, are any two of them agreed in their objections to the remedy proposed, or in the proper one to be substituted? Let them speak for themselves. This one tells us that the proposed constitution ought to be rejected, because it is not a confederation of the states, but a government over individuals. Another admits that it ought to be a government over individu-

105 als, to a certain extent, but by no means to the extent proposed. A third does not object to the government over individuals, or to the extent proposed, but to the want of a bill of rights. A fourth concurs in the absolute necessity of a bill of rights, but contends that it ought to be declaratory not of the personal rights of individuals, but of the rights reserved to the states in their political capacity. A fifth

110 is of opinion that a bill of rights of any sort would be superfluous and misplaced, and that the plan would be unexceptionable, but for the fatal power of regulating the times and places of election. An objector in a large state exclaims loudly against the unreasonable equality of representation in the senate. An objector in a small state is equally loud against the dangerous inequality in the house of rep-

115 resentatives. From this quarter we are alarmed with the amazing expence from the number of persons who are to administer the new government. From another quarter, and sometimes from the same quarter, on another occasion, the cry is, that the congress will be but the shadow of a representation, and that the government would be far less objectionable, if the number and the expence were dou-

120 bled. A patriot in a state that does not import or export, discerns insuperable objections against the power of direct taxation. The patriotic adversary in a state of great exports and imports, is not less dissatisfied that the whole burden of taxes may be thrown on consumption. This politician discovers in the constitution a direct and irresistible tendency to monarchy. That is equally sure, it will end in

125 aristocracy. Another is puzzled to say which of these shapes it will ultimately assume, but sees clearly it must be one or other of them. Whilst a fourth is not wanting who with no less confidence affirms that the constitution is so far from having a bias towards either of these dangers, that the weight on that side will not be sufficient to keep it upright and firm against its opposite propensities. With

130 another class of adversaries to the constitution, the language is that the legislative, executive and judiciary departments are intermixed in such a manner as to contradict all the ideas of regular government, and all the requisite precautions in favour of liberty. Whilst this objection circulates in vague and general expressions, there are not a few who lend their sanction to it. Let each one come for-

135 ward with his particular explanation and scarce any two are exactly agreed on the subject. In the eyes of one the junction of the senate with the president in the responsible function of appointing to offices, instead of vesting this executive power in the executive, alone, is the vicious part of the organization. To another,

the exclusion of the house of representatives whose numbers alone could be a due security against corruption and partiality in the exercise of such a power, is *140* equally obnoxious. With another, the admission of the president into any share of a power which must ever be a dangerous engine in the hands of the executive magistrate, is an unpardonable violation of the maxims of republican jealousy. No part of the arrangement according to some is more admissible than the trial of impeachments by the senate, which is alternately a member both of the legislative *145* and executive departments, when this power so evidently belonged to the judiciary department. We concur fully, reply others, in the objection to this part of the plan, but we can never agree that a reference of impeachments to the judiciary authority would be an amendment of the error. Our principal dislike to the organisation arises from the extensive powers already lodged in that department. Even among *150* the zealous patrons of a council of state, the most irreconcilable variance is discovered concerning the mode in which it ought to be constituted. The demand of one gentleman is that the council should consist of a small number, to be appointed by the most numerous branch of the legislature. Another would prefer a larger number, and considers it as a fundamental condition that the appointment should be *155* made by the president himself.

As it can give no umbrage to the writers against the plan of the federal constitution, let us suppose that as they are the most zealous, so they are also the most sagacious of those who think the late convention were unequal to the task assigned them, and that a wiser and better plan might and ought to be substituted. *160* Let us further suppose that their country should concur both in this favorable opinion of their merits, and in their unfavorable opinion of the convention, and should accordingly proceed to form them into a second convention, with full powers and for the express purpose of revising and remoulding the work of the first. Were the experiment to be seriously made, though it requires some effort to *165* view it seriously even in fiction, I leave it to be decided by the sample of opinions just exhibited, whether with all their enmity to their predecessors, they would in any one point depart so widely from their example, as in the discord and ferment that would mark their own deliberations; and whether the constitution, now before the public, would not stand as fair a chance for immortality, as Lycurgus *170* gave to that of Sparta, by making its change to depend on his own return from exile and death, if it were to be immediately adopted, and were to continue in force, not until a BETTER, but until ANOTHER should be agreed upon by this new assembly of Lawgivers.

It is a matter both of wonder and regret, that those who raise so many objec- *175* tions against the new constitution, should never call to mind the defects of that which is to be exchanged for it. It is not necessary that the former should be perfect; it is sufficient that the latter is more imperfect. No man would refuse to give brass for silver or gold, because the latter had some alloy in it. No man would refuse to quit a shattered and tottering habitation, for a firm and commodious *180* building, because the latter had not a porch to it; or because some of the rooms might be a little larger or smaller, or the ceiling a little higher or lower than his

fancy would have planned them. But waving illustrations of this sort, is it not manifest that most of the capital objections urged against the new system, lie
185 with tenfold weight against the existing confederation? Is an indefinite power to raise money dangerous in the hands of a federal government? The present congress can make requisitions to any amount they please; and the states are constitutionally bound to furnish them; they can emit bills of credit as long as they will pay for the paper; they can borrow both abroad and at home, as long as a shilling
190 will be lent. Is an indefinite power to raise troops dangerous? The confederation gives to congress that power also; and they have already begun to make use of it. Is it improper and unsafe to intermix the different powers of government in the same body of men? Congress, a single body of men, are the sole depository of all the federal powers. Is it particularly dangerous to give the keys of the treasury,
195 and the command of the army, into the same hands? The confederation places them both in the hands of congress. Is a Bill of Rights essential to liberty? The confederation has no Bill of Rights. Is it an objection against the new constitution, that it empowers the senate with the concurrence of the executive to make treaties which are to be the laws of the land? The existing congress, without any
200 such controul, can make treaties which they themselves have declared, and most of the states have recognized, to be the supreme law of the land. Is the importation of slaves permitted by the new constitution for twenty years? By the old, it is permitted for ever.

I shall be told that however dangerous this mixture of powers may be in the-
205 ory, it is rendered harmless by the dependence of congress on the states for the means of carrying them into practice: That however large the mass of powers may be, it is in fact a lifeless mass. Then say I in the first place, that the confederation is chargeable with the still greater folly of declaring certain powers in the federal government to be absolutely necessary, and at the same time rendering
210 them absolutely nugatory: And in the next place, that if the union is to continue, and no better government be substituted, effective powers must either be granted to or assumed by the existing congress, in either of which events the contrast just stated will hold good. But this is not all. Out of this lifeless mass has already grown an excrescent power, which tends to realize all the dangers that can be ap-
215 prehended from a defective construction of the supreme government of the union. It is now no longer a point of speculation and hope that the Western territory is a mine of vast wealth to the United States, and although it is not of such a nature as to extricate them from their present distresses, or for some time to come, to yield any regular supplies for the public expences, yet must it hereafter
220 be able under proper management both to effect a gradual discharge of the domestic debt, and to furnish for a certain period, liberal tributes to the federal

---

Lines 216–42 The Ordinance of 1787 was a sweeping exercise of power for so debilitated a body as the dying Congress; it laid down conditions for territorial government and eventual statehood in the vast areas of the Ohio Valley. See note to No. 7, lines 10–44.

treasury. A very large proportion of this fund has been already surrendered by individual states; and it may with reason be expected, that the remaining states will not persist in withholding similar proofs of their equity and generosity. We may calculate therefore that a rich and fertile country, of an area equal to the inhabitated extent of the United States, will soon become a national stock. Congress have assumed the administration of this stock. They have begun to render it productive. Congress have undertaken to do more; they have proceeded to form new states; to erect temporary governments; to appoint officers for them; and to prescribe the conditions on which such states shall be admitted into the confederacy. All this has been done; and done without the least colour of constitutional authority. Yet no blame has been whispered; no alarm has been sounded. A GREAT and INDEPENDENT fund of revenue is passing into the hands of a SINGLE BODY of men, who can RAISE TROOPS to an INDEFINITE NUMBER, and appropriate money to their support for an INDEFINITE PERIOD OF TIME. And yet there are men who have not only been silent spectators of this prospect; but who are advocates for the system which exhibits it; and at the same time urge against the new system the objections which we have heard. Would they not act with more consistency in urging the establishment of the latter, as no less necessary to guard the union against the future powers and resources of a body constructed like the existing congress, than to save it from the dangers threatened by the present impotency of that assembly?

I mean not by any thing here said to throw censure on the measures which have been pursued by congress. I am sensible they could not have done otherwise. The public interest, the necessity of the case, imposed upon them the task of overleaping their constitutional limits. But is not the fact an alarming proof of the danger resulting from a government which does not possess regular powers commensurate to its objects? A dissolution or usurpation is the dreadful dilemma to which it is continually exposed.

PUBLIUS.

THIRTY-NINE
{NO. 38 IN NEWSPAPERS}

JAMES MADISON

January 16, 1788

The Conformity of the Plan to Republican Principles:

An Objection in Respect to the Powers of the Convention, Examined

To the People of the State of New York.

The last paper having concluded the observations which were meant to introduce a candid survey of the plan of government reported by the convention, we
now proceed to the execution of that part of our undertaking.

The first question that offers itself is, whether the general form and aspect of
the government be strictly-republican? It is evident that no other form would be
reconcileable with the genius of the people of America; with the fundamental
principles of the revolution; or with that honorable determination, which animates every votary of freedom, to rest all our political experiments on the capacity of mankind for self-government. If the plan of the convention therefore be
found to depart from the republican character, its advocates must abandon it as
no longer defensible.

What then are the distinctive characters of the republican form? Were an answer to this question to be sought, not by recurring to principles, but in the application of the term by political writers, to the constitutions of different states,
no satisfactory one would ever be found. Holland, in which no particle of the
supreme authority is derived from the people, has passed almost universally
under the denomination of a republic. The same title has been bestowed on
Venice, where absolute power over the great body of the people, is exercised in
the most absolute manner, by a small body of hereditary nobles. Poland, which is
a mixture of aristocracy and of monarchy in their worst forms, has been dignified

---

Lines 12–50 There was no consensus on the meaning of "republic." Johnson's *Dictionary* had defined it as "Commonwealth; state in which the power is lodged in
more than one." This would have made Britain a republic. Madison, concerned with
formal definitions, remarks the government of England has "one republican branch
only," meaning of course the House of Commons. The *Encyclopaedia Britannica*
(1771) also called a republic a commonwealth, but added that it was a popular
government or a state in which the people had the government "in their own hands."
The vagueness of definition has considerable bearing on the problem of interpreting
the Constitution's guarantee to each state of "a Republican Form of Government"
(Art. IV, Sect. 4), which could mean almost anything.

with the same appellation. The government of England, which has one republican branch only, combined with a hereditary aristocracy and monarchy, has with equal impropriety been frequently placed on the list of republics. These examples, which are nearly as dissimilar to each other as to a genuine republic, shew the extreme inaccuracy with which the term has been used in political disquisitions.

If we resort for a criterion, to the different principles on which different forms of government are established, we may define a republic to be, or at least may bestow that name on, a government which derives all its powers directly or indirectly from the great body of the people; and is administered by persons holding their offices during pleasure, for a limited period, or during good behaviour. It is *essential* to such a government, that it be derived from the great body of the society, not from an inconsiderable proportion, or a favored class of it; otherwise a handful of tyrannical nobles, exercising their oppressions by a delegation of their powers, might aspire to the rank of republicans, and claim for their government the honorable title of republic. It is *sufficient* for such a government, that the persons administering it be appointed, either directly or indirectly, by the people; and that they hold their appointments by either of the tenures just specified; otherwise every government in the United States, as well as every other popular government that has been or can be well organized or well executed, would be degraded from the republican character. According to the constitution of every state in the union, some or other of the officers of government are appointed indirectly only by the people. According to most of them the chief magistrate himself is so appointed. And according to one, this mode of appointment is extended to one of the co-ordinate branches of the legislature. According to all the constitutions also, the tenure of the highest offices is extended to a definite period, and in many instances, both within the legislative and executive departments, to a period of years. According to the provisions of most of the constitutions, again, as well as according to the most respectable and received opinions on the subject, the members of the judiciary department are to retain their offices by the firm tenure of good behaviour.

On comparing the constitution planned by the convention, with the standard here fixed, we perceive at once that it is in the most rigid sense conformable to it. The house of representatives, like that of one branch at least of all the state legislatures, is elected immediately by the great body of the people. The senate, like the present congress, and the senate of Maryland, derives its appointment indirectly from the people. The president is indirectly derived from the choice of the people, according to the example in most of the states. Even the judges, with all other officers of the union, will, as in the several states, be the choice, though a remote choice, of the people themselves. The duration of the appointments is equally conformable to the republican standard, and to the model of the state constitutions. The house of representatives is periodically elective as in all the states: and for the period of two years as in the state of South-Carolina. The senate is elective for the period of six years; which is but one year more than the period of the senate of Maryland; and but two more than that of the senates of New-York

65 and Virginia. The president is to continue in office for the period of four years; as in New-York and Delaware, the chief magistrate is elected for three years, and in South-Carolina for two years. In the other states the election is annual. In several of the states however, no explicit provision is made for the impeachment of the chief magistrate. And in Delaware and Virginia, he is not impeachable till out of

70 office. The president of the United States is impeachable at any time during his continuance in office. The tenure by which the judges are to hold their places, is, as it unquestionably ought to be, that of good behaviour. The tenure of the ministerial offices generally will be a subject of legal regulation, conformably to the reason of the case, and the example of the state constitutions.

75 Could any further proof be required of the republican complexion of this system, the most decisive one might be found in its absolute prohibition of titles of nobility, both under the federal and the state governments; and in its express guarantee of the republican form to each of the latter.

But it was not sufficient, say the adversaries of the proposed constitution, for

80 the convention to adhere to the republican form. They ought, with equal care, to have preserved the *federal* form, which regards the union as a *confederacy* of sovereign states; instead of which, they have framed a *national* government, which regards the union as a *consolidation* of the states. And it is asked by what authority this bold and radical innovation was undertaken. The handle which has been

85 made of this objection requires, that it should be examined with some precision.

Without enquiring into the accuracy of the distinction on which the objection is founded, it will be necessary to a just estimate of its force, first to ascertain the real character of the government in question; secondly, to enquire how far the convention were authorised to propose such a government; and thirdly, how far the

90 duty they owed to their country, could supply any defect of regular authority.

First. In order to ascertain the real character of the government it may be considered in relation to the foundation on which it is to be established; to the sources from which its ordinary powers are to be drawn; to the operation of those powers; to the extent of them; and to the authority by which future changes in

95 the government are to be introduced.

On examining the first relation, it appears on one hand that the constitution is to be founded on the assent and ratification of the people of America, given by deputies elected for the special purpose; but on the other, that this assent and ratification is to be given by the people, not as individuals composing one entire nation;

100 but as composing the distinct and independent states to which they respectively belong. It is to be the assent and ratification of the several states, derived from the supreme authority in each state, the authority of the people themselves. The act therefore establishing the constitution, will not be a *national* but a *federal* act.

Line 103 By "federal," Madison means pertaining to a confederation, as *opposed* to a nation. The Federalists have appropriated the word from their anti-nationalist opponents, now reduced to being known as "Anti-Federalists." See note on No. 15, lines 25–26.

That it will be a federal and not a national act, as these terms are understood by the objectors, the act of the people as forming so many independent states, not as forming one aggregate nation, is obvious from this single consideration that it is to result neither from the decision of a *majority* of the people of the union, nor from that of a *majority* of the states. It must result from the *unanimous* assent of the several states that are parties to it, differing no other wise from their ordinary assent than in its being expressed, not by the legislative authority, but by that of the people themselves. Were the people regarded in this transaction as forming one nation, the will of the majority of the whole people of the United States, would bind the minority; in the same manner as the majority in each state must bind the minority; and the will of the majority must be determined either by a comparison of the individual votes; or by considering the will of the majority of the states, as evidence of the will of a majority of the people of the United States. Neither of these rules has been adopted. Each state in ratifying the constitution, is considered as a sovereign body independent of all others, and only to be bound by its own voluntary act. In this relation then the new constitution will, if established, be a *federal* and not a *national* constitution.

The next relation is to the sources from which the ordinary powers of government are to be derived. The house of representatives will derive its powers from the people of America, and the people will be represented in the same proportion, and on the same principle, as they are in the legislature of a particular state. So far the government is *national* not *federal*. The senate on the other hand will derive its powers from the states, as political and co-equal societies; and these will be represented on the principle of equality in the senate, as they now are in the existing congress. So far the government is *federal*, not *national*. The executive power will be derived from a very compound source. The immediate election of the president is to be made by the states in their political characters. The votes allotted to them, are in a compound ratio, which considers them partly as distinct and co-equal societies; partly as unequal members of the same society. The eventual election, again is to be made by that branch of the legislature which consists of the national representatives; but in this particular act, they are to be thrown into the form of individual delegations from so many distinct and co-equal bodies politic. From this aspect of the government, it appears to be of a mixed character presenting at least as many *federal* as *national* features.

105
110
115
120
125
130
135

Lines 104–20 Notwithstanding the argument of this paragraph, the Constitution undeniably *converted* the people of the states into the people of the United States. The opening of the preamble, "We the People of the United States" said as much, as was clearly so understood by its opponents. Patrick Henry attacked the preamble on this point in his speech in the Virginia Ratifying Convention. It was only in the *process* of ratification that the Constitution would be a "*federal*, and not a *national* constitution" (in the old sense of "federal").

The difference between a federal and national government as it relates to the *operation of the government,* is, by the adversaries of the plan of the convention,
140 to consist in this, that in the former, the powers operate on the political bodies composing the confederacy, in their political capacities: In the latter, on the individual citizens, composing the nation, in their individual capacities. On trying the constitution by this criterion, it falls under the *national,* not the *federal* character; though perhaps not so compleatly, as has been understood. In several cases and
145 particularly in the trial of controversies to which states may be parties, they must be viewed and proceeded against in their collective and political capacities only. But the operation of the government on the people in their individual capacities, in its ordinary and most essential proceedings, will on the whole, in the sense of its opponents, designate it in this relation, a *national* government.

150 But if the government be national with regard to the *operation* of its powers, it changes its aspect again when we contemplate it in relation to the *extent* of its powers. The idea of a national government involves in it, not only an authority over the individual citizens; but an indefinite supremacy over all persons and things, so far as they are objects of lawful government. Among a people consoli-
155 dated into one nation, this supremacy is compleatly vested in the national legislature. Among communities united for particular purposes, it is vested partly in the general, and partly in the municipal legislatures. In the former case, all local authorities are subordinate to the supreme; and may be controuled, directed or abolished by it at pleasure. In the latter the local or municipal authorities form
160 distinct and independent portions of the supremacy, no more subject within their respective spheres to the general authority, than the general authority is subject to them, within its own sphere. In this relation then the proposed government cannot be deemed a *national* one; since its jurisdiction extends to certain enumerated objects only, and leaves to the several states a residuary and
165 inviolable sovereignty over all other objects. It is true that in controversies relating to the boundary between the two jurisdictions, the tribunal which is ultimately to decide, is to be established under the general government. But this does not change the principle of the case. The decision is to be impartially made, according to the rules of the constitution; and all the usual and most effectual
170 precautions are taken to secure this impartiality. Some such tribunal is clearly essential to prevent an appeal to the sword, and a dissolution of the compact; and that it ought to be established under the general, rather than under the local

---

Lines 164–65 The introduction of the phrase "residuary . . . sovereignty" continues the process hinted at in No. 9 and noted in No. 32, in which Hamilton had conceded certain features of sovereignty to the states. This was hardly compatible with the view that sovereignty was indivisible, and divided sovereignty a "solecism in theory" (see note to No. 9, line 143; and No. 20). By admitting immediately that the "tribunal" with ultimate power to decide will be under the general government, Madison effectively recognizes that power is lodged in national institutions.

governments; or to speak more properly, that it could be safely established under the first alone, is a position not likely to be combated.

If we try the constitution by its last relation, to the authority by which amend-   *175*
ments are to be made, we find it neither wholly *national*, nor wholly *federal*. Were it wholly national, the supreme and ultimate authority would reside in the *majority* of the people of the union; and this authority would be competent at all times, like that of a majority of every national society, to alter or abolish its established government. Were it wholly federal on the other hand, the concurrence of   *180*
each state in the union would be essential to every alteration that would be binding on all. The mode provided by the plan of the convention is not founded on either of these principles. In requiring more than a majority, and particularly, in computing the proportion by *states*, not by *citizens*, it departs from the *national*, and advances towards the *federal* character: In rendering the concurrence of less   *185*
than the whole number of states sufficient, it loses again the *federal*, and partakes of the *national* character.

The proposed constitution therefore, even when tested by the rules laid down by its antagonists, is in strictness neither a national nor a federal constitution; but a composition of both. In its foundation, it is federal, not national; in the sources   *190*
from which the ordinary powers of the government are drawn, it is partly federal, and partly national: in the operation of these powers, it is national, not federal: In the extent of them again, it is federal, not national: And finally, in the authoritative mode of introducing amendments, it is neither wholly federal, nor wholly national.   *195*

PUBLIUS.

Lines 188–95 This paragraph is a hinge in the course of the debate about the character of the federal government. Publius at last admits—or claims—that a government *can* be partly federal, partly national, a statement that stands, perhaps rather reluctantly, as a virtually new position in political thought. The unspoken question was, however, could the balance be maintained, and if not, which way would the new republic move? Anti-Federalists were convinced that it would contain a dynamic toward national concentration of power—at the expense of liberty.

FORTY
{NO. 39 IN NEWSPAPERS}

JAMES MADISON
January 18, 1788
The Same Objection Further Examined

To the People of the State of New York.

The *second* point to be examined is, whether the convention were authorised to frame and propose this mixed constitution.

The powers of the convention ought in strictness to be determined, by an inspection of the commissions given to the members by their respective con-
5   stituents. As all of these however had reference, either to the recommendation from the meeting at Annapolis in September, 1786, or to that from congress in February, 1787, it will be sufficient to recur to these particular acts.

The act from Annapolis recommends the "appointment of commissioners to take into consideration, the situation of the United States, to devise *such further*
10   *provisions* as shall appear to them necessary to render the constitution of the federal government *adequate to the exigencies of the union*; and to report such an act for that purpose, to the United States in congress assembled, as when agreed to by them, and afterwards confirmed by the legislature of every state, will effectually provide for the same."

15   The recommendatory act of congress is in the words following: "Whereas there is provision in the articles of confederation and perpetual union, for making alterations therein, by the assent of a congress of the United States, and of the legislatures of the several states: And whereas experience hath evinced, that there are defects in the present confederation, as a mean to remedy which, several of
20   the states, and *particularly the state of New-York*, by express instructions to their delegates in congress, have suggested a convention for the purposes expressed in the following resolution; and such convention appearing to be the most probable mean of establishing in these states, *a firm national government*.

"Resolved, That in the opinion of congress, it is expedient, that on the 2d
25   Monday in May next, a convention of delegates, who shall have been appointed

---

Lines 4–5 The "respective constituents" were the state legislatures—not the voters at large.

Lines 8–14 The quotation from Annapolis is from *Proceedings of Commissioners to Remedy Defects of the Federal Government,* September 11, 1786.

Lines 15–30 The resolution of Congress is in *Journals of the Continental Congress* xxxii, 71–74.

by the several states, be held at Philadelphia for the sole and express purpose of *revising the articles of confederation*, and reporting to congress and the several legislatures, such *alterations and provisions therein*, as shall, when agreed to in congress, and confirmed by the states, render the federal constitution *adequate to the exigencies of government and the preservation of the union.*" 30

From these two acts it appears, 1st. that the object of the convention was to establish in these states, *a firm national government*; 2d. that this government was to be such as would be *adequate to the exigencies of government* and *the preservation of the union*; 3d. that these purposes were to be effected by *alterations and provisions in the articles of confederation*, as it is expressed in the act of congress, 35 or by *such further provisions as should appear necessary*, as it stands in the recommendatory act from Annapolis; 4th. that the alterations and provisions were to be reported to congress, and to the states, in order to be agreed to by the former, and confirmed by the latter.

From a comparison and fair construction of these several modes of expression, is to be deduced the authority, under which the convention acted. They 40 were to frame a *national government*, adequate to the *exigencies of government* and *of the union*, and to reduce the articles of confederation into such form as to accomplish these purposes.

There are two rules of construction dictated by plain reason, as well as 45 founded on legal axioms. The one is, that every part of the expression ought, if possible, to be allowed some meaning, and be made to conspire to some common end. The other is, that where the several parts cannot be made to coincide, the less important should give way to the more important part; the means should be sacrificed to the end, rather than the end to the means. 50

Suppose then that the expressions defining the authority of the convention, were irreconcileably at variance with each other; that a *national* and *adequate government* could not possibly, in the judgment of the convention, be effected by *alterations* and *provisions* in the *articles of confederation*, which part of the definition ought to have been embraced, and which rejected? Which was the more 55 important, which the less important part? Which the end, which the means? Let the most scrupulous expositors of delegated powers: Let the most inveterate objectors against those exercised by the convention, answer these questions. Let them declare, whether it was of most importance to the happiness of the people of America, that the articles of confederation should be disregarded, and an 60 adequate government be provided, and the union preserved; or that an adequate government should be omitted, and the articles of confederation preserved. Let

---

Lines 51–67 The New Jersey Plan, which would have been more in keeping with the aim of strengthening the Articles as opposed to setting up a new *form* of government, had, in fact, been offered as an alternative to the Virginia Plan, but had been rejected by the Convention. See Farrand, *Records of the Federal Convention of 1787* I, 276–80 for comparison of the Virginia and New Jersey plans; for debate, 282–313.

them declare, whether the preservation of these articles was the end for securing which a reform of the government was to be introduced as the means; or whether the establishment of a government, adequate to the national happiness, was the end at which these articles themselves originally aimed, and to which they ought, as insufficient means, to have been sacrificed.

But is it necessary to suppose that these expressions are absolutely irreconcileable to each other; that no *alterations* or *provisions* in *the articles of the confederation*, could possibly mould them into a national and adequate government; into such a government as has been proposed by the convention?

No stress it is presumed will in this case be laid on the *title*, a change of that could never be deemed an exercise of ungranted power. *Alterations* in the body of the instrument, are expressly authorised. *New provisions* therein are also expressly authorised. Here then is a power to change the title; to insert new articles; to alter old ones. Must it of necessity be admitted that this power is infringed, so long as a part of the old articles remain? Those who maintain the affirmative, ought at least to mark the boundary between authorised and usurped innovations, between that degree of change, which lies within the compass of *alterations and further provisions*; and that which amounts to a *transmutation* of the government. Will it be said that the alterations ought not to have touched the substance of the confederation? The states would never have appointed a convention with so much solemnity, nor described its objects with so much latitude, if some *substantial* reform had not been in contemplation. Will it be said that the *fundamental principles* of the confederation were not within the purview of the convention, and ought not to have been varied? I ask what are these principles? do they require that in the establishment of the constitution, the states should be regarded as distinct and independent sovereigns? They are so regarded by the constitution proposed. Do they require that the members of the government should derive their appointment from the legislatures, not from the people of the state? One branch of the new government is to be appointed by these legislatures; and under the confederation the delegates to congress *may all* be appointed immediately by the people, and in two states* are actually so appointed. Do they require that the powers of the government should act on the states, and not immediately on individuals? In some instances, as has been shewn, the powers of the new government will act on the states in their collective characters. In some instances also those of the existing government act immediately on individuals. In cases of capture, of piracy, of the post-office, of coins, weights and

* Connecticut and Rhode-island.

Lines 98–107 The Articles of Confederation refer to the post office in Article IX, declaring the powers of the Congress. The intercolonial post office had originally been set up under an act of Parliament of 1712—an early case of *internal* legislation by Parliament, to which no constitutional objections were raised either then or later.

measures, of trade with the Indians, of claims under grants of land by different states, and above all, in the case of trials by courts-martial in the army and navy, by which death may be inflicted without the intervention of a jury, or even of a civil magistrate; in all these cases the powers of the confederation operate immediately on the persons and interests of individual citizens. Do these fundamental principles require particularly, that no tax should be levied without the intermediate agency of the states? The confederation itself authorises a direct tax to a certain extent on the post-office. The power of coinage has been so construed by congress, as to levy a tribute immediately from that source also. But pretermitting these instances, was it not an acknowledged object of the convention, and the universal expectation of the people, that the regulation of trade should be submitted to the general government in such a form as would render it an immediate source of general revenue? Had not congress repeatedly recommended this measure as not inconsistent with the fundamental principles of the confederation? Had not every state but one, had not New-York herself, so far complied with the plan of congress, as to recognize the *principle* of the innovation? Do these principles in fine require that the powers of the general government should be limited, and that beyond this limit, the states should be left in possession of their sovereignty and independence? We have seen that in the new government as in the old, the general powers are limited, and that the states in all unenumerated cases, are left in the enjoyment of their sovereign and independent jurisdiction.

The truth is, that the great principles of the constitution proposed by the convention, may be considered less as absolutely new, than as the expansion of principles which are found in the articles of confederation. The misfortune under the latter system has been, that these principles are so feeble and confined as to justify all the charges of inefficiency which have been urged against it; and to require a degree of enlargement which gives to the new system, the aspect of an entire transformation of the old.

In one particular it is admitted that the convention have departed from the tenor of their commission. Instead of reporting a plan requiring the confirmation *of all the states*, they have reported a plan which is to be confirmed and may be carried into effect by *nine states only*. It is worthy of remark, that this objection, though the most plausible, has been the least urged in the publications which

---

The colonies could not have done this for themselves: an intercolonial authority was essential. From the British point of view, colonial defense involved the same principle. Benjamin Franklin became postmaster general of the colonies in 1751 and improved the service. The next power mentioned, that of coinage, was an attribute of sovereignty enumerated by Jean Bodin in his *Six Books of the Commonwealthe* (1576). (See note on No. 9, lines 142–43.) The measure "repeatedly recommended" (line 111) by Congress was contained in both the impost and finance plans, and the one state (line 113) was Rhode Island. The paragraph ends with another reference to the sovereignty left over to the states. More of this will occur in No. 42 and No. 45.

have swarmed against the convention. The forbearance can only have proceeded from an irresistible conviction of the absurdity of subjecting the fate of twelve states, to the perverseness or corruption of a thirteenth; from the example of inflex-
135 ible opposition given by *a majority* of one sixtieth of the people of America, to a measure approved and called for by the voice of twelve states comprising fifty-nine sixtieths of the people; an example still fresh in the memory and indignation of every citizen who has felt for the wounded honor and prosperity of his country. As this objection, therefore, has been in a manner waved by those who have criticised
140 the powers of the convention, I dismiss it without further observation.

The *third* point to be enquired into is, how far considerations of duty arising out of the case itself, could have supplied any defect of regular authority.

In the preceding enquiries, the powers of the convention have been analised and tried with the same rigour, and by the same rules, as if they had been real
145 and final powers, for the establishment of a constitution for the United States. We have seen, in what manner they have borne the trial, even on that supposition. It is time now to recollect, that the powers were merely advisory and recommendatory; that they were so meant by the states, and so understood by the convention; and that the latter have accordingly planned and proposed a consti-
150 tution, which is to be of no more consequence than the paper on which it is written, unless it be stamped with the approbation of those to whom it is addressed. This reflection places the subject in a point of view altogether different, and will enable us to judge with propriety of the course taken by the convention.

Let us view the ground on which the convention stood. It may be collected
155 from their proceedings, that they were deeply and unanimously impressed with the crisis which had led their country almost with one voice to make so singular and solemn an experiment, for correcting the errors of a system by which this crisis had been produced; that they were no less deeply and unanimously convinced, that such a reform as they have proposed, was absolutely necessary to
160 effect the purposes of their appointment. It could not be unknown to them, that the hopes and expectations of the great body of citizens, throughout this great empire, were turned with the keenest anxiety, to the event of their deliberations. They had every reason to believe that the contrary sentiments agitated the minds and bosoms of every external and internal foe to the liberty and prosperity of the
165 United States. They had seen in the origin and progress of the experiment, the alacrity with which the *proposition* made by a single state (Virginia) towards a partial amendment of the confederation, had been attended to and promoted.

Lines 147–48 "[M]erely advisory and recommendatory" was stretching a point. The call had been to strengthen the Articles, so state legislatures had not felt obliged to declare how they would view a plan to supersede the Articles with a completely new instrument. For example, Delaware's delegates at the Convention had been constrained by their instructions from agreeing to any change in the "one state-one vote" principle, though they were willing to agree on the need for a new constitution.

They had seen the *liberty assumed* by a *very few* deputies, from a *very few* states, convened at Annapolis, of recommending a great and critical object, wholly foreign to their commission, not only justified by the public opinion, but actually *170* carried into effect, by twelve out of the thirteen states. They had seen in a variety of instances, assumptions by congress, not only of recommendatory, but of operative powers, warranted in the public estimation, by occasions and objects infinitely less urgent than those by which their conduct was to be governed. They must have reflected, that in all great changes of established governments, forms *175* ought to give way to substance; that a rigid adherence in such cases to the former, would render nominal and nugatory, the transcendent and precious right of the people to "abolish or alter their governments as to them shall seem most likely to effect their safety and happiness,"* since it is impossible for the people spontaneously and universally, to move in concert towards their object; and it is *180* therefore essential, that such changes be instituted by some *informal and unauthorised propositions*, made by some patriotic and respectable citizen or number of citizens. They must have recollected that it was by this irregular and assumed privilege of proposing to the people plans for their safety and happiness, that the states were first united against the danger with which they were threatened by *185* their antient government; that committees and congresses, were formed for concentrating their efforts, and defending their rights; and that *conventions* were *elected* in *the several states*, for establishing the constitutions under which they are now governed; nor could it have been forgotten that no little ill-timed scruples, no zeal for adhering to ordinary forms, were any where seen, except in those *190* who wished to indulge under these masks, their secret enmity to the substance contended for. They must have borne in mind, that as the plan to be framed and proposed, was to be submitted *to the people themselves*, the disapprobation of this supreme authority would destroy it for ever; its approbation blot out all antecedent errors and irregularities. It might even have occurred to them, that *195* where a disposition to cavil prevailed, their neglect to execute the degree of power vested in them, and still more their recommendation of any measure whatever not warranted by their commission, would not less excite animadversion, than a recommendation at once of a measure fully commensurate to the national exigencies. *200*

Had the convention under all these impressions, and in the midst of all these considerations, instead of exercising a manly confidence in their country, by whose confidence they had been so peculiarly distinguished, and of pointing out a system capable in their judgment of securing its happiness, taken the cold and sullen resolution of disappointing its ardent hopes of sacrificing substance to *205* forms, of committing the dearest interests of their country to the uncertainties of delay, and the hazard of events; let me ask the man, who can raise his mind to one elevated conception; who can awaken in his bosom, one patriotic emotion,

---

* *Declaration of Independence.*

what judgment ought to have been pronounced by the impartial world, by the
210   friends of mankind, by every virtuous citizen, on the conduct and character of
this assembly, or if there be a man whose propensity to condemn, is susceptible
of no controul, let me then ask what sentence he has in reserve for the twelve
states, who *usurped the power* of sending deputies to the convention, a body utterly unknown to their constitutions; for congress, who recommended the ap-
215   pointment of this body, equally unknown to the confederation; and for the state
of New-York in particular, who first urged and then complied with this unauthorised interposition.

But that the objectors may be disarmed of every pretext, it shall be granted for
a moment, that the convention were neither authorised by their commission, nor
220   justified by circumstances, in proposing a constitution for their country: Does it
follow that the constitution ought for that reason alone to be rejected? If according to the noble precept it be lawful to accept good advice even from an enemy,
shall we set the ignoble example of refusing such advice even when it is offered
by our friends? The prudent enquiry in all cases, ought surely to be not so much
225   *from whom* the advice comes, as whether the advice be *good*.

The sum of what has been here advanced and proved, is that the charge
against the convention of exceeding their powers, except in one instance little
urged by the objectors, has no foundation to support it; that if they had exceeded
their powers, they were not only warranted but required, as the confidential ser-
230   vants of their country, by the circumstances in which they were placed, to exercise the liberty which they assumed, and that finally, if they had violated both
their powers, and their obligations in proposing a constitution, this ought nevertheless to be embraced, if it be calculated to accomplish the views and happiness
of the people of America. How far this character is due to the constitution, is the
235   subject under investigation.

PUBLIUS.

FORTY-ONE
{NO. 40 IN NEWSPAPERS}

JAMES MADISON

January 19, 1788

General View of the Powers Proposed to Be Vested in the Union

To the People of the State of New York.

The constitution proposed by the convention may be considered under two general points of view. The FIRST relates to the sum or quantity of power which it vests in the government, including the restraints imposed on the states. The SECOND, to the particular structure of the government, and the distribution of this power, among its several branches.

Under the first view of the subject two important questions arise;—1. Whether any part of the powers transferred to the general government be unnecessary or improper?—2. Whether the entire mass of them be dangerous to the portion of jurisdiction left in the several states?

Is the aggregate power of the general government greater than ought to have been vested in it? This is the first question.

It cannot have escaped those who have attended with candour to the arguments employed against the extensive powers of the government, that the authors of them have very little considered how far these powers were necessary means of attaining a necessary end. They have chosen rather to dwell on the inconveniences which must be unavoidably blended with all political advantages; and on the possible abuses which must be incident to every power or trust of which a beneficial use can be made. This method of handling the subject cannot impose on the good sense of the people of America. It may display the subtlety of the writer; it may open a boundless field for rhetoric and declamation; it may inflame the passions of the unthinking, and may confirm the prejudices of the misthinking. But cool and candid people will at once reflect, that the purest of human blessings must have a portion of alloy in them, that the choice must always be made, if not of the lesser evil, at least of the GREATER, not the PERFECT good; and that in every political institution, a power to advance the public happiness, involves discretion which may be misapplied and abused. They will see therefore that in all cases, where power is to be conferred, the point first to be decided is whether such a power be necessary to the public good; as the next will be, in case of an affirmative decision, to guard as effectually as possible against a perversion of the power to the public detriment.

That we may form a correct judgment on this subject, it will be proper to review the several powers conferred on the government of the union; and that this

may be the more conveniently done, they may be reduced into different classes as they relate to the following different objects;—1. security against foreign dan-
35 ger;—2. Regulation of the intercourse with foreign nations;—3. Maintenance of harmony and proper intercourse among the states;—4. Certain miscellaneous objects of general utility;—5. Restraint of the states from certain injurious acts;— 6. Provisions for giving due efficacy to all these powers.

The powers falling within the first class, are those of declaring war, and grant-
40 ing letters of marque; of providing armies and fleets; of regulating and calling forth the militia; of levying and borrowing money.

Security against foreign danger is one of the primitive objects of civil society. It is an avowed and essential object of the American union. The powers requisite for attaining it, must be effectually confided to the federal councils.

45 Is the power of declaring war necessary? No man will answer this question in the negative. It would be superfluous therefore to enter into a proof of the affirma-tive. The existing confederation establishes this power in the most ample form.

Is the power of raising armies, and equipping fleets necessary? This is involved in the foregoing power. It is involved in the power of self-defence.

50 But was it necessary to give an INDEFINITE POWER of raising TROOPS, as well as providing fleets; and of maintaining both in PEACE, as well as in WAR?

The answer to these questions has been too far anticipated, in another place, to admit an extensive discussion of them in this place. The answer indeed seems to be so obvious and conclusive as scarcely to justify such a discussion in any
55 place. With what colour of propriety could the force necessary for defence, be limited by those who cannot limit the force of offence? If a federal constitution could chain the ambition, or set bounds to the exertions of all other nations: then indeed might it prudently chain the discretion of its own government, and set bounds to the exertions for its own safety.

60 How could a readiness for war in time of peace be safely prohibited, unless we could prohibit in like manner the preparations and establishments of every hostile nation? The means of security can only be regulated by the means and the danger of attack. They will in fact be ever determined by these rules, and by no others. It is in vain to oppose constitutional barriers to the impulse of self-preservation. It
65 is worse than in vain; because it plants in the constitution itself necessary usurpa-tions of power, every precedent of which is a germ of unnecessary and multiplied repetitions. If one nation maintains constantly a disciplined army ready for the service of ambition or revenge, it obliges the most pacific nations, who may be within the reach of its enterprizes, to take corresponding precautions. The fif-
70 teenth century was the unhappy epoch of military establishments in time of

---

Line 50–51 The restraint on support for standing armies is in Article I, Section 8.

peace. They were introduced by Charles VII. of France. All Europe has followed, or been forced into the example. Had the example not been followed by other nations, all Europe must long ago have worne the chains of a universal monarch. Were every nation except France now to disband its peace establishment, the same event might follow. The veteran legions of Rome were an overmatch for the undisciplined valour of all other nations, and rendered her mistress of the world.

Not less true is it, that the liberties of Rome proved the final victim to her military triumphs, and that the liberties of Europe, as far as they ever existed, have with few exceptions been the price of her military establishments. A standing force therefore is a dangerous, at the same time that it may be a necessary provision. On the smallest scale it has its inconveniences. On an extensive scale, its consequences may be fatal. On any scale, it is an object of laudable circumspection and precaution. A wise nation will combine all these considerations; and whilst it does not rashly preclude itself from any resource which may become essential to its safety, will exert all its prudence in diminishing both the necessity and the danger of resorting to one which may be inauspicious to its liberties.

The clearest marks of this prudence are stamped on the proposed constitution. The union itself which it cements and secures, destroys every pretext for a military establishment which could be dangerous. America, united with a handful of troops, or without a single soldier, exhibits a more forbidding posture to foreign ambition, than America disunited, with an hundred thousand veterans ready for combat. It was remarked on a former occasion, that the want of this pretext had saved the liberties of one nation in Europe. Being rendered by her insular situation and her maritime resources, impregnable to the armies of her neighbours, the rulers of Great-Britain have never been able, by real or artificial dangers, to cheat the public into an extensive peace establishment. The distance of the United States from the powerful nations of the world, gives them the same happy security. A dangerous establishment can never be necessary or plausible, so long as they continue a united people. But let it never for a moment be forgotten, that they are indebted for this advantage to their union alone. The moment of its dissolution will be the date of a new order of things. The fears of the weaker or the ambition of the stronger states or confederacies, will set the same

---

Lines 71–76 Charles VII of France invaded Italy in 1494, an event that destroyed the ancient independence of the city-state republics and that many historians regard as having been decisive in the shaping of modern history.

Lines 77–79 "[T]he liberties of Rome. . . . " Madison is presumably thinking of the collapse of the republic; after Augustus, however, they fell victim to the lack of a constitutional system for electing or restraining the emperors as much as from military triumphs. But the reference to "Europe" does not seem to include Britain; an exception might also have been made of the Netherlands, whose *naval* power contributed to the provinces' liberties.

See note on No. 26, lines 42–65.

example in the new, as Charles VII. did in the old world. The example will be followed here from the same motives which produced universal imitation there.
105 Instead of deriving from our situation the precious advantage which Great-Britain has derived from hers, the face of America will be but a copy of that of the continent of Europe. It will present liberty every where crushed between standing armies and perpetual taxes. The fortunes of disunited America will be even more disastrous than those of Europe. The sources of evil in the latter are con-
110 fined to her own limits. No superior powers of another quarter of the globe intrigue among her rival nations, inflame their mutual animosities, and render them the instruments of foreign ambition, jealousy and revenge. In America, the miseries springing from her internal jealousies, contentions and wars, would form a part only of her lot. A plentiful addition of evils would have their source in
115 that relation in which Europe stands to this quarter of the earth, and which no other quarter of the earth bears to Europe.

This picture of the consequences of disunion cannot be too highly coloured, or too often exhibited. Every man who loves peace, every man who loves his country, every man who loves liberty, ought to have it ever before his eyes, that
120 he may cherish in his heart a due attachment to the union of America, and be able to set a due value on the means of preserving it.

Next to the effectual establishment of the union, the best possible precaution against danger from standing armies, is a limitation of the term for which revenue may be appropriated to their support. This precaution the constitution has
125 prudently added. I will not repeat here the observations, which I flatter myself have placed this subject in a just and satisfactory light. But it may not be improper to take notice of an argument against this part of the constitution, which has been drawn from the policy and practice of Great-Britain. It is said that the continuance of an army in that kingdom, requires an annual vote of the legisla-
130 ture; whereas the American constitution has lengthened this critical period to two years. This is the form in which the comparison is usually stated to the public: But is it a just form? Is it a fair comparison? Does the British constitution restrain the Parliamentary discretion to one year? Does the American impose on the congress appropriations for two years? On the contrary, it cannot be un-
135 known to the authors of the fallacy themselves, that the British constitution fixes no limit whatever to the discretion of the legislature, and that the American ties down the legislature to two years, as the longest admissible term.

Had the argument from the British example been truly stated, it would have stood thus: The term for which supplies may be appropriated to the army estab-
140 lishment, though unlimited by the British constitution, has nevertheless in practice been limited by parliamentary discretion, to a single year. Now if in

---

Lines 141–51 After a period of triennial parliaments marked by great political turbulence, following the Glorious Revolution, seven-year parliaments were introduced by the Septennial Act of 1716. The measure aroused bitter controversy but

Great-Britain, where the house of commons is elected for seven years; where so great a proportion of the members are elected by so small a proportion of the people; where the electors are so corrupted by the representatives, and the representatives so corrupted by the crown, the representative body can possess a power 145 to make appropriations to the army for an indefinite term, without desiring, or without daring, to extend the term beyond a single year; ought not suspicion herself to blush in pretending that the representatives of the United States, elected FREELY, by the WHOLE BODY of the people, every SECOND YEAR, cannot be safely entrusted with a discretion over such appropriations, expressly limited 150 to the short period of TWO YEARS?

A bad cause seldom fails to betray itself. Of this truth, the management of the opposition to the federal government is an unvaried exemplification. But among all the blunders which have been committed, none is more striking than the attempt to enlist on that side, the prudent jealousy entertained by the people, of 155 standing armies. The attempt has awakened fully the public attention to that important subject; and has led to investigations which must terminate in a thorough and universal conviction, not only that the constitution has provided the most effectual guards against danger from that quarter, but that nothing short of a constitution fully adequate to the national defence, and the preservation of the 160 union, can save America from as many standing armies as it may be split into states or confederacies; and from such a progressive augmentation of these establishments in each, as will render them as burdensome to the properties and ominous to the liberties of the people; as any establishment that can become necessary, under a united and efficient government, must be tolerable to the for- 165 mer, and safe to the latter.

The palpable necessity of the power to provide and maintain a navy has protected that part of the constitution against a spirit of censure, which has spared few other parts. It must indeed be numbered among the greatest blessings of America, that as her union will be the only source of her maritime strength, so this will be a 170 principal source of her security against danger from abroad. In this respect our situation bears another likeness to the insular advantage of Great-Britain. The batteries most capable of repelling foreign enterprizes on our safety, are happily such as can never be turned by a perfidious government against our liberties.

The inhabitants of the Atlantic frontier are all of them deeply interested in 175 this provision for naval protection, and if they have hitherto been suffered to

---

was followed by much greater political stability. The term of a parliament was reduced to five years in 1911.

The allegation that British electors were corrupted by their representatives presumably referred to free spending by candidates on elections; Madison should have recognized the practice: much the same sort of thing happened in Virginia. Corruption of representatives by the Crown was an old British "Country party" or Whig theme, and referred to the practice of conferring public offices or pensions.

sleep quietly in their beds; if their property has remained safe against the predatory spirit of licencious adventurers; if their maritime towns have not yet been
compelled to ransome themselves from the terrors of a conflagration, by yielding
180 to the exactions of daring and sudden invaders, these instances of good fortune
are not to be ascribed to the capacity of the existing government for the protection of those from whom it claims allegiance, but to causes that are fugitive and
fallacious. If we except perhaps Virginia and Maryland, which are peculiarly vulnerable on their Eastern frontiers, no part of the union ought to feel more anxi-
185 ety on this subject than New-York. Her sea coast is extensive. The very important
district of the state is an island. The state itself is penetrated by a large navigable
river for more than fifty leagues. The great emporium of its commerce, the great
reservoir of its wealth, lies every moment at the mercy of events, and may almost
be regarded as a hostage, for ignominious compliances with the dictates of a for-
190 eign enemy, or even with the rapacious demands of pirates and barbarians.
Should a war be the result of the precarious situation of European affairs, and all
the unruly passions attending it, be let loose on the ocean, our escape from insults and depredations, not only on that element but every part of the other bordering on it, will be truly miraculous. In the present condition of America, the
195 states more immediately exposed to these calamities, have nothing to hope from
the phantom of a general government which now exists; and if their single resources were equal to the task of fortifying themselves against the danger, the object to be protected would be almost consumed by the means of protecting them.
The power of regulating and calling forth the militia has been already suffi-
200 ciently vindicated and explained.
The power of levying and borrowing money, being the sinew of that which is
to be exerted in the national defence, is properly thrown into the same class with
it. This power also has been examined already with much attention, and has I
trust been clearly shewn to be necessary both in the extent and form given to it by
205 the constitution. I will address one additional reflection only to those who contend that the power ought to have been restrained to external taxation, by which
they mean taxes on articles imported from other countries. It cannot be doubted
that this will always be a valuable source of revenue, that for a considerable time,
it must be a principle source, that at this moment it is an essential one. But we
210 may form very mistaken ideas on this subject, if we do not call to mind in our
calculations, that the extent of revenue drawn from foreign commerce, must vary
with the variations both in the extent and the kind of imports, and that these variations do not correspond with the progress of population, which must be the general measure of the publick wants. As long as agriculture continues the sole field
215 of labour, the importation of manufactures must increase as the consumers mul-

---

Lines 214–15 Agriculture actually accounted for about eighty per cent of the economic activities of Americans.

tiply. As soon as domestic manufactures are begun by the hands not called for by agriculture, the imported manufactures will decrease as the numbers of people increase. In a more remote stage, the imports may consist in considerable part of raw materials which will be wrought into articles for exportation, and will therefore require rather the encouragement of bounties, than to be loaded with discouraging duties. A system of government, meant for duration, ought to contemplate these revolutions, and be able to accommodate itself to them. *220*

Some who have not denied the necessity of the power of taxation, have grounded a very fierce attack against the constitution on the language in which it is defined. It has been urged and echoed, that the power "to lay and collect taxes, *225* duties, imposts and excises, to pay the debts and provide for the common defence and general welfare of the United States," amounts to an unlimited commission to exercise every power which may be alledged to be necessary for the common defence or general welfare. No stronger proof could be given of the distress under which these writers labour for objections, than their stooping to such *230* a misconstruction.

Had no other enumeration or definition of the powers of the congress been found in the constitution, than the general expression just cited, the authors of the objection might have had some colour for it; though it would have been difficult to find a reason for so awkward a form of describing an authority to legislate *235* in all possible cases. A power to destroy the freedom of the press, the trial by jury or even to regulate the course of descents, or the forms of conveyances, must be very singularly expressed by the terms "to raise money for the general welfare."

But what colour can the objection have, when a specification of the objects alluded to by these general terms, immediately follows; and is not even separated *240* by a longer pause than a semicolon. If the different parts of the same instrument ought to be so expounded as to give meaning to every part which will bear it; shall one part of the same sentence be excluded altogether from a share in the meaning; and shall the more doubtful and indefinite terms be retained in their full extent and the clear and precise expressions, be denied any signification *245* whatsoever? For what purpose could the enumeration of particular powers be inserted, if these and all others were meant to be included in the preceding general power? Nothing is more natural or common than first to use a general phrase, and then to explain and qualify it by a recital of particulars. But the idea of an enumeration of particulars, which neither explain nor qualify the general mean- *250* ing, and can have no other effect than to confound and mislead, is an absurdity which as we are reduced to the dilemma of charging either on the authors of the objection, or on the authors of the constitution, we must take the liberty of supposing, had not its origin with the latter.

The objection here is the more extraordinary, as it appears, that the language *255* used by the convention is a copy from the articles of confederation. The objects

---

Lines 223–31 The taxing power is in Article 1, Section 8.

of the union among the states as described in article 3d. are, "their common defence, security of their liberties, and mutual and general welfare." The terms of
article 8th. are still more identical. "All charges of war, and all other expences,
260 that shall be incurred for the common defence or general welfare, and allowed
by the United States in congress, shall be defrayed out of a common treasury
&c." A similar language again occurs in art. 9. Construe either of these articles by
the rules which would justify, the construction put on the new constitution, and
they vest in the existing congress a power to legislate in all cases whatsoever. But
265 what would have been thought of that assembly, if attaching themselves to these
general expressions, and disregarding the specifications, which ascertain and
limit their import, they had exercised an unlimited power of providing for the
common defence and general welfare? I appeal to the objectors themselves,
whether they would in that case have employed the same reasoning in justifica-
270 tion of congress, as they now make use of against the convention. How difficult it
is for error to escape its own condemnation!

PUBLIUS.

FORTY-TWO
{NO. 41 IN NEWSPAPERS}

JAMES MADISON
January 22, 1788
The Same View Continued

To the People of the State of New York.

The *second* class of powers lodged in the general government, consists of those which regulate the intercourse with foreign nations, to wit, to make treaties; to send and receive ambassadors, other public ministers and consuls; to define and punish piracies and felonies committed on the high seas, and offences against the law of nations; to regulate foreign commerce, including a power to prohibit   5
after the year 1808, the importation of slaves, and to lay an intermediate duty of ten dollars per head, as a discouragement to such importations.

This class of powers forms an obvious and essential branch of the federal administration. If we are to be one nation in any respect, it clearly ought to be in respect to other nations.   10

The powers to make treaties and to send and receive ambassadors, speak their own propriety.—Both of them are comprized in the articles of confederation; with this difference only, that the former is disembarrassed by the plan of the convention of an exception, under which treaties might be substantially frustrated by regulations of the states; and that a power of appointing and receiving   15
"other public ministers and consuls," is expressly and very properly added to the former provision concerning ambassadors. The term ambassador, if taken strictly, as seems to be required by the second of the articles of confederation, comprehends the highest grade only of public ministers; and excludes the grades which the United States will be most likely to prefer where foreign embassies   20
may be necessary. And under no latitude of construction will the term comprehend consuls. Yet it has been found expedient, and has been the practice of congress to employ the inferior grades of public ministers; and to send and receive consuls. It is true that where treaties of commerce stipulate for the mutual appointment of consuls, whose functions are connected with commerce, the admission of foreign consuls may fall within the power of making commercial treaties; and that where no such treaties exist, the mission of American consuls into foreign countries, may *perhaps* be covered under the authority given by the   25

Lines 17–24 Jefferson and John Adams were ministers, not formally ambassadors, to the French and British courts, respectively.

9th article of the confederation, to appoint all such civil officers as may be necessary for managing the general affairs of the United States. But the admission of
consuls into the United States, where no previous treaty has stipulated it, seems to
have been no where provided for. A supply of the omission is one of the lesser instances in which the convention have improved on the model before them. But
the most minute provisions become important when they tend to obviate the necessity or the pretext for gradual and unobserved usurpations of power; a list of the
cases in which congress have been betrayed, or forced by the defects of the confederation into violations of their chartered authorities, would not a little surprize
those who have paid no attention to the subject; and would be no inconsiderable
argument in favor of the new constitution, which seems to have provided no less
studiously for the lesser, than the more obvious and striking defects of the old.

The power to define and punish piracies and felonies committed on the high
seas, and offences against the law of nations, belongs with equal propriety to the
general government; and is a still greater improvement on the articles of confederation. These articles contain no provision for the case of offences against the
law of nations; and consequently leave it in the power of any indiscreet member
to embroil the confederacy with foreign nations. The provision of the federal articles on the subject of piracies and felonies, extends no farther than to the establishment of courts for the trial of these offences. The definition of piracies might
perhaps without inconveniency, be left to the law of nations; though a legislative
definition of them, is found in most municipal codes. A definition of felonies on
the high seas is evidently requisite. Felony is a term of loose signification even in
the common law of England; and of various import in the statute law of that
kingdom. But neither the common, nor the statute law of that or of any other nation ought to be a standard for the proceedings of this, unless previously made its
own by legislative adoption. The meaning of the term as defined in the codes of
the several states, would be as impracticable as the former would be a dishonorable and illegitimate guide. It is not precisely the same in any two of the states;
and varies in each with every revision of its criminal laws. For the sake of certainty and uniformity therefore, the power of defining felonies in this case, was in
every respect necessary and proper.

The regulation of foreign commerce, having fallen within several views
which have been taken of this subject, has been too fully discussed to need additional proofs here of its being properly submitted to the federal administration.

Lines 41–60 Under common law deriving from medieval England, felony had originally meant crimes punishable by death with forfeiture of goods. Felony was loosely
defined but always serious. But common law was subject to anomalies: theft was always felony, fraud only misdemeanor. Next, Madison raises an issue that was to become highly contentious—the status of common law in America when not
sanctioned by local statute. Most of the new state constitutions provided for the continuation of English common law unless repealed by state statute.

It were doubtless to be wished that the power of prohibiting the importation of slaves, had not been postponed until the year 1808, or rather that it had been suffered to have immediate operation. But it is not difficult to account either for this restriction on the general government, or for the manner in which the whole clause is expressed. It ought to be considered as a great point gained in favor of humanity, that a period of twenty years may terminate for ever within these states, a traffic which has so long and so loudly upbraided the barbarism of modern policy; that within that period it will receive a considerable discouragement from the federal government, and may be totally abolished by a concurrence of the few states which continue the unnatural traffic, in the prohibitory example which has been given by so great a majority of the union. Happy would it be for the unfortunate Africans, if an equal prospect lay before them, of being redeemed from the oppressions of their European brethren!

Attempts have been made to pervert this clause into an objection against the constitution, by representing it on one side as a criminal toleration of an illicit practice, and on another, as calculated to prevent voluntary and beneficial emigrations from Europe to America. I mention these misconstructions, not with a view to give them an answer, for they deserve none; but as specimens of the manner and spirit in which some have thought fit to conduct their opposition to the proposed government.

The powers included in the *third* class, are those which provide for the harmony and proper intercourse among the states.

Under this head might be included the particular restraints imposed on the authority of the states, and certain powers of the judicial department; but the former are reserved for a distinct class, and the latter will be particularly examined when we arrive at the structure and organization of the government. I shall confine myself to a cursory review of the remaining powers comprehended under this third description, to wit, to regulate commerce among the several states and the Indian tribes; to coin money, regulate the value thereof and of foreign coin; to provide for the punishment of counterfeiting the current coin, and securities of the United States; to fix the standard of weights and measures; to establish an uniform rule of naturalization, and uniform laws of bankruptcy; to prescribe the manner in which the public acts, records and judicial proceedings of each state

---

Lines 64–76 The strong antislavery tone of this passage reminds us of the antislavery feeling expressed by some delegates, including George Mason of Virginia, in the Convention. But one may wonder whether Madison would have thought it prudent to publish these reservations if *The Federalist* essays had been appearing in his home state of Virginia rather than New York. Madison does not make clear how he expected the federal government to discourage the slave trade. Virginia, where the ratio of blacks to whites was causing anxiety, had attempted to prohibit slave importations in the late 1760s but had met with a veto by the crown. South Carolina also imposed a ban on slave importations in the 1770s mainly to conserve currency.

shall be proved, and the effect they shall have in other states; and to establish post-offices, and post-roads.

The defect of power in the existing confederacy, to regulate the commerce between its several members, is in the number of those which have been clearly pointed out by experience. To the proofs and remarks which former papers have brought into view on this subject, it may be added, that without this supplemental provision, the great and essential power of regulating foreign commerce, would have been incompleat, and ineffectual. A very material object of this power was the relief of the states which import and export through other states, from the improper contributions levied on them by the latter. Were these at liberty to regulate the trade between state and state, it must be foreseen that ways would be found out, to load the articles of import and export, during the passage through their jurisdiction, with duties which would fall on the makers of the latter, and the consumers of the former. We may be assured by past experience, that such a practice would be introduced by future contrivances; and both by that and a common knowledge of human affairs, that it would nourish unceasing animosities, and not improbably terminate in serious interruptions of the public tranquility. To those who do not view the question through the medium of passion or of interest, the desire of the commercial states to collect in any form, an indirect revenue from their uncommercial neighbours, must appear not less impolitic than it is unfair; since it would stimulate the injured party, by resentment as well as interest, to resort to less convenient channels for their foreign trade. But the mild voice of reason, pleading the cause of an enlarged and permanent interest, is but too often drowned before public bodies as well as individuals, by the clamours of an impatient avidity for immediate and immoderate gain.

The necessity of a superintending authority over the reciprocal trade of confederated states has been illustrated by other examples as well as our own. In Switzerland, where the union is so very slight, each canton is obliged to allow to merchandizes, a passage through its jurisdiction into other cantons, without an augmentation of the tolls. In Germany, it is a law of the empire, that the princes and states shall not lay tolls or customs on bridges, rivers, or passages, without the consent of the emperor and diet; though it appears from a quotation in an antecedent paper, that the practice in this as in many other instances in that confederacy, has not followed the law, and has produced there the mischiefs which have been foreseen here. Among the restraints imposed by the union of the Netherlands, on its members, one is, that they shall not establish imposts disadvantageous to their neighbors, without the general permission.

The regulation of commerce with the Indian tribes is very properly unfettered from two limitations in the articles of confederation, which render the provision

---

Lines 128–29 An example of the rapid composition of the essays: no such quotation appears in an earlier "antecedent paper." Publius had discussed the German empire in No. 19.

obscure and contradictory. The power is there restrained to Indians, not members of any of the states, and is not to violate or infringe the legislative right of any state within its own limits. What description of Indians are to be deemed members of a state, is not yet settled; and has been a question of frequent perplexity and contention in the federal councils. And how the trade with Indians, though not members of a state, yet residing within its legislative jurisdiction, can be regulated by an external authority, without so far intruding on the internal rights of legislation, is absolutely incomprehensible. This is not the only case in which the articles of confederation have inconsiderately endeavored to accomplish impossibilities; to reconcile a partial sovereignty in the union, with compleat sovereignty in the states; to subvert a mathematical axiom, by taking away a part, and letting the whole remain.

All that need be remarked on the power to coin money, regulate the value thereof, and of foreign coin, is that by providing for this last case, the constitution has supplied a material omission in the articles of confederation. The authority of the existing congress is restrained to the regulation of coin *struck* by their own authority, or that of the respective states. It must be seen at once, that the proposed uniformity in the *value* of the current coin might be destroyed by subjecting that of foreign coin to the different regulations of the different states.

The punishment of counterfeiting the public securities as well as of the current coin, is submitted of course to that authority, which is to secure the value of both.

The regulation of weights and measures is transferred from the articles of confederation, and is founded on like considerations with the preceding power of regulating coin.

The dissimilarity in the rules of naturalization, has long been remarked as a fault in our system, and as laying a foundation for intricate and delicate questions. In the 4th article of the confederation, it is declared "that the *free inhabitants* of each of these states, paupers, vagabonds, and fugitives from justice excepted, shall be entitled to all privileges and immunities of *free citizens*, in the several states, and *the people* of each state, shall in every other, enjoy all the privileges of trade and commerce, &c." There is a confusion of language here, which is remarkable. Why the terms *free inhabitants*, are used in one part of the article; *free citizens* in another, and *people* in another, or what was meant by superadding "to all privileges and immunities of free citizens," — "all the privileges of trade and commerce," cannot easily be determined. It seems to be a construction scarcely avoidable, however, that those who come under the denomination of *free inhabitants* of a state, although not citizens of such state, are entitled in every other state to all the privileges of *free citizens* of the latter; that is, to greater privileges

---

Lines 148–54 As previously remarked, the power to mint coinage was a classical mark of sovereignty, which the Congress did not possess under the Confederation. The Congress did, of course, issue paper money, in huge quantities and deteriorating values. Publius's concern here is evidently with policy rather than formal theory.

than they may be entitled to in their own state; so that it may be in the power of a particular state, or rather every state is laid under a necessity, not only to confer the rights of citizenship in other states upon any whom it may admit to such rights within itself; but upon any whom it may allow to become inhabitants within its jurisdiction. But were an exposition of the term "inhabitants" to be admitted, which would confine the stipulated privileges to citizens alone, the difficulty is diminished only, not removed. The very improper power would still be retained by each state, of naturalizing aliens in every other state. In one state residence for a short term confers all the rights of citizenship. In another qualifications of greater importance are required. An alien therefore legally incapacitated for certain rights in the latter, may by previous residence only in the former, elude his incapacity; and thus the law of one state, be preposterously rendered paramount to the law of another, within the jurisdiction of the other. We owe it to mere casualty, that very serious embarrassments on this subject, have been hitherto escaped. By the laws of several states, certain descriptions of aliens who had rendered themselves obnoxious, were laid under interdicts inconsistent, not only with the rights of citizenship, but with the privileges of residence. What would have been the consequence, if such persons, by residence or otherwise, had acquired the character of citizens under the laws of another state, and then asserted their rights as such, both to residence and citizenship within the state proscribing them? Whatever the legal consequences might have been, other consequences would probably have resulted of too serious a nature, not to be provided against. The new constitution has accordingly with great propriety made provision against them, and all others proceeding from the defect of the confederation, on this head, by authorising the general government to establish an uniform rule of naturalization throughout the United States.

The power of establishing uniform laws of bankruptcy, is so intimately connected with the regulation of commerce, and will prevent so many frauds where the parties or their property may lie or be removed into different states, that the expediency of it seems not likely to be drawn into question.

The power of prescribing by general laws the manner in which the public acts, records and judicial proceedings of each state shall be proved, and the effect they shall have in other states, is an evident and valuable improvement on the clause relating to this subject in the articles of confederation. The meaning of the latter is extremely indeterminate; and can be of little importance under any interpretation which it will bear. The power here established, may be rendered a very convenient instrument of justice, and be particularly beneficial on the borders of contiguous states, where the effects liable to justice, may be suddenly and secretly translated in any stage of the process, within a foreign jurisdiction.

Line 187 "Casualty" means chance.

The power of establishing post-roads, must in every view be a harmless power; and may perhaps, by judicious management, become productive of great public conveniency. Nothing which tends to facilitate the intercourse between the *215* states, can be deemed unworthy of the public care.

PUBLIUS.

Lines 213–16 The power of establishing posts (stages or relay points for couriers located at intervals on certain roads), a Federal power that followed from British colonial power, originally exercised in an act of Parliament in 1712.

FORTY-THREE
{NO. 42 IN NEWSPAPERS}

JAMES MADISON
January 23, 1788
The Same View Continued

To the People of the State of New York.

The *fourth* class comprises the following miscellaneous powers: 1. A power "to promote the progress of science and useful arts, by securing for a limited time, to authors and inventors, the exclusive right, to their respective writings and discoveries."

The utility of this power will scarcely be questioned. The copy right of authors
5 has been solemnly adjudged in Great Britain to be a right at common law. The right to useful inventions, seems with equal reason to belong to the inventors. The public good fully coincides in both cases, with the claims of individuals. The states cannot separately make effectual provision for either of the cases, and most of them have anticipated the decision of this point, by laws passed at the in-
10 stance of congress.

2. "To exercise exclusive legislation in all cases whatsoever, over such district (not exceeding ten miles square) as may by cession of particular states and the acceptance of congress, become the seat of the government of the United States; and to exercise like authority over all places purchased by the consent of the leg-
15 islature of the states, in which the same shall be, for the erection of forts, magazines, arsenals, dockyards and other needful buildings."

The indispensible necessity of compleat authority at the seat of government carries its own evidence with it. It is a power exercised by every legislature of the

---

Lines 4–10 Authors' copyright in Britain was based on the limited statutory protection afforded since 1710 by Act of Parliament, 8 Anne c. 21. This was considerably amplified by Mansfield LCJ in *Millar v. Taylor* in 1769; Mansfield felt strongly about authors' rights to their work, both before and after publication. Madison may have had this case in mind, but if so, he overlooked the fact that the judgment (unusually, for Mansfield) was overruled by the House of Lords only a few years later, in 1774, in *Donaldson v. Becket* (on which there is a large literature). However, in the closely related matter of trademark, common law protection prevailed. Compare *Greenough v. Lambertson* (1777) and others. For authoritative comment see James Oldham, *The Mansfield Manuscripts and the Growth of English Law in the Eighteenth Century* (Chapel Hill, N.C., 1992), 723–29.

Lines 11–40 The new republic would need a capital, a matter of keen competition among some of the states (Philadelphia, New York, and Trenton, N.J., were competi-

union, I might say of the world, by virtue of its general supremacy. Without it, not only the public authority might be insulted and its proceedings be inter- *20* rupted, with impunity; but a dependence of the members of the general government, on the state comprehending the seat of the government for protection in the exercise of their duty, might bring on the national councils an imputation of awe or influence, equally dishonorable to the government, and dissatisfactory to the other members of the confederacy. This consideration has the more weight *25* as the gradual accumulation of public improvements at the stationary residence of the government, would be both too great a public pledge to be left in the hands of a single state; and would create so many obstacles to a removal of the government, as still further to abridge its necessary independence. The extent of this federal district is sufficiently circumscribed to satisfy every jealousy of an *30* opposite nature. And as it is to be appropriated to this use with the consent of the state ceding it; as the state will no doubt provide in the compact for the rights, and the consent of the citizens inhabiting it; as the inhabitants will find sufficient inducements of interest to become willing parties to the cession; as they will have had their voice in the election of the government which is to exercise au- *35* thority over them; as a municipal legislature for local purposes, derived from their own suffrages, will of course be allowed them; and as the authority of the legislature of the state, and of the inhabitants of the ceded part of it, to concur in the cession, will be derived from the whole people of the state, in their adoption of the constitution, every imaginable objection seems to be obviated. *40*

The necessity of a like authority over forts, magazines &c. established by the general government is not less evident. The public money expended on such places, and the public property deposited in them, require that they should be exempt from the authority of the particular state. Nor would it be proper for the places on which the security of the entire union may depend, to be in any de- *45* gree dependent on a particular member of it. All objections and scruples are here also obviated by requiring the concurrence of the states concerned, in every such establishment.

3. "To declare the punishment of treason, but no attainder of treason shall work corruption of blood, or forfeiture, except during the life of the person attainted." *50*

---

tors). It seemed preferable, however, to avoid placing the federal capital within the boundaries of any one state, and after the Convention had reached the compromise decision to locate it on the banks of the Potomac, the choice of site was left to the first president.

Lines 19–21 The proceedings of the old Congress had indeed been interrupted and insulted by mutinous soldiers of the Continental army demanding pay and pension rights in the summer of 1783.

Lines 49–58 Section 3 of No. 43 introduces a republican and individualist principle. In countries of feudal legacy, treason was rebellion against the monarch, and led

As treason may be committed against the United States, the authority of the United States ought to be enabled to punish it. But as new-fangled and artificial treasons, have been the great engines, by which violent factions, the natural off-spring of free governments, have usually wreaked their alternate malignity on each other, the convention have with great judgment opposed a barrier to this peculiar danger, by inserting a constitutional definition of the crime, fixing the proof necessary for conviction of it, and restraining the congress, even in punishing it, from extending the consequences of guilt beyond the person of its author.

4. "To admit new states into the union; but no new state, shall be formed or erected within the jurisdiction of any other state; nor any state be formed by the junction of two or more states, or parts of states, without the consent of the legislatures of the states concerned, as well as of the congress."

In the articles of confederation no provision is found on this important subject. Canada was to be admitted of right on her joining in the measures of the United States; and the other *colonies*, by which were evidently meant, the other British colonies, at the discretion of nine states. The eventual establishment of *new states*, seems to have been overlooked by the compilers of that instrument. We have seen the inconvenience of this omission, and the assumption of power into which congress have been led by it. With great propriety therefore has the new system supplied the defect. The general precaution that no new states shall be formed without the concurrence of the federal authority and that of the states concerned, is consonant to the principles which ought to govern such transactions. The particular precaution against the erection of new states, by the partition of a state without its consent, quiets the jealousy of the larger states; as that of the smaller is quieted by a like precaution against a junction of states without their consent.

5. "To dispose of and make all needful rules and regulations respecting the territory or other property belonging to the United States, with a proviso that nothing in the constitution shall be so construed as to prejudice any claims of the United States, as of any particular state."

This is a power of very great importance, and required by considerations similar to those which shew the propriety of the former. The proviso annexed is proper in itself, and was probably rendered absolutely necessary, by jealousies and questions concerning the Western territory, sufficiently known to the public.

---

to attainder, with consequent reversion of possessions and lands to the crown. It would have been out of keeping with the individualist ethos of American republicanism to make the heirs to an estate suffer for the crimes of their parents. Responsibility and punishment stopped with the individual.

Line 52 Here "new-fangled and artificial" means newly invented and trumped up.

Lines 53–54 The remark that "violent factions" were "the natural offspring of free government" looks back to Shays's rebellion in Massachusetts, but may remind modern readers of the so-called "militia" groups.

6. "To guarantee to every state in the union a republican form of government; *85* to protect each of them against invasion; and on application of the legislature; or of the executive (when the legislature cannot be convened) against domestic violence."

In a confederacy founded on republican principles, and composed of republican members, the superintending government ought clearly to possess author- *90* ity to defend the system against aristocratic or monarchical innovations. The more intimate the nature of such a union may be, the greater interest have the members in the political institutions of each other; and the greater right to insist that the forms of government under which the compact was entered into, should be *substantially* maintained. But a right implies a remedy; and where else could *95* the remedy be deposited, than where it is deposited by the constitution? governments of dissimilar principles and forms have been found less adapted to a federal coalition of any sort, than those of a kindred nature. "As the confederate republic of Germany," says Montesquieu, "consists of free cities and petty states subject to different princes, experience shews us that it is more imperfect than *100* that of Holland and Switzerland." "Greece was undone" he adds, "as soon as the king of Macedon obtained a seat among the Amphyctions." In the latter case, no doubt, the disproportionate force, as well as the monarchical form of the new confederate, had its share of influence on the events. It may possibly be asked what need there could be of such a precaution, and whether it may not become *105* a pretext for alterations in the state governments, without the concurrence of the states themselves. These questions admit of ready answers. If the interposition of the general government should not be needed, the provision for such an event will be a harmless superfluity only in the constitution. But who can say what experiments may be produced by the caprice of particular states, by the ambition of *110* enterprizing leaders, or by the intrigues and influence of foreign powers? To the second question it may be answered, that if the general government should

---

Line 85 The question of what the Constitution meant by offering protection to republican forms of government came to a crisis in Rhode Island when Dorr's rebellion broke out in 1841 against an unrepresentative government still under the same constitutional form as existed in 1787. In *Luther v. Borden* (1849), the Supreme Court declined to take responsibility for imposing an interpretation, which it held to be the responsibility of Congress.

Lines 89–111 The establishment of new states (which might also entail alterations to existing states) may have been overlooked by the framers of the Articles, but the Continental Congress had in fact commissioned the ordinances of 1784 and 1785, and enacted that of 1787. Maine (1820) and West Virginia (1863) were admitted on the principle of consent on the part of the state that was to be divided; in the latter case—Virginia—the consent was largely fictitious.

Lines 98–102 Montesquieu's quoted remark is in *The Spirit of the Laws* Book IX chapter 2.

interpose by virtue of this constitutional authority, it will be of course bound to pursue the authority. But the authority extends no farther than to a guaranty of a
115 republican form of government, which supposes a pre-existing government of the form which is to be guaranteed. As long therefore as the existing republican forms are continued by the states, they are guaranteed by the federal constitution. Whenever the states may chuse to substitute other republican forms, they have a right to do so, and to claim the federal guaranty for the latter. The only re-
120 striction imposed on them is, that they shall not exchange republican for anti-republican constitutions; a restriction which it is presumed will hardly be considered as a grievance.

A protection against invasion is due from every society to the parts composing it. The latitude of the expression here used, seems to secure each state not only
125 against foreign hostility, but against ambitious or vindictive enterprizes of its more powerful neighbours. The history both of antient and modern confederacies, proves that the weaker members of the union ought not to be insensible to the policy of this article.

Protection against domestic violence is added with equal propriety. It has been
130 remarked that even among the Swiss cantons, which properly speaking are not under one government, provision is made for this object; and the history of that league informs us, that mutual aid is frequently claimed and afforded; and as well by the most democratic, as the other cantons. A recent and well known event among ourselves, has warned us to be prepared for emergencies of a like nature.
135 At first view it might seem not to square with the republican theory, to suppose either that a majority have not the right, or that a minority will have the force to subvert a government; and consequently that the federal interposition can never be required but when it would be improper. But theoretic reasoning in this, as in most other cases, must be qualified by the lessons of practice. Why may not illicit
140 combinations for purposes of violence be formed as well by a majority of a state, especially a small state, as by a majority of a county or a district of the same state; and if the authority of the state ought in the latter case to protect the local magistracy, ought not the federal authority in the former to support the state authority? Besides, there are certain parts of the state constitutions which are so
145 interwoven with the federal constitution, that a violent blow cannot be given to the one without communicating the wound to the other. Insurrections in a state will rarely induce a federal interposition, unless the number concerned in them, bear some proportion to the friends of government. It will be much better that the violence in such cases should be repressed by the superintending power,

---

Lines 114–22 As previously remarked (see note on No. 9, line 112), the concept of republican government lacked any clear definition or consensus.

While forms of government might be similar, the social structures differed widely between the New England states and those of the South.

Lines 139–48 Another reference to Shays.

than that the majority should be left to maintain their cause by a bloody and obstinate contest. The existence of a right to interpose will generally prevent the necessity of exerting it.

Is it true that force and right are necessarily on the same side in republican governments? May not the minor party possess such a superiority of pecuniary resources, of military talents and experience, or of secret succours from foreign powers, as will render it superior also in an appeal to the sword? May not a more compact and advantageous position turn the scale on the same side against a superior number so situated as to be less capable of a prompt and collected exertion of its strength? Nothing can be more chimerical than to imagine that in a trial of actual force, victory may be calculated by the rules which prevail in a census of the inhabitants, or which determine the event of an election! May it not happen in fine that the minority of citizens may become a majority of persons, by the accession of alien residents, of a casual concourse of adventurers, or of those whom the constitution of the state has not admitted to the rights of suffrage? I take no notice of an unhappy species of population abounding in some of the states, who during the calm of regular government are sunk below the level of men; but who in the tempestuous scenes of civil violence may emerge into the human character, and give a superiority of strength to any party with which they may associate themselves.

In cases where it may be doubtful on which side justice lies, what better umpires could be desired by two violent factions, flying to arms and tearing a state to pieces, than the representatives of confederate states not heated by the local flame? To the impartiality of judges they would unite the affection of friends. Happy would it be if such a remedy for its infirmities, could be enjoyed by all free governments; if a project equally effectual could be established for the universal peace of mankind.

Should it be asked what is to be the redress for an insurrection pervading all the states, and comprizing a superiority of the entire force, though not a constitutional right; the answer must be, that such a case, as it would be without the compass of human remedies, so it is fortunately not within the compass of human probability; and that it is a sufficient recommendation of the federal constitution, that it diminishes the risk of a calamity, for which no possible constitution can provide a cure.

Among the advantages of a confederate republic enumerated by Montesquieu, an important one is, "that should a popular insurrection happen in one of the states, the others are able to quell it. Should abuses creep into one part, they are reformed by those that remain sound."

Line 165 "I take no notice . . ." is *The Federalist's* first explicit reference to the racial issue. The implication is that black men will fight for their liberties when opportunity arises. The prognostication was to be borne out a very few years later with the slave uprising on Saint Domingue led by Toussaint L'Ouverture.

7. "To consider all debts contracted and engagements entered into, before the adoption of this constitution, as being no less valid against the United States under this constitution, than under the confederation."

This can only be considered as a declaratory proposition; and may have been inserted, among other reasons, for the satisfaction of the foreign creditors of the United States, who cannot be strangers to the pretended doctrine that a change in the political form of civil society, has the magical effect of dissolving its moral obligations.

Among the lesser criticisms which have been exercised on the constitution, it has been remarked that the validity of engagements ought to have been asserted in favour of the United States, as well as against them; and in the spirit which usually characterizes little critics, the omission has been transformed and magnified into a plot against the national rights. The authors of this discovery may be told, what few others need be informed of, that as engagements are in their nature reciprocal, an assertion of their validity on one side necessarily involves a validity on the other side; and that as the article is merely declaratory, the establishment of the principle in one case is sufficient for every case. They may be further told that every constitution must limit its precautions to dangers that are not altogether imaginary; and that no real danger can exist that the government would dare, with or even without this constitutional declaration before it, to remit the debts justly due to the public, on the pretext here condemned.

8. "To provide for amendments to be ratified by three-fourths of the states, under two exceptions only."

That useful alterations will be suggested by experience, could not but be foreseen. It was requisite therefore that a mode for introducing them should be provided. The mode preferred by the convention seems to be stamped with every mark of propriety. It guards equally against that extreme facility which would render the constitution too mutable; and that extreme difficulty which might perpetuate its discovered faults. It moreover equally enables the general and the state governments to originate the amendment of errors as they may be pointed out by the experience on one side or on the other. The exception in favour of the equality of suffrage in the senate was probably meant as a palladium to the residuary sovereignty of the states, implied and secured by that principle of representation in one branch of the legislature; and was probably insisted on by the states particularly attached to that equality. The other exception must have been admitted on the same considerations which produced the privilege defended by it.

9. "The ratification of the conventions of nine states shall be sufficient for the establishment of this constitution between the states ratifying the same."

Lines 220–21 Another reference to "the residuary sovereignty of the states" (see No. 39, lines 164–65). Publius's "probably" is a disclaimer of personal presence at the Convention in his persona of anonymity.

This article speaks for itself. The express authority of the people alone could give due validity to the constitution. To have required the unanimous ratification of the thirteen states, would have subjected the essential interests of the whole to the caprice or corruption of a single member. It would have marked a want of foresight in the convention, which our own experience would have rendered inexcusable.

Two questions of a very delicate nature present themselves on this occasion. 1. On what principle the confederation, which stands in the solemn form of a compact among the states, can be superceded without the unanimous consent of the parties to it? 2. What relation is to subsist between the nine or more states ratifying the constitution, and the remaining few who do not become parties to it.

The first question is answered at once by recurring to the absolute necessity of the case; to the great principle of self-preservation; to the transcendent law of nature and of nature's God, which declares that the safety and happiness of society are the objects at which all political institutions aim, and to which all such institutions must be sacrificed. Perhaps also an answer may be found without searching beyond the principles of the compact itself. It has been heretofore noted among the defects of the confederation, that in many of the states, it had received no higher sanction than a mere legislative ratification. The principle of reciprocality seems to require, that its obligation on the other states should be reduced to the same standard. A compact between independent sovereigns, founded on acts of legislative authority, can pretend to no higher validity than a league or treaty between the parties. It is an established doctrine on the subject of treaties, that all the articles are mutually conditions of each other; that a breach of any one article is a breach of the whole treaty; and that a breach committed by either of the parties absolves the others; and authorises them, if they please, to pronounce the compact violated and void. Should it unhappily be necessary to appeal to these delicate truths for a justification for dispensing with the consent of particular states to a dissolution of the federal pact, will not the complaining parties find it a difficult task to answer the multiplied and important infractions with which they may be confronted? The time has been when it was incumbent on us all to veil the ideas which this paragraph exhibits. The scene is now changed, and with it, the part which the same motives dictate.

The second question is not less delicate; and the flattering prospect of its being merely hypothetical, forbids an over-curious discussion of it. It is one of

---

Line 238 The existence of a "transcendent law" under the Confederation would not seem to rule out a higher law under the Constitution, when similar ends might be in view.

Line 246 "A compact between independent sovereigns" is of course the Articles of Confederation.

those cases which must be left to provide for itself. In general it may be observed, that although no political relation can subsist between the assenting and dissenting states, yet the moral relations will remain uncancelled. The claims of justice, both on one side and on the other, will be in force, and must be fulfilled; the *265* rights of humanity must in all cases be duly and mutually respected; whilst considerations of a common interest, and above all the remembrance of the endearing scenes which are past, and the anticipation of a speedy triumph over the obstacles to re-union, will, it is hoped, not urge in vain moderation on one side, and prudence on the other.

PUBLIUS.

FORTY-FOUR
{NO. 43 IN NEWSPAPERS}

JAMES MADISON
January 25, 1788
The Same View Continued and Concluded

To the People of the State of New York.

A *fifth* class of provisions in favor of the federal authority, consists of the following restrictions on the authority of the several states:

1. "No state shall enter into any treaty, alliance or confederation, grant letters of marque and reprisal, coin money, emit bills of credit, make any thing but gold and silver a legal tender in payment of debt; pass any bill of attainder, ex post facto law, or law impairing the obligation of contracts, or grant any title of nobility."   *5*

The prohibition against treaties, alliances and confederations, makes a part of the existing articles of union; and for reasons which need no explanation, is copied into the new constitution. The prohibition of letters of marque is another part of the old system, but is somewhat extended in the new. According to the for-   *10* mer, letters of marque could be granted by the states after a declaration of war. According to the latter, these licences must be obtained as well during war as previous to its declaration, from the government of the United States. This alter-ation is fully justified by the advantage of uniformity in all points which relate to foreign powers; and of immediate responsibility to the nation in all those, for   *15* whose conduct the nation itself is to be responsible.

The right of coining money, which is here taken from the states, was left in their hands by the confederation as a concurrent right with that of congress, under an exception in favor of the exclusive right of congress to regulate the alloy and value. In this instance also the new provision is an improvement on the old.   *20* Whilst the alloy and value depended on the general authority, a right of coinage in the particular states could have no other effect than to multiply expensive mints, and diversify the forms and weights of the circulating pieces. The latter in-conveniency defeats one purpose for which the power was originally submitted to the federal head. And as far as the former might prevent an inconvenient re-   *25* mittance of gold and silver to the central mint for recoinage, the end can be as well attained, by local mints established under the general authority.

The extension of the prohibition to bills of credit must give pleasure to every citizen in proportion to his love of justice, and his knowledge of the true springs

---

Lines 28–50 On paper money, see comment on No. 7, line 156.

30   of public prosperity. The loss which America has sustained since the peace, from the pestilent effects of paper money, on the necessary confidence between man and man; on the necessary confidence in the public councils; on the industry and morals of the people, and on the character of republican government, constitutes an enormous debt against the states chargeable with this unadvised meas-

35   ure, which must long remain unsatisfied; or rather an accumulation of guilt, which can be expiated no otherwise than by a voluntary sacrifice on the altar of justice, of the power which has been the instrument of it. In addition to these persuasive considerations, it may be observed that the same reasons which shew the necessity of denying to the states the power of regulating coin, prove with

40   equal force that they ought not to be at liberty to substitute a paper medium in the place of coin. Had every state a right to regulate the value of its coin, there might be as many different currencies as states; and thus the intercourse among them would be impeded; retrospective alterations in its value might be made, and thus the citizens of other states be injured; and animosities be kindled

45   among the states themselves. The subjects of foreign powers might suffer from the same cause, and hence the union be discredited and embroiled by the indiscretion of a single member. No one of these mischiefs is less incident to a power in the states to emit paper money than to coin gold or silver. The power to make any thing but gold and silver a tender in payment of debts, is withdrawn from the

50   states, on the same principle with that of striking of paper currency.

     Bills of attainder, ex post facto laws, and laws impairing the obligation of contracts, are contrary to the first principles of the social compact, and to every principle of sound legislation. The two former are expressly prohibited by the declarations prefixed to some of the state constitutions, and all of them are pro-

55   hibited by the spirit and scope of these fundamental charters. Our own experience has taught us nevertheless, that additional fences against these dangers ought not to be omitted. Very properly therefore have the convention added this constitutional bulwark in favor of personal security and private rights; and I am much deceived if they have not in so doing as faithfully consulted the genuine sentiments,

60   as the undoubted interests of their constituents. The sober people of America are weary of the fluctuating policy which has directed the public councils. They have seen with regret and with indignation, that sudden changes and legislative interferences in cases affecting personal rights, become jobs in the hands of enterprizing and influential speculators; and snares to the more industrious and less

---

Lines 51–60 Bills of attainder belonged to feudal law, which depended on the concept of allegiance; American law was held to be based on the principle of social compact or individual contract. The individualistic ethos of the Constitution is further implicit in the emphasis on "personal security and private rights."

Line 63 "Jobs": in 18th century parlance, a job was always a corrupt arrangement designed to promote a private or factional interest. Edmund Burke once said in Parliament that the Board of Trade originated in a "job." The word appears to have

informed part of the community. They have seen, too, that one legislative interfer- 65
ence, is but the first link of a long chain of repetitions; every subsequent interference being naturally produced by the effects of the preceding. They very rightly
infer, therefore, that some thorough reform is wanting which will banish speculations on public measures, inspire a general prudence and industry, and give a regular course to the business of society. The prohibition with respect to titles of 70
nobility, is copied from the articles of confederation, and needs no comment.

2. "No state shall, without the consent of the congress, lay any imposts or duties on imports or exports, except what may be absolutely necessary for executing
its inspection laws, and the neat produce of all duties and imposts laid by any
state on imports or exports, shall be for the use of the treasury of the United 75
States; and all such laws shall be subject to the revision and controul of the congress. No state shall, without the consent of congress, lay any duty on tonnage,
keep troops or ships of war in time of peace; enter into any agreement or compact with another state, or with a foreign power, or engage in war unless actually
invaded, or in such imminent danger as will not admit of delay." 80

The restraint on the power of the states over imports and exports is enforced
by all the arguments which prove the necessity of submitting the regulation of
trade to the federal councils. It is needless therefore to remark further on this
head, than that the manner in which the restraint is qualified, seems well calculated at once to secure to the states a reasonable discretion in providing for the 85
conveniency of their imports and exports; and to the United States a reasonable
check against the abuse of this discretion. The remaining particulars of this
clause, fall within reasonings which are either so obvious, or have been so fully
developed, that they may be passed over without remark.

The sixth and last class consists of the several powers and provisions by which 90
efficacy is given to all the rest.

1. "Of these the first is the power to make all laws which shall be necessary
and proper for carrying into execution the foregoing powers, and all other powers
vested by this constitution in the government of the United States."

Few parts of the constitution have been assailed with more intemperance 95
than this; yet on a fair investigation of it, as has been elsewhere shown, no part
can appear more compleatly invulnerable. Without the *substance* of this power,
the whole constitution would be a dead letter. Those who object to the article
therefore as a part of the constitution, can only mean that the *form* of the provision is improper. But have they considered whether a better form could have 100
been substituted?

---

undergone a radical change of meaning, though we can still speak of "jobbery,"
meaning corruption.

Lines 92–96 Publius has already expounded the "necessary and proper" clause in
No. 33.

There are four other possible methods which the convention might have taken on this subject. They might have copied the second article of the existing confederation which would have prohibited the exercise of any power not *expressly* delegated; they might have attempted a positive enumeration of the powers comprehended under the general terms "necessary and proper"; they might have attempted a negative enumeration of them, by specifying the powers excepted from the general definition: They might have been altogether silent on the subject; leaving these necessary and proper powers, to construction and inference.

Had the convention taken the first method of adopting the second article of confederation; it is evident that the new congress would be continually exposed as their predecessors have been, to the alternative of construing the term *"expressly"* with so much rigour as to disarm the government of all real authority whatever, or with so much latitude as to destroy altogether the force of the restriction. It would be easy to shew if it were necessary, that no important power, delegated by the articles of confederation, has been or can be executed by congress, without recurring more or less to the doctrine of *construction* or *implication*. As the powers delegated under the new system are more extensive, the government which is to administer it would find itself still more distressed with the alternative of betraying the public interest by doing nothing; or of violating the constitution by exercising powers, indispensably necessary and proper; but at the same time, not *expressly* granted.

Had the convention attempted a positive enumeration of the powers necessary and proper for carrying their other powers into effect; the attempt would have involved a complete digest of laws on every subject to which the constitution relates; accommodated too not only to the existing state of things, but to all the possible changes which futurity may produce: For in every new application of a general power, the *particular powers*, which are the means of attaining the *object* of the general power, must always necessarily vary with that object; and be often properly varied whilst the object remains the same.

Had they attempted to enumerate the particular powers or means, not necessary or proper for carrying the general powers into execution, the task would have been no less chimerical; and would have been liable to this further objection; that every defect in the enumeration, would have been equivalent to a positive grant of authority. If to avoid this consequence they had attempted a partial enumeration of the exceptions, and described the residue by the general terms, *not necessary or proper:* It must have happened that the enumeration would comprehend a few of the excepted powers only; that these would be such as would be least likely to be assumed or tolerated, because the enumeration would of course select such as would be least necessary or proper, and that the unnecessary and improper powers included in the residuum, would be less forcibly excepted, than if no partial enumeration had been made.

Had the constitution been silent on this head, there can be no doubt that all the particular powers, requisite as means of executing the general powers, would have resulted to the government, by unavoidable implication. No axiom is more clearly established in law, or in reason, than that wherever the end is required, the means are authorised; wherever a general power to do a thing is given, every particular power necessary for doing it, is included. Had this last method there-fore been pursued by the convention, every objection now urged against their plan, would remain in all its plausibility; and the real inconveniency would be incurred, of not removing a pretext which may be seized on critical occasions for drawing into question the essential powers of the union. *150*

If it be asked, what is to be the consequence, in case the congress shall mis-construe this part of the constitution, and exercise powers not warranted by its true meaning? I answer the same as if they should misconstrue or enlarge any *155* other power vested in them, as if the general power had been reduced to particu-lars, and any one of these were to be violated; the same in short, as if the state leg-islatures should violate their respective constitutional authorities. In the first instance, the success of the usurpation will depend on the executive and judici-ary departments, which are to expound and give effect to the legislative acts; and *160* in the last resort, a remedy must be obtained from the people, who can by the election of more faithful representatives, annul the acts of the usurpers. The truth is, that this ultimate redress may be more confided in against unconstitu-tional acts of the federal than of the state legislatures, for this plain reason, that as every such act of the former, will be an invasion of the rights of the latter, these *165* will be ever ready to mark the innovation, to sound the alarm to the people, and to exert their local influence in effecting a change of federal representatives. There being no such intermediate body between the state legislatures and the people, interested in watching the conduct of the former, violations of the state constitution are more likely to remain unnoticed and unredressed. *170*

2. "This constitution and the laws of the United States which shall be made in pursuance thereof, and all treaties made, or which shall be made, under the au-thority of the United States, shall be the supreme law of the land, and the judges in every state shall be bound thereby, any thing in the constitution or laws of any state to the contrary notwithstanding." *175*

The indiscreet zeal of the adversaries to the constitution, has betrayed them into an attack on this part of it also, without which it would have been evidently and radically defective. To be fully sensible of this we need only suppose for a moment, that the supremacy of the state constitutions had been left compleat by a saving clause in their favor. *180*

Lines 159–60 There is a hint here of the judiciary as an agency of legislative action, suggesting a less than complete formulation of the separation of powers in Publius's mind.

Line 173 Article 6, second paragraph; "the supreme law of the land" is taken from the Magna Carta.

Lines 176–78 "Centinel" Letter I, October 1787 is one such attack.

In the first place, as these constitutions invest the state legislatures with absolute sovereignty, in all cases not excepted by the existing articles of confederation, all the authorities contained in the proposed constitution, so far as they exceed those enumerated in the confederation, would have been annulled, and the new congress would have been reduced to the same impotent condition with their predecessors.

In the next place, as the constitutions of some of the states do not even expressly and fully recognize the existing powers of the confederacy, an express saving of the supremacy of the former, would in such states have brought into question, every power contained in the proposed constitution.

In the third place, as the constitutions of the states differ much from each other, it might happen that a treaty or national law of great and equal importance to the states, would interfere with some and not with other constitutions, and would consequently be valid in some of the states at the same time that it would have no effect in others.

In fine, the world would have seen for the first time, a system of government founded on an inversion of the fundamental principles of all government; it would have seen the authority of the whole society every where subordinate to the authority of the parts; it would have seen a monster in which the head was under the direction of the members.

3. "The senators and representatives, and the members of the several state legislatures; and all executive and judicial officers, both of the United States, and the several states shall be bound by oath or affirmation, to support this constitution."

It has been asked, why it was thought necessary, that the state magistracy should be bound to support the federal constitution, and unnecessary, that a like oath should be imposed on the officers of the United States in favor of the state constitutions?

Several reasons might be assigned for the distinctions. I content myself with one which is obvious and conclusive. The members of the federal government will have no agency in carrying the state constitutions into effect. The members and officers of the state governments, on the contrary, will have an essential agency in giving effect to the federal constitution. The election of the president and senate, will depend in all cases, on the legislatures of the several states. And the election of the house of representatives, will equally depend on the same authority in the first instance; and will probably, for ever be conducted by the officers and according to the laws of the states.

4. Among the provisions for giving efficacy to the federal powers, might be added, those which belong to the executive and judiciary departments: But as these are reserved for particular examination in another place, I pass them over in this.

We have now reviewed in detail all the articles composing the sum or quantity of power delegated by the proposed constitution to the federal government; and

are brought to this undeniable conclusion, that no part of the power is unnecessary or improper for accomplishing the necessary objects of the union. The ques- 225
tion therefore, whether this amount of power shall be granted or not, resolves
itself into another question, therefore, whether or not a government commensurate to the exigencies of the union, shall be established, or in other words,
whether the union itself shall be preserved.

PUBLIUS.

FORTY-FIVE
{NO. 44 IN NEWSPAPERS}

JAMES MADISON
January 26, 1788
A Further Discussion of the Supposed Danger from the
Powers of the Union, to the State Governments

To the People of the State of New York.

Having shewn that no one of the powers transferred to the federal government is unnecessary or improper, the next question to be considered is whether the whole mass of them will be dangerous to the portion of authority left in the several states.

5   The adversaries to the plan of the convention instead of considering in the first place what degree of power was absolutely necessary for the purposes of the federal government, have exhausted themselves in a secondary enquiry into the possible consequences of the proposed degree of power, to the governments of the particular states. But if the union, as has been shewn, be essential, to the se-
10   curity of the people of America against foreign danger; if it be essential to their security against contentions and wars among the different states; if it be essential to guard them against those violent and oppressive factions which embitter the blessings of liberty, and against those military establishments which must gradually poison its very fountain; if, in a word the union be essential to the happiness
15   of the people of America, is it not preposterous, to urge as an objection to a government without which the objects of the union cannot be attained, that such a government may derogate from the importance of the governments of the individual states? Was then the American revolution effected, was the American confederacy formed, was the precious blood of thousands spilt, and the hard earned
20   substance of millions lavished, not that the people of America should enjoy peace, liberty and safety; but that the governments of the individual states, that particular municipal establishments, might enjoy a certain extent of power, and be arrayed with certain dignities and attributes of sovereignty? We have heard of the impious doctrine in the old world that the people were made for kings, not
25   kings for the people. Is the same doctrine to be revived in the new, in another shape, that the solid happiness of the people is to be sacrificed to the views of political institutions of a different form? It is too early for politicians to presume on our forgetting that the public good, the real welfare of the great body of the people is the supreme object to be pursued; and that no form of government
30   whatever, has any other value, than as it may be fitted for the attainment of this object. Were the plan of the convention adverse to the public happiness, my

voice would be, reject the plan. Were the union itself inconsistent with the public happiness, it would be, abolish the union. In like manner as far as the sovereignty of the states cannot be reconciled to the happiness of the people, the voice of every good citizen must be, let the former be sacrificed to the latter. How far the sacrifice is necessary, has been shewn. How far the unsacrificed residue will be endangered, is the question before us.

Several important considerations have been touched in the course of these papers, which discountenance the supposition that the operation of the federal government will by degrees prove fatal to the state governments. The more I revolve the subject the more fully I am persuaded that the balance is much more likely to be disturbed by the preponderancy of the last than of the first scale.

We have seen in all the examples of antient and modern confederacies, the strongest tendency continually betraying itself in the members to despoil the general government of its authorities, with a very ineffectual capacity in the latter to defend itself against the encroachments. Although in most of these examples, the system has been so dissimilar from that under consideration, as greatly to weaken any inference concerning the latter from the fate of the former; yet as the states will retain under the proposed constitution a very extensive portion of active sovereignty, the inference ought not to be wholly disregarded. In the Achaean league, it is probable that the federal head had a degree and species of power, which gave it a considerable likeness to the government framed by the convention. The Lycian confederacy, as far as its principles and form are transmitted, must have borne a still greater analogy to it. Yet history does not inform us that either of them ever degenerated or tended to degenerate into one consolidated government. On the contrary, we know that the ruin of one of them proceeded from the incapacity of the federal authority to prevent the dissentions, and finally the disunion of the subordinate authorities. These cases are the more worthy of our attention, as the external causes by which the component parts were pressed together, were much more numerous and powerful than in our case; and consequently, less powerful ligaments within, would be sufficient to bind the members to the head, and to each other.

In the feudal system we have seen a similar propensity exemplified. Notwithstanding the want of proper sympathy in every instance between the local

---

Lines 33–37 The language of this argument suggests the idea that "residual" sovereignty is somehow not the real thing—a note that is in keeping with Publius's, and all conventional, opinion.

Lines 48–50 However, "a very extensive portion of active sovereignty" returns to the compromise position in keeping with that of Nos. 32, 39, and 42. For the Lycian Confederacy, see note on No. 9, lines 147–58.

Lines 63–70 It is difficult to comment on so sweeping and nonspecific a statement, but the situation in which a king offered protection to the common people against their barons could also characterize medieval monarchy.

65 sovereigns and the people, and the sympathy in some instances between the general sovereign and the latter; it usually happened that the local sovereigns prevailed in the rivalship for encroachments. Had no external dangers, enforced internal harmony and subordination; and particularly had the local sovereigns possessed the affections of the people, the great kingdoms in Europe, would at this time con-
70 sist of as many independent princes as there were formerly feudatory barons.

The state governments will have the advantage of the federal government, whether we compare them in respect to the immediate dependence of the one on the other; to the weight of personal influence which each side will possess; to the powers respectively vested in them; to the predilection and probable support
75 of the people; to the disposition and faculty of resisting and frustrating the measures of each other.

The state governments may be regarded as constituent and essential parts of the federal government; whilst the latter is nowise essential to the operation or organisation of the former. Without the intervention of the state legislatures, the
80 president of the United States cannot be elected at all. They must in all cases have a great share in his appointment, and will perhaps in most cases of themselves determine it. The senate will be elected absolutely and exclusively by the state legislatures. Even the house of representatives, though drawn immediately from the people, will be chosen very much under the influence of that class of
85 men, whose influence over the people obtains for themselves an election into the state legislatures. Thus each of the principal branches of the federal government will owe its existence more or less to the favor of the state governments, and must consequently feel a dependence, which is much more likely to beget a disposition too obsequious, than too overbearing towards them. On the other side,
90 the component parts of the state governments will in no instance be indebted for their appointment to the direct agency of the federal government, and very little if at all, to the local influence of its members.

The number of individuals employed under the constitution of the United States, will be much smaller, than the number employed under the particular
95 states. There will consequently be less of personal influence on the side of the former, than of the latter. The members of the legislative, executive and judiciary departments of thirteen and more states; the justices of peace, officers of militia, ministerial officers of justice, with all the county corporation and town-officers, for three millions and more of people, intermixed and having particular ac-
100 quaintance with every class and circle of people, must exceed beyond all proportion, both in number and influence, those of every description who will be

---

Lines 77–92 This paragraph reflects (as well as argues for the ongoing necessity of) "deference" in American political life.

Lines 93–128 In its early years, the Department of State employed only a handful of clerks and two interpreters. By 1792, the federal administration as a whole (excluding deputy postmasters) employed 780 civil servants; 660 of these were under the treasury.

employed in the administration of the federal system. Compare the members of the three great departments, of the thirteen states, excluding from the judiciary department the justices of peace, with the members of the corresponding departments of the single government of the union; compare the militia officers of three millions of people, with the military and marine officers of any establishment which is within the compass of probability, or I may add, of possibility, and in this view alone, we may pronounce the advantage of the states to be decisive. If the federal government is to have collectors of revenue, the state governments will have theirs also. And as those of the former will be principally on the sea-coast, and not very numerous; whilst those of the latter will be spread over the face of the country, and will be very numerous, the advantage in this view also lies on the same side. It is true that the confederacy is to possess, and may exercise, the power of collecting internal as well as external taxes throughout the states: But it is probable that this power will not be resorted to, except for supplemental purposes of revenue; that an option will then be given to the states to supply their quotas by previous collections of their own; and that the eventual collection under the immediate authority of the union, will generally be made by the officers, and according to the rules, appointed by the several states. Indeed it is extremely probable that in other instances, particularly in the organisation of the judicial power, the officers of the states will be cloathed with the correspondent authority of the union. Should it happen however that separate collectors of internal revenue should be appointed under the federal government, the influence of the whole number would not be a comparison with that of the multitude of state officers in the opposite scale. Within every district, to which a federal collector would be allotted, there would not be less than thirty or forty or even more officers of different descriptions and many of them persons of character and weight, whose influence would lie on the side of the state.

The powers delegated by the proposed constitution to the federal government, are few and defined. Those which are to remain in the state governments are numerous and indefinite. The former will be exercised principally on external objects, as war, peace, negociation, and foreign commerce; with which last the power of taxation will for the most part be connected. The powers reserved to the several states will extend to all the objects, which, in the ordinary course of affairs, concern the lives, liberties and properties of the people; and the internal order, improvement, and prosperity of the state.

The operations of the federal government will be most extensive and important in times of war and danger; those of the state governments, in times of peace and security. As the former periods will probably bear a small proportion to the

---

Lines 109–28 Protection was not a policy and tariffs were not envisaged as a major source of government income. Note that there is no expectation of protective tariffs.

Line 130 In view of the debate over the "necessary and proper" clause (see Nos. 33 and 44), "few and defined" is clearly designed to soothe.

140 latter, the state governments will here enjoy another advantage over the federal government. The more adequate indeed the federal powers may be rendered to the national defence, the less frequent will be those scenes of danger which might favour their ascendency over the governments of the particular states.

If the new constitution be examined with accuracy and candour, it will be 145 found that the change which it proposes, consists much less in the addition of NEW POWERS to the union, than in the invigoration of its ORIGINAL POWERS. The regulation of commerce, it is true, is a new power; but that seems to be an addition which few oppose, and from which no apprehensions are entertained. The powers relating to war and peace, armies and fleets, treaties and fi-150 nance, with the other more considerable powers, are all vested in the existing congress by the articles of confederation. The proposed change does not enlarge these powers; it only substitutes a more effectual mode of administering them. The change relating to taxation, may be regarded as the most important: And yet the present congress have as compleat authority to REQUIRE of the states indef-155 inite supplies of money for the common defence and general welfare, as the future congress will have to require them of individual citizens; and the latter will be no more bound than the states themselves have been, to pay the quotas respectively taxed on them. Had the states complied punctually with the articles of confederation, or could their compliance have been enforced by as peaceable 160 means as may be used with success towards single persons, our past experience is very far from countenancing an opinion that the state governments would have lost their constitutional powers, and have gradually undergone an entire consolidation. To maintain that such an event would have ensued, would be to say at once, that the existence of the state governments is incompatible with any system 165 whatever that accomplishes the essential purposes of the union.

PUBLIUS.

Lines 144–65 This paragraph is again clearly designed to pacify Anti-Federalist fears by minimizing the changes and glossing over the *structural* differences between the Articles and the Constitution.

FORTY-SIX
{NO. 45 IN NEWSPAPERS}

JAMES MADISON
January 29, 1788

**The Subject of the Last Paper Resumed; with an Examination of the
Comparative Means of Influence of the Federal and State Governments**

To the People of the State of New York.

Resuming the subject of the last paper, I proceed to enquire whether the federal
government or the state governments will have the advantage with regard to the
predilection and support of the people. Notwithstanding the different modes in
which they are appointed, we must consider both of them, as substantially dependent on the great body of the citizens of the United States. I assume this po-   5
sition here as it respects the first, reserving the proofs for another place. The
federal and state governments are in fact but different agents and trustees of the
people, instituted with different powers, and designated for different purposes.
The adversaries of the constitution seem to have lost sight of the people altogether in their reasonings on this subject; and to have viewed these different es-   10
tablishments, not only as mutual rivals and enemies, but as uncontrouled by any
common superior in their efforts to usurp the authorities of each other. These
gentlemen must here be reminded of their error. They must be told that the ultimate authority, wherever the derivative may be found, resides in the people
alone; and that it will not depend merely on the comparative ambition or address   15
of the different governments, whether either, or which of them, will be able to
enlarge its sphere of jurisdiction at the expence of the other. Truth no less than
decency requires, that the event in every case, should be supposed to depend on
the sentiments and sanction of their common constituents.

Many considerations, besides those suggested on a former occasion, seem to   20
place it beyond doubt, that the first and most natural attachment of the people
will be to the governments of their respective states. Into the administration of
these, a greater number of individuals will expect to rise. From the gift of these a
greater number of offices and emoluments will flow. By the superintending care
of these, all the more domestic, and personal interests of the people will be regu-   25
lated and provided for. With the affairs of these, the people will be more famil-
iarly and minutely conversant. And with the members of these, will a greater
proportion of the people have the ties of personal acquaintance and friendship,
and of family and party attachments; on the side of these therefore the popular
bias, may well be expected most strongly to incline.   30

Experience speaks the same language in this case. The federal administration, though hitherto very defective, in comparison with what may be hoped under a better system, had during the war, and particularly, whilst the independent fund of paper emissions was in credit, an activity and importance as great as it can well
35 have, in any future circumstances whatever. It was engaged too in a course of measures, which had for their object, the protection of every thing that was dear, and the acquisition of every thing that could be desireable to the people at large. It was nevertheless, invariably found, after the transient enthusiasm for the early congresses was over, that the attention and attachment of the people were turned
40 anew to their own particular governments; that the federal council, was at no time the idol of popular favor; and that opposition to proposed enlargements of its powers and importance, was the side usually taken by the men who wished to build their political consequence on the prepossessions of their fellow citizens.

If therefore, as has been elsewhere remarked, the people should in future be-
45 come more partial to the federal than to the state governments, the change can only result, from such manifest and irresistible proofs of a better administration, as will overcome all their antecedent propensities. And in that case, the people ought not surely to be precluded from giving most of their confidence where they may discover it to be most due: But even in that case, the state governments
50 could have little to apprehend, because it is only within a certain sphere, that the federal power can, in the nature of things, be advantageously administered.

The remaining points on which I proposed to compare the federal and state governments, are the disposition, and the faculty they may respectively possess, to resist and frustrate the measures of each other.
55 It has been already proved, that the members of the federal will be more dependent on the members of the state governments, than the latter will be on the former. It has appeared also, that the prepossessions of the people on whom both will depend, will be more on the side of the state governments, than of the federal government. So far as the disposition of each, towards the other, may be in-
60 fluenced by these causes, the state governments must clearly have the advantage. But in a distinct and very important point of view, the advantage will lie on the same side. The prepossessions which the members themselves will carry into the federal government, will generally be favorable to the states; whilst it will rarely happen, that the members of the state governments will carry into the public
65 councils, a bias in favor of the general government. A local spirit will infallibly prevail much more in the members of the congress, than a national spirit will prevail in the legislatures of the particular states. Every one knows that a great proportion of the errors committed by the state legislatures proceeds from the

---

Lines 55–96 This paragraph appeals to memory rather than to written history. Madison himself had been a member of the Virginia delegation to Congress and then, when his three-year term of service expired, a representative in the House of Delegates.

disposition of the members to sacrifice the comprehensive and permanent interest of the state, to the particular and separate views of the counties or districts in   *70*
which they reside. And if they do not sufficiently enlarge their policy to embrace
the collective welfare of their particular state, how can it be imagined, that they
will make the aggregate prosperity of the union, and the dignity and respectability of its government, the objects of their affections and consultations? For the
same reason, that the members of the state legislatures, will be unlikely to attach   *75*
themselves sufficiently to national objects, the members of the federal legislature
will be likely to attach themselves too much to local objects. The states will be to
the latter, what counties and towns are to the former. Measures will too often be
decided according to their probable effect, not on the national prosperity and
happiness, but on the prejudices, interests and pursuits of the governments and   *80*
people of the individual states. What is the spirit that has in general characterized
the proceedings of congress? A perusal of their journals as well as the candid acknowledgments of such as have had a seat in that assembly, will inform us, that the
members have but too frequently displayed the character, rather of partizans of
their respective states, than of impartial guardians of a common interest; that   *85*
where, on one occasion improper sacrifices have been made of local considerations to the aggrandizement of the federal government; the great interests of the nation have suffered on an hundred, from an undue attention to the local prejudices,
interests and views of the particular states. I mean not by these reflections to insinuate, that the new federal government will not embrace a more enlarged plan of   *90*
policy than the existing government may have pursued, much less that its views
will be as confined as those of the state legislatures; but only that it will partake sufficiently of the spirit of both, to be disinclined to invade the rights of the individual
states, or the prerogatives of their governments. The motives on the part of the state
governments, to augment their prerogatives by defalcations from the federal gov-   *95*
ernment, will be overruled by no reciprocal predispositions in the members.

Were it admitted however that the federal government may feel an equal disposition with the state governments to extend its power beyond the due limits,
the latter would still have the advantage in the means of defeating such encroachments. If an act of a particular state, though unfriendly to the national   *100*
government, be generally popular in that state, and should not too grossly violate
the oaths of the state officers, it is executed immediately and of course, by means
on the spot, and depending on the state alone. The opposition of the federal government, or the interposition of federal officers, would but inflame the zeal of all
parties on the side of the state, and the evil could not be prevented or repaired, if   *105*
at all, without the employment of means which must always be resorted to with
reluctance and difficulty. On the other hand, should an unwarrantable measure

---

Lines 97–117 See No. 45. Though remaining anonymous, Madison obviously
speaks from experience.

of the federal government be unpopular in particular states, which would seldom fail to be the case, or even a warrantable measure be so, which may sometimes be the case, the means of opposition to it are powerful and at hand. The
disquietude of the people, their repugnance and perhaps refusal to co-operate
with the officers of the union, the frowns of the executive magistracy of the state,
the embarrassments created by legislative devices, which would often be added
on such occasions, would oppose in any state difficulties not to be despised;
would form in a large state very serious impediments, and where the sentiments
of several adjoining states happened to be in unison, would present obstructions
which the federal government would hardly be willing to encounter.

But ambitious encroachments of the federal government, on the authority of
the state governments, would not excite the opposition of a single state or of a
few states only. They would be signals of general alarm. Every government
would espouse the common cause. A correspondence would be opened. Plans of
resistance would be concerted. One spirit would animate and conduct the
whole. The same combination in short would result from an apprehension of the
federal, as was produced by the dread of a foreign yoke; and unless the projected
innovations should be voluntarily renounced, the same appeal to a trial of force
would be made in the one case, as was made in the other. But what degree of
madness could ever drive the federal government to such an extremity? In the
contest with Great Britain, one part of the empire was employed against the
other. The more numerous part invaded the rights of the less numerous part.
The attempt was unjust and unwise; but it was not in speculation absolutely
chimerical. But what would be the contest in the case we are supposing? Who
would be the parties? A few representatives of the people, would be opposed to
the people themselves; or rather one set of representatives would be contending
against thirteen sets of representatives, with the whole body of their common
constituents on the side of the latter.

The only refuge left for those who prophecy the downfall of the state governments, is the visionary supposition that the federal government may previously
accumulate a military force for the projects of ambition. The reasonings contained in these papers must have been employed to little purpose indeed, if it
could be necessary now to disprove the reality of this danger. That the people
and the states should for a sufficient period of time elect an uninterrupted succession of men ready to betray both; that the traitors should throughout this
period, uniformly and systematically pursue some fixed plan for the extension of
the military establishment; that the governments and the people of the states
should silently and patiently behold the gathering storm, and continue to supply
the materials, until it should be prepared to burst on their own heads, must appear to every one more like the incoherent dreams of a delirious jealousy, or the
misjudged exaggerations of a counterfeit zeal, than like the sober apprehensions
of genuine patriotism. Extravagant as the supposition is, let it however be made.
Let a regular army, fully equal to the resources of the country be formed; and let
it be entirely at the devotion of the federal government; still it would not be going

too far to say, that the state governments with the people on their side would be able to repel the danger. The highest number to which, according to the best computation, a standing army can be carried in any country, does not exceed one hundredth part of the whole number of souls; or one twenty-fifth part of the number able to bear arms. This proportion would not yield in the United States an army of more than twenty-five or thirty thousand men. To these would be opposed a militia amounting to near half a million of citizens with arms in their hands, officered by men chosen from among themselves, fighting for their common liberties, and united and conducted by governments possessing their affections and confidence. It may well be doubted whether a militia thus circumstanced could ever be conquered by such a proportion of regular troops. Those who are best acquainted with the late successful resistance of this country against the British arms will be most inclined to deny the possibility of it. Besides the advantage of being armed, which the Americans possess over the people of almost every other nation, the existence of subordinate governments to which the people are attached, and by which the militia officers are appointed, forms a barrier against the enterprizes of ambition, more insurmountable than any which a simple government of any form can admit of. Notwithstanding the military establishments in the several kingdoms of Europe, which are carried as far as the public resources will bear, the governments are afraid to trust the people with arms. And it is not certain that with this aid alone, they would not be able to shake off their yokes. But were the people to possess the additional advantages of local governments chosen by themselves, who could collect the national will, and direct the national force; and of officers appointed out of the militia, by these governments and attached both to them and to the militia, it may be affirmed with the greatest assurance, that the throne of every tyranny in Europe would be speedily overturned, in spite of the legions which surround it. Let us not insult the free and gallant citizens of America with the suspicion that they would be less able to defend the rights of which they would be in actual possession, than the debased subjects of arbitrary power would be to rescue theirs from the hands of their oppressors. Let us rather no longer insult them with the supposition, that they can ever reduce themselves to the necessity of making the experiment, by a blind and tame submission to the long train of insidious measures, which must precede and produce it.

Lines 157–85 The reference to the militia as a safeguard of liberty was, of course, to official, state-sponsored bodies, to which men brought their own firearms. Madison oversteps his knowledge on the bearing of arms in Europe. The militia was an English local institution long before it was an American one. Ordinary British farmers normally kept firearms for shooting animals; it seems probable that the same was true of many French peasants. (All this has nothing whatever to do with the question of whether the government has constitutional power to ban such weapons as semi-automatic weapons and assault rifles.)

The argument under the present head may be put into a very concise form, which appears altogether conclusive. Either the mode in which the federal government is to be constructed will render it sufficiently dependant on the people, or it will not. On the first supposition, it will be restrained by that dependence from forming schemes obnoxious to their constituents. On the other supposition it will not possess the confidence of the people, and its schemes of usurpation will be easily defeated by the state governments; who will be supported by the people.

On summing up the considerations stated in this and the last paper, they seem to amount to the most convincing evidence, that the powers proposed to be lodged in the federal government, are as little formidable to those reserved to the individual states, as they are indispensibly necessary to accomplish the purposes of the union; and that all those alarms which have been sounded, of a meditated and consequential annihilation of the state governments, must, on the most favorable interpretation, be ascribed to the chimerical fears of the authors of them.

PUBLIUS.

FORTY-SEVEN
{NO. 46 IN NEWSPAPERS}

JAMES MADISON
January 30, 1788
The Meaning of the Maxim, Which Requires a Separation of the Departments of Power, Examined and Ascertained

To the People of the State of New York.

Having reviewed the general form of the proposed government, and the general mass of power allotted to it: I proceed to examine the particular structure of this government, and the distribution of this mass of power among its constituent parts.

One of the principal objections inculcated by the more respectable adversaries to the constitution, is its supposed violation of the political maxim, that the leg- islative, executive and judiciary departments ought to be separate and distinct. In the structure of the federal government, no regard, it is said, seems to have been paid to this essential precaution in favor of liberty. The several departments of power are distributed and blended in such a manner, as at once to destroy all sym- metry and beauty of form; and to expose some of the essential parts of the edifice to the danger of being crushed by the disproportionate weight of other parts.

No political truth is certainly of greater intrinsic value or is stamped with the authority of more enlightened patrons of liberty than that on which the objection is founded. The accumulation of all powers legislative, executive and judiciary in the same hands, whether of one, a few or many, and whether hereditary, self ap- pointed, or elective, may justly be pronounced the very definition of tyranny. Were the federal constitution therefore really chargeable with this accumulation of power or with a mixture of powers having a dangerous tendency to such an

5

10

15

Lines 4–11 This paragraph introduces discussion of the principle of the separation of powers. Both sides were agreed that there were three functions of government: legislative, executive, and judicial; and they agreed on the vital importance to politi- cal liberty of keeping these functions in separate hands. They differed as to whether separation was adequately embodied in the Constitution. The principle of separation is nowhere stated in the Constitution, but it is implied by the way in which the three branches of government are separately established and their powers and duties laid down. It may here be observed that the Constitution of the United States incorpo- rated this principle in more extreme form than that of any other existing state, then or since. A very great deal of time and resources are expended in the process of Ameri- can government in circumventing the obstacles to efficient government created by the principle of separation.

accumulation, no further arguments would be necessary to inspire a universal
20   reprobation of the system. I persuade myself however, that it will be made apparent to every one, that the charge cannot be supported, and that the maxim on
which it relies, has been totally misconceived and misapplied. In order to form
correct ideas on this important subject, it will be proper to investigate the sense,
in which the preservation of liberty requires, that the three great departments of
25   power should be separate and distinct.

The oracle who is always consulted and cited on this subject, is the celebrated
Montesquieu. If he be not the author of this invaluable precept in the science of
politics, he has the merit at least of displaying, and recommending it most effectually to the attention of mankind. Let us endeavour in the first place to ascertain
30   his meaning on this point.

The British constitution was to Montesquieu, what Homer has been to the di-
dactic writers on epic poetry. As the latter have considered the work of the im-
mortal bard, as the perfect model from which the principles and rules of the epic
art were to be drawn, and by which all similar works were to be judged; so this
35   great political critic appears to have viewed the constitution of England, as the
standard, or to use his own expression, as the mirror of political liberty; and to
have delivered in the form of elementary truths, the several characteristic principles of that particular system. That we may be sure then not to mistake his meaning in this case, let us recur to the source from which the maxim was drawn.

Lines 26–30 Montesquieu develops his theme on the separation of powers in *The
Spirit of the Laws*, Book XI Chapter 6, where he propounds the Whig principle "that
every man invested with power is apt to abuse it." This would later appear in Lord
Acton's celebrated dictum, "Power tends to corrupt, and absolute power corrupts
absolutely." American Whigs in this period already felt they had immediate experience of the truth of this from George III. This had been possible because the king's
government was believed by both the British opposition and by Americans to have
corrupted the legislature by conferring office on members of Parliament. (Opposition
members had in fact introduced "place" bills to check this practice at intervals in the
18th century, but to no avail.) Montesquieu extols England as the one country "that
has for the direct end of its constitution political liberty." He distinguishes as the
three branches of government "the legislative; the executive in respect to things dependent on the law of nations; and the executive, in respect to things that depend on
the civil laws." He then defines the latter as "the judiciary power." Montesquieu sat-
isfies himself as to the *forms* of the English constitution but admits that he has not enquired into the substance. Judicial independence of the crown had been established
by the Act of Settlement, 1701 (not mentioned by Montesquieu). Later specialists
have noted the possible influence of the ancient philosopher Polybius on theories of
the mixed constitution, which may account for Madison's doubt about whether
Montesquieu is the author of the doctrine. From the American point of view, if a
government as nearly perfect as England's could be subverted, it was all the more
important to make the separation as nearly absolute as was compatible with the necessary degree of cooperation between the branches.

On the slightest view of the British constitution we must perceive, that the leg- *40*
islative, executive and judiciary departments are by no means totally separate
and distinct from each other. The executive magistrate forms an integral part of
the legislative authority. He alone has the prerogative of making treaties with foreign sovereigns, which when made have, under certain limitations, the force of
legislative acts. All the members of the judiciary department are appointed by *45*
him; can be removed by him on the address of the two houses of Parliament, and
form, when he pleases to consult them, one of his constitutional councils. One
branch of the legislative department forms also, a great constitutional council to
the executive chief; as on another hand, it is the sole depositary of judicial power
in cases of impeachment, and is invested with the supreme appellate jurisdic- *50*
tion, in all other cases. The judges again are so far connected with the legislative
department, as often to attend and participate in its deliberations, though not admitted to a legislative vote.

From these facts by which Montesquieu was guided it may clearly be inferred,
that in saying "there can be no liberty where the legislative and executive powers *55*
are united in the same person, or body of magistrates," or "if the power of judging
be not separated from the legislative and executive powers," he did not mean that
these departments ought to have no *partial agency* in, or no *controul* over the acts
of each other. His meaning, as his own words import, and still more conclusively
as illustrated by the example in his eye, can amount to no more than this, that *60*
where the *whole* power of one department is exercised by the same hands which
possess the *whole* power of another department, the fundamental principles of a
free constitution, are subverted. This would not have been the case in the constitution examined by him, if the king who is the sole executive magistrate, had possessed also the compleat legislative power, or the supreme administration of *65*
justice; or if the entire legislative body, had possessed the supreme judiciary, or
the supreme executive authority. This however is not among the vices of that
constitution. The magistrate in whom the whole executive power resides cannot
of himself make a law, though he can put a negative on every law, nor administer
justice in person, though he has the appointment of those who do administer it. *70*
The judges can exercise no executive prerogative, though they are shoots from

---

Lines 45–58 Madison exaggerates the dependence of British judges. It would have
been extraordinarily difficult to get both houses of Parliament to draw up an address
demanding a judge's resignation, and it did not happen. The Americans instituted a
somewhat similar impeachment procedure (which was unsuccessfully used against
Supreme Court Justice Samuel Chase during Jefferson's presidency). In Britain, the
monarch, however, retained considerable initiative over the choice of prime minister, though he was constrained by the need to choose a man who could command
the respect of the House of Commons. The House of Lords was—and still is—the
highest court of appeal. (This function is now performed by its judicial committee,
consisting of very senior lawyers. But as this goes to press, the establishment of a
new Supreme Court is contemplated.)

the executive stock, nor any legislative function, though they may be advised with by the legislative councils. The entire legislature, can perform no judiciary act, though by the joint act of two of its branches, the judges may be removed from their offices; and though one of its branches is possessed of the judicial power in the last resort. The entire legislature again can exercise no executive prerogative, though one of its branches constitutes the supreme executive magistracy; and another, on the impeachment of a third, can try and condemn all the subordinate officers in the executive department.

The reasons on which Montesquieu grounds his maxim are a further demonstration of his meaning. "When the legislative and executive powers are united in the same person or body" says he, "there can be no liberty, because apprehensions may arise lest *the same* monarch or senate should *enact* tyrannical laws, to *execute* them in a tyrannical manner." Again "Were the power of judging joined with the legislative, the life and liberty of the subject would be exposed to arbitrary controul, for *the judge* would then be *the legislator*. Were it joined to the executive power, *the judge* might behave with all the violence of *an oppressor*." Some of these reasons are more fully explained in other passages; but briefly stated as they are here, they sufficiently establish the meaning which we have put on this celebrated maxim of this celebrated author.

If we look into the constitutions of the several states we find that notwithstanding the emphatical, and in some instances, the unqualified terms in which this axiom has been laid down, there is not a single instance in which the several departments of power have been kept absolutely separate and distinct. New-Hampshire, whose constitution was the last formed, seems to have been fully aware of the impossibility and inexpediency of avoiding any mixture whatever of these departments; and has qualified the doctrine by declaring "that the legislative, executive and judiciary powers ought to be kept as separate from, and independent of each other *as the nature of a free government will admit; or as is consistent with that chain of connection, that binds the whole fabric of the constitution in one indissoluble bond of unity and amity*." Her constitution accordingly mixes these departments in several respects. The senate which is a branch of the legislative department is also a judicial tribunal for the trial of impeachments. The president who is the head of the executive department, is the presiding member also of the senate; and besides an equal vote in all cases, has a casting vote in case of a tie. The executive head is himself eventually elective every year by the legislative department; and his council is every year chosen by and from the members of the same department. Several of the officers of state are also appointed by the legislature. And the members of the judiciary department are appointed by the executive department.

Line 95; Lines 111–16 The date of the New Hampshire Constitution was 1784, that of Massachusetts, 1780. Notwithstanding these stringent provisions, plural office holding continued in Massachusetts.

The constitution of Massachusetts has observed a sufficient though less pointed caution in expressing this fundamental article of liberty. It declares "that the legislative department shall never exercise the executive and judicial powers, or either of them: The executive shall never exercise the legislative and judicial powers, or either of them: The judicial shall never exercise the legislative and executive powers, or either of them." This declaration corresponds precisely with the doctrine of Montesquieu as it has been explained, and is not in a single point violated by the plan of the convention. It goes no farther than to prohibit any one of the entire departments from exercising the powers of another department. In the very constitution to which it is prefixed, a partial mixture of powers has been admitted. The executive magistrate has a qualified negative on the legislative body; and the senate, which is a part of the legislature, is a court of impeachment for members both of the executive and judiciary departments. The members of the judiciary department again are appointable by the executive department, and removeable by the same authority, on the address of the two legislative branches. Lastly, a number of the officers of government are annually appointed by the legislative department. As the appointment to offices, particularly executive offices, is in its nature an executive function, the compilers of the constitution have in this last point at least, violated the rule established by themselves.

I pass over the constitutions of Rhode-Island and Connecticut, because they were formed prior to the revolution; and even before the principle under examination had become an object of political attention.

The constitution of New-York contains no declaration on this subject; but appears very clearly to have been framed with an eye to the danger of improperly blending the different departments. It gives nevertheless to the executive magistrate a partial controul over the legislative department; and what is more, gives a like controul to the judiciary department, and even blends the executive and judiciary departments in the exercise of this controul. In its council of appointment, members of the legislative are associated with the executive authority in the appointment of officers both executive and judiciary. And its court for the trial of impeachments and correction of errors, is to consist of one branch of the legislature and the principal members of the judiciary department.

The constitution of New-Jersey has blended the different powers of government more than any of the preceding. The governor, who is the executive magistrate, is appointed by the legislature; is chancellor and ordinary or surrogate of the state; is a member of the supreme court of appeals, and president with a casting vote, of one of the legislative branches. The same legislative branch acts again as executive council to the governor, and with him constitutes the court of

115

120

125

130

135

140

145

Lines 130–32 Rhode Island and Connecticut were satisfied with their existing charters and did not embark on new constitutions.

Lines 133–204 The constitution of New York was adopted in 1777; Massachusetts in 1780; the other state constitutions in 1776 or 1777.

appeals. The members of the judiciary department are appointed by the legislative department, and removeable by one branch of it, on the impeachment of
the other.

According to the constitution of Pennsylvania, the president, who is head of
the executive department, is annually elected by a vote in which the legislative
department predominates. In conjunction with an executive council, he appoints the members of the judiciary department, and forms a court of impeachments for trial of all officers, judiciary as well as executive. The judges of the
supreme court, and justices of the peace, seem also to be removeable by the legislature; and the executive power of pardoning in certain cases to be referred to
the same department. The members of the executive council are made EX
OFFICIO justices of peace throughout the state.

In Delaware, the chief executive magistrate is annually elected by the legislative department. The speakers of the two legislative branches are vice-presidents
in the executive department. The executive chief, with six others, appointed
three by each of the legislative branches, constitute the supreme court of appeals: He is joined with the legislative department in the appointment of the
other judges. Throughout the states it appears that the members of the legislature may at the same time be justices of the peace. In this state, the members of
one branch of it are EX OFFICIO justices of peace; as are also the members of
the executive council. The principal officers of the executive department are appointed by the legislative; and one branch of the latter forms a court of impeachments. All officers may be removed on address of the legislature.

Maryland has adopted the maxim in the most unqualified terms; declaring
that the legislative, executive and judicial powers of government, ought to be forever separate and distinct from each other. Her constitution, notwithstanding
makes the executive magistrate appointable by the legislative department; and
the members of the judiciary, by the executive department.

The language of Virginia is still more pointed on this subject. Her constitution declares, "that the legislative, executive and judiciary departments, shall be
separate and distinct; so that neither exercise the powers properly belonging to
the other; nor shall any person exercise the powers of more than one of them at
the same time; except that the justices of the county courts shall be eligible to either house of assembly." Yet we find not only this express exception, with respect
to the members of the inferior courts; but that the chief magistrate with his executive council are appointable by the legislature; that two members of the latter
are triennially displaced at the pleasure of the legislature; and that all the principal offices, both executive and judiciary, are filled by the same department. The
executive prerogative of pardon, also is in one case vested in the legislative
department.

The constitution of North-Carolina, which declares, "that the legislative, executive and supreme judicial powers of government, ought to be forever separate
and distinct from each other," refers at the same time to the legislative depart-

ment, the appointment not only of the executive chief, but all the principal officers within both that and the judiciary department.

In South-Carolina, the constitution makes the executive magistracy eligible
by the legislative department. It gives to the latter also the appointment of the
members of the judiciary department, including even justices of the peace and
sheriffs; and the appointment of officers in the executive department, down to
captains in the army and navy of the state.

In the constitution of Georgia, where it is declared, "that the legislative, executive and judiciary departments shall be separate and distinct, so that neither
exercise the powers properly belonging to the other." We find that the executive department is to be filled by appointments of the legislature; and the
executive prerogative of pardon, to be finally exercised by the same authority.
Even justices of the peace are to be appointed by the legislature.

In citing these cases in which the legislative, executive and judiciary departments, have not been kept totally separate and distinct, I wish not to be regarded
as an advocate for the particular organizations of the several state governments. I
am fully aware that among the many excellent principles which they exemplify,
they carry strong marks of the haste, and still stronger of the inexperience, under
which they were framed. It is but too obvious that in some instances, the fundamental principle under consideration has been violated by too great a mixture,
and even an actual consolidation of the different powers; and that in no instance
has a competent provision been made for maintaining in practice the separation
delineated on paper. What I have wished to evince is, that the charge brought
against the proposed constitution, of violating a sacred maxim of free government, is warranted neither by the real meaning annexed to that maxim by its author; nor by the sense in which it has hitherto been understood in America. This
interesting subject will be resumed in the ensuing paper.

PUBLIUS.

FORTY-EIGHT
{NO. 47 IN NEWSPAPERS}

JAMES MADISON
February 1, 1788
**The Same Subject continued, with a View to the Means of
Giving Efficacy in Practice to That Maxim**

To the People of the State of New York.

It was shewn in the last paper, that the political apothegm there examined, does not require that the legislative, executive and judiciary departments should be wholly unconnected with each other. I shall undertake in the next place, to shew that unless these departments be so far connected and blended, as to give to each
5   a constitutional controul over the others, the degree of separation which the maxim requires as essential to a free government, can never in practice, be duly maintained.

It is agreed on all sides, that the powers properly belonging to one of the departments, ought not to be directly and compleatly administered by either of the other
10   departments. It is equally evident, that neither of them ought to possess directly or indirectly, an overruling influence over the others in the administration of their respective powers. It will not be denied, that power is of an encroaching nature, and that it ought to be effectually restrained from passing the limits assigned to it. After discriminating therefore in theory, the several classes of power, as they may in their
15   nature be legislative, executive, or judiciary; the next and most difficult task, is to provide some practical security for each against the invasion of the others. What this security ought to be, is the great problem to be solved.

Will it be sufficient to mark with precision the boundaries of these departments in the constitution of the government, and to trust to these parchment bar-
20   riers against the encroaching spirit of power? This is the security which appears to have been principally relied on by the compilers of most of the American constitutions. But experience assures us, that the efficacy of the provision has been greatly over-rated; and that some more adequate defence is indispensibly necessary for the more feeble, against the more powerful members of the government.
25   The legislative department is every where extending the sphere of its activity, and drawing all power into its impetuous vortex.

The founders of our republics have so much merit for the wisdom which they have displayed, that no task can be less pleasing than that of pointing out the errors into which they have fallen. A respect for truth however obliges us to remark,
30   that they seem never for a moment to have turned their eyes from the danger to liberty from the overgrown and all-grasping prerogative of an hereditary magis-

trate, supported and fortified by an hereditary branch of the legislative authority. They seem never to have recollected the danger from legislative usurpations; which by assembling all power in the same hands, must lead to the same tyranny as is threatened by executive usurpations.   35

In a government, where numerous and extensive prerogatives are placed in the hands of a hereditary monarch, the executive department is very justly regarded as the source of danger, and watched with all the jealousy which a zeal for liberty ought to inspire. In a democracy, where a multitude of people exercise in person the legislative functions, and are continually exposed by their incapac-   40
ity for regular deliberation and concerted measures, to the ambitious intrigues of their executive magistrates, tyranny may well be apprehended on some favorable emergency, to start up in the same quarter. But in a representative republic, where the executive magistracy is carefully limited both in the extent and the duration of its power; and where the legislative power is exercised by an assembly,   45
which is inspired by a supposed influence over the people with an intrepid confidence in its own strength; which is sufficiently numerous to feel all the passions which actuate a multitude; yet not so numerous as to be incapable of pursuing the objects of its passions, by means which reason prescribes; it is against the enterprising ambition of this department, that the people ought to indulge all   50
their jealousy and exhaust all their precautions.

The legislative department derives a superiority in our governments from other circumstances. Its constitutional powers being at once more extensive and less susceptible of precise limits, it can with the greater facility, mask under complicated and indirect measures, the encroachments which it makes on the co-   55
ordinate departments. It is not unfrequently a question of real nicety in legislative bodies, whether the operation of a particular measure, will, or will not extend beyond the legislative sphere. On the other side, the executive power being restrained within a narrower compass, and being more simple in its nature; and the judiciary being described by land marks, still less uncertain, projects of usurpa-   60
tion by either of these departments, would immediately betray and defeat themselves. Nor is this all: As the legislative department alone has access to the pockets of the people, and has in some constitutions full discretion, and in all, a prevailing influence over the pecuniary rewards of those who fill the other departments, a dependence is thus created in the latter, which gives still greater fa-   65
cility to encroachments of the former.

Lines 39–43 The Constitution provides for a *representative* form of government, which contemporaries did not identify as *democracy*. Direct democracy had a very dubious reputation, on account of the ease with which the populace could be swayed by demagogues (see No. 6) and of the only too well-known tendency of democracies to degenerate into mob rule, followed by dictatorship.

I have appealed to our own experience for the truth of what I advance on this subject. Were it necessary to verify this experience by particular proofs, they might be multiplied without end. I might collect vouchers in abundance from the records and archives of every state in the union. But as a more concise and at the same time, equally satisfactory evidence, I will refer to the example of two states, attested by two unexceptionable authorities.

The first example is that of Virginia, a state which, as we have seen, has expressly declared in its constitution, that the three great departments ought not to be intermixed. The authority in support of it is Mr. Jefferson, who, besides his other advantages for remarking the operation of the government, was himself the chief magistrate of it. In order to convey fully the ideas with which his experience had impressed him on this subject, it will be necessary to quote a passage of some length from his very interesting "Notes on the state of Virginia." (p. 195.) "All the powers of government, legislative, executive and judiciary, result to the legislative body. The concentrating these in the same hands is precisely the definition of despotic government. It will be no alleviation that these powers will be exercised by a plurality of hands, and not by a single one. One hundred and seventy-three despots would surely be as oppressive as one. Let those who doubt it turn their eyes on the republic of Venice. As little will it avail us that they are chosen by ourselves. An *elective despotism*, was not the government we fought for; but one which should not only be founded on free principles, but in which the powers of government should be so divided and balanced among several bodies of magistracy, as that no one could transcend their legal limits, without being effectually checked and restrained by the others. For this reason that convention which passed the ordinance of government, laid its foundation on this basis, that the legislative, executive and judiciary departments should be separate and distinct, so that no person should exercise the powers of more than one of them at

---

Lines 67–72 Both state legislatures and Congress published their records. Publius is here within the realm of public memory.

Lines 73–102 This paragraph enlists Jefferson in the case for separation of powers. Jefferson was governor of Virginia at the time referred to (but not when the Virginia constitution and declaration of rights were adopted in 1776). Jefferson's *Notes on the State of Virginia*, published originally in Paris in 1785, was composed in response to a circularized request for information about the states, in the form of enumerated queries, from François Marbois, secretary to the French legation in Philadelphia. Marbois's request, originating in 1780, was happily passed to Governor Jefferson, who made exhaustive inquiries of various correspondents and revised and enlarged his work several times before permitting publication (which he had not initially intended). *Notes on the State of Virginia* remained the only publication authorized by Jefferson during his lifetime.

The burden of the argument of this paragraph is that state legislatures are exceeding their legitimate *legislative* powers and have trespassed into the judicial role. This is an abuse typical of the excesses of democracy.

the same time. *But no barrier was provided between these several powers.* The judiciary and executive members were left dependent on the legislative for their sub- *95* sistence in office, and some of them for their continuance in it. If therefore the legislature assumes executive and judiciary powers, no opposition is likely to be made; nor if made can be effectual; because in that case, they may put their proceeding into the form of an act of assembly, which will render them obligatory on the other branches. They have accordingly *in many* instances *decided rights* *100* which should have been left to *judiciary controversy*; and *the direction of the executive during the whole time of their session, is becoming habitual and familiar."*

The other state which I shall have for an example, is Pennsylvania; and the other authority the council of censors which assembled in the years 1783 and 1784. A part of the duty of this body, as marked out by the constitution was, "to *105* enquire whether the constitution had been preserved inviolate in every part; and whether the legislative and executive branches of government had performed their duty as guardians of the people, or assumed to themselves, or exercised other or greater powers than they are entitled to by the constitution." In the execution of this trust, the council were necessarily led to a comparison, of both the *110* legislative and executive proceedings, with the constitutional powers of these departments; and from the facts enumerated, and to the truth of most of which, both sides in the council subscribed, it appears that the constitution had been flagrantly violated by the legislature in a variety of important instances.

A great number of laws had been passed violating without any apparent neces- *115* sity, the rule requiring that all bills of a public nature, shall be previously printed for the consideration of the people; although this is one of the precautions chiefly relied on by the constitution, against improper acts of the legislature.

The constitutional trial by jury had been violated; and powers assumed, which had not been delegated by the constitution. *120*

Executive powers had been usurped.

The salaries of the judges, which the constitution expressly requires to be fixed, had been occasionally varied; and cases belonging to the judiciary department, frequently drawn within legislative cognizance and determination.

Those who wish to see the several particulars falling under each of these *125* heads, may consult the journals of the council which are in print. Some of them, it will be found may be imputable to peculiar circumstances connected with the war: But the greater part of them may be considered as the spontaneous shoots of an ill-constituted government.

Lines 103–43 This account of the democratic excesses of the Pennsylvania legislature, which provides evidence to sustain the argument of lines 73–102, is also an attack on the conduct of the Pennsylvania radicals, who had seized power in the spring and summer of 1776. The records were available through the policy, provided for in the revolutionary state constitution, of publishing legislative proceedings in the interests of more open government.

130   It appears also, that the executive department had not been innocent of frequent breaches of the constitution. There are three observations however, which ought to be made on this head. *First.* A great proportion of the instances, were either immediately produced by the necessities of the war, or recommended by congress or the commander in chief. *Second.* In most of the other instances, they

135 conformed either to the declared or the known sentiments of the legislative department. *Third.* The executive department of Pennsylvania is distinguished from that of the other states, by the number of members composing it. In this respect it has as much affinity to a legislative assembly, as to an executive council. And being at once exempt from the restraint of an individual responsibility for

140 the acts of the body, and deriving confidence from mutual example and joint influence; unauthorized measures would of course be more freely hazarded, than where the executive department is administered by a single hand or by a few hands.

     The conclusion which I am warranted in drawing from these observations is,

145 that a mere demarkation on parchment of the constitutional limits of the several departments, is not a sufficient guard against those encroachments which lead to a tyrannical concentration of all the powers of government in the same hands.

     PUBLIUS.

FORTY-NINE
{NO. 48 IN NEWSPAPERS}

JAMES MADISON
February 2, 1788
The Same Subject Continued with the Same View

To the People of the State of New York.

The author of the "Notes on the state of Virginia," quoted in the last paper, has subjoined to that valuable work, the draught of a constitution which had been prepared in order to be laid before a convention expected to be called in 1783 by the legislature, for the establishment of a constitution for that commonwealth. The plan, like every thing from the same pen, marks a turn of thinking original, comprehensive and accurate; and is the more worthy of attention, as it equally displays a fervent attachment to republican government, and an enlightened view of the dangerous propensities against which it ought to be guarded. One of the precautions which he proposes, and on which he appears ultimately to rely as a palladium to the weaker departments of power, against the invasions of the stronger, is perhaps altogether his own, and as it immediately relates to the subject of our present enquiry, ought not to be overlooked.

His proposition is, "that whenever any two of the three branches of government shall concur in opinion, each by the voices of two thirds of their whole number, that a convention is necessary for altering the constitution or *correcting breaches of it*, a convention shall be called for the purpose."

As the people are the only legitimate fountain of power, and it is from them that the constitutional charter, under which the several branches of government hold their power, is derived; it seems strictly consonant to the republican theory, to recur to the same original authority, not only whenever it may be necessary to enlarge, diminish, or new-model the powers of government; but also whenever any one of the departments may commit encroachments on the chartered authorities of the others. The several departments being perfectly co-ordinate by the terms of their common commission, neither of them, it is evident, can pretend to an exclusive or superior right of settling the boundaries between their respective powers; and how are the encroachments of the stronger to be prevented, or the wrongs of the weaker to be redressed, without an appeal to the people themselves; who, as the grantors of the commission, can alone declare its true meaning and enforce its observance?

There is certainly great force in this reasoning, and it must be allowed to prove, that a constitutional road to the decision of the people, ought to be marked out, and kept open, for certain great and extraordinary occasions. But there appear to

be insuperable objections against the proposed recurrence to the people, as a provision in all cases for keeping the several departments of power within their
35   constitutional limits.

In the first place, the provision does not reach the case of a combination of two of the departments against a third. If the legislative authority, which possesses so many means of operating on the motives of the other departments, should be able to gain to its interest either of the others, or even one-third of its
40   members, the remaining department could derive no advantage from this remedial provision. I do not dwell however on this objection, because it may be thought to lie rather against the modification of the principle, than against the principle itself.

In the next place, it may be considered as an objection inherent in the princi-
45   ple, that as every appeal to the people would carry an implication of some defect in the government, frequent appeals would in great measure deprive the government of that veneration, which time bestows on every thing, and without which perhaps the wisest and freest governments would not possess the requisite stability. If it be true that all governments rest on opinion, it is no less true that the
50   strength of opinion in each individual, and its practical influence on his conduct, depend much on the number which he supposes to have entertained the same opinion. The reason of man, like man himself is timid and cautious, when left alone; and acquires firmness and confidence, in proportion to the number with which it is associated. When the examples, which fortify opinion, are
55   *antient* as well as *numerous*, they are known to have a double effect. In a nation of philosophers, this consideration ought to be disregarded. A reverence for the laws, would be sufficiently inculcated by the voice of an enlightened reason. But a nation of philosophers is as little to be expected as the philosophical race of kings wished for by Plato. And in every other nation, the most rational govern-
60   ment will not find it a superfluous advantage, to have the prejudices of the community on its side.

The danger of disturbing the public tranquility by interesting too strongly the public passions, is a still more serious objection against a frequent reference of constitutional questions, to the decision of the whole society. Notwithstanding
65   the success which has attended the revisions of our established forms of government, and which does so much honour to the virtue and intelligence of the people of America, it must be confessed, that the experiments are of too ticklish a nature to be unnecessarily multiplied. We are to recollect that all the existing

---

Line 49 The source for the observation that "all governments rest on opinion" is David Hume's essay "On the First Principles of Government," first published in his *Essays Moral and Political* (1741).

Lines 58–59 The reference is to the philosopher–kings of Plato's *Republic*.

Line 65 The "revisions" were the new state constitutions formed in the revolutionary era.

constitutions were formed in the midst of a danger which repressed the passions most unfriendly to order and concord; of an enthusiastic confidence of the people in their patriotic leaders, which stifled the ordinary diversity of opinions on great national questions; of a universal ardor for new and opposite forms, produced by a universal resentment and indignation against the antient government; and whilst no spirit of party, connected with the changes to be made, or the abuses to be reformed, could mingle its leaven in the operation. The future situations in which we must expect to be usually placed, do not present any equivalent security against the danger which is apprehended.

But the greatest objection of all is, that the decisions which would probably result from such appeals, would not answer the purpose of maintaining the constitutional equilibrium of the government. We have seen that the tendency of republican governments is to an aggrandizement of the legislative, at the expence of the other departments. The appeals to the people therefore would usually be made by the executive and judiciary departments. But whether made by one side or the other, would each side enjoy equal advantages on the trial? Let us view their different situations. The members of the executive and judiciary departments, are few in number, and can be personally known to a small part only of the people. The latter by the mode of their appointment, as well as, by the nature and permanency of it, are too far removed from the people to share much in their prepossessions. The former are generally the objects of jealousy: And their administration is always liable to be discoloured and rendered unpopular. The members of the legislative department, on the other hand, are numerous. They are distributed and dwell among the people at large. Their connections of blood, of friendship and of acquaintance, embrace a great proportion of the most influencial part of the society. The nature of their public trust implies a personal influence among the people, and that they are more immediately the confidential guardians of the rights and liberties of the people. With these advantages, it can hardly be supposed that the adverse party would have an equal chance for a favorable issue.

But the legislative party would not only be able to plead their cause most successfully with the people. They would probably be constituted themselves the judges. The same influence which had gained them an election into the legislature, would gain them a seat in the convention. If this should not be the case with all, it would probably be the case with many, and pretty certainly with those leading characters, on whom every thing depends in such bodies. The convention in short would be composed chiefly of men, who had been, who actually were, or who expected to be, members of the department whose conduct was arraigned. They would consequently be parties to the very question to be decided by them.

It might however sometimes happen, that appeals would be made under circumstances less adverse to the executive and judiciary departments. The usurpations of the legislature might be so flagrant and so sudden, as to admit of no specious colouring. A strong party among themselves might take side with the

other branches. The executive power might be in the hands of a peculiar favorite of the people. In such a posture of things, the public decision might be less
115 swayed by prepossessions in favor of the legislative party. But still it could never be expected to turn on the true merits of the question. It would inevitably be connected with the spirit of pre-existing parties, or of parties springing out of the question itself. It would be connected with persons of distinguished character and extensive influence in the community. It would be pronounced by the very
120 men who had been agents in, or opponents of the measures, to which the decision would relate. The *passions* therefore not *the reason*, of the public, would sit in judgment. But it is the reason of the public alone that ought to controul and regulate the government. The passions ought to be controuled and regulated by the government.
125 We found in the last paper that mere declarations in the written constitution, are not sufficient to restrain the several departments within their legal limits. It appears in this, that occasional appeals to the people would be neither a proper nor an effectual provision, for that purpose. How far the provisions of a different nature contained in the plan above quoted, might be adequate, I do not exam-
130 ine. Some of them are unquestionably founded on sound political principles, and all of them are framed with singular ingenuity and precision.

PUBLIUS.

Lines 121–24 This expression of anxiety that the passions may dominate the faculty of reason is a key to the moral structure of *The Federalist* as well as to its political purpose. Eighteenth-century psychology inherited an ancient tradition that divided the mind into faculties. Publius's strategy was to replicate the mental faculties in the structure of society; the cool, measured, reasoning element was represented in the educated and leisured classes, which had time for deep reading, for reflection, and for taking account of the long-term interests of society (always compatible with those of property). The well-intentioned but less-well-educated populace were susceptible to the sway of passion, but could be induced to accept the guidance of the reasoning classes, given time, and through political institutions that were needed to assist this process. The separation of powers was designed to prevent any one faction (see No. 10) from obtaining power over the whole operation of government. The emphatic differentiation between reason and the passions suggests that Madison had been influenced by Hume's moral philosophy, as for example in his *Essay on Human Nature* (1739), in addition to his political essays.

FIFTY
{NO. 49 IN NEWSPAPERS}

JAMES MADISON
February 5, 1788
The Same Subject Continued with the Same View

To the People of the State of New York.

It may be contended perhaps, that instead of *occasional* appeals to the people, which are liable to the objections urged against them, *periodical* appeals are the proper and adequate means *of preventing and correcting infractions of the constitution.*

It will be attended to, that in the examination of these expedients, I confine myself to their aptitude for *enforcing* the constitution by keeping the several departments of power within their due bounds, without particularly considering them, as provisions for *altering* the constitution itself. In the first view, appeals to the people at fixed periods, appear to be nearly as ineligible, as appeals on particular occasions as they emerge. If the periods be separated by short intervals, the measures to be reviewed and rectified, will have been of recent date, and will be connected with all the circumstances which tend to viciate and pervert the result of occasional revisions. If the periods be distant from each other, the same remark will be applicable to all recent measures, and in proportion as the remoteness of the others may favor a dispassionate review of them, this advantage is inseparable from inconveniencies which seem to counterbalance it. In the first place, a distant prospect of public censure would be a very feeble restraint on power from those excesses, to which it might be urged by the force of present motives. Is it to be imagined, that a legislative assembly, consisting of a hundred or two hundred members, eagerly bent on some favorite object, and breaking through the restraints of the constitution in pursuit of it, would be arrested in their career, by considerations drawn from a censorial revision of their conduct at the future distance of ten, fifteen or twenty years? In the next place, the abuses would often have compleated their mischievous effects, before the remedial provision would be applied. And in the last place, where this might not be the case, they would be of long standing, would have taken deep root, and would not easily be extirpated.

The scheme of revising the constitution in order to correct recent breaches of it, as well as for other purposes, has been actually tried in one of the states. One of the objects of the council of censors, which met in Pennsylvania, in 1783 and

5

10

15

20

25

Lines 28–37 The Council of Censors was introduced in the Pennsylvania constitution of 1776 as a means of trying to make sure that legislation had not departed from

30 1784 was, as we have seen, to enquire "whether the constitution had been violated, and whether the legislative and executive departments had encroached on
each other." This important and novel experiment in politics, merits in several
points of view, very particular attention. In some of them it may perhaps, as a
single experiment, made under circumstances somewhat peculiar, be thought to
35 be not absolutely conclusive. But as applied to the case under consideration, it
involves some facts which I venture to remark, as a compleat and satisfactory
illustration of the reasoning which I have employed.

First. It appears from the names of the gentlemen, who composed the council, that some at least of its most active and leading members, had also been ac-
40 tive and leading characters in the parties which pre-existed in the state.

Second. It appears that the same active and leading members of the council,
had been active and influential members of the legislative and executive
branches, within the period to be reviewed; and even patrons or opponents of the
very measures to be thus brought to the test of the constitution. Two of the mem-
45 bers had been vice-presidents of the state, and several others, members of the
executive council, within the seven preceding years. One of them had been
speaker, and a number of others distinguished members of the legislative assembly, within the same period.

Third. Every page of their proceedings witnesses the effect of all these cir-
50 cumstances on the temper of their deliberations. Throughout the continuance of
the council, it was split into two fixed and violent parties. The fact is acknowledged and lamented by themselves. Had this not been the case, the face of their
proceedings exhibit a proof equally satisfactory. In all questions, however unim-

---

the constitution's first principles. (This was an old republican precept which can be
found in Machiavelli.) The Council was elective, with two members from each
county; it was to meet every seven years. But it had no powers of enforcement, was
riven by party controversy, and served only to demonstrate the futility of such efforts.
One provision of the constitution was an oath of loyalty to be sworn by voters. Since
the constitution itself was at the center of violent party controversy, and both the
Constitutionalist (i.e., radical) and Republican (i.e., conservative) parties were represented on the Council, its deliberations reverberated with party accusations and
countercharges. Its only long-term effect may have been to strengthen the Republican case for a state constitutional convention, which came about in 1790. The radical constitution was overthrown and a bicameral legislature was established in
Pennsylvania. Madison, of course, could not yet know that this would happen; but
he had served on the Congress sitting in Philadelphia and had had every opportunity
for observing the conduct of Pennsylvania politics.

Lines 41–48 Elections to fill Council vacancies in 1783 brought in some new
members, including the former vice president of the state, Judge George Bryan, a
prominent radical and contributor to the framing of the constitution, and the constitutionalist James Potter, who was the other former vice president. The former speaker
was the more conservative Frederick A. C. Muhlenberg.

portant in themselves, or unconnected with each other, the same names, stand invariably contrasted on the opposite columns. Every unbiassed observer, may infer without danger of mistake, and at the same time, without meaning to reflect on either party, or any individuals of either party, that unfortunately *passion*, not *reason*, must have presided over their decisions. When men exercise their reason coolly and freely, on a variety of distinct questions, they inevitably fall into different opinions, on some of them. When they are governed by a common passion, their opinions if they are so to be called, will be the same.

Fourth. It is at least problematical, whether the decisions of this body, do not, in several instances, misconstrue the limits prescribed for the legislative and executive departments, instead of reducing and limiting them within their constitutional places.

Fifth. I have never understood that the decisions of the council on constitutional questions, whether rightly or erroneously formed, have had any effect in varying the practice founded on legislative constructions. It even appears, if I mistake not, that in one instance, the contemporary legislature denied the constructions of the council, and actually prevailed in the contest.

This censorial body therefore, proves at the same time, by its researches, the existence of the disease; and by its example, the inefficacy of the remedy.

This conclusion cannot be invalidated by alledging that the state in which the experiment was made, was at that crisis, and had been for a long time before, violently heated and distracted by the rage of party. Is it to be presumed, that at any future septennial epoch, the same state will be free from parties? Is it to be presumed that any other state, at the same or any other given period, will be exempt from them? Such an event ought to be neither presumed nor desired; because an extinction of parties necessarily implies either a universal alarm for the public safety, or an absolute extinction of liberty.

Were the precaution taken of excluding from the assemblies elected by the people to revise the preceding administration of the government, all persons who should have been concerned in the government within the given period, the difficulties would not be obviated. The important task would probably devolve on men, who with inferior capacities, would in other respects, be little better qualified. Although they might not have been personally concerned in the administration, and therefore not immediately agents in the measures to be examined; they would probably have been involved in the parties connected with these measures, and have been elected under their auspices.

PUBLIUS.

Lines 68–70 Madison does not identify the incident, and his "if I mistake not" does not inspire confidence, but if right, he does demonstrate the inability of this sort of institution to enforce its own rulings. Clearly, such a council would not serve the purposes of the United States.

FIFTY-ONE
{NO. 50 IN NEWSPAPERS}

JAMES MADISON
February 6, 1788
The Same Subject Continued with the Same View, and Concluded

To the People of the State of New York.

To what expedient then shall we finally resort for maintaining in practice the necessary partition of power among the several departments, as laid down in the constitution? The only answer that can be given is, that as all these exterior provisions are found to be inadequate, the defect must be supplied, by so contriving
5 the interior structure of the government, as that its several constituent parts may, by their mutual relations, be the means of keeping each other in their proper places. Without presuming to undertake a full developement of this important idea, I will hazard a few general observations, which may perhaps place it in a clearer light, and enable us to form a more correct judgment of the principles
10 and structure of the government planned by the convention.

In order to lay a due foundation for that separate and distinct exercise of the different powers of government, which to a certain extent, is admitted on all hands to be essential to the preservation of liberty, it is evident that each department should have a will of its own; and consequently should be so constituted, that the
15 members of each should have as little agency as possible in the appointment of the members of the others. Were this principle rigorously adhered to, it would require that all the appointments for the supreme executive, legislative, and judiciary magistracies, should be drawn from the same fountain of authority, the people, through channels, having no communication whatever with one another.
20 Perhaps such a plan of constructing the several departments would be less difficult in practice than it may in contemplation appear. Some difficulties however, and some additional expence, would attend the execution of it. Some deviations therefore from the principle must be admitted. In the constitution of the judici-

---

Attribution: Jacob E. Cooke gives Madison, with Hamilton in square brackets. I see no internal reason for doubting Madison's authorship. The argument of this essay is closely related to that of No. 10, which is by Madison, and reintroduces an echo of Montesquieu (see note on lines 39–40), whom Madison has apparently been reading for this series of essays (see No. 47).

Lines 13–14 The thought that "each department should have a will of its own" again invokes the faculty psychology underlying *The Federalist* (see No. 49, note for lines 121–24).

ary department in particular, it might be inexpedient to insist rigorously on the principle; first, because peculiar qualifications being essential in the members, the primary consideration ought to be to select that mode of choice, which best secures these qualifications; secondly, because the permanent tenure by which the appointments are held in that department, must soon destroy all sense of dependence on the authority conferring them.

It is equally evident that the members of each department should be as little dependent as possible on those of the others, for the emoluments annexed to their offices. Were the executive magistrate, or the judges, not independent of the legislature in this particular, their independence in every other would be merely nominal.

But the great security against a gradual concentration of the several powers in the same department, consists in giving to those who administer each department, the necessary constitutional means, and personal motives, to resist encroachments of the others. The provision for defence must in this, as in all other cases, be made commensurate to the danger of attack. Ambition must be made to counteract ambition. The interest of the man must be connected with the constitutional rights of the place. It may be a reflection on human nature, that such devices should be necessary to controul the abuses of government. But what is government itself but the greatest of all reflections on human nature? If men were angels, no government would be necessary. If angels were to govern men, neither external nor internal controuls on government would be necessary. In framing a government which is to be administered by men over men, the great difficulty lies in this: You must first enable the government to controul the governed; and in the next place, oblige it to controul itself. A dependence on the people is no doubt the primary controul on the government; but experience has taught mankind the necessity of auxiliary precautions.

This policy of supplying by opposite and rival interests, the defect of better motives, might be traced through the whole system of human affairs, private as well as public. We see it particularly displayed in all the subordinate distributions of power; where the constant aim is to divide and arrange the several offices in such a manner as that each may be a check on the other; that the private interest of every individual, may be a centinel over the public rights. These inventions of prudence cannot be less requisite in the distribution of the supreme powers of the state.

Lines 39–40 "Ambition must be made to counteract ambition. . . . " Compare Montesquieu, *Spirit of the Laws*: "Constant experience shows us, that every man invested with power is apt to abuse it. . . . To prevent the abuse of power, 'tis necessary that by the very disposition of things power should be a check to power" (book XI, chapter IV).

Lines 44–45 "If men were angels. . . . " Compare Jean-Jacques Rousseau, *The Social Contract* (1762): "If there were a people of gods, they would govern themselves democratically. So perfect a government does not suit itself to men" (book III, chapter IV).

But it is not possible to give to each department an equal power of self defence. In republican government the legislative authority necessarily predominates. The remedy for this inconveniency is, to divide the legislature into
different branches; and to render them by different modes of election, and different principles of action, as little concerned with each other, as the nature of their
common functions, and their common dependence on the society, will admit. It
may even be necessary to guard against dangerous encroachments by still further
precautions. As the weight of the legislative authority requires that it should be
thus divided, the weakness of the executive may require, on the other hand, that
it should be fortified. An absolute negative, on the legislature, appears at first
view to be the natural defence with which the executive magistrate should be
armed. But perhaps it would be neither altogether safe, nor alone sufficient. On
ordinary occasions, it might not be exerted with the requisite firmness; and on extraordinary occasions, it might be perfidiously abused. May not this defect of an
absolute negative be supplied, by some qualified connection between this
weaker department, and the weaker branch of the stronger department, by which
the latter may be led to support the constitutional rights of the former, without
being too much detached from the rights of its own department?

If the principles on which these observations are founded be just, as I persuade myself they are, and they be applied as a criterion, to the several state constitutions, and to the federal constitution, it will be found, that if the latter does
not perfectly correspond with them, the former are infinitely less able to bear
such a test.

There are moreover two considerations particularly applicable to the federal
system of America, which place that system in a very interesting point of view.

First. In a single republic, all the power surrendered by the people is submitted to the administration of a single government; and the usurpations are
guarded against by a division of the government into distinct and separate departments. In the compound republic of America, the power surrendered by the
people, is first divided between two distinct governments, and then the portion
allotted to each, subdivided among distinct and separate departments. Hence a
double security arises to the rights of the people. The different governments will
controul each other; at the same time that each will be controuled by itself.

Second. It is of great importance in a republic, not only to guard the society
against the oppression of its rulers; but to guard one part of the society against the
injustice of the other part. Different interests necessarily exist in different classes
of citizens. If a majority be united by a common interest, the rights of the minority will be insecure. There are but two methods of providing against this evil: The

---

Lines 60–61 In laying down that "in republican government the legislative authority
necessarily predominates," Madison gives Publius's keynote definition of republican
government. It is because of this predominance that all the other checks and balances are necessary. See also No. 22, lines 80–82, and No. 39, lines 12–40.

one by creating a will in the community independent of the majority, that is, of the society itself; the other by comprehending in the society so many separate descriptions of citizens, as will render an unjust combination of a majority of the whole, very improbable, if not impracticable. The first method prevails in all governments possessing an hereditary or self-appointed authority. This at best is but a precarious security; because a power independent of the society may as well espouse the unjust views of the major, as the rightful interests, of the minor party, and may possibly be turned against both parties. The second method will be exemplified in the federal republic of the United States. Whilst all authority in it will be derived from and dependent on the society, the society itself will be broken into so many parts, interests and classes of citizens, that the rights of individuals or of the minority, will be in little danger from interested combinations of the majority. In a free government, the security for civil rights must be the same as that for religious rights. It consists in the one case in the multiplicity of interests, and in the other, in the multiplicity of sects. The degree of security in both cases will depend on the number of interests and sects; and this may be presumed to depend on the extent of country and number of people comprehended under the same government. This view of the subject must particularly recommend a proper federal system to all the sincere and considerate friends of republican government: Since it shews that in exact proportion as the territory of the union may be formed into more circumscribed confederacies or states, oppressive combinations of a majority will be facilitated, the best security under the republican form, for the rights of every class of citizens, will be diminished; and consequently, the stability and independence of some member of the government, the only other security, must be proportionally increased. Justice is the end of government. It is the end of civil society. It ever has been, and ever will be pursued, until it be obtained, or until liberty be lost in the pursuit. In a society under the forms of which the stronger faction can readily unite and oppress the weaker, anarchy may as truly be said to reign, as in a state of nature where the weaker individual is not secured against the violence of the stronger: And as in the latter

100

105

110

115

120

125

Lines 109–16 The idea that religious freedom can be secured by a multiplicity of sects could have derived historically from England in the 1640s. What was undoubtedly uppermost in Madison's thoughts, however, was the experience of Virginia in the previous few years, when he himself (with a large Baptist element in his own constituency) had steered Jefferson's draft of the Statute for Religious Freedom through the legislature in 1786.

The comparison with the security for civil rights from a multiplicity of interests is continuous with the argument of No. 10. The next step in the argument returns to Montesquieu (see No. 9, lines 82–119).

Lines 121–22 Justice had been defined by Locke, as copied by Johnson, as "The virtue by which we give to every man what is his due."

The ultimate derivation is from Aristotle's *Nicomachean Ethics*, Book V.

state even the stronger individuals are prompted by the uncertainty of their condition, to submit to a government which may protect the weak as well as themselves: So in the former state, will the more powerful factions or parties be
130 gradually induced by a like motive, to wish for a government which will protect all parties, the weaker as well as the more powerful. It can be little doubted, that if the state of Rhode Island was separated from the confederacy, and left to itself, the insecurity of rights under the popular form of government within such narrow limits, would be displayed by such reiterated oppressions of factious majori-
135 ties, that some power altogether independent of the people would soon be called for by the voice of the very factions whose misrule had proved the necessity of it. In the extended republic of the United States, and among the great variety of interests, parties and sects which it embraces, a coalition of a majority of the whole society could seldom take place on any other principles than those of justice and
140 the general good: Whilst there being thus less danger to a minor from the will of the major party, there must be less pretext also, to provide for the security of the former, by introducing into the government a will not dependent on the latter; or in other words, a will independent of the society itself. It is no less certain than it is important, notwithstanding the contrary opinions which have been enter-
145 tained, that the larger the society, provided it lie within a practicable sphere, the more duly capable it will be of self government. And happily for the *republican cause*, the practicable sphere may be carried to a very great extent, by a judicious modification and mixture of the *federal principle*.

PUBLIUS.

Lines 131–36 Madison later returns to Rhode Island as a model of legislative misrule. The example was all the more ominous because it was an *outcome* of the American Revolution occurring within the framework of American institutions.

FIFTY-TWO
{NO. 51 IN NEWSPAPERS}

JAMES MADISON

February 8, 1788

Concerning the House of Representatives, with a View to the Qualifications of the Electors and Elected, and the Time of Service of the Members

To the People of the State of New York.

From the more general enquiries pursued in the four last papers, I pass on to a more particular examination of the several parts of the government. I shall begin with the house of representatives.

The first view to be taken of this part of the government, relates to the qualifi- 5
cations of the electors and the elected. Those of the former are to be the same with those of the electors of the most numerous branch of the state legislatures. The definition of the right of suffrage is very justly regarded as a fundamental ar- ticle of republican government. It was incumbent on the convention therefore to define and establish this right, in the constitution. To have left it open for the oc- casional regulation of the congress, would have been improper for the reason 10 just mentioned. To have submitted it to the legislative discretion of the states, would have been improper for the same reason; and for the additional reason, that it would have rendered too dependent on the state governments, that branch of the federal government, which ought to be dependent on the people alone. To have reduced the different qualifications in the different states, to one uniform 15 rule, would probably have been as dissatisfactory to some of the states, as it would have been difficult to the convention. The provision made by the convention ap- pears therefore, to be the best that lay within their option. It must be satisfactory to every state; because it is conformable to the standard already established, or which may be established by the state itself. It will be safe to the United States; 20 because, being fixed by the state constitutions, it is not alterable by the state gov- ernments, and it cannot be feared that the people of the states will alter this part

---

Lines 4–24 Only in the provision that the suffrage in each state shall be the same for the legislature as for the electoral college does the Constitution "define" the right of suffrage. In leaving these qualifications to the individual states the Convention per- mitted a potential departure from the underlying principle of individual political equality. Property, racial, and gender restrictions were normal in state constitutions. Nevertheless, suffrage was more widespread than in any other known jurisdiction in the period.

of their constitutions, in such a manner as to abridge the rights secured to them by the federal constitution.

25   The qualifications of the elected being less carefully and properly defined by the state constitutions, and being at the same time more susceptible of uniformity, have been very properly considered and regulated by the convention. A representative of the United States must be of the age of twenty-five years; must have been seven years a citizen of the United States, must at the time of his elec-
30   tion, be an inhabitant of the state he is to represent, and during the time of his service must be in no office under the United States. Under these reasonable limitations, the door of this part of the federal government, is open to merit of every description, whether native or adoptive, whether young or old, and without regard to poverty or wealth, or to any particular profession of religious faith.

35   The term for which the representatives are to be elected, falls under a second view which may be taken of this branch. In order to decide on the propriety of this article, two questions must be considered; first, whether biennial elections will, in this case, be safe; secondly, whether they be necessary or useful.

    First. As it is essential to liberty that the government in general, should have a
40   common interest with the people; so it is particularly essential that the branch of it under consideration, should have an immediate dependence on, and an intimate sympathy with the people. Frequent elections are unquestionably the only policy by which this dependence and sympathy can be effectually secured. But what particular degree of frequency may be absolutely necessary for the purpose,
45   does not appear to be susceptible of any precise calculation; and must depend on a variety of circumstances with which it may be connected. Let us consult experience, the guide that ought always to be followed, whenever it can be found.

    The scheme of representation, as a substitute for a meeting of the citizens in person, being at most but very imperfectly known to ancient polity; it is in more
50   modern times only, that we are to expect instructive examples. And even here, in order to avoid a research too vague and diffusive, it will be proper to confine ourselves to the few examples which are best known, and which bear the greatest analogy to our particular case. The first to which this character ought to be applied, is the house of commons in Great Britain. The history of this branch of the
55   English constitution, anterior to the date of Magna Charta, is too obscure to yield instruction. The very existence of it has been made a question among political antiquaries. The earliest records of subsequent date prove, that Parliaments were to *sit* only, every year; not that they were to be *elected* every year. And even these annual sessions were left so much at the discretion of the monarch, that

---

Line 55 "Magna Charta" is a common but erroneous spelling of *Magna Carta*. Madison seems to have had an imperfect set of English statutes (see note for No. 84, line 79).

Lines 57–61 Annual parliaments as a means of restoring the dependence of members of the House of Commons on their electors had become an issue in British pol-

under various pretexts, very long and dangerous intermissions, were often con-   *60*
trived by royal ambition. To remedy this grievance, it was provided by a statute in
the reign of Charles II that the intermissions should not be protracted beyond a
period of three years. On the accession of William III, when a revolution took
place in the government, the subject was still more seriously resumed, and it was
declared to be among the fundamental rights of the people, that Parliaments   *65*
ought to be held *frequently*. By another statute which passed a few years later in
the same reign, the term 'frequently' which had alluded to the triennial period
settled in the time of Charles II is reduced to a precise meaning, it being expressly enacted that a new parliament shall be called within three years after the
determination of the former. The last change from three to seven years is well   *70*
known to have been introduced pretty early in the present century, under an
alarm for the Hanoverian succession. From these facts it appears, that the greatest frequency of elections which has been deemed necessary in that kingdom, for
binding the representatives to their constituents, does not exceed a triennial return of them. And if we may argue from the degree of liberty retained even under   *75*
septennial elections, and all the other vicious ingredients in the parliamentary
constitution, we cannot doubt that a reduction of the period from seven to three
years, with the other necessary reforms, would so far extend the influence of the
people over their representatives, as to satisfy us, that biennial elections under
the federal system, cannot possibly be dangerous to the requisite dependence of   *80*
the house of representatives on their constituents.

Elections in Ireland till of late were regulated entirely by the discretion of the
crown, and were seldom repeated except on the accession of a new prince, or
some other contingent event. The parliament which commenced with George
IId. was continued throughout his whole reign, a period of about thirty-five years.   *85*
The only dependence of the representatives on the people consisted, in the right
of the latter to supply occasional vacancies, by the election of new members, and
in the chance of some event which might produce a general new election. The
ability also of the Irish parliament, to maintain the rights of their constituents, so
far as the disposition might exist, was extremely shackled by the controul of the   *90*

---

itics in the 1770s. But the annual parliaments of antiquity were a product of Whig
political mythology.

Lines 61–63 The Triennial Act apparently referred to must be 16 Ch. II cap. 1, 1664,
the main purpose of which was to repeal and replace one passed in 1641; but no
further such act was passed under Charles II.

Lines 66–72 Madison must be thinking of the Triennial Act that followed the Glorious Revolution (6 and 7 Will. and Mary cap. 2, 1694). The Septennial Act (I Geo. I
St. 2 c. 38) was passed in 1716 (see No. 41, lines 141–51). Madison's vagueness on
relevant English history suggests hasty composition.

Lines 82–99 The latest act affecting the Irish Parliament had been passed as recently
as 1782 (23 Geo. III cap. 28). But it had no provision for octennial parliaments.

crown over the subjects of their deliberation. Of late these shackles, if I mistake not, have been broken; and octennial parliaments have besides been established. What effect may be produced by this partial reform, must be left to further expe- rience. The example of Ireland, from this view of it, can throw but little light on
95 the subject. As far as we can draw any conclusion from it, it must be, that if the people of that country have been able, under all these disadvantages, to retain any liberty whatever, the advantage of biennial elections would secure to them every degree of liberty which might depend on a due connection between their representatives and themselves.

100 Let us bring our enquiries nearer home. The example of these states when British colonies claims particular attention; at the same time that it is so well known, as to require little to be said on it. The principle of representation, in one branch of the legislature at least, was established in all of them. But the periods of election were different. They varied from one to seven years. Have we any rea-
105 son to infer from the spirit and conduct of the representatives of the people, prior to the revolution, that biennial elections would have been dangerous to the pub- lic liberties? The spirit which every where displayed itself at the commencement of the struggle; and which vanquished the obstacles to independence, is the best of proofs that a sufficient portion of liberty had been every where enjoyed to in-
110 spire both a sense of its worth, and a zeal for its proper enlargement. This remark holds good as well with regard to the then colonies, whose elections were least frequent, as to those whose elections were most frequent. Virginia was the colony which stood first in resisting the parliamentary usurpations of Great-Britain: it was the first also in espousing by public act, the resolution of independence. In
115 Virginia nevertheless, if I have not been misinformed, elections under the for- mer government were septennial. This particular example is brought into view, not as a proof of any peculiar merit, for the priority in those instances, was prob- ably accidental; and still less of any advantage in *septennial* elections, for when compared with a greater frequency they are inadmissible: but merely as a proof,
120 and I conceive it to be a very substantial proof, that the liberties of the people can be in no danger from *biennial* elections.

The conclusion resulting from these examples will be not a little strength- ened by recollecting three circumstances. The first is that the federal legislature will possess a part only of that supreme legislative authority which is vested com-
125 pletely in the British parliament, and which with a few exceptions was exercised

---

Lines 114–16 Madison seems to have been writing without access to Virginia statutes. Elections under the colonial regime were not in fact septennial; the best es- timate is that the length of life of any one House of Burgesses was about three years. In 1715 the House attempted to enact a triennial bill but was vetoed by Governor Spottswood; an attempt by the House of Burgesses in 1762 to bring Virginia into line with Britain by instituting septennial legislatures was disallowed by the Crown as an infringement of the royal prerogative.

by the colonial assemblies and the Irish legislature. It is a received and well founded maxim, that, where no other circumstances affect the case, the greater the power is, the shorter ought to be its duration; and, conversely, the smaller the power, the more safely may its duration be protracted. In the second place, it has, on another occasion, been shewn that the federal legislature will not only be re- *130* strained by its dependence on the people as other legislative bodies are; but that it will be moreover watched and controuled by the several collateral legislatures, which other legislative bodies are not. And in the third place, no comparison can be made between the means that will be possessed by the more permanent branches of the federal government for seducing, if they should be disposed to se- *135* duce, the house of representatives from their duty to the people; and the means of influence over the popular branch, possessed by the other branches of the governments above cited. With less power therefore to abuse, the federal representatives, can be less tempted on one side, and will be doubly watched on the other.

PUBLIUS.

FIFTY-THREE
{NO. 52 IN NEWSPAPERS}

JAMES MADISON
February 9, 1788
The Same Subject Continued, with a View of the
Term of Service of the Members

To the People of the State of New York.

I shall here perhaps be reminded of a current observation, "that where annual elections end, tyranny begins." If it be true as has often been remarked, that sayings which become proverbial, are generally founded in reason, it is not less true that when once established, they are often applied to cases to which the reason of
5   them does not extend. I need not look for a proof beyond the case before us. What is the reason on which this proverbial observation is founded? No man will subject himself to the ridicule of pretending that any natural connection subsists between the sun or the seasons, and the period within which human virtue can bear the temptations of power. Happily for mankind, liberty is not in this respect
10   confined to any single point of time; but lies within extremes, which afford sufficient latitude for all the variations which may be required by the various situations and circumstances of civil society. The election of magistrates might be, if it were found expedient, as in some instances it actually has been, daily, weekly, or monthly, as well as annual; and if circumstances may require a deviation from
15   the rule on one side, why not also on the other side? Turning our attention to the periods established among ourselves, for the election of the most numerous branches of the state legislatures, we find them by no means coinciding any more in this instance, than in the elections of other civil magistrates. In Connecticut and Rhode-Island, the periods are half-yearly. In the other states, South-
20   Carolina excepted, they are annual. In South-Carolina, they are biennial; as is proposed in the federal government. Here is a difference, as four to one, between the longest and shortest periods; and yet it would be not easy to shew that Connecticut or Rhode-Island is better governed, or enjoys a greater share of rational liberty than South-Carolina; or that either the one or the other of these states are
25   distinguished in these respects, and by these causes, from the states whose elections are different from both.

Lines 1–2 This slogan had been current in later colonial years, and even appeared on newspaper mastheads.

In searching for the grounds of this doctrine, I can discover but one, and that is wholly inapplicable to our case. The important distinction so well understood in America between a constitution established by the people, and unalterable by the government; and a law established by the government, and alterable by the government, seems to have been little understood and less observed in any other country. Wherever the supreme power of legislation has resided, has been supposed to reside also, a full power to change the form of the government. Even in Great-Britain, where the principles of political and civil liberty have been most discussed; and where we hear most of the rights of the constitution, it is maintained that the authority of the parliament is transcendent and uncontroulable, as well with regard to the constitution, as the ordinary objects of legislative provision. They have accordingly, in several instances, actually changed, by legislative acts, some of the most fundamental articles of the government. They have in particular, on several occasions, changed the period of election; and on the last occasion, not only introduced septennial, in place of triennial elections; but by the same act continued themselves in place four years beyond the term for which they were elected by the people. An attention to these dangerous practices has produced a very natural alarm in the votaries of free government, of which frequency of elections is the corner stone; and has led them to seek for some security to liberty against the danger to which it is exposed. Where no constitution paramount to the government, either existed or could be obtained, no constitutional security similar to that established in the United States, was to be attempted. Some other security therefore was to be sought for; and what better security would the case admit, than that of selecting and appealing to some simple and familiar portion of time, as a standard for measuring the danger of innovations, for fixing the national sentiment, and for uniting the patriotic exertions. The most simple and familiar portion of time, applicable to the subject, was that of a year; and hence the doctrine has been inculcated by a laudable zeal to erect some barrier against the gradual innovations of an unlimited government, that the advance towards tyranny was to be calculated by the distance of departure from the fixed point of annual elections. But what necessity can there be of applying this expedient to a government, limited as the federal government will be, by the authority of a paramount constitution? Or who will pretend that the liberties of the people of America will not be more secure under biennial elections, unalterably fixed by such a constitution, than those of any other nation would be, where elections were annual or even more frequent, but subject to alterations by the ordinary power of the government?

Lines 39–43 Parliament's power over its own duration was exercised in the triennial and septennial acts and in the Parliament Act of 1911 (see No. 52, lines 57–72). Early in the Second World War, Parliament extended its life for the duration of the war; a general election would have been due in 1940 but took place in 1945.

The second question stated is, whether biennial elections be necessary or useful? The propriety of answering this question in the affirmative will appear from several very obvious considerations.

No man can be a competent legislator who does not add to an upright intention and a sound judgment, a certain degree of knowledge of the subjects on which he is to legislate. A part of this knowledge may be acquired by means of information which lie within the compass of men in private as well as public stations. Another part can only be attained, or at least thoroughly attained, by actual experience in the station which requires the use of it. The period of service ought therefore in all such cases to bear some proportion to the extent of practical knowledge, requisite to the due performance of the service. The period of legislative service established in most of the states for the more numerous branch is, as we have seen, one year. The question then may be put into this simple form; does the period of two years bear no greater proportion to the knowledge requisite for federal legislation, than one year does to the knowledge requisite for state legislation? The very statement of the question in this form, suggests the answer that ought to be given to it.

In a single state the requisite knowledge, relates to the existing laws which are uniform throughout the state, and with which all the citizens are more or less conversant; and to the general affairs of the state, which lie within a small compass, are not very diversified, and occupy much of the attention and conversation of every class of people. The great theatre of the United States presents a very different scene. The laws are so far from being uniform, that they vary in every state; whilst the public affairs of the union are spread throughout a very extensive region, and are extremely diversified by the local affairs connected with them, and can with difficulty be correctly learnt in any other place, than in the central councils, to which a knowledge of them will be brought by the representatives of every part of the empire. Yet some knowledge of the affairs, and even of the laws of all the states, ought to be possessed by the members from each of the states. How can foreign trade be properly regulated by uniform laws, without some acquaintance with the commerce, the ports, the usages, and the regulations, of the different states? How can the trade between the different states be duly regulated without some knowledge of their relative situations in these and other points? How can taxes be judiciously imposed, and effectually collected, if they be not accommodated to the different laws and local circumstances relating to these objects in the different states? How can uniform regulations for the militia be duly provided without a similar knowledge of some internal circumstances by which the states are distinguished from each other? These are the principal objects of federal legislation, and suggest most forceably, the extensive information which the representatives ought to acquire. The other inferior objects will require a proportional degree of information with regard to them.

It is true that all these difficulties will by degrees be very much diminished. The most laborious task will be the proper inauguration of the government, and the primeval formation of a federal code. Improvements on the first draught will every year become both easier and fewer. Past transactions of the government will be a ready and accurate source of information to new members. The affairs of the union will become more and more objects of curiosity and conversation among the citizens at large. And the increased intercourse among those of different states will contribute not a little to diffuse a mutual knowledge of their affairs, as this again will contribute to a general assimilation of their manners and laws. But with all these abatements the business of federal legislation must continue so far to exceed both in novelty and difficulty, the legislative business of a single state as to justify the longer period of service assigned to those who are to transact it.

A branch of knowledge which belongs to the acquirements of a federal representative, and which has not been mentioned, is that of foreign affairs. In regulating our own commerce he ought to be not only acquainted with the treaties between the United States and other nations, but also with the commercial policy and laws of other nations. He ought not to be altogether ignorant of the law of nations, for that as far as it is a proper object of municipal legislation is submitted to the federal government. And although the house of representatives is not immediately to participate in foreign negotiations and arrangements, yet from the necessary connection between the several branches of public affairs, those particular branches will frequently deserve attention in the ordinary course of legislation, and will sometimes demand particular legislative sanction and cooperation. Some portion of this knowledge may no doubt be acquired in a man's closet; but some of it also can only be derived from the public sources of information; and all of it will be acquired to best effect by a practical attention to the subject during the period of actual service in the legislature.

There are other considerations of less importance perhaps, but which are not unworthy of notice. The distance which many of the representatives will be obliged to travel, and the arrangements rendered necessary by that circumstance, might be much more serious objections with fit men to this service if limited to a single year than if extended to two years. No argument can be drawn on this subject from the case of the delegates to the existing congress. They are elected annually it is true; but their re-election is considered by the legislative assemblies almost as a matter of course. The election of the representatives by the people would not be governed by the same principle.

A few of the members, as happens in all such assemblies, will possess superior talents, will by frequent re-elections, become members of long standing; will be thoroughly masters of the public business, and perhaps not unwilling to avail themselves of those advantages. The greater the proportion of new members, and the less the information of the bulk of the members, the more apt will they be to fall into the snares that may be laid for them. This remark is no less applicable to the relation which will subsist between the house of representatives and the senate.

It is an inconvenience mingled with the advantages of our frequent elections, even in single states where they are large and hold but one legislative session in the year, that spurious elections cannot be investigated and annulled in time for

the decision to have its due effect. If a return can be obtained, no matter by what unlawful means, the irregular member, who takes his seat of course, is sure of holding it a sufficient time, to answer his purposes. Hence a very pernicious en-
155 couragement is given to the use of unlawful means for obtaining irregular returns. Were elections for the federal legislature to be annual, this practice might become a very serious abuse, particularly in the more distant states. Each house is, as it necessarily must be, the judge of the elections, qualifications and returns of its members, and whatever improvements may be suggested by experience for
160 simplifying and accelerating the process in disputed cases. So great a portion of a year would unavoidably elapse, before an illegitimate member could be dispossessed of his seat, that the prospect of such an event, would be little check to unfair and illicit means of obtaining a seat.

All these considerations taken together warrant us in affirming that biennial
165 elections will be as useful to the affairs of the public, as we have seen that they will be safe to the liberties of the people.

PUBLIUS.

FIFTY-FOUR
{NO. 53 IN NEWSPAPERS}

JAMES MADISON
February 12, 1788
The Same Subject Continued with a View to the Ratio of Representation

To the People of the State of New York.

The next view which I shall take of the house of representatives, relates to the apportionment of its members to the several states, which is to be determined by the same rule with that of direct taxes.

It is not contended that the number of people in each state ought not to be the standard for regulating the proportion of those who are to represent the people of each state. The establishment of the same rule for the apportionment of taxes, will probably be as little contested; though the rule itself in this case, is by no means founded on the same principle. In the former case, the rule is understood to refer to the personal rights of the people, with which it has a natural and universal connection. In the latter, it has reference to the proportion of wealth, of which it is in no case a precise measure, and in ordinary cases a very unfit one. But notwithstanding the imperfection of the rule as applied to the relative wealth and contributions of the states, it is evidently the least exceptionable among the practicable rules; and had too recently obtained the general sanction of America, not to have found a ready preference with the convention.

All this is admitted, it will perhaps be said: But does it follow from an admission of numbers for the measure of representation, or of slaves combined with free citizens, as a ratio of taxation, that slaves ought to be included in the numerical rule of representation? Slaves are considered as property, not as persons. They ought therefore to be comprehended in estimates of taxation which are founded on property, and to be excluded from representation which is regulated by a census of persons. This is the objection, as I understand it, stated in its full force. I shall be equally candid in stating the reasoning which may be offered on the opposite side.

We subscribe to the doctrine, might one of our southern brethren observe, that representation relates more immediately to persons, and taxation more immediately to property, and we join in the application of this distinction to the case of our slaves. But we must deny the fact that slaves are considered merely as

---

Lines 16–22 Publius here assumes a New York persona.

295

property, and in no respect whatever as persons. The true state of the case is, that they partake of both these qualities; being considered by our laws, in some respects, as persons, and in other respects, as property. In being compelled to labor not for himself, but for a master; in being vendible by one master to another master; and in being subject at all times to be restrained in his liberty, and chastised in his body, by the capricious will of another, the slave may appear to be degraded from the human rank, and classed with those irrational animals, which fall under the legal denomination of property. In being protected on the other hand in his life and in his limbs, against the violence of all others, even the master of his labor and his liberty; and in being punishable himself for all violence committed against others; the slave is no less evidently regarded by the law as a member of the society; not as a part of the irrational creation; as a moral person, not as a mere article of property. The federal constitution therefore, decides with great propriety on the case of our slaves, when it views them in the mixt character of persons and of property. This is in fact their true character. It is the character bestowed on them by the laws under which they live; and it will not be denied that these are the proper criterion; because it is only under the pretext that the laws have transformed the negroes into subjects of property, that a place is disputed them in the computation of numbers; and it is admitted that if the laws were to restore the rights which have been taken away, the negroes could no longer be refused an equal share of representation with the other inhabitants.

This question may be placed in another light. It is agreed on all sides, that numbers are the best scale of wealth and taxation, as they are the only proper scale of representation. Would the convention have been impartial or consistent, if they had rejected the slaves from the list of inhabitants when the shares of representation were to be calculated; and inserted them on the lists when the tariff of contributions was to be adjusted? Could it be reasonably expected that the southern states would concur in a system which considered their slaves in some degree as men, when burdens were to be imposed, but refused to consider them in the same light when advantages were to be conferred? Might not some surprize also be expressed that those who reproach the southern states with the barbarous policy of considering as property a part of their human brethren, should themselves contend that the government to which all the states are to be parties, ought to consider this unfortunate race more compleatly in the unnatural light of property, than the very laws of which they complain!

It may be replied perhaps that slaves are not included in the estimate of representatives in any of the states possessing them. They neither vote themselves, nor increase the votes of their masters. Upon what principle then ought they to

---

Lines 41–49 This view had been adopted at the opening of the First Continental Congress in 1774, not so much as a matter of principle, but as the only practical way to proceed on voting rights.

be taken into the federal estimate of representation? In rejecting them altogether, the constitution would in this respect have followed the very laws which have been appealed to, as the proper guide.

This objection is repelled by a single observation. It is a fundamental principle of the proposed constitution, that as the aggregate number of representatives allotted to the several states, is to be determined by a federal rule founded on the aggregate number of inhabitants, so the right of choosing this allotted number in each state is to be exercised by such part of the inhabitants, as the state itself may designate. The qualifications on which the right of suffrage depend, are not perhaps the same in any two states. In some of the states the difference is very material. In every state, a certain proportion of inhabitants are deprived of this right by the constitution of the state, who will be included in the census by which the federal constitution apportions the representatives. In this point of view, the southern states might retort the complaint, by insisting, that the principle laid down by the convention required that no regard should be had to the policy of particular states towards their own inhabitants; and consequently, that the slaves as inhabitants should have been admitted into the census according to their full number, in like manner with other inhabitants, who by the policy of other states, are not admitted to all the rights of citizens. A rigorous adherence however to this principle is waved by those who would be gainers by it. All that they ask is, that equal moderation be shewn on the other side. Let the case of the slaves be considered as it is in truth a peculiar one. Let the compromising expedient of the constitution be mutually adopted, which regards them as inhabitants, but as debased by servitude below the equal level of free inhabitants, which regards the *slave* as divested of two fifth of the *man*.

After all may not another ground be taken on which this article of the constitution, will admit of a still more ready defence? We have hitherto proceeded on the idea that representation related to persons only, and not at all to property. But is it a just idea? Government is instituted no less for protection of the property, than of the persons of individuals. The one as well as the other, therefore may be considered as represented by those who are charged with the government. Upon this principle it is, that in several of the states, and particularly in the state of New-York, one branch of the government is intended more especially to be the

---

Lines 92–104 The most articulate statement of the principle that government acts on persons *and* property, which therefore deserve separate representation, appeared in a Massachusetts pamphlet, *The Result of a Convention Holden in Essex County*, usually reduced to *The Essex Result* (1780). The author was Theophilus Parsons, a prominent conservative lawyer and later a judge. Most state constitutions had adopted some method of differentiating on property grounds either between voters for the upper and lower houses (as in New York) or between members of those bodies (as in Massachusetts).

100 guardian of property, and is accordingly elected by that part of the society which is most interested in this object of government. In the federal constitution, this policy does not prevail. The rights of property are committed into the same hands with the personal rights. Some attention ought therefore to be paid to property in the choice of those hands.

105 For another reason the votes allowed in the federal legislature to the people of each state, ought to bear some proportion to the comparative wealth of the states. States have not like individuals, an influence over each other arising from superior advantages of fortune. If the law allows an opulent citizen but a single vote in the choice of his representative, the respect and consequence which he derives

110 from his fortunate situation, very frequently guide the votes of others to the objects of his choice; and through this imperceptible channel the rights of property are conveyed into the public representation. A state possesses no such influence over other states. It is not probable that the richest state in the confederacy will ever influence the choice of a single representative in any other state. Nor will

115 the representatives of the larger and richer states possess any other advantage in the federal legislature over the representatives of other states, than what may result from their superior number alone; as far therefore as their superior wealth and weight may justly entitle them to any advantage, it ought to be secured to them by a superior share of representation. The new constitution is in this re-

120 spect materially different from the existing confederation, as well as from that of the United Netherlands, and other similar confederacies. In each of the latter the efficacy of the federal resolutions depends on the subsequent and voluntary resolutions of the states composing the union. Hence the states, though possessing an equal vote in the public councils, have an unequal influence, corresponding

125 with the unequal importance of these subsequent and voluntary resolutions. Under the proposed constitution, the federal acts will take effect without the necessary intervention of the individual states. They will depend merely on the majority of votes in the federal legislature, and consequently each vote whether proceeding from a larger or a smaller state, or a state more or less wealthy or pow-

130 erful, will have an equal weight and efficacy; in the same manner as the votes individually given in a state legislature, by the representatives of unequal counties or other districts, have each a precise equality of value and effect; or if there be any difference in the case, it proceeds from the difference in the personal character of the individual representative, rather than from any regard to the extent of

135 the district from which he comes.

Such is the reasoning which an advocate for the southern interests might employ on this subject: And although it may appear to be a little strained in some

---

Lines 137–38 The admission contained in the words "a little strained in some points" marks Madison's, and Publius's, discomfort with this intellectually inconsistent and morally unconscionable argument.

points, yet on the whole, I must confess, that it fully reconciles me to the scale of representation, which the convention have established.

In one respect the establishment of a common measure for representation and taxation will have a very salutary effect. As the accuracy of the census to be obtained by the congress, will necessarily depend in a considerable degree on the disposition, if not the cooperation of the states, it is of great importance that the states should feel as little bias as possible to swell or to reduce the amount of their numbers. Were their share of representation alone to be governed by this rule they would have an interest in exaggerating their inhabitants. Were the rule to decide their share of taxation alone, a contrary temptation would prevail. By extending the rule to both objects, the states will have opposite interests, which will controul and ballance each other; and produce the requisite impartiality.

PUBLIUS.

FIFTY-FIVE
{NO. 54 IN NEWSPAPERS}

JAMES MADISON
February 13, 1788
The Same Subject Continued in Relation to the Total Number of the Body

To the People of the State of New York.

The number of which the house of representatives is to consist, forms another, and a very interesting point of view under which this branch of the federal legislature may be contemplated. Scarce any article indeed in the whole constitution seems to be rendered more worthy of attention, by the weight of character and the apparent force of argument, with which it has been assailed. The charges exhibited against it are, first, that so small a number of representatives will be an unsafe depositary of the public interests; secondly, that they will not possess a proper knowledge of the local circumstances of their numerous constituents; thirdly, that they will be taken from that class of citizens which will sympathize least with the feelings of the mass of the people, and be most likely to aim at a permanent elevation of the few on the depression of the many; fourthly, that defective as the number will be in the first instance, it will be more and more disproportionate, by the increase of the people, and the obstacles which will prevent a correspondent increase of the representatives.

In general it may be remarked on this subject, that no political problem is less susceptible of a precise solution, than that which relates to the number most convenient for a representative legislature: Nor is there any point on which the policy of the several states is more at variance; whether we compare their legislative assemblies directly with each other, or consider the proportions which they respectively bear to the number of their constituents. Passing over the difference between the smallest and largest states, as Delaware, whose most numerous branch consists of twenty-one representatives, and Massachusetts, where it amounts to between three and four hundred; a very considerable difference is

---

Lines 1–3 The size and likely composition of the House of Representatives were attacked by practically all leading Anti-Federalist spokesmen: Centinel, Federal Farmer, the Pennsylvania Convention minority, Patrick Henry, Impartial Examiner, and Melancton Smith.

Lines 20–33 There were as yet no official census returns. Such matters as taxation and militia service had called for some of the calculations on which these estimates could have been based.

observable among states nearly equal in population. The number of representatives in Pennsylvania is not more than one-fifth of that in the state last mentioned. New-York, whose population is to that of South-Carolina as six to five, has little more than one third of the number of representatives. As great a disparity prevails between the states of Georgia and Delaware, or Rhode-Island. In Pennsylvania the representatives do not bear a greater proportion to their constituents than of one for every four or five thousand. In Rhode-Island, they bear a proportion of at least one for every thousand. And according to the constitution of Georgia, the proportion may be carried to one for every ten electors; and must unavoidably far exceed the proportion in any of the other states.

Another general remark to be made is, that the ratio between the representatives and the people, ought not to be the same where the latter are very numerous, as where they are very few. Were the representatives in Virginia to be regulated by the standard in Rhode-Island, they would at this time amount to between four and five hundred; and twenty or thirty years hence, to a thousand. On the other hand, the ratio of Pennsylvania, if applied to the state of Delaware, would reduce the representative assembly of the latter to seven or eight members. Nothing can be more fallacious than to found our political calculations on arithmetical principles. Sixty or seventy men, may be more properly trusted with a given degree of power than six or seven. But it does not follow, that six or seven hundred would be proportionally a better depositary. And if we carry on the supposition to six or seven thousand, the whole reasoning ought to be reversed. The truth is, that in all cases a certain number at least seems to be necessary to secure the benefits of free consultation and discussion, and to guard against too easy a combination for improper purposes: As on the other hand, the number ought at most to be kept within a certain limit, in order to avoid the confusion and intemperance of a multitude. In all very numerous assemblies, of whatever characters composed, passion never fails to wrest the sceptre from reason. Had every Athenian citizen been a Socrates; every Athenian assembly would still have been a mob.

It is necessary also to recollect here the observations which were applied to the case of biennial elections. For the same reason that the limited powers of the congress and the controul of the state legislatures, justify less frequent elections than the public safety might otherwise require; the members of the congress need be less numerous than if they possessed the whole power of legislation, and were under no other than the ordinary restraints of other legislative bodies.

With these general ideas in our minds, let us weigh the objections which have been stated against the number of members proposed for the house of

---

Lines 50–52 Passion is again represented in the mob (which is derived etymologically from "mobility"); reason, in the upper, propertied, leisured classes. The memorable closing sentence of this paragraph is Publius's only explicit reference to Socrates (but see No. 63, lines 76–77), and almost his only invocation of ancient philosophy. Earlier references to Athens by Hamilton were almost entirely disparaging. See No. 6.

representatives. It is said in the first place, that so small a number cannot be safely trusted with so much power.

The number of which this branch of the legislature is to consist at the outset of the government, will be sixty five. Within three years a census is to be taken, when the number may be augmented to one for every thirty thousand inhabitants; and within every successive period of ten years, the census is to be renewed, and augmentations may continue to be made under the above limitation. It will not be thought an extravagant conjecture, that the first census, will, at the rate of one for every thirty thousand raise the number of representatives to at least one hundred. Estimating the negroes in the proportion of three fifths, it can scarcely be doubted that the population of the United States will by that time, if it does not already, amount to three millions. At the expiration of twenty five years, according to the computed rate of increase, the number of representatives will amount to two hundred; and of fifty years to four hundred. This is a number which I presume will put an end to all fears arising from the smallness of the body. I take for granted here what I shall in answering the fourth objection hereafter shew, that the number of representatives will be augmented from time to time in the manner provided by the constitution. On a contrary supposition, I should admit the objection to have very great weight indeed.

The true question to be decided then is whether the smallness of the number, as a temporary regulation, be dangerous to the public liberty: Whether sixty five members for a few years, and a hundred or two hundred for a few more, be a safe depositary for a limited and well guarded power of legislating for the United States? I must own that I could not give a negative answer to this question, without first obliterating every impression which I have received with regard to the present genius of the people of America, the spirit, which actuates the state legislatures, and the principles which are incorporated with the political character of every class of citizens. I am unable to conceive that the people of America in their present temper, or under any circumstances which can speedily happen, will chuse, and every second year repeat the choice of sixty-five or an hundred men, who would be disposed to form and pursue a scheme of tyranny or treachery. I am unable to conceive that the state legislatures which must feel so many motives to watch, and which possess so many means of counteracting the federal legislature, would fail either to detect or to defeat a conspiracy of the latter against the liberties of their common constituents. I am equally unable to conceive that there are at this time, or can be in any short time, in the United States any sixty-five or an hundred men capable of recommending themselves to the choice of the people at large, who would either desire or dare within the short space of two years, to betray the solemn trust committed to them. What change of circumstances time and a fuller population of our country may produce, requires a prophetic spirit to declare, which makes no part of my pretensions. But judging from the circumstances now before us, and from the probable state of them within a moderate period of time, I must pronounce that the liberties of America cannot be unsafe in the number of hands proposed by the federal constitution.

From what quarter can the danger proceed? Are we afraid of foreign gold? If *105* foreign gold could so easily corrupt our federal rulers, and enable them to ensnare and betray their constituents, how has it happened that we are at this time a free and independent nation? The congress which conducted us through the revolution were a less numerous body than their successors will be; they were not chosen by nor responsible to their fellow citizens at large; though appointed from *110* year to year, and recallable at pleasure, they were generally continued for three years; and prior to the ratification of the federal articles, for a still longer term; they held their consultations always under the veil of secrecy; they had the sole transaction of our affairs with foreign nations; through the whole course of the war, they had the fate of their country more in their hands, than it is to be hoped *115* will ever be the case with our future representatives; and from the greatness of the prize at stake and the eagerness of the party which lost it, it may well be supposed, that the use of other means than force would not have been scrupled; yet we know by happy experience that the public trust was not betrayed; nor has the purity of our public councils in this particular ever suffered even from the whis- *120* pers of calumny.

Is the danger apprehended from the other branches of the federal government? But where are the means to be found by the president or the senate, or both? Their emoluments of office it is to be presumed will not, and without a previous corruption of the house of representatives cannot, more than suffice for *125* very different purposes: Their private fortunes, as they must all be American citizens, cannot possibly be sources of danger. The only means then which they can possess, will be in the dispensation of appointments. Is it here that suspicion rests her charge? Sometimes we are told that this fund of corruption is to be exhausted by the president in subduing the virtue of the senate. Now the fidelity of the *130* other house is to be the victim. The improbability of such a mercenary and perfidious combination of the several members of government standing on as different foundations as republican principles will well admit, and at the same time accountable to the society over which they are placed, ought alone to quiet this apprehension. But fortunately the constitution has provided a still further safe- *135* guard. The members of the congress are rendered ineligible to any civil offices that may be created or of which the emoluments may be increased, during the term of their election. No offices therefore can be dealt out to the existing members, but such as may become vacant by ordinary casualties; and to suppose that these would be sufficient to purchase the guardians of the people, selected by the *140* people themselves, is to renounce every rule by which events ought to be calculated, and to substitute an indiscriminate and unbounded jealousy, with which all reasoning must be vain. The sincere friends of liberty who give themselves up

---

Lines 136–38 Article 1, Section 6 prohibits members of Congress from holding civil office.

to the extravagancies of this passion are not aware of the injury they do their own
145 cause. As there is a degree of depravity in mankind which requires a certain degree of circumspection and distrust: So there are other qualities in human nature, which justify a certain portion of esteem and confidence. Republican
government presupposes the existence of these qualities in a higher degree than
any other form. Were the pictures which have been drawn by the political jeal-
150 ousy of some among us, faithful likenesses of the human character, the inference
would be that there is not sufficient virtue among men for self-government; and
that nothing less than the chains of despotism can restrain them from destroying
and devouring one another.

PUBLIUS.

Lines 146–53 This conclusion offers one of Publius's rare concessions to the better
side of human nature. But virtue as well as precautions will be needed in a republic;
hints of virtue in the American people have occurred to date in Nos. 36 and 49.

FIFTY-SIX
{NO. 55 IN NEWSPAPERS}

JAMES MADISON
February 16, 1788
The Same Subject Continued in Relation to the Same Point

To the People of the State of New York.

The *second* charge against the house of representatives is, that it will be too small to possess a due knowledge of the interests of its constituents.

As this objection evidently proceeds from a comparison of the proposed number of representatives, with the great extent of the United States, the number of their inhabitants, and the diversity of their interests, without taking into view at the same time the circumstances which will distinguish the congress from other legislative bodies, the best answer that can be given to it, will be a brief explanation of these peculiarities.

It is a sound and important principle that the representative ought to be acquainted with the interests and circumstances of his constituents. But this principle can extend no farther than to those circumstances and interests, to which the authority and care of the representative relate. An ignorance of a variety of minute and particular objects, which do not lie within the compass of legislation, is consistent with every attribute necessary to a due performance of the legislative trust. In determining the extent of information required in the exercise of a particular authority, recourse then must be had to the objects within the purview of that authority.

What are to be the objects of federal legislation? Those which are of most importance, and which seem most to require local knowledge, are commerce, taxation, and the militia.

A proper regulation of commerce requires much information, as has been elsewhere remarked; but as far as this information relates to the laws and local situation of each individual state, a very few representatives would be very sufficient vehicles of it to the federal councils.

Taxation will consist, in great measure, of duties which will be involved in the regulation of commerce. So far the preceding remark is applicable to this object. As far as it may consist of internal collections, a more diffusive knowledge of the circumstances of the state may be necessary. But will not this also be possessed in sufficient degree by a very few intelligent men diffusively elected within the state. Divide the largest state into ten or twelve districts, and it will be found that there will be no peculiar local interest in either, which will not be within the knowledge of the representative of the district. Besides this source of information, the laws of the state framed by representatives from every part of it, will be almost of themselves a sufficient guide. In every state there have been made, and must continue to be made, regulations on this subject, which will in many cases leave little more to be done by the federal legislature, than to review the different laws, and reduce them into one general act. A skilful individual in his closet, with all the local codes before him, might compile a law on some subjects of taxation for the whole union, without any aid from oral information; and it may be expected, that whenever internal taxes may be necessary, and particularly in cases requiring uniformity throughout the states, the more simple objects will be preferred. To be fully sensible of the facility which will be given to this branch of federal legislation, by the assistance of the state codes, we need only suppose for a moment, that this or any other state were divided into a number of parts, each having and exercising within itself a power of local legislation. Is it not evident that a degree of local information and preparatory labour would be found in the several volumes of their proceedings, which would very much shorten the labours of the general legislature, and render a much smaller number of members sufficient for it? The federal councils will derive great advantage from another circumstance. The representatives of each state will not only bring with them a considerable knowledge of its laws, and a local knowledge of their respective districts; but will probably in all cases have been members, and may even at the very time be members of the state legislature, where all the local information and interests of the state are assembled, and from whence they may easily be conveyed by a very few hands into the legislature of the United States.

With regard to the regulation of the militia, there are scarcely any circumstances in reference to which local knowledge can be said to be necessary. The general face of the country, whether mountainous or level, most fit for the operations of infantry or cavalry, is almost the only consideration of this nature that can occur. The art of war teaches general principles of organization, movement and discipline, which apply universally.

The attentive reader will discern that the reasoning here used to prove the sufficiency of a moderate number of representatives, does not in any respect contradict what was urged on another occasion with regard to the extensive information which the representatives ought to possess, and the time that might be necessary for acquiring it. This information, so far as it may relate to local objects, is rendered necessary and difficult, not by a difference of laws and local circumstances within a single state; but of those among different states. Taking each state by itself, its laws are the same, and its interests but little diversified. A few men therefore will possess all the knowledge requisite for a proper representation of them. Were the interests and affairs of each individual state, perfectly simple and uniform, a knowledge of them in one part would involve a knowledge of them in every other, and the whole state might be competently represented, by a single member taken from any part of it. On a comparison of the different states together, we find a great dissimilarity in their laws, and in many other circumstances connected with the objects of federal legislation, with all of which the

federal representatives ought to have some acquaintance. Whilst a few representatives therefore from each state may bring with them a due knowledge of their
own state, every representative will have much information to acquire concerning all the other states. The changes of time, as was formerly remarked, on the   *80*
comparative situation of the different states, will have an assimilating effect. The
effect of time on the internal affairs of the states taken singly, will be just the contrary. At present some of the states are little more than a society of husbandmen.
Few of them have made much progress in those branches of industry, which give
a variety and complexity to the affairs of a nation. These however will in all of   *85*
them be the fruits of a more advanced population; and will require on the part of
each state a fuller representation. The foresight of the convention has accordingly taken care that the progress of population may be accompanied with a
proper increase of the representative branch of the government.

The experience of Great Britain which presents to mankind so many political   *90*
lessons, both of the monitory and exemplary kind, and which has been frequently consulted in the course of these enquiries, corroborates the result of the
reflections which we have just made. The number of inhabitants in the two kingdoms of England and Scotland, cannot be stated at less than eight millions. The
representatives of these eight millions in the house of commons, amount to five   *95*
hundred fifty-eight. Of this number one ninth are elected by three hundred and
sixty four persons, and one half by five thousand seven hundred and twenty three
persons.* It cannot be supposed that the half thus elected, and who do not even
reside among the people at large, can add any thing either to the security of the
people against the government; or to the knowledge of their circumstances and   *100*
interests, in the legislative councils. On the contrary it is notorious that they are

---

* Burgh's Political Disquisitions.

Lines 98–108 Many British boroughs had become depopulated over the centuries
while continuing to be represented in Parliament. Wealthy landowners in many
cases owned property that gave them the power to place their protégés in these
seats. Rich merchants returning from years in India, known ironically as "nabobs,"
and seeking the social prestige associated with membership of Parliament, bought
themselves seats in the House of Commons based on these "rotten boroughs." Great
influence fell into the hands of wealthy patrons, often themselves members of the
aristocracy. The situation was chaotic and had lost touch with its original claims to
represent borough corporations; but it was defended on the pragmatic grounds that
an able man could usually find himself a seat. The whole system was eventually reformed by the Great Reform Act of 1832.

Madison's Footnote James Burgh's *Political Disquisitions,* in three volumes, which
had appeared in London in 1774, was a vast compilation of information and opinion
used as source material by Whig politicians and thinkers.

more frequently the representatives and instruments of the executive magistrate, than the guardians and advocates of the popular rights. They might therefore with great propriety be considered as something more than a mere deduction
105 from the real representatives of the nation. We will however consider them, in this light alone, and will not extend the deduction, to a considerable number of others, who do not reside among their constituents, are very faintly connected with them, and have very little particular knowledge of their affairs. With all these concessions two hundred and seventy nine persons only will be the depos-
110 itory of the safety, interest and happiness of eight millions; that is to say: There will be one representative only to maintain the rights and explain the situation of *twenty eight thousand six hundred and seventy* constituents, in an assembly exposed to the whole force of executive influence, and extending its authority to every object of legislation within a nation whose affairs are in the highest degree
115 diversified and complicated. Yet it is very certain not only that a valuable portion of freedom has been preserved under all these circumstances, but that the defects in the British code are chargeable in a very small proportion, on the ignorance of the legislature concerning the circumstances of the people. Allowing to this case the weight which is due to it: And comparing it with that of the house of
120 representatives as above explained, it seems to give the fullest assurance that a representative for every *thirty thousand inhabitants* will render the latter both a safe and competent guardian of the interests which will be confided to it.

PUBLIUS.

FIFTY-SEVEN
{NO. 56 IN NEWSPAPERS}

JAMES MADISON
February 19, 1788
**The Same Subject Continued in Relation to the Supposed Tendency
of the Plan of the Convention to Elevate the Few Above the Many**

To the People of the State of New York.

The third charge against the house of representatives is, that it will be taken from that class of citizens which will have least sympathy with the mass of the people, and be most likely to aim at an ambitious sacrifice of the many to the aggrandizement of the few.

Of all the objections which have been framed against the federal constitution, this is perhaps the most extraordinary. Whilst the objection itself is levelled against a pretended oligarchy, the principle of it strikes at the very root of republican government.

The aim of every political constitution is or ought to be first to obtain for rulers, men who possess most wisdom to discern, and most virtue to pursue the common good of the society; and in the next place, to take the most effectual precautions for keeping them virtuous, whilst they continue to hold their public trust. The elective mode of obtaining rulers is the characteristic policy of republican government. The means relied on in this form of government for preventing their degeneracy are numerous and various. The most effectual one is such a limitation of the term of appointments, as will maintain a proper responsibility to the people.

Let me now ask what circumstance there is in the constitution of the house of representatives, that violates the principles of republican government; or favors the elevation of the few on the ruins of the many? Let me ask whether every circumstance is not, on the contrary, strictly conformable to these principles; and scrupulously impartial to the rights and pretensions of every class and description of citizens?

Who are to be the electors of the federal representatives? Not the rich more than the poor; not the learned more than the ignorant; not the haughty heirs of

---

Lines 9–16 The implication is that the proposed system will enable the people to select the ablest and most virtuous citizens to represent them. The argument does not explain how the people will know who the ablest and most virtuous are, and it implies a good deal of continuity with traditional notions of social deference.

Lines 23–28 This paragraph redresses the balance.

25 distinguished names, more than the humble sons of obscure and unpropitious fortune. The electors are to be the great body of the people of the United States. They are to be the same who exercise the right in every state of electing the correspondent branch of the legislature of the state.

Who are to be the objects of popular choice? Every citizen whose merit may 30 recommend him to the esteem and confidence of his country. No qualification of wealth, of birth, of religious faith, or of civil profession, is permitted to fetter the judgment or disappoint the inclination of the people.

If we consider the situation of the men on whom the free suffrages of their fellow citizens may confer the representative trust, we shall find it involving every 35 security which can be devised or desired for their fidelity to their constituents.

In the first place, as they will have been distinguished by the preference of their fellow citizens, we are to presume, that in general, they will be somewhat distinguished also, by those qualities which entitle them to it, and which promise a sincere and scrupulous regard to the nature of their engagements.

40 In the second place, they will enter into the public service under circumstances which cannot fail to produce a temporary affection at least to their constituents. There is in every breast a sensibility to marks of honor, of favor, of esteem, and of confidence, which, apart from all considerations of interest, is some pledge for grateful and benevolent returns. Ingratitude is a common topic 45 of declamation against human nature; and it must be confessed, that instances of it are but too frequent and flagrant both in public and in private life. But the universal and extreme indignation which it inspires, is itself a proof of the energy and prevalence of the contrary sentiment.

In the third place, those ties which bind the representative to his constituents 50 are strengthened by motives of a more selfish nature. His pride and vanity attach him to a form of government which favors his pretensions, and gives him a share in its honors and distinctions. Whatever hopes or projects might be entertained by a few aspiring characters, it must generally happen that a great proportion of the men deriving their advancement from their influence with the people, 55 would have more to hope from a preservation of the favor, than from innovations in the government subversive of the authority of the people.

All these securities however would be found very insufficient without the restraint of frequent elections. Hence, in the fourth place, the house of representatives is so constituted as to support in the members an habitual recollection of 60 their dependence on the people. Before the sentiments impressed on their minds

---

Lines 30–32 "No qualification of wealth . . . " ignores the existence of property qualifications (see No. 52, lines 4–24 and note; also No. 54, lines 92–104 and note). It is fair to say that such requirements for suffrage were generally low. By "birth," Madison means social rank or privilege; interestingly, it does not occur to him that race, color, or gender might be matters of birth. Actually, free Negroes were not excluded from the vote in New England states, New York, Pennsylvania, or, curiously, North Carolina.

by the mode of their elevation, can be effaced by the exercise of power, they will be compelled to anticipate the moment when their power is to cease, when their exercise of it is to be reviewed, and when they must descend to the level from which they were raised; there for ever to remain, unless a faithful discharge of their trust shall have established their title to a renewal of it.   65

I will add as a fifth circumstance in the situation of the house of representatives, restraining them from oppressive measures, that they can make no law which will not have its full operation on themselves and their friends, as well as on the great mass of the society. This has always been deemed one of the strongest bonds by which human policy can connect the rulers and the people   70
together. It creates between them that communion of interests and sympathy of sentiments of which few governments have furnished examples; but without which every government degenerates into tyranny. If it be asked what is to restrain the house of representatives from making legal discriminations in favor of themselves and a particular class of the society? I answer, the genius of the whole   75
system, the nature of just and constitutional laws, and above all the vigilant and manly spirit which actuates the people of America, a spirit which nourishes freedom, and in return is nourished by it.

If this spirit shall ever be so far debased as to tolerate a law not obligatory on the legislature as well as on the people, the people will be prepared to tolerate   80
anything but liberty.

Such will be the relation between the house of representatives and their constituents. Duty, gratitude, interest, ambition itself, are the cords by which they will be bound to fidelity and sympathy with the great mass of the people. It is possible that these may all be insufficient to controul the caprice and wickedness of   85
man. But are they not all that government will admit, and that human prudence can devise? Are they not the genuine and the characteristic means by which republican government provides for the liberty and happiness of the people? Are they not the identical means on which every state government in the union, relies for the attainment of these important ends? What then are we to understand   90
by the objection which this paper has combated? What are we to say to the men who profess the most flaming zeal for republican government, yet boldly impeach the fundamental principle of it; who pretend to be champions for the right and the capacity of the people to chuse their own rulers, yet maintain that they will prefer those only who will immediately and infallibly betray the trust com-   95
mitted to them?

Were the objection to be read by one who had not seen the mode prescribed by the constitution for the choice of representatives, he could suppose nothing less than that some unreasonable qualification of property was annexed to the

---

Lines 66–69 That the representatives can pass no law from which they themselves are exempt is another key republican, or Whig, principle.

100 right of suffrage; or that the right of eligibility was limited to persons of particular families or fortunes; or at least that the mode prescribed by the state constitutions was in some respect or other very grossly departed from. We have seen how far such a supposition would err as to the two first points. Nor would it in fact be less erroneous as to the last. The only difference discoverable between the two cases,
105 is, that each representative of the United States will be elected by five or six thousand citizens; whilst in the individual states the election of a representative is left to about as many hundred. Will it be pretended that this difference is sufficient to justify an attachment to the state governments and an abhorrence to the federal government? If this be the point on which the objection turns, it deserves to
110 be examined.

Is it supported by *reason?* This cannot be said, without maintaining that five or six thousand citizens are less capable of chusing a fit representative, or more liable to be corrupted by an unfit one, than five or six hundred. Reason, on the contrary assures us, that as in so great a number, a fit representative would be
115 most likely to be found, so the choice would be less likely to be diverted from him, by the intrigues of the ambitious, or the bribes of the rich.

Is the *consequence* from this doctrine admissible? If we say that five or six hundred citizens are as many as can jointly exercise their right of suffrage, must we not deprive the people of the immediate choice of their public servants in every
120 instance where the administration of the government does not require as many of them as will amount to one for that number of citizens?

Is the doctrine warranted by *facts?* It was shewn in the last paper, that the real representation in the British house of commons very little exceeds the proportion of one for every thirty thousand inhabitants. Besides a variety of powerful
125 causes, not existing here, and which favor in that country, the pretensions of rank and wealth, no person is eligible as a representative of a county, unless he possess real estate of the clear value of six hundred pounds sterling per year; nor of a city or borough, unless he possess a like estate of half that annual value. To this qualification on the part of the county representatives, is added another on the part of
130 the county electors, which restrains the right of suffrage to persons having a freehold estate of the annual value of more than twenty pounds sterling according to the present rate of money. Notwithstanding these unfavorable circumstances, and notwithstanding some very unequal laws in the British code, it cannot be said that the representatives of the nation have elevated the few on the ruins of
135 the many.

Lines 111 "Reason" appears again as a cardinal element in the argument of *The Federalist.* Its use here means more than the ability to think logically; it invokes *reasonableness,* a qualitative as well as an efficient faculty.

Lines 122–35 See No. 56, lines 90–122.

The landed property qualification of £600 had been introduced in 1710 by 9 Anne cap. 5.

But we need not resort to foreign experience on this subject. Our own is explicit and decisive. The districts in New-Hampshire in which the senators are chosen immediately by the people are nearly as large as will be necessary for her representatives in the congress. Those of Massachusetts are larger, than will be necessary for that purpose. And those of New-York still more so. In the last state the members of assembly, for the cities and counties of New-York and Albany, are elected by very nearly as many voters, as will be entitled to a representative in the congress, calculating on the number of sixty-five representatives only. It makes no difference that in these senatorial districts and counties, a number of representatives are voted for by each elector at the same time. If the same electors, at the same time are capable of choosing four or five representatives, they cannot be incapable of choosing one. Pennsylvania is an additional example. Some of her counties which elect her state representatives, are almost as large as her districts will be by which her federal representatives will be elected. The city of Philadelphia is supposed to contain between fifty and sixty thousand souls. It will therefore form nearly two districts for the choice of federal representatives. It forms however but one county, in which every elector votes for each of its representatives in the state legislature. And what may appear to be still more directly to our purpose, the whole city actually elects a *single member* for the executive council. This is the case in all the other counties of the state.

Are not these facts the most satisfactory proofs of the fallacy which has been employed against the branch of the federal government under consideration? Has it appeared on trial that the senators of New-Hampshire, Massachusetts, and New-York; or the executive council of Pennsylvania; or the members of the assembly in the two last states, have betrayed any peculiar disposition to sacrifice the many to the few; or are in any respect less worthy of their places than the representatives and magistrates appointed in other states, by very small divisions of the people?

But there are cases of a stronger complexion than any which I have yet quoted. One branch of the legislature of Connecticut is so constituted that each member of it is elected by the whole state. So is the governor of that state, of Massachusetts, and of this state, and the president of New-Hampshire. I leave every man to decide whether the result of any one of these experiments can be said to countenance a suspicion that a diffusive mode of chusing representatives of the people tends to elevate traitors, and to undermine the public liberty.

PUBLIUS.

Lines 136–70 For state constitutions, see Thorpe, *American Charters,* cited in the note examining No. 24, lines 11–15.

FIFTY-EIGHT
{NO. 57 IN NEWSPAPERS}

JAMES MADISON
February 20, 1788
The Same Subject Continued in Relation to the
Future Augmentation of the Members

To the People of the State of New York.

The remaining charge against the house of representatives which I am to examine, is grounded on a supposition that the number of members will not be augmented from time to time, as the progress of population may demand.

It has been admitted that this objection, if well supported, would have great
5 weight. The following observations will shew that like most other objections against the constitution, it can only proceed from a partial view of the subject; or from a jealousy which discolours and disfigures every object which is beheld.

1. Those who urge the objection seem not to have recollected that the federal constitution will not suffer by a comparison with the state constitutions, in the se-
10 curity provided for a gradual augmentation of the number of representatives. The number which is to prevail in the first instance is declared to be temporary. Its duration is limited to the short term of three years.

Within every successive term of ten years, a census of inhabitants is to be repeated. The unequivocal objects of these regulations are, first, to readjust from
15 time to time the apportionment of representatives to the number of inhabitants; under the single exception that each state shall have one representative at least; Secondly, to augment the number of representatives at the same periods; under the sole limitation, that the whole number shall not exceed one for every thirty thousand inhabitants. If we review the constitutions of the several states, we shall find
20 that some of them contain no determinate regulations on this subject; that others correspond pretty much on this point with the federal constitution; and that the most effectual security in any of them is resolvable into a mere directory provision.

2. As far as experience has taken place on this subject, a gradual increase of representatives under the state constitutions, has at least kept pace with that of
25 the constituents; and it appears that the former have been as ready to concur in such measures, as the latter have been to call for them.

3. There is a peculiarity in the federal constitution which ensures a watchful attention in a majority both of the people and of their representatives, to a constitutional augmentation of the latter. The peculiarity lies in this, that one
30 branch of the legislature is a representation of citizens; the other of the states: in the former consequently the larger states will have most weight; in the latter, the

advantage will be in favour of the smaller states. From this circumstance it may with certainty be inferred, that the larger states will be strenuous advocates for increasing the number and weight of that part of the legislature in which their influence predominates. And it so happens that four only of the largest, will have a majority of the whole votes in the house of representatives. Should the representatives or people therefore of the smaller states oppose at any time a reasonable addition of members, a coalition of a very few states will be sufficient to overrule the opposition; a coalition, which notwithstanding the rivalship and local prejudices which might prevent it on ordinary occasions, would not fail to take place, when not merely prompted by common interest, but justified by equity and the principles of the constitution.

It may be alledged, perhaps, that the senate would be prompted by like motives to an adverse coalition; and as their concurrence would be indispensable, the just and constitutional views of the other branch might be defeated. This is the difficulty which has probably created the most serious apprehensions in the jealous friends of a numerous representation. Fortunately it is among the difficulties which, existing only in appearance, vanish on a close and accurate inspection. The following reflections will, if I mistake not, be admitted to be conclusive and satisfactory on this point.

Notwithstanding the equal authority which will subsist between the two houses on all legislative subjects, except the originating of money bills, it cannot be doubted that the house composed of the greater number of members, when supported by the more powerful states, and speaking the known and determined sense of a majority of the people, will have no small advantage in a question depending on the comparative firmness of the two houses.

This advantage must be increased by the consciousness felt by the same side, of being supported in its demands, by right, by reason, and by the constitution; and the consciousness on the opposite side, of contending against the force of all these solemn considerations.

It is farther to be considered that in the gradation between the smallest and largest states, there are several which, though most likely in general to arrange themselves among the former, are too little removed in extent and population from the latter, to second an opposition to their just and legitimate pretensions. Hence it is by no means certain that a majority of votes, even in the senate, would be unfriendly to proper augmentations in the number of representatives.

It will not be looking too far to add, that the senators from all the new states may be gained over to the just views of the house of representatives, by an expedient too obvious to be overlooked. As these states will for a great length of time advance in population with peculiar rapidity, they will be interested in frequent reapportionments of the representatives to the number of inhabitants. The large states therefore, who will prevail in the house of representatives, will have nothing to do, but to make reapportionments and augmentations mutually conditions of each other; and the senators from all the most growing states will be bound to contend for the latter, by the interest which their states will feel in the former.

These considerations seem to afford ample security on this subject; and ought alone to satisfy all the doubts and fears which have been indulged with regard to it. Admitting however that, they should all be insufficient to subdue the unjust policy of the smaller states, or their predominant influence in the councils of the
80 senate; a constitutional and infallible resource, still remains with the larger states, by which they will be able at all times to accomplish their just purposes. The house of representatives can not only refuse, but they alone can propose the supplies requisite for the support of government. They in a word hold the purse; that powerful instrument by which we behold in the history of the British consti-
85 tution, an infant and humble representation of the people, gradually enlarging the sphere of its activity and importance, and finally reducing, as far as it seems to have wished, all the overgrown prerogatives of the other branches of the government. This power over the purse, may in fact be regarded as the most compleat and effectual weapon with which any constitution can arm the immediate
90 representatives of the people, for obtaining a redress of every grievance, and for carrying into effect every just and salutary measure.

But will not the house of representatives be as much interested as the senate in maintaining the government in its proper functions, and will they not therefore be unwilling to stake its existence for its reputation on the pliancy of the senate?
95 Or if such a trial of firmness between the two branches were hazarded, would not the one be as likely first to yield as the other? These questions will create no difficulty with those who reflect, that in all cases the smaller the number and the more permanent and conspicuous the station of men in power, the stronger must be the interest which they will individually feel in whatever concerns the government.
100 Those who represent the dignity of their country in the eyes of other nations, will be particularly sensible to every prospect of public danger, or of a dishonorable stagnation in public affairs. To those causes we are to ascribe the continual triumph of the British house of commons over the other branches of the government, whenever the engine of a money bill has been employed. An absolute
105 inflexibility on the side of the latter, although it could not have failed to involve every department of the state in the general confusion, has neither been apprehended nor experienced. The utmost degree of firmness that can be displayed by the federal senate or president will not be more than equal to a resistance in which they will be supported by constitutional and patriotic principles.
110 In this review of the constitution of the house of representatives, I have passed over the circumstance of economy which in the present state of affairs might have had some effect in lessening the temporary number of representatives; and

---

Lines 82–91 The privilege of the House of Representatives in voting on taxes is based on the traditions of the British House of Commons. The principle is that which Americans adopted as "No taxation without representation." The House of Commons is the representative body; the House of Lords is not.

a disregard of which would probably have been as rich a theme of declamation against the constitution as has been furnished by the smallness of the number proposed. I omit also any remarks on the difficulty which might be found, under present circumstances, in engaging in the federal service, a large number of such characters as the people will probably elect. One observation however, I must be permitted to add on this subject, as claiming in my judgment a very serious attention. It is, that in all legislative assemblies, the greater the number composing them may be, the fewer will be the men who will in fact direct their proceedings. In the first place, the more numerous any assembly may be, of whatever characters composed, the greater is known to be the ascendancy of passion over reason. In the next place, the larger the number, the greater will be the proportion of members of limited information and of weak capacities. Now it is precisely on characters of this description that the eloquence and address of the few are known to act with all their force. In the antient republics, where the whole body of the people assembled in person, a single orator, or an artful statesman, was generally seen to rule with as compleat a sway, as if a sceptre had been placed in his single hands. On the same principle the more multitudinous a representative assembly may be rendered, the more it will partake of the infirmities incident to collective meetings of the people. Ignorance will be the dupe of cunning; and passion the slave of sophistry and declamation. The people can never err more than in supposing that by multiplying their representatives, beyond a certain limit, they strengthen the barrier against the government of a few. Experience will forever admonish them that on the contrary, *after securing a sufficient number for the purposes of safety, of local information, and of diffusive sympathy with the whole society*, they will counteract their own views by every addition to their representatives. The countenance of the government may become more democratic; but the soul that animates it will be more oligarchic. The machine will be enlarged, but the fewer and often, the more secret will be the springs by which its motions are directed.

As connected with the objection against the number of representatives, may properly be here noticed, that which has been suggested against the number made competent for legislative business. It has been said that more than a majority ought to have been required for a quorum, and in particular cases, if not in

---

Lines 119–41 The greater influence of a small number of experienced legislators in a large assembly should have been well known to Madison; through most of the 18th century, the colonial House of Burgesses in Virginia was dominated by a group of committees filled almost entirely from a handful of great families.

The source for the remark about the influence of speakers in the ancient republics (lines 125–29) is probably Thucydides.

It may be noted that nothing in this essay anticipates the emergence of the committee system or the privileges of seniority that came to dominate the procedures of the House of Representatives.

all, more than a majority of a quorum for a decision. That some advantages might have resulted from such a precaution, cannot be denied. It might have been an additional shield to some particular interests, and another obstacle generally to hasty and partial measures. But these considerations are outweighed by

150 the inconveniencies in the opposite scale. In all cases where justice or the general good might require new laws to be passed, or active measures to be pursued, the fundamental principle of free government would be reversed. It would be no longer the majority that would rule; the power would be transferred to the minority. Were the defensive privilege limited to particular cases, an interested mi-

155 nority might take advantage of it to screen themselves from equitable sacrifices to the general weal, or in particular emergencies to extort unreasonable indulgences. Lastly, it would facilitate and foster the baneful practice of secessions; a practice which has shewn itself even in states where a majority only is required; a practice subversive of all the principles of order and regular government; a

160 practice which leads more directly to public convulsions, and the ruin of popular governments, than any other which has yet been displayed among us.

PUBLIUS.

FIFTY-NINE
{NO. 58 IN NEWSPAPERS}

ALEXANDER HAMILTON
February 22, 1788
Concerning the Regulation of Elections

To the People of the State of New York.

The natural order of the subject leads us to consider in this place, that provision of the constitution which authorises the national legislature to regulate in the last resort the election of its own members. It is in these words—"The *times, places* and *manner* of holding elections for senators and representatives, shall be prescribed in each state by the legislature thereof; but the congress may at any time   5
by law, make or alter *such regulations* except as to *places* of choosing senators."* This provision has not only been declaimed against by those who condemn the constitution in the gross; but it has been censured by those, who have objected with less latitude and greater moderation; and in one instance, it has been thought exceptionable by a gentleman who has declared himself the advocate of   10
every other part of the system.

   I am greatly mistaken, notwithstanding, if there be any article in the whole plan more completely defensible than this. Its propriety rests upon the evidence of this plain proposition, that *every government ought to contain in itself the means of its own preservation.* Every just reasoner will at first sight, approve an   15
adherence to this rule, in the work of the convention; and will disapprove every deviation from it, which may not appear to have been dictated by the necessity of incorporating into the work some particular ingredient, with which a rigid conformity to the rule was incompatible. Even in this case, though he may acquiesce in the necessity; yet he will not cease to regard a departure from so fundamental   20

---

* 1st Clause, 4th Section of the 1st Article.

Lines 9–11 In *Essay No. IV* (*New York Journal,* November 29, 1787), Brutus had expressed anxiety that this clause would take control from the people and give Congress the power to determine what type of men should be chosen as representatives. This might be done, for example, by making the whole of a state into one election district. Patrick Henry warned that electors might have to vote for total strangers. The Pennsylvania minority also attacked the clause.

   The "gentleman" (line 10) is not identified; originally Brutus, but can he be said to have been "an advocate of every other part of the system"? See also No. 78, note for lines 1–2.

a principle, as a portion of imperfection in the system which may prove the seed of future weakness and perhaps anarchy.

It will not be alledged that an election law could have been framed and inserted into the constitution, which would have been applicable to every probable change in the situation of the country; and it will therefore not be denied that a discretionary power over elections ought to exist somewhere. It will, I presume, be as readily conceded, that there were only three ways, in which this power could have been reasonably modified and disposed, that it must either have been lodged wholly in the national legislature, or wholly in the state legislatures, or primarily in the latter, and ultimately in the former. The last mode has with reason been preferred by the convention. They have submitted the regulation of elections for the federal government in the first instance to the local administrations; which in ordinary cases, and when no improper views prevail, may be both more convenient and more satisfactory; but they have reserved to the national authority a right to interpose, whenever extraordinary circumstances might render that interposition necessary to its safety.

Nothing can be more evident, than that an exclusive power of regulating elections for the national government, in the hands of the state legislatures, would leave the existence of the union entirely at their mercy. They could at any moment annihilate it, by neglecting to provide for the choice of persons to administer its affairs. It is to little purpose to say that a neglect or omission of this kind, would not be likely to take place. The constitutional possibility of the thing, without an equivalent for the risk, is an unanswerable objection. Nor has any satisfactory reason been yet assigned for incurring that risk. The extravagant surmises of a distempered jealousy can never be dignified with that character. If we are in a humour to presume abuses of power, it is as fair to presume them on the part of the state governments, as on the part of the general government. And as it is more consonant to the rules of a just theory to intrust the union with the care of its own existence, than to transfer that care to any other hands; if abuses of power are to be hazarded, on the one side, or on the other, it is more rational to hazard them where the power would naturally be placed, than where it would unnaturally be placed.

Suppose an article had been introduced into the constitution, empowering the United States to regulate the elections for the particular states, would any man have hesitated to condemn it, both as an unwarrantable transposition of power, and as a premeditated engine for the destruction of the state governments? The violation of principle in this case would have required no comment; and to an unbiassed observer, it will not be less apparent in the project of subjecting the existence of the national government, in a similar respect to the pleasure of the state governments. An impartial view of the matter cannot fail to result in a conviction, that each, as far as possible, ought to depend on itself for its own preservation.

As an objection to this position, it may be remarked, that the constitution of the national senate, would involve in its full extent the danger which it is sug-

gested might flow from an exclusive power in the state legislatures to regulate the 65
federal elections. It may be alledged, that by declining the appointment of senators they might at any time give a fatal blow to the union; and from this, it may be
inferred, that as its existence would be thus rendered dependent upon them in so
essential a point, there can be no objection to entrusting them with it, in the particular case under consideration. The interest of each state, it may be added, to 70
maintain its representation in the national councils, would be a complete security against an abuse of the trust.

    This argument though specious, will not upon examination be found solid. It
is certainly true, that the state legislatures, by forbearing the appointment of senators, may destroy the national government. But it will not follow, that because 75
they have the power to do this in one instance, they ought to have it in every
other. There are cases in which the pernicious tendency of such a power may be
far more decisive, without any motive, equally cogent with that which must have
regulated the conduct of the convention, in respect to the construction of the
senate, to recommend their admission into the system. So far as that construction 80
may expose the union to the possibility of injury from the state legislatures, it is
an evil; but it is an evil, which could not have been avoided without excluding
the states, in their political capacities, wholly from a place in the organization of
the national government. If this had been done, it would doubtless have been interpreted into an entire dereliction of the federal principle; and would certainly 85
have deprived the state governments of that absolute safe-guard, which they will
enjoy under this provision. But however wise it may have been, to have submitted in this instance to an inconvenience, for the attainment of a necessary advantage, or a greater good, no inference can be drawn from thence to favor an
accumulation of the evil, where no necessity urges, nor any greater good invites. 90

    It may easily be discerned also, that the national government would run a
much greater risk from a power in the state legislatures over the elections of its
house of representatives, than from their power of appointing the members of its
senate. The senators are to be chosen for the period of six years; there is to be a
rotation, by which the seats of a third part of them are to be vacated, and replen- 95
ished every two years; and no state is to be entitled to more than two senators: A
quorum of the body is to consist of sixteen members. The joint result of these circumstances would be, that a temporary combination of a few states, to intermit
the appointment of senators, could neither annul the existence nor impair the
activity of the body: And it is not from a general or permanent combination of 100
the states, that we can have any thing to fear. The first might proceed from sinister designs in the leading members of a few of the state legislatures; the last
would suppose a fixed and rooted disaffection in the great body of the people;
which will either never exist at all, or will in all probability proceed from an experience of the inaptitude of the general government to the advancement of 105
their happiness; in which event no good citizen could desire its continuance.

    But with regard to the federal house of representatives, there is intended to be
a general election of members once in two years. If the state legislatures were to

be invested with an exclusive power of regulating these elections, every period of making them would be a delicate crisis in the national situation; which might issue in a dissolution of the union, if the leaders of a few of the most important states should have entered into a previous conspiracy to prevent an election.

I shall not deny that there is a degree of weight in the observation, that the interest of each state to be represented in the federal councils will be a security against the abuse of a power over its elections in the hands of the state legislatures. But the security will not be considered as complete, by those who attend to the force of an obvious distinction between the interest of the people in the public felicity, and the interest of their local rulers in the power and consequence of their offices. The people of America may be warmly attached to the government of the union at times, when the particular rulers of particular states, stimulated by the natural rivalship of power and by the hopes of personal aggrandisement, and supported by a strong faction in each of those states, may be in a very opposite temper. This diversity of sentiment, between a majority of the people and the individuals who have the greatest credit in their councils, is exemplified in some of the states, at the present moment, on the present question. The scheme of separate confederacies, which will always multiply the chances of ambition, will be a never failing bait to all such influential characters in the state administrations as are capable of preferring their own emolument and advancement to the public weal. With so effectual a weapon in their hands as the exclusive power of regulating elections for the national government a combination of a few such men, in a few of the most considerable states, where the temptation will always be the strongest, might accomplish the destruction of the union, by seizing the opportunity of some casual dissatisfaction among the people (and which perhaps they may themselves have excited) to discontinue the choice of members for the federal house of representatives. It ought never to be forgotten, that a firm union of this country, under an efficient government, will probably be an encreasing object of jealousy to more than one nation of Europe; and that enterprises to subvert it will sometimes originate in the intrigues of foreign powers, and will seldom fail to be patronised and abetted by some of them. Its preservation therefore ought in no case, that can be avoided, to be committed to the guardianship of any but those, whose situation will uniformly beget an immediate interest in the faithful and vigilant performance of the trust.

PUBLIUS.

SIXTY
{NO. 59 IN NEWSPAPERS}

ALEXANDER HAMILTON
February 23, 1788
The Same Subject Continued

To the People of the State of New York.

We have seen that an incontrolable power over the elections for the federal government could not without hazard be committed to the state legislatures. Let us now see what would be the dangers on the other side; that is, from confiding the ultimate right of regulating its own elections to the union itself. It is not pretended, that this right would ever be used for the exclusion of any state from its 5 share in the representation. The interest of all would in this respect at least be the security of all. But it is alledged that it might be employed in such a manner as to promote the election of some favourite class of men in exclusion of others; by confining the places of election to particular districts, and rendering it impracticable to the citizens at large to partake in the choice. Of all chimerical sup- 10 positions, this seems to be the most chimerical. On the one hand no rational calculation of probabilities would lead us to imagine, that the disposition, which a conduct so violent and extraordinary would imply, could ever find its way into the national councils; and on the other, it may be concluded with certainty, that if so improper a spirit should ever gain admittance into them, it would display it- 15 self in a form altogether different and far more decisive.

The improbability of the attempt may be satisfactorily inferred from this single reflection, that it could never be made without causing an immediate revolt of the great body of the people,—headed and directed by the state governments. It is not difficult to conceive that this characteristic right of freedom may, 20 in certain turbulent and factious seasons, be violated in respect to a particular class of citizens by a victorious majority; but that so fundamental a privilege, in a country situated and enlightened as this is, should be invaded to the prejudice of the great mass of the people, by the deliberate policy of the government; without occasioning a popular revolution, is altogether inconceivable and incredible. 25

In addition to this general reflection, there are considerations of a more precise nature, which forbid all apprehension on the subject. The dissimilarity in the ingredients, which will compose the national government, and still more in the manner in which they will be brought into action in its various branches must form a powerful obstacle to a concert of views, in any partial scheme of elections. 30 There is sufficient diversity in the state of property, in the genius, manners, and habits of the people of the different parts of the union to occasion a material

diversity of disposition in their representatives towards the different ranks and conditions in society. And though an intimate intercourse under the same gov-
35 ernment will promote a gradual assimilation, of temper and sentiment, yet there are causes as well physical as moral, which may in a greater or less degree permanently nourish different propensities and inclinations in this particular. But the circumstance, which will be likely to have the greatest influence in the matter, will be the dissimilar modes of constituting the several component parts of
40 the government. The house of representatives being to be elected immediately by the people; the senate by the state legislatures; the president by electors chosen for that purpose by the people; there would be little probability of a common interest to cement these different branches in a predilection for any particular class of electors.

45 As to the senate it is impossible that any regulation of "time and manner," which is all that is proposed to be submitted to the national government in respect to that body, can affect the spirit which will direct the choice of its members. The collective sense of the state legislatures can never be influenced by extraneous circumstances of that sort: A consideration, which alone ought to sat-
50 isfy us that the discrimination apprehended would never be attempted. For what inducement could the senate have to concur in a preference, in which itself would not be included? Or to what purpose would it be established in reference to one branch of the legislature; if it could not be extended to the other? The composition of the one would in this case counteract that of the other. And we
55 can never suppose that it would embrace the appointments to the senate, unless we can at the same time suppose the voluntary co-operation of the state legislatures. If we make the latter supposition, it then becomes immaterial where the power in question is placed; whether in their hands or in those of the union.

But what is to be the object of this capricious partiality in the national councils?
60 Is it to be exercised in a discrimination between the different departments of industry, or between the different kinds of property, or between the different degrees of property? Will it lean in favor of the landed interest, or the monied interest, or the mercantile interest, or the manufacturing interest? Or to speak in the fashionable language of the adversaries of the constitution, will it court the elevation
65 of the "wealthy and the well born" to the exclusion and debasement of all the rest of the society?

If this partiality is to be exerted in favor of those who are concerned in any particular description of industry or property, I presume it will readily be admitted that the competition for it will lie between landed men and merchants. And I
70 scruple not to affirm, that it is infinitely less likely, that either of them should gain an ascendant in the national councils, than that the one or the other of them

---

Line 62 The "monied interest" is an addition to the usual enumeration of interests, and not one that later Jeffersonian Republicans would regard as very respectable.

should predominate in all the local councils. The inference will be, that a conduct tending to give an undue preference to either is much less to be dreaded from the former than from the latter.

The several states are in various degrees addicted to agriculture and commerce. In most, if not all of them, agriculture is predominant. In a few of them, however, commerce nearly divides its empire, and in most of them has a considerable share of influence. In proportion as either prevails, it will be conveyed into the national representation, and for the very reason that this will be an emanation from a greater variety of interests, and in much more various proportions, than are to be found in any single state, it will be much less apt to espouse either of them, with a decided partiality, than the representation of any single state.

In a country consisting chiefly of the cultivators of land where the rules of an equal representation obtain the landed interest must upon the whole preponderate in the government. As long as this interest prevails in most of the state legislatures, so long it must maintain a correspondent superiority in the national senate, which will generally be a faithful copy of the majorities of those assemblies. It cannot therefore be presumed that a sacrifice of the landed to the mercantile class will ever be a favorite object of this branch of the federal legislature. In applying thus particularly to the senate a general observation suggested by the situation of the country, I am governed by the consideration, that the credulous votaries of state power, cannot upon their own principles suspect that the state legislatures would be warped from their duty by any external influence. But as in reality the same situation must have the same effect in the primitive composition at least of the federal house of representatives; an improper byass towards the mercantile class is as little to be expected from this quarter or from the other.

In order perhaps to give countenance to the objection at any rate, it may be asked, is there not danger of an opposite byass in the national government, which may dispose it to endeavour to secure a monopoly of the federal administration to the landed class? As there is little likelihood that the supposition of such a byass will have any terrors for those who would be immediately injured by it, a laboured answer to this question will be dispensed with. It will be sufficient to remark, first, that for the reasons elsewhere assigned, it is less likely that any decided partiality should prevail in the councils of the union than in those of any of its members. Secondly that there would be no temptation to violate the constitution in favor of the landed class, because that class would in the natural course of things enjoy as great a preponderancy as itself could desire. And thirdly that men accustomed to investigate the sources of public prosperity, upon a large scale,

---

Lines 75–78 Commerce had a prominent place in the economies of Massachusetts, New York, and Pennsylvania; Charleston merchants had significant economic and political influence in South Carolina.

Lines 97–114 It may be noted that the conflicts anticipated here are between *interests*, not *classes*.

must be too well convinced of the utility of commerce, to be inclined to inflict
110 upon it so deep a wound as would be occasioned by the entire exclusion of those
who would best understand its interest from a share in the management of them.
The importance of commerce in the view of revenue alone must effectually
guard it against the enmity of a body which would be continually importuned in
its favour by the urgent calls of public necessity.

115 I rather consult brevity in discussing the probability of a preference founded
upon a discrimination between the different kinds of industry and property; because, as far as I understand the meaning of the objectors, they contemplate a
discrimination of another kind. They appear to have in view, as the objects of the
preference with which they endeavour to alarm us, those whom they designate
120 by the description of the "wealthy and the well born." These, it seems, are to be
exalted to an odious pre-eminence over the rest of their fellow citizens. At one
time however their elevation is to be a necessary consequence of the smallness of
the representative body; at another time it is to be effected by depriving the
people at large of the opportunity of exercising their right of suffrage in the
125 choice of that body.

But upon what principle is the discrimination of the places of election to be
made in order to answer the purpose of the meditated preference? Are the
wealthy and the well born, as they are called, confined to particular spots in the
several states? Have they by some miraculous instinct or foresight set apart in
130 each of them a common place of residence? Are they only to be met with in the
towns or cities? Or are they, on the contrary, scattered over the face of the country as avarice or chance may have happened to cast their own lot, or that of their
predecessors? If the latter is the case, (as every intelligent man knows it to be*) is
it not evident that the policy of confining the places of elections to particular dis-
135 tricts would be as subversive of its own aim as it would be exceptionable on every
other account? The truth is that there is no method of securing to the rich the
preference apprehended, but by prescribing qualifications of property either for
those who may elect, or be elected.

But this forms no part of the power to be conferred upon the national govern-
140 ment. Its authority would be expressly restricted to the regulation of the *times*,
the *places*, and the *manner* of elections. The qualifications of the persons who
may choose or be chosen, as has been remarked upon another occasion, are defined and fixed in the constitution; and are unalterable by the legislature.

Let it however be admitted, for argument sake, that the expedient suggested
145 might be successful; and let it at the same time be equally taken for granted that

* Particularly in the Southern States and in this State.

Line 120 "[T]he 'wealthy and the well born.'" Hamilton does not specify a source
for this phrase, but the theme was familiar in Anti-Federalist argument.

all the scruples which a sense of duty or an apprehension of the danger of the experiment might inspire, were overcome in the breasts of the national rulers; still, I imagine, it will hardly be pretended, that they could ever hope to carry such an enterprise into execution, without the aid of a military force sufficient to subdue, the resistance of the great body of the people. The improbability of the existence of a force equal to that object, has been discussed and demonstrated in different parts of these papers; but that the futility of the objection under consideration may appear in the strongest light, it shall be conceded for a moment that such a force might exist; and the national government shall be supposed to be in the actual possession of it. What will be the conclusion? With a disposition to invade the essential rights of the community, and with the means of gratifying that disposition, is it presumable that the persons who were actuated by it would amuse themselves in the ridiculous task of fabricating election laws for securing a preference to a favourite class of men? Would they not be likely to prefer a conduct better adapted to their own immediate aggrandisement? Would they not rather boldly resolve to perpetuate themselves in office by one decisive act of usurpation, than to trust to precarious expedients, which in spite of all the precautions that might accompany them, might terminate in the dismission, disgrace and ruin of their authors? Would they not fear that citizens not less tenacious than conscious of their rights would flock from the remotest extremes of their respective states to the places of election, to overthrow their tyrants, and to substitute men who would be disposed to avenge the violated majesty of the people?

PUBLIUS.

Lines 155–67 This reasoning at the conclusion of this essay did not prove equal to the task of saving African American citizens from almost universal disfranchisement in the ex-Confederate states at the end of the 19th century.

Lines 151–52 "[I]n different parts of these papers . . . " may refer to the weighing of arguments in Nos. 24 to 27.

SIXTY-ONE
{NO. 60 IN NEWSPAPERS}

ALEXANDER HAMILTON
February 26, 1788
The Same Subject Continued and Concluded

To the People of the State of New York.

The more candid opposers of the provision respecting elections contained in the plan of the convention, when pressed in argument, will sometimes concede the propriety of that provision; with this qualification however that it ought to have been accompanied with a declaration that all elections should be had in the
5 counties where the electors resided. This say they, was a necessary precaution against an abuse of the power. A declaration of this nature, would certainly have been harmless: So far as it would have had the effect of quieting apprehensions, it might not have been undesirable. But it would in fact have afforded little or no additional security against the danger apprehended; and the want of it will never be
10 considered by an impartial and judicious examiner as a serious, still less, as an insuperable objection to the plan. The different views taken of the subject in the two preceding papers must be sufficient to satisfy all dispassionate and discerning men, that if the public liberty should ever be the victim of the ambition of the national rulers, the power under examination at least will be guiltless of the sacrifice.
15 If those who are inclined to consult their jealousy only would exercise it in a careful inspection of the several state constitutions, they would find little less room for disquietude and alarm from the latitude which most of them allow in respect to elections, than from the latitude which is proposed to be allowed to the national government in the same respect. A review of their situation, in this
20 particular, would tend greatly to remove any ill impressions which may remain in regard to this matter. But as that review would lead into lengthy and tedious details, I shall content myself with the single example of the state in which I write. The constitution of New-York makes no other provision for *locality* of elections, than that the members of the assembly shall be elected in the *counties*,
25 those of the senate in the great districts into which the state is or may be divided; these at present are four in number, and comprehend each from two to six counties. It may readily be perceived that it would not be more difficult to the legislature of New-York to defeat the suffrages of the citizens of New-York by confining

---

Lines 23–27 On the constitution of New York, see Thorpe, *American Charters,* cited in the note examining No. 24, lines 11–15.

elections to particular places, than to the legislature of the United States to defeat the suffrages of the citizens of the union, by the like expedient. Suppose for instance, the city of Albany was to be appointed the sole place of election for the county and district of which it is a part, would not the inhabitants of that city speedily become the only electors of the members both of the senate and assembly, for that county and district? Can we imagine that the electors who reside in the remote subdivisions of the county of Albany, Saratoga, Cambridge, &c. or in any part of the county of Montgomery, would take the trouble to come to the city of Albany to give their votes for members of the assembly or senate, sooner than they would repair to the city of New-York to participate in the choice of the members of the federal house of representatives? The alarming indifference discoverable in the exercise of so invaluable a privilege under the existing laws, which afford every facility to it, furnishes a ready answer to this question. And, abstracted from any experience on the subject, we can be at no loss to determine that when the place of election is at an *inconvenient distance* from the elector, the effect upon his conduct will be the same whether that distance be twenty miles or twenty thousand miles. Hence it must appear that objections to the particular modification of the federal power of regulating elections will in substance apply with equal force to the modification of the like power in the constitution of this state; and for this reason it will be impossible to acquit the one and to condemn the other. A similar comparison would lead to the same conclusion in respect to the constitutions of most of the other states.

If it should be said that defects in the state constitutions furnish no apology for those which are to be found in the plan proposed; I answer, that as the former have never been thought chargeable with inattention to the security of liberty, where the imputations thrown on the latter can be shown to be applicable to them also, the presumption is that they are rather the cavilling refinements of a predetermined opposition, than the well founded inferences of a candid research after truth. To those who are disposed to consider, as innocent omissions in the state constitutions, what they regard as unpardonable blemishes in the plan of the convention, nothing can be said; or at most they can only be asked to assign some substantial reason why the representatives of the people in a single state should be more impregnable to the lust of power or other sinister motives, than the representatives of the people of the United States? If they cannot do this, they ought at least to prove to us, that it is easier to subvert the liberties of three millions of people, with the advantage of local governments to head their opposition, than of two hundred thousand people, who are destitute of that advantage. And in relation to the point immediately under consideration, they ought to convince us that it is less probable a predominant faction in a single state, should, in order to maintain its superiority, incline to a preference of a particular class of electors, than that a similar spirit should take possession of the representatives of thirteen states spread over a vast region, and in several respects distinguishable from each other by a diversity of local circumstances, prejudices and interests.

Hitherto my observations have only aimed at a vindication of the provision in question, on the ground of theoretic propriety, on that of the danger of placing the power elsewhere, and on that of the safety of placing it in the manner proposed. But there remains to be mentioned a positive advantage which will accrue from this disposition, and which could not as well have been obtained from any other: I allude to the circumstance of uniformity in the time of elections for the federal house of representatives. It is more than possible, that this uniformity may be found by experience to be of great importance to the public welfare; both as a security against the perpetuation of the same spirit in the body; and as a cure for the diseases of faction. If each state may choose its own time of election, it is possible there may be at least as many different periods as there are months in the year. The times of election in the several states as they are now established for local purposes, vary between extremes as wide as March and November. The consequence of this diversity would be, that there could never happen a total dissolution or renovation of the body at one time. If an improper spirit of any kind should happen to prevail in it, that spirit would be apt to infuse itself into the new members as they come forward in succession. The mass would be likely to remain nearly the same; assimilating constantly to itself its gradual accretions. There is a contagion in example which few men have sufficient force of mind to resist. I am inclined to think that treble the duration in office, with the condition of a total dissolution of the body at the same time, might be less formidable to liberty, than one third of that duration, subject to gradual and successive alterations.

Uniformity in the time of elections seems not less requisite for executing the idea of a regular rotation in the senate; and for conveniently assembling the legislature at a stated period in each year.

It may be asked, why then could not a time have been fixed in the constitution? As the most zealous adversaries of the plan of the convention in this state, are in general not less zealous admirers of the constitution of the state, the question may be retorted, and it may be asked, why was not a time for the like purpose fixed in the constitution of this state? No better answer can be given, than that it was a matter which might safely be entrusted to legislative discretion, and that if a time had been appointed, it might upon experiment have been found less convenient than some other time. The same answer may be given to the question put on the other side. And it may be added, that the supposed danger of a gradual change being merely speculative, it would have been hardly adviseable upon that speculation to establish, as a fundamental point, what would deprive several states of the convenience of having the elections for their own governments, and for the national government, at the same epoch.

PUBLIUS.

Lines 82–83 Each state does now choose its own time for *primary* elections.

SIXTY-TWO
{NO. 61 IN NEWSPAPERS}

JAMES MADISON

February 27, 1788

**Concerning the Constitution of the Senate, with Regard to the
Qualifications of the Members, the Manner of Appointing Them, the
Equality of Representation, the Number of the Senators and the
Duration of Their Appointments**

To the People of the State of New York.

Having examined the constitution of the house of representatives, and answered
such of the objections against it as seemed to merit notice, I enter next on the examination of the senate. The heads into which this member of the government
may be considered, are—I. the qualifications of senators—II. the appointment of
them by the state legislatures—III. the equality of representation in the senate—   5
IV. the number of senators, and the term for which they are to be elected—V. the
powers vested in the senate.

    I. The qualifications proposed for senators, as distinguished from those of rep-
resentatives, consist in a more advanced age, and a longer period of citizenship. A
senator must be thirty years of age at least; as a representative, must be twenty-five.   10
And the former must have been a citizen nine years; as seven years are required for
the latter. The propriety of these distinctions is explained by the nature of the senatorial trust; which requiring greater extent of information and stability of character, requires at the same time that the senator should have reached a period of life
most likely to supply these advantages; and which participating immediately in   15
transactions with foreign nations, ought to be exercised by none who are not thoroughly weaned from the prepossessions and habits incident to foreign birth and
education. The term of nine years appears to be a prudent mediocrity between a

---

Lines 8–9 Article 1, Section 3 prescribes age qualifications for the Senate. The age
qualification should be understood in relation to the general age distribution in the
American population, which by modern standards was extraordinarily young. By
the time of Jefferson's election in 1800, about half the population had been born
since the Declaration of Independence. Thus men of thirty-five were older in proportion to the population than they would be now. One is reminded of the derivation of the word "Senate," which is related to "senior" and "senescence," not to
mention "senility."

Line 18 "Mediocrity," a word that has slipped, was a term of approbation, which literally referred to the medium; often "a happy mediocrity."

total exclusion of adopted citizens, whose merit and talents may claim a share in
20 the public confidence; and an indiscriminate and hasty admission of them,
which might create a channel for foreign influence on the national councils.

II. It is equally unnecessary to dilate on the appointment of senators by the
state legislatures. Among the various modes which might have been devised for
constituting this branch of the government, that which has been proposed by the
25 convention is probably the most congenial with the public opinion. It is recommended by the double advantage of favouring a select appointment, and of giving to the state governments such an agency in the formation of the federal
government, as must secure the authority of the former; and may form a convenient link between the two systems.

30 III. The equality of representation in the senate is another point, which, being
evidently the result of compromise between the opposite pretensions of the large
and the small states, does not call for much discussion. If indeed it be right that
among a people thoroughly incorporated into one nation, every district ought to
have a *proportional* share in the government; and that among independent and
35 sovereign states bound together by a simple league, the parties however unequal
in size, ought to have an *equal* share in the common councils, it does not appear
to be without some reason, that in a compound republic partaking both of the
national and federal character, the government ought to be founded on a mixture of the principles of proportional and equal representation. But it is superflu-
40 ous to try by the standard of theory, a part of the constitution which is allowed on
all hands to be the result not of theory, but "of a spirit of amity, and that mutual
deference and concession which the peculiarity of our political situation rendered indispensable." A common government with powers equal to its objects, is
called for by the voice, and still more loudly by the political situation of America.
45 A government founded on principles more consonant to the wishes of the larger
states, is not likely to be obtained from the smaller states. The only option then
for the former lies between the proposed government and a government still
more objectionable. Under this alternative the advice of prudence must be, to
embrace the lesser evil; and instead of indulging a fruitless anticipation of the
50 possible mischiefs which may ensue, to contemplate rather the advantageous
consequences which may qualify the sacrifice.

In this spirit it may be remarked, that the equal vote allowed to each state, is at
once a constitutional recognition of the portion of sovereignty remaining in the
individual states, and an instrument for preserving that residuary sovereignty. So
55 far the equality ought to be no less acceptable to the large than to the small

---

Lines 36–37 "[I]t does not appear to be without some reason" is an expression notably lacking in enthusiasm. Neither Hamilton nor Madison liked this provision,
which Madison had strenuously resisted in the Convention.

Lines 41–43 "Of a spirit of amity . . . " Publius omits to credit this quotation.

states; since they are not less solicitous to guard by every possible expedient against an improper consolidation of the states into one simple republic.

Another advantage accruing from this ingredient in the constitution of the senate, is the additional impediment it must prove against improper acts of legislation. No law or resolution can now be passed without the concurrence first of a majority of the people, and then of a majority of the states. It must be acknowledged that this complicated check on legislation may in some instances be injurious as well as beneficial; and that the peculiar defence which it involves in favour of the smaller states would be more rational, if any interests common to them, and distinct from those of the other states, would otherwise be exposed to peculiar danger. But as the larger states will always be able by their power over the supplies to defeat unreasonable exertions of this prerogative of the lesser states; and as the facility and excess of law-making seem to be the diseases to which our governments are most liable, it is not impossible that this part of the constitution may be more convenient in practice than it appears to many in contemplation.

IV. The number of senators and the duration of their appointment come next to be considered. In order to form an accurate judgment on both these points, it will be proper to enquire into the purposes which are to be answered by a senate; and in order to ascertain these it will be necessary to review the inconveniencies which a republic must suffer from the want of such an institution.

First. It is a misfortune incident to republican government, though in a less degree than to other governments, that those who administer it, may forget their obligations to their constituents, and prove unfaithful to their important trust. In this point of view, a senate, as a second branch of the legislative assembly, distinct from, and dividing the power with, a first, must be in all cases a salutary check on the government. It doubles the security to the people, by requiring the concurrence of two distinct bodies in schemes of usurpation or perfidy, where the ambition or corruption of one, would otherwise be sufficient. This is a precaution founded on such clear principles, and now so well understood in the United States, that it would be more than superfluous to enlarge on it. I will barely remark that as the improbability of sinister combinations will be in proportion to the dissimilarity in the genius of the two bodies; it must be politic to distinguish them from each other by every circumstance which will consist with a due harmony in all proper measures, and with the genuine principles of republican government.

Line 66 "But as the larger states" makes the best of the compromise.

Lines 76–89 Bicameral legislatures were adopted in every state except Pennsylvania and Georgia. The Pennsylvania radicals believed in unicameralism on grounds of democratic principle; a second house was traditionally an "upper" house, deriving its status from comparison with the House of Lords. The people *en masse* needed only one chamber to represent them. As it happened, the arrangement was in line with tradition, since the colonial Pennsylvania council was so enfeebled that the province was virtually unicameral, as was Georgia.

90   *Second.* The necessity of a senate is not less indicated by the propensity of all single and numerous assemblies, to yield to the impulse of sudden and violent passions, and to be seduced by factious leaders, into intemperate and pernicious resolutions. Examples on this subject might be cited without number; and from proceedings within the United States, as well as from the history of other nations.

95   But a position that will not be contradicted need not be proved. All that need be remarked is that a body which is to correct this infirmity ought itself be free from it, and consequently ought to be less numerous. It ought moreover to possess great firmness, and consequently ought to hold its authority by a tenure of considerable duration.

100   *Third.* Another defect to be supplied by a senate lies in a want of due acquaintance with the objects and principles of legislation. It is not possible that an assembly of men called for the most part from pursuits of a private nature, continued in appointment for a short time, and led by no permanent motive to devote the intervals of public occupation to a study of the laws, the affairs and the

105   comprehensive interests of their country, should, if left wholly to themselves, escape a variety of important errors in the exercise of their legislative trust. It may be affirmed, on the best grounds, that no small share of the present embarrassments of America is to be charged on the blunders of our governments; and that these have proceeded from the heads rather than the hearts of most of the au-

110   thors of them. What indeed are all the repealing, explaining and amending laws, which fill and disgrace our voluminous codes, but so many monuments of deficient wisdom; so many impeachments exhibited by each succeeding, against each preceding session; so many admonitions to the people of the value of those aids which may be expected from a well constituted senate?

115   A good government implies two things; first, fidelity to the object of government, which is the happiness of the people; secondly, a knowledge of the means by which that object can be best attained. Some governments are deficient in both these qualities: Most governments are deficient in the first. I scruple not to assert that in the American governments, too little attention has been paid to the

120   last. The federal constitution avoids this error; and what merits particular notice, it provides for the last in a mode which increases the security for the first.

       Fourth. The mutability in the public councils, arising from a rapid succession of new members, however qualified they may be, points out in the strongest manner, the necessity of some stable institution in the government. Every new

125   election in the states, is found to change one half of the representatives. From this change of men must proceed a change of opinions; and from a change of opinions, a change of measures. But a continual change even of good measures is inconsistent with every rule of prudence, and every prospect of success. The remark is verified in private life, and becomes more just as well as more impor-

130   tant, in national transactions.

Lines 115–21 The object of government is now seen to be expressly utilitarian.

To trace the mischievous effects of a mutable government would fill a volume. I will hint a few only, each of which will be perceived to be a source of innumerable others.

In the first place it forfeits the respect and confidence of other nations, and all the advantages connected with national character. An individual who is observed *135* to be inconstant to his plans, or perhaps to carry on his affairs without any plan at all, is marked at once by all prudent people as a speedy victim to his own unsteadiness and folly. His more friendly neighbours may pity him; but all will decline to connect their fortunes with his; and not a few will seize the opportunity of making their fortunes out of his. One nation is to another what one individual is to another; *140* with this melancholy distinction perhaps, that the former with fewer of the benevolent emotions than the latter, are under fewer restraints also from taking undue advantage of the indiscretions of each other. Every nation consequently whose affairs betray a want of wisdom and stability, may calculate on every loss which can be sustained from the more systematic policy of its wiser neighbours. But the best *145* instruction on this subject is unhappily conveyed to America by the example of her own situation. She finds that she is held in no respect by her friends; that she is the derision of her enemies; and that she is a prey to every nation which has an interest in speculating on her fluctuating councils and embarrassed affairs.

The internal effects of a mutable policy are still more calamitous. It poisons the *150* blessings of liberty itself. It will be of little avail to the people that the laws are made by men of their own choice, if the laws be so voluminous that they cannot be read, or so incoherent that they cannot be understood; if they be repealed or revised before they are promulged, or undergo such incessant changes that no man who knows what the law is to-day can guess what it will be to-morrow. Law is defined to *155* be a rule of action; but how can that be a rule, which is little known and less fixed?

Another effect of public instability is the unreasonable advantage it gives to the sagacious, the enterprising and the moneyed few, over the industrious and uninformed mass of the people. Every new regulation concerning commerce or revenue, or in any manner affecting the value of the different species of property, *160* presents a new harvest to those who watch the change, and can trace its consequences; a harvest reared not by themselves but by the toils and cares of the great body of their fellow citizens. This is a state of things in which it may be said with some truth that laws are made for the *few* not for the *many*.

In another point of view great injury results from an unstable government. *165* The want of confidence in the public councils damps every useful undertaking;

Lines 150–56 Jefferson, who believed that the law should be revised every nineteen years, to correspond to a generation, would not have agreed with this.

Lines 157–64 The social differentiation indicated here is another sign of the marked sense in which Publius's political thought relies on the leadership of the educated elite.

Line 165 State governments are implied here.

the success and profit of which may depend on a continuance of existing arrangements. What prudent merchant will hazard his fortunes in any new branch of commerce, when he knows not but that his plans may be rendered unlawful before they can be executed? What farmer or manufacturer will lay himself out for the encouragement given to any particular cultivation or establishment, when he can have no assurance that his preparatory labors and advances will not render him a victim to an inconstant government? In a word no great improvement or laudable enterprise, can go forward, which requires the auspices of a steady system of national policy.

But the most deplorable effect of all is that diminution of attachment and reverence which steals into the hearts of the people, towards a political system which betrays so many marks of infirmity, and disappoints so many of their flattering hopes. No government any more than an individual will long be respected, without being truly respectable, nor be truly respectable without possessing a certain portion of order and stability.

PUBLIUS.

SIXTY-THREE
{NO. 62 IN NEWSPAPERS}

JAMES MADISON
March 1, 1788
**A Further View of the Constitution of the Senate, in Regard
to the Duration of Appointment of its Members**

To the People of the State of New York.

A fifth desideratum illustrating the utility of a senate, is the want of a due sense of
national character. Without a select and stable member of the government, the
esteem of foreign powers will not only be forfeited by an unenlightened and variable policy, proceeding from the causes already mentioned; but the national councils will not possess that sensibility to the opinion of the world, which is perhaps not   5
less necessary in order to merit, than it is to obtain, its respect and confidence.

An attention to the judgment of other nations is important to every government for two reasons: The one is, that independently of the merits of any particular plan or measure, it is desireable on various accounts, that it should appear to
other nations as the offspring of a wise and honorable policy: The second is, that   10
in doubtful cases, particularly where the national councils may be warped by
some strong passion, or momentary interest, the presumed or known opinion of
the impartial world, may be the best guide that can be followed. What has not
America lost by her want of character with foreign nations? And how many errors
and follies would she not have avoided, if the justice and propriety of her meas-   15
ures had in every instance been previously tried by the light in which they would
probably appear to the unbiassed part of mankind?

Yet however requisite a sense of national character may be, it is evident that it
can never be sufficiently possessed by a numerous and changeable body. It can only
be found in a number so small, that a sensible degree of the praise and blame of   20
public measures may be the portion of each individual; or in an assembly so

---

Lines 7–17 This paragraph draws attention to the numerous and humiliating failures
on the part of Americans to honor international obligations. Publius probably had
particularly in mind the pre-war debts of American planters to British merchants, re-
payment of which was stipulated in the Treaty of Paris that had ended the war, but on
which British plaintiffs had great difficulty in getting favorable judgments in the
courts. Virginia was a prominent culprit. Britain retaliated by retaining control of certain northern forts located on the New York–Canadian frontier, which should have
been relinquished under the treaty.

Line 14 Here "want of character" means lack of good reputation.

durably invested with public trust, that the pride and consequence of its members may be sensibly incorporated with the reputation and prosperity of the community. The half-yearly representatives of Rhode-Island, would probably have
25   been little affected in their deliberations on the iniquitous measures of that state, by arguments drawn from the light in which such measures would be viewed by foreign nations, or even by the sister states; whilst it can scarcely be doubted, that if the concurrence of a select and stable body had been necessary, a regard to national character alone, would have prevented the calamities under which that
30   misguided people is now labouring.

I add as a *sixth* defect, the want in some important cases of a due responsibility in the government to the people, arising from that frequency of elections, which in other cases produces this responsibility. The remark will perhaps appear not only new but paradoxical. It must nevertheless be acknowledged, when
35   explained, to be as undeniable as it is important.

Responsibility in order to be reasonable must be limited to objects within the power of the responsible party; and in order to be effectual, must relate to operations of that power, of which a ready and proper judgment can be formed by the constituents. The objects of government may be divided into two general classes;
40   the one depending on measures which have singly an immediate and sensible operation; the other depending on a succession of well chosen and well connected measures, which have a gradual and perhaps unobserved operation. The importance of the latter description to the collective and permanent welfare of every country needs no explanation. And yet it is evident, that an assembly
45   elected for so short a term as to be unable to provide more than one or two links in a chain of measures, on which the general welfare may essentially depend, ought not to be answerable for the final result, any more than a steward or tenant, engaged for one year, could be justly made to answer for places or improvements, which could not be accomplished in less than half a dozen years. Nor is
50   it possible for the people to estimate the *share* of influence which their annual assemblies may respectively have on events resulting from the mixed transactions of several years. It is sufficiently difficult at any rate to preserve a personal responsibility in the members of a *numerous* body, for such acts of the body as have an immediate, detached and palpable operation on its constituents.

55   The proper remedy for this defect must be an additional body in the legislative department, which, having sufficient permanency to provide for such objects as require a continued attention, and a train of measures, may be justly and effectually answerable for the attainment of those objects.

Thus far I have considered the circumstances which point out the necessity of
60   a well constructed senate, only as they relate to the representatives of the people. To a people as little blinded by prejudice, or corrupted by flattery, as those whom I address, I shall not scruple to add, that such an institution may be sometimes necessary, as a defence to the people against their own temporary errors and

delusions. As the cool and deliberate sense of the community ought in all governments, and actually will in all free governments ultimately prevail over the views of its rulers; so there are particular moments in public affairs, when the people stimulated by some irregular passion, or some illicit advantage, or misled by the artful misrepresentations of interested men, may call for measures which they themselves will afterwards be the most ready to lament and condemn. In these critical moments, how salutary will be the interference of some temperate and respectable body of citizens, in order to check the misguided career, and to suspend the blow meditated by the people against themselves, until reason, justice and truth, can regain their authority over the public mind? What bitter anguish would not the people of Athens have often escaped, if their government had contained so provident a safeguard against the tyranny of their own passions? Popular liberty might then have escaped the indelible reproach of decreeing to the same citizens, the hemlock on one day, and statues on the next.

It may be suggested that a people spread over an extensive region, cannot like the crowded inhabitants of a small district, be subject to the infection of violent passions; or to the danger of combining in the pursuit of unjust measures. I am far from denying that this is a distinction of peculiar importance. I have on the contrary endeavoured in a former paper, to shew that it is one of the principal recommendations of a confederated republic. At the same time this advantage ought not to be considered as superseding the use of auxiliary precautions. It may even be remarked that the same extended situation which will exempt the people of America from some of the dangers incident to lesser republics, will expose them to the inconveniency of remaining for a longer time, under the influence of those misrepresentations which the combined industry of interested men may succeed in distributing among them.

It adds no small weight to all these considerations, to recollect, that history informs us of no long lived republic which had not a senate. Sparta, Rome and Carthage are in fact the only states to whom that character can be applied. In each of the two first there was a senate for life. The constitution of the senate in the last, is less known. Circumstantial evidence makes it probable that it was not different in this particular from the two others. It is at least certain that it had

---

Lines 61–73 Once again, reason, in the form of the cool, judicious deliberations of a Senate, is called in to restrain the passions of the uninstructed multitudes. Reason, justice, and truth, three highly abstract concepts, are preeminently the qualities of the educated elite; it is apparently only the upper ranks of society who can be relied on to be guided by these qualities.

Lines 76–77 This sentence recalls No. 55 lines 29–44, but refers to the Athenian assembly's verdict on Socrates and their sentencing him to death.

Lines 90–102 For sources, see note on No. 18, lines 1–5.

some quality or other which rendered it an anchor against popular fluctuations; and that a smaller council drawn out of the senate was appointed not only for life; but filled up vacancies itself. These examples, though as unfit for the imitation, as they are repugnant to the genius of America, are notwithstanding, when

100 compared with the fugitive and turbulent existence of other antient republics, very instructive proofs of the necessity of some institution that will blend stability with liberty. I am not unaware of the circumstances which distinguish the American from other popular governments, as well antient as modern; and which render extreme circumspection necessary in reasoning from the one case to the

105 other. But after allowing due weight to this consideration, it may still be maintained that there are many points of similitude which render these examples not unworthy of our attention. Many of the defects as we have seen, which can only be supplied by a senatorial institution, are common to a numerous assembly frequently elected by the people, and to the people themselves. There are others pe-

110 culiar to the former, which require the controul of such an institution. The people can never wilfully betray their own interests: But they may possibly be betrayed by the representatives of the people; and the danger will be evidently greater where the whole legislative trust is lodged in the hands of one body of men, than where the concurrence of separate and dissimilar bodies is required in

115 every public act.

The difference most relied on between the American and other republics, consists in the principle of representation, which is the pivot on which the former move, and which is supposed to have been unknown to the latter, or at least to the antient part of them. The use which has been made of this difference, in reason-

120 ings contained in former papers, will have shewn that I am disposed neither to deny its existence nor to undervalue its importance. I feel the less restraint therefore in observing that the position concerning the ignorance of the antient government on the subject of representation is by no means precisely true in the latitude commonly given to it. Without entering into a disquisition which here

125 would be misplaced, I will refer to a few known facts in support of what I advance.

In the most pure democracies of Greece, many of the executive functions were performed not by the people themselves but by officers elected by the people, and *representing* the people in their *executive* capacity.

Prior to the reform of Solon, Athens was governed by nine Archons, annually

130 *elected by the people at large.* The degree of power delegated to them seems to be left in great obscurity. Subsequent to that period, we find an assembly first of four

---

Lines 121–48 No. 10 opened up, and No. 14 developed, the distinction between democracies, exemplified by the Greek city-states, and republics, characterized by representative institutions. Here Publius seems, however, to backtrack from the view that representation was unknown in the ancient world.

Lines 129–38 On Athens, the source is Plutarch's essay on Solon. On Carthage, the source is possibly Polybius.

and afterwards of six hundred members, annually *elected by the people*; and *partially* representing them in their *legislative* capacity; since they were not only associated with the people in the function of making laws; but had the exclusive right of originating legislative propositions to the people. The senate of Carthage   *135* also, whatever might be its power or the duration of its appointment, appears to have been *elective* by the suffrages of the people. Similar instances might be traced in most if not all the popular governments of antiquity.

Lastly in Sparta, we meet with the Ephori, and in Rome with the Tribunes; two bodies, small indeed in number, but annually *elected by the whole body of the peo-*   *140* *ple*, and considered as the *representatives* of the people, almost in their *plenipotentiary* capacity. The Cosmi of Crete were also annually *elected by the people*; and have been considered by some authors as an institution analogous to those of Sparta and Rome; with this difference only that in the election of that representative body, the right of suffrage was communicated to a part only of the people.   *145*

From these facts, to which many others might be added, it is clear that the principle of representation was neither unknown to the antients, nor wholly overlooked in their political constitutions. The true distinction between these and the American governments lies *in the total exclusion of the people in their collective capacity* from any share in the *latter*, and not in the *total exclusion* of the *repre-*   *150* *sentatives of the people*, from the administration of the *former*. The distinction however thus qualified must be admitted to leave a most advantageous superiority in favor of the United States. But to ensure to this advantage its full effect, we must be careful not to separate it from the other advantage, of an extensive territory. For it cannot be believed that any form of representative government, could   *155* have succeeded within the narrow limits occupied by the democracies of Greece.

In answer to all these arguments, suggested by reason, illustrated by examples, and enforced by our own experience, the jealous adversary of the constitution will probably content himself with repeating, that a senate appointed not immediately by the people, and for the term of six years, must gradually acquire a   *160* dangerous pre-eminence in the government, and finally transform it into a tyrannical aristocracy.

To this general answer the general reply ought to be sufficient; that liberty may be endangered by the abuses of liberty, as well as by the abuses of power; that there are numerous instances of the former as well as of the latter; and that   *165* the former rather than the latter is apparently most to be apprehended by the United States. But a more particular reply may be given.

Before such a revolution can be effected, the senate, it is to be observed, must in the first place corrupt itself; must next corrupt the state legislatures, must then

---

Lines 139–45 See No. 18.

Lines 163–64 The point that "liberty may be endangered by the abuses of liberty" strikes a note all too familiar in modern debate.

170 corrupt the house of representatives, and must finally corrupt the people at large. It is evident that the senate must be first corrupted, before it can attempt an establishment of tyranny. Without corrupting the state legislatures, it cannot prosecute the attempt, because the periodical change of members would otherwise regenerate the whole body. Without exerting the means of corruption with equal
175 success on the house of representatives, the opposition of that co-equal branch of the government would inevitably defeat the attempt; and without corrupting the people themselves, a succession of new representatives would speedily restore all things to their pristine order. Is there any man who can seriously persuade himself, that the proposed senate can, by any possible means within the compass of
180 human address, arrive at the object of a lawless ambition, through all these obstructions?

If reason condemns the suspicion, the same sentence is pronounced by experience. The constitution of Maryland furnishes the most apposite example. The senate of that state is elected, as the federal senate will be, indirectly by the peo-
185 ple; and for a term less by one year only, than the federal senate. It is distinguished also by the remarkable prerogative of filling up its own vacancies within the term of its appointment: and at the same time, is not under the controul of any such rotation, as is provided for the federal senate. There are some other lesser distinctions, which would expose the former to colorable objections that
190 do not lie against the latter. If the federal senate therefore really contained the danger which has been so loudly proclaimed, some symptoms at least of a like danger ought by this time to have been betrayed by the senate of Maryland; but no such symptoms have appeared. On the contrary the jealousies at first entertained by men of the same description with those who view with terror the cor-
195 respondent part of the federal constitution, have been gradually extinguished by the progress of the experiment; and the Maryland constitution is daily deriving from the salutary operations of this part of it, a reputation in which it will probably not be rivalled by that of any state in the union.

But if any thing could silence the jealousies on this subject, it ought to be the
200 British example. The senate there, instead of being elected for a term of six years, and of being unconfined to particular families or fortunes, is an hereditary assembly of opulent nobles. The house of representatives, instead of being elected for two years and by the whole body of the people, is elected for seven years; and in very great proportion, by a very small proportion of the people. Here unques-
205 tionably ought to be seen in full display, the aristocratic usurpations and tyranny, which are at some future period to be exemplified in the United States. Unfortunately however for the antifederal argument the British history informs us, that this hereditary assembly has not even been able to defend itself against the continual encroachments of the house of representatives; and that it no sooner lost

---

Lines 206–11 These lines apparently refer to the abolition of the House of Lords under Oliver Cromwell (1599–1658).

the support of the monarch, than it was actually crushed by the weight of the   *210*
popular branch.

As far as antiquity can instruct us on this subject, its examples support the reasoning which we have employed. In Sparta the Ephori, the annual representatives of the people, were found an overmatch for the senate for life, continually
gained on its authority, and finally drew all power into their own hands. The trib-   *215*
unes of Rome, who were the representatives of the people, prevailed, it is well
known, in almost every contest with the senate for life, and in the end gained the
most complete triumph over it. This fact is the more remarkable, as unanimity
was required in every act of the tribunes, even after their number was augmented
to ten. It proves the irresistable force possessed by that branch of a free govern-   *220*
ment, which has the people on its side. To these examples might be added that of
Carthage, whose senate, according to the testimony of Polybius, instead of drawing all power into its vortex, had at the commencement of the second punic war,
lost almost the whole of its original portion.

Besides the conclusive evidence resulting from this assemblage of facts, that   *225*
the federal senate will never be able to transform itself, by gradual usurpations,
into an independent and aristocratic body; we are warranted in believing that if
such a revolution should ever happen from causes which the foresight of man
cannot guard against, the house of representatives with the people on their side
will at all times be able to bring back the constitution to its primitive form and   *230*
principles. Against the force of the immediate representatives of the people,
nothing will be able to maintain even the constitutional authority of the senate,
but such a display of enlightened policy, and attachment to the public good, as
will divide with that branch of the legislature, the affections and support of the
entire body of the people themselves.   *235*

PUBLIUS.

Line 222 For Polybius, see the note examining No. 34 lines 14–15.

SIXTY-FOUR
{NO. 63 IN NEWSPAPERS}

JOHN JAY

March 5, 1788

A Further View of the Constitution of the Senate, in Regard to the Power of Making Treaties

To the People of the State of New York.

It is a just and not a new observation, that enemies to particular persons and opponents to particular measures, seldom confine their censures to such things only in either, as are worthy of blame. Unless on this principle it is difficult to explain the motives of their conduct, who condemn the proposed constitution in the ag-
5   gregate, and treat with severity some of the most unexceptionable articles in it.

The 2d. section gives power to the president *"by and with the advice and consent of the senate to make treaties* PROVIDED TWO THIRDS OF THE SENATORS PRESENT CONCUR."

The power of making treaties is an important one, especially as it relates to
10 war, peace and commerce; and it should not be delegated but in such a mode, and with such precautions, as will afford the highest security, that it will be exercised by men the best qualified for the purpose, and in the manner most conducive to the public good. The convention appears to have been attentive to both these points—they have directed the president to be chosen by select bodies
15 of electors to be deputed by the people for that express purpose; and they have committed the appointment of senators to the state legislatures. This mode has in such cases, vastly the advantage of elections by the people in their collective capacity, where the activity of party zeal taking advantage of the supineness, the ignorance, and the hopes and fears of the unwary and interested, often places
20 men in office by the votes of a small proportion of the electors.

As the select assemblies for choosing the president, as well as the state legislatures who appoint the senators will in general be composed of the most enlightened and respectable citizens, there is reason to presume that their attention and their votes will be directed to those men only who have become the most distin-
25 guished by their abilities and virtue, and in whom the people perceive just grounds for confidence. The constitution manifests very particular attention to this object. By excluding men under thirty five from the first office, and those

---

Lines 6–8 This gift of executive power reflects the royal prerogative—modified by the powers of the Senate. See Hamilton's discussion at No. 69, lines 110–38 (and the note on lines 111–33), and in No. 75.

under thirty from the second, it confines the elections to men of whom the people have had time to form a judgment, and with respect to whom they will not be liable to be deceived by those brilliant appearances of genius and patriotism, which like transient meteors sometimes mislead as well as dazzle. If the observation be well founded, that wise kings will always be served by able ministers, it is fair to argue that as an assembly of select electors possess in a greater degree than kings, the means of extensive and accurate information relative to men and characters, so will their appointments bear at least equal marks of discretion and discernment. The inference which naturally results from these considerations is this, that the president and senators so chosen will always be of the number of those who best understand our national interests, whether considered in relation to the several states or to foreign nations, who are best able to promote those interests, and whose reputation for integrity inspires and merits confidence. With such men the power of making treaties may be safely lodged.

Although the absolute necessity of system in the conduct of any business, is universally known and acknowledged, yet the high importance of it in national affairs has not yet become sufficiently impressed on the public mind. They who wish to commit the power under consideration to a popular assembly, composed of members constantly coming and going in quick succession, seem not to recollect that such a body must necessarily be inadequate to the attainment of those great objects, which require to be steadily contemplated in all their relations and circumstances, and which can only be approached and achieved by measures, which not only talents, but also exact information and often much time are necessary to concert and to execute. It was wise therefore in the convention to provide not only that the power of making treaties should be committed to able and honest men, but also that they should continue in place a sufficient time to become perfectly acquainted with our national concerns, and to form and introduce a system for the management of them. The duration prescribed is such as will give them an opportunity of greatly extending their political informations and of rendering their accumulating experience more and more beneficial to their country. Nor has the convention discovered less prudence in providing for the frequent elections of senators in such a way, as to obviate the inconvenience of periodically transferring those great affairs entirely to new men, for by leaving a considerable residue of the old ones in place, uniformity and order, as well as a constant succession of official information, will be preserved.

There are few who will not admit that the affairs of trade and navigation should be regulated by a system cautiously formed and steadily pursued; and that both our treaties and our laws should correspond with, and be made to promote it. It is of much consequence that this correspondence and conformity be carefully maintained, and they who assent to the truth of this position, will see and confess that it is well provided for by making the concurrence of the senate necessary both to treaties and to laws.

It seldom happens in the negociation of treaties of whatever nature, but that perfect *secrecy* and immediate *dispatch* are sometimes requisite. There are cases where the most useful intelligence may be obtained, if the persons possessing it can be relieved from apprehensions of discovery. Those apprehensions will operate on those persons whether they are actuated by mercenary or friendly motives, and there doubtless are many of both descriptions, who would rely on the secrecy of the president, but who would not confide in that of the senate, and still less in that of a large popular assembly. The convention have done well therefore in so disposing of the power of making treaties, that although the president must in forming them act by the advice and consent of the senate, yet he will be able to manage the business of intelligence in such manner as prudence may suggest.

They who have turned their attention to the affairs of men, must have perceived that there are tides in them. Tides, very irregular in their duration, strength and direction, and seldom found to run twice exactly in the same manner or measure. To discern and to profit by these tides in national affairs, is the business of those who preside over them; and they who have had much experience on this head inform us, that there frequently are occasions when days, nay even when hours are precious. The loss of a battle, the death of a prince, the removal of a minister, or other circumstances intervening to change the present posture and aspect of affairs, may turn the most favorable tide into a course opposite to our wishes. As in the field, so in the cabinet, there are moments to be seized as they pass, and they who preside in either, should be left in capacity to improve them. So often and so essentially have we heretofore suffered from the want of secrecy and dispatch, that the constitution would have been inexcusably defective if no attention had been paid to those objects. Those matters which in negociations usually require the most secrecy and the most dispatch, are those preparatory and auxiliary measures which are no otherways important in a national view, than as they tend to facilitate the attainment of the objects of the negociation. For these the president will find no difficulty to provide, and should any circumstance occur which requires the advice and consent of the senate, he may at any time convene them. Thus we see that the constitution provides that our negociations for treaties shall have every advantage which can be derived from talents, information, integrity, and deliberate investigations on the one hand, and from secrecy and dispatch on the other.

But to this plan as to most others that have ever appeared, objections are contrived and urged.

Some are displeased with it, not on account of any errors or defects in it, but because as the treaties when made are to have the force of laws, they should be made only by men invested with legislative authority. These gentlemen seem not to consider that the judgments of our courts, and the commissions constitution-

---

Lines 81–90 A pale reflection of Brutus in Shakespeare's *Julius Caesar*: "There is a tide in the affairs of men / Which taken at the flood leads on to fortune; / Omitted, all the voyage of their life / Is bound in shallows and in miseries" 4.3.

ally given by our governor, are as valid and as binding on all persons whom they   *110*
concern, as the laws passed by our legislature are. All constitutional acts of
power, whether in the executive or in the judicial departments, have as much
legal validity and obligation as if they proceeded from the legislature, and therefore whatever name be given to the power of making treaties, or however obligatory they may be when made, certain it is that the people may with much   *115*
propriety commit the power to a distinct body from the legislature, the executive
or the judicial. It surely does not follow that because they have given the power of
making laws to the legislature, that therefore they should likewise give them
power to do every other act of sovereignty by which the citizens are to be bound
and affected.   *120*

Others, though content that treaties should be made in the mode proposed,
are averse to their being the *supreme* laws of the land. They insist and profess to
believe, that treaties, like acts of assembly, should be repealable at pleasure. This
idea seems to be new and peculiar to this country, but new errors as well as new
truths often appear. These gentlemen would do well to reflect that a treaty is only   *125*
another name for a bargain; and that it would be impossible to find a nation who
would make any bargain with us, which should be binding on them *absolutely*,
but on us only so long and so far as we may think proper to be bound by it. They
who make laws may without doubt amend or repeal them, and it will not be disputed that they who make treaties may alter or cancel them; but still let us not   *130*
forget that treaties are made not by only one of the contracting parties, but by
both, and consequently that as the consent of both was essential to their formation at first, so must it ever afterwards be to alter or cancel them. The proposed
constitution therefore has not in the least extended the obligation of treaties.
They are just as binding, and just as far beyond the lawful reach of legislative acts   *135*
now, as they will be at any future period, or under any form of government.

However useful jealousy may be in republics, yet when, like bile in the natural, it abounds too much in the body politic; the eyes of both become very liable
to be deceived by the delusive appearances which that malady casts on surrounding objects. From this cause probably proceed the fears and apprehensions   *140*
of some, that the president and senate may make treaties without an equal eye to
the interests of all the states. Others suspect that the two-thirds will oppress the
remaining third, and ask whether those gentlemen are made sufficiently responsible for their conduct—whether if they act corruptly they can be punished; and
if they make disadvantageous treaties, how are we to get rid of those treaties?   *145*

As all the states are equally represented in the senate, and by men the most
able and the most willing to promote the interests of their constituents, they will
all have an equal degree of influence in that body, especially while they continue
to be careful in appointing proper persons, and to insist on their punctual attendance. In proportion as the United States assume a national form, and a national   *150*
character, so will the good of the whole be more and more an object of attention;
and the government must be a weak one indeed, if it should forget that the good
of the whole can only be promoted by advancing the good of each of the parts or

members which compose the whole. It will not be in the power of the president and senate to make any treaties, by which they and their families and estates will not be equally bound and affected with the rest of the community; and having no private interest distinct from that of the nation, they will be under no temptations to neglect the latter.

As to corruption, the case is not supposable, he must either have been very unfortunate in his intercourse with the world, or possess a heart very susceptible of such impressions, who can think it probable that the president and two-thirds of the senate will ever be capable of such unworthy conduct. The idea is too gross and too invidious to be entertained. But in such a case, if it should ever happen, the treaty so obtained from us would, like all other fraudulent contracts, be null and void by the laws of nations.

With respect to their responsibility, it is difficult to conceive how it could be encreased. Every consideration that can influence the human mind, such as honor, oaths, reputation, conscience, the love of country, and family affections and attachments, afford security for their fidelity. In short, as the constitution has taken the utmost care that they shall be men of talents and integrity, we have reason to be persuaded that the treaties they make will be as advantageous as all circumstances considered could be made; and so far as the fear of punishment and disgrace can operate, that motive to good behaviour is amply afforded by the article on the subject of impeachments.

PUBLIUS.

SIXTY-FIVE
{NO. 65 IN NEWSPAPERS}

ALEXANDER HAMILTON
March 7, 1788
A Further View of the Constitution of the Senate, in Relation to Its Capacity as a Court for the Trial of Impeachments

To the People of the State of New York.

The remaining powers, which the plan of the convention allots to the senate, in a distinct capacity, are comprised in their participation with the executive in the appointment to offices, and in their judicial character as a court for the trial of impeachments. As in the business of appointments the executive will be the principal agent, the provisions relating to it will most properly be discussed in   5
the examination of that department. We will therefore conclude this head with a view of the judicial character of the senate.

A well constituted court for the trial of impeachments, is an object not more to be desired than difficult to be obtained in a government wholly elective. The subjects of its jurisdiction are those offenses which proceed from the misconduct   10
of public men, or in other words from the abuse or violation of some public trust. They are of a nature which may with peculiar propriety be denominated

---

Lines 8–11 ff Impeachment was a form of trial with medieval origins by which persons, usually though not necessarily holding great offices of state, could be tried for alleged crimes against crown or state. There was usually a political element, just as there was later to be in the impeachment of President Andrew Johnson. In English history, it had usually ended in the disgrace and death of the accused, followed by the forfeiture of his estate. Americans had used impeachments against loyalists during the Revolution, and had developed their own forms; thus impeachment as laid down in the Constitution had more precise limits than in England. In England almost anyone except members of the royal family could be impeached, and punishments depended on the will of Parliament; the Constitution made only public officers liable, and punishment was limited to removal and disqualification from office. The concurrent trial before the House of Lords of Warren Hastings (1732–1818), governor-general of the East India Company, on charges of corruption and tyrannical conduct in his administration in India, does not seem to have been prominent in American thinking. But prosecution by members of the Commons and trial by the full House of Lords was closely replicated by the American procedure of trial by the Senate on indictment by the House. New York included impeachment procedures in its constitution of 1777; see Thorpe, *American Charters,* V, 2635. Impeachment became obsolete in Britain soon after the drafting of the Constitution.

POLITICAL, as they relate chiefly to injuries done immediately to the society itself. The prosecution of them, for this reason, will seldom fail to agitate the passions of the whole community, and to divide it into parties, more or less friendly or inimical, to the accused. In many cases, it will connect itself with the preexisting factions, and will inlist all their animosities, partialities, influence and interest on one side, or on the other; and in such cases there will always be the greatest danger, that the decision will be regulated more by the comparative strength of parties than by the real demonstrations of innocence or guilt.

The delicacy and magnitude of a trust, which so deeply concerns the political reputation and existence of every man engaged in the administration of public affairs, speak for themselves. The difficulty of placing it rightly in a government resting entirely on the basis of periodical elections will as readily be perceived, when it is considered that the most conspicuous characters in it will, from that circumstance, be too often the leaders, or the tools of the most cunning or the most numerous faction; and on this account can hardly be expected to possess the requisite neutrality towards those, whose conduct may be the subject of scrutiny.

The convention, it appears, thought the senate the most fit depositary of this important trust. Those who can best discern the intrinsic difficulty of the thing will be least hasty in condemning that opinion; and will be most inclined to allow due weight to the arguments which may be supposed to have produced it.

What it may be asked is the true spirit of the institution itself? Is it not designed as a method of NATIONAL INQUEST into the conduct of public men? If this be the design of it, who can so properly be the inquisitors for the nation, as the representatives of the nation themselves? It is not disputed that the power of originating the inquiry, or in other words of preferring the impeachment ought to be lodged in the hands of one branch of the legislative body; will not the reasons which indicate the propriety of this arrangement, strongly plead for an admission of the other branch of that body to a share of the inquiry? The model, from which the idea of this institution has been borrowed, pointed out that course to the convention: In Great Britain, it is the province of the house of commons to prefer the impeachment; and of the house of lords to decide upon it. Several of the state constitutions have followed the example. As well the latter as the former seem to have regarded the practice of impeachments, as a bridle in the hands of the legislative body upon the executive servants of the government. Is not this the true light in which it ought to be regarded?

Where else, than in the senate could have been found a tribunal sufficiently dignified, or sufficiently independent? What other body would be likely to feel *confidence enough in its own situation,* to preserve unawed and uninfluenced the necessary impartiality between an *individual* accused, and the *representatives of the people, his accusers?*

Could the supreme court have been relied upon as answering this description? It is much to be doubted whether the members of that tribunal would, at all times, be endowed with so eminent a portion of fortitude, as would be called for in the execution of so difficult a task; and it is still more to be doubted, whether they would possess the degree of credit and authority, which might, on certain occasions, be indispensable, towards reconciling the people to a decision, that should happen to clash with an accusation brought by their immediate represen- 60 tatives. A deficiency in the first would be fatal to the accused; in the last, danger- ous to the public tranquillity. The hazard in both these respects could only be avoided, if at all, by rendering that tribunal more numerous than would consist with a reasonable attention to economy. The necessity of a numerous court for the trial of impeachments is equally dictated by the nature of the proceeding. 65 This can never be tied down by such strict rules, either in the delineation of the offence by the prosecutors, or in the construction of it by the judges, as in com- mon cases serve to limit the discretion of courts in favor of personal security. There will be no jury to stand between the judges, who are to pronounce the sentence of the law and the party who is to receive or suffer it. The awful discre- 70 tion, which a court of impeachments must necessarily have, to doom to honor or to infamy the most confidential and the most distinguished characters of the community, forbids the commitment of the trust to a small number of persons.

These considerations seem alone sufficient to authorise a conclusion, that the supreme court would have been an improper substitute for the senate, as a court 75 of impeachments. There remains a further consideration which will not a little strengthen this conclusion. It is this—The punishment, which may be the con- sequence of conviction upon impeachment, is not to terminate the chastisement of the offender. After having been sentenced to a perpetual ostracism from the es- teem and confidence, and honors and emoluments of his country; he will still be 80 liable to prosecution and punishment in the ordinary course of law. Would it be proper that the persons, who had disposed of his fame and his most valuable rights as a citizen in one trial, should in another trial, for the same offence, be also the disposers of his life and his fortune? Would there not be the greatest rea- son to apprehend, that error in the first sentence would be the parent of error in 85 the second sentence? That the strong bias of one decision would be apt to over- rule the influence of any new lights, which might be brought to vary the com- plexion of another decision? Those, who know any thing of human nature, will not hesitate to answer these questions in the affirmative; and will be at no loss to perceive, that by making the same persons judges in both cases, those who might 90 happen to be the objects of prosecution would in a great measure be deprived of the double security, intended them by a double trial. The loss of life and estate would often be virtually included in a sentence, which, in its terms, imported nothing more than dismission from a present, and disqualification for a future of- fice. It may be said, that the intervention of a jury, in the second instance, would 95 obviate the danger. But juries are frequently influenced by the opinions of judges. They are sometimes induced to find special verdicts which refer the main question to the decision of the court. Who would be willing to stake his life and his estate upon the verdict of a jury, acting under the auspices of judges, who had predetermined his guilt? 100

Would it have been an improvement of the plan, to have united the supreme court with the senate, in the formation of the court of impeachments? This union would certainly have been attended with several advantages; but would they not have been overballanced by the signal disadvantage, already stated, aris-
105 ing from the agency of the same judges in the double prosecution to which the offender would be liable? To a certain extent, the benefits of that union will be obtained from making the chief Justice of the supreme court the president of the court of impeachments, as is proposed to be done in the plan of the convention; while the inconveniences of an intire incorporation of the former into the latter
110 will be substantially avoided. This was perhaps the prudent mean. I forbear to re-mark upon the additional pretext for clamour, against the judiciary, which so considerable an augmentation of its authority would have afforded.

Would it have been desirable to have composed the court for the trial of im-peachments of persons wholly distinct from the other departments of the govern-
115 ment? There are weighty arguments, as well against, as in favor of such a plan. To some minds, it will not appear a trivial objection, that it would tend to increase the complexity of the political machine; and to add a new spring to the govern-ment, the utility of which would at best be questionable. But an objection, which will not be thought by any unworthy of attention, is this—A court formed upon
120 such a plan would either be attended with heavy expence, or might in practice be subject to a variety of casualties and inconveniencies. It must either consist of permanent officers stationary at the seat of government, and of course entitled to fixed and regular stipends, or of certain officers of the state governments, to be called upon whenever an impeachment was actually depending. It will not be
125 easy to imagine any third mode materially different, which could rationally be proposed. As the court, for reasons already given, ought to be numerous; the first scheme will be reprobated by every man, who can compare the extent of the public wants, with the means of supplying them; the second will be espoused with caution by those, who will seriously consider the difficulty of collecting
130 men dispersed over the whole union; the injury to the innocent, from the pro-crastinated determination of the charges which might be brought against them; the advantage to the guilty, from the opportunities which delay would afford to intrigue and corruption; and in some cases the detriment to the state, from the prolonged inaction of men, whose firm and faithful execution of their duty
135 might have exposed them to the persecution of an intemperate or designing ma-jority in the house of representatives. Though this latter supposition may seem harsh, and might not be likely often to be verified; yet it ought not to be forgot-ten, that the demon of faction will at certain seasons extend his sceptre over all numerous bodies of men.
140 But though one or the other of the substitutes which have been examined, or some other that might be devised, should be thought preferable to the plan, in this respect, reported by the convention, it will not follow, that the constitution ought for this reason to be rejected. If mankind were to resolve to agree in no in-stitution of government, until every part of it had been adjusted to the most exact

standard of perfection, society would soon become a general scene of anarchy,   *145*
and the world a desert. Where is the standard of perfection to be found? Who
will undertake to unite the discordant opinions of a whole community, in the
same judgment of it; and to prevail upon one conceited projector to renounce
his *infallible* criterion, for the *fallible* criterion of his more *conceited neighbor?* To
answer the purpose of the adversaries of the constitution, they ought to prove, not   *150*
merely, that particular provisions in it are not the best, which might have been
imagined; but that the plan upon the whole is bad and pernicious.

PUBLIUS.

SIXTY-SIX
{NO. 65 IN NEWSPAPERS}

ALEXANDER HAMILTON
March 8, 1788
The Same Subject Continued

To the People of the State of New York.

A review of the principal objections that have appeared against the proposed court for the trial of impeachments, will not improbably eradicate the remains of any unfavourable impressions, which may still exist, in regard to this matter.

The *first* of these objections is, that the provision in question confounds leg- islative and judiciary authorities in the same body; in violation of that important and well established maxim, which requires a separation between the different departments of power. The true meaning of this maxim has been discussed and ascertained in another place, and has been shewn to be entirely compatible with a partial intermixture of those departments for special purposes, preserving them in the main distinct and unconnected. This partial intermixture is even in some cases not only proper, but necessary to the mutual defence of the several mem- bers of the government, against each other. An absolute or qualified negative in the executive, upon the acts of the legislative body, is admitted by the ablest adepts in political science, to be an indefensible barrier against the encroach- ments of the latter upon the former. And it may perhaps with not less reason be contended that the powers relating to impeachments are as before intimated, an essential check in the hands of that body upon the encroachments of the execu- tive. The division of them between the two branches of the legislature; assigning to one the right of accusing, to the other the right of judging; avoids the incon- venience of making the same persons both accusers and judges; and guards against the danger of persecution from the prevalency of a factious spirit in either of those branches. As the concurrence of two-thirds of the senate will be requisite to a condemnation, the security to innocence, from this additional circum- stance, will be as complete as itself can desire.

It is curious to observe with what vehemence this part of the plan is assailed, on the principle here taken notice of, by men who profess to admire without ex- ception the constitution of this state; while that constitution makes the senate, to- gether with the chancellor and judges of the supreme court, not only a court of impeachments, but the highest judicatory in the state in all causes, civil and criminal. The proportion, in point of numbers, of the chancellor and judges to the senators, is so inconsiderable, that the judiciary authority of New-York in the last resort may, with truth, be said to reside in its senate. If the plan of the convention be in this respect chargeable with a departure from the celebrated maxim which has been so often mentioned, and seems to be so little understood, how much more culpable must be the constitution of New-York?* 35

A *second* objection to the senate, as a court of impeachments, is, that it contributes to an undue accumulation of power in that body, tending to give to the government a countenance too aristocratic. The senate, it is observed, is to have concurrent authority with the executive in the formation of treaties, and in the appointment to offices: If, say the objectors, to these prerogatives is added that of 40 determining in all cases of impeachment, it will give a decided predominancy to senatorial influence. To an objection so little precise in itself, it is not easy to find a very precise answer. Where is the measure or criterion to which we can appeal, for estimating what will give the senate too much, too little, or barely the proper degree of influence? Will it not be more safe, as well as more simple, to dismiss 45 such vague and uncertain calculations, to examine each power by itself, and to decide on general principles where it may be deposited with most advantage and least inconvenience?

If we take this course it will lead to a more intelligible, if not to a more certain result. The disposition of the power of making treaties, which has obtained in the 50 plan of the convention, will then, if I mistake not, appear to be fully justified by the considerations stated in a former number, and by others which will occur under the next head of our enquiries. The expediency of the junction of the senate with the executive, in the power of appointing to offices will, I trust, be placed in a light not less satisfactory, in the disquisitions under the same head. 55 And I flatter myself the observations in my last paper must have gone no inconsiderable way towards proving that it was not easy, if practicable, to find a more fit receptacle for the power of determining impeachments, than that which has been chosen. If this be truly the case, the hypothetical danger of the too great weight of the senate ought to be discarded from our reasonings. 60

But this hypothesis, such as it is has already been refuted in the remarks applied to the duration in office prescribed for the senators. It was by them shewn, as well on the credit of historical examples, as from the reason of the thing, that the most *popular* branch of every government, partaking of the republican genius, by being generally the favorite of the people, will be as generally a full 65 match, if not an overmatch, for every other member of the government.

But independent of this most active and operative principle; to secure the equilibrium of the national house of representatives, the plan of the convention has provided in its favor, several important counterpoises to the additional

* In that of New-Jersey also the final judiciary authority is in a branch of the legislature. In New-Hampshire, Massachusetts, Pennsylvania, and South-Carolina, one branch of the legislature is the court for the trial of impeachments.

70 authorities, to be conferred upon the senate. The exclusive privilege of originating money bills will belong to the house of representatives. The same house will possess the sole right of instituting impeachments: Is not this a complete counterballance to that of determining them? The same house will be the umpire in all elections of the president, which do not unite the suffrages of a majority of the
75 whole number of electors; a case which it cannot be doubted will sometimes, if not frequently, happen. The constant possibility of the thing must be a fruitful source of influence to that body. The more it is contemplated, the more important will appear this ultimate, though contingent power of deciding the competitions of the most illustrious citizens of the union, for the first office in it. It would
80 not perhaps be rash to predict, that as a mean of influence it will be found to outweigh all the peculiar attributes of the senate.

A *third* objection to the senate as a court of impeachments is drawn from the agency they are to have in the appointments to office. It is imagined that they would be too indulgent judges of the conduct of men, in whose official creation
85 they had participated. The principle of this objection would condemn a practice, which is to be seen in all the state governments, if not in all the governments, with which we are acquainted: I mean that of rendering those, who hold office during pleasure, dependent on the pleasure of those, who appoint them. With equal plausibility might it be alledged in this case that the favoritism of the latter
90 would always be an asylum for the misbehavior of the former. But that practice, in contradiction to this principle, proceeds upon the presumption, that the responsibility of those who appoint, for the fitness and competency of the persons, on whom they bestow their choice, and the interest they have in the respectable and prosperous administration of affairs, will inspire a sufficient disposition, to
95 dismiss from a share in it, all such, who, by their conduct, may have proved themselves unworthy of the confidence reposed in them. Though facts may not always correspond with this presumption, yet if it be in the main just, it must destroy the supposition, that the senate, who will merely sanction the choice of the executive, should feel a byass towards the objects of that choice, strong enough to
100 blind them to the evidences of guilt so extraordinary as to have induced the representatives of the nation to become its accusers.

If any further argument were necessary to evince the improbability of such a byass, it might be found in the nature of the agency of the senate, in the business of appointments. It will be the office of the president to *nominate*, and with the
105 advice and consent of the senate to *appoint*. There will of course be no exertion of *choice* on the part of the senate. They may defeat one choice of the executive, and oblige him to make another; but they cannot themselves *choose* — they can only ratify or reject the choice, he may have made. They might even entertain a preference to some other person, at the very moment they were assenting to the

---

Lines 70–71 Money bills originate in the House, which has a popular basis of representation; likewise, they originate in the House of Commons. See No. 58, lines 82–91.

one proposed; because there might be no positive ground of opposition to him; and they could not be sure, if they withheld their assent, that the subsequent nomination would fall upon their own favorite, or upon any other person in their estimation more meritorious than the one rejected. Thus it could hardly happen that the majority of the senate would feel any other complacency towards the object of an appointment, than such, as the appearances of merit, might inspire, and the proofs of the want of it, destroy.

A *fourth* objection to the senate, in the capacity of a court of impeachments, is derived from their union with the executive in the power of making treaties. This, it has been said, would constitute the senators their own judges, in every case of a corrupt or perfidious execution of that trust. After having combined with the executive in betraying the interests of the nation in a ruinous treaty, what prospect, it is asked, would there be of their being made to suffer the punishment, they would deserve, when they were themselves to decide upon the accusation brought against them for the treachery of which they had been guilty?

This objection has been circulated with more earnestness and with greater show of reason, than any other which has appeared against this part of the plan; and yet I am deceived if it does not rest upon an erroneous foundation.

The security essentially intended by the constitution against corruption and treachery in the formation of treaties, is to be sought for in the numbers and characters of those who are to make them. The JOINT AGENCY of the chief magistrate of the union, and of two-thirds of the members of a body selected by the collective wisdom of the legislatures of the several states, is designed to be the pledge for the fidelity of the national councils in this particular. The convention might with propriety have meditated the punishment of the executive, for a deviation from the instructions of the senate, or a want of integrity in the conduct of the negociations committed to him: They might also have had in view the punishment of a few leading individuals in the senate, who should have prostituted their influence in that body, as the mercenary instruments of foreign corruption: But they could not with more or with equal propriety have contemplated the impeachment and punishment of two-thirds of the senate, consenting to an improper treaty, than of a majority of that or of the other branch of the national legislature, consenting to a pernicious or unconstitutional law: a principle which I believe has never been admitted into any government. How in fact could a majority of the house of representatives impeach themselves? Not better, it is evident, than two-thirds of the senate might try themselves. And yet what reason is there, that a majority of the house of representatives, sacrificing the interests of the society, by an unjust and tyrannical act of legislation, should escape with impunity more than two-thirds of the senate, sacrificing the same interests in an injurious treaty with a foreign power? The truth is, that in all such cases it is essential to the freedom and to the necessary independence of the deliberations of the body, that the members of it should be exempt from punishment for acts done in a collective capacity; and the security to the society must depend on the care which is taken to confide the trust to proper hands, to make it their interest

to execute it with fidelity, and to make it as difficult as possible for them to com-
155 bine in any interest opposite to that of the public good.

So far as might concern the misbehaviour of the executive in perverting the
instructions, or contravening the views of the senate, we need not be apprehensive of the want of a disposition in that body to punish the abuse of their confidence, or to vindicate their own authority. We may thus far count upon their
160 pride, if not upon their virtue. And so far even as might concern the corruption
of leading members, by whose arts and influence the majority may have been in-
veigled into measures odious to the community; if the proofs of that corruption
should be satisfactory, the usual propensity of human nature will warrant us in
concluding, that there would be commonly no defect of inclination in the body,
165 to divert the public resentment from themselves, by a ready sacrifice of the authors of their mismanagement and disgrace.

PUBLIUS.

SIXTY-SEVEN
{NO. 66 IN NEWSPAPERS}

ALEXANDER HAMILTON
March 11, 1788
Concerning the Constitution of the President; A Gross Attempt to Misrepresent this Part of the Plan Detected

To the People of the State of New York.

The constitution of the executive department of the proposed government claims next our attention.

There is hardly any part of the system which could have been attended with greater difficulty in the arrangement of it than this; and there is perhaps none, which has been inveighed against with less candor, or criticised with less judgment. 5

Here the writers against the constitution seem to have taken pains to signalize their talent of misrepresentation. Calculating upon the aversion of the people to monarchy, they have endeavoured to inlist all their jealousies and apprehensions in opposition to the intended president of the United States; not merely as the embryo but as the full grown progeny of that detested parent. To establish the 10 pretended affinity they have not scrupled to draw resources even from the regions of fiction. The authorities of a magistrate, in few instances greater, and in some instances less, than those of a governor of New-York, have been magnified into more than royal prerogatives. He has been decorated with attributes superior in dignity and splendor to those of a king of Great-Britain. He has been shown to 15 us with the diadem sparkling on his brow, and the imperial purple flowing in his train. He has been seated on a throne surrounded with minions and mistresses; giving audience to the envoys of foreign potentates, in all the supercilious pomp of majesty. The images of Asiatic despotism and voluptuousness have scarcely been wanting to crown the exaggerated scene. We have been almost taught to 20 tremble at the terrific visages of murdering janizaries; and to blush at the unveiled mysteries of a future seraglio.

Attempts so extravagant as these to disfigure, or it might rather be said, to metamorphose the object, render it necessary to take an accurate view of its real nature and form; in order as well to ascertain its true aspect and genuine appear- 25 ance, as to unmask the disingenuity and expose the fallacy of the counterfeit resemblances which have been so insidiously as well as industriously propagated.

In the execution of this task there is no man, who would not find it an arduous effort, either to behold with moderation or to treat with seriousness the devices, not less weak than wicked, which have been contrived to pervert the 30 public opinion in relation to the subject. They so far exceed the usual, though

unjustifiable, licenses of party-artifice, that even in a disposition the most candid and tolerant they must force the sentiments which favor an indulgent construction of the conduct of political adversaries to give place to a voluntary and unre-
35 served indignation. It is impossible not to bestow the imputation of deliberate imposture and deception upon the gross pretence of a similitude between a king of Great-Britain and a magistrate of the character marked out for that of the president of the United States. It is still more impossible to withhold that imputation from the rash and barefaced expedients which have been employed to give
40 success to the attempted imposition.

In one instance, which I cite as a sample of the general spirit, the temerity has proceeded so far as to ascribe to the president of the United States a power, which by the instrument reported is *expressly* allotted to the executives of the individual states. I mean the power of filling casual vacancies in the senate.
45 This bold experiment upon the discernment of his countrymen, has been hazarded by a writer who (whatever may be his real merit) has had no inconsiderable share in the applauses of his party;* and who upon his false and unfounded suggestion, has built a series of observations equally false and unfounded. Let him now be confronted with the evidence of the fact; and let him,
50 if he be able, justify or extenuate the shameful outrage he has offered to the dictates of truth and to the rules of fair dealing.

The second clause of the second section of the second article empowers the president of the United States "to nominate, and by and with the advice and consent of the senate to appoint ambassadors, other public ministers and consuls,
55 judges of the supreme court, and all other *officers* of the United States, whose appointments are *not* in the constitution *otherwise provided for*, and *which shall be established by law.*" Immediately after this clause follows another in these words—"The president shall have power to fill up all *vacancies* that may happen *during the recess of the senate*, by granting commissions which shall *expire at the*
60 *end of their next session.*" It is from this last provision that the pretended power of the president to fill vacancies in the senate has been deduced. A slight attention to the connection of the clauses and to the obvious meaning of the terms will satisfy us that the deduction is not even colorable.

* See Cato No. 5.

Lines 45–51 *Cato* was the pseudonym of George Clinton (1739–1812), governor of New York and head of one of the most effectively organized parties in American politics of the period. (He was later to be Madison's vice president.) His letters appeared from November 1787 to January 1788. He was picking up the pseudonym used earlier in the century by the English anti-establishment pamphleteers John Trenchard (1662–1723) and Thomas Gordon (?–1750), whose essays helped to formulate anti-British opinion in the colonies. Cato the Roman statesman (95–46 B.C.) had a reputation for integrity and intransigence.

The first of these two clauses it is clear only provides a mode for appointing such officers, "whose appointments are *not otherwise provided for* in the constitu- 65 tion, and which *shall be established by law*"; of course it cannot extend to the appointment of senators; whose appointments are *otherwise provided for* in the constitution,* and who are *established by the constitution,* and will not require a future establishment by law. This position will hardly be contested.

The last of these two clauses, it is equally clear, cannot be understood to com- 70 prehend the power of filling vacancies in the senate, for the following reasons— *First.* The relation in which that clause stands to the other, which declares the general mode of appointing officers of the United States, denotes it to be nothing more than a supplement to the other; for the purpose of establishing an auxiliary method of appointment in cases, to which the general method was inadequate. 75 The ordinary power of appointment is confided to the president and senate *jointly,* and can therefore only be exercised during the session of the senate; but as it would have been improper to oblige this body to be continually in session for the appointment of officers; and as vacancies might happen *in their recess,* which it might be necessary for the public service to fill without delay, the suc- 80 ceeding clause is evidently intended to authorise the president *singly* to make temporary appointments "during the recess of the senate, by granting commissions which should expire at the end of their next session." *Second.* If this clause is to be considered as supplementary to the one which precedes, the *vacancies* of which it speaks must be construed to relate to the "officers" described in the pre- 85 ceding one; and this we have seen excludes from its description the members of the senate. *Third.* The time within which the power is to operate "during the recess of the senate" and the duration of the appointments "to the end of the next session" of that body, conspire to elucidate the sense of the provision; which if it had been intended to comprehend senators would naturally have referred the 90 temporary power of filling vacancies to the recess of the state legislatures, who are to make the permanent appointments, and not to the recess of the national senate, who are to have no concern in those appointments; and would have extended the duration in office of the temporary senators to the next session of the legislature of the state, in whose representation the vacancies had happened, 95 instead of making it to expire at the end of the ensuing session of the national senate. The circumstances of the body authorised to make the permanent appointments, would of course have governed the modification of a power which related to the temporary appointments; and as the national senate is the body whose situation is alone contemplated in the clause upon which the suggestion 100 under examination has been founded, the vacancies to which it alludes can only be deemed to respect those officers, in whose appointment that body has a concurrent agency with the president. But, *lastly,* the first and second clauses of the

---

* Article 1. Sec. 3. Clause I.

third section of the first article, not only obviate the possibility of doubt, but destroy the pretext of misconception. The former provides that "the senate of the United States shall be composed of two senators from each state, chosen *by the legislature thereof* for six years," and the latter directs that "if vacancies in that body should happen by resignation or otherwise *during the recess of the legislature of* ANY STATE, the executive THEREOF may make temporary appointments until the *next meeting of the legislature,* which shall then fill such vacancies." Here is an express power given, in clear and unambiguous terms, to the state executives to fill the casual vacancies in the senate by temporary appointments; which not only invalidates the supposition, that the clause before considered could have been intended to confer that power upon the president of the United States; but proves that this supposition, destitute as it is even of the merit of plausibility, must have originated in an intention to deceive the people, too palpable to be obscured by sophistry, and too atrocious to be palliated by hypocrisy.

I have taken the pains to select this instance of misrepresentation, and to place it in a clear and strong light, as an unequivocal proof of the unwarrantable arts which are practised to prevent a fair and impartial judgment of the real merits of the constitution submitted to the consideration of the people. Nor have I scrupled in so flagrant a case to allow myself in a severity of animadversion little congenial with the general spirit of these papers. I hesitate not to submit it to the decision of any candid and honest adversary of the proposed government, whether language can furnish epithets of too much asperity for so shameless and so prostitute an attempt to impose on the citizens of America.

PUBLIUS.

SIXTY-EIGHT
{NO. 67 IN NEWSPAPERS}

ALEXANDER HAMILTON
March 12, 1788
The View of the Constitution of the President Continued,
in Relation to the Mode of Appointment

To the People of the State of New York.

The mode of appointment of the chief magistrate of the United States is almost the only part of the system, of any consequence, which has escaped without severe censure, or which has received the slightest mark of approbation from its opponents. The most plausible of these, who has appeared in print, has even deigned to admit, that the election of the president is pretty well guarded.* I venture somewhat further, and hesitate not to affirm, that if the manner of it be not perfect, it is at least excellent. It unites in an eminent degree all the advantages, the union of which was to be desired. 5

It was desireable, that the sense of the people should operate in the choice of the person to whom so important a trust was to be confided. This end will be answered by committing the right of making it, not to any pre-established body, but to men, chosen by the people for the special purpose, and at the particular conjuncture. 10

It was equally desirable, that the immediate election should be made by men most capable of analizing the qualities adapted to the station, and acting under circumstances favourable to deliberation and to a judicious combination of all the reasons and inducements, that were proper to govern their choice. A small number of persons, selected by their fellow citizens from the general mass, will be most likely to possess the information and discernment requisite to so complicated an investigation. 15

It was also peculiarly desirable, to afford as little opportunity as possible to tumult and disorder. This evil was not least to be dreaded in the election of a magistrate, who was to have so important an agency in the administration of the government, as the president of the United States. But the precautions which have been so happily concerted in the system under consideration, promise an effectual security against this mischief. The choice of *several* to form an intermediate 25

* Vide Federal Farmer.

Hamilton's footnote The Federal Farmer, cited here, is Richard Henry Lee (1732–1794) of Virginia.

body of electors, will be much less apt to convulse the community, with any extraordinary or violent movements, than the choice of *one* who was himself to be the final object of the public wishes. And as the electors, chosen in each state,
30 are to assemble and vote in the state, in which they are chosen, this detached and divided situation will expose them much less to heats and ferments, which might be communicated from them to the people, than if they were all to be convened at one time, in one place.

Nothing was more to be desired, than that every practicable obstacle should
35 be opposed to cabal, intrigue and corruption. These most deadly adversaries of republican government might naturally have been expected to make their approaches from more than one quarter, but chiefly from the desire in foreign powers to gain an improper ascendant in our councils. How could they better gratify this, than by raising a creature of their own to the chief magistracy of the union?
40 But the convention have guarded against all danger of this sort with the most provident and judicious attention. They have not made the appointment of the president to depend on any pre-existing bodies of men who might be tampered with beforehand to prostitute their votes; but they have referred it in the first instance to an immediate act of the people of America, to be exerted in the choice
45 of persons for the temporary and sole purpose of making the appointment. And they have excluded from eligibility to this trust, all those who from situation might be suspected of too great devotion to the president in office. No senator, representative, or other person holding a place of trust or profit under the United States, can be of the number of the electors. Thus, without corrupting the body
50 of the people, the immediate agents in the election will at least enter upon the task, free from any sinister byass. Their transient existence, and their detached situation, already taken notice of, afforded a satisfactory prospect of their continuing so, to the conclusion of it. The business of corruption, when it is to embrace so considerable a number of men, requires time, as well as means. Nor
55 would it be found easy suddenly to embark them, dispersed as they would be over thirteen states, in any combinations founded upon motives, which though they could not properly be denominated corrupt, might yet be of a nature to mislead them from their duty.

Another and no less important desideratum was, that the executive should be
60 independent for his continuance in office on all, but the people themselves. He might otherwise be tempted to sacrifice his duty to his complaisance for those whose favor was necessary to the duration of his official consequence. This advantage will also be secured, by making his re-election to depend on a special

---

Lines 40–58 The object of the precautions mentioned in this paragraph is to guard against the corruption of members of Congress by the executive similar to the corruption that both British and American radical Whigs perceived in British politics.

body of representatives, deputed by the society for the single purpose of making the important choice.   65

All these advantages will be happily combined in the plan devised by the convention; which is, that the people of each state shall choose a number of persons as electors, equal to the number of senators and representatives of such state in the national government, who shall assemble within the state and vote for some fit person as president. Their votes, thus given, are to be transmitted to the seat of   70 the national government, and the person who may happen to have a majority of the whole number of votes will be the president. But as a majority of the votes might not always happen to centre on one man, and as it might be unsafe to permit less than a majority to be conclusive, it is provided, that in such a contingency, the house of representatives shall elect out of the candidates, who shall   75 have the five highest numbers of votes, the man who in their opinion may be best qualified for the office.

This process of election affords a moral certainty, that the office of president, will seldom fall to the lot of any man, who is not in an eminent degree endowed with the requisite qualifications. Talents for low intrigue and the little arts of pop-   80 ularity may alone suffice to elevate a man to the first honors in a single state, but it will require other talents and a different kind of merit to establish him in the esteem and confidence of the whole union, or of so considerable a portion of it as would be necessary to make him a successful candidate for the distinguished office of president of the United States. It will not be too strong to say, that there   85 will be a constant probability of seeing the station filled by characters preeminent for ability and virtue. And this will be thought no inconsiderable recommendation of the constitution, by those, who are able to estimate the share, which the executive in every government must necessarily have in its good or ill administration. Though we cannot acquiesce in the political heresy of the poet   90 who says—

"For forms of government let fools contest—That which is best administered is best."

—yet we may safely pronounce, that the true test of a good government is its aptitude and tendency to produce a good administration.   95

The vice-president is to be chosen in the same manner with the president; with this difference, that the senate is to do, in respect to the former, what is to be done by the house of representatives, in respect to the latter.

Lines 78–87 When the British political scientist and recent ambassador to the United States James Bryce (1838–1922; later Lord Bryce) came to write *The American Commonwealth* one hundred years later (1888), he included a chapter discussing why great men do *not* become president!

Line 92 The quotation is from Alexander Pope's (1688–1744) *Essay on Man* (1733–1734). See the note examining No. 27 lines 13–16.

The appointment of an extraordinary person, as vice president, has been ob-
100   jected to as superfluous, if not mischievous. It has been alledged, that it would
have been preferable to have authorised the senate to elect out of their own body
an officer, answering to that description. But two considerations seem to justify
the ideas of the convention in this respect. One is, that to secure at all times the
possibility of a definitive resolution of the body, it is necessary that the president
105   should have only a casting vote. And to take the senator of any state from his seat
as senator, to place him in that of president of the senate, would be to exchange,
in regard to the state from which he came, a constant for a contingent vote. The
other consideration is, that as the vice-president may occasionally become a
substitute for the president, in the supreme executive magistracy, all the reasons,
110   which recommend the mode of election prescribed for the one, apply with great,
if not with equal force to the manner of appointing the other. It is remarkable,
that in this as in most other instances, the objection, which is made, would lie
against the constitution of this state. We have a lieutenant governor chosen by
the people at large, who presides in the senate, and is the constitutional substi-
115   tute for the governor in casualties similar to those, which would authorise the
vice-president to exercise the authorities and discharge the duties of the president.

PUBLIUS.

SIXTY-NINE
{NO. 68 IN NEWSPAPERS}

ALEXANDER HAMILTON
March 14, 1788
The Same View Continued, with a Comparison Between the President and the King of Great-Britain on the One Hand, and the Governor of New-York on the Other

To the People of the State of New York.

I proceed now to trace the real characters of the proposed executive as they are marked out in the plan of the convention. This will serve to place in a strong light the unfairness of the representations which have been made in regard to it.

    The first thing which strikes our attention is that the executive authority, with few exceptions, is to be vested in a single magistrate. This will scarcely, however,   *5* be considered as a point upon which any comparison can be grounded; for if in this particular there be a resemblance to the king of Great-Britain, there is not less a resemblance to the Grand Signior, to the Khan of Tartary, to the man of the seven mountains, or to the governor of New-York.

    That magistrate is to be elected for *four* years; and is to be re-eligible as often   *10* as the people of the United States shall think him worthy of their confidence. In these circumstances, there is a total dissimilitude between *him* and a king of Great-Britain; who is an *hereditary* monarch, possessing the crown as a patrimony descendible to his heirs forever; but there is a close analogy between *him* and a governor of New-York, who is elected for *three* years, and is re-eligible without   *15* limitation or intermission. If we consider how much less time would be requisite for establishing a dangerous influence in a single state, than for establishing a like influence throughout the United States, we must conclude that a duration of

---

Lines 8–9 The referent of Hamilton's "the Grand Signior" is not clear, nor do we have an identity for the obviously mythical "man of the seven mountains"; the "Khan of Tartary" (Mongolia) is Genghis Khan.

Lines 10–11 See note on No. 72, lines 35–41.

Lines 11–14 Since the Glorious Revolution, Parliament had certified the authenticity of the heir's claim to the throne. This was designed to prevent substitutions, which had been alleged on the proclaimed birth of James II's son. It was the Convention Parliament that had proclaimed and sanctioned William of Orange and his wife, Mary, who was James's daughter. Parliament therefore could claim to have a lawful role in determining the succession—which it would certainly do if there were rival claimants.

four years for the chief magistrate of the union, is a degree of permanency far less
to be dreaded in that office, than a duration of *three* years for a correspondent office in a single state.

The president of the United States would be liable to be impeached, tried,
and upon conviction of treason, bribery, or other high crimes or misdemeanors,
removed from office; and would afterwards be liable to prosecution and punishment in the ordinary course of law. The person of the king of Great-Britain is sacred and inviolable: There is no constitutional tribunal to which he is amenable;
no punishment to which he can be subjected without involving the crisis of a national revolution. In this delicate and important circumstance of personal responsibility, the president of confederated America would stand upon no better
ground than a governor of New-York, and upon worse ground than the governors
of Virginia and Delaware.

The president of the United States is to have power to return a bill, which
shall have passed the two branches of the legislature, for re-consideration; but the
bill so returned is not to become a law, unless upon that re-consideration it be
approved by two thirds of both houses. The king of Great Britain, on his part, has
an absolute negative upon the acts of the two houses of Parliament. The disuse of
that power for a considerable time past, does not affect the reality of its existence;
and is to be ascribed wholly to the crown's having found the means of substituting influence to authority, or the art of gaining a majority in one or the other of
the two houses, to the necessity of exerting a prerogative which could seldom be
exerted without hazarding some degree of national agitation. The qualified negative of the president differs widely from this absolute negative of the British sovereign; and tallies exactly with the revisionary authority of the council of revision
of this state, of which the governor is a constituent part. In this respect, the power
of the president would exceed that of the governor of New-York; because the former would possess singly what the latter shares with the chancellor and judges:
But it would be precisely the same with that of the governor of Massachusetts,
whose constitution, as to this article, seems to have been the original from which
the convention have copied.

The president is to be the "commander in chief of the army and navy of the
United States, and of the militia of the several states, when called into the actual
service of the United States. He is to have power to grant reprieves and pardons

---

Lines 25–28 The restraints placed on George III during his bouts of apparent insanity call this inviolability into question. The constitutional point not made by Hamilton is that the king's ministers could be removed though the king remained.

Lines 35–41 The argument pursued here about the royal veto, or negative, is in-
valid. The disuse of the power since 1708 in the reign of Queen Anne amounted to
a convention of the constitution; its reuse would have provoked a constitutional crisis.

Lines 50–60 Here we begin to see evidence of the need to circumvent the separation of powers.

for offences against the United States, *except in cases of impeachment*; to recommend to the consideration of congress such measures as he shall judge necessary and expedient; to convene on extraordinary occasions both houses of the legislature, or either of them, and in case of disagreement between them *with respect to the time of adjournment*, to adjourn them to such time as he shall think proper; to take care that the laws be faithfully executed; and to commission all officers of the United States." In most of these particulars the power of the president will resemble equally that of the king of Great-Britain and of the governor of New-York. The most material points of difference are these:—First. The president will have only the occasional command of such part of the militia of the nation, as by legislative provision may be called into the actual service of the union. The king of Great-Britain and the governor of New-York have at all times the entire command of all the militia within their several jurisdictions. In this article therefore the power of the president would be inferior to that of either the monarch or the governor. Second. The president is to be commander in chief of the army and navy of the United States. In this respect his authority would be nominally the same with that of the king of Great-Britain, but in substance much inferior to it. It would amount to nothing more than the supreme command and direction of the military and naval forces, as first general and admiral of the confederacy; while that of the British king extends to the *declaring* of war and to the *raising* and *regulating* of fleets and armies; all which by the constitution under consideration would appertain to the legislature.* The governor of New-York on the other hand, is by the constitution of the state vested only with the command of its militia and navy. But the constitutions of several of the states, expressly declare their governors to be commanders in chief as well of the army as navy; and it may well be a question whether those of New-Hampshire and Massachusetts, in particular, do not in this instance confer larger powers upon their respective governors, than could be claimed by a president of the United States. Third. The power of the president in respect to pardons would extend to all cases, *except those of impeachment*. The governor of New-York may pardon in all cases, even in those of impeachment, except for treason and murder. Is not the power of the

---

* A writer in a Pennsylvania paper, under the signature of Tamony has asserted that the king of Great-Britain owes his prerogatives as commander in chief to an annual mutiny bill. The truth is on the contrary that his prerogative in this respect is immemorial, and was only disputed "contrary to all reason and precedent," as Blackstone, vol. 1, p. 262, expresses it, by the long parliament of Charles I; but by the statute the 13th, of Charles II, chap. 6, it was declared to be in the king alone, for that the sole supreme government and command of the militia within his Majesty's realms and dominions, and of all forces by sea and land, and of all forts and places of strength, EVER WAS AND IS the undoubted right of his Majesty and his royal predecessors kings and queens of England, and that both or either house of Parliament cannot nor ought to pretend to the same.

governor in this article, on a calculation of political consequences, greater than
that of the president? All conspiracies and plots against the government, which
have not been matured into actual treason, may be screened from punishment of
every kind, by the interposition of the prerogative of pardoning. If a governor of
New-York therefore should be at the head of any such conspiracy, until the design had been ripened into actual hostility, he could ensure his accomplices and
adherents an entire impunity. A president of the union on the other hand,
though he may even pardon treason, when prosecuted in the ordinary course of
law, could shelter no offender in any degree from the effects of impeachment &
conviction. Would not the prospect of a total indemnity for all the preliminary
steps be a greater temptation to undertake and persevere in an enterprise against
the public liberty than the mere prospect of an exemption from death and con-
fiscation, if the final execution of the design, upon an actual appeal to arms,
should miscarry? Would this last expectation have any influence at all, when the
probability was computed that the person who was to afford that exemption
might himself be involved in the consequences of the measure; and might be incapacitated by his agency in it, from affording the desired impunity? The better
to judge of this matter, it will be necessary to recollect that by the proposed constitution the offence of treason is limited "to levying war upon the United States,
and adhering to their enemies, giving them aid and comfort," and that by the
laws of New-York it is confined within similar bounds. Fourth. The president can
only adjourn the national legislature in the single case of disagreement about the
time of adjournment. The British monarch may prorogue or even dissolve the
Parliament. The governor of New-York may also prorogue the legislature of this
state for a limited time; a power which in certain situations may be employed to
very important purposes.

The president is to have power with the advice and consent of the senate to
make treaties; provided two thirds of the senators present concur. The king of
Great-Britain is the sole and absolute representative of the nation in all foreign
transactions. He can of his own accord make treaties of peace, commerce, alliance, and of every other description. It has been insinuated, that his authority
in this respect is not conclusive, and that his conventions with foreign powers are
subject to the revision, and stand in need of the ratification of Parliament. But I

Lines 106–107 George III had dissolved Parliament and called for a general election
in the autumn of 1774, confident that he could get a parliament that would stand by
him during the forthcoming American crisis. His calculations proved correct.

Lines 111–33 The prerogative of making treaties rested in the crown, but this really
meant the ministry, as Hamilton fails to make clear. The tendency of this essay is
to exaggerate the role of the monarch as autocrat; he did possess very extensive powers, but they were hedged by shared responsibilities and processes of
consultation.

believe this doctrine was never heard of till it was broached upon the present occasion. Every jurist* of that kingdom, and every other man acquainted with its constitution knows, as an established fact, that the prerogative of making treaties exists in the crown in its utmost plenitude; and that the compacts entered into by the royal authority have the most complete legal validity and perfection, independent of any other sanction. The Parliament, it is true, is sometimes seen employing itself in altering the existing laws to conform them to the stipulations in a new treaty; and this may have possibly given birth to the imagination that its cooperation was necessary to the obligatory efficacy of the treaty. But this parliamentary interposition proceeds from a different cause; from the necessity of adjusting a most artificial and intricate system of revenue and commercial laws to the changes made in them by the operation of the treaty; and of adapting new provisions and precautions to the new state of things, to keep the machine from running into disorder. In this respect therefore, there is no comparison between the intended power of the president, and the actual power of the British sovereign. The one can perform alone, what the other can only do with the concurrence of a branch of the legislature. It must be admitted that in this instance the power of the federal executive would exceed that of any state executive. But this arises naturally from the exclusive possession by the union of that part of the sovereign power, which relates to treaties. If the confederacy were to be dissolved, it would become a question, whether the executives of the several states were not solely invested with that delicate and important prerogative.

The president is also to be authorised to receive ambassadors and other public ministers. This, though it has been a rich theme of declamation, is more a matter of dignity than of authority. It is a circumstance, which will be without consequence in the administration of the government; and it was far more convenient that it should be arranged in this manner, than that there should be a necessity of convening the legislature, or one of its branches, upon every arrival of a foreign minister; though it were merely to take the place of a departed predecessor.

The president is to nominate and *with the advice and consent of the senate* to appoint ambassadors and other public ministers, judges of the supreme court, and in general all officers of the United States established by law and whose appointments are not otherwise provided for by the constitution. The king of Great-Britain is emphatically and truly stiled the fountain of honor. He not only

* Vide Blackstone's Commentaries, vol. 1, page 257.

Lines 139–45 The Anti-Federalists objected to receiving ambassadors on the republican grounds that ambassadors were by custom sent by monarchs to one another's courts. This is why the nations of the present-day Commonwealth are represented by high commissioners; the queen of Great Britain cannot send an ambassador to herself as queen of New Zealand.

appoints to all offices, but can create offices. He can confer titles of nobility at pleasure; and has the disposal of an immense number of church preferments. There is evidently a great inferiority, in the power of the president in this particular, to that of the British king; nor is it equal to that of the governor of New-York,
155 if we are to interpret the meaning of the constitution of the state by the practice which has obtained under it. The power of appointment is with us lodged in a council composed of the governor and four members of the senate chosen by the assembly. The governor *claims* and has frequently *exercised* the right of nomination, and is *entitled* to a casting vote in the appointment. If he really has the right
160 of nominating, his authority is in this respect equal to that of the president, and exceeds it in the article of the casting vote. In the national government, if the senate should be divided, no appointment could be made: In the government of New-York, if the council should be divided the governor can turn the scale and confirm his own nomination.* If we compare the publicity which must necessar-
165 ily attend the mode of appointment by the president and an entire branch of the national legislature, with the privacy in the mode of appointment by the governor of New-York, closeted in secret apartment with at most four, and frequently with only two persons; and if we at the same time consider how much more easy it must be to influence the small number of which a council of appointment con-
170 sist than the considerable number of which the national senate would consist, we cannot hesitate to pronounce, that the power of the chief magistrate of this state in the disposition of offices must in practice be greatly superior to that of the chief magistrate of the union.

Hence it appears, that except as to the concurrent authority of the president in
175 the article of treaties, it would be difficult to determine whether that magistrate would in the aggregate, possess more or less power than the governor of New-York. And it appears yet more unequivocally that there is no pretence for the parallel which has been attempted between him and the king of Great-Britain. But to render the contrast, in this respect, still more striking, it may be of use to throw
180 the principal circumstances of dissimilitude into a closer groupe.

* Candor however demands an acknowledgment; that I do not think the claim of the governor to a right of nomination well founded. Yet it is always justifiable to reason from the practice of a government till its propriety has been constitutionally questioned. And independent of this claim, when we take into view the other considerations and pursue them through all their consequences, we shall be inclined to draw much the same conclusion.

Lines 174–77 It was George Clinton who, as governor of New York, was alleged to have abused the power of patronage. His opposition to the Constitution was well known, so this remark, appearing in a New York newspaper, was probably political in motive.

The president of the United States would be an officer elected by the people for *four* years. The king of Great-Britain is a perpetual and *hereditary* prince. The one would be amenable to personal punishment and disgrace: The person of the other is sacred and inviolable. The one would have a *qualified* negative upon the acts of the legislative body: The other has an *absolute* negative. The one would have a right to command the military and naval forces of the nation: The other in addition to this right, possesses that of *declaring* war, and of *raising* and *regulating* fleets and armies by his own authority. The one would have a concurrent power with a branch of the legislature in the formation of treaties: The other is the *sole possessor* of the power of making treaties. The one would have a like concurrent authority in appointing to offices: The other is the sole author of all appointments. The one can confer no privileges whatever: The other can make denizens of aliens, noblemen of commoners, can erect corporations with all the rights incident to corporate bodies. The one can prescribe no rules concerning the commerce or currency of the nation: The other is in several respects the arbiter of commerce, and in this capacity can establish markets and fairs, can regulate weights and measures, can lay embargoes for a limited time, can coin money, can authorise or prohibit the circulation of foreign coin. The one has no particle of spiritual jurisdiction: The other is the supreme head and governor of the national church! What answer shall we give to those who would persuade us that things so unlike resemble each other? The same that ought to be given to those who tell us, that a government, the whole power of which would be in the hands of the elective and periodical servants of the people, is an aristocracy, a monarchy, and a despotism.

PUBLIUS.

Line 184 This is the second use of an exaggerated "sacred and inviolable." Actually, Charles I had been beheaded and James II forced from the throne, and the later years of the reign of George III were to pass in a regency. (Hence London's Regent Street and Regent's Park.)

SEVENTY
{NO. 69 IN NEWSPAPERS}

ALEXANDER HAMILTON
March 15, 1788
The Same View Continued in Relation to the UNITY of the Executive,
with an Examination of the Project of an Executive Council

To the People of the State of New York.

There is an idea, which is not without its advocates, that a vigorous executive is inconsistent with the genius of republican government. The enlightened well wishers to this species of government must at least hope that the supposition is destitute of foundation; since they can never admit its truth, without at the same time admitting the condemnation of their own principles. Energy in the executive is a leading character in the definition of good government. It is essential to the protection of the community against foreign attacks: It is not less essential to the steady administration of the laws, to the protection of property against those irregular and high handed combinations, which sometimes interrupt the ordinary course of justice, to the security of liberty against the enterprises and assaults of ambition, of faction and of anarchy. Every man the least conversant in Roman story knows how often that republic was obliged to take refuge in the absolute power of a single man, under the formidable title of dictator, as well against the intrigues of ambitious individuals, who aspired to the tyranny, and the seditions of whole classes of the community, whose conduct threatened the existence of all government, as against the invasions of external enemies, who menaced the conquest and destruction of Rome.

There can be no need however to multiply arguments or examples on this head. A feeble executive implies a feeble execution of the government. A feeble execution is but another phrase for a bad execution: And a government ill executed, whatever it may be in theory, must be in practice a bad government.

Taking it for granted, therefore, that all men of sense will agree in the necessity of an energetic executive; it will only remain to inquire, what are the ingredients which constitute this energy—how far can they be combined with those other ingredients which constitute safety in the republican sense? And how far does this combination characterise the plan, which has been reported by the convention?

The ingredients which constitute energy in the executive are, unity—duration—an adequate provision for its support—competent powers.

The ingredients which constitute safety in the republican sense are, a due dependence on the people—a due responsibility.

Those politicians and statesmen, who have been the most celebrated for the soundness of their principles, and for the justness of their views, have declared in favor of a single executive and a numerous legislature. They have with great propriety considered energy as the most necessary qualification of the former, and have regarded this as most applicable to power in a single hand; while they have with equal propriety considered the latter as best adapted to deliberation and wisdom, and best calculated to conciliate the confidence of the people and to secure their privileges and interests.   35

That unity is conducive to energy will not be disputed. Decision, activity, secrecy, and dispatch will generally characterise the proceedings of one man, in a much more eminent degree, than the proceedings of any greater number; and in proportion as the number is increased, these qualities will be diminished.   40

This unity may be destroyed in two ways; either by vesting the power in two or more magistrates of equal dignity and authority; or by vesting it ostensibly in one man, subject in whole or in part to the controul and co-operation of others, in the capacity of counsellors to him. Of the first the two consuls of Rome may serve as an example; of the last we shall find examples in the constitutions of several of the states. New-York and New-Jersey, if I recollect right, are the only states, which have entrusted the executive authority wholly to single men.* Both these methods of destroying the unity of the executive have their partisans; but the votaries of an executive council are the most numerous. They are both liable, if not to equal, to similar objections; and may in most lights be examined in conjunction.   45, 50

The experience of other nations will afford little instruction on this head. As far however as it teaches any thing, it teaches us not to be inamoured of plurality in the executive. We have seen that the Achaeans on an experiment of two praetors, were induced to abolish one. The Roman history records many instances of mischiefs to the republic from the dissentions between the consuls, and between   55

* New-York has no council except for the single purpose of appointing to offices; New-Jersey has a council, whom the governor may consult. But I think from the terms of the constitution their resolutions do not bind him.

Lines 47–48 In the Roman republic, the office of consul was normally held for one year, and was often followed by appointment as a provincial governor. The consuls (usually two) were elected by the people on presentation by the senate; there was a convention, not closely followed, that one of the two should be a plebeian. The consuls were effectively heads of government during their term of office, and their responsibilities included military authority. Under the empire, after ca. 27 B.C., nominations to the office increasingly came into the hands of the emperors, and consulships were sometimes held only for a few months. The multiple executive referred to in the new states consisted of the governor and council, the latter being a rather distant replica of the king's privy council.

Lines 56–57 See No. 18, lines 83–91 for the previous mention, and note on No. 18, lines 1–ff for probable source.

the military tribunes, who were at times substituted to the consuls. But it gives us no specimens of any peculiar advantages derived to the state, from the plurality of those magistrates. That the dissentions between them were not more frequent, or more fatal, is matter of astonishment; until we advert to the singular position in which the republic was almost continually placed and to the prudent policy pointed out by the circumstances of the state, and pursued by the consuls, of making a division of the government between them. The Patricians engaged in a perpetual struggle with the Plebians for the preservation of their antient authorities and dignities; the consuls, who were generally chosen out of the former body, were commonly united by the personal interest they had in the defence of the privileges of their order. In addition to this motive of union, after the arms of the republic had considerably expanded the bounds of its empire, it became an established custom with the consuls to divide the administration between themselves by lot; one of them remaining at Rome to govern the city and its environs; the other taking the command in the more distant provinces. This expedient must no doubt have had great influence in preventing those collisions and rivalships, which might otherwise have embroiled the republic.

But quitting the dim light of historical research, and attaching ourselves purely to the dictates of reason and good sense, we shall discover much greater cause to reject than to approve the idea of plurality in the executive, under any modification whatever.

Wherever two or more persons are engaged in any common enterprize or pursuit, there is always danger of difference of opinion. If it be a public trust or office in which they are cloathed with equal dignity and authority, there is peculiar danger of personal emulation and even animosity. From either and especially from all these causes, the most bitter dissentions are apt to spring. Whenever these happen, they lessen the respectability, weaken the authority, and distract the plans and operations of those whom they divide. If they should unfortunately assail the supreme executive magistracy of a country, consisting of a plurality of persons, they might impede or frustrate the most important measures of the government, in the most critical emergencies of the state. And what is still worse, they might split the community into the violent and irreconcilable factions, adhering differently to the different individuals who composed the magistracy.

Men often oppose a thing merely because they have had no agency in planning it, or because it may have been planned by those whom they dislike. But if they have been consulted and have happened to disapprove, opposition then becomes in their estimation an indispensable duty of self love. They seem to think themselves bound in honor, and by all the motives of personal infallibility to defeat the success of what has been resolved upon, contrary to their sentiments. Men of upright, benevolent tempers have too many opportunities of remarking with horror, to what desperate lengths this disposition is sometimes carried, and

---

Lines 76–79 Hamilton perhaps senses that he is placing a strain on the patience of practical readers.

how often the great interests of society are sacrificed to the vanity, to the conceit *100*
and to the obstinacy of individuals, who have credit enough to make their passions and their caprices interesting to mankind. Perhaps the question now before
the public may in its consequences afford melancholy proofs of the effects of this
despicable frailty, or rather detestable vice in the human character.

Upon the principles of a free government, inconveniencies from the source *105*
just mentioned must necessarily be submitted to in the formation of the legislature; but it is unnecessary and therefore unwise to introduce them into the constitution of the executive. It is here too that they may be most pernicious. In the
legislature, promptitude of decision is oftener an evil than a benefit. The differences of opinion, and the jarrings of parties in that department of the govern- *110*
ment, though they may sometimes obstruct salutary plans, yet often promote
deliberation and circumspection; and serve to check excesses in the majority.
When a resolution too is once taken, the opposition must be at an end. That resolution is a law, and resistance to it punishable. But no favourable circumstances
palliate or atone for the disadvantages of dissention in the executive department. *115*
Here they are pure and unmixed. There is no point at which they cease to operate. They serve to embarrass and weaken the execution of the plan or measure, to
which they relate, from the first step to the final conclusion of it. They constantly
counteract those qualities in the executive, which are the most necessary ingredients in its composition, vigour and expedition, and this without any counter- *120*
ballancing good. In the conduct of war, in which the energy of the executive is
the bulwark of the national security, every thing would be to be apprehended
from its plurality.

It must be confessed that these observations apply with principal weight to the
first case supposed, that is to a plurality of magistrates of equal dignity and au- *125*
thority; a scheme the advocates for which are not likely to form a numerous sect:
But they apply, though not with equal, yet with considerable weight, to the project of a council, whose concurrence is made constitutionally necessary to the operations of the ostensible executive. An artful cabal in that council would be able
to distract and to enervate the whole system of administration. If no such cabal *130*
should exist, the mere diversity of views and opinions would alone be sufficient
to tincture the exercise of the executive authority with a spirit of habitual feebleness and dilatoriness.

But one of the weightiest objections to a plurality in the executive, and which
lies as much against the last as the first plan, is that it tends to conceal faults, and *135*
destroy responsibility. Responsibility is of two kinds, to censure and to punishment.
The first is the most important of the two; especially in an elective office. Men, in
public trust, will much oftener act in such a manner as to render them unworthy of
being any longer trusted, than in such a manner as to make them obnoxious to
legal punishment. But the multiplication of the executive adds to the difficulty of *140*

Lines 134–50 This paragraph has an alarmingly modernistic sound.

detection in either case. It often becomes impossible, amidst mutual accusations, to determine on whom the blame or the punishment of a pernicious measure, or series of pernicious measures ought really to fall. It is shifted from one to another with so much dexterity, and under such plausible appearances, that the public

145 opinion is left in suspense about the real author. The circumstances which may have led to any national miscarriage or misfortune are sometimes so complicated, that where there are a number of actors who may have had different degrees and kinds of agency, though we may clearly see upon the whole that there has been mismanagement, yet it may be impracticable to pronounce to whose account the

150 evil which may have been incurred is truly chargeable.

"I was overruled by my council. The council were so divided in their opinions, that it was impossible to obtain any better resolution on the point." These and similar pretexts are constantly at hand, whether true or false. And who is there that will either take the trouble or incur the odium of a strict scrutiny into the secret springs

155 of the transaction? Should there be found a citizen zealous enough to undertake the unpromising task, if there happen to be a collusion between the parties concerned, how easy is it to cloath the circumstances with so much ambiguity, as to render it uncertain what was the precise conduct of any of those parties?

In the single instance in which the governor of this state is coupled with a

160 council, that is in the appointment to offices, we have seen the mischiefs of it in the view now under consideration. Scandalous appointments to important offices have been made. Some cases indeed have been so flagrant, that ALL PARTIES have agreed in the impropriety of the thing. When enquiry has been made, the blame has been laid by the governor on the members of the council; who on

165 their part have charged it upon his nomination: While the people remain altogether at a loss to determine by whose influence their interests have been committed to hands so unqualified, and so manifestly improper. In tenderness to individuals, I forbear to descend to particulars.

It is evident from these considerations, that the plurality of the executive tends

170 to deprive the people of the two greatest securities they can have for the faithful exercise of any delegated power; first, the restraints of public opinion, which lose their efficacy as well on account of the division of the censure attendant on bad measures among a number, as on account of the uncertainty on whom it ought to fall; and secondly, the opportunity of discovering with facility and clearness

175 the misconduct of the persons they trust, in order either to their removal from office, or to their actual punishment, in cases which admit of it.

In England the king is a perpetual magistrate; and it is a maxim, which has obtained for the sake of the public peace, that he is unaccountable for his administration, and his person sacred. Nothing therefore can be wiser in that king-

180 dom than to annex to the king a constitutional council, who may be responsible

---

Line 180 The nearest equivalent to the "constitutional council" referred to here was in fact the cabinet. Such a body was unheard of in England at the time of the Glorious Revolution in 1688–1689, but it had grown up under William III, and developed

to the nation for the advice they give. Without this there would be no responsibility whatever in the executive department; an idea inadmissible in a free government. But even there the king is not bound by the resolutions of his council, though they are answerable for the advice they give. He is the absolute master of his own conduct, in the exercise of his office; and may observe or disregard the counsel given to him at his sole discretion.

185

But in a republic, where every magistrate ought to be personally responsible for his behaviour in office, the reason which in the British constitution dictates the propriety of a council not only ceases to apply, but turns against the institution. In the monarchy of Great-Britain, it furnishes a substitute for the prohibited responsibility of the chief magistrate; which serves in some degree as a hostage to the national justice for his good behaviour. In the American republic it would serve to destroy, or would greatly diminish the intended and necessary responsibility of the chief magistrate himself.

190

The idea of a council to the executive, which has so generally obtained in the state constitutions, has been derived from that maxim of republican jealousy, which considers power as safer in the hands of a number of men than of a single man. If the maxim should be admitted to be applicable to the case, I should contend that the advantage on that side would not counterballance the numerous disadvantages on the opposite side. But I do not think the rule at all applicable to the executive power. I clearly concur in opinion in this particular with a writer whom the celebrated Junius pronounces to be "deep, solid and ingenious," that,

195

200

---

into a permanent institution under George I, at least in part because of their absences in their own countries—Holland and Hanover, respectively. Since each minister was appointed by and answerable to the king but had to work under the prime minister (known until the mid-18th century only in his capacity of First Lord of the Treasury), the institution of cabinet government was constitutionally difficult to define, and seems not to have been very clearly understood in America. Hamilton goes too far in calling the king "absolute master" in line 184. Although he had the power to appoint and dismiss ministers, the king could only govern for any length of time through a majority in Parliament, and this really meant the House of Commons. The government at any particular time was always the king's government, but to a large extent it was the prime minister's in practice. (The British government is still known officially as Her Majesty's Government.)

Lines 195–98 The governor's council in the new states was the republican successor to the colonial governor's council, but formed an elective basis.

Line 202 Junius was the pseudonym of an anonymous political publicist who contributed a series of letters to Henry Woodfall's London paper *The Public Advertiser* between 1769 and 1772. His purpose was to discredit George III's government and unite the opposition factions. Junius was trenchant, extremely well informed, sometimes libellous, widely read, and still more widely discussed. Interest was stimulated—and still is—by intense speculation about his identity. The most likely identification is Sir Philip Francis (1740–1818), a well-placed civil servant.

"the executive power is more easily confined when it is one":* That it is far more safe there should be a single object for the jealousy and watchfulness of the
205 people; and in a word that all multiplication of the executive is rather dangerous than friendly to liberty.

A little consideration will satisfy us, that the species of security sought for in the multiplication of the executive is unattainable. Numbers must be so great as to render combination difficult; or they are rather a source of danger than of se-
210 curity. The united credit and influence of several individuals must be more formidable to liberty than the credit and influence of either of them separately. When power therefore is placed in the hands of so small a number of men, as to admit of their interests and views being easily combined in a common enterprise, by an artful leader, it becomes more liable to abuse and more dangerous when
215 abused, than if it be lodged in the hands of one man; who from the very circumstance of his being alone will be more narrowly watched and more readily suspected, and who cannot unite so great a mass of influence as when he is associated with others. The decemvirs of Rome, whose name denotes their number,† were more to be dreaded in their usurpation than any ONE of them
220 would have been. No person would think of proposing an executive much more numerous than that body, from six to a dozen have been suggested for the number of the council. The extreme of these numbers is not too great for an easy combination; and from such a combination America would have more to fear, than from the ambition of any single individual. A council to a magistrate, who is
225 himself responsible for what he does, are generally nothing better than a clog upon his good intentions; are often the instruments and accomplices of his bad, and are almost always a cloak to his faults.

I forbear to dwell upon the subject of expence; though it be evident that if the council should be numerous enough to answer the principal end, aimed at by
230 the institution, the salaries of the members, who must be drawn from their homes

* De Lolme.
† *Ten.*

Lines 207–27 It is to be noted that there is no discussion of the concept of an American cabinet. Contention would arise as to whether an American secretary of a department, whose appointment was owed to the Senate on the president's nomination, could be dismissed by the president without the Senate's consent. On this see No. 77, lines 1–15.

Hamilton's Footnote Jean Louis de Lolme (1741–1806, about whose life little is known) was a Genevan democrat who, after living in England, wrote a widely read and much quoted book, *The Constitution of England,* first published in French in Amsterdam in 1771 but translated into English in 1775. De Lolme remained basically democratic in sentiment, but was impressed by the continuing and restraining power of the monarchy. This may have been the source of Hamilton's views on the power of the crown.

to reside at the seat of government, would form an item in the catalogue of public expenditures, too serious to be incurred for an object of equivocal utility.

I will only add, that prior to the appearance of the constitution, I rarely met with an intelligent man from any of the states, who did not admit as the result of experience, that the UNITY of the executive of this state was one of the best of the distinguishing features of our constitution.

235

PUBLIUS.

SEVENTY-ONE
{NO. 70 IN NEWSPAPERS}

ALEXANDER HAMILTON
March 18, 1788
The Same View Continued in Regard to the Duration of the Office

To the People of the State of New York.

Duration in office has been mentioned as the second requisite to the energy of
the executive authority. This has relation to two objects: To the personal firmness
of the executive magistrate in the employment of his constitutional powers; and
to the stability of the system of administration which may have been adopted
under his auspices. With regard to the first, it must be evident, that the longer the
duration in office, the greater will be the probability of obtaining so important an
advantage. It is a general principle of human nature, that a man will be interested
in whatever he possesses, in proportion to the firmness or precariousness of the
tenure, by which he holds it; will be less attached to what he holds by a momentary or uncertain title, than to what he enjoys by a durable or certain title; and of
course will be willing to risk more for the sake of the one, than for the sake of the
other. This remark is not less applicable to a political privilege, or honor, or trust,
than to any article of ordinary property. The inference from it is, that a man acting in the capacity of chief magistrate, under a consciousness, that in a very short
time he *must* lay down his office, will be apt to feel himself too little interested in
it, to hazard any material censure or perplexity, from the independent exertion of
his powers, or from encountering the ill-humors, however transient, which may
happen to prevail either in a considerable part of the society itself, or even in a
predominant faction in the legislative body. If the case should only be, that he
might lay it down, unless continued by a new choice; and if he should be desirous of being continued, his wishes conspiring with his fears would tend still
more powerfully to corrupt his integrity, or debase his fortitude. In either case
feebleness and irresolution must be the characteristics of the station.

There are some, who would be inclined to regard the servile pliancy of the
executive to a prevailing current, either in the community, or in the legislature,
as its best recommendation. But such men entertain very crude notions, as well
of the purposes for which government was instituted, as of the true means by
which the public happiness may be promoted. The republican principle demands, that the deliberate sense of the community should govern the conduct of
those to whom they entrust the management of their affairs; but it does not require an unqualified complaisance to every sudden breese of passion, or to every
transient impulse which the people may receive from the arts of men, who flatter

their prejudices to betray their interests. It is a just observation, that the people commonly *intend* the PUBLIC GOOD. This often applies to their very errors. But their good sense would despise the adulator, who should pretend that they always *reason right* about the *means* of promoting it. They know from experience, that they sometimes err; and the wonder is, that they so seldom err as they do; beset as they continually are by the wiles of parasites and sycophants, by the snares of the ambitious, the avaricious, the desperate; by the artifices of men, who possess their confidence more than they deserve it, and of those who seek to possess, rather than to deserve it. When occasions present themselves in which the interests of the people are at variance with their inclinations, it is the duty of the persons whom they have appointed to be the guardians of those interests, to withstand the temporary delusion, in order to give them time and opportunity for more cool and sedate reflection. Instances might be cited, in which a conduct of this kind has saved the people from very fatal consequences of their own mistakes, and has procured lasting monuments of their gratitude to the men, who had courage and magnanimity enough to serve them at the peril of their displeasure.

But however inclined we might be to insist upon an unbounded complaisance in the executive to the inclinations of the people, we can with no propriety contend for a like complaisance to the humors of the legislature. The latter may sometimes stand in opposition to the former; and at other times the people may be entirely neutral. In either supposition, it is certainly desirable that the executive should be in a situation to dare to act his own opinion with vigor and decision.

The same rule, which teaches the propriety of a partition between the various branches of power, teaches likewise that this partition ought to be so contrived as to render the one independent of the other. To what purpose separate the executive, or the judiciary, from the legislative, if both the executive and the judiciary are so constituted as to be at the absolute devotion of the legislative? Such a separation must be merely nominal and incapable of producing the ends for which it was established. It is one thing to be subordinate to the laws, and another to be dependent on the legislative body. The first comports with, the last violates, the fundamental principles of good government; and whatever may be the forms of the constitution, unites all power in the same hands. The tendency of the legislative authority to absorb every other, has been fully displayed and illustrated by examples, in some preceding numbers. In governments purely republican, this tendency is almost irresistable. The representatives of the people, in a popular assembly, seem sometimes to fancy that they are the people themselves; and betray strong symptoms of impatience and disgust at the least sign of opposition from any other quarter; as if the exercise of its rights by either the executive or judiciary, were a breach of their privilege and an outrage to their dignity. They often appear disposed to exert an imperious controul over the other

---

Lines 56–57 See No. 51.

departments; and as they commonly have the people on their side, they always
75 act with such momentum as to make it very difficult for the other members of
the government to maintain the balance of the constitution.

It may perhaps be asked how the shortness of the duration in office can affect
the independence of the executive on the legislature, unless the one were possessed of the power of appointing or displacing the other? One answer to this en-
80 quiry may be drawn from the principle already remarked, that is from the slender
interest a man is apt to take in a short lived advantage, and the little inducement
it affords him to expose himself on account of it to any considerable inconvenience or hazard. Another answer, perhaps more obvious, though not more conclusive, will result from the consideration of the influence of the legislative body
85 over the people, which might be employed to prevent the re-election of a man,
who by an upright resistance to any sinister project of that body, should have
made himself obnoxious to its resentment.

It may be asked also whether a duration of four years would answer the end
proposed, and if it would not, whether a less period which would at least be rec-
90 ommended by greater security against ambitious designs, would not for that reason be preferable to a longer period, which was at the same time too short for the
purpose of inspiring the desired firmness and independence of the magistrate?

It cannot be affirmed, that a duration of four years or any other limited duration would completely answer the end proposed; but it would contribute towards
95 it in a degree which would have a material influence upon the spirit and character of the government. Between the commencement and termination of such a
period there would always be a considerable interval, in which the prospect of
annihilation would be sufficiently remote not to have an improper effect upon
the conduct of a man endued with a tolerable portion of fortitude; and in which
100 he might reasonably promise himself, that there would be time enough, before it
arrived, to make the community sensible of the propriety of the measures he
might incline to pursue. Though it be probable, that as he approached the moment when the public were by a new election to signify their sense of his conduct, his confidence and with it, his firmness would decline; yet both the one
105 and the other would derive support from the opportunities, which his previous
continuance in the station had afforded him of establishing himself in the esteem and good will of his constituents. He might then hazard with safety, in proportion to the proofs he had given of his wisdom and integrity, and to the title he
had acquired to the respect and attachment of his fellow citizens. As on the one
110 hand, a duration of four years will contribute to the firmness of the executive in
a sufficient degree to render it a very valuable ingredient in the composition; so
on the other, it is not long enough to justify any alarm for the public liberty. If a

---

Lines 112–23 This passage takes a step in the direction of recognizing the con-
straints on monarchical power in Britain. The abolition of royalty and aristocracy
refer to events in and following the English civil wars of the 1640s.

British house of commons, from the most feeble beginnings, *from the mere power of assenting or disagreeing to the imposition of a new tax*, have by rapid strides, reduced the prerogatives of the crown and the privileges of the nobility within the limits they conceived to be compatible with the principles of a free government; while they raised themselves to the rank and consequence of a co-equal branch of the legislature; if they have been able in one instance to abolish both the royalty and the aristocracy, and to overturn all the ancient establishments as well in the church as state; if they have been able on a recent occasion to make the monarch tremble at the prospect of an innovation* attempted by them; what would be to be feared from an elective magistrate of four years duration, with the confined authorities of a president of the United States? What but that he might be unequal to the task which the constitution assigns him?—I shall only add that if his duration be such as to leave a doubt of his firmness, that doubt is inconsistent with a jealousy of his encroachments.

PUBLIUS.

---

* This was the case with respect to Mr. Fox's India bill which was carried in the house of commons, and rejected in the house of lords, to the entire satisfaction, as it is said, of the people.

Hamilton's Footnote Charles James Fox's (1749–1896) India bill (1749–1806) proposed to set up a commission to run the affairs of the East India Company from London. Having passed in the Commons, it was defeated in the Lords (in 1783), leading to the fall of the Fox-North coalition administration, but only when the king had assured himself that he could form a new government more to his own liking.

SEVENTY-TWO
{NO. 71 IN NEWSPAPERS}

ALEXANDER HAMILTON
March 19, 1788
The Same View Continued in Regard to the Re-eligibility of the President

To the People of the State of New York.

The administration of government, in its largest sense, comprehends all the operations of the body politic, whether legislative, executive or judiciary, but in its most usual and perhaps in its most precise signification, it is limited to executive details, and falls peculiarly within the province of the executive department. The
5   actual conduct of foreign negotiations, the preparatory plans of finance, the application and disbursement of the public monies, in conformity to the general appropriations of the legislature, the arrangement of the army and navy, the direction of the operations of war; these and other matters of a like nature constitute what seems to be most properly understood by the administration of
10   government. The persons therefore, to whose immediate management these different matters are committed, ought to be considered as the assistants or deputies of the chief magistrate; and, on this account, they ought to derive their offices from his appointment, at least from his nomination, and ought to be subject to his superintendence. This view of the subject will at once suggest to us the inti-
15   mate connection between the duration of the executive magistrate in office, and the stability of the system of administration. To reverse and undo what has been done by a predecessor is very often considered by a successor, as the best proof he can give of his own capacity and desert; and, in addition to this propensity, where the alteration has been the result of public choice, the person substituted is war-
20   ranted in supposing, that the dismission of his predecessor has proceeded from a dislike to his measures, and that the less he resembles him the more he will recommend himself to the favor of his constituents. These considerations, and the influence of personal confidences and attachments, would be likely to induce every new president to promote a change of men to fill the subordinate stations;
25   and these causes together could not fail to occasion a disgraceful and ruinous mutability in the administration of the government.
        With a positive duration of considerable extent, I connect the circumstance of re-eligibility. The first is necessary to give the officer himself the inclination and the resolution to act his part well, and to the community time and leisure to ob-
30   serve the tendency of his measures, and thence to form an experimental estimate of their merits. The last is necessary to enable the people, when they see reason to approve of his conduct, to continue him in the station, in order to prolong the

utility of his talents and virtues, and to secure to the government, the advantage of permanency in a wise system of administration.

Nothing appears more plausible at first sight, nor more ill founded upon close inspection, than a scheme, which in relation to the present point has had some respectable advocates—I mean that of continuing the chief magistrate in office for a certain time, and then excluding him from it, either for a limited period, or for ever after. This exclusion whether temporary or perpetual would have nearly the same effects; and these effects would be for the most part rather pernicious than salutary.

One ill effect of the exclusion would be a diminution of the inducements to good behaviour. There are few men who would not feel much less zeal in the discharge of a duty, when they were conscious that the advantage of the station, with which it was connected, must be relinquished at a determinate period, then when they were permitted to entertain a hope of *obtaining* by *meriting* a continuance of them. This position will not be disputed, so long as it is admitted that the desire of reward is one of the strongest incentives of human conduct, or that the best security for the fidelity of mankind is to make their interest coincide with their duty. Even the love of fame, the ruling passion of the noblest minds, which would prompt a man to plan and undertake extensive and arduous enterprises for the public benefit, requiring considerable time to mature and perfect them, if he could flatter himself with the prospect of being allowed to finish what he had begun, would on the contrary deter him from the undertaking, when he foresaw that he must quit the scene, before he could accomplish the work, and must commit that, together with his own reputation, to hands which might be unequal or unfriendly to the task. The most to be expected from the generality of men, in such a situation, is the negative merit of not doing harm instead of the positive merit of doing good.

Another ill effect of the exclusion would be the temptation to sordid views, to peculation, and in some instances, to usurpation. An avaricious man, who might happen to fill the offices, looking forward to a time when he must at all events yield up the advantages he enjoyed, would feel a propensity, not easy to be resisted by such a man, to make the best use of his opportunities, while they lasted; and might not scruple to have recourse to the most corrupt expedients to make the harvest as abundant as it was transitory; though the same man probably, with a different prospect before him, might content himself with the regular emoluments

---

Lines 35–41 The two-term limit was finally introduced by the 22nd Amendment in 1951, after Franklin Roosevelt had been elected four times.

Line 50 The phrase "the ruling passion of the noblest minds" recalls Milton's poem *Lycidas,* though Hamilton has perhaps unconsciously altered the sense: "Fame is the spur that the clear spirit doth raise, / (That last infirmity of noble mind). . . . "

of his station, and might even be unwilling to risk the consequences of an abuse of his opportunities. His avarice might be a guard upon his avarice. Add to this,
70 that the same man might be vain or ambitious as well as avaricious. And if he could expect to prolong his honors, by his good conduct, he might hesitate to sacrifice his appetite for them to his appetite for gain. But with the prospect before him of approaching and inevitable annihilation, his avarice would be likely to get the victory over his caution, his vanity or his ambition.

75   An ambitious man too, finding himself seated on the summit of his country's honors, looking forward to the time at which he must descend from the exalted eminence forever; and reflecting that no exertion of merit on his part could save him from the unwelcome reverse, would be much more violently tempted to embrace a favorable conjuncture for attempting the prolongation of his power, at
80 every personal hazard, than if he had the probability of answering the same end by doing his duty.

     Would it promote the peace of the community, or the stability of the government, to have half a dozen men who had had credit enough to raise themselves to the seat of the supreme magistracy, wandering among the people like dis-
85 contented ghosts, and sighing for a place which they were destined never more to possess?

     A third ill effect of the exclusion would be the depriving the community of the advantage of the experience gained by the chief magistrate in the exercise of his office. That experience is the parent of wisdom is an adage, the truth of which is
90 recognized by the wisest as well as the simplest of mankind. What more desirable or more essential than this quality in the governors of nations? Where more desirable or more essential than in the first magistrate of a nation? Can it be wise to put this desirable and essential quality under the ban of the constitution; and to declare that the moment it is acquired, its possessor shall be compelled to aban-
95 don the station in which it was acquired, and to which it is adapted? This nevertheless is the precise import of all those regulations, which exclude men from serving their country, by the choice of their fellow citizens, after they have, by a course of service fitted themselves for doing it with a greater degree of utility.

     A fourth ill effect of the exclusion would be the banishing men from stations,
100 in which in certain emergencies of the state their presence might be of the greatest moment to the public interest or safety. There is no nation which has not at one period or another experienced an absolute necessity of the services of particular men, in particular situations, perhaps it would not be too strong to say, to the preservation of its political existence. How unwise therefore must be every such

---

Lines 82–86 The error in this reasoning is that a president never admits that his own program is bad policy.

Lines 99–101 Such an emergency led to the third-time election of Franklin Roosevelt in 1940.

self-denying ordinance, as serves to prohibit a nation from making use of its own 105
citizens, in the manner best suited to its exigences and circumstances! Without
supposing the personal essentiality of the man, it is evident that a change of the
chief magistrate, at the breaking out of a war, or any similar crisis, for another
even of equal merit, would at all times be detrimental to the community; inasmuch as it would substitute inexperience to experience and would tend to un- 110
hinge and set afloat the already settled train of the administration.

A fifth ill effect of the exclusion would be, that it would operate as a constitutional interdiction of stability in the administration. *By necessitating* a change of
men, in the first office in the nation, it would necessitate a mutability of measures.
It is not generally to be expected, that men will vary; and measures remain uni- 115
form. The contrary is the usual course of things. And we need not be apprehensive
there will be too much stability, while there is even the option of changing; nor
need we desire to prohibit the people from continuing their confidence, where
they think it may be safely placed, and where by constancy on their part they may
obviate the fatal inconveniences of fluctuating councils and a variable policy. 120

These are some of the disadvantages, which would flow from the principle of
exclusion. They apply most forcibly to the scheme of a perpetual exclusion; but
when we consider that even a partial one would always render the re-admission
of the person a remote and precarious object, the observations which have been
made will apply nearly as fully to one case as to the other. 125

What are the advantages promised to counterballance these disadvantages?
They are represented to be—1st. Greater independence in the magistrate: 2d.
Greater security to the people. Unless the exclusion be perpetual there will be no
pretence to infer the first advantage. But even in that case, may he have no object beyond his present station to which he may sacrifice his independence? May 130
he have no connections, no friends, for whom he may sacrifice it? May he not be
less willing, by a firm conduct, to make personal enemies, when he acts under
the impression, that a time is fast approaching, on the arrival of which he not
only MAY, but MUST be exposed to their resentments, upon an equal, perhaps
upon an inferior footing? It is not an easy point to determine whether his inde- 135
pendence would be most promoted or impaired by such an arrangement.

As to the second supposed advantage, there is still greater reason to entertain
doubts concerning it, especially if the exclusion were to be perpetual, a man of
irregular ambition, of whom alone there could be reason in any case to entertain
apprehensions, would with infinite reluctance yield to the necessity of taking his 140
leave forever of a post, in which his passion for power and pre-eminence had
acquired the force of habit. And if he had been fortunate or adroit enough to
conciliate the good will of the people he might induce them to consider as a very
odious and unjustifiable restraint upon themselves, a provision which was calculated to debar them of the right of giving a fresh proof of their attachment to a 145
favorite. There may be conceived circumstances, in which this disgust of the
people, seconding the thwarted ambition of such a favourite, might occasion
greater danger to liberty, than could ever reasonably be dreaded from the possi-

bility of a perpetuation in office, by the voluntary suffrages of the community, ex-
150   ercising a constitutional privilege.

There is an excess of refinement in the idea of disabling the people to continue in office men, who had entitled themselves, in their opinion, to approbation and confidence; the advantages of which are at best speculative and equivocal; and are overbalanced by disadvantages far more certain and decisive.

PUBLIUS.

SEVENTY-THREE
{NO. 72 IN NEWSPAPERS}

ALEXANDER HAMILTON
March 21, 1788
**The Same View Continued, in Relation to the Provision
Concerning Support, and the Power of the Negative**

To the People of the State of New York.

The third ingredient towards constituting the vigor of the executive authority is an adequate provision for its support. It is evident that without proper attention to this article, the separation of the executive from the legislative department would be merely nominal and nugatory. The legislature, with a discretionary power over the salary and emoluments of the chief magistrate, could render him as 5 obsequious to their will, as they might think proper to make him. They might in most cases either reduce him by famine, or tempt him by largesses, to surrender at discretion his judgment to their inclinations. These expressions taken in all the latitude of the terms would no doubt convey more than is intended. There are men who could neither be distressed nor won into a sacrifice of their duty; 10 but this stern virtue is the growth of few soils: And in the main it will be found, that a power over a man's support is a power over his will. If it were necessary to confirm so plain a truth by facts, examples would not be wanting, even in this country, of the intimidation or seduction of the executive by the terrors, or allurements, of the pecuniary arrangements of the legislative body. 15

It is not easy therefore to commend too highly the judicious attention which has been paid to this subject in the proposed constitution. It is there provided that "The president of the United States shall, at stated times, receive for his services a compensation, *which shall neither be increased nor diminished, during the period for which he shall have been elected, and he shall not receive within that pe-* 20 *riod any other emolument* from the United States or any of them." It is impossible to imagine any provision which would have been more eligible than this. The legislature on the appointment of a president is once for all to declare what shall be the compensation for his services during the time for which he shall have been elected. This done, they will have no power to alter it either by increase or 25 diminution, till a new period of service by a new election commences. They can neither weaken his fortitude by operating upon his necessities; nor corrupt his integrity, by appealing to his avarice. Neither the union nor any of its members will be at liberty to give, nor will he be at liberty to receive any other emolument, than that which may have been determined by the first act. He can of course 30 have no pecuniary inducement to renounce or desert the independence intended for him by the constitution.

The last of the requisites to energy which have been enumerated are competent powers. Let us proceed to consider those which are proposed to be vested in the president of the United States.

The first thing that offers itself to our observation, is the qualified negative of the president upon the acts or resolutions of the two houses of the legislature; or in other words his power of returning all bills with objections; to have the effect of preventing their becoming laws, unless they should afterwards be ratified by two thirds of each of the component members of the legislative body.

The propensity of the legislative department to intrude upon the rights and to absorb the powers of the other departments, has been already more than once suggested; the insufficiency of a mere parchment delineation of the boundaries of each, has also been remarked upon; and the necessity of furnishing each with constitutional arms for its own defence, has been inferred and proved. From these clear and indubitable principles results the propriety of a negative, either absolute or qualified, in the executive, upon the acts of the legislative branches. Without the one or the other the former would be absolutely unable to defend himself against the depredations of the latter. He might gradually be stripped of his authorities by successive resolutions, or annihilated by a single vote. And in the one mode or the other, the legislative and executive powers might speedily come to be blended in the same hands. If even no propensity had ever discovered itself in the legislative body, to invade the rights of the executive, the rules of just reasoning and theoretic propriety would of themselves teach us, that the one ought not to be left at the mercy of the other, but ought to possess a constitutional and effectual power of self defence.

But the power in question has a further use. It not only serves as a shield to the executive, but it furnishes an additional security against the enaction of improper laws. It establishes a salutary check upon the legislative body calculated to guard the community against the effects of faction, precipitancy, or of any impulse unfriendly to the public good, which may happen to influence a majority of that body.

The propriety of a negative, has upon some occasions been combated by an observation, that it was not to be presumed a single man would possess more virtue or wisdom, than a number of men; and that unless this presumption should be entertained, it would be improper to give the executive magistrate any species of controul over the legislative body.

But this observation when examined will appear rather specious than solid. The propriety of the thing does not turn upon the supposition of superior wis-

---

Lines 36–40 The presidential power of veto recalls to life the royal veto, disused since 1708. Americans of this generation would also recall the power of the privy council, acting in the name of the crown, to disallow colonial laws.

dom or virtue in the executive: But upon the supposition that the legislative will   *70*
not be infallible: That the love of power may sometimes betray it into a disposition to encroach upon the rights of the other members of the government; that a
spirit of faction may sometimes pervert its deliberations; that impressions of the
moment may sometimes hurry it into measures which itself on maturer reflection would condemn. The primary inducement to conferring the power in ques-   *75*
tion upon the executive, is to enable him to defend himself; the secondary one is
to encrease the chances in favor of the community, against the passing of bad
laws, through haste, inadvertence, or design. The oftener a measure is brought
under examination, the greater the diversity in the situations of those who are to
examine it, the less must be the danger of those errors which flow from want of   *80*
due deliberation, or of those missteps which proceed from the contagion of some
common passion or interest. It is far less probable, that culpable views of any
kind should infect all the parts of the government, at the same moment and in
relation to the same object, than that they should by turns govern and mislead
every one of them.   *85*

It may perhaps be said, that the power of preventing bad laws includes that of
preventing good ones; and may be used to the one purpose as well as to the other.
But this objection will have little weight with those who can properly estimate
the mischiefs of that inconstancy and mutability in the laws, which form the
greatest blemish in the character and genius of our governments. They will con-   *90*
sider every institution calculated to restrain the excess of law-making, and to keep
things in the same state in which they may happen to be at any given period, as
much more likely to do good than harm; because it is favorable to greater stability in the system of legislation. The injury which may possibly be done by defeating a few good laws will be amply compensated by the advantage of preventing a   *95*
number of bad ones.

Nor is this all. The superior weight and influence of the legislative body in a
free government, and the hazard to the executive in a trial of strength with that
body, afford a satisfactory security, that the negative would generally be employed with great caution, and that there would oftener be room for a charge of   *100*
timidity than of rashness, in the exercise of it. A king of Great-Britain, with all his
train of sovereign attributes, and with all the influence he draws from a thousand
sources, would at this day hesitate to put a negative upon the joint resolutions of
the two houses of Parliament. He would not fail to exert the utmost resources of
that influence to strangle a measure disagreeable to him, in its progress to the   *105*
throne, to avoid being reduced to the dilemma of permitting it to take effect, or

---

Lines 86–96 "Good" and "bad" seem here to be treated as objective categories, dis-
entangled from the political circumstances that gave rise to the laws in question.
Whether or not the laws passed by Congress might be inconsistent with the executive views of good policy is not considered.

of risking the displeasure of the nation, by an opposition to the sense of the legislative body. Nor is it probable that he would ultimately venture to exert his
prerogative, but in a case of manifest propriety, or extreme necessity. All well
110 informed men in that kingdom will accede to the justness of this remark. A very
considerable period has elapsed since the negative of the crown has been
exercised.

If a magistrate, so powerful and so well fortified as a British monarch, would
have scruples about the exercise of the power under consideration, how much
115 greater caution may be reasonably expected in a president of the United States,
cloathed for the short period of four years with the executive authority of a government wholly and purely republican?

It is evident that there would be greater danger of his not using his power
when necessary, than of his using it too often, or too much. An argument indeed
120 against its expediency has been drawn from this very source. It has been represented on this account as a power odious in appearance; useless in practice. But
it will not follow, that because it might be rarely exercised, it would never be exercised. In the case for which it is chiefly designed, that of an immediate attack
upon the constitutional rights of the executive, or in a case in which the public
125 good was evidently and palpably sacrificed, a man of tolerable firmness would
avail himself of his constitutional means of defence, and would listen to the admonitions of duty and responsibility. In the former supposition, his fortitude
would be stimulated by his immediate interest in the power of his office; in the
latter by the probability of the sanction of his constituents; who though they
130 would naturally incline to the legislative body in a doubtful case, would hardly
suffer their partiality to delude them in a very plain case. I speak now with an eye
to a magistrate possessing only a common share of firmness. There are men, who
under any circumstances will have the courage to do their duty at every hazard.

But the convention have pursued a mean in this business; which will both fa-
135 cilitate the exercise of the power vested in this respect in the executive magistrate, and make its efficacy to depend on the sense of a considerable part of the
legislative body. Instead of an absolute negative, it is proposed to give the executive the qualified negative already described. This is a power, which would be
much more readily exercised than the other. A man who might be afraid to de-
140 feat a law by his single VETO, might not scruple to return it for re-consideration;
subject to being finally rejected only in the event of more than one third of each
house concurring in the sufficiency of his objections. He would be encouraged
by the reflection, that if his opposition should prevail, it would embark in it a
very respectable proportion of the legislative body, whose influence would be
145 united with his in supporting the propriety of his conduct, in the public opinion.
A direct and categorical negative has something in the appearance of it more
harsh, and more apt to irritate, than the mere suggestion of argumentative objections to be approved or disapproved, by those to whom they are addressed. In
proportion as it would be less apt to offend, it would be more apt to be exercised;
150 and for this very reason it may in practice be found more effectual. It is to be

hoped that it will not often happen, that improper views will govern so large a proportion as two-thirds of both branches of the legislature at the same time; and this too in defiance of the counterpoising weight of the executive. It is at any rate far less probable, that this should be the case, than that such views should taint the resolutions and conduct of a bare majority. A power of this nature, in the ex-   155
ecutive, will often have a silent and unperceived though forcible operation. When men engaged in unjustifiable pursuits are aware, that obstructions may come from a quarter which they cannot controul, they will often be restrained, by the bare apprehension of opposition, from doing what they would with eagerness rush into, if no such external impediments were to be feared.   160

This qualified negative, as has been elsewhere remarked, is in this state vested in a council, consisting of the governor, with the chancellor and judges of the supreme court, or any two of them. It has been freely employed upon a variety of occasions, and frequently with success. And its utility has become so apparent, that persons who in compiling the constitution were violent opposers of it, have   165
from experience become its declared admirers.*

I have in another place remarked, that the convention in the formation of this part of their plan, had departed from the model of the constitution of this state, in favor of that of Massachusetts:—two strong reasons may be imagined for this preference. One is that the judges, who are to be the interpreters of the law,   170
might receive an improper bias from having given a previous opinion in their re-visionary capacities. The other is that by being often associated with the executive they might be induced to embark too far in the political views of that magistrate, and thus a dangerous combination might by degrees be cemented between the executive and judiciary departments. It is impossible to keep the   175
judges too distinct from every other avocation than that of expounding the laws. It is peculiarly dangerous to place them in a situation to be either corrupted or influenced by the executive.

PUBLIUS.

* Mr. Abraham Yates, a warm opponent of the plan of the convention, is of this number.

Lines 161–64 A prominent case in point was the Trespass Act of 1783, under which a citizen might sue an occupant of his property if the occupation took place while the property was behind British lines. The Mayor's Court voided this act on the ground that it violated the law of nations in regard to the rights of forces of occupation. This amounts to a very early case of judicial review.

Lines 167–69 The constitution of Massachusetts was drawn up by a convention meeting in Boston in the winter of 1779–1780 and ratified by the towns (and with the help of some creative arithmetic) in 1780. For the point made here, see No. 47.

Hamilton's Footnote Abraham Yates (1724–1796) had been a member of the New York provincial convention at the time of the Declaration of Independence.

SEVENTY-FOUR
{NO. 73 IN NEWSPAPERS}

ALEXANDER HAMILTON
March 25, 1788
The Same View Continued, in Relation to the Command
of the National Forces, and Power of Pardoning

To the People of the State of New York.

The president of the United States is to be "commander in chief of the army and navy of the United States, and of the militia of the several states *when called into the actual service* of the United States." The propriety of this provision is so evident in itself; and it is at the same time so consonant to the precedents of the

5   state constitutions in general, that little need be said to explain or enforce it. Even those of them, which have in other respects coupled the chief magistrate with a council, have for the most part concentred the military authority in him alone. Of all the cares or concerns of government, the direction of war most peculiarly demands those qualities which distinguish the exercise of power by a

10   single hand. The direction of war implies the direction of the common strength; and the power of directing and employing the common strength, forms an usual and essential part in the definition of the executive authority.

"The president may require the opinion in writing of the principal officer in each of the executive departments upon any subject relating to the duties of their

15   respective offices." This I consider as a mere redundancy in the plan; as the right for which it provides would result of itself from the office.

He is also to be authorised "to grant reprieves and pardons for offences against the United States *except in cases of impeachment.*" Humanity and good policy conspire to dictate, that the benign prerogative of pardoning should be as little as

20   possible fettered or embarrassed. The criminal code of every country partakes so much of necessary severity, that without an easy access to exceptions in favor of unfortunate guilt, justice would wear a countenance too sanguinary and cruel.

Lines 17–18 The presidential powers here mirror those of the royal prerogative of clemency. Whether the monarch had power of pardon in cases of impeachment is dubious territory; in only one case, that of the impeachment of the earl of Danby in 1679, had a monarch—Charles II—tried to block an impeachment by a royal pardon, and in that case the point remained moot because of the dissolution of Parliament. No such power had been exercised by Charles I in the capital cases of the 1640s. He feared that to intervene would cost him the throne.

As the sense of responsibility is always strongest in proportion as it is undivided, it may be inferred that a single man would be most ready to attend to the force of those motives, which might plead for a mitigation of the rigor of the law, and least apt to yield to considerations, which were calculated to shelter a fit object of its vengeance. The reflection, that the fate of a fellow creature depended on his *sole fiat*, would naturally inspire scrupulousness and caution: The dread of being accused of weakness or connivance would beget equal circumspection, though of a different kind. On the other hand, as men generally derive confidence from their numbers, they might often encourage each other in an act of obduracy, and might be less sensible to the apprehension of suspicion or censure for an injudicious or affected clemency. On these accounts, one man appears to be a more eligible dispenser of the mercy of the government than a body of men.

The expediency of vesting the power of pardoning in the president has, if I mistake not, been only contested in relation to the crime of treason. This, it has been urged, ought to have depended upon the assent of one or both of the branches of the legislative body. I shall not deny that there are strong reasons to be assigned for requiring in this particular the concurrence of that body or of a part of it. As treason is a crime levelled at the immediate being of the society, when the laws have once ascertained the guilt of the offender, there seems a fitness in referring the expediency of an act of mercy towards him to the judgment of the legislature. And this ought the rather to be the case, as the supposition of the connivance of the chief magistrate ought not to be entirely excluded. But there are also strong objections to such a plan. It is not to be doubted that a single man of prudence and good sense, is better fitted, in delicate conjunctures, to balance the motives, which may plead for and against the remission of the punishment, than any numerous body whatever. It deserves particular attention, that treason will often be connected with seditions, which embrace a large proportion of the community; as lately happened in Massachusetts. In every such case, we might expect to see the representation of the people tainted with the same spirit, which had given birth to the offense. And when parties were pretty equally matched, the secret sympathy of the friends and favorers of the condemned, availing itself of the good nature and weakness of others, might frequently bestow impunity where the terror of an example was necessary. On the other hand, when the sedition had proceeded from causes which had inflamed the resentments of the major party, they might often be found obstinate and inexorable, when policy demanded a conduct of forbearance and clemency. But the principal argument for reposing the power of pardoning in this case in the chief magistrate is this; in seasons of insurrection or rebellion, there are often critical moments, when a well timed offer of pardon to the insurgents or rebels may

---

Line 50 The phrase "as lately happened in Massachusetts" is, of course, another reference to Shays's rebellion.

restore the tranquility of the commonwealth; and which, if suffered to pass unimproved, it may never be possible afterwards to recall. The dilatory process of convening the legislature, or one of its branches, for the purpose of obtaining its
65   sanction to the measure, would frequently be the occasion of letting slip the
golden opportunity. The loss of a week, a day, an hour, may sometimes be fatal.
If it should be observed that a discretionary power with a view to such contingencies might be occasionally conferred upon the president; it may be answered
in the first place, that it is questionable whether, in a limited constitution, that
70   power could be delegated by law; and in the second place, that it would generally be impolitic before-hand to take any step which might hold out the prospect
of impunity. A proceeding of this kind, out of the usual course, would be likely to
be construed into an argument of timidity or of weakness, and would have a tendency to embolden guilt.

PUBLIUS.

SEVENTY-FIVE
{NO. 74 IN NEWSPAPERS}

ALEXANDER HAMILTON
March 26, 1788
The Same View Continued in Relation to the Power of Making Treaties

To the People of the State of New York.

The president is to have power "by and with the advice and consent of the senate, to make treaties, provided two-thirds of the senators present concur." Though this provision has been assailed on different grounds, with no small degree of vehemence, I scruple not to declare my firm persuasion, that it is one of the best digested and most unexceptionable parts of the plan. One ground of objection is, the trite topic of the intermixture of powers; some contending that the president ought alone to possess the power of making treaties; and others, that it ought to have been exclusively deposited in the senate. Another source of objection is derived from the small number of persons by whom a treaty may be made: Of those who espouse this objection, a part are of opinion that the house of representatives ought to have been associated in the business, while another part seem to think that nothing more was necessary than to have substituted two-thirds of *all* the members of the senate to two-thirds of the members *present*. As I flatter myself the observations made in a preceding number, upon this part of the plan, must have sufficed to place it to a discerning eye in a very favourable light, I shall here content myself with offering only some supplementary remarks, principally with a view to the objections which have been just stated.

With regard to the intermixture of powers, I shall rely upon the explanations already given, in other places of the true sense of the rule, upon which that objection is founded; and shall take it for granted, as an inference from them, that the union of the executive with the senate, in the article of treaties, is no infringement of that rule I venture to add that the particular nature of the power of making treaties indicates a peculiar propriety in that union. Though several writers on the subject of government place that power in the class of executive authorities, yet this is evidently an arbitrary disposition: For if we attend carefully to its operation, it will be found to partake more of the legislative than of the executive character, though it does not seem strictly to fall within the definition of either of them. The essence of the legislative authority is to enact laws, or in other words to prescribe rules for the regulation of the society. While the execution of the laws and the employment of the common strength, either for this purpose or for the common defence, seem to comprise all the functions of the executive magistrate. The power of making treaties is plainly neither the one nor the other.

It relates neither to the execution of the subsisting laws, nor to the enaction of new ones, and still less to an exertion of the common strength. Its objects are
35 CONTRACTS with foreign nations, which have the force of law, but derive it from the obligations of good faith. They are not rules prescribed by the sovereign to the subject, but agreements between sovereign and sovereign. The power in question seems therefore to form a distinct department, and to belong properly neither to the legislative nor to the executive. The qualities elsewhere detailed,
40 as indispensable in the management of foreign negotiations, point out the executive as the most fit agent in-those transactions; while the vast importance of the trust, and the operation of treaties as laws, plead strongly for the participation of the whole or a part of the legislative body in the office of making them.

However proper or safe it may be in governments where the executive magis-
45 trate is an hereditary monarch, to commit to him the entire power of making treaties, it would be utterly unsafe and improper to entrust that power to an elective magistrate of four years duration. It has been remarked upon another occasion, and the remark is unquestionably just, that an hereditary monarch, though often the oppressor of his people, has personally too much at stake in the govern-
50 ment to be in any material danger of being corrupted by foreign powers. But a man raised from the station of a private citizen to the rank of chief magistrate, possessed of but a moderate or slender fortune, and looking forward to a period not very remote, when he may probably be obliged to return to the station from which he was taken, might sometimes be under temptations to sacrifice his duty
55 to his interest, which it would require superlative virtue to withstand. An avaricious man might be tempted to betray the interests of the state to the acquisition of wealth. An ambitious man might make his own aggrandizement, by the aid of a foreign power, the price of his treachery to his constituents. The history of human conduct does not warrant that exalted opinion of human virtue which
60 would make it wise in a nation to commit interests of so delicate and momentous a kind as those which concern its intercourse with the rest of the world to the sole disposal of a magistrate, created and circumstanced, as would be a president of the United States.

To have entrusted the power of making treaties to the senate alone, would
65 have been to relinquish the benefits of the constitutional agency of the president, in the conduct of foreign negotiations. It is true, that the senate would in that case have the option of employing him in this capacity; but they would also have the option of letting it alone; and pique or cabal might induce the latter rather than the former. Besides this, the ministerial servant of the senate could not be

---

Line 35 For references to contract, see No. 7, lines 156–66.

Lines 36–43 It would appear that in the treaty-making context, sovereignty resides in the conjunction of the executive with the Senate; this is not a view sustained elsewhere in American jurisprudence, and it implies that the United States has different attributes of sovereignty vis-à-vis other nations than in its internal aspect.

expected to enjoy the confidence and respect of foreign powers in the same de- *70*
gree with the constitutional representative of the nation; and of course would not
be able to act with an equal degree of weight or efficacy. While the union would
from this cause lose a considerable advantage in the management of its external
concerns, the people would lose the additional security, which would result from
the co-operation of the executive. Though it would be imprudent to confide in *75*
him solely so important a trust; yet it cannot be doubted, that his participation in
it would materially add to the safety of the society. It must indeed be clear to a
demonstration, that the joint possession of the power in question by the president
and senate would afford a greater prospect of security, than the separate possession of it by either of them. And whoever has maturely weighed the circum- *80*
stances, which must concur in the appointment of a president will be satisfied,
that the office will always bid fair to be filled by men of such characters as to render their concurrence in the formation of treaties peculiarly desirable, as well on
the score of wisdom as on that of integrity.

The remarks made in a former number, which has been alluded to in another *85*
part of this paper, will apply with conclusive force against the admission of the
house of representatives to a share in the formation of treaties. The fluctuating,
and taking its future increase into the account, the multitudinous composition of
that body, forbid us to expect in it those qualities which are essential to the
proper execution of such a trust. Accurate and comprehensive knowledge of for- *90*
eign politics; a steady and systematic adherence to the same views; a nice and
uniform sensibility to national character, decision, *secrecy* and dispatch; are incompatible with the genius of a body so variable and so numerous. The very
complication of the business by introducing a necessity of the concurrence of so
many different bodies, would of itself afford a solid objection. The greater fre- *95*
quency of the calls upon the house of representatives, and the greater length of
time which it would often be necessary to keep them together when convened,
to obtain their sanction in the progressive stages of a treaty, would be source of so
great inconvenience and expence, as alone ought to condemn the project.

The only objection which remains to be canvassed is that which would sub- *100*
stitute the proportion of two thirds of all the members composing the senatorial
body to that of two thirds of the members *present*. It has been shewn under the
second head of our inquiries that all provisions which require more than the majority of any body to its resolutions have a direct tendency to embarrass the operations of the government and an indirect one to subject the sense of the majority *105*
to that of the minority. This consideration seems sufficient to determine our
opinion, that the convention have gone as far in the endeavour to secure the advantage of numbers in the formation of treaties as could have been reconciled either with the activity of the public councils or with a reasonable regard to the
major sense of the community. If two thirds of the whole number of members *110*
had been required, it would in many cases from the non attendance of a part
amount in practice to a necessity of unanimity. And the history of every political
establishment in which this principle has prevailed is a history of impotence,

perplexity and disorder. Proofs of this position might be adduced from the examples
115 of the Roman tribuneship, the Polish diet and the states general of the Netherlands; did not an example at home render foreign precedents unnecessary.

To require a fixed proportion of the whole body would not in all probability
contribute to the advantages of a numerous agency, better than merely to require
a proportion of the attending members. The former by increasing the difficulty
120 of resolutions disagreeable to the minority diminishes the motives to punctual
attendance. The latter by making the capacity of the body to depend on a *proportion* which may be varied by the absence or presence of a single member, has
the contrary effect. And as, by promoting punctuality, it tends to keep the body
complete, there is great likelihood that its resolutions would generally be dic-
125 tated by as great a number in this case as in the other; while there would be
much fewer occasions of delay. It ought not to be forgotten that under the existing confederation two members *may* and usually *do* represent a state; whence it
happens that congress, who now are solely invested with *all the powers* of the
union, rarely consists of a greater number of persons than would compose the in-
130 tended senate. If we add to this, that as the members vote by states, and that
where there is only a single member present from a state, his vote is lost, it will
justify a supposition that the active voices in the senate, where the members are
to vote individually, would rarely fall short in number of the active voices in the
existing congress. When in addition to these considerations we take into view the
135 co-operation of the president, we shall not hesitate to infer that the people of
America would have greater security against an improper use of the power of
making treaties, under the new constitution, than they now enjoy under the confederation. And when we proceed still one step further, and look forward to the
probable augmentation of the senate, by the erection of new states, we shall not
140 only perceive ample ground of confidence in the sufficiency of the numbers, to
whose agency that power will be entrusted; but we shall probably be led to conclude that a body more numerous than the senate would be likely to become,
would be very little fit for the proper discharge of the trust.

PUBLIUS.

Lines 114–16 The Roman tribunes were established to protect the liberties of the
plebeians but failed to stand up against the rise of the Caesars. On Poland, see No.
19, lines 126–31; on the Netherlands, see No. 20, lines 1–96.

SEVENTY-SIX
{NO. 75 IN NEWSPAPERS}

ALEXANDER HAMILTON
April 1, 1788
The Same View Continued, in Relation to the Appointment
of the Officers of the Government

To the People of the State of New York.

The president is "to *nominate* and by and with the advice and consent of the senate to appoint ambassadors, other public ministers and consuls, judges of the
supreme court, and all other officers of the United States, whose appointments
are not otherwise provided for in the constitution. But the congress may by law
vest the appointment of such inferior officers as they think proper in the president   5
alone, or in the courts of law, or in the heads of departments. The president shall
have power to fill up *all vacancies* which may happen *during the recess of the senate*, by granting commissions which shall *expire* at the end of their next session."

It has been observed in a former paper, "that the true test of a good government is its aptitude and tendency to produce a good administration." If the just-   10
ness of this observation be admitted, the mode of appointing the officers of the
United States contained in the foregoing clauses, must when examined be allowed to be entitled to particular commendation. It is not easy to conceive a plan
better calculated than this, to promote a judicious choice of men for filling the
offices of the union; and it will not need proof, that on this point must essentially   15
depend the character of its administration.

It will be agreed on all hands, that the power of appointment in ordinary cases
can be properly modified only in one of three ways. It ought either to be vested in
a single man—or in a *select* assembly of a moderate number—or in a single man
with the concurrence of such an assembly. The exercise of it by the people at   20
large, will be readily admitted to be impracticable; as, waving every other consideration it would leave them little time to do any thing else. When therefore
mention is made in the subsequent reasonings of an assembly or body of men,
what is said must be understood to relate to a select body or assembly of the description already given. The people collectively from their number and from   25
their dispersed situation cannot be regulated in their movements by that systematic spirit of cabal and intrigue, which will be urged as the chief objections to
reposing the power in question in a body of men.

Those who have themselves reflected upon the subject, or who have attended
to the observations made in other parts of these papers, in relation to the ap-   30
pointment of the president, will I presume agree to the position that there would

always be great probability of having the place supplied by a man of abilities, at least respectable. Premising this, I proceed to lay it down as a rule, that one man of discernment is better fitted to analise and estimate the peculiar qualities
35   adapted to particular offices, than a body of men of equal, or perhaps even of superior discernment.

    The sole and undivided responsibility of one man will naturally beget a livelier sense of duty and a more exact regard to reputation. He will on this account feel himself under stronger obligations, and more interested to investigate with
40   care the qualities requisite to the stations to be filled, and to prefer with impartiality the persons who may have the fairest pretentions to them. He will have *fewer* personal attachments to gratify than a body of men, who may each be supposed to have an equal number, and will be so much the less liable to be misled by the sentiments of friendship and of affection. There is nothing so apt to agitate
45   the passions of mankind as personal considerations, whether they relate to ourselves or to others, who are to be the objects of our choice or preference. Hence, in every exercise of the power of appointing to offices by an assembly of men, we must expect to see a full display of all the private and party likings and dislikes, partialities and antipathies, attachments and animosities, which are felt by those
50   who compose the assembly. The choice which may at any time happen to be made under such circumstances will of course be the result either of a victory gained by one party over the other, or of a compromise between the parties. In either case, the intrinsic merit of the candidate will be too often out of sight. In the first, the qualifications best adapted to uniting the suffrages of the party will be
55   more considered than those which fit the person for the station. In the last the coalition will commonly turn upon some interested equivalent—"Give us the man we wish for this office, and you shall have the one you wish for that." This will be the usual condition of the bargain. And it will rarely happen that the advancement of the public service will be the primary object either of party vic-
60   tories or of party negociations.

    The truth of the principles here advanced seems to have been felt by the most intelligent of those who have found fault with the provision made in this respect by the convention. They contend that the president ought solely to have been authorized to make the appointments under the federal government. But it is easy to shew
65   that every advantage to be expected from such an arrangement would in substance be derived from the power of *nomination*, which is proposed to be conferred upon him; while several disadvantages which might attend the absolute power of appointment in the hands of that officer, would be avoided. In the act of nomination his judgment alone would be exercised; and as it would be his sole duty to point
70   out the man, who with the approbation of the senate should fill an office, his responsibility would be as complete as if he were to make the final appointment. There can in this view be no difference between nominating and appointing. The same motives which would influence a proper discharge of his duty in one case would exist in the other. And as no man could be appointed, but upon his previous
75   nomination, every man who might be appointed would be in fact his choice.

But his nomination may be overruled:—this it certainly may, yet it can only be to make place for another nomination by himself. The person ultimately appointed must be the object of his preference, though perhaps not in the first degree. It is also not very probable that his nomination would often be overruled. The senate could not be tempted by the preference they might feel to another to reject the one proposed; because they could not assure themselves that the person they might wish would be brought forward by a second or by any subsequent nomination. They could not even be certain that a future nomination would present a candidate in any degree more acceptable to them: And as their dissent might cast a kind of stigma upon the individual rejected; and might have the appearance of a reflection upon the judgment of the chief magistrate; it is not likely that their sanction would often be refused, where there were not special and strong reasons for the refusal.

To what purpose then require the co-operation of the senate? I answer that the necessity of their concurrence would have a powerful, though in general a silent operation. It would be an excellent check upon a spirit of favoritism in the president, and would tend greatly to preventing the appointment of unfit characters from state prejudice, from family connection, from personal attachment, or from a view to popularity. And, in addition to this, it would be an efficacious source of stability in the administration.

It will readily be comprehended, that a man, who had himself the sole disposition of offices, would be governed much more by his private inclinations and interests, than when he was bound to submit the propriety of his choice to the discussion and determination of a different and independent body; and that body an entire branch of the legislature. The possibility of rejection would be a strong motive to care in proposing. The danger to his own reputation, and, in the case of an elective magistrate, to his political existence, from betraying a spirit of favoritism, or an unbecoming pursuit of popularity, to the observation of a body, whose opinion would have great weight in forming that of the public, could not fail to operate as a barrier to the one and to the other. He would be both ashamed and afraid to bring forward for the most distinguished or lucrative stations, candidates who had no other merit, than that of coming from the same state to which he particularly belonged, or of being in some way or other personally allied to him, or of possessing the necessary insignificance and pliancy to render them the obsequious instruments of his pleasure.

To this reasoning, it has been objected, that the president by the influence of the power of nomination may secure the complaisance of the senate to his views. The supposition of universal venality in human nature is little less an error in political reasoning than the supposition of universal rectitude. The institution of delegated power implies that there is a portion of virtue and honor among mankind, which may be a reasonable foundation of confidence. And experience justifies the theory: It has been found to exist in the most corrupt periods of the most corrupt governments. The venality of the British house of commons has been long a topic of accusation against that body, in the country to which they

120   belong, as well as in this; and it cannot be doubted that the charge is to a considerable extent well founded. But it is as little to be doubted that there is always a
large proportion of the body, which consists of independent and public spirited
men, who have an influential weight in the councils of the nation. Hence it is
(the present reign not excepted) that the sense of that body is often seen to con-
125   troul the inclinations of the monarch, both with regard to men and to measures.
Though it might therefore be allowable to suppose, that the executive might occasionally influence some individuals in the senate; yet the supposition that he
could in general purchase the integrity of the whole body would be forced and
improbable. A man disposed to view human nature as it is, without either flatter-
130   ing its virtues or exaggerating its vices, will see sufficient ground of confidence in
the probity of the senate, to rest satisfied not only that it will be impracticable to
the executive to corrupt or seduce a majority of its members; but that the necessity of its co-operation in the business of appointments will be a considerable and
salutary restraint upon the conduct of that magistrate. Nor is the integrity of the
135   senate the only reliance. The constitution has provided some important guards
against the danger of executive influence upon the legislative body: It declares
that "No senator, or representative shall, during the time *for which he was elected,*
be appointed to any civil office under the United States, which shall have been
created, or the emoluments whereof shall have been encreased during such
140   time; and no person holding any office under the United States shall be a member
of either house during his continuance in office."

    PUBLIUS.

SEVENTY-SEVEN
{NO. 76 IN NEWSPAPERS}

ALEXANDER HAMILTON
April 2, 1788
**The View of the Constitution of the President Concluded,
with a Further Consideration of the Power of Appointment,
and a Concise Examination of His Remaining Powers**

To the People of the State of New York.

It has been mentioned as one of the advantages to be expected from the co-operation of the senate, in the business of appointments, that it would contribute to the stability of the administration. The consent of that body would be necessary to displace as well as to appoint. A change of the chief magistrate therefore would not occasion so violent or so general a revolution in the officers of the government, as might be expected if he were the sole disposer of offices. Where a man in any station had given satisfactory evidence of his fitness for it, a new president would be restrained from attempting a change, in favour of a person more agreeable to him, by the apprehension that the discountenance of the senate might frustrate the attempt, and bring some degree of discredit upon himself. Those who can best estimate the value of a steady administration will be most disposed to prize a provision, which connects the official existence of public men with the approbation or disapprobation of that body, which from the greater permanency of its own composition, will in all probability be less subject to inconstancy, than any other member of the government.

To this union of the senate with the president, in the article of appointments, it has in some cases been objected, that it would serve to give the president an undue influence over the senate; and in others, that it would have an opposite tendency; a strong proof that neither suggestion is true.

To state the first in its proper form is to refute it. It amounts to this—The president would have an improper *influence* over the senate; because the senate would have the power of *restraining* him. This is an absurdity in terms. It cannot admit of a doubt that the intire power of appointment would enable him much more effectually to establish a dangerous empire over that body, than a mere power of nomination subject to their controul.

Let us take a view of the converse of the proposition—"The senate would influence the executive." As I have had occasion to remark in several other instances,

---

Line 5 The "revolution" referred to here would be in the officeholders, not in the state.

the indistinctness of the objection forbids a precise answer. In what manner is
this influence to be exerted? In relation to what objects? The power of influenc-
30 ing a person, in the sense in which it is here used, must imply a power of conferring a benefit upon him. How could the senate confer a benefit upon the
president by the manner of employing their right of negative upon his nominations? If it be said they might sometimes gratify him by an acquiescence in a favorite choice, when public motives might dictate a different conduct; I answer
35 that the instances in which the president could be personally interested in the result, would be too few to admit of his being materially affected by the compliances of the senate. Besides this, it is evident that the POWER which can
originate the disposition of honors and emoluments, is more likely to attract than
to be attracted by the POWER which can merely obstruct their course. If by in-
40 fluencing the president be meant *restraining* him, this is precisely what must
have been intended. And it has been shewn that the restraint would be salutary,
at the same time that it would not be such as to destroy a single advantage to be
looked for from the uncontrouled agency of that magistrate. The right of nomination would produce all the good, without the ill.

45   Upon a comparison of the plan for the appointment of the officers of the proposed government with that which is established by the constitution of this state
a decided preference must be given to the former. In that plan the power of nomination is unequivocally vested in the executive. And as there would be a necessity for submitting each nomination to the judgement of an entire branch of the
50 legislature, the circumstances attending an appointment, from the mode of conducting it, would naturally become matters of notoriety; and the public could be
at no loss to determine what part had been performed by the different actors. The
blame of a bad nomination would fall upon the president singly and absolutely.
The censure of rejecting a good one would lie entirely at the door of the senate;
55 aggravated by the consideration of their having counteracted the good intentions
of the executive. If an ill appointment should be made the executive for nominating and the senate for approving would participate though in different degrees
in the opprobrium and disgrace.

The reverse of all this characterises the manner of appointment in this state.
60 The council of appointment consists of from three to five persons, of whom the
governor is always one. This small body, shut up in a private apartment, impene-
trable to the public eye, proceed to the execution of the trust committed to them.
It is known that the governor claims the right of nomination, upon the strength of
some ambiguous expressions in the constitution; but it is not known to what extent,
65 or in what manner he exercises it; nor upon what occasions he is contradicted or

---

Lines 53–58 The question of "good" or "bad" appointments here would usually be
a matter of political judgment and, often, of policy; the argument seems strained.

Lines 59–82 Hamilton is here, at home, criticizing George Clinton's administration
of the State of New York.

opposed. The censure of a bad appointment, on account of the uncertainty of its author, and for want of a determinate object, has neither poignancy nor duration. And while an unbounded field for cabal and intrigue lies open, all idea of responsibility is lost. The most that the public can know is, that the governor claims the right of nomination: That *two* out of the considerable number of *four* men can too often be managed without much difficulty: That if some of the members of a particular council should happen to be of an uncomplying character, it is frequently not impossible to get rid of their opposition, by regulating the times of meeting in such a manner as to render their attendance inconvenient: And that, from whatever cause it may proceed, a great number of very improper appointments are from time to time made. Whether a governor of this state avails himself of the ascendant he must necessarily have, in this delicate and important part of the administration, to prefer to offices men who are best qualified for them: Or whether he prostitutes that advantage to the advancement of persons, whose chief merit is their implicit devotion to his will, and to the support of a despicable and dangerous system of personal influence, are questions which unfortunately for the community can only be the subjects of speculation and conjecture.

Every mere council of appointment, however constituted, will be a conclave, in which cabal and intrigue will have their full scope. Their number, without an unwarrantable increase of expence, cannot be large enough to preclude a facility of combination. And as each member will have his friends and connections to provide for, the desire of mutual gratification will beget a scandalous bartering of votes and bargaining for places. The private attachments of one man might easily be satisfied; but to satisfy the private attachments of a dozen, or of twenty men, would occasion a monopoly of all the principal employments of the government, in a few families, and would lead more directly to an aristocracy or an oligarchy, than any measure that could be contrived. If to avoid an accumulation of offices, there was to be a frequent change in the persons, who were to compose the council, this would involve the mischiefs of a mutable administration in their full extent. Such a council would also be more liable to executive influence than the senate, because they would be fewer in number, and would act less immediately under the public inspection. Such a council in fine as a substitute for the plan of the convention, would be productive of an increase of expence, a multiplication of the evils which spring from favouritism and intrigue in the distribution of the public honors, a decrease of stability in the administration of the government, and a diminution of the security against an undue influence of the executive. And yet such a council has been warmly contended for as an essential amendment in the proposed constitution.

I could not with propriety conclude my observations on the subject of appointments, without taking notice of a scheme, for which there has appeared some, though but a few advocates; I mean that of uniting the house of representatives in the power of making them. I shall however do little more than mention it, as I cannot imagine that it is likely to gain the countenance of any considerable part of the community. A body so fluctuating, and at the same time so

110 numerous, can never be deemed proper for the exercise of that power. Its unfitness will appear manifest to all, when it is recollected that in half a century it may
consist of three or four hundred persons. All the advantages of the stability, both
of the executive and of the senate, would be defeated by this union; and infinite
delays and embarrassments would be occasioned. The example of most of the
115 states in their local constitutions, encourages us to reprobate the idea.

The only remaining powers of the executive, are comprehended in giving information to congress of the state of the union; in recommending to their consideration such measures as he shall judge expedient; in convening them, or
either branch, upon extraordinary occasions; in adjourning them when they can-
120 not themselves agree upon the time of adjournment; in receiving ambassadors
and other public ministers; in faithfully executing the laws; and in commissioning all the officers of the United States.

Except some cavils about the power of convening *either* house of the legislature and that of receiving ambassadors, no objection has been made to this class
125 of authorities; nor could they possibly admit of any. It required indeed an insa-
tiable avidity for censure to invent exceptions to the parts which have been excepted to. In regard to the power of convening either house of the legislature, I
shall barely remark, that in respect to the senate at least, we can readily discover
a good reason for it. As this body has a concurrent power with the executive in
130 the article of treaties, it might often be necessary to call it together with a view to
this object, when it would be unnecessary and improper to convene the house of
representatives. As to the reception of ambassadors, what I have said in a former
paper will furnish a sufficient answer.

We have now compleated a survey of the structure and powers of the execu-
135 tive department, which, I have endeavoured to show, combines, as far as republican principles will admit, all the requisites to energy. The remaining enquiry is:
does it also combine the requisites to safety in the republican sense—a due dependence on the people—a due responsibility? The answer to this question has
been anticipated in the investigation of its other characteristics, and is satisfacto-
140 rily deducible from these circumstances, the election of the president once in
four years by persons immediately chosen by the people for that purpose; and his
being at all times liable to impeachment, trial, dismission from office, incapacity
to serve in any other; and to the forfeiture of life and estate by subsequent prosecution in the common course of law. But these precautions, great as they are, are
145 not the only ones, which the plan of the convention has provided in favor of the
public security. In the only instances in which the abuse of the executive
authority was materially to be feared, the chief magistrate of the United States
would by that plan be subjected to the controul of a branch of the legislative
body. What more can an enlightened and reasonable people desire?

PUBLIUS.

Line 124 On receiving ambassadors, see No. 69, lines 139–45.

SEVENTY-EIGHT

ALEXANDER HAMILTON
May 28, 1788
A View of the Constitution of the Judicial Department,
in Relation to the Tenure of Good Behaviour

To the People of the State of New York.

We proceed now to an examination of the judiciary department of the proposed government.

In unfolding the defects of the existing confederation, the utility and necessity of a federal judicature have been clearly pointed out. It is the less necessary to recapitulate the considerations there urged; as the propriety of the institution in   *5* the abstract is not disputed: The only questions which have been raised being relative to the manner of constituting it, and to its extent. To these points therefore our observations shall be confined.

The manner of constituting it seems to embrace these several objects—1st. The mode of appointing the judges.—2d. The tenure by which they are to hold   *10* their places.—3d. The partition of the judiciary authority between different courts, and their relations to each other.

First. As to the mode of appointing the judges: This is the same with that of appointing the officers of the union in general, and has been so fully discussed in the two last numbers, that nothing can be said here which would not be useless   *15* repetition.

Lines 1–2 The essay initiated here is a fundamental statement generally considered the authoritative interpretation of the doctrine that a century later came to be known as judicial review. It was not scheduled in the draft plan of *The Federalist,* but was composed in reply to a series of cogently argued and well-informed attacks on the proposed judicial power by "Brutus," probably Robert Yates (1738–1801) of New York. They appeared in *The New York Journal* and *Weekly Register* between December 27, 1787, and March 20, 1788.

For previous references to aspects of judicial power, see No. 7, lines 51–60; No. 16, lines 118–37; and No. 44, lines 153–62.

Lines 13–16 In England, judicial appointments were made by the crown, which in effect meant by the government of the day—though always from the ranks of trained lawyers. (This is still the case.) The American Constitution breaks new ground in engaging the Senate in the process. The check on the executive is an important instance in which separation of powers is not the controlling principle.

Second. As to the tenure by which the judges are to hold their places: This chiefly concerns their duration in office; the provisions for their support; and the precautions for their responsibility.

20   According to the plan of the convention, all the judges who may be appointed by the United States are to hold their offices *during good behaviour,* which is conformable to the most approved of the state constitutions; and among the rest, to that of this state. Its propriety having been drawn into question by the adversaries of that plan, is no light symptom of the rage for objection which disorders their
25   imaginations and judgments. The standard of good behaviour for the continuance in office of the judicial magistracy is certainly one of the most valuable of the modern improvements in the practice of government. In a monarchy it is an excellent barrier to the despotism of the prince: In a republic it is a no less excellent barrier to the encroachments and oppressions of the representative body.
30   And it is the best expedient which can be devised in any government, to secure a steady, upright and impartial administration of the laws.

Whoever attentively considers the different departments of power must perceive, that in a government in which they are separated from each other, the judiciary, from the nature of its functions, will always be the least dangerous to the
35   political rights of the constitution; because it will be least in a capacity to annoy or injure them. The executive not only dispenses the honors, but holds the sword of the community. The legislature not only commands the purse, but prescribes the rules by which the duties and rights of every citizen are to be regulated. The judiciary on the contrary has no influence over either the sword or the purse, no
40   direction either of the strength or of the wealth of the society, and can take no active resolution whatever. It may truly be said to have neither FORCE nor WILL, but merely judgment; and must ultimately depend upon the aid of the executive arm even for the efficacy of its judgments.

This simple view of the matter suggests several important consequences. It
45   proves incontestibly that the judiciary is beyond comparison the weakest of the

---

Line 21 The concept of tenure *"during good behavior"* (*quamdiu se bene gesserint*), which replaced that of "during the king's pleasure" (*durante bene placito*), secured the independence of the judiciary by putting the judges beyond the reach of the will of the reigning monarch. A judge could thenceforth be removed only by a joint vote of the two houses of Parliament. These reforms were introduced by the Act of Settlement, 1701, and may be said to have rounded off the constitutional settlement of 1688–1689 (though the fact that they had to wait twelve years suggests that they came as a late addition to the agenda).

Lines 32–43 This paragraph, from which Alexander Bickel borrowed the title of his influential book *The Least Dangerous Branch* (Indianapolis, 1962), is interesting from a modern point of view for the perspective it yields on the seemingly limited powers of the judiciary. The concept of denoted by the title *Government by Judiciary"* (Louis Boudin, 1932), or of a Supreme Court that continually intervenes in political policy and virtually acts as a superior legislative body, plays no part in

three departments of power;* that it can never attack with success either of the other two; and that all possible care is requisite to enable it to defend itself against their attacks. It equally proves, that though individual oppression may now and then proceed from the courts of justice, the general liberty of the people can never be endangered from that quarter: I mean, so long as the judiciary remains truly distinct from both the legislative and executive. For I agree that "there is no liberty, if the power of judging be not separated from the legislative and executive powers."† And it proves, in the last place, that as liberty can have nothing to fear from the judiciary alone, but would have every thing to fear from its union with either of the other departments; that as all the effects of such an union must ensue from a dependence of the former on the latter, notwithstanding a nominal and apparent separation; that as from the natural feebleness of the judiciary, it is in continual jeopardy of being overpowered, awed or influenced by its co-ordinate branches; and that as nothing can contribute so much to its firmness and independence, as permanency in office, this quality may therefore be justly regarded as an indispensable ingredient in its constitution; and in a great measure as the citadel of the public justice and the public security.

The complete independence of the courts of justice is peculiarly essential in a limited constitution. By a limited constitution I understand one which contains certain specified exceptions to the legislative authority; such for instance as

---

* The celebrated Montesquieu speaking of them says, "of the three powers above mentioned, the JUDICIARY is next to nothing." Spirit of Laws, vol. 1, page 186.
† Idem. page 181.

Publius's constitutional thought, or the thinking he attributes to the Convention. This interpretation is undoubtedly correct; the debates give little sign that members feared an interventionist judiciary. In faculty psychology language, the Court possesses judgment but lacks will; in practical terms, it lacks force. The point was illustrated by President Andrew Jackson when, disagreeing with a Supreme Court decision on Native American rights, he reputedly declared, "John Marshall has made his decision; now let him enforce it" (*Worcester v. Georgia*, 1832). This weakness of the judiciary is actually consistent with traditional thought on the subject, both Locke and Montesquieu having considered the judiciary as subordinate to both the executive and legislature. But contrast this with the deep foreboding of Brutus, to whom Hamilton is here replying, and who says, "I question whether the world ever saw, in any period of it, a court of justice invested with such immense powers, and yet placed in a situation so little responsible" (*New York Journal*, March 20, 1788).

Lines 63–70 This paragraph introduces the first specific mention of judicial review. But it is generally expected that review will in fact be restricted to a narrow range of cases arising immediately from the structure of the Constitution. The politicization of the Supreme Court essentially began after its controversial decision in *Dred Scott v. Sanford* (1857); but it was only after the passage of the 14th Amendment that judicial review became an active political issue.

that it shall pass no bills of attainder, no *ex post facto* laws, and the like. Limitations of this kind can be preserved in practice no other way than through the medium of the courts of justice; whose duty it must be to declare all acts contrary to the manifest tenor of the constitution void. Without this, all the reservations of
70 particular rights or privileges would amount to nothing.

Some perplexity respecting the right of the courts to pronounce legislative acts void, because contrary to the constitution, has arisen from an imagination that the doctrine would imply a superiority of the judiciary to the legislative power. It is urged that the authority which can declare the acts of another void,
75 must necessarily be superior to the one whose acts may be declared void. As this doctrine is of great importance in all the American constitutions, a brief discussion of the grounds on which it rests cannot be unacceptable.

There is no position which depends on clearer principles, than that every act of a delegated authority, contrary to the tenor of the commission under which it
80 is exercised, is void. No legislative act therefore contrary to the constitution can be valid. To deny this would be to affirm that the deputy is greater than his principal; that the servant is above his master; that the representatives of the people are superior to the people themselves; that men acting by virtue of powers may do not only what their powers do not authorise, but what they forbid.

85 If it be said that the legislative body are themselves the constitutional judges of their own powers, and that the construction they put upon them is conclusive upon the other departments, it may be answered, that this cannot be the natural presumption, where it is not to be collected from any particular provisions in the constitution. It is not otherwise to be supposed that the constitution could intend
90 to enable the representatives of the people to substitute their *will* to that of their constituents. It is far more rational to suppose that the courts were designed to be an intermediate body between the people and the legislature, in order, among

---

Lines 78–84 This paragraph addresses the classical view of the matter from a conflict-of-laws point of view. There is as yet no bill of rights, so little room exists for potential conflict between political policies and principles embodied in constitutional structure. On these terms, the argument seems irrefutable. The comment above (on lines 63–70), however, alters the perspective; what Hamilton's argument lacks at this stage is a concept of the organic character of law that makes it susceptible to interpretation—a point applying equally to the apparent, but deceptive, rigidity of constitutional law. (But for the emergence of this concept, see No. 82, lines 1–7.) Madison's observation in No. 37, lines 123–51 about the uncertainty and obscurity of language has a bearing on this problem because it will mean that constitutional principles will in most cases require interpretation in the light of the facts of the case.

Lines 85–101 Hamilton's development of the argument for constitutional ascendancy as an expression of democratic values deserves scrutiny. The assumption is that the will of the people as manifested in 1788 is permanently superior to that of a majority of the legislature, though democratically elected, at any future date. (Constitutional amendment, the only remedy, will not always be practicable.)

other things, to keep the latter within the limits assigned to their authority. The interpretation of the laws is the proper and peculiar province of the courts. A constitution is in fact, and must be, regarded by the judges as a fundamental law. *95* It therefore belongs to them to ascertain its meaning as well as the meaning of any particular act proceeding from the legislative body. If there should happen to be an irreconcileable variance between the two, that which has the superior obligation and validity ought of course to be preferred; or in other words, the constitution ought to be preferred to the statute, the intention of the people to the *100* intention of their agents.

Nor does this conclusion by any means suppose a superiority of the judicial to the legislative power. It only supposes that the power of the people is superior to both; and that where the will of the legislature declared in its statutes, stands in opposition to that of the people declared in the constitution, the judges ought to *105* be governed by the latter, rather than the former. They ought to regulate their decisions by the fundamental laws, rather than by those which are not fundamental.

This exercise of judicial discretion in determining between two contradictory laws, is exemplified in a familiar instance. It not uncommonly happens, that there are two statutes existing at one time, clashing in whole or in part with each *110* other, and neither of them containing any repealing clause or expression. In such a case, it is the province of the courts to liquidate and fix their meaning and operation: So far as they can by any fair construction be reconciled to each other; reason and law conspire to dictate that this should be done. Where this is impracticable, it becomes a matter of necessity to give effect to one, in exclusion of *115* the other. The rule which has obtained in the courts for determining their relative validity is that the last in order of time shall be preferred to the first. But this is mere rule of construction, not derived from any positive law, but from the nature and reason of the thing. It is a rule not enjoined upon the courts by legislative provision, but adopted by themselves, as consonant to truth and propriety, *120* for the direction of their conduct as interpreters of the law. They thought it reasonable, that between the interfering acts of an *equal* authority, that which was the last indication of its will, should have the preference.

But in regard to the interfering acts of a superior and subordinate authority, of an original and derivative power, the nature and reason of the thing indicate the *125* converse of that rule as proper to be followed. They teach us that the prior act of a superior ought to be preferred to the subsequent act of an inferior and subordinate authority; and that, accordingly, whenever a particular statute contravenes the constitution, it will be the duty of the judicial tribunals to adhere to the latter, and disregard the former. *130*

Lines 93–94; 108–23 Here Hamilton recognizes the necessity for judicial interpretation.

It can be of no weight to say, that the courts on the pretence of a repugnancy, may substitute their own pleasure to the constitutional intentions of the legislature. This might as well happen in the case of two contradictory statutes; or it might as well happen in every adjudication upon any single statute. The courts
135   must declare the sense of the law; and if they should be disposed to exercise WILL instead of JUDGMENT, the consequence would equally be the substitution of their pleasure to that of the legislative body. The observation, if it proved any thing, would prove that there ought to be no judges distinct from that body.

If then the courts of justice are to be considered as the bulwarks of a limited
140   constitution against legislative encroachments, this consideration will afford a strong argument for the permanent tenure of judicial offices, since nothing will contribute so much as this to that independent spirit in the judges, which must be essential to the faithful performance of so arduous a duty.

This independence of the judges is equally requisite to guard the constitution
145   and the rights of individuals from the effects of those ill humours which the arts of designing men, or the influence of particular conjunctures, sometimes disseminate among the people themselves, and which, though they speedily give place to better information and more deliberate reflection, have a tendency in the mean time to occasion dangerous innovations in the government, and seri-
150   ous oppressions of the minor party in the community. Though I trust the friends of the proposed constitution will never concur with its enemies* in questioning that fundamental principle of republican government, which admits the right of the people to alter or abolish the established constitution whenever they find it inconsistent with their happiness; yet it is not to be inferred from this principle,
155   that the representatives of the people, whenever a momentary inclination happens to lay hold of a majority of their constituents incompatible with the provisions in the existing constitution, would on that account be justifiable in a violation of those provisions; or that the courts would be under a greater obligation to connive at infractions in this shape, than when they had proceeded
160   wholly from the cabals of the representative body. Until the people have by some solemn and authoritative act annulled or changed the established form, it is binding upon themselves collectively, as well as individually; and no presumption, or even knowledge of their sentiments, can warrant their representatives in a departure from it, prior to such an act. But it is easy to see that it would require
165   an uncommon portion of fortitude in the judges to do their duty as faithful guardians of the constitution, where legislative invasions of it had been instigated by the major voice of the community.

But it is not with a view to infractions of the constitution only that the independence of the judges may be an essential safeguard against the effects of occa-
170   sional ill humours in the society. These sometimes extend no farther than to the injury of the private rights of particular classes of citizens, by unjust and partial

* Vide Protest of the minority of the convention of Pennsylvania, Martin's speech, &c.

laws. Here also the firmness of the judicial magistracy is of vast importance in mitigating the severity, and confining the operation of such laws. It not only serves to moderate the immediate mischiefs of those which may have been passed, but it operates as a check upon the legislative body in passing them; who, perceiving *175* that obstacles to the success of an iniquitous intention are to be expected from the scruples of the courts, are in a manner compelled by the very motives of the injustice they meditate, to qualify their attempts. This is a circumstance calculated to have more influence upon the character of our governments, than but few may be aware of. The benefits of the integrity and moderation of the judici- *180* ary have already been felt in more states than one; and though they may have displeased those whose sinister expectations they may have disappointed, they must have commanded the esteem and applause of all the virtuous and disinterested. Considerate men of every description ought to prize whatever will tend to beget or fortify that temper in the courts; as no man can be sure that he may not be to- *185* morrow the victim of a spirit of injustice, by which he may be a gainer to-day. And every man must now feel that the inevitable tendency of such a spirit is to sap the foundations of public and private confidence, and to introduce in its stead, universal distrust and distress.

That inflexible and uniform adherence to the rights of the constitution and of *190* individuals, which we perceive to be indispensable in the courts of justice, can certainly not be expected from judges who hold their offices by a temporary commission. Periodical appointments, however regulated, or by whomsoever made, would in some way or other be fatal to their necessary independence. If the power of making them was committed either to the executive or legislature, there *195* would be danger of an improper complaisance to the branch which possessed it; if to both, there would be an unwillingness to hazard the displeasure of either; if to the people, or to persons chosen by them for the special purpose, there would be too great a disposition to consult popularity, to justify a reliance that nothing would be consulted but the constitution and the laws. *200*

Lines 180–83 There were several cases that Hamilton might have had in mind in which state courts had already refused to enforce legislation on constitutional grounds. Chronologically, they are *Holmes v. Walton* (N.J., 1780); *Commonwealth v. Caton*, (Vir., 1782); *Rutgers v. Waddington* (N.Y., 1784), which is not a clear precedent; and most clearly, *Trevett v. Weedon* (R.I., 1786) and *Bayard v. Singleton* (N.C., 1787). Another possibility is the New York Mayor's Court case referred to above, No. 73 lines 161–64. The concept could also be traced to a local Virginia decision of 1766 in which the word "unconstitutional" appears to have been used for the first time; and more generally to the colonists' experience of having their legislation subjected to review by the privy council in London. In *Dr. Bonham's Case* (1610), Sir Edward Coke (1552–1634), Chief Justice of the King's Bench, had declared in famous but controversial words that if an act of parliament was "against common right and reason, or repugnant, or impossible to be performed" the common law would "control" such an act and declare it to be void.

There is yet a further and a weighty reason for the permanency of the judicial offices; which is deducible from the nature of the qualifications they require. It has been frequently remarked with great propriety, that a voluminous code of laws is one of the inconveniences necessarily connected with the advantages of a free government. To avoid an arbitrary discretion in the courts, it is indispensable that they should be bound down by strict rules and precedents, which serve to define and point out their duty in every particular case that comes before them; and it will readily be conceived from the variety of controversies which grow out of the folly and wickedness of mankind, that the records of those precedents must unavoidably swell to a very considerable bulk, and must demand long and laborious study to acquire a competent knowledge of them. Hence it is that there can be but few men in the society, who will have sufficient skill in the laws to qualify them for the stations of judges. And making the proper deductions for the ordinary depravity of human nature, the number must be still smaller of those who unite the requisite integrity with the requisite knowledge. These considerations apprise us, that the government can have no great option between fit characters; and that a temporary duration in office, which would naturally discourage such characters from quitting a lucrative line of practice to accept a seat on the bench, would have a tendency to throw the administration of justice into hands less able, and less well qualified to conduct it with utility and dignity. In the present circumstances of this country, and in those in which it is likely to be for a long time to come, the disadvantages on this score would be greater than they may at first sight appear; but it must be confessed that they are far inferior to those which present themselves under the other aspects of the subject.

Upon the whole there can be no room to doubt that the convention acted wisely in copying from the models of those constitutions which have established *good behaviour* as the tenure of their judicial offices in point of duration; and that so far from being blameable on this account, their plan would have been inexcuseably defective if it had wanted this important feature of good government. The experience of Great Britain affords an illustrious comment on the excellence of the institution.

PUBLIUS.

Line 230 The "illustrious comment" Hamilton had in mind might have been *Wilkes v. Wood* 3 George III 1763, Howell, *State Trials*, 1167; and *Entick v. Carrington*, 3 George III 1765, *State Trials*, 1044. In these cases Sir Charles Pratt (1714–1794; by 1765 Lord Chief Justice Camden), handed down resounding declarations of the liberty of British subjects against intrusion into their own homes, and corresponding rebukes to ministers of the crown who, claiming crown (executive) privilege, overstepped their powers at common law. The 4th Amendment and similar clauses in several state constitutions are direct descendants of these judgments. The common law had never been more valuable as an instrument of liberty, a point not lost on the colonists.

SEVENTY-NINE

ALEXANDER HAMILTON
May 28, 1788
A Further View of the Judicial Department, in Relation to the
Provisions for the Support and Responsibility of the Judges

To the People of the State of New York.

Next to permanency in office, nothing can contribute more to the independence of the judges than a fixed provision for their support. The remark made in relation to the president, is equally applicable here. In the general course of human nature, *a power over a man's subsistence amounts to a power over his will.* And we can never hope to see realised in practice the complete separation of the judicial 5 from the legislative power, in any system, which leaves the former dependent for pecuniary resources on the occasional grants of the latter. The enlightened friends to good government, in every state, have seen cause to lament the want of precise and explicit precautions in the state constitutions on this head. Some of these indeed have declared that *permanent** salaries should be established for 10 the judges; but the experiment has in some instances shewn that such expressions are not sufficiently definite to preclude legislative evasions. Something still more positive and unequivocal has been evinced to be requisite. The plan of the convention accordingly has provided, that the judges of the United States "shall at *stated* times receive for their services a compensation, which shall not be 15 *diminished* during their continuance in office."

This, all circumstances considered, is the most eligible provision that could have been devised. It will readily be understood, that the fluctuations in the value of money, and in the state of society, rendered a fixed rate of compensation in the constitution inadmissible. What might be extravagant to day, might in half 20 a century become penurious and inadequate. It was therefore necessary to leave it to the discretion of the legislature to vary its provisions in conformity to the variations in circumstances; yet under such restrictions as to put it out of the power of that body to change the condition of the individual for the worse. A man may then be sure of the ground upon which he stands, and can never be de- 25 terred from his duty by the apprehension of being placed in a less eligible situation. The clause which has been quoted combines both advantages. The salaries

---

* Vide Constitution of Massachusetts, Chap. 2, Sect. 1. Art. 13.

Lines 1–44 The violent inflation of both state and continental currencies during the war years lay behind the economic realism of these remarks on judicial salaries.

of judicial offices may from time to time be altered, as occasion shall require, yet
so as never to lessen the allowance with which any particular judge comes into
office, in respect to him. It will be observed that a difference has been made by
the convention between the compensation of the president and of the judges.
That of the former can neither be increased nor diminished. That of the latter
can only not be diminished. This probably arose from the difference in the
duration of the respective offices. As the president is to be elected for no more
than four years, it can rarely happen that an adequate salary, fixed at the commencement of that period, will not continue to be such to the end of it. But with
regard to the judges, who, if they behave properly, will be secured in their places
for life, it may well happen, especially in the early stages of the government, that
a stipend, which would be very sufficient at their first appointment, would become too small in the progress of their service.

This provision for the support of the judges bears every mark of prudence and
efficacy; and it may be safely affirmed that, together with the permanent tenure
of their offices, it affords a better prospect of their independence than is discoverable in the constitutions of any of the states, in regard to their own judges.

The precautions for their responsibility are comprised in the article respecting
impeachments. They are liable to be impeached for mal-conduct by the house
of representatives, and tried by the senate, and if convicted, may be dismissed
from office and disqualified for holding any other. This is the only provision on
the point, which is consistent with the necessary independence of the judicial
character, and is the only one which we find in our own constitution in respect
to our own judges.

The want of a provision for removing the judges on account of inability, has
been a subject of complaint. But all considerate men will be sensible that such a
provision would either not be practiced upon, or would be more liable to abuse
than calculated to answer any good purpose. The mensuration of the faculties of
the mind has, I believe, no place in the catalogue of known arts. An attempt to fix
the boundary between the regions of ability and inability, would much oftener
give scope to personal and party attachments and enmities, than advance the interests of justice, or the public good. The result, except in the case of insanity,
must for the most part be arbitrary; and insanity without any formal or express
provision, may be safely pronounced to be a virtual disqualification.

The constitution of New-York, to avoid investigations that must forever be
vague and dangerous, has taken a particular age as the criterion of inability. No
man can be a judge beyond sixty. I believe there are few at present, who do not
disapprove of this provision. There is no station in relation to which it is less
proper than to that of a judge. The deliberating and comparing faculties generally preserve their strength much beyond that period, in men who survive it; and

---

Lines 62–64 This requirement of New York's constitution was to be the cause of
Chancellor James Kent's (1763–1847) premature retirement in the mid-1820s.

when in addition to this circumstance, we consider how few there are who out-
live the season of intellectual vigour, and how improbable it is that any considerable proportion of the bench, whether more or less numerous, should be in such   70
a situation at the same time, we shall be ready to conclude that limitations of this
sort have little to recommend them. In a republic, where fortunes are not afflu-
ent, and pensions not expedient, the dismission of men from stations in which
they have served their country long and usefully, on which they depend for subsistence, and from which it will be too late to resort to any other occupation for a   75
livelihood, ought to have some better apology to humanity, than is to be found in
the imaginary danger of a superannuated bench.

PUBLIUS.

EIGHTY

ALEXANDER HAMILTON
May 28, 1788
**A Further View of the Judicial Department,
in Relation to the Extent of Its Powers**

To the People of the State of New York.

To judge with accuracy of the proper extent of the federal judicature, it will be necessary to consider in the first place what are its proper objects.

It seems scarcely to admit of controversy that the judiciary authority of the union ought to extend to these several descriptions of causes. 1st. To all those which arise out of the laws of the United States, passed in pursuance of their just and constitutional powers of legislation; 2d. to all those which concern the execution of the provisions expressly contained in the articles of union; 3d. to all those in which the United States are a party; 4th. to all those which involve the PEACE of the CONFEDERACY, whether they relate to the intercourse between the United States and foreign nations, or to that between the states themselves; 5th. to all those which originate on the high seas, and are of admiralty or maritime jurisdiction; and lastly, to all those in which the state tribunals cannot be supposed to be impartial and unbiassed.

The first point depends upon this obvious consideration that there ought always to be a constitutional method of giving efficacy to constitutional provisions. What for instance would avail restrictions on the authority of the state legislatures, without some constitutional mode of enforcing the observance of them? The states, by the plan of the convention are prohibited from doing a variety of things; some of which are incompatible with the interests of the union, and others with the principles of good government. The imposition of duties on imported articles, and the emission of paper money, are specimens of each kind. No man of sense will believe that such prohibitions would be scrupulously regarded, without some effectual power in the government to restrain or correct the infractions of them. This power must either be a direct negative on the state laws, or an authority in the federal courts, to over-rule such as might be in manifest contravention of the articles of union. There is no third course that I can imagine. The latter appears to have been thought by the convention preferable to the former, and I presume will be most agreeable to the states.

As to the second point, it is impossible by any argument or comment to make it clearer than it is in itself. If there are such things as political axioms, the propriety of the judicial power of a government being co-extensive with its legislative, may be ranked among the number. The mere necessity of uniformity in the interpretation of the national laws, decides the question. Thirteen independent courts of final jurisdiction over the same causes, arising upon the same laws, is a hydra in government, from which nothing but contradiction and confusion can proceed. 35

Still less need be said in regard to the third point. Controversies between the nation and its members or citizens, can only be properly referred to the national tribunals. Any other plan would be contrary to reason, to precedent, and to decorum.

The fourth point rests on this plain proposition, that the peace of the WHOLE ought not to be left at the disposal of a PART. The union will undoubtedly be answerable to foreign powers for the conduct of its members. And the responsibility for an injury ought ever to be accompanied with the faculty of preventing it. As the denial or perversion of justice by the sentences of courts, as well as in any other manner, is with reason classed among the just causes of war, it will follow that the federal judiciary ought to have cognizance of all causes in which the citizens of other countries are concerned. This is not less essential to the preservation of the public faith, than to the security of the public tranquility. A distinction may perhaps be imagined between cases arising upon treaties and the laws of nations, and those which may stand merely on the footing of the municipal law. The former kind may be supposed proper for the federal jurisdiction, the latter for that of the states. But it is at least problematical whether an unjust sentence against a foreigner, where the subject of controversy was wholly relative to the *lex loci*, would not, if unredressed, be an aggression upon his sovereign, as well as one which violated the stipulations in a treaty or the general laws of nations. And a still greater objection to the distinction would result from the immense difficulty, if not impossibility, of a practical discrimination between the cases of one complection and those of the other. So great a proportion of the cases in which foreigners are parties involve national questions, that it is by far most safe and most expedient to refer all those in which they are concerned to the national tribunals. 60

The power of determining causes between two states, between one state and the citizens of another, and between the citizens of different states, is perhaps not less essential to the peace of the union than that which has been just examined. History gives us a horrid picture of the dissentions and private wars which distracted and desolated Germany prior to the institution of the IMPERIAL CHAMBER by Maximilian, towards the close of the fifteenth century; and informs us at the same time of the vast influence of that institution in appeasing the disorders and establishing the tranquility of the empire. This was a court invested with authority to decide finally all differences between the members of the Germanic body. 70

A method of terminating territorial disputes between the states, under the authority of the federal head, was not unattended to, even in the imperfect system by which they have been hitherto held together But there are many other

---

Lines 65–71 For organization of the German Empire, see No. 19, lines 89–97.

75 sources, besides interfering claims of boundary, from which bickerings and animosities may spring up among the members of the union. To some of these we have been witnesses in the course of our past experience. It will readily be conjectured that I allude to the fraudulent laws which have been passed in too many of the states. And though the proposed constitution establishes particular guards
80 against the repetition of those instances which have heretofore made their appearance, yet it is warrantable to apprehend that the spirit which produced them will assume new shapes that could not be foreseen, nor specifically provided against. Whatever practices may have a tendency to disturb the harmony between the states, are proper objects of federal superintendence and control.
85 It may be esteemed the basis of the union, that "the citizens of each state shall be entitled to all the privileges and immunities of citizens of the several states." And if it be a just principle that every government *ought to possess the means of executing its own provisions by its own authority*, it will follow, that in order to the inviolable maintenance of that equality of privileges and immunities to which
90 the citizens of the union will be entitled, the national judiciary ought to preside in all cases in which one state or its citizens are opposed to another state or its citizens. To secure the full effect of so fundamental a provision against all evasion and subterfuge, it is necessary that its construction should be committed to that tribunal, which, having no local attachments, will be likely to be impartial be-
95 tween the different states and their citizens, and which, owing its official existence to the union, will never be likely to feel any bias inauspicious to the principles on which it is founded.

The fifth point will demand little animadversion. The most bigotted idolizers of state authority have not thus far shewn a disposition to deny the national judi-
100 ciary the cognizance of maritime causes. These so generally depend on the laws of nations, and so commonly affect the rights of foreigners, that they fall within the considerations which are relative to the public peace. The most important part of them are by the present confederation submitted to federal jurisdiction.

The reasonableness of the agency of the national courts in cases in which the
105 state tribunals cannot be supposed to be impartial, speaks for itself. No man ought certainly to be a judge in his own cause, or in any cause in respect to which he has the least interest or bias. This principle has no inconsiderable weight in designating the federal courts as the proper tribunals for the determination of controversies between different states and their citizens. And it ought to
110 have the same operation in regard to some cases between the citizens of the same state. Claims to land under grants of different states, founded upon adverse pretensions of boundary, are of this description. The courts of neither of the granting states could be expected to be unbiassed. The laws may have even prejudged

Line 78 The "fraudulent laws" are the recent state laws authorizing the issue of paper money.
Lines 104–17 See note on No. 7 lines 53–60.

the question, and tied the courts down to decisions in favour of the grants of the state to which they belonged. And even where this had not been done, it would *115* be natural that the judges, as men, should feel a strong predilection to the claims of their own government.

Having thus laid down and discussed the principles which ought to regulate the constitution of the federal judiciary, we will proceed to test, by these principles, the particular powers of which, according to the plan of the convention, it is *120* to be composed. It is to comprehend, "all cases in law and equity arising under the constitution, the laws of the United States, and treaties made, or which shall be made under their authority; to all cases affecting ambassadors, other public ministers and consuls; to all cases of admiralty and maritime jurisdiction; to controversies to which the United States shall be a party; to controversies be- *125* tween two or more states, between a state and citizens of another state, between citizens of different states, between citizens of the same state claiming lands under grants of different states, and between a state or the citizens thereof, and foreign states, citizens and subjects." This constitutes the entire mass of the judicial authority of the union. Let us now review it in detail. It is then to extend, *130*

First. To all cases in law and equity *arising under the constitution and the laws of the United States.* This corresponds to the two first classes of causes which have been enumerated as proper for the jurisdiction of the United States. It has been asked what is meant by "cases arising under the constitution," in contradistinction from those "arising under the laws of the United States." The differ- *135* ence has been already explained. All the restrictions upon the authority of the state legislatures, furnish examples of it. They are not, for instance, to emit paper money; but the interdiction results from the constitution, and will have no connection with any law of the United States. Should paper money, notwithstanding, be emitted, the controversies concerning it would be cases arising upon the con- *140* stitution, and not upon the laws of the United States, in the ordinary signification of the terms. This may serve as a sample of the whole.

It has also been asked, what need of the word "equity"? What equitable causes can grow out of the constitution and laws of the United States? There is hardly a

---

Lines 137–39 The makers of the Constitution, in forbidding states to coin money, seem to have overlooked the possibility that state legislatures might charter banks with power to issue their own notes, which would—and soon did—circulate as paper money.

Lines 143–60 Equity, administered by the Court of Chancery, developed in England to grant relief when the common law proved too strict or inflexible to satisfy the demand for fairness in individual cases. In colonial legal history, very few colonies had chancery courts, partly because they were suspected of being agents of proprietary interests (Pennsylvania), but largely, no doubt, because the common law courts acted more like chancery courts, and the distinction became somewhat blurred. Hamilton explains the function of equity later in this paragraph (lines 148–60).

145 subject of litigation between individuals, which may not involve those ingredients of *fraud, accident, trust* or *hardship*, which would render the matter an object of equitable, rather than of legal jurisdiction, as the distinction is known and established in several of the states. It is the peculiar province, for instance, of a court of equity to relieve against what are called hard bargains: These are con-
150 tracts, in which, though there may have been no direct fraud or deceit, sufficient to invalidate them in a court of law; yet there may have been some undue and unconscionable advantage taken of the necessities or misfortunes of one of the parties, which a court of equity would not tolerate. In such cases, where foreigners were concerned on either side, it would be impossible for the federal judica-
155 tories to do justice without an equitable, as well as a legal jurisdiction. Agreements to convey lands claimed under the grants of different states, may afford another example of the necessity of an equitable jurisdiction in the federal courts. This reasoning may not be so palpable in those states where the formal and technical distinction between LAW and EQUITY is not maintained as in
160 this state, where it is exemplified by every day's practice.

The judiciary authority of the union is to extend—

Second. To treaties made, or which shall be made under the authority of the United States, and to all cases affecting ambassadors, other public ministers and consuls. These belong to the fourth class of the enumerated cases, as they have
165 an evident connection with the preservation of the national peace.

Third. To cases of admiralty and maritime jurisdiction. These form altogether the fifth of the enumerated classes of causes proper for the cognizance of the national courts.

Fourth. To controversies to which the United States shall be a party. These
170 constitute the third of those classes.

Fifth. To controversies between two or more states, between a state and citizens of another state, between citizens of different states. These belong to the fourth of those classes, and partake in some measure of the nature of the last.

Sixth. To cases between the citizens of the same state, *claiming lands under*
175 *grants of different states.* These fall within the last class, and *are the only instance in which the proposed constitution directly contemplates the cognizance of disputes between the citizens of the same state.*

Seventh. To cases between a state and the citizens thereof, and foreign states, citizens, or subjects. These have been already explained to belong to the fourth
180 of the enumerated classes, and have been shewn to be in a peculiar manner the proper subjects of the national judicature.

From this review of the particular powers of the federal judiciary, as marked out in the constitution, it appears, that they are all conformable to the principles which ought to have governed the structure of that department, and which were
185 necessary to the perfection of the system. If some partial inconveniencies should appear to be connected with the incorporation of any of them into the plan, it ought to be recollected that the national legislature will have ample authority to

make such *exceptions* and to prescribe such regulations as will be calculated to obviate or remove these inconveniencies. The possibility of particular mischiefs can never be viewed by a well-informed mind as a solid objection to a general principle, which is calculated to avoid general mischiefs, and to obtain general advantages. *190*

PUBLIUS.

EIGHTY-ONE

ALEXANDER HAMILTON
May 28, 1788
A Further View of the Judicial Department,
in Relation to the Distribution of Its Authority

To the People of the State of New York.

Let us now return to the partition of the judiciary authority between different courts, and their relations to each other.

"The judicial power of the United States is (by the plan of the convention) to be vested in one supreme court, and in such inferior courts as the congress may
5 from time to time ordain and establish."*

That there ought to be one court of supreme and final jurisdiction is a proposition which has not been, and is not likely to be contested. The reasons for it have been assigned in another place, and are too obvious to need repetition. The only question that seems to have been raised concerning it, is whether it ought to
10 be a distinct body, or a branch of the legislature. The same contradiction is observable in regard to this matter, which has been remarked in several other cases. The very men who object to the senate as a court of impeachments, on the ground of an improper intermixture of powers, advocate, by implication at least, the propriety of vesting the ultimate decision of all causes in the whole, or in a
15 part of the legislative body.

The arguments or rather suggestions, upon which this charge is founded, are to this effect: "The authority of the proposed supreme court of the United States, which is to be a separate and independent body, will be superior to that of the legislature. The power of construing the laws, according to the *spirit* of the con-
20 stitution, will enable that court to mould them into whatever shape it may think proper; especially as its decisions will not be in any manner subject to the revi-

---

* Article 3. Sec. I.

Lines 6–7 This judicial function dates from the middle ages, when Parliament was itself the High Court of Parliament. In the 18th century the whole House of Lords would convene to hear great causes like the impeachment of Warren Hastings (1732–1818). Today the judicial function is carried out by a highly select committee of senior judges, who are members of the House and are known as the law lords. Unlike the justices of the Supreme Court of the United States, they are selected on grounds of legal qualifications without reference to politics.

sion or correction of the legislative body. This is as unprecedented as it is dangerous. In Britain, the judicial power in the last resort, resides in the house of lords, which is a branch of the legislature; and this part of the British government has been imitated in the state constitutions in general. The parliament of Great-Britain, and the legislatures of the several states, can at any time rectify by law, the exceptionable decisions of their respective courts. But the errors and usurpations of the supreme court of the United States will be uncontrolable and remediless." This, upon examination, will be found to be altogether made up of false reasoning upon misconceived fact.

In the first place, there is not a syllable in the plan under consideration, which *directly* empowers the national courts to construe the laws according to the spirit of the constitution, or which gives them any greater latitude in this respect, than may be claimed by the courts of every state. I admit however, that the constitution ought to be the standard of construction for the laws, and that wherever there is an evident opposition, the laws ought to give place to the constitution. But this doctrine is not deducible from any circumstance peculiar to the plan of the convention; but from the general theory of a limited constitution; and as far as it is true, is equally applicable to most, if not to all the state governments. There can be no objection therefore, on this account, to the federal judicature, which will not lie against the local judicatures in general, and which will not serve to condemn every constitution that attempts to set bounds to the legislative discretion.

But perhaps the force of the objection may be thought to consist in the particular organization of the proposed supreme court; in its being composed of a distinct body of magistrates, instead of being one of the branches of the legislature, as in the government of Great-Britain and in that of this state. To insist upon this point, the authors of the objection must renounce the meaning they have laboured to annex to the celebrated maxim requiring a separation of the departments of power. It shall nevertheless be conceded to them, agreeably to the interpretation given to that maxim in the course of these papers, that it is not violated by vesting the ultimate power of judging in a *part* of the legislative body. But though this be not an absolute violation of that excellent rule; yet it verges so nearly upon it, as on this account alone to be less eligible than the mode preferred by the convention. From a body which had had even a partial agency in passing bad laws, we could rarely expect a disposition to temper and moderate them in the application. The same spirit, which had operated in making them,

25

30

35

40

45

50

55

In the colonies, the governor's council served similarly as a final court of appeal; the function was carried over to the powers of the councils in the new state constitutions. For methods of appointment in state constitutions, see Thorpe, *American Charters* (cited in the note examining No. 24, lines 11–15.): Delaware, vol. I, 564; Georgia, I, 780; Massachusetts, III, 1902; New Hampshire, IV, 2453; North Carolina, V, 2791; Pennsylvania, V, 3087; South Carolina, VI, 3246.

would be too apt to operate in interpreting them: Still less could it be expected, that men who had infringed the constitution, in the character of legislators, would be disposed to repair the breach, in the character of judges. Nor is this all:

60 Every reason, which recommends the tenure of good behaviour for judicial offices, militates against placing the judiciary power in the last resort in a body composed of men chosen for a limited period. There is an absurdity in referring the determination of causes in the first instance to judges of permanent standing, and in the last to those of a temporary and mutable constitution. And there is a

65 still greater absurdity in subjecting the decisions of men selected for their knowledge of the laws, acquired by long and laborious study, to the revision and control of men, who for want of the same advantage cannot but be deficient in that knowledge. The members of the legislature will rarely be chosen with a view to those qualifications which fit men for the stations of judges; and as on this ac-

70 count there will be great reason to apprehend all the ill consequences of defective information; so on account of the natural propensity of such bodies to party divisions, there will be no less reason to fear, that the pestilential breath of faction may poison the fountains of justice. The habit of being continually marshalled on opposite sides, will be too apt to stifle the voice both of law and of equity.

75 These considerations teach us to applaud the wisdom of those states, who have committed the judicial power in the last resort, not to a part of the legislature, but to distinct and independent bodies of men. Contrary to the supposition of those, who have represented the plan of the convention in this respect as novel and unprecedented, it is but a copy of the constitutions of New-Hampshire,

80 Massachusetts, Pennsylvania, Delaware, Maryland, Virginia, North-Carolina, South-Carolina and Georgia; and the preference which has been given to these models is highly to be commended.

It is not true, in the second place, that the parliament of Great Britain, or the legislatures of the particular states, can rectify the exceptionable decisions of their

85 respective courts, in any other sense than might be done by a future legislature of the United States. The theory neither of the British, nor the state constitutions, authorises the revisal of a judicial sentence, by a legislative act. Nor is there any thing in the proposed constitution more than in either of them, by which it is forbidden. In the former as well as in the latter, the impropriety of the thing, on the

90 general principles of law and reason, is the sole obstacle. A legislature without exceeding its province cannot reverse a determination once made, in a particular case; though it may prescribe a new rule for future cases. This is the principle, and it applies in all its consequences, exactly in the same manner and extent, to the state governments, as to the national government, now under consideration. Not

95 the least difference can be pointed out in any view of the subject.

It may in the last place be observed that the supposed danger of judiciary encroachments on the legislative authority, which has been upon many occasions reiterated, is in reality a phantom. Particular misconstructions and contraventions of the will of the legislature may now and then happen; but they can never

100 be so extensive as to amount to an inconvenience, or in any sensible degree to

affect the order of the political system. This may be inferred with certainty from the general nature of the judicial power; from the objects to which it relates; from the manner in which it is exercised; from its comparative weakness, and from its total incapacity to support its usurpations by force. And the inference is greatly fortified by the consideration of the important constitutional check,   *105* which the power of instituting impeachments, in one part of the legislative body, and of determining upon them in the other, would give to that body upon the members of the judicial department This is alone a complete security. There never can be danger that the judges, by a series of deliberate usurpations on the authority of the legislature, would hazard the united resentment of the body en-   *110* trusted with it, while this body was possessed of the means of punishing their presumption by degrading them from their stations. While this ought to remove all apprehensions on the subject, it affords at the same time a cogent argument for constituting the senate a court for the trial of impeachments.

Having now examined, and I trust removed the objections to the distinct and   *115* independent organization of the supreme court, I proceed to consider the propriety of the power of constituting inferior courts,* and the relations which will subsist between these and the former.

The power of constituting inferior courts is evidently calculated to obviate the necessity of having recourse to the supreme court, in every case of federal cog-   *120* nizance. It is intended to enable the national government to institute or *authorise* in each state or district of the United States, a tribunal competent to the determination of matters of national jurisdiction within its limits.

But why, it is asked, might not the same purpose have been accomplished by the instrumentality of the state courts? This admits of different answers. Though   *125* the fitness and competency of those courts should be allowed in the utmost latitude; yet the substance of the power in question, may still be regarded as a necessary part of the plan, if it were only to empower the national legislature to commit to them the cognizance of causes arising out of the national constitution. To confer the power of determining such causes upon the existing courts of   *130* the several states, would perhaps be as much "to constitute tribunals," as to create new courts with the like power. But ought not a more direct and explicit provision to have been made in favour of the state courts? There are, in my opinion, substantial reasons against such a provision: The most discerning cannot foresee how far the prevalency of a local spirit may be found to disqualify the local tri-   *135* bunals for the jurisdiction of national causes; whilst every man may discover that

---

* This power has been absurdly represented as intended to abolish all the county courts in the several states, which are commonly called inferior courts. But the expressions of the constitution are to constitute "tribunals INFERIOR TO THE SUPREME COURT," and the evident design of the provision is to enable the institution of local courts subordinate to the supreme, either in states or larger districts. It is ridiculous to imagine that county courts were in contemplation.

courts constituted like those of some of the states, would be improper channels of the judicial authority of the union. State judges, holding their offices during pleasure, or from year to year, will be too little independent to be relied upon for
140 an inflexible execution of the national laws. And if there was a necessity for confiding the original cognizance of causes arising under those laws to them, there would be a correspondent necessity for leaving the door of appeal as wide as possible. In proportion to the grounds of confidence in, or diffidence of the subordinate tribunals, ought to be the facility or difficulty of appeals. And well satisfied
145 as I am of the propriety of the appellate jurisdiction in the several classes of causes to which it is extended by the plan of the convention, I should consider every thing calculated to give in practice, an *unrestrained course* to appeals as a source of public and private inconvenience.

I am not sure but that it will be found highly expedient and useful to divide
150 the United States into four or five, or half a dozen districts; and to institute a federal court in each district, in lieu of one in every state. The judges of these courts, with the aid of the state judges, may hold circuits for the trial of causes in the several parts of the respective districts. Justice through them may be administered with ease and dispatch; and appeals may be safely circumscribed within a very
155 narrow compass. This plan appears to me at present the most eligible of any that could be adopted, and in order to it, it is necessary that the power of constituting inferior courts should exist in the full extent in which it is to be found in the proposed constitution.

These reasons seem sufficient to satisfy a candid mind, that the want of such a
160 power would have been a great defect in the plan. Let us now examine in what manner the judicial authority is to be distributed between the supreme and the inferior courts of the union.

The supreme court is to be invested with original jurisdiction, only "in cases affecting ambassadors, other public ministers and consuls, and those in which A
165 STATE shall be a party." Public ministers of every class, are the immediate representatives of their sovereigns. All questions in which they are concerned, are so directly connected with the public peace, that as well for the preservation of this, as out of respect to the sovereignties they represent, it is both expedient and proper, that such questions should be submitted in the first instance to the high-
170 est judiciary of the nation. Though consuls have not in strictness a diplomatic character, yet as they are the public agents of the nations to which they belong, the same observation is in a great measure applicable to them. In cases in which a state might happen to be a party, it would ill suit its dignity to be turned over to an inferior tribunal.

175 Though it may rather be a digression from the immediate subject of this paper, I shall take occasion to mention here, a supposition which has excited some alarm upon very mistaken grounds: It has been suggested that an assignment of the public securities of one state to the citizens of another, would enable them to prosecute that state in the federal courts for the amount of those securities. A sug-
180 gestion which the following considerations prove to be without foundation.

It is inherent in the nature of sovereignty, not to be amenable to the suit of an individual *without its consent*. This is the general sense and the general practice of mankind; and the exemption, as one of the attributes of sovereignty, is now enjoyed by the government of every state in the union. Unless therefore, there is a surrender of this immunity in the plan of the convention, it will remain with the *185* states, and the danger intimated must be merely ideal. The circumstances which are necessary to produce an alienation of state sovereignty, were discussed in considering the article of taxation, and need not be repeated here. A recurrence to the principles there established will satisfy us, that there is no colour to pretend that the state governments, would by the adoption of that plan, be divested of the priv- *190* ilege of paying their own debts in their own way, free from every constraint but that which flows from the obligations of good faith. The contracts between a nation and individuals are only binding on the conscience of the sovereign, and have no pretensions to a compulsive force. They confer no right of action independent of the sovereign will. To what purpose would it be to authorise suits *195* against states, for the debts they owe? How could recoveries be enforced? It is evident that it could not be done without waging war against the contracting state; and to ascribe to the federal courts, by mere implication, and in destruction of a pre-existing right of the state governments, a power which would involve such a consequence, would be altogether forced and unwarrantable. *200*

Let us resume the train of our observations; we have seen that the original jurisdiction of the supreme court would be confined to two classes of causes, and those of a nature rarely to occur. In all other causes of federal cognizance, the original jurisdiction would appertain to the inferior tribunals, and the supreme court would have nothing more than an appellate jurisdiction, "with such *excep-* *205* *tions*, and under such *regulations* as the congress shall make."

The propriety of this appellate jurisdiction has been scarcely called in question in regard to matters of law; but the clamours have been loud against it as applied to matters of fact. Some well intentioned men in this state, deriving their notions from the language and forms which obtain in our courts, have been induced to *210* consider it as an implied supersedure of the trial by jury, in favour of the civil law

---

Lines 181–200 In *Chisholm v. Georgia* 2 Dallas 419 (1793), the first great case determined by the Supreme Court, which arose from an action by a citizen of South Carolina against the State of Georgia, the Court ignored Publius and sustained the action. Old Anti-Federalist fears of consolidation were reawakened by the Court's claim that for the purposes of the Constitution, states were not sovereignties. The further result was the passage of the 11th Amendment in 1798, which declared that states could not be sued by citizens of other states, or of foreign states.

Lines 207–29 This paragraph raises an old controversy about the powers of juries. The legal profession in general maintained that the role of the jury was confined to determining matters of fact (e.g., whether an alleged act had occurred or not). It was for the court to determine any question of law. This, of course, involved interpreting

mode of trial, which prevails in our courts of admiralty, probates and chancery. A technical sense has been affixed to the term "appellate", which in our law parlance is commonly used in reference to appeals in the course of the civil law. But if I am not misinformed, the same meaning would not be given to it in any part of New-England. There an appeal from one jury to another is familiar both in language and practice, and is even a matter of course, until there have been two verdicts on one side. The word "appellate" therefore will not be understood in the same sense in New-England as in New-York, which shews the impropriety of a technical interpretation derived from the jurisprudence of any particular state. The expression taken in the abstract, denotes nothing more than the power of one tribunal to review the proceedings of another, either as to the law or fact, or both. The mode of doing it may depend on ancient custom or legislative provision, (in a new government it must depend on the latter) and may be with or without the aid of a jury, as may be judged adviseable. If therefore the re-examination of a fact, once determined by a jury, should in any case be admitted under the proposed constitution, it may be so regulated as to be done by a second jury, either by remanding the cause to the court below for a second trial of the fact, or by directing an issue immediately out of the supreme court.

But it does not follow that the re-examination of a fact once ascertained by a jury, will be permitted in the supreme court. Why may it not be said, with the strictest propriety, when a writ of error is brought from an inferior to a superior court

---

the character of the act: criminally, whether a homicide was murder or manslaughter, or whether a publication was fair comment or seditious libel. For many people of republican tendencies, this threatened to take fundamental liberties out of the hands of the people, represented by the jury, and place them in the hands of judges, who were sometimes believed to be agents of government. The issue was no less contentious in Britain, where it was resolved by the passage of Fox's Libel Act in 1792, which settled the matter in the jury's favor. In New York in the early years of the 19th century, a prosecution at common law for conspiracy (in the absence of local statutes) was conducted against trade unionists, for conspiring to raise their wages, notwithstanding the statutory liberalization of British common law, on which the prosecutions in principle rested.

Hamilton's remark about the system in Massachusetts of appeal from one jury to another (on which, by his own "if I am not misinformed" [line 215], he has no documentary information), is by no means clear. But he presumably means only that a successful appeal normally led to a retrial before a second jury. During the 18th century, increasing numbers of criminal cases were heard before juries, who acquitted much more often than magistrates had. Jury trials in civil cases declined. However, controversies over juries in the ten or twelve years before the battle of Lexington nearly all involved civil cases.

Line 232 A "writ of error" is a writ issued by an appellate court to a court of record, ordering it to send up the record of a trial so that the appellate court may determine whether alleged errors occurred during the trial. The appellate court may reverse, correct, or affirm the earlier judgment but will not conduct a new trial.

of law in this state, that the latter has jurisdiction of the fact, as well as the law? It is true it cannot institute a new enquiry concerning the fact, but it takes cognizance of it as it appears upon the record, and pronounces the law arising upon it.* This is jurisdiction of both fact and law, nor is it even possible to separate them. Though the common law courts of this state ascertain disputed facts by a jury, yet they unquestionably have jurisdiction of both fact and law; and accordingly, when the former is agreed in the pleadings, they have no recourse to a jury, but proceed at once to judgment. I contend therefore on this ground, that the expressions, "appellate jurisdiction, both as to law and fact," do not necessarily imply a re-examination in the supreme court of facts decided by juries in the inferior courts.

The following train of ideas may well be imagined to have influenced the convention in relation to this particular provision. The appellate jurisdiction of the supreme court (may it have been argued) will extend to causes determinable in different modes, some in the course of the COMMON LAW, and others in the course of the CIVIL LAW. In the former, the revision of the law only, will be, generally speaking, the proper province of the supreme court; in the latter, the re-examination of the fact is agreeable to usage, and in some cases, of which prize causes are an example, might be essential to the preservation of the public peace. It is therefore necessary, that the appellate jurisdiction should, in certain cases, extend in the broadest sense to matters of fact. It will not answer to make an express exception of cases, which shall have been originally tried by a jury, because in the courts of some of the states, *all causes* are tried in this mode;† and

235

240

245

250

* This word is a compound of JUS and DICTIO, juris, dictio, or a speaking or pronouncing of the law.

† I hold that the states will have concurrent jurisdiction with the subordinate federal judicatories, in many cases of federal cognizance, as will be explained in my next paper.

Lines 243–44 The Convention appears from the records to have spent considerably more time on the method of making judicial appointments than on questions of jurisdiction. The jurisdiction of the Supreme Court is recorded, without reported discussion, in Max Farrand, *Records of the Federal Convention of 1787* (New Haven, 1937, reprinted 1966), I, 120, 132, 220, 232, 238–39. Madison expressed himself as opposed to appointment by the legislature "or any numerous body," since such bodies were subject to bargains and intrigues (see Farrand, I, 120).

Lines 244–61 Common law was the body of law and legal procedure generally received into the colonies from England, though variously adapted in different colonies. It was still in force unless specifically repealed by local legislation. Civil law is defined by *Black's Law Dictionary* (St. Paul: West Publishing, 1983) as "The body of law which every particular nation, commonwealth, or city has established peculiarly for itself; more properly called 'municipal law,' to distinguish it from the 'law of nature,' or international law." Hamilton, a New York lawyer, was presumably familiar with both procedures. The aim of the argument is to justify a general power of review in the Supreme Court.

255 such an exception would preclude the revision of matters of fact, as well where it might be proper, as where it might be improper. To avoid all inconveniencies, it will be safest to declare generally, that the supreme court shall possess appellate jurisdiction, both as to law and *fact*, and that this jurisdiction shall be subject to such *exceptions* and regulations as the national legislature may prescribe. This
260 will enable the government to modify it in such a manner as will best answer the ends of public justice and security.

This view of the matter, at any rate puts it out of all doubt that the supposed *abolition* of the trial by jury, by the operation of this provision, is fallacious and untrue. The legislature of the United States would certainly have full power to
265 provide that in appeals to the supreme court there should be no re-examination of facts where they had been tried in the original causes by juries. This would certainly be an authorised exception; but if for the reason already intimated it should be thought too extensive, it might be qualified with a limitation to such causes only as are determinable at common law in that mode of trial.

270 The amount of the observations hitherto made on the authority of the judicial department is this—that it has been carefully restricted to those causes which are manifestly proper for the cognizance of the national judicature, that in the partition of this authority a very small portion of original jurisdiction has been reserved to the supreme court, and the rest consigned to the subordinate
275 tribunals—that the supreme court will possess an appellate jurisdiction both as to law and fact in all the cases referred to them, but subject to any *exceptions* and *regulations* which may be thought adviseable; that this appellate jurisdiction does in no case *abolish* the trial by jury, and that an ordinary degree of prudence and integrity in the national councils will insure us solid advantages from the es-
280 tablishment of the proposed judiciary, without exposing us to any of the inconveniencies which have been predicted from that source.

PUBLIUS.

EIGHTY-TWO

ALEXANDER HAMILTON
May 28, 1788
**A Further View of the Judicial Department,
in Reference to Some Miscellaneous Questions**

To the People of the State of New York.

The erection of a new government, whatever care or wisdom may distinguish the work, cannot fail to originate questions of intricacy and nicety; and these may in a particular manner be expected to flow from the establishment of a constitution founded upon the total or partial incorporation of a number of distinct sovereignties. 'Tis time only that can mature and perfect so compound a system, can liquidate the meaning of all the parts, and can adjust them to each other in a harmonious and consistent WHOLE.

Such questions accordingly have arisen upon the plan proposed by the convention, and particularly concerning the judiciary department. The principal of these respect the situation of the state courts in regard to those causes, which are to be submitted to federal jurisdiction. Is this to be exclusive, or are those courts to possess a concurrent jurisdiction? If the latter, in what relation will they stand to the national tribunals? These are inquiries which we meet with in the mouths of men of sense, and which are certainly intitled to attention.

The principles established in a former paper* teach us, that the states will retain all *pre-existing* authorities, which may not be exclusively delegated to the federal head; and that this exclusive delegation can only exist in one of three cases; where an exclusive authority is in express terms granted to the union; or where a particular authority is granted to the union, and the exercise of a like authority is prohibited to the states, or where an authority is granted to the union with which a similar authority in the states would be utterly incompatible. Though these principles may not apply with the same force to the judiciary as to the legislative power; yet I am inclined to think that they are in the main just with respect to the former as well as the latter. And under this impression I shall

* Vol. 1, No. XXXII.

Lines 1–7 This paragraph has general interpretative significance, since it implicitly recognizes the organic, unfixed character of the Constitution. Note the archaic "liquidate" (elucidate), which has connotations that are quite incompatible with the concept of a structure that is rigid by its essence, and raises serious difficulties for modern appeals to "original intent."

25   lay it down as a rule that the state courts will *retain* the jurisdiction they now have, unless it appears to be taken away in one of the enumerated modes.

    The only thing in the proposed constitution, which wears the appearance of confining the causes of federal cognizance to the federal courts is contained in this passage — "The JUDICIAL POWER of the United States *shall be vested* in

30   one supreme court, and in *such* inferior courts as the congress shall from time to time ordain and establish." This might either be construed to signify, that the supreme and subordinate courts of the union should alone have the power of deciding those causes, to which their authority is to extend; or simply to denote that the organs of the national judiciary should be one supreme court and as many

35   subordinate courts as congress should think proper to appoint, or in other words, that the United States should exercise the judicial power with which they are to be invested through one supreme tribunal and a certain number of inferior ones to be instituted by them. The first excludes, the last admits the concurrent jurisdiction of the state tribunals: And as the first would amount to an alienation of

40   state power by implication, the last appears to me the most natural and the most defensible construction.

    But this doctrine of concurrent jurisdiction is only clearly applicable to those descriptions of causes of which the state courts have previous cognizance. It is not equally evident in relation to cases which may grow out of, and be *peculiar* to

45   the constitution to be established: For not to allow the state courts a right of jurisdiction in such cases can hardly be considered as the abridgement of a preexisting authority. I mean not therefore to contend that the United States in the course of legislation upon the objects entrusted to their direction may not commit the decision of causes arising upon a particular regulation to the federal

50   courts solely, if such a measure should be deemed expedient; but I hold that the state courts will be divested of no part of their primitive jurisdiction, further than may relate to an appeal; and I am even of opinion, that in every case in which they were not expressly excluded by the future acts of the national legislature, they will of course take cognizance of the causes to which those acts may give

55   birth. This I infer from the nature of judiciary power, and from the general genius of the system. The judiciary power of every government looks beyond its own local or municipal laws, and in civil cases lays hold of all subjects of litigation between parties within its jurisdiction though the causes of dispute are relative to the laws of the most distant part of the globe. Those of Japan not less than

60   of New-York may furnish the objects of legal discussion to our courts. When in addition to this, we consider the state governments and the national governments as they truly are, in the light of kindred systems and as parts of ONE WHOLE, the inference seems to be conclusive that the state courts would have a concurrent jurisdiction in all cases arising under the laws of the union, where it was not

65   expressly prohibited.

Lines 29–31 Article 3, Section 1.

Here another question occurs—what relation would subsist between the national and state courts in these instances of concurrent jurisdiction? I answer that an appeal would certainly lie from the latter to the supreme court of the United States. The constitution in direct terms, gives an appellate jurisdiction to the supreme court in all the enumerated cases of federal cognizance, in which it is not to have an original one; without a single expression to confine its operation to the inferior federal courts. The objects of appeal, not the tribunals from which it is to be made, are alone contemplated. From this circumstance and from the reason of the thing it ought to be construed to extend to the state tribunals. Either this must be the case, or the local courts must be excluded from a concurrent jurisdiction in matters of national concern, else the judiciary authority of the union may be eluded at the pleasure of every plaintiff or prosecutor. Neither of these consequences ought without evident necessity to be involved; the latter would be entirely inadmissible, as it would defeat some of the most important and avowed purposes of the proposed government, and would essentially embarrass its measures. Nor do I perceive any foundation for such a supposition. Agreeably to the remark already made, the national and state systems are to be regarded as ONE WHOLE. The courts of the latter will of course be natural auxiliaries to the execution of the laws of the union, and an appeal from them will as naturally lie to that tribunal, which is destined to unite and assimilate the principles of national justice and the rules of national decisions. The evident aim of the plan of the convention is that all the causes of the specified classes, shall for weighty public reasons receive their original or final determination in the courts of the union. To confine therefore the general expressions giving appellate jurisdiction to the supreme court to appeals from the subordinate federal courts, instead of allowing their extension to the state courts, would be to abridge the latitude of the terms, in subversion of the intent, contrary to every sound rule of interpretation.

But could an appeal be made to lie from the state courts to the subordinate federal judicatories? This is another of the questions which have been raised, and of greater difficulty than the former. The following considerations countenance the affirmative. The plan of the convention in the first place authorises the national legislature "to constitute tribunals inferior to the supreme court."* It declares in the next place that, "the JUDICIAL POWER of the United States *shall be vested* in one supreme court and in such inferior courts as congress shall ordain and establish"; and it then proceeds to enumerate the cases to which this judicial power shall extend. It afterwards divides the jurisdiction of the supreme court into original and appellate, but gives no definition of that of the subordinate courts. The only outlines described for them are that they shall be "inferior to the supreme court" and that they shall not exceed the specified limits of the

* Section 8th, Article 1st.

federal judiciary. Whether their authority shall be original or appellate or both is not declared. All this seems to be left to the discretion of the legislature. And this being the case, I perceive at present no impediment to the establishment of an appeal from the state courts to the subordinate national tribunals; and many advantages attending the power of doing it may be imagined. It would diminish the motives to the multiplication of federal courts, and would admit of arrangements calculated to contract the appellate jurisdiction of the supreme court. The state tribunals may then be left with a more entire charge of federal causes; and appeals in most cases in which they may be deemed proper instead of being carried to the supreme court, may be made to lie from the state courts to district courts of the union.

PUBLIUS.

EIGHTY-THREE

ALEXANDER HAMILTON
May 28, 1788
**A Further View of the Judicial Department,
in Relation to the Trial By Jury**

To the People of the State of New York.

The objection to the plan of the convention, which has met with most success in
this state, and perhaps in several of the other states, is *that* relative to *the want of
a constitutional provision* for the trial by jury in civil cases. The disingenuous
form in which this objection is usually stated, has been repeatedly adverted to
and exposed; but continues to be pursued in all the conversations and writings of   5
the opponents of the plan. The mere silence of the constitution in regard to *civil
causes*, is represented as an abolition of the trial by jury; and the declamations to
which it has afforded a pretext, are artfully calculated to induce a persuasion that
this pretended abolition is complete and universal; extending not only to every
species of civil, but even to *criminal causes*. To argue with respect to the latter,   10
would, however, be as vain and fruitless, as to attempt the serious proof of the *existence* of *matter*, or to demonstrate any of those propositions which by their own
internal evidence force conviction, when expressed in language adapted to convey their meaning.

With regard to civil causes, subtleties almost too contemptible for refutation,   15
have been adopted to countenance the surmise that a thing, which is only *not
provided for*, is entirely *abolished*. Every man of discernment must at once perceive the wide difference between *silence* and *abolition*. But as the inventors of
this fallacy have attempted to support it by certain *legal maxims* of interpretation,
which they have perverted from their true meaning, it may not be wholly useless   20
to explore the ground they have taken.

The maxims on which they rely are of this nature, "a specification of particulars is an exclusion of generals"; or, "the expression of one thing is the exclusion
of another." Hence, say they, as the constitution has established the trial by jury
in criminal cases, and is silent in respect to civil, this silence is an implied prohi-   25
bition of trial by jury in regard to the latter.

The rules of legal interpretation are rules of *common sense*, adopted by the
courts in the construction of the laws. The true test therefore, of a just application of them, is its conformity to the source from which they are derived. This

---

Lines 1–14 See, for example, Brutus, Essay II, November 1, 1787.

30 being the case, let me ask if it is consistent with reason or common sense to suppose, that a provision obliging the legislative power to commit the trial of criminal causes to juries, is a privation of its right to authorise or permit that mode of trial in other cases? Is it natural to suppose, that a command to do one thing, is a prohibition to the doing of another, which there was a previous power to do, and which is

35 not incompatible with the thing commanded to be done? If such a supposition would be unnatural and unreasonable, it cannot be rational to maintain that an injunction of the trial by jury in certain cases is an interdiction of it in others.

A power to constitute courts, is a power to prescribe the mode of trial; and consequently, if nothing was said in the constitution on the subject of juries, the

40 legislature would be at liberty either to adopt that institution, or to let it alone. This discretion in regard to criminal causes is abridged by the express injunction of trial by jury in all such cases; but it is of course left at large in relation to civil causes, there being a total silence on this head. The specification of an obligation to try all criminal causes in a particular mode, excludes indeed the obliga-

45 tion or necessity of employing the same mode in civil causes, but does not abridge *the power* of the legislature to exercise that mode if it should be thought proper. The pretence therefore, that the national legislature would not be at full liberty to submit all the civil causes of federal cognizance to the determination of juries, is a pretence destitute of all just foundation.

50 From these observations, this conclusion results, that the trial by jury in civil cases would not be abolished, and that the use attempted to be made of the maxims which have been quoted, is contrary to reason and common sense, and therefore not admissible. Even if these maxims had a precise technical sense, corresponding with the ideas of those who employ them upon the present occa-

55 sion, which, however, is not the case, they would still be inapplicable to a constitution of government. In relation to such a subject, the natural and obvious sense of its provisions, apart from any technical rules, is the true criterion of construction.

Having now seen that the maxims relied upon will not bear the use made of them, let us endeavour to ascertain their proper use and true meaning. This will

60 be best done by examples. The plan of the convention declares that the power of congress or in other words of the *national legislature,* shall extend to certain enumerated cases. This specification of particulars evidently excludes all pretension to a general legislative authority; because an affirmative grant of special powers would be absurd as well as useless, if a general authority was intended.

65 In like manner, the judicial authority of the federal judicatures, is declared by the constitution to comprehend certain cases particularly specified. The expression of those cases marks the precise limits beyond which the federal courts cannot extend their jurisdiction; because the objects of their cognizance being enumerated, the specification would be nugatory if it did not exclude all ideas of

70 more extensive authority.

These examples might be sufficient to elucidate the maxims which have been mentioned, and designate the manner in which they should be used. But that there may be no possibility of misapprehension upon this subject I shall add one case more, to demonstrate the proper use of these maxims, and the abuse which has been made of them.   *75*

Let us suppose that by the laws of this state, a married woman was incapable of conveying her estate, and that the legislature, considering this as an evil, should enact that she might dispose of her property by deed executed in the presence of a magistrate. In such a case there can be no doubt but the specification would amount to an exclusion of any other mode of conveyance; because the woman *80* having no previous power to alienate her property, the specification determines the particular mode which she is, for that purpose, to avail herself of. But let us further suppose that in a subsequent part of the same act it should be declared that no woman should dispose of any estate of a determinate value without the consent of three of her nearest relations, signified by their signing the deed; could it be in- *85* ferred from this regulation that a married woman might not procure the approba- tion of her relations to a deed for conveying property of inferior value? The position is too absurd to merit a refutation, and yet this is precisely the position which those must establish who contend that the trial by juries, in civil cases, is abolished, because it is expressly provided for in cases of a criminal nature.   *90*

From these observations it must appear unquestionably true that trial by jury is in no case abolished by the proposed constitution, and it is equally true that in those controversies between individuals in which the great body of the people are likely to be interested, that institution will remain precisely in the same situ- ation in which it is placed by the state constitutions, and will be in no degree al- *95* tered or influenced by the adoption of the plan under consideration. The foundation of this assertion is that the national judiciary will have no cognizance of them, and of course they will remain determinable as heretofore by the state courts only, and in the manner which the state constitutions and laws prescribe. All land causes, except where claims under the grants of different states come *100* into question, and all other controversies between the citizens of the same state, unless where they depend upon positive violations of the articles of union by acts of the state legislatures, will belong exclusively to the jurisdiction of the state tri- bunals. Add to this that admiralty causes, and almost all those which are of equity jurisdiction are determinable under our own government without the interven- *105* tion of a jury, and the inference from the whole will be that this institution, as it exists with us at present, cannot possibly be affected to any great extent by the proposed alteration in our system of government.

The friends and adversaries of the plan of the convention, if they agree in nothing else, concur at least in the value they set upon the trial by jury: Or if *110* there is any difference between them, it consists in this; the former regard it as a valuable safeguard to liberty, the latter represent it as the very palladium of free government. For my own part, the more the operation of the institution has fallen

---

Lines 113–28 Here Hamilton almost discards the collective identity and speaks as a professional lawyer.

under my observation, the more reason I have discovered for holding it in high
estimation; and it would be altogether superfluous to examine to what extent it
deserves to be esteemed useful or essential in a representative republic, or how
much more merit it may be entitled to as a defence against the oppressions of an
hereditary monarch, than as a barrier to the tyranny of popular magistrates in a
popular government. Discussions of this kind would be more curious than beneficial, as all are satisfied of the utility of the institution, and of its friendly aspect
to liberty. But I must acknowledge that I cannot readily discern the inseparable
connection between the existence of liberty and the trial by jury in civil cases. Arbitrary impeachments, arbitrary methods of prosecuting pretended offences, and
arbitrary punishments upon arbitrary convictions have ever appeared to me to be
the great engines of judicial despotism; and these have all relation to criminal
proceedings. The trial by jury in criminal cases, aided by the *habeas corpus* act,
seems therefore to be alone concerned in the question. And both of these are
provided for in the most ample manner in the plan of the convention.

It has been observed, that trial by jury is a safeguard against an oppressive exercise of the power of taxation. This observation deserves to be canvassed.

It is evident that it can have no influence upon the legislature, in regard to the
amount of the taxes to be laid, to the *objects* upon which they are to be imposed,
or to the *rule* by which they are to be apportioned. If it can have any influence
therefore, it must be upon the mode of collection, and the conduct of the officers
entrusted with the execution of the revenue laws.

As to the mode of collection in this state, under our own constitution, the trial
by jury is in most cases out of use. The taxes are usually levied by the more summary proceeding of distress and sale, as in cases of rent. And it is acknowledged
on all hands, that this is essential to the efficacy of the revenue laws. The dilatory
course of a trial at law to recover the taxes imposed on individuals, would neither
suit the exigencies of the public, nor promote the convenience of the citizens. It
would often occasion an accumulation of costs, more burthensome than the
original sum of the tax to be levied.

And as to the conduct of the officers of the revenue, the provision in favor of
trial by jury in criminal cases, will afford the security aimed at. Wilful abuses of a
public authority, to the oppression of the subject, and every species of official ex-
tortion, are offences against the government; for which, the persons who commit
them, may be indicted and punished according to the circumstances of the case.

The excellence of the trial by jury in civil cases, appears to depend on circumstances foreign to the preservation of liberty. The strongest argument in its
favour is, that it is a security against corruption. As there is always more time and
better opportunity to tamper with a standing body of magistrates than with a jury

---

Lines 129–30 Hamilton does not offer a citation for this observation, and juries did
not customarily assess taxes.

summoned for the occasion, there is room to suppose, that a corrupt influence would more easily find its way to the former than to the latter. The force of this consideration, is however, diminished by others. The sheriff who is the sum- *155* moner of ordinary juries, and the clerks of courts who have the nomination of special juries, are themselves standing officers, and acting individually, may be supposed more accessible to the touch of corruption than the judges, who are a collective body. It is not difficult to see that it would be in the power of those of- ficers to select jurors who would serve the purpose of the party as well as a cor- *160* rupted bench. In the next place, it may fairly be supposed that there would be less difficulty in gaining some of the jurors promiscuously taken from the public mass, than in gaining men who had been chosen by the government for their probity and good character. But making every deduction for these considerations the trial by jury must still be a valuable check upon corruption. It greatly multi- *165* plies the impediments to its success. As matters now stand, it would be necessary to corrupt both court and jury; for where the jury have gone evidently wrong, the court will generally grant a new trial, and it would be in most cases of little use to practice upon the jury, unless the court could be likewise gained. Here then is a double security; and it will readily be perceived that this complicated agency *170* tends to preserve the purity of both institutions. By increasing the obstacles to success it discourages attempts to seduce the integrity of either. The temptations to prostitution, which the judges might have to surmount, must certainly be much fewer while the co-operation of a jury is necessary, than they might be if they had themselves the exclusive determination of all causes. *175*

Notwithstanding therefore the doubts I have expressed as to the essentiality of trial by jury, in civil cases, to liberty, I admit that it is in most cases, under proper regulations, an excellent method of determining questions of property; and that on this account alone it would be entitled to a constitutional provision in its favour, if it were possible to fix the limits within which it ought to be compre- *180* hended. There is however, in all cases, great difficulty in this; and men not blinded by enthusiasm, must be sensible that in a federal government which is a composition of societies whose ideas and institutions in relation to the matter materially vary from each other, that difficulty must be not a little augmented. For my own part, at every new view I take of the subject, I become more con- *185* vinced of the reality of the obstacles, which we are authoritatively informed, pre- vented the insertion of a provision on this head in the plan of the convention.

The great difference between the limits of the jury trial in different states is not generally understood. And as it must have considerable influence on the sen- tence we ought to pass upon the omission complained of, in regard to this point, *190* an explanation of it is necessary. In this state our judicial establishments resemble more nearly, than in any other, those of Great-Britain. We have courts of com- mon law, courts of probates (analogous in certain matters to the spiritual courts

---

Line 193 "Spiritual courts" refers to ecclesiastical courts.

in England) a court of admiralty, and a court of chancery. In the courts of common law only the trial by jury prevails, and this with some exceptions. In all the
others a single judge presides and proceeds in general either according to the
course of the cannon or civil law, without the aid of a jury.* In New-Jersey there
is a court of chancery which proceeds like ours, but neither courts of admiralty,
nor of probates, in the sense in which these last are established with us. In that
state the courts of common law have the cognizance of those causes, which with
us are determinable in the courts of admiralty and of probates, and of course the
jury trial is more extensive in New-Jersey than in New-York. In Pennsylvania this
is perhaps still more the case, for there is no court of chancery in that state, and
its common law courts have equity jurisdiction. It has a court of admiralty, but
none of probates, at least on the plan of ours. Delaware has in these respects imitated Pennsylvania. Maryland approaches more nearly to New-York, as does also
Virginia, except that the latter has a plurality of chancellors. North-Carolina
bears most affinity to Pennsylvania; South-Carolina to Virginia. I believe however that in some of those states which have distinct courts of admiralty, the
causes depending in them are triable by juries. In Georgia there are none but
common law courts, and an appeal of course lies from the verdict of one jury to
another, which is called a special jury, and for which a particular mode of appointment is marked out. In Connecticut they have no distinct courts, either of
chancery or of admiralty, and their courts of probates have no jurisdiction of causes.
Their common law courts have admiralty, and to a certain extent, equity jurisdiction. In cases of importance their general assembly is the only court of chancery.
In Connecticut therefore the trial by jury extends in *practice* further than in
any other state yet mentioned. Rhode-Island is I believe in this particular pretty
much in the situation of Connecticut. Massachusetts and New-Hampshire,
in regard to the blending of law, equity and admiralty, jurisdictions are in a
similar predicament. In the four eastern states the trial by jury not only stands
upon a broader foundation than in the other states, but it is attended with a peculiarity unknown in its full extent to any of them. There is an appeal *of course*
from one jury to another till there have been two verdicts out of three on one
side.

From this sketch it appears, that there is a material diversity as well in the
modification as in the extent of the institution of trial by jury in civil cases in the
several states; and from this fact, these obvious reflections flow. First, that no general rule could have been fixed upon by the convention which would have cor-
responded with the circumstances of all the states; and secondly, that more, or at
least as much might have been hazarded, by taking the system of any one state

---

* It has been erroneously insinuated, with regard to the court of chancery, that this
court generally tries disputed facts by a jury. The truth is, that references to a jury in
that court rarely happen, and are in no case necessary, but where the validity of a
devise of land comes into question.

for a standard, as by omitting a provision altogether, and leaving the matter as it has been left, to legislative regulation.

The propositions which have been made for supplying the omission, have rather served to illustrate than to obviate the difficulty of the thing. The minority of Pennsylvania have proposed this mode of expression for the purpose—"trial by jury shall be as heretofore"—and this I maintain would be absolutely senseless and nugatory. The United States, in their united or collective capacity, are the OBJECT to which all general provisions in the constitution must necessarily be construed to refer. Now it is evident, that though trial by jury with various limitations is known in each state individually, yet in the United States *as such*, it is at this time altogether unknown, because the present federal government has no judiciary power whatever; and consequently there is no proper antecedent or previous establishment to which the term *heretofore* could relate. It would therefore be destitute of a precise meaning, and inoperative from its uncertainty.

As on the one hand, the form of the provision would not fulfil the intent of its proposers, so on the other, if I apprehend that intent rightly, it would be in itself inexpedient. I presume it to be, that causes in the federal courts should be tried by jury, if in the state where the courts sat, that mode of trial would obtain in a similar case in the state courts—that is to say admiralty causes should be tried in Connecticut by a jury, and in New-York without one. The capricious operation of so dissimilar a method of trial in the same cases, under the same government, is of itself sufficient to indispose every well regulated judgment towards it. Whether the cause should be tried with or without a jury, would depend in a great number of cases, on the accidental situation of the court and parties.

But this is not in my estimation the greatest objection. I feel a deep and deliberate conviction, that there are many cases in which the trial by jury is an ineligible one. I think it so particularly in cases which concern the public peace with foreign nations; that is in most cases where the question turns wholly on the laws of nations. Of this nature among others are all prize causes. Juries cannot be supposed competent to investigations, that require a thorough knowledge of the laws and usages of nations, and they will sometimes be under the influence of impressions which will not suffer them to pay sufficient regard to those considerations of public policy which ought to guide their enquiries. There would of course be always danger that the rights of other nations might be infringed by their decisions, so as to afford occasions of reprisal and war. Though the proper province of juries be to determine matters of fact, yet in most cases legal consequences are complicated with fact in such a manner as to render a separation impracticable.

It will add great weight to this remark in relation to prize causes to mention that the method of determining them has been thought worthy of particular regulation in various treaties between different powers of Europe, and that pursuant to such treaties they are determinable in Great-Britain in the last resort before the king himself in his privy council, where the fact as well as the law undergoes a re-examination. This alone demonstrates the impolicy of inserting a fundamental

235

240

245

250

255

260

265

270

275

provision in the constitution which would make the state systems a standard for the national government in the article under consideration, and the danger of incumbering the government with any constitutional provisions, the propriety of which is not indisputable.

280   My convictions are equally strong that great advantages result from the separation of the equity from the law jurisdiction; and that the causes which belong to the former would be improperly committed to juries. The great and primary use of a court of equity is to give relief *in extraordinary cases,* which are *exceptions** to general rules. To unite the jurisdiction of such cases with the ordinary
285 jurisdiction must have a tendency to unsettle the general rules and to subject every case that arises to a *special* determination. While the separation of the one from the other has the contrary effect of rendering one a sentinel over the other, and of keeping each within the expedient limits. Besides this the circumstances that constitute cases proper for courts of equity, are in many instances so nice
290 and intricate, that they are incompatible with the genius of trials by jury. They require often such long, deliberate and critical investigation as would be impracticable to men called from their occupations and obliged to decide before they were permitted to return to them. The simplicity and expedition which form the distinguishing characters of this mode of trial require that the matter to be de-
295 cided should be reduced to some single and obvious point; while the litigations usual in chancery frequently comprehend a long train of minute and independent particulars.

    It is true that the separation of the equity from the legal jurisdiction is peculiar to the English system of jurisprudence; which is the model that has been fol-
300 lowed in several of the states. But it is equally true, that the trial by jury has been unknown in every case in which they have been united. And the separation is essential to the preservation of that institution in its pristine purity. The nature of a court of equity will readily permit the extension of its jurisdiction to matters of law, but it is not a little to be suspected, that the attempt to extend the jurisdiction
305 of the courts of law to matters of equity will not only be unproductive of the advantages which may be derived from courts of chancery, on the plan upon which they are established in this state, but will tend gradually to change the nature of the courts of law, and to undermine the trial by jury, by introducing questions too complicated for a decision in that mode.

310   These appear to be conclusive reasons against incorporating the systems of all the states in the formation of the national judiciary; according to what may be conjectured to have been the intent of the Pennsylvania minority. Let us now examine how far the proposition of Massachusetts is calculated to remedy the supposed defect.

---

* It is true that the principles by which that relief is governed are now reduced to a regular system, but it is not the less true that they are in the main, applicable to SPECIAL circumstances which form exceptions to general rules.

It is in this form—"In civil actions between citizens of different states, every issue of fact, arising in *actions at common law*, may be tried by a jury, if the parties, or either of them, request it."

This at best is a proposition confined to one description of causes; and the inference is fair either that the Massachusetts convention considered that as the only class of federal causes, in which the trial by jury would be proper; or that if desirous of a more extensive provision, they found it impracticable to devise one which would properly answer the end. If the first, the omission of a regulation respecting so partial an object, can never be considered as a material imperfection in the system. If the last, it affords a strong corroboration of the extreme difficulty of the thing.

But this is not all: If we advert to the observations already made respecting the courts that subsist in the several states of the union, and the different powers exercised by them, it will appear, that there are no expressions more vague and indeterminate than those which have been employed to characterise *that* species of causes which it is intended shall be entitled to a trial by jury. In this state the boundaries between actions at common law and actions of equitable jurisdiction are ascertained in conformity to the rules which prevail in England upon that subject. In many of the other states, the boundaries are less precise. In some of them, every cause is to be tried in a court of common law, and upon that foundation every action may be considered as an action at common law, to be determined by a jury, if the parties or either of them chuse it. Hence the same irregularity and confusion would be introduced by a compliance with this proposition, that I have already noticed as resulting from the regulation proposed by the Pennsylvania minority. In one state a cause would receive its determination from a jury, if the parties or either of them requested it; but in another state a cause exactly similar to the other must be decided without the intervention of a jury, because the state judicatories varied as to common law jurisdiction.

It is obvious therefore that the Massachusetts proposition, upon this subject, cannot operate as a general regulation until some uniform plan, with respect to the limits of common law and equitable jurisdictions shall be adopted by the different states. To devise a plan of that kind is a task arduous in itself, and which it would require much time and reflection to mature. It would be extremely difficult, if not impossible, to suggest any general regulation that would be acceptable to all the states in the union, or that would perfectly quadrate with the several state institutions.

It may be asked, why could not a reference have been made to the constitution of this state, taking that, which is allowed by me to be a good one, as a standard for the United States? I answer that it is not very probable the other states should entertain the same opinion of our institutions which we do ourselves. It is

315

320

325

330

335

340

345

350

Lines 315–17 See F. N. Thorpe, *American Charters*, cited in No. 24, lines 11–15.

355 natural to suppose that they are hitherto more attached to their own, and that each would struggle for the preference. If the plan of taking one state as a model for the whole had been thought of in the convention, it is to be presumed that the adoption of it in that body, would have been rendered difficult by the predilection of each representation in favour of its own government; and it must
360 be uncertain which of the states would have been taken as the model. It has been shewn that many of them would be improper ones. And I leave it to conjecture whether, under all circumstances, it is most likely that New-York or some other state would have been preferred. But admit that a judicious selection could have been effected in the convention, still there would have been great danger of jeal-
365 ousy and disgust in the other states, at the partiality which had been shewn to the institutions of one. The enemies of the plan would have been furnished with a fine pretext for raising a host of local prejudices against it, which perhaps might have hazarded in no inconsiderable degree, its final establishment.

To avoid the embarrassments of a definition of the cases which the trial by
370 jury ought to embrace, it is some times suggested by men of enthusiastic tempers, that a provision might have been inserted for establishing it in all cases whatsoever. For this I believe no precedent is to be found in any member of the union; and the considerations which have been stated in discussing the proposition of the minority of Pennsylvania, must satisfy every sober mind that the estab-
375 lishment of the trial by jury in all cases, would have been an unpardonable error in the plan.

In short, the more it is considered, the more arduous will appear the task of fashioning a provision in such a form, as not to express too little to answer the purpose, or too much to be adviseable; or which might not have opened other
380 sources of opposition to the great and essential object of introducing a firm national government.

I cannot but persuade myself on the other hand, that the different lights in which the subject has been placed in the course of these observations, will go far towards removing in candid minds, the apprehensions they may have enter-
385 tained on the point. They have tended to shew that the security of liberty is materially concerned only in the trial by jury in criminal cases, which is provided for in the most ample manner in the plan of the convention; that even in far the greatest proportion of civil cases, and those in which the great body of the community is interested, that mode of trial will remain in its full force, as established
390 in the state constitutions, untouched and unaffected by the plan of the convention: That it is in no case abolished* by that plan; and that there are great if not insurmountable difficulties in the way of making any precise and proper provision for it in a constitution for the United States.

* Vide No. LXXXI, in which the supposition of its being abolished by the appellate jurisdiction in matters of fact being vested in the supreme court is examined and refuted.

The best judges of the matter will be the least anxious for a constitutional establishment of the trial by jury in civil cases, and will be the most ready to admit that the changes which are continually happening in the affairs of society, may render a different mode of determining questions of property, preferable in many cases, in which that mode of trial now prevails. For my own part, I acknowledge myself to be convinced that even in this state, it might be advantageously extended to some cases to which it does not at present apply, and might as advantageously be abridged in others. It is conceded by all reasonable men, that it ought not to obtain in all cases. The examples of innovations which contract its ancient limits, as well in these states as in Great-Britain, afford a strong presumption that its former extent has been found inconvenient; and give room to suppose that future experience may discover the propriety and utility of other exceptions. I suspect it to be impossible in the nature of the thing, to fix the salutary point at which the operation of the institution ought to stop; and this is with me a strong argument for leaving the matter to the discretion of the legislature.

This is now clearly understood to be the case in Great-Britain, and it is equally so in the state of Connecticut; and yet it may be safely affirmed, that more numerous encroachments have been made upon the trial by jury in this state since the revolution, though provided for by a positive article of our constitution, than has happened in the same time either in Connecticut or Great-Britain. It may be added that these encroachments have generally originated with the men who endeavour to persuade the people they are the warmest defenders of popular liberty, but who have rarely suffered constitutional obstacles to arrest them in a favourite career. The truth is that the general GENIUS of a government is all that can be substantially relied upon for permanent effects. Particular provisions, though not altogether useless, have far less virtue and efficacy than are commonly ascribed to them; and the want of them will never be with men of sound discernment a decisive objection to any plan which exhibits the leading characters of a good government.

It certainly sounds not a little harsh and extraordinary to affirm that there is no security for liberty in a constitution which expressly establishes the trial by jury in criminal cases, because it does not do it in civil also; while it is a notorious fact that Connecticut, which has been always regarded as the most popular state in the union, can boast of no constitutional provision for either.

PUBLIUS.

EIGHTY-FOUR

ALEXANDER HAMILTON
May 28, 1788
Concerning Several Miscellaneous Objections

To the People of the State of New York.

In the course of the foregoing review of the constitution I have taken notice of, and endeavoured to answer, most of the objections which have appeared against it. There however remain a few which either did not fall naturally under any particular head, or were forgotten in their proper places. These shall now be discussed; but as the subject has been drawn into great length, I shall so far consult brevity as to comprise all my observations on these miscellaneous points in a single paper.

The most considerable of these remaining objections is, that the plan of the convention contains no bill of rights. Among other answers given to this, it has been upon different occasions remarked, that the constitutions of several of the states are in a similar predicament. I add, that New-York is of this number. And yet the opposers of the new system in this state, who profess an unlimited admiration for its constitution, are among the most intemperate partizans of a bill of rights. To justify their zeal in this matter, they alledge two things; one is, that though the constitution of New-York has no bill of rights prefixed to it, yet it contains in the body of it various provisions in favour of particular privileges and rights, which in substance amount to the same thing; the other is, that the constitution adopts in their full extent the common and statute law of Great-Britain, by which many other rights not expressed in it are equally secured.

To the first I answer, that the constitution proposed by the convention contains, as well as the constitution of this state, a number of such provisions.

Independent of those, which relate to the structure of the government, we find the following:—Article I. section 3. clause 7. "Judgment in cases of impeachment shall not extend further than to removal from office, and disqualification to hold and enjoy any office of honour, trust or profit under the United

---

Lines 7–8 This is one of the commonest of Anti-Federalist complaints. See, for example, Brutus, Essay I, November 1, 1787, where the issues involved—and in some cases remedied by the Bill of Rights—are canvassed; and Essay IX, January 17, 1788. See also the *Address of the Minority of the Convention of Pennsylvania*, 3.11.32, December 18, 1787; and Agrippa, VI, November 13, 1787, who argues that a bill of rights, unlike the common law, will not be susceptible to change by the legislature. The arguments were to continue after the publication of this essay with Patrick Henry's speech in the Virginia Convention on June 5.

States; but the party convicted shall nevertheless be liable and subject to indict- 25
ment, trial, judgment and punishment, according to law."—Section 9. of the
same article, clause 2. "The privilege of the writ of *habeas corpus* shall not be suspended, unless when in cases of rebellion or invasion the public safety may require it."—Clause 3. "No bill of attainder or *ex post facto* law shall be
passed."—Clause 7. "No title of nobility shall be granted by the United States: 30
And no person holding any office of profit or trust under them, shall, without the
consent of the congress, accept of any present, emolument, office or title, of any
kind whatever, from any king, prince or foreign state."—Article III. section 2.
clause 3. "The trial of all crimes, except in cases of impeachment, shall be by
jury; and such trial shall be held in the state where the said crimes shall have 35
been committed; but when not committed within any state, the trial shall be at
such place or places as the congress may by law have directed."—Section 3, of
the same article, "Treason against the United States shall consist only in levying
war against them, or in adhering to their enemies, giving them aid and comfort.
No person shall be convicted of treason unless on the testimony of two witnesses 40
to the same overt act, or on confession in open court." And clause 3, of the same
section. "The congress shall have power to declare the punishment of treason,
but no attainder of treason shall work corruption of blood, or forfeiture, except
during the life of the person attainted."

It may well be a question whether these are not upon the whole, of equal im- 45
portance with any which are to be found in the constitution of this state. The establishment of the writ of *habeas corpus*, the prohibition of *ex post facto* laws, and
of TITLES OF NOBILITY, *to which we have no corresponding provisions in our
constitution*, are perhaps greater securities to liberty and republicanism than any
it contains. The creation of crimes after the commission of the fact, or in other 50
words, the subjecting of men to punishment for things which, when they were
done, were breaches of no law, and the practice of arbitrary imprisonments have
been in all ages the favourite and most formidable instruments of tyranny. The observations of the judicious Blackstone* in reference to the latter, are well worthy
of recital. "To bereave a man of life (says he) or by violence to confiscate his es- 55
tate, without accusation or trial, would be so gross and notorious an act of despotism, as must at once convey the alarm of tyranny throughout the whole nation;
but confinement of the person by secretly hurrying him to goal, where his suffer-
ings are unknown or forgotten, is a less public, a less striking, and therefore *a more
dangerous engine* of arbitrary government." And as a remedy for this fatal evil, he 60
is every where peculiarly emphatical in his encomiums on the *habeas corpus* act,
which in one place he calls "the BULWARK of the British constitution."†

---

* Vide Blackstone's Commentaries; vol. 1, page 136.

† Idem, vol. 4, page 438.

Nothing need be said to illustrate the importance of the prohibition of titles of nobility. This may truly be denominated the corner stone of republican govern-
65 ment; for so long as they are excluded, there can never be serious danger that the government will be any other than that of the people.

To the second, that is, to the pretended establishment of the common and statute law by the constitution, I answer, that they are expressly made subject "to such alterations and provisions as the legislature shall from time to time make
70 concerning the same." They are therefore at any moment liable to repeal by the ordinary legislative power, and of course have no constitutional sanction. The only use of the declaration was to recognize the ancient law, and to remove doubts which might have been occasioned by the revolution. This consequently can be considered as no part of a declaration of rights, which under our constitu-
75 tions must be intended as limitations of the power of the government itself.

It has been several times truly remarked, that bills of rights are in their origin, stipulations between kings and their subjects, abridgments of prerogative in favor of privilege, reservations of rights not surrendered to the prince. Such was MAGNA CHARTA, obtained by the Barons, sword in hand, from king John.
80 Such were the subsequent confirmations of that charter by subsequent princes. Such was the *petition of right* assented to by Charles the First, in the beginning of his reign. Such also was the declaration of right presented by the lords and commons to the prince of Orange in 1688, and afterwards thrown into the form of an act of parliament, called the bill of rights. It is evident, therefore, that ac-

---

Line 79 Magna Charta is incorrect spelling for the Latin "Magna Carta" or "the Great Charter" (as noted in the comment to No. 52, line 55). Often held by subsequent generations of common lawyers (instigated by Sir Edward Coke in the early 17th century), and later ideologues of liberty as the foundation document of the rights and liberties of the English people, it was wrested from King John at Runnymede in 1215 by rebellious barons and clergy. Although the charter was more interested in baronial privileges than the liberties of common people, it contained clauses that did extend more general principles of protection to common people—all "free men"—against arbitrary abuses of power and deprivations of customary sources of livelihood. Note the famous clause 30 (in the reissue of 1225): "To none will we sell, or deny, or delay, right or justice." This clause also contains the origins of the 5th Amendment's guarantee of "due process."

Line 81 The Petition of Right was a parliamentary protest addressed to Charles I in 1628, against arbitrary arrest and imprisonment, unparliamentary taxation, billeting of soldiers on civilians, and martial law over civilians; Charles accepted these conditions in return for a grant of supplies. But in 1629 he dissolved Parliament and ruled without recalling it until 1640.

Line 82 The Declaration of Right, which was later incorporated into the formal Bill of Rights of 1689, was presented to and accepted by William of Orange, by both houses of Parliament in 1688, as the conditions on which he would be elevated to the throne of England.

cording to their primitive signification, they have no application to constitutions 85
professedly founded upon the power of the people, and executed by their immediate representatives and servants. Here, in strictness, the people surrender nothing, and as they retain every thing, they have no need of particular reservations.
"WE THE PEOPLE of the United States, to secure the blessings of liberty to
ourselves and our posterity, do *ordain* and *establish* this constitution for the 90
United States of America." Here is a better recognition of popular rights than volumes of those aphorisms which make the principal figure in several of our state
bills of rights, and which would sound much better in a treatise of ethics than in
a constitution of government.

But a minute detail of particular rights is certainly far less applicable to a con- 95
stitution like that under consideration, which is merely intended to regulate the
general political interests of the nation, than to a constitution which has the regulation of every species of personal and private concerns. If therefore the loud
clamours against the plan of the convention on this score, are well founded, no
epithets of reprobation will be too strong for the constitution of this state. But the 100
truth is, that both of them contain all, which in relation to their objects, is reasonably to be desired.

I go further, and affirm that bills of rights, in the sense and in the extent in
which they are contended for, are not only unnecessary in the proposed constitution, but would even be dangerous. They would contain various exceptions to 105
powers which are not granted; and on this very account, would afford a
colourable pretext to claim more than were granted. For why declare that things
shall not be done which there is no power to do? Why for instance, should it be
said, that the liberty of the press shall not be restrained, when no power is given
by which restrictions may be imposed? I will not contend that such a provision 110
would confer a regulating power; but it is evident that it would furnish, to men
disposed to usurp, a plausible pretence for claiming that power. They might urge
with a semblance of reason, that the constitution ought not to be charged with
the absurdity of providing against the abuse of an authority, which was not given,
and that the provision against restraining the liberty of the press afforded a clear 115
implication, that a power to prescribe proper regulations concerning it, was intended to be vested in the national government. This may serve as a specimen of
the numerous handles which would be given to the doctrine of constructive powers, by the indulgence of an injudicious zeal for bills of rights.

On the subject of the liberty of the press, as much has been said, I cannot for- 120
bear adding a remark or two: In the first place, I observe that there is not a syllable concerning it in the constitution of this state, and in the next, I contend that
whatever has been said about it in that of any other state, amounts to nothing.

Lines 120–30 Historically, constitutional protection did not stand up particularly
well in light of the numerous prosecutions conducted under the Sedition Act of
1798—and that was *after* the passage of the 1st Amendment.

125 What signifies a declaration that "the liberty of the press shall be inviolably preserved?" What is the liberty of the press? Who can give it any definition which would not leave the utmost latitude for evasion? I hold it to be impracticable; and from this, I infer, that its security, whatever fine declarations may be inserted in any constitution respecting it, must altogether depend on public opinion, and on the general spirit of the people and of the government.* And here, after all, as inti-130 mated upon another occasion, must we seek for the only solid basis of all our rights.

There remains but one other view of this matter to conclude the point. The truth is, after all the declamation we have heard, that the constitution is itself in every rational sense, and to every useful purpose, A BILL OF RIGHTS. The several bills of rights, in Great-Britain, form its constitution, and conversely the con-135 stitution of each state is its bill of rights. And the proposed constitution, if adopted, will be the bill of rights of the union. Is it one object of a bill of rights to declare and specify the political privileges of the citizens in the structure and administration of the government? This is done in the most ample and precise manner in the plan of the convention, comprehending various precautions for 140 the public security, which are not to be found in any of the state constitutions. Is another object of a bill of rights to define certain immunities and modes of proceeding, which are relative to personal and private concerns? This we have seen has also been attended to, in a variety of cases, in the same plan. Adverting therefore to the substantial meaning of a bill of rights, it is absurd to allege that it is not

---

* To show that there is a power in the constitution by which the liberty of the press may be affected, recourse has been had to the power of taxation. It is said that duties may be laid upon publications so high as to amount to a prohibition. I know not by what logic it could be maintained that the declarations in the state constitutions, in favour of the freedom of the press, would be a constitutional impediment to the imposition of duties upon publications by the state legislatures. It cannot certainly be pretended that any degree of duties, however low, would be an abrigement of the liberty of the press. We know that newspapers are taxed in Great-Britain, and yet it is notorious that the press no where enjoys greater liberty than in that country. And if duties of any kind may be laid without a violation of that liberty, it is evident that the extent must depend on legislative discretion, regulated by public opinion; so that after all, general declarations respecting the liberty of the press will give it no greater security than it will have without them. The same invasions of it may be effected under the state constitutions which contain those declarations through the means of taxation, as under the proposed constitution which has nothing of the kind. It would be quite as significant to declare that government ought to be free, that taxes ought not to be excessive, &c., as that the liberty of the press ought not to be restrained.

Lines 125–29 Hamilton's observation that the liberty of the press would depend on public opinion was to prove a prophetic insight into the powers and limitations of constitutional government.

to be found in the work of the convention. It may be said that it does not go far 145
enough, though it will not be easy to make this appear; but it can with no propriety be contended that there is no such thing. It certainly must be immaterial
what mode is observed as to the order of declaring the rights of the citizens, if
they are to be found in any part of the instrument which establishes the government. And hence it must be apparent that much of what has been said on this 150
subject rests merely on verbal and nominal distinctions, which are entirely foreign from the substance of the thing.

Another objection, which has been made, and which from the frequency of
its repetition it is to be presumed is relied on, is of this nature: — It is improper
(say the objectors) to confer such large powers, as are proposed, upon the na- 155
tional government; because the seat of that government must of necessity be too
remote from many of the states to admit of a proper knowledge on the part of the
constituent, of the conduct of the representative body. This argument, if it proves
any thing, proves that there ought to be no general government whatever. For the
powers which it seems to be agreed on all hands, ought to be vested in the union, 160
cannot be safely intrusted to a body which is not under every requisite controul.
But there are satisfactory reasons to shew that the objection is in reality not well
founded. There is in most of the arguments which relate to distance a palpable
illusion of the imagination. What are the sources of information by which the
people in Montgomery county must regulate their judgment of the conduct of 165
their representatives in the state legislature? Of personal observation they can
have no benefit. This is confined to the citizens on the spot. They must therefore
depend on the information of intelligent men, in whom they confide—and how
must these men obtain their information? Evidently from the complection of
public measures, from the public prints, from correspondences with their repre- 170
sentatives, and with other persons who reside at the place of their deliberation.
This does not apply to Montgomery county only, but to all the counties, at any
considerable distance from the seat of government.

It is equally evident that the same sources of information would be open to
the people, in relation to the conduct of their representatives in the general gov- 175
ernment; and the impediments to a prompt communication which distance may
be supposed to create, will be overballanced by the effects of the vigilance of the
state governments. The executive and legislative bodies of each state will be so
many centinels over the persons employed in every department of the national
administration; and as it will be in their power to adopt and pursue a regular and 180
effectual system of intelligence, they can never be at a loss to know the behaviour
of those who represent their constituents in the national councils, and can readily communicate the same knowledge to the people. Their disposition to apprise
the community of whatever may prejudice its interests from another quarter, may
be relied upon, if it were only from the rivalship of power. And we may conclude 185
with the fullest assurance, that the people, through that channel, will be better
informed of the conduct of their national representatives, than they can be by
any means they now possess of that of their state representatives.

It ought also to be remembered, that the citizens who inhabit the country at and near the seat of government, will in all questions that affect the general liberty and prosperity, have the same interest with those who are at a distance; and that they will stand ready to sound the alarm when necessary, and to point out the actors in any pernicious project. The public papers will be expeditious messengers of intelligence to the most remote inhabitants of the union.

Among the many extraordinary objections which have appeared against the proposed constitution, the most extraordinary and the least colourable one, is derived from the want of some provision respecting the debts due *to* the United States. This has been represented as a tacit relinquishment of those debts, and as a wicked contrivance to screen public defaulters. The newspapers have teemed with the most inflammatory railings on this head; and yet there is nothing clearer than that the suggestion is entirely void of foundation, and is the offspring of extreme ignorance or extreme dishonesty. In addition to the remarks I have made upon the subject in another place, I shall only observe, that as it is a plain dictate of common sense, so it is also an established doctrine of political law, that *"states neither lose any of their rights, nor are discharged from any of their obligations by a change in the form of their civil government."* *

The last objection of any consequence which I at present recollect, turns upon the article of expence. If it were even true that the adoption of the proposed government would occasion a considerable increase of expence, it would be an objection that ought to have no weight against the plan. The great bulk of the citizens of America, are with reason convinced that union is the basis of their political happiness. Men of sense of all parties now, with few exceptions, agree that it cannot be preserved under the present system, nor without radical alterations; that new and extensive powers ought to be granted to the national head, and that these require a different organization of the federal government, a single body being an unsafe depository of such ample authorities. In conceding all this, the question of expence must be given up, for it is impossible, with any degree of safety, to narrow the foundation upon which the system is to stand. The two branches of the legislature are in the first instance, to consist of only sixty-five persons, which is the same number of which congress, under the existing confederation, may be composed. It is true that this number is intended to be increased; but this is to keep pace with the increase of the population and resources of the country. It is evident, that a less number would, even in the first instance, have been unsafe; and that a continuance of the present number would, in a more advanced stage of population, be a very inadequate representation of the people.

Whence is the dreaded augmentation of expence to spring? One source pointed out, is the multiplication of offices under the new government. Let us examine this a little.

---

* Vide Rutherford's Institutes, vol. 2. book II, chap. x. sect. xiv. and xv.—Vide also Grotius, book II, chap. ix. sect. viii. and ix.

It is evident that the principal departments of the administration under the   *230*
present government, are the same which will be required under the new. There
are now a secretary at war, a secretary for foreign affairs, a secretary for domestic
affairs, a board of treasury consisting of three persons, a treasurer, assistants,
clerks, &c. These offices are indispensable under any system, and will suffice
under the new as well as under the old. As to ambassadors and other ministers   *235*
and agents in foreign countries, the proposed constitution can make no other difference, than to render their characters, where they reside, more respectable,
and their services more useful. As to persons to be employed in the collection of
the revenues, it is unquestionably true that these will form a very considerable
addition to the number of federal officers; but it will not follow, that this will oc-   *240*
casion an increase of public expence. It will be in most cases nothing more than
an exchange of state officers for national officers. In the collection of all duties,
for instance, the persons employed will be wholly of the latter description. The
states individually will stand in no need of any for this purpose. What difference
can it make in point of expence, to pay officers of the customs appointed by the   *245*
state, or those appointed by the United States? There is no good reason to suppose, that either the number or the salaries of the latter, will be greater than those
of the former.

Where then are we to seek for those additional articles of expence which are
to swell the account to the enormous size that has been represented to us? The   *250*
chief item which occurs to me, respects the support of the judges of the United
States. I do not add the president, because there is now a president of congress,
whose expences may not be far, if any thing, short of those which will be incurred on account of the president of the United States. The support of the
judges will clearly be an extra expence, but to what extent will depend on the   *255*
particular plan which may be adopted in practice in regard to this matter. But it
can upon no reasonable plan amount to a sum which will be an object of material consequence.

Let us now see what there is to counterballance any extra expences that may
attend the establishment of the proposed government. The first thing that pres-   *260*
ents itself is, that a great part of the business, which now keeps congress sitting
through the year, will be transacted by the president. Even the management of
foreign negociations will naturally devolve upon him according to general principles concerted with the senate, and subject to their final concurrence. Hence it
is evident, that a portion of the year will suffice for the session of both the senate   *265*
and the house of representatives: We may suppose about a fourth for the latter,
and a third or perhaps a half for the former. The extra business of treaties and appointments may give this extra occupation to the senate. From this circumstance
we may infer, that until the house of representatives shall be increased greatly

---

Lines 230–40 The official staff of the departments of state were a handful of clerks
and secretaries.

270 beyond its present number, there will be a considerable saving of expence from the difference between the constant session of the present, and the temporary session of the future congress.

But there is another circumstance, of great importance in the view of economy. The business of the United States has hitherto occupied the state legisla-
275 tures as well as congress. The latter has made requisitions which the former have had to provide for. Hence it has happened that the sessions of the state legislatures have been protracted greatly beyond what was necessary for the execution of the mere local business of the states. More than half their time has been frequently employed in matters which related to the United States. Now the mem-
280 bers who compose the legislatures of the several states amount to two thousand and upwards; which number has hitherto performed what under the new system will be done in the first instance by sixty-five persons, and probably at no future period by above a fourth or a fifth of that number. The congress under the proposed government will do all the business of the United States themselves, with-
285 out the intervention of the state legislatures, who thenceforth will have only to attend to the affairs of their particular states, and will not have to sit in any proportion as long as they have heretofore done. This difference, in the time of the sessions of the state legislatures, will be all clear gain, and will alone form an article of saving, which may be regarded as an equivalent for any additional objects
290 of expence that may be occasioned by the adoption of the new system.

The result from these observations is, that the sources of additional expence from the establishment of the proposed constitution are much fewer than may have been imagined, that they are counterbalanced by considerable objects of saving, and that while it is questionable on which side the scale will preponder-
295 ate, it is certain that a government less expensive would be incompetent to the purposes of the union.

PUBLIUS.

EIGHTY-FIVE

ALEXANDER HAMILTON
May 28, 1788
Conclusion

To the People of the State of New York.

According to the formal division of the subject of these papers, announced in my
first number, there would appear still to remain for discussion, two points, "the
analogy of the proposed government to your own state constitution," and "the
additional security, which its adoption will afford to republican government, to
liberty and to property." But these heads have been so fully anticipated and ex-   5
hausted in the progress of the work, that it would now scarcely be possible to do
any thing more than repeat, in a more dilated form, what has been heretofore
said; which the advanced stage of the question, and the time already spent upon
it conspire to forbid.

It is remarkable, that the resemblance of the plan of the convention to the act   10
which organizes the government of this state holds, not less with regard to many
of the supposed defects, than to the real excellencies of the former. Among the
pretended defects, are the re-eligibility of the executive, the want of a council,
the omission of a formal bill of rights, the omission of a provision respecting the
liberty of the press: These and several others, which have been noted in the   15
course of our inquiries, are as much chargeable on the existing constitution of
this state, as on the one proposed for the union. And a man must have slender
pretensions to consistency, who can rail at the latter for imperfections which he
finds no difficulty in excusing in the former. Nor indeed can there be a better
proof of the insincerity and affectation of some of the zealous adversaries of the   20
plan of the convention among us, who profess to be the devoted admirers of the
government under which they live, than the fury with which they have attacked
that plan, for matters in regard to which our own constitution is equally, or perhaps more vulnerable.

The additional securities to republican government, to liberty and to property,   25
to be derived from the adoption of the plan under consideration, consist chiefly
in the restraints which the preservation of the union will impose on local factions
and insurrections, and on the ambition of powerful individuals in single states,
who might acquire credit and influence enough, from leaders and favorites, to become the despots of the people; in the diminution of the opportunities to foreign   30
intrigue, which the dissolution of the confederacy would invite and facilitate; in
the prevention of extensive military establishments, which could not fail to grow
out of wars between the states in a disunited situation; in the express guarantee of

461

a republican form of government to each; in the absolute and universal exclusion
of titles of nobility; and in the precautions against the repetition of those practices
on the part of the state governments, which have undermined the foundations of
property and credit, have planted mutual distrust in the breasts of all classes of citizens, and have occasioned an almost universal prostration of morals.

Thus have I, my fellow citizens, executed the task I had assigned to myself;
with what success, your conduct must determine. I trust at least you will admit,
that I have not failed in the assurance I gave you respecting the spirit with which
my endeavours should be conducted. I have addressed myself purely to your
judgments, and have studiously avoided those asperities which are too apt to disgrace political disputants of all parties, and which have been not a little provoked
by the language and conduct of the opponents of the constitution. The charge of
a conspiracy against the liberties of the people, which has been indiscriminately
brought against the advocates of the plan, has something in it too wanton and too
malignant not to excite the indignation of every man who feels in his own bosom
a refutation of the calumny. The perpetual changes which have been rung upon
the wealthy, the well-born and the great, have been such as to inspire the disgust
of all sensible men. And the unwarrantable concealments and misrepresentations which have been in various ways practiced to keep the truth from the
public eye, have been of a nature to demand the reprobation of all honest men.
It is not impossible that these circumstances may have occasionally betrayed me
into intemperances of expression which I did not intend: It is certain that I have
frequently felt a struggle between sensibility and moderation, and if the former
has in some instances prevailed, it must be my excuse that it has been neither
often nor much.

Let us now pause and ask ourselves whether, in the course of these papers, the
proposed constitution has not been satisfactorily vindicated from the aspersions
thrown upon it, and whether it has not been shewn to be worthy of the public
approbation, and necessary to the public safety and prosperity. Every man is
bound to answer these questions to himself, according to the best of his conscience and understanding, and to act agreeably to the genuine and sober dictates
of his judgment. This is a duty, from which nothing can give him a dispensation.—'Tis one that he is called upon, nay, constrained by all the obligations that
form the bands of society, to discharge sincerely and honestly.—No partial motive, no particular interest, no pride of opinion, no temporary passion or prejudice, will justify to himself, to his country or to his posterity, an improper election
of the part he is to act. Let him beware of an obstinate adherence to party.—Let
him reflect that the object upon which he is to decide is not a particular interest

---

Lines 35–38 This passage refers principally to state legislative issues of paper
money.

of the community, but the very existence of the nation.—And let him remember that a majority of America has already given its sanction to the plan, which he is to approve or reject.

I shall not dissemble, that I feel an intire confidence in the arguments, which recommend the proposed system to your adoption; and that I am unable to discern any real force in those by which it has been opposed. I am persuaded, that it is the best which our political situation, habits and opinions will admit, and superior to any the revolution has produced.

Concessions on the part of the friends of the plan, that it has not a claim to absolute perfection, have afforded matter of no small triumph to its enemies. Why, say they, should we adopt an imperfect thing? Why not amend it, and make it perfect before it is irrevocably established? This may be plausible enough, but it is only plausible. In the first place I remark, that the extent of these concessions has been greatly exaggerated. They have been stated as amounting to an admission, that the plan is radically defective; and that, without material alterations, the rights and the interests of the community cannot be safely confided to it. This, as far as I have understood the meaning of those who make the concessions, is an intire perversion of their sense. No advocate of the measure can be found who will not declare as his sentiment, that the system, though it may not be perfect in every part, is upon the whole a good one, is the best that the present views and circumstances of the country will permit, and is such an one as promises every species of security which a reasonable people can desire.

I answer in the next place, that I should esteem it the extreme of imprudence to prolong the precarious state of our national affairs, and to expose the union to the jeopardy of successive experiments, in the chimerical pursuit of a perfect plan. I never expect to see a perfect work from imperfect man. The result of the deliberations of all collective bodies must necessarily be a compound as well of the errors and prejudices, as of the good sense and wisdom of the individuals of whom they are composed. The compacts which are to embrace thirteen distinct states, in a common bond of amity and union, must as necessarily be a compromise of as many dissimilar interests and inclinations. How can perfection spring from such materials?

The reasons assigned in an excellent little pamphlet lately published in this city* are unanswerable to shew the utter improbability of assembling a new convention, under circumstances in any degree so favourable to a happy issue, as

75

80

85

90

95

100

105

---

* Intitled "An Address to the people of the state of New-York."

Lines 72–74 It is now late in the debate, and the concluding sentence of the paragraph reminds us that these essays were composed in the course of an ongoing argument.

those in which the late convention met, deliberated and concluded. I will not repeat the arguments there used, as I presume the production itself has had an extensive circulation. It is certainly well worthy the perusal of every friend to his
110 country. There is however one point of light in which the subject of amendments still remains to be considered; and in which it has not yet been exhibited
to public view. I cannot resolve to conclude, without first taking a survey of it in
this aspect.

It appears to me susceptible of absolute demonstration, that it will be far more
115 easy to obtain subsequent than previous amendments to the constitution. The
moment an alteration is made in the present plan, it becomes, to the purpose of
adoption, a new one, and must undergo a new decision of each state. To its complete establishment throughout the union, it will therefore require the concurrence of thirteen states. If, on the contrary, the constitution proposed should once
120 be ratified by all the states as it stands, alterations in it may at any time be effected
by nine states. Here then the chances are as thirteen to nine* in favour of subsequent amendments, rather than of the original adoption of an intire system.

This is not all. Every constitution for the United States must inevitably consist
of a great variety of particulars, in which thirteen independent states are to be ac-
125 commodated in their interests or opinions of interest. We may of course expect to
see, in any body of men charged with its original formation, very different combinations of the parts upon different points. Many of those who form the majority on one question may become the minority on a second, and an association
dissimilar to either may constitute the majority on a third. Hence the necessity of
130 moulding and arranging all the particulars which are to compose the whole in
such a manner as to satisfy all the parties to the compact; and hence also an immense multiplication of difficulties and casualties in obtaining the collective assent to a final act. The degree of that multiplication must evidently be in a ratio
to the number of particulars and the number of parties.

135 But every amendment to the constitution, if once established, would be a single proposition, and might be brought forward singly. There would then be no necessity for management or compromise, in relation to any other point, no giving
nor taking. The will of the requisite number would at once bring the matter to a
decisive issue. And consequently whenever nine† or rather ten states, were united
140 in the desire of a particular amendment, that amendment must infallibly take
place. There can therefore be no comparison between the facility of effecting an
amendment, and that of establishing in the first instance a complete constitution.

In opposition to the probability of subsequent amendments it has been urged,
that the persons delegated to the administration of the national government, will

---

* It may rather be said TEN, for though two-thirds may set on foot the measure,
three-fourths must ratify.

† It may rather be said TEN, for though two-thirds may set on foot the measure,
three-fourths must ratify.

always be disinclined to yield up any portion of the authority of which they were   *145*
once possessed. For my own part I acknowledge a thorough conviction that any
amendments which may, upon mature consideration, be thought useful, will be
applicable to the organization of the government, not to the mass of its powers;
and on this account alone, I think there is no weight in the observation just
stated. I also think there is little weight in it on another account. The intrinsic   *150*
difficulty of governing THIRTEEN STATES at any rate, independent of calculations upon an ordinary degree of public spirit and integrity, will, in my opinion,
constantly *impose* on the national rulers the *necessity* of a spirit of accommodation to the reasonable expectations of their constituents. But there is yet a further
consideration, which proves beyond the possibility of doubt, that the observation   *155*
is futile. It is this, that the national rulers, whenever nine states concur, will have
no option upon the subject. By the fifth article of the plan the congress will be
obliged, "on the application of the legislatures of two-thirds of the states, (which
at present amounts to nine) to call a convention for proposing amendments,
which *shall be valid* to all intents and purposes, as part of the constitution, when   *160*
ratified by the legislatures of three-fourths of the states, or by conventions in
three-fourths thereof." The words of this article are peremptory. The congress
"*shall* call a convention." Nothing in this particular is left to the discretion of that
body. And of consequence all the declamation about their disinclination to a
change, vanishes in air. Nor however difficult it may be supposed to unite two-   *165*
thirds or three-fourths of the state legislatures, in amendments which may affect
local interests, can there be any room to apprehend any such difficulty in a
union on points which are merely relative to the general liberty or security of the
people. We may safely rely on the disposition of the state legislatures to erect barriers against the encroachments of the national authority.   *170*

If the foregoing argument is a fallacy, certain it is that I am myself deceived by
it; for it is, in my conception, one of those rare instances in which a political
truth can be brought to the test of mathematical demonstration. Those who see
the matter in the same light with me, however zealous they may be for amendments, must agree in the propriety of a previous adoption, as the most direct road   *175*
to their own object.

The zeal for attempts to amend, prior to the establishment of the constitution,
must abate in every man, who, is ready to accede to the truth of the following
observations of a writer, equally solid and ingenious: "To balance a large state or
society (says he) whether monarchial or republican, on general laws, is a work of   *180*
so great difficulty, that no human genius, however comprehensive, is able by the

---

Lines 177–85 This final reference to the Scottish philosopher David Hume, who
had died in 1776—and on whom Madison had relied in No. 10—is a further and
final reminder that the Constitution will be organic in character: a framework surely,
but not an iron cage, whose parts and their relationships will be subject to the
processes and vicissitudes of time.

mere dint of reason and reflection, to effect it. The judgments of many must unite in the work: EXPERIENCE must guide their labour: TIME must bring it to perfection: And the FEELING of inconveniences must correct the mistakes
185 which they *inevitably* fall into, in their first trials and experiments."* These judicious reflections contain a lesson of moderation to all the sincere lovers of the union, and ought to put them upon their guard against hazarding anarchy, civil war, a perpetual alienation of the states from each other, and perhaps the military despotism of a victorious demagogue, in the pursuit of what they are not
190 likely to obtain, but from TIME and EXPERIENCE. It may be in me a defect of political fortitude, but I acknowledge, that I cannot entertain an equal tranquillity with those who affect to treat the dangers of a longer continuance in our present situation as imaginary. A NATION without a NATIONAL GOVERNMENT is, in my view, an awful spectacle. The establishment of a constitution, in time of
195 profound peace, by the voluntary consent of a whole people, is a PRODIGY, to the completion of which I look forward with trembling anxiety. I can reconcile it to no rules of prudence to let go the hold we now have, in so arduous an enterprise, upon seven out of the thirteen states; and after having passed over so considerable a part of the ground to recommence the course. I dread the more the
200 consequences of new attempts, because I KNOW that POWERFUL INDIVID-UALS, in this and in other states, are enemies to a general national government, in every possible shape.

PUBLIUS.

---

* Hume's Essays, vol. I, page 128. — The rise of arts and sciences.

THE ARTICLES OF CONFEDERATION[1]

To all to whom these Presents shall come, we the undersigned Delegates of the States affixed to our Names send greeting.

Articles of Confederation and perpetual Union between the states of New Hampshire, Massachusetts-bay, Rhode Island and Providence Plantations, Connecticut, New York, New Jersey, Pennsylvania, Delaware, Maryland, Virginia, North Carolina, South Carolina and Georgia.

Article I

The Stile of this Confederacy shall be "The United States of America."

Article II

Each state retains its sovereignty, freedom, and independence, and every power, jurisdiction, and right, which is not by this Confederation expressly delegated to the United States, in Congress assembled.

Article III

The said States hereby severally enter into a firm league of friendship with each other, for their common defence, the security of their liberties, and their mutual and general welfare, binding themselves to assist each other, against all force offered to, or attacks made upon them, or any of them, on account of religion, sovereignty, trade, or any other pretence whatever.

Article IV

The better to secure and perpetuate mutual friendship and intercourse among the people of the different States in this Union, the free inhabitants of each of these States, paupers, vagabonds, and fugitives from justice excepted, shall be entitled to all privileges and immunities of free citizens in the several States; and the people of each State shall free ingress and regress to and from any other State, and shall enjoy therein all the privileges of trade and commerce, subject to the same duties, impositions, and restrictions as the inhabitants thereof respectively, provided that such restrictions shall not extend so far as to prevent the removal of

[1] Congress agreed to these Articles November 15, 1777 and ratified them March 1, 1781.

property imported into any State, to any other State, of which the owner is an inhabitant; provided also that no imposition, duties or restriction shall be laid by any State, on the property of the United States, or either of them.

If any person guilty of, or charged with, treason, felony, or other high misdemeanor in any State, shall flee from justice, and be found in any of the United States, he shall, upon demand of the Governor or executive power of the State from which he fled, be delivered up and removed to the State having jurisdiction of his offense.

Full faith and credit shall be given in each of these States to the records, acts, and judicial proceedings of the courts and magistrates of every other State.

Article V

For the most convenient management of the general interests of the United States, delegates shall be annually appointed in such manner as the legislatures of each State shall direct, to meet in Congress on the first Monday in November, in every year, with a power reserved to each State to recall its delegates, or any of them, at any time within the year, and to send others in their stead for the remainder of the year.

No State shall be represented in Congress by less than two, nor more than seven members; and no person shall be capable of being a delegate for more than three years in any term of six years; nor shall any person, being a delegate, be capable of holding any office under the United States, for which he, or another for his benefit, receives any salary, fees or emolument of any kind.

Each State shall maintain its own delegates in a meeting of the States, and while they act as members of the committee of the States.

In determining questions in the United States in Congress assembled, each State shall have one vote.

Freedom of speech and debate in Congress shall not be impeached or questioned in any court or place out of Congress, and the members of Congress shall be protected in their persons from arrests or imprisonments, during the time of their going to and from, and attendence on Congress, except for treason, felony, or breach of the peace.

Article VI

No State, without the consent of the United States in Congress assembled, shall send any embassy to, or receive any embassy from, or enter into any conference, agreement, alliance or treaty with any King, Prince or State; nor shall any person holding any office of profit or trust under the United States, or any of them, accept any present, emolument, office or title of any kind whatever from any King, Prince or foreign State; nor shall the United States in Congress assembled, or any of them, grant any title of nobility.

No two or more States shall enter into any treaty, confederation or alliance whatever between them, without the consent of the United States in Congress assembled, specifying accurately the purposes for which the same is to be entered into, and how long it shall continue.

No State shall lay any imposts or duties, which may interfere with any stipulations in treaties, entered into by the United States in Congress assembled, with any King, Prince or State, in pursuance of any treaties already proposed by Congress, to the courts of France and Spain.

No vessel of war shall be kept up in time of peace by any State, except such number only, as shall be deemed necessary by the United States in Congress assembled, for the defence of such State, or its trade; nor shall any body of forces be kept up by any State in time of peace, except such number only, as in the judgement of the United States in Congress assembled, shall be deemed requisite to garrison the forts necessary for the defence of such State; but every State shall always keep up a well-regulated and disciplined militia, sufficiently armed and accoutered, and shall provide and constantly have ready for use, in public stores, a due number of filed pieces and tents, and a proper quantity of arms, ammunition and camp equipage.

No State shall engage in any war without the consent of the United States in Congress assembled, unless such State be actually invaded by enemies, or shall have received certain advice of a resolution being formed by some nation of Indians to invade such State, and the danger is so imminent as not to admit of a delay till the United States in Congress assembled can be consulted; nor shall any State grant commissions to any ships or vessels of war, nor letters of marque or reprisal, except it be after a declaration of war by the United States in Congress assembled, and then only against the Kingdom or State and the subjects thereof, against which war has been so declared, and under such regulations as shall be established by the United States in Congress assembled, unless such State be infested by pirates, in which case vessels of war may be fitted out for that occasion, and kept so long as the danger shall continue, or until the United States in Congress assembled shall determine otherwise.

Article VII

When land forces are raised by any State for the common defence, all officers of or under the rank of colonel, shall be appointed by the legislature of each State respectively, by whom such forces shall be raised, or in such manner as such State shall direct, and all vacancies shall be filled up by the State which first made the appointment.

Article VIII

All charges of war, and all other expenses that shall be incurred for the common defence or general welfare, and allowed by the United States in Congress assembled, shall be defrayed out of a common treasury, which shall be supplied by the several States in proportion to the value of all land within each State, granted or surveyed for any person, as such land and the buildings and improvements thereon shall be estimated according to such mode as the United States in Congress assembled, shall from time to time direct and appoint.

The taxes for paying that proportion shall be laid and levied by the authority and direction of the legislatures of the several States within the time agreed upon by the United States in Congress assembled.

Article IX

The United States in Congress assembled, shall have the sole and exclusive right and power of determining on peace and war, except in the cases mentioned in the sixth article—of sending and receiving ambassadors—entering into treaties and alliances, provided that no treaty of commerce shall be made whereby the legislative power of the respective States shall be restrained from imposing such imposts and duties on foreigners, as their own people are subjected to, or from prohibiting the exportation or importation of any species of goods or commodities whatsoever—of establishing rules for deciding in all cases, what captures on land or water shall be legal, and in what manner prizes taken by land or naval forces in the service of the United States shall be divided or appropriated—of granting letters of marque and reprisal in times of peace—appointing courts for the trial of piracies and felonies committed on the high seas and establishing courts for receiving and determining finally appeals in all cases of captures, provided that no member of Congress shall be appointed a judge of any of the said courts.

The United States in Congress assembled shall also be the last resort on appeal in all disputes and differences now subsisting or that hereafter may arise between two or more States concerning boundary, jurisdiction or any other causes whatever; which authority shall always be exercised in the manner following. Whenever the legislative or executive authority or lawful agent of any State in controversy with another shall present a petition to Congress stating the matter in question and praying for a hearing, notice thereof shall be given by order of Congress to the legislative or executive authority of the other State in controversy, and a day assigned for the appearance of the parties by their lawful agents, who shall then be directed to appoint by joint consent, commissioners or judges to constitute a court for hearing and determining the matter in question: but if they cannot agree, Congress shall name three persons out of each of the United States, and from the list of such persons each party shall alternately strike out one, the petitioners beginning, until the number shall be reduced to thirteen; and from that number not less than seven, nor more than nine names as Congress shall direct, shall in the presence of Congress be drawn out by lot, and the persons whose names shall be so drawn or any five of them, shall be commissioners or judges, to hear and finally determine the controversy, so always as a major part of the judges who shall hear the cause shall agree in the determination: and if either party shall neglect to attend at the day appointed, without showing reasons, which Congress shall judge sufficient, or being present shall refuse to strike, the Congress shall proceed to nominate three persons out of each State, and the secretary of Congress shall strike in behalf of such party absent or refusing; and the judgement and sentence of the court to be appointed, in the manner before prescribed, shall be final and conclusive; and if any of the parties shall refuse to submit to the authority of such court, or to appear or defend their claim or cause, the court shall nevertheless proceed to pronounce sentence, or judgement, which shall in like manner be final and decisive, the judgement or sentence and other proceedings being in either case transmitted to Congress, and lodged among the acts of Congress for the security of the parties concerned: provided that every commissioner, before he sits in judgement, shall take an oath to be administered by one of the judges of the supreme or superior court of the State, where the cause shall be tried, "well and truly to hear and determine the matter in question, according to the best of his judgement, without favor, affection or hope of reward": provided also, that no State shall be deprived of territory for the benefit of the United States.

All controversies concerning the private right of soil claimed under different grants of two or more States, whose jurisdictions as they may respect such lands, and the States which passed such grants are adjusted, the said grants or either of them being at the same time claimed to have originated antecedent to such settlement of jurisdiction, shall on the petition of either party to the Congress of the United States, be finally determined as near as may be in the same manner as is before prescribed for deciding disputes respecting territorial jurisdiction between different States.

The United States in Congress assembled shall also have the sole and exclusive right and power of regulating the alloy and value of coin struck by their own authority, or by that of the respective States—fixing the standards of weights and measures throughout the United States—regulating the trade and managing all affairs with the Indians, not members of any of the States, provided that the legislative right of any State within its own limits be not infringed or violated—establishing or regulating post offices from one State to another, throughout all the United States, and exacting such postage on the papers passing through the same as may be requisite to defray the expenses of the said office—appointing all officers of the land forces, in the service of the United States, excepting regimental officers—appointing all the officers of the naval forces, and commissioning all officers whatever in the service of the United States—making rules for the government and regulation of the said land and naval forces, and directing their operations.

The United States in Congress assembled shall have authority to appoint a committee, to sit in the recess of Congress, to be denominated "A Committee of the States," and to consist of one delegate from each State; and to appoint such other committees and civil officers as may be necessary for managing the general affairs of the United States under their direction—to appoint one of their members to preside, provided that no person be allowed to serve in the office of president more than one year in any term of three years; to ascertain the necessary sums of money to be raised for the service of the United States, and to appropriate and apply the same for defraying the public expenses—to borrow money, or emit bills on the credit of the United States, transmitting every half-year to the respective States an account of the sums of money so borrowed or emitted—to build and equip a navy—to agree upon the number of land forces, and to make requisitions from each State for its quota, in proportion to the number of white inhabitants in such State; which requisition shall be binding, and thereupon the legislature of each State shall appoint the regimental officers, raise the men and cloath, arm and equip them in a solid-like manner, at the expense of the United States; and the officers and men so cloathed, armed and equipped shall march to the place appointed, and within the time agreed on by the United States in Congress assembled. But if the United States in Congress assembled shall, on consideration of circumstances judge proper that any State should not raise men, or should raise a smaller number of men than the quota thereof, such extra number shall be raised, officered, cloathed, armed and equipped in the same manner as the quota of each State, unless the legislature of such State shall judge that such extra number cannot be safely spread out in the same, in which case they shall raise, officer, cloath, arm and equip as many of such extra number as they judge can be safely spared. And the officers and men so cloathed, armed, and equipped, shall march to the place appointed, and within the time agreed on by the United States in Congress assembled.

The United States in Congress assembled shall never engage in a war, nor grant letters of marque or reprisal in time of peace, nor enter into any treaties or alliances, nor coin money, nor regulate the value thereof, nor ascertain the sums and expenses necessary for the defence and welfare of the United States, or any of them, nor emit bills, nor borrow money on the credit of the United States, nor appropriate money, nor agree upon the number of vessels of war, to be built or purchased, or the number of land or sea forces to be raised, nor appoint a commander in chief of the army or navy, unless nine States assent to the same: nor shall a question on any other point, except for adjourning from day to day be determined, unless by the votes of the majority of the United States in Congress assembled.

The Congress of the United States shall have power to adjourn to any time within the year, and to any place within the United States, so that no period of adjournment be for a longer duration than the space of six months, and shall publish the journal of their proceedings monthly, except such parts thereof relating to treaties, alliances or military operations, as in their judgement require secrecy; and the yeas and nays of the delegates of each State on any question shall be entered on the journal, when it is desired by any delegates of a State, or any of them, at his or their request shall be furnished with a transcript of the said journal, except such parts as are above excepted, to lay before the legislatures of the several States.

Article X

The Committee of the States, or any nine of them, shall be authorized to execute, in the recess of Congress, such of the powers of Congress as the United States in Congress assembled, by the consent of the nine States, shall from time to time think expedient to vest them with; provided that no power be delegated to the said Committee, for the exercise of which, by the Articles of Confederation, the voice of nine States in the Congress of the United States assembled be requisite.

Article XI

Canada acceding to this confederation, and adjoining in the measures of the United States, shall be admitted into, and entitled to all the advantages of this Union; but no other colony shall be admitted into the same, unless such admission be agreed to by nine States.

Article XII

All bills of credit emitted, monies borrowed, and debts contracted by, or under the authority of Congress, before the assembling of the United States, in pursuance of the present confederation, shall be deemed and considered as a charge against the United States, for payment and satisfaction whereof the said United States, and the public faith are hereby solemnly pledged.

Article XIII

Every State shall abide by the determination of the United States in Congress assembled, on all questions which by this confederation are submitted to them. And the Articles of this Confederation shall be inviolably observed by every State, and the Union shall be perpetual; nor shall any alteration at any time hereafter be made in any of them; unless such alteration be agreed to in a Congress of the United States, and be afterwards confirmed by the legislatures of every State.

And Whereas it hath pleased the Great Governor of the World to incline the hearts of the legislatures we respectively represent in Congress, to approve of, and to authorize us to ratify the said Articles of Confederation and perpetual Union. Know Ye that we the undersigned delegates, by virtue of the power and authority to us given for that purpose, do by these presents, in the name and in behalf of our respective constituents, fully and entirely ratify and confirm each and every of the said Articles of Confederation and perpetual Union, and all and singular the matters and things therein contained: And we do further solemnly plight and engage the faith of our respective constituents, that they shall abide by the determinations of the United States in Congress assembled, on all questions, which by the said Confederation are submitted to them. And that the Articles thereof shall be inviolably observed by the States we respectively represent, and that the Union shall be perpetual.

In Witness whereof we have hereunto set our hands in Congress. Done at Philadelphia in the State of Pennsylvania the ninth day of July in the Year of our Lord One Thousand Seven Hundred and Seventy-Eight, and in the Third Year of the independence of America.

THE CONSTITUTION OF THE UNITED STATES[1]

We the People of the United States, in Order to form a more perfect Union, establish Justice, insure domestic Tranquility, provide for the common defence, promote the general Welfare, and secure the Blessings of Liberty to ourselves and our Posterity, do ordain and establish this Constitution for the United States of America.

Article I

Section 1. All legislative Powers herein granted shall be vested in a Congress of the United States, which shall consist of a Senate and House of Representatives. [45][2]

Section 2. The House of Representatives shall be composed of Members chosen every second Year by the People of the several States, and the Electors in each State shall have the Qualifications requisite for Electors of the most numerous Branch of the State Legislature. [39, 45, 52–53, 57, 70]

No Person shall be a Representative who shall not have attained to the Age of twenty five Years, and been seven Years a Citizen of the United States, and who shall not, when elected, be an Inhabitant of that State in which he shall be chosen. [52, 60]

Representatives and direct Taxes shall be apportioned among the several States which may be included within this Union, according to their respective Numbers, which shall be determined by adding to the whole Number of free Persons, including those bound to Service for a Term of Years, and excluding Indians not taxed, three fifths of all other Persons.[3] The actual Enumeration shall be made within three Years after the first Meeting of the Congress of the United States, and within every subsequent Term of ten Years, in such Manner as they shall by Law direct. The Number of Representatives shall not exceed one for every thirty Thousand, but each State shall have at Least one Representative; and until such enumeration shall be made, the State of New Hampshire shall be

---

[1] The Constitution was adopted by a convention of the States on September 17, 1787, and was finally ratified on June 21, 1788.

[2] The bracketed numbers following each clause refer to specific Federalist papers.

[3] The part of this Clause relating to the mode of apportionment of representatives among the several States was altered by Section 2 of the 14th Amendment (see p. 489), and as to taxes on incomes without apportionment, by the 16th Amendment (see p. 490).

474

entitled to chuse three, Massachusetts eight, Rhode-Island and Providence Plantations one, Connecticut five, New-York six, New Jersey four, Pennsylvania eight, Delaware one, Maryland six, Virginia ten, North Carolina five, South Carolina five, and Georgia three. [53–58]

When vacancies happen in the Representation from any State, the Executive Authority thereof shall issue Writs of Election to fill such Vacancies.

The House of Representatives shall chuse their Speaker and other Officers; and shall have the sole Power of Impeachment. [80]

Section 3. The Senate of the United States shall be composed of two Senators from each State, chosen by the Legislature thereof,[4] for six Years; and each Senator shall have one Vote. [39, 45, 60, 62–63]

Immediately after they shall be assembled in Consequence of the first Election, they shall be divided as equally as may be into three Classes. The Seats of the Senators of the first Class shall be vacated at the Expiration of the second Year, of the second Class at the Expiration of the fourth Year, and of the third Class at the Expiration of the sixth Year, so that one third may be chosen every second Year; and if Vacancies happen by Resignation, or otherwise, during the Recess of the Legislature of any State, the Executive thereof may make temporary Appointments until the next Meeting of the Legislature, which shall then fill such Vacancies.[5] [59, 68]

No Person shall be a Senator who shall not have attained to the Age of thirty Years, and been nine Years a Citizen of the United States, and who shall not, when elected, be an Inhabitant of that State for which he shall be chosen. [62, 64]

The Vice President of the United States shall be President of the Senate, but shall have no Vote, unless they be equally divided.

The Senate shall chuse their other Officers, and also a President pro tempore, in the Absence of the Vice President, or when he shall exercise the Office of President of the United States.

The Senate shall have the sole Power to try all Impeachments. When sitting for that Purpose, they shall be on Oath or Affirmation. When the President of the United States is tried, the Chief Justice shall preside: And no Person shall be convicted without the Concurrence of two thirds of the Members present. [39, 65–66, 80]

Judgment in Cases of Impeachment shall not extend further than to removal from Office, and disqualification to hold and enjoy any Office of honor, Trust or Profit under the United States: but the Party convicted shall nevertheless be liable and subject to Indictment, Trial, Judgment and Punishment, according to Law. [84]

---

[4] This Clause was altered by Clause 1 of the 17th Amendment (see p. 490).

[5] This Clause was altered by Clause 2 of the 18th Amendment (see pp. 490–91).

Section 4. The Times, Places and Manner of holding Elections for Senators and Representatives, shall be prescribed in each State by the Legislature thereof; but the Congress may at any time by Law make or alter such Regulations, except as to the Places of chusing Senators. [59–61]

The Congress shall assemble at least once in every Year, and such Meeting shall be on the first Monday in December,[6] unless they shall by Law appoint a different Day.

Section 5. Each House shall be the Judge of the Elections, Returns and Qualifications of its own Members, and a Majority of each shall constitute a Quorum to do Business; but a smaller Number may adjourn from day to day, and may be authorized to compel the Attendance of absent Members, in such Manner, and under such Penalties as each House may provide.

Each House may determine the Rules of its Proceedings, punish its Members for disorderly Behaviour, and, with the Concurrence of two thirds, expel a Member.

Each House shall keep a Journal of its Proceedings, and from time to time publish the same, excepting such Parts as may in their Judgment require Secrecy; and the Yeas and Nays of the Members of either House on any question shall, at the Desire of one fifth of those Present, be entered on the Journal.

Neither House, during the Session of Congress, shall, without the Consent of the other, adjourn for more than three days, nor to any other Place than that in which the two Houses shall be sitting.

Section 6. The Senators and Representatives shall receive a Compensation for their Services, to be ascertained by Law, and paid out of the Treasury of the United States.[7] They shall in all Cases, except Treason, Felony and Breach of the Peace, be privileged from Arrest during their Attendance at the Session of their respective Houses, and in going to and returning from the same; and for any Speech or Debate in either House, they shall not be questioned in any other Place.

No Senator or Representative shall, during the Time for which he was elected, be appointed to any civil Office under the Authority of the United States, which shall have been created, or the Emoluments whereof shall have been encreased during such time; and no Person holding any Office under the United States, shall be a Member of either House during his Continuance in Office. [55, 76–77]

Section 7. All Bills for raising Revenue shall originate in the House of Representatives; but the Senate may propose or concur with Amendments as on other Bills. [66]

Every Bill which shall have passed the House of Representatives and the Senate, shall, before it become a Law, be presented to the President of the United States; If he approve he shall sign it, but if not he shall return it, with his Objec-

---

[6] This Clause was altered by the 20th Amendment (see pp. 491–92).

[7] This Clause was altered by the 27th Amendment, (see p. 494).

tions to that House in which it shall have originated, who shall enter the Objections at large on their Journal, and proceed to reconsider it. If after such Reconsideration two thirds of that House shall agree to pass the Bill, it shall be sent, together with the Objections, to the other House, by which it shall likewise be reconsidered, and if approved by two thirds of that House, it shall become a Law. But in all such Cases the Votes of both Houses shall be determined by yeas and Nays, and the Names of the Persons voting for and against the Bill shall be entered on the Journal of each House respectively. If any Bill shall not be returned by the President within ten Days (Sundays excepted) after it shall have been presented to him, the Same shall be a Law, in like Manner as if he had signed it, unless the Congress by their Adjournment prevent its Return, in which Case it shall not be a Law. [69, 73]

Every Order, Resolution, or Vote to which the Concurrence of the Senate and House of Representatives may be necessary (except on a question of Adjournment) shall be presented to the President of the United States; and before the Same shall take Effect, shall be approved by him, or being disapproved by him, shall be repassed by two thirds of the Senate and House of Representatives, according to the Rules and Limitations prescribed in the Case of a Bill. [69, 73]

Section 8. The Congress shall have Power To lay and collect Taxes, Duties, Imposts and Excises, to pay the Debts and provide for the common Defence and general Welfare of the United States; but all Duties, Imposts and Excises shall be uniform throughout the United States; [30–36, 41, 56]

To borrow Money on the credit of the United States;

To regulate Commerce with foreign Nations, and among the several States, and with the Indian Tribes; [40, 42, 45]

To establish an uniform Rule of Naturalization, and uniform Laws on the subject of Bankruptcies throughout the United States; [32, 42–44]

To coin Money, regulate the Value thereof, and of foreign Coin, and fix the Standard of Weights and Measures; [42]

To provide for the Punishment of counterfeiting the Securities and current Coin of the United States; [42]

To establish Post Offices and post Roads; [42]

To promote the Progress of Science and useful Arts, by securing for limited Times to Authors and Inventors the exclusive Right to their respective Writings and Discoveries; [43]

To constitute Tribunals inferior to the supreme Court; [81]

To define and punish Piracies and Felonies committed on the high Seas, and Offences against the Law of Nations; [42]

To declare War, grant Letters of Marque and Reprisal, and make Rules concerning Captures on Land and Water; [41]

To raise and support Armies, but no Appropriation of Money to that Use shall be for a longer Term than two Years; [23–24, 26, 41]

To provide and maintain a Navy; [41]

To make Rules for the Government and Regulation of the land and naval Forces;

To provide for calling forth the Militia to execute the Laws of the Union, suppress Insurrections and repel Invasions; [29]

To provide for organizing, arming, and disciplining, the Militia, and for governing such Part of them as may be employed in the Service of the United States, reserving to the States respectively, the Appointment of the Officers, and the Authority of training the Militia according to the discipline prescribed by Congress; [29, 56]

To exercise exclusive Legislation in all Cases whatsoever, over such District (not exceeding ten Miles square) as may, by Cession of particular States, and the Acceptance of Congress, become the Seat of the Government of the United States, and to exercise like Authority over all Places purchased by the Consent of the Legislature of the State in which the Same shall be, for the Erection of Forts, Magazines, Arsenals, dock-Yards, and other needful Buildings;—And [32, 43]

To make all Laws which shall be necessary and proper for carrying into Execution the foregoing Powers, and all other Powers vested by this Constitution in the Government of the United States, or in any Department or Officer thereof. [29, 31, 33, 44]

Section 9. The Migration or Importation of such Persons as any of the States now existing shall think proper to admit, shall not be prohibited by the Congress prior to the Year one thousand eight hundred and eight, but a Tax or duty may be imposed on such Importation, not exceeding ten dollars for each Person. [42]

The Privilege of the Writ of Habeas Corpus shall not be suspended, unless when in Cases of Rebellion or Invasion the public Safety may require it. [83–84]

No Bill of Attainder or ex post facto Law shall be passed. [84]

No Capitation, or other direct, Tax shall be laid, unless in Proportion to the Census or Enumeration herein before directed to be taken.[8]

No Tax or Duty shall be laid on Articles exported from any State.

No Preference shall be given by any Regulation of Commerce or Revenue to the Ports of one State over those of another: nor shall Vessels bound to, or from, one State, be obliged to enter, clear, or pay Duties in another. [32]

No Money shall be drawn from the Treasury, but in Consequence of Appropriations made by Law; and a regular Statement and Account of the Receipts and Expenditures of all public Money shall be published from time to time.

No Title of Nobility shall be granted by the United States: And no Person holding any Office of Profit or Trust under them, shall, without the Consent of the Congress, accept of any present, Emolument, Office, or Title, of any kind whatever, from any King, Prince, or foreign State. [39, 84]

---

[8] This Clause was altered by the 16th Amendment (see p. 490).

Section 10. No State shall enter into any Treaty, Alliance, or Confederation; grant Letters of Marque and Reprisal; coin Money; emit Bills of Credit; make any Thing but gold and silver Coin a Tender in Payment of Debts; pass any Bill of Attainder, ex post facto Law, or Law impairing the Obligation of Contracts, or grant any Title of Nobility. [33, 41, 44]

No State shall, without the Consent of the Congress, lay any Imposts or Duties on Imports or Exports, except what may be absolutely necessary for executing its inspection Laws: and the net Produce of all Duties and Imposts, laid by any State on Imports or Exports, shall be for the Use of the Treasury of the United States; and all such Laws shall be subject to the Revision and Controul of the Congress. [32, 44]

No State shall, without the Consent of Congress, lay any Duty of Tonnage, keep Troops, or Ships of War in time of Peace, enter into any Agreement or Compact with another State, or with a foreign Power, or engage in War, unless actually invaded, or in such imminent Danger as will not admit of delay. [44]

Article II

Section 1. The executive Power shall be vested in a President of the United States of America. He shall hold his Office during the Term of four Years, and, together with the Vice President, chosen for the same Term, be elected, as follows [39, 68, 70–72, 84]

Each State shall appoint, in such Manner as the Legislature thereof may direct, a Number of Electors, equal to the whole Number of Senators and Representatives to which the State may be entitled in the Congress: but no Senator or Representative, or Person holding an Office of Trust or Profit under the United States, shall be appointed an Elector. [39, 45, 68, 77]

The Electors shall meet in their respective States, and vote by Ballot for two Persons, of whom one at least shall not be an Inhabitant of the same State with themselves. And they shall make a List of all the Persons voted for, and of the Number of Votes for each; which List they shall sign and certify, and transmit sealed to the Seat of the Government of the United States, directed to the President of the Senate. The President of the Senate shall, in the Presence of the Senate and House of Representatives, open all the Certificates, and the Votes shall then be counted. The Person having the greatest Number of Votes shall be the President, if such Number be a Majority of the whole Number of Electors appointed; and if there be more than one who have such Majority, and have an equal Number of Votes, then the House of Representatives shall immediately chuse by Ballot one of them for President; and if no Person have a Majority, then from the five highest on the List the said House shall in like Manner chuse the President. But in chusing the President, the Votes shall be taken by States, the Representation from each State having one Vote; A quorum for this Purpose shall consist of a Member or Members from two thirds of the States, and a Majority of all the States shall be necessary to a Choice. In every Case, after the

Choice of the President, the Person having the greatest Number of Votes of the Electors shall be the Vice President. But if there should remain two or more who have equal Votes, the Senate shall chuse from them by Ballot the Vice President.[9] [66]

The Congress may determine the Time of chusing the Electors, and the Day on which they shall give their Votes; which Day shall be the same throughout the United States.

No Person except a natural born Citizen, or a Citizen of the United States, at the time of the Adoption of this Constitution, shall be eligible to the Office of President; neither shall any Person be eligible to that Office who shall not have attained to the Age of thirty five Years, and been fourteen Years a Resident within the United States. [64]

In Case of the Removal of the President from Office, or of his Death, Resignation, or Inability to discharge the Powers and Duties of the said Office, the Same shall devolve on the Vice President, and the Congress may by Law provide for the Case of Removal, Death, Resignation or Inability, both of the President and Vice President, declaring what Officer shall then act as President, and such Officer shall act accordingly, until the Disability be removed, or a President shall be elected.[10]

The President shall, at stated Times, receive for his Services, a Compensation, which shall neither be encreased nor diminished during the Period for which he shall have been elected, and he shall not receive within that Period any other Emolument from the United States, or any of them. [73, 79]

Before he enter on the Execution of his Office, he shall take the following Oath or Affirmation: — "I do solemnly swear (or affirm) that I will faithfully execute the Office of President of the United States, and will to the best of my Ability, preserve, protect and defend the Constitution of the United States."

Section 2. The President shall be Commander in Chief of the Army and Navy of the United States, and of the Militia of the several States, when called into the actual Service of the United States; he may require the Opinion, in writing, of the principal Officer in each of the executive Departments, upon any Subject relating to the Duties of their respective Offices, and he shall have Power to grant Reprieves and Pardons for Offences against the United States, except in Cases of Impeachment. [69, 74]

He shall have Power, by and with the Advice and Consent of the Senate, to make Treaties, provided two thirds of the Senators present concur; and he shall nominate, and by and with the Advice and Consent of the Senate, shall appoint Ambassadors, other public Ministers and Consuls, Judges of the supreme Court, and all other Officers of the United States, whose Appointments are not herein otherwise provided for, and which shall be established by Law: but the Congress

---

[9] This Clause was superseded by the 12th Amendment (see p. 488).

[10] This Clause was altered by the 25th Amendment (see pp. 493–94).

may by Law vest the Appointment of such inferior Officers, as they think proper, in the President alone, in the Courts of Law, or in the Heads of Departments. [42, 64, 66, 69, 76–77]

The President shall have Power to fill up all Vacancies that may happen during the Recess of the Senate, by granting Commissions which shall expire at the End of their next Session. [67, 76]

Section 3. He shall from time to time give to the Congress Information of the State of the Union, and recommend to their Consideration such Measures as he shall judge necessary and expedient; he may, on extraordinary Occasions, convene both Houses, or either of them, and in Case of Disagreement between them, with Respect to the Time of Adjournment, he may adjourn them to such Time as he shall think proper; he shall receive Ambassadors and other public Ministers; he shall take Care that the Laws be faithfully executed, and shall Commission all the Officers of the United States. [42, 69, 77–78]

Section 4. The President, Vice President and all civil Officers of the United States, shall be removed from Office on Impeachment for, and Conviction of, Treason, Bribery, or other high Crimes and Misdemeanors. [39, 69]

Article III

Section 1. The judicial Power of the United States, shall be vested in one supreme Court, and in such inferior Courts as the Congress may from time to time ordain and establish. The Judges, both of the supreme and inferior Courts, shall hold their Offices during good Behaviour, and shall, at stated Times, receive for their Services, a Compensation, which shall not be diminished during their Continuance in Office. [65, 78–79, 81–83]

Section 2. The judicial Power shall extend to all Cases, in Law and Equity, arising under this Constitution, the Laws of the United States, and Treaties made, or which shall be made, under their Authority;—to all Cases affecting Ambassadors, other public Ministers and Consuls;—to all Cases of admiralty and maritime Jurisdiction;—to Controversies to which the United States shall be a Party;—to Controversies between two or more States;—between a State and Citizens of another State;—between Citizens of different States,—between Citizens of the same State claiming Lands under Grants of different States, and between a State, or the Citizens thereof, and foreign States, Citizens or Subjects.[11] [80]

In all Cases affecting Ambassadors, other public Ministers and Consuls, and those in which a State shall be Party, the supreme Court shall have original Jurisdiction. In all the other Cases before mentioned, the supreme Court shall have appellate Jurisdiction, both as to Law and Fact, with such Exceptions, and under such Regulations as the Congress shall make. [81]

---

[11] This Clause was altered by the 11th Amendment (see p. 487).

The Trial of all Crimes, except in Cases of Impeachment, shall be by Jury; and such Trial shall be held in the State where the said Crimes shall have been committed; but when not committed within any State, the Trial shall be at such Place or Places as the Congress may by Law have directed. [83]

Section 3. Treason against the United States, shall consist only in levying War against them, or in adhering to their Enemies, giving them Aid and Comfort. No Person shall be convicted of Treason unless on the Testimony of two Witnesses to the same overt Act, or on Confession in open Court. [43, 84]

The Congress shall have Power to declare the Punishment of Treason, but no Attainder of Treason shall work Corruption of Blood, or Forfeiture except during the Life of the Person attainted. [43, 84]

Article IV

Section 1. Full Faith and Credit shall be given in each State to the public Acts, Records, and judicial Proceedings of every other State. And the Congress may by general Laws prescribe the Manner in which such Acts, Records and Proceedings shall be proved, and the Effect thereof. [42]

Section 2. The Citizens of each State shall be entitled to all Privileges and Immunities of Citizens in the several States. [80]

A Person charged in any State with Treason, Felony, or other Crime, who shall flee from Justice, and be found in another State, shall on Demand of the executive Authority of the State from which he fled, be delivered up, to be removed to the State having Jurisdiction of the Crime.

No Person held to Service or Labour in one State, under the Laws thereof, escaping into another, shall, in Consequence of any Law or Regulation therein, be discharged from such Service or Labour, but shall be delivered up on Claim of the Party to whom such Service or Labour may be due.[12]

Section 3. New States may be admitted by the Congress into this Union; but no new State shall be formed or erected within the Jurisdiction of any other State; nor any State be formed by the Junction of two or more States, or Parts of States, without the Consent of the Legislatures of the States concerned as well as of the Congress. [43]

The Congress shall have Power to dispose of and make all needful Rules and Regulations respecting the Territory or other Property belonging to the United States; and nothing in this Constitution shall be so construed as to Prejudice any Claims of the United States, or of any particular State. [43]

---

[12] This Clause was altered by the 13th Amendment (see p. 488).

Section 4. The United States shall guarantee to every State in this Union a Republican Form of Government, and shall protect each of them against Invasion; and on Application of the Legislature, or of the Executive (when the Legislature cannot be convened) against domestic Violence. [39, 43]

Article V

The Congress, whenever two thirds of both Houses shall deem it necessary, shall propose Amendments to this Constitution, or, on the Application of the Legislatures of two thirds of the several States, shall call a Convention for proposing Amendments, which, in either Case, shall be valid to all Intents and Purposes, as Part of this Constitution, when ratified by the Legislatures of three fourths of the several States, or by Conventions in three fourths thereof, as the one or the other Mode of Ratification may be proposed by the Congress; Provided that no Amendment which may be made prior to the Year One thousand eight hundred and eight shall in any Manner affect the first and fourth Clauses in the Ninth Section of the first Article; and that no State, without its Consent, shall be deprived of its equal Suffrage in the Senate. [39, 43, 85]

Article VI

All Debts contracted and Engagements entered into, before the Adoption of this Constitution, shall be as valid against the United States under this Constitution, as under the Confederation. [43]

This Constitution, and the Laws of the United States which shall be made in Pursuance thereof; and all Treaties made, or which shall be made, under the Authority of the United States, shall be the supreme Law of the Land; and the Judges in every State shall be bound thereby, any Thing in the Constitution or Laws of any State to the Contrary notwithstanding. [27, 33, 39, 44, 64]

The Senators and Representatives before mentioned, and the Members of the several State Legislatures, and all executive and judicial Officers, both of the United States and of the several States, shall be bound by Oath or Affirmation, to support this Constitution; but no religious Test shall ever be required as a Qualification to any Office or public Trust under the United States. [27, 44]

Article VII

The Ratification of the Conventions of nine States, shall be sufficient for the Establishment of this Constitution between the States so ratifying the Same. [39–40, 43]

Done in Convention by the Unanimous Consent of the States present the Seventeenth Day of September in the Year of our Lord one thousand seven hundred and Eighty seven and of the Independence of the United States of America the Twelfth In witness whereof We have hereunto subscribed our Names,

Go WASHINGTON—Presidt. and deputy from Virginia

[Signed also by the deputies of twelve States.]

Delaware

Geo: Read
Gunning Bedford jun
John Dickinson
Richard Bassett
Jaco: Broom

Maryland

James MCHenry
Dan of ST ThoS. Jenifer
DanL Carroll.

Virginia

John Blair—
James Madison Jr.

North Carolina

WM Blount
RichD. Dobbs Spaight.
Hu Williamson

South Carolina

J. Rutledge
Charles Cotesworth Pinckney
Charles Pinckney
Pierce Butler.

Georgia

William Few
Abr Baldwin

New Hampshire

John Langdon
Nicholas Gilman

Massachusetts

Nathaniel Gorham
Rufus King

Connecticut

WM. SamL. Johnson
Roger Sherman

New York

Alexander Hamilton

New Jersey

Wil: Livingston
David Brearley.
WM. Paterson.
Jona: Dayton

Pennsylvania

B Franklin
Thomas Mifflin
RobT Morris
Geo. Clymer
ThoS. FitzSimons
Jared Ingersoll
James Wilson.
Gouv Morris
Attest William Jackson Secretary

AMENDMENTS TO THE CONSTITUTION OF THE UNITED STATES

Articles in addition to, and Amendment of, the Constitution of the United States of America, proposed by Congress, and ratified by the several States, pursuant to the fifth Article of the original Constitution.

Amendment I

Congress shall make no law respecting an establishment of religion, or prohibiting the free exercise thereof; or abridging the freedom of speech, or of the press; or the right of the people peaceably to assemble, and to petition the Government for a redress of grievances.[1]

Amendment II

A well regulated Militia, being necessary to the security of a free State, the right of the people to keep and bear Arms, shall not be infringed.

Amendment III

No Soldier shall, in time of peace, be quartered in any house, without the consent of the Owner, nor in time of war, but in a manner to be prescribed by law.

Amendment IV

The right of the people to be secure in their persons, houses, papers, and effects, against unreasonable searches and seizures, shall not be violated, and no Warrants shall issue, but upon probable cause, supported by Oath or affirmation, and particularly describing the place to be searched, and the persons or things to be seized.

Amendment V

No person shall be held to answer for a capital, or otherwise infamous crime, unless on a presentment or indictment of a Grand Jury, except in cases arising in the land or naval forces, or in the Militia, when in actual service in time of War

---

[1] The first ten amendments —of twelve proposed—to the Constitution were ratified in 1791. See note 21.

or public danger; nor shall any person be subject for the same offence to be twice put in jeopardy of life or limb; nor shall be compelled in any criminal case to be a witness against himself, nor be deprived of life, liberty, or property, without due process of law; nor shall private property be taken for public use, without just compensation.

Amendment VI

In all criminal prosecutions, the accused shall enjoy the right to a speedy and public trial, by an impartial jury of the State and district wherein the crime shall have been committed, which district shall have been previously ascertained by law, and to be informed of the nature and cause of the accusation; to be confronted with the witnesses against him; to have compulsory process for obtaining witnesses in his favor, and to have the Assistance of Counsel for his defence.

Amendment VII

In Suits at common law, where the value in controversy shall exceed twenty dollars, the right of trial by jury shall be preserved, and no fact tried by a jury, shall be otherwise re-examined in any Court of the United States, than according to the rules of the common law.

Amendment VIII

Excessive bail shall not be required, nor excessive fines imposed, nor cruel and unusual punishments inflicted.

Amendment IX

The enumeration in the Constitution, of certain rights, shall not be construed to deny or disparage others retained by the people.

Amendment X

The powers not delegated to the United States by the Constitution, nor prohibited by it to the States, are reserved to the States respectively, or to the people.

Amendment XI[2]

The Judicial power of the United States shall not be construed to extend to any suit in law or equity, commenced or prosecuted against one of the United States by Citizens of another State, or by Citizens or Subjects of any Foreign State.

[2] Ratified 1795.

Amendment XII[3]

The Electors shall meet in their respective states and vote by ballot for President and Vice-President, one of whom, at least, shall not be an inhabitant of the same state with themselves; they shall name in their ballots the person voted for as President, and in distinct ballots the person voted for as Vice-President, and they shall make distinct lists of all persons voted for as President, and of all persons voted for as Vice-President, and of the number of votes for each, which lists they shall sign and certify, and transmit sealed to the seat of the government of the United States, directed to the President of the Senate;—The President of the Senate shall, in the presence of the Senate and House of Representatives, open all the certificates and the votes shall then be counted;—The person having the greatest Number of votes for President, shall be the President, if such number be a majority of the whole number of Electors appointed; and if no person have such majority, then from the persons having the highest numbers not exceeding three on the list of those voted for as President, the House of Representatives shall choose immediately, by ballot, the President. But in choosing the President, the votes shall be taken by states, the representation from each state having one vote; a quorum for this purpose shall consist of a member or members from two-thirds of the states, and a majority of all the states shall be necessary to a choice. And if the House of Representatives shall not choose a President whenever the right of choice shall devolve upon them, before the fourth day of March next following, then the Vice-President shall act as President, as in the case of the death or other constitutional disability of the President[4]—The person having the greatest number of votes as Vice-President, shall be the Vice-President, if such number be a majority of the whole number of Electors appointed, and if no person have a majority, then from the two highest numbers on the list, the Senate shall choose the Vice-President; a quorum for the purpose shall consist of two-thirds of the whole number of Senators, and a majority of the whole number shall be necessary to a choice. But no person constitutionally ineligible to the office of President shall be eligible to that of Vice-President of the United States.

Amendment XIII[5]

Section 1. Neither slavery nor involuntary servitude, except as a punishment for crime whereof the party shall have been duly convicted, shall exist within the United States, or any place subject to their jurisdiction.

Section 2. Congress shall have power to enforce this article by appropriate legislation.

---

[3] Ratified 1804. This amendment was rejected by Delaware and Connecticut.

[4] This was altered by the 20th Amendment (see pp. 491–92).

[5] Ratified 1865. This amendment was rejected by Kentucky and Mississippi.

Amendment XIV[6]

Section 1. All persons born or naturalized in the United States and subject to the jurisdiction thereof, are citizens of the United States and of the State wherein they reside. No State shall make or enforce any law which shall abridge the privileges or immunities of citizens of the United States; nor shall any State deprive any person of life, liberty, or property, without due process of law; nor deny to any person within its jurisdiction the equal protection of the laws.

Section 2. Representatives shall be apportioned among the several States according to their respective numbers, counting the whole number of persons in each State, excluding Indians not taxed. But when the right to vote at any election for the choice of electors for President and Vice President of the United States, Representatives in Congress, the Executive and Judicial officers of a State, or the members of the Legislature thereof, is denied to any of the male inhabitants of such State, being twenty-one years of age, and citizens of the United States, or in any way abridged, except for participation in rebellion, or other crime, the basis of representation therein shall be reduced in the proportion which the number of such male citizens shall bear to the whole number of male citizens twenty-one years of age in such State.[7]

Section 3. No person shall be a Senator or Representative in Congress, or elector of President and Vice President, or hold any office, civil or military, under the United States, or under any State, who, having previously taken an oath, as a member of Congress, or as an officer of the United States, or as a member of any State legislature, or as an executive or judicial officer of any State, to support the Constitution of the United States, shall have engaged in insurrection or rebellion against the same, or given aid or comfort to the enemies thereof. But Congress may by a vote of two-thirds of each House, remove such disability.

Section 4. The validity of the public debt of the United States, authorized by law, including debts incurred for payment of pensions and bounties for services in suppressing insurrection or rebellion, shall not be questioned. But neither the United States nor any State shall assume or pay any debt or obligation incurred in aid of insurrection or rebellion against the United States, or any claim for the loss or emancipation of any slave; but all such debts, obligations and claims shall be held illegal and void.

Section 5. The Congress shall have power to enforce, by appropriate legislation, the provisions of this article.

---

[6] Ratified 1868. This amendment was rejected (and not subsequently ratified) by Kentucky.

[7] This section was altered by the 19th Amendment (see p. 491).

Amendment XV[8]

Section 1. The right of citizens of the United States to vote shall not be denied or abridged by the United States or by any State on account of race, color, or previous condition of servitude.

Section 2. The Congress shall have power to enforce this article by appropriate legislation.

Amendment XVI[9]

The Congress shall have power to lay and collect taxes on incomes, from whatever source derived, without apportionment among the several States, and without regard to any census or enumeration.

Amendment XVII[10]

The Senate of the United States shall be composed of two Senators from each State, elected by the people thereof, for six years; and each Senator shall have one vote. The electors in each State shall have the qualifications requisite for electors of the most numerous branch of the State legislatures.

When vacancies happen in the representation of any State in the Senate, the executive authority of such State shall issue writs of election to fill such vacancies: Provided, That the legislature of any State may empower the executive thereof to make temporary appointments until the people fill the vacancies by election as the legislature may direct.

This amendment shall not be so construed as to affect the election or term of any Senator chosen before it becomes valid as part of the Constitution.

Amendment XVIII[11]

Section 1. After one year from the ratification of this article the manufacture, sale, or transportation of intoxicating liquors within, the importation thereof into, or the exportation thereof from the United States and all territory subject to the jurisdiction thereof for beverage purposes is hereby prohibited.

[8] Ratified 1870. This amendment was rejected (and not subsequently ratified) by Kentucky, Maryland, and Tennessee.

[9] Ratified 1913. This amendment was rejected (and not subsequently ratified) by Connecticut, Rhode Island, and Utah.

[10] Ratified 1913. This amendment was rejected by Utah.

[11] Ratified 1919. By its terms this amendment did not become effective until one year after ratification. This amendment was later repealed by the 21st Amendment (see p. 492).

Section 2. The Congress and the several States shall have concurrent power to enforce this article by appropriate legislation.

Section 3. This article shall be inoperative unless it shall have been ratified as an amendment to the Constitution by the legislatures of the several States, as provided in the Constitution, within seven years from the date of the submission hereof to the States by the Congress.

Amendment XIX[12]

The right of citizens of the United States to vote shall not be denied or abridged by the United States or by any State on account of sex.

Congress shall have power to enforce this article by appropriate legislation.

Amendment XX[13]

Section 1. The terms of the President and Vice President shall end at noon on the 20th day of January, and the terms of Senators and Representatives at noon on the 3d day of January, of the years in which such terms would have ended if this article had not been ratified; and the terms of their successors shall then begin.

Section 2. The Congress shall assemble at least once in every year, and such meeting shall begin at noon on the 3d day of January, unless they shall by law appoint a different day.

Section 3. If, at the time fixed for the beginning of the term of the President, the President elect shall have died, the Vice President elect shall become President. If a President shall not have been chosen before the time fixed for the beginning of his term, or if the President elect shall have failed to qualify, then the Vice President elect shall act as President until a President shall have qualified; and the Congress may by law provide for the case wherein neither a President elect nor a Vice President elect shall have qualified, declaring who shall then act as President, or the manner in which one who is to act shall be selected, and such person shall act accordingly until a President or Vice President shall have qualified.

Section 4. The Congress may by law provide for the case of the death of any of the persons from whom the House of Representatives may choose a President whenever the right of choice shall have devolved upon them, and for the case of the death of any of the persons from whom the Senate may choose a Vice President whenever the right of choice shall have devolved upon them.

Section 5. Sections 1 and 2 shall take effect on the 15th day of October following the ratification of this article.

---

[12] Ratified 1920. This amendment was rejected (and not subsequently ratified) by South Carolina, Maryland, and Mississippi.

[13] Ratified 1933.

Section 6. This article shall be inoperative unless it shall have been ratified as an amendment to the Constitution by the legislatures of three-fourths of the several States within seven years from the date of its submission.

Amendment XXI[14]

Section 1. The eighteenth article of amendment to the Constitution of the United States is hereby repealed.

Section 2. The transportation or importation into any State, Territory, or possession of the United States for delivery or use therein of intoxicating liquors, in violation of the laws thereof, is hereby prohibited.

Section 3. This article shall be inoperative unless it shall have been ratified as an amendment to the Constitution by conventions in the several States, as provided in the Constitution, within seven years from the date of the submission hereof to the States by the Congress.

Amendment XXII[15]

Section 1. No person shall be elected to the office of the President more than twice, and no person who has held the office of President, or acted as President, for more than two years of a term to which some other person was elected President shall be elected to the office of the President more than once. But this Article shall not apply to any person holding the office of President, when this Article was proposed by the Congress, and shall not prevent any person who may be holding the office of President, or acting as President, during the term within which this Article becomes operative from holding the office of President or acting as President during the remainder of such term.

Section 2. This article shall be inoperative unless it shall have been ratified as an amendment to the Constitution by the legislatures of three-fourths of the several States within seven years from the date of its submission to the States by the Congress.

Amendment XXIII[16]

Section 1. The District constituting the seat of Government of the United States shall appoint in such manner as the Congress may direct:

---

[14] Ratified 1933. This amendment was rejected by South Carolina and the electorate of North Carolina did not vote upon it.

[15] Ratified 1951.

[16] Ratified 1961.

A number of electors of President and Vice President equal to the whole number of Senators and Representatives in Congress to which the District would be entitled if it were a State, but in no event more than the least populous State; they shall be in addition to those appointed by the States, but they shall be considered, for the purposes of the election of President and Vice President, to be electors appointed by a State; and they shall meet in the District and perform such duties as provided by the twelfth article of amendment.

Section 2. The Congress shall have power to enforce this article by appropriate legislation.

Amendment XXIV[17]

Section 1. The right of citizens of the United States to vote in any primary or other election for President or Vice President, for electors for President or Vice President, or for Senator or Representative in Congress, shall not be denied or abridged by the United States or any State by reason of failure to pay any poll tax or other tax.

Section 2. The Congress shall have power to enforce this article by appropriate legislation.

Amendment XXV[18]

Section 1. In case of the removal of the President from office or of his death or resignation, the Vice President shall become President.

Section 2. Whenever there is a vacancy in the office of the Vice President, the President shall nominate a Vice President who shall take office upon confirmation by a majority vote of both Houses of Congress.

Section 3. Whenever the President transmits to the President pro tempore of the Senate and the Speaker of the House of Representatives his written declaration that he is unable to discharge the powers and duties of his office, and until he transmits to them a written declaration to the contrary, such powers and duties shall be discharged by the Vice President as Acting President.

Section 4. Whenever the Vice President and a majority of either the principal officers of the executive departments or of such other body as Congress may by law provide, transmit to the President pro tempore of the Senate and the Speaker of the House of Representatives their written declaration that the President is unable to discharge the powers and duties of his office, the Vice President shall immediately assume the powers and duties of the office as Acting President.

---

[17] Ratified 1964.
[18] Ratified 1965.

Thereafter, when the President transmits to the President pro tempore of the Senate and the Speaker of the House of Representatives has written declaration that no inability exists, he shall resume the powers and duties of his office unless the Vice President and a majority of either the principal officers of the executive department or of such other body as Congress may by law provide, transmit within four days to the President pro tempore of the Senate and the Speaker of the House of Representatives their written declaration that the President is unable to discharge the powers and duties of his office. Thereupon Congress shall decide the issue, assembling within forty-eight hours for that purpose if not in session. If the Congress, within twenty-one days after receipt of the latter written declaration, or, if Congress is not in session, within twenty-one days after Congress is required to assemble, determines by two-thirds vote of both Houses that the President is unable to discharge the powers and duties of his office, the Vice President shall continue to discharge the same as Acting President; otherwise, the President shall resume the powers and duties of his office.

Amendment XXVI[19]

Section 1. The right of citizens of the United States, who are eighteen years of age or older, to vote shall not be denied or abridged by the United States or by any State on account of age.

Section 2. The Congress shall have power to enforce this article by appropriate legislation.

Amendment XXVII[20]

No law varying the compensation for the services of the Senators and Representatives shall take effect, until an election of Representatives shall have intervened.

[19] Ratified 1971.

[20] Originally proposed—but not ratified—by Congress in 1789 as part of the Bill of Rights. Ratified 1992.

INDEX

As authorship of each paper is cited in the letter's heading, all are addressed to the people of New York State, and all are signed "Publius," these references have been omitted for the sake of clarity. Brief glosses are included for many entries.